CENSUS OF INDIA 1911

Owing to the antiquity and rarity of this book, certain pages are regrettably absent, and readability is compromised due to the blurring of the original text. If you possess any insights regarding the availability of these missing sections, kindly inform us. Your assistance is crucial in ensuring thc completion of this significant work for the benefit of future generations.

CENSUS OF INDIA, 1911

VOLUME - VIII

BOMBAY

(TOWN AND ISLAND)

PART I & II - REPORT AND TABLES

P. J. MEAD AND **G. LAIRD MACGREGOR**

GYAN

Published by

Gyan Publishing House
5, Ansari Road
Daryaganj, New Delhi-110002
Phone: 011-47034999, 9811692060
E-mail: books@gyanbooks.com

Distribution Network
gyanbooks.com
India, USA, Canada, UK, Australia

ISBN: 978-81-212-7127-1 (Set) 23 Vols. In 41 Bindings

ISBN: 978-81-212-7475-3 (PB) Vol. VIII, Pt. I, II

First Published, 1912

2nd Impression 2024

Printed at: Gyan Press, Delhi.

CENSUS OF INDIA 1911

CENSUS OF INDIA, 1911.

VOLUME VIII.

BOMBAY

(TOWN AND ISLAND).

PARTS I AND II.

REPORT AND TABLES.

BY

P. J. MEAD AND G. LAIRD MACGREGOR

OF THE INDIAN CIVIL SERVICE,

IN CHARGE CENSUS OPERATIONS.

BOMBAY:
PRINTED AT THE GOVERNMENT CENTRAL PRESS.
1912

CONTENTS.

I

REPORT.

ERRATA.

Page	7,	Table III—Note, line 1	*after*	Esplanade	*read*	"there are"
"	"	" " " 4	*for*	"togethers a"	"	"together as"
"	12,	" IV-B—Hindu married persons—70 and over (column 8)...	"	1,304	"	1,305
"	"	" " Do. Total—Hindu (column 8) ..	"	404,481	"	404,482
"	14,	" " F—Christian population—Males 0—1 (column 3) ...	"	497	"	407
"	24,	" V—Khetwadi—Zoroastrian—Total—persons 20 and over, last line (column 2)	"	694	"	4,694
"	38,	" VI—E Ward—males—Multan (S. No. 119) (column 13)	"	42	"	24
"	102,	" XIII—Grand Total Bombay City—number of occupied buildings (column 10)	"	32,992	"	32,902

B 1638—*a*

II

TABLES.

INTRODUCTION.

The Census of the Town and Island of Bombay was taken as part of the Census of India on the night of the 10th March 1911. Although the condition of the City was not abnormal on that date, the unfortunate circumstances under which the Census was taken in 1901 with a virulent epidemic of plague raging through the City preclude the drawing of comparisons between 1901 and 1911. This review of the Census figures will therefore be confined generally to an exegesis on the statical and not the dynamical aspect of the statistics.

The final test shows that the population of our City is 979,445, just over 203,000 more than in 1901, and 1,623 more than the figures revealed by the Municipal Census taken in 1906 by the Health Department of the Municipality who required something more authentic than the vitiated statistics of the Imperial Census for the proper administration of their department. This is the first instance in India of a quinquennial census being taken, but it is unlikely that it will be repeated, although a census every five years is recommended by the statisticians of Europe.

The preliminary record was complete five days before the Census night, having been prepared by Dr. J. A. Turner, the Executive Health Officer of the Municipality, this being his second census. Mr. P. P. Vágh had the direct supervision of the arrangements. It may not be out of place to mention that this was the third census, with the direction of which Mr. Vágh had been closely connected. His experience on previous occasions conduced in no small measure to the smoothness with which all details were carried out. For the last five days with the aid of Government servants, volunteers and scholastic institutions the schedules were carefully checked and everything was ready for the final check on the night of March 10th. In 1901, thanks to the initiative of Mr. E. D. Talati, school-boys carefully trained into census squads were utilized for the first time. There was a great extension of this on the present occasion and sixteen schools took part in the final enumeration and the previous five days of checking. By this agency 97,962 persons, just over 10 per cent. of the population, were enumerated. The work was of course not equal, some of it was much better done than the rest, but there is no doubt that a well-trained squad working under supervision is a most useful adjunct to the means available for enumeration.

In addition to the schools some nineteen mercantile firms, both European and Indian, lent the services of clerks for the final enumeration. In several other instances volunteers came forward and agreed to take complete charge of the enumeration of certain areas, providing their own staff.

The innovation of using a general schedule, and filling in the details by means of enumerators instead of permitting the householder to fill in the entries himself, was made in 1901 with some diffidence, and trouble was anticipated in some of the turbulent quarters of the City. Thanks, however, to the personal influence of Mr. Edwardes, there was no difficulty. Since then there has been a Municipal Census in 1906 and the Musalmán population are getting accustomed to enumerations and no trouble was anticipated. But to make assurance doubly sure Mr. Edwardes' kind offices were again enlisted and the cooperation of the heads of the Jamáts obtained beforehand.

The Police took charge of the enumeration of the homeless. All railway arches, maidans and alleys were searched and the sleepers marshalled into gangs and taken off to fixed enumeration stations where their particulars were recorded and they were allowed to go away armed with a slip of paper to show that they had been enumerated.

The floating population was enumerated by the agency of the Royal Indian Marine and Mr. C. R. Watkins of the Preventive Service.

The abstraction and compilation work was done in the Poona office.

It is impossible to say yet what the cost of this Census of the City will be, as the composition charges are not yet known, but it is not likely to exceed the sum set apart by the Municipality and an equal contribution from the Government of India.

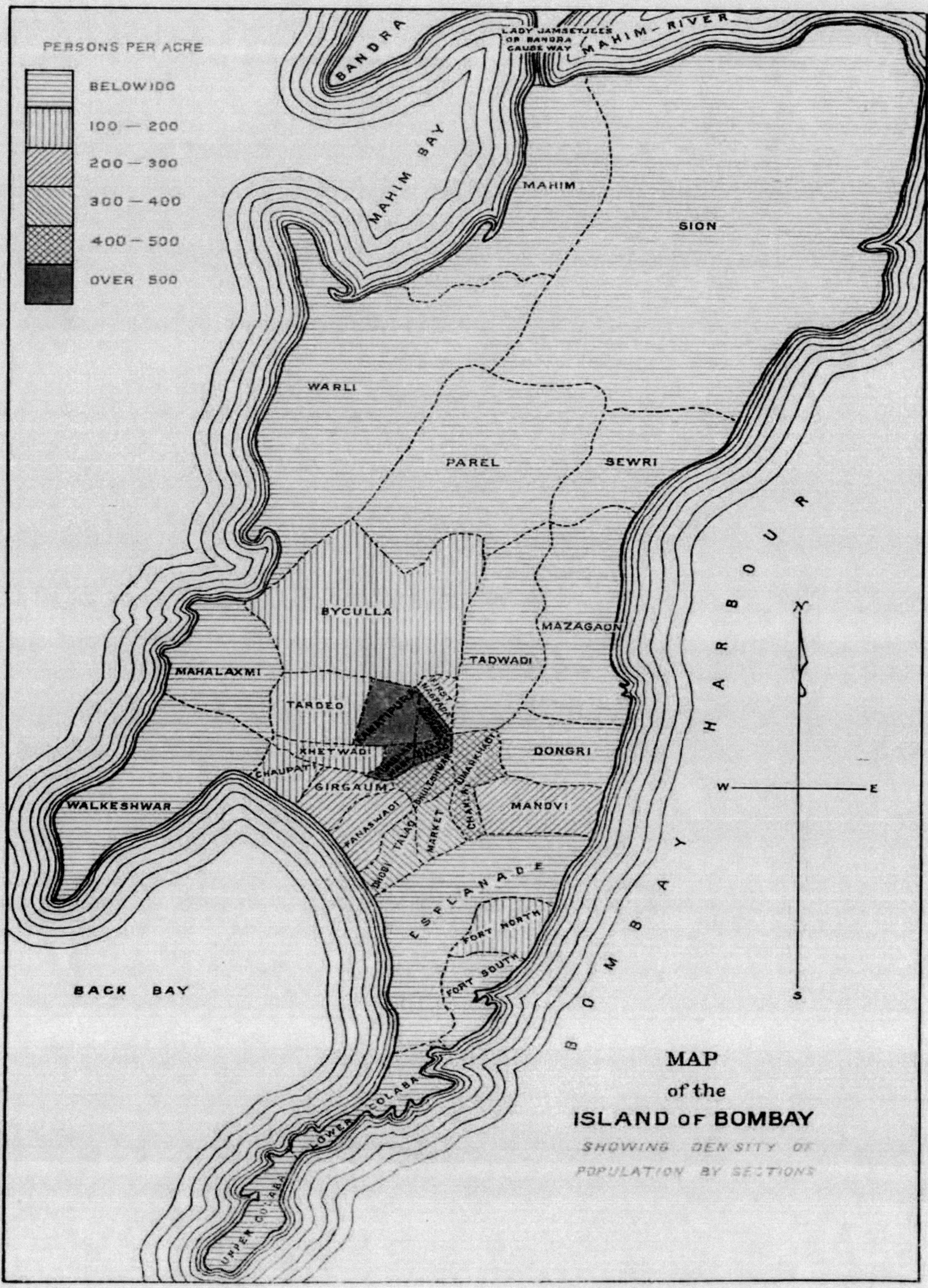
PERSONS PER ACRE
BELOW 100
100 — 200
200 — 300
300 — 400
400 — 500
OVER 500
BANDRA
LADY JAMSETJEES OR BANDRA CAUSE WAY
MAHIM-RIVER
MAHIM BAY
MAHIM
SION
WARLI
PAREL
SEWRI
BYCULLA
MAZAGAON
TADWADI
MAHALAXMI
TARDEO
KHETWADI
CHAUPATI
GIRGAUM
DONGRI
WALKESHWAR
MANDVI
FANASWADI
TALAO
BHULESHWAR
MARKET
CHAKLA
UMARKHADI
DHOBI
ESPLANADE
FORT NORTH
FORT SOUTH
BACK BAY
BOMBAY HARBOUR
LOWER COLABA
UPPER COLABA
N
W
E
S
MAP
of the
ISLAND OF BOMBAY
SHOWING DENSITY OF
POPULATION BY SECTIONS

CHAPTER I.

POPULATION OF THE ISLAND.

1. The population of the Town and Island of Bombay on the night of the 10th March was 979,445. When it is remembered that the Census was taken at a time when many had gone off to their homes for the Holi holidays and when there was great depression in the textile industry and many mills had closed down owing to the prohibitive cost of the raw material, it may be taken for granted that except for these interferences the population would have exceeded a million. The area of the island is 14,575½ acres or 330 acres more than it was ten years ago. The increase is due to reclamation from the sea at Colaba, Fort North, Mazagaon and Sewri with the big schemes in progress or in the air. This rate of increase is likely to be maintained. **Population.**

2. The details of area, houses and population arranged by wards and sections will be found in Table I of the Tables which are printed at the end of this report. The population is most concentrated in 2nd Nagpáda, Kumbhárwáda, Kámátipura and Khára Talao, all of which have more than 550 persons per acre, and most scattered in Sion, Upper Colába and Walkeshwar, where there are less than 20 to the acre. The reason of this will be evident to any one who knows Bombay; Sion is still largely unreclaimed rice swamps (of which the land won by the G. I. P. Railway for their workshops is only a very small fraction) or salt works, neither of which are capable of supporting a crowded population. Upper Colába is practically a military reservation and Walkeshwar contains the residential suburb of Malabar Hill. The explanation of the density of 2nd Nagpáda and Khára Talao has been given by Mr. Edwardes in the last Census report as being due to their being Muhammadan centres and Muhammadans do not run away from plague. Moreover the Sons of the Prophet have a knack of packing closely together into one quarter, even in mofussil towns. Other overcrowded sections are Bhuleshwar, Chakla, Umarkhádi, all of which show a large Musalman population. These seven sections have been the mostly densly populated for the last thirty years, but recently there has been some re-arrangement of the order of precedence. Second Nagpáda now holds the unenviable pride of place and has increased 136 per acre since 1881. **Density.**

3. The population of Calcutta (excluding Howrah) is 896,067 and subsequent to the census Glasgow has been attempting to manipulate its boundaries so as to include a large area of suburbs. Whether the attempt be successful or not, it is certain that so long as the present census figures are current Bombay still justifies her proud boast of being the first city in India and the second in the Empire. **Urbs prima in India.**

4. The number of occupied houses is 37,932, giving an average of 21 persons in each house. There was no difference in the definition of a house, which was, as in 1901, 'the whole of a building under one undivided roof.' For a detailed disquisition on the term house the reader is referred to page 13 of Mr. Edwardes' Report on the Census of Bombay City in 1901. The largest number of houses are to be found in the northern sections, Warli, Mahim and Sion, but many of these are huts and do not indicate overcrowding. The **Houses.**

fewest houses are to be found in 1st Nagpáda where many small buildings have been pulled down by the operations of the Improvement Trust; Upper Colába where the military quarters take up much of the room and Fort South, which is a business quarter with residential flats.

The number of empty houses has fallen by nearly one thousand, while the total number has risen over 6,000 which testifies to the greatness of the exodus in 1901. The largest number of unoccupied houses is to be found in F and G wards in the north of the island and in Tadwadi, Byculla, and Mazagon but many of these are huts. Lower Colába also shows a large number of untenanted dwellings and so do Walkeshwar and Mahalaxmi.

Harbour, Docks, etc.

5. The Harbour, Docks, Railways, Military and Homeless show an increase of 7,000, but this is not proportionately greater than the increase of the population and a number would be accounted for by the Port Trust workers. Vagrants have in all probability decreased.

Subjoined below will be found three subsidiary tables giving the

Density of each section in persons per acre since 1881 ;
Average number of houses per acre ;
Number of houses, occupied and unoccupied, on March 10th, 1911.

The density is graphically represented in the map which faces this Chapter.

Subsidiary Table I.

Showing by sections the density per acre.

Section.	1881.	1891.	1901.	1911.
Upper Colaba	20·3	30·3	27·4	10·8
Lower Colaba	55·5	52·3	49·0	69·7
Fort South	27·0	30·0	25·1	26·3
Fort North	258·2	246·9	170·9	157·5
Esplanade	20·9	15·9	15·6	26·2
Chakla	726·4	624·2	472·7	469·8
Mandvi	261·4	226·5	190·7	201·6
Umarkhadi	525·5	498·1	460·2	433·7
Dongri	118·0	106·2	90·3	95·4
Market	558·2	502·2	318·8	338·6
Dhobi Talao	402·1	400·7	296·4	338·0
Fanaswadi	188·7	192·2	130·5	218·8
Bhuleshwar	508·0	506·2	398·8	481·1
Kumbharwada	777·5	699·3	598·0	601·5
Khara Talao	699·8	649·3	556·2	551·8
Khetwadi	175·2	169·2	159·4	187·5
Girgaum	205·8	216·7	119·3	247·0
Chaupati	99·7	103·0	60·2	102·0
Walkeshwar	21·2	24·1	19·8	19·5
Mahalaxmi	16·9	45·6	28·1	40·9
Tardeo	89·7	83·0	91·6	121·4
Kamatipura	437·7	441·5	403·7	555·7
First Nagpada	323·1	376·1	357·3	216·7
Second Nagpada	482·4	552·0	546·7	638·2
Byculla	29·0	50·7	112·6	147·3
Tadwadi	30·7	44·4	38·4	59·3
Mazagaon	49·2	58·6	45·4	41·3
Parel	16·9	25·9	60·4	82·3
Sewri	13·1	14·2	20·8	37·7
Sion	4·1	4·6	5·9	7·2
Mahim	18·8	9·9	21·2	23·7
Warli	10·0	17·2	25·1	49·4
Mean density ...	54·	58·	51·	67·

Subsidiary Table II.

Showing by sections the average number of total and occupied houses per acre.

Section.	Number of houses per acre. Total.	Occupied.
Upper Colaba	0·79	0·53
Lower Colaba	3·83	2·53
Fort South	3·14	3·00
Fort North	7·61	7·20
Esplanade	1·12	0·85
Chakla	17·66	17·33
Mandvi	6·86	6·69
Umarkhadi	10·98	10·45
Dongri	2·31	2·06
Market	14·11	11·69
Dhobi Talao	13·86	12·63
Fanaswadi	7·42	6·63
Bhuleshwar	17·42	16·33
Kumbharwada	15·46	14·83
Khara Talao	16·33	15·71
Khetwadi	8·05	7·28
Girgaum	9·61	8·95
Chaupati	7·15	6·54
Walkeshwar	2·85	2·22
Mahalaxmi	2·75	2·30
Tardeo	4·08	3·24
Kamatipura	17·33	16·53
First Nagpada	3·75	3·38
Second Nagpada	15·94	14·65
Byculla	5·20	4·57
Tadwadi	3·63	2·00
Mazagaon	2·87	2·39
Parel	3·72	2·97
Sewri	3·25	2·77
Sion	0·79	0·56
Mahim	3·18	2·38
Warli	2·72	2·13

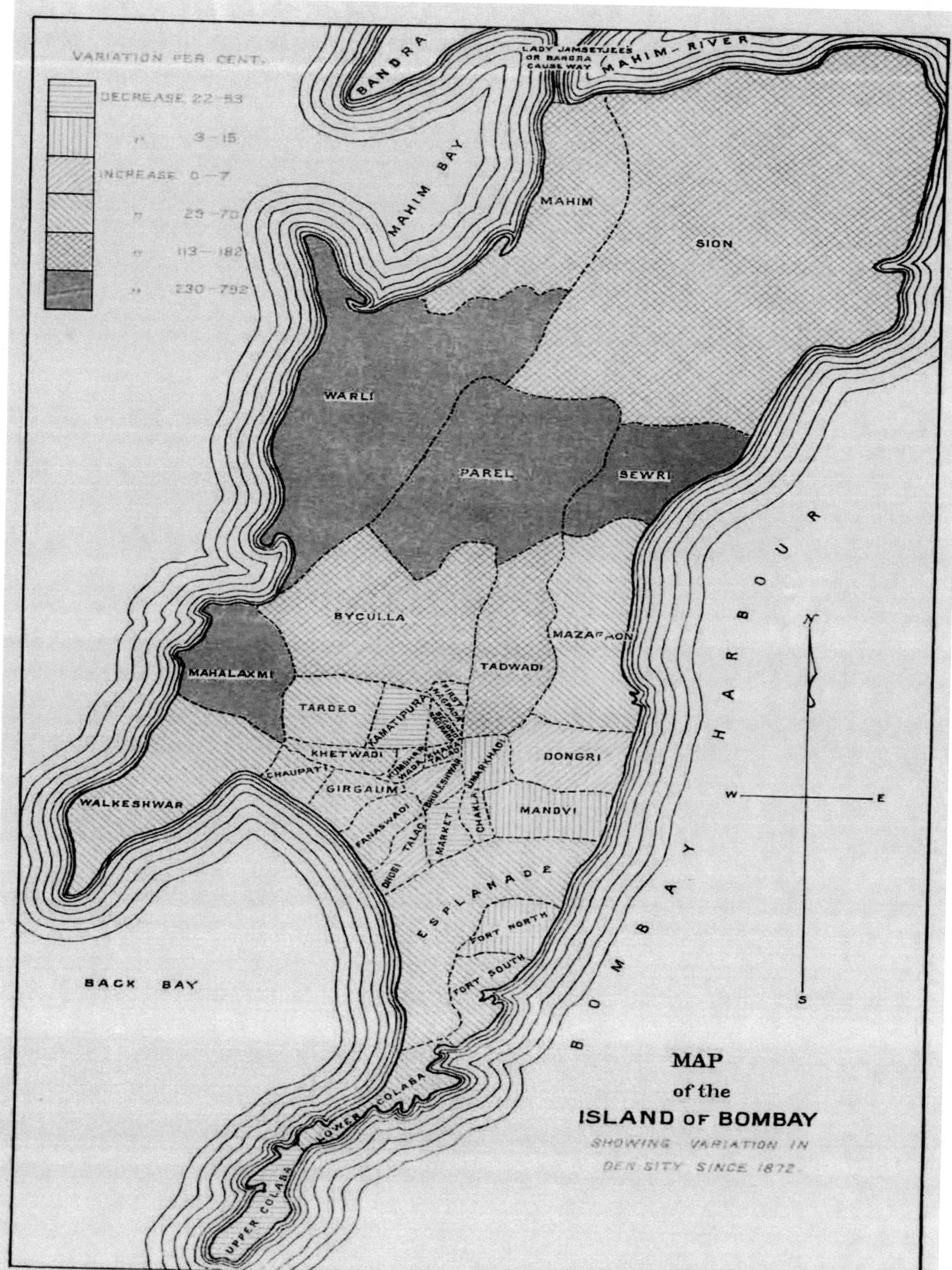

MAP
of the
ISLAND OF BOMBAY
SHOWING VARIATION IN DENSITY SINCE 1872.

CHAPTER II.

VARIATION IN POPULATION SINCE 1872.

6. Imperial Table II shows the increase or decrease of each section since 1872, which are well exemplified in the map facing this page. Variation since 1872. Map—Variation.

The Island generally shows an increase of 52 per cent. in the forty years. The centres of habitation have however changed. Twenty-four sections (including the harbour, docks, etc.) show an increase, while 9 show a diminished population. The highest percentage increases are Warli (792), Mahalaxmi (509), Sewri (327), Parel (230), Tadwadi (182), Byculla (169), Sion (165) and Mahim (130). Byculla, Tadwadi and Warli are the three biggest mill centres in the Island, while Parel and Sion, if they have not many mills, come next in the matter of workshops, the G. I. P. Railway shops in particular employing a large number of hands. Sewri, Mahalaxmi and Mahim also have mills and workshops, though they are also residential areas. All these sections lie to the north of the densely congested areas of Kamatipura, Umarkhadi and second Nagpada.

7. The principal decreases are to be found in Upper Colaba (53), Esplanade (34), First Nagpada (32), Kamatipura (22) and Fort South (15). The decrease in Upper Colaba is misleading and due to the inclusion of the military in the figures of 1901 and their exclusion on the present occasion. Decreases.

Esplanade and Fort South are big mercantile centres and have not many residential buildings for their size, the Government offices along Back Bay take up a great deal of space, and it is not surprising that the population is receding. The loss in First Nagpada represents the removal of a number of insanitary rookeries and is not a matter for regret.

8. There is clearly a tendency to move out towards the opener and clearer parts in the North of the Island. This tendency has probably been increased by the arrival of plague and will be very rapidly developed when the Eastern Avenue with its better tramway facilities make Sion more accessible as a residential centre. It was once the royal seat of Raja Bimb and possibly it may once again become a residential quarter. Northward movement of residents.

The variations in Tardeo and First and Second Nagpadas are calculated from 1881 only; before that date they formed portions of other sections and were not separately enumerated.

Subsidiary Table IV at the end of this Chapter gives the percentage and details of variations by sections.

It will not be out of place to conclude this chapter with a few remarks on the effect of plague on the City. Since it broke out in 1896 it has been always with us, some years the epidemic has been serious as in 1903 and 1901, at other times it has fallen as low as 3,656 deaths which were recorded in 1910. Plague has accounted for 114,506 deaths in the decennium, and it is permissible to hope that this severe lesson is not being lost on the well-to-do. If plague leads to suburbanization it will have had one good result. So long as a city refuses inoculation its only safety lies in evacuation.

Birth-place and Immigration.

Reasons for low birth-rate.

9. While the above variations show the great increase in the population of the City, it must be remembered that the growth of Bombay is entirely due to the stream of immigrants that replace the wastage inseparable from a big city. In the intercensual period the births registered in Bombay averaged 18,643 annually, while the deaths during the same ten years averaged 44,850. There are several causes for this. In the first place there is a great shortage of married women of child-bearing age compared with the number that there ought to be in a normal community. The number of married women aged 15 to 40 is 150,000. We can take this figure roughly as the number of potential mothers, 27 per cent., of the total married population, whereas the figure for the whole of the Presidency is 35. Secondly, there is a well-established and entirely salutary custom of sending a prospective mother home to her parents, where the baby has a better chance of life. This, however, decreases the birth-rate of the City. And, lastly, if the child is born in Bombay, the fearful child mortality which amounted in 1910 to 288 per 1,000 children, in the first year of life, does not give the infant a fair chance. The mortality on the *registered* births is even greater, 380 per 1,000, but the adjusted figures are here taken as being more in accordance with the real facts. Even these figures, it may be noted, are an improvement on recent years.

Sources of Immigration.

10. Having thus seen that the population is only kept up by a constant supply of humanity from outside it will be of some interest to examine whence it comes. Imperial Table XI, Part III, of the Census Report of the province will be found reproduced here as Table VI, Part III. It gives the place of origin of immigrants from the principal districts that contribute to the city population combined with details of certain occupations.

Of the 979,445 persons which constitute the population of the City, only 191,581 or less than 20 per cent. were born in Bombay. This is less than the number sent here by Ratnágiri which is over 22 per cent. The principal districts of the Presidency which keep Bombay supplied are shown in the marginal table, which needs little comment.

Districts or States.	Numbers.	Percentage of population.
DISTRICTS.		
Ratnágiri	216,060	22·06
Poona	71,188	7·27
Sátára	56,754	5·80
Kolába	37,119	3·79
Surat	35,073	3·58
NATIVE STATES.		
Káthiáwár	50,615	5·17
Cutch	36,470	3·72

From Ratnágiri come most of the salaried menials, the office hamáls and pattáválas of the principal firms, the bulk of the City Police, and lascars. Twenty-seven per cent. of the Ratnágiri born are mill-hands, and D, E, F and G wards are the localities they chiefly favour. Poona and Sátára supply chiefly coolies, cartmen and mill-hands. These are the people who are collectively termed Ghátis and may some day develop into a separate caste. The Poona people haunt B and E wards, while the Sátára-born congregate in C, E and G. Kolába sends to E and G wards coolies, mill-hands and artizans of various kinds. From Surat come the Surati domestics of A ward and also artizans, coolies and shop-keepers, most of whom are to be found in C and D wards. From the Native States in Káthiáwár and from Cutch come the shop-keepers and artizans of B and C wards.

11. Outside the Presidency the principal stream of immigration sets in from the United Provinces which send us over 50,000, principally to the mills of Byculla and Tadwadi. Most of them come from the districts of Allahabad, Jaunpur and Azamghar. Rájputána is a poor second with 12,000, mostly shop-keepers in C ward from Jodhpur and Jaipur. The news that there was money to be made in keeping a shop in C ward seems to have spread to the neighbouring district of Merwára. We now find 6,000 immigrants from there, more than half of whom keep shops in C ward, whereas in 1891 the total immigrants into the Presidency from Ajmer-Merwára amounted to less than 2,000. Immigration from outside.

One more important source which Bombay taps is Goa. As is to be expected, the principal occupation of the 30,000 Goanese is domestic service. They are well distributed throughout the City but are found in the largest number in C Ward.

12. Of those born outside India nearly 6,000 come from the United Kingdom, over 2,000 each from Persia and Arabia and 1,000 from Afghanistan. With the exception of our own nationality the remaining European nations are but poorly represented; Germany with 257, Austria-Hungary with 206, Italy with 175 and France with 135 being the principal contributors. Full proportionate details of immigrants by wards will be found in Subsidiary Table V at the end of this Chapter. Europeans.

13. The proportion in Bombay-born has decreased from 23 per cent. in 1901 to under 20 per cent. This is not difficult to understand. In the plague exodus of ten years ago the immigrants who had homes near by to go to and who had only come in search of casual employment, naturally returned to them. The Bombay-born having no other home to go to, stayed where he was, or if he was wise removed to a plague camp in Mahim, Sewri or Sion. In either case he came within the enumerator's net. With the absence of dislocation from plague on the present occasion the foreign-born reasserted their supremacy. Decrease in Bombay born.

Subsidiary Table IV.

Showing the percentage of Increase (+) or Decrease (—) by Sections.

Section.	Variation per cent. since 1872.
Upper Colaba	— 53·49
Lower Colaba	+ 48·49
Fort South	+ 46·51
Fort North	— 14·57
Esplanade	+ 69·73
Chakla	— 34·06
Mandvi	— 5·41
Umarkhadi	— 8·41
Dongri	+ 6·61
Market	— 30·15
Dhobi Talao	+ 2·03
Fanaswadi	+ 32 00
Bhuleshwar	+ 1·19
Kumbharwada	+ 0·40
Khara talao	— 2·79
Khetwadi	+ 28·69
Girgaon	+ 44·95
Chaupati	+ 51·33
Walkeshwar	+ 37·45
Mahalaxmi	+509·27
Tardeo	+ 36·87
Kamatipura	— 21·80
First Nagpada	— 31·56
Second Nagpada	+ 36·29
Byculla	+158·79
Tadwadi	+181·90
Mazagaon	+ 43·40
Parel	+230·17
Sewri	+327·51
Sion	+165·12
Mahim	+113·08
Warli	+792·86
Harbour docks, etc.	+ 95·96
Town and Island	+ 51·99

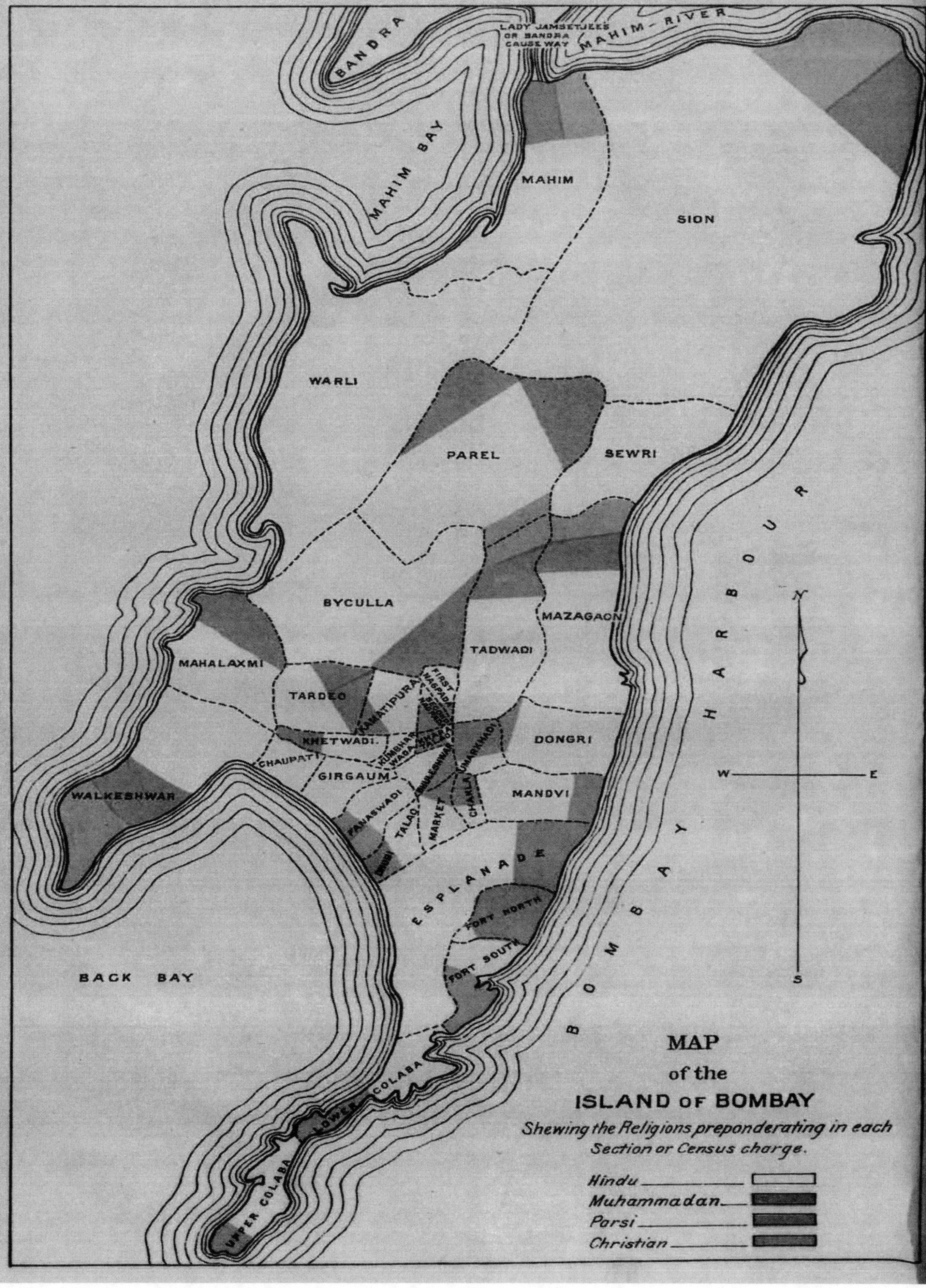

MAP
of the
ISLAND OF BOMBAY
Shewing the Religions preponderating in each Section or Census charge.

CHAPTER III.

Religion.

14. Table III contains the details of the various religions followed by the inhabitants of the Island, and an attempt has been made to represent the same pictorially in the map in the opposite page. It must not however be thought that the location of each religion shown in a section is exactly where it is depicted. For instance the Parsis of Parel are not all huddled up in the north-western corner of the section, nor are they separated by a deep gulf of Hindus from the Christians who are closing up with their co-religionists of Tadwadi. All that is meant by the colouring is that the coloured area represents proportionately the strength of the two or three principal religions in each section which may be either widely diffused throughout the area or closely massed in one locality The percentage and population of each religion will be found in the margin. The religions of the Island.

Table showing strength of each religion.

Religion.	Population.	Percentage of total population of Island.
Hindu	664,042	67·80
Musalman	179,346	18·31
Christian	57,355	5·85
Jain	20,460	2·09
Zoroastrian	50,931	5·20
Jew and others ...	7,311	0·75

Hindus constitute 68 per cent. of the total population, Muhammadans 18 per cent., Christians 6 per cent. and Zoroastrians 5 per cent. Two per cent. of the remainder are Jains and 1 per cent. Jews and others.

Whereas in 1901 Hindus had decreased from 66·1 to 65·5 per cent. of the total number they have now increased again to 67·8. A large portion of this increment must be due to the return of plague refugees. Hindus are represented in strength in every section and practically monopolize Warli, Sewri, Kumbharwada, Girgaon and Chaupati.

The Muhammadans now represent 18·31 per cent. of the people, a slight falling off from the 18·9 that they constituted in 1891 and a good deal less than the 20·07 that they registered in 1901. But as stated by Mr. Edwardes when others ran away from the plague they stood firm. They are to be found in greatest strength in the crowded quarters of Second Nagpada, Khara Talao, Umarkhadi, Chakla and Byculla. The number of Musalmán women per 1,000 males has fallen off from 617 to 507 which shows that either many of the unattached fled in 1901 or that many men unaccompanied by their womenfolk have since entered the island. The followers of Islam are weakest in Girgaum and Fanaswadi where they do not amount to 1 and 2 per cent. respectively.

The Christian and the Jew are gaining ground at the expense of the Parsi, slowly of course, but the advance is perceptible as the subjoined figures will show :—

	1881.	1891.	1901.	1911.
Christian	5·5	5·5	5·8	5·85
Parsi	6·3	5·8	5·9	5·20
Jew	0·5	0·6	0·6	0·67

It is not so much that the Christian is increasing as that the Parsi is decreasing. They have the lowest birth rate of any race and their numbers are only kept up by the lowness of their death rate.

Local distribution of religions.

15. Christians show in greatest number in Fort South, Colaba, Walkeshwar and Dhobi Talao, Mazagaon and Tadwadi, in all of which they exceed 10 per cent. of the population. They are also in strength in the Harbour, Docks and Military sections where they total nearly 5,000. They seem to avoid the Musalman quarter. The homeless Christians have increased from 119 to 186. The home of the Parsis is in the North Fort, Dhobi Talao and Khetwadi, where they number about 25 per cent. of the residents. Their numbers are negligible in B Ward, the Nagpadas and Sewri. The care they take of their poor is evinced by there being only 13 homeless Parsis on Census night.

Jains are found in strength only in the Market and Mandvi, where they constitute 15 and 8 per cent. respectively of the inhabitants. There are also a good number in Bhuleshwar and Umarkhadi. There were only 8 Jains returned as having no homes.

The Jews show an increase of 23 per cent. on the figures of 1901, but there has been a falling off in the proportions, so that it is possible that many males retired to their homes in Kolaba or Janjira, where the Bane Israel are numerous, on the outbreak of plague in 1901. They are found in largest numbers in Umarkhadi, Byculla and First Nagpada, but except in the last named, where they constitute 12 per cent. of the population, they are not numerous enough to affect the sectional totals.

Minor religions.

16. It remains to give a hasty glance at the other religions returned. There are 578 Buddhists ; they show an increase of 50 per cent. principally in Tardeo and Kamatipura. There are only 107 Sikhs, nearly all in Fort North and Walkeshwar. Of weird and uncommon religions less than usual were returned, only 29 altogether. The Brahmo and Arya Samaj seem to make but little footing in Bombay, though they are doing better in Sind. The reason is probably that caste rules are so lax in this city that the incentive to shed caste by joining one of these theistic religions is not present.

The number of females to 1,000 males in each religion is shown in the subjoined table.

SUBSIDIARY TABLE VI.

Proportion of females to 1,000 males of each religion.

Religion.	No. of females to 1,000 males.
Hindu	521·21
Musalman	507·31
Christian	486·54
Buddhist	360·00
Jain	329·00
Sikh	150·54
Zoroastrian	902·97
Jews and Others	880·78

CHAPTER IV.

AGE, SEX AND CIVIL CONDITION.

17. The particulars of Age, Sex and Civil Condition are given in Table IV. Owing to the prevalence of illiteracy the age return is very inaccurate, and there is a marked tendency to plump on round numbers which is not unknown in Europe. All multiples of ten are favourites, in a lesser degree the multiples of five and of four. In addition to these accidental mistakes there is the case of the Hindu spinster who ought to be married and is over 12 whose age is wilfully 'corrected' to a more decent figure. Age.

The series in a great city owing to the disturbing factors of children being born outside and immigrants being mostly over 20 when they come in is quite different to the age pyramid of the rural areas. In the latter if there are no disturbing factors and the population is either stationary or progressive the largest class should be the age group 0—5, and each succeeding age group should be less than the one preceding it. In a city it is different. Children are born outside and those that are born within the city precincts have a poorer chance of life. Therefore the age class 0—5 is smaller; immigrants come in after the age of 20 and therefore the age classes 20—30 are greater. The series in fact grows to a maximum and then decreases again. One curious fact is that old women are proportionately nearer to old men in number; in the mofussil they actually exceed them. The explanation is said to be that women are notorious for exaggerating their ages, but this theory is somehow not very convincing.

18. So much for the general population. The sex proportions are interesting and Subsidiary Table VII at the end of this chapter shows the proportion throughout the several age periods. As in the mofussil, more boys are born than girls, but being more delicate they are in defect during the first four years of life. After that, however, males are always the more numerous. The disproportion is very great between the ages of 10 and 50, the females frequently not amounting to 50 per cent. of the males. The causes are as follows:— Sex.

(*a*) There is a natural defect in women in the age class 10—15, due to early marriage and premature motherhood and unskilful midwifery; (*b*) when on the top of this women are sent away to their fathers' homes for their *accouchement* this defect becomes still more pronounced; and (*c*) the disparity is increased by the immigration of able-bodied males who have not brought their women-folk with them.

There is a curious proportion of the sexes at age period 20—25. In the mofussil women are actually in excess at that age, though they quickly revert to inferiority, and the same tendency is to be seen, though equality even is not reached, in the figures for Bombay. What the explanation is it is difficult to say. One might hazard a guess that the age period 20—25, when the young man is going out into the world or when the young able-bodied stranger enters the city, is the great change in his life as maternity is in a woman's, and that the change proves too much for him.

Sex proportion by religion.

19. The sex proportions of the different religions are given in Subsidiary Table VI at the end of the last chapter. It will be seen that the Pársis with 903 per 1,000 are easily first. They are inveterate town dwellers and their women probably hold a position with regard to men which is only equalled in the European races. There is no early marriage and there are excellent Pársi hospitals and maternity wards, all of which are factors in prolonging female life.

The Jews are very similarly situated, and the race has always been known to have a large proportion of females, and is permanently established in Bombay.

A long way behind comes the Hindu. These figures, as well as those for Muhammadans who come next, are kept low by the large number of immigrants. Probably, if the natural population only were taken, the positions of the Hindu and the Musalmán would be reversed; widow-marriage and adult marriage generally lead to a higher percentage of females amongst Muhammadans than amongst Hindus.

The shortage of Christian women is due to the disparity of the sexes among the European and kindred races, in which the males outnumber the females by two to one. With the Armenians—there are only 39 of them—the disparity is nearly three to one, and the Anglo-Indian community is not strong enough numerically to help in redressing the balance. The Goanese too does not bring his wife to service in Bombay.

The shortage in Jains is due to their being mostly birds of passage, who come down here to make a living by shop-keeping, and then return to Rájputána or Gujarát. The bulk of them do not make their homes here.

The other religions are too poorly represented to be worth examining.

There are 853 females per 1,000 males among the city-born and 529 among the foreign-born population.

Sex proportion by locality.

20. Subsidiary Table VIII shows by sections the proportion of females to 1,000 males and the same is represented pictorially in the map opposite this page.

The sex proportions in Upper Colába are a little difficult to understand, but it must be borne in mind that the troops are not included in the section but are classed with the harbour, docks, railways and homeless population. In Máhim the high proportion of females is due to the residential portion being largely agricultural, while the railway construction with its female carriers of earth that was then in progress in the north of the island is responsible for the figures in Sion. Both these sections also are havens of refuge for the Bombay-born, among whom the proportion of females is comparatively high. In the next class—from 600-650 per acre—Sewri has a large number of females on account of reclamation work; Dongri, Umarkhádi, Kámátipura and Second Nágpáda have many low-caste Hindus which always means a high proportion of females; Khetwádi and Tárdeo are large industrial centres in which women also are employed; Chaupáti and Girgaum are residential areas and Fort North is a Pársi area; Fort South, a mercantile and non-residential shopping centre, has naturally fewest females.

21. Let us now examine the civil condition of the whole population. Thirty-five per cent. is unmarried, 57 per cent. married and 8 per cent. widowed. Details by religion are given in the margin. It will be seen that the Hindu has the largest proportion of married and the Pársi the least. The Musalmán and the Jain, both of whom encourage adult marriage, come next, and the Christian and the Pársi tail off. A curious feature is the absence of Jain widows. Jains do not go in for widow re-marriage and should show a larger number than the Pársis, Musalmáns and Christians who allow it and the Hindus who do not universally disapprove of it. **Civil condition.**

Number per 1,000 of each religion who are

	Unmarried.	Married.	Widowed.
Hindu	31	61	8
Musalmán	37	55	8
Christian	52	41	7
Jain	37	58	5
Pársi	54	37	9
Total ...	35	57	9

22. In the marginal table will be found the variations of the population as a whole by civil condition during the last 30 years. The fluctuations are extreme, but it will be seen that there is very little change between the figures of 1891 and of 1911. It is necessary to ignore the figures of 1901, as the circumstances were abnormal, and the decrease in the married is probably due to the higher proportion of Musalmáns enumerated, who have a lower proportion of wives to husbands. **Fluctuations of the last 30 year.**

Table showing the unmarried, married and widowed per 1,000 of the population since 1881.

	1881.	1891.	1901.	1911.
Unmarried ...	336	349	354	345
Married ..	575	565	548	573
Widowed ...	89	86	98	82

23. Subsidiary Table IX shows the percentage of the population who are married, unmarried or widowed at each age period. Of the 56 infants who are married in the first year of life 42 are Hindus, 11 are Muhamadans; Pársis, Jains and Christians have one representative each. It may be noticed that there are 79 Christians under the age of 10 who are married. It may possibly be that they (or rather their parents) are recent converts and that the marriage was celebrated before their conversion. But if this theory is incorrect these early marriages show the influence of Hinduism on the other religions which are found in its midst. There are 25 per cent. more married Christians at this age (0-10) than Pársis. **Civil condition by religion.**

Of child-widows there are 80 under 10, and 23 widowers. Hindus, 65 and 19, provide the bulk of them. There are three Pársi and three Christian widows and 9 Muhammadans.

Subsidiary Table VII.

Showing the number of females per 1,000 males at each age period.

Age.	No. of females to 1,000 males at each age period.
0—1	900
1—2	1,010
2—3	1,030
3—4	1,056
4—5	962
0—5	990
5—10	915
10—15	582
15—20	553
20—25	531
25—30	416
30—35	388
35—40	346
40—45	450
45—50	507
50—55	629
55—60	636
60 and over	835

Subsidiary Table VIII.

Showing the number of females to 1,000 males.

Sections.	Number of females to 1,000 males.
Upper Colába	791·71
Lower Colába	45[illegible]·19
Fort South	225·49
Fort North	681·97
Esplanade	415·90
Chakla	536·72
Mándvi	423·94
Umarkhádi	603·28
Dongri	604·12
Market	370·77
Dhobi Tálao	568·06
Fanaswádi	511 89
Bhuleshwár	475·30
Kumbhárwáda	546·96
Khará Tálao	526·64
Khetwádi	608·92
Girgaum	606·76
Chaupáti	607·93
Walkeshwar	545·84
Mahalaxmi	583·69
Tardeo	610·00
Kámátipura	631·71
First Nágpáda	533·72
Second Nágpáda	629·01
Byculla	580·55
Tádwádi	566·84
Mazagaon	550·42
Parel	575·78
Sewri	610·25
Sion	661·70
Máhim	668·87
Warli	532·87
Harbours, Docks etc.	125·52
Bombay Town and Island	529·69

SUBSIDIARY TABLE IX.

Showing percentage of unmarried, married and widowed at each age period to total population of the Island.

Age.	Unmarried.	Married.	Widowed.
0—1	1·40	......	......
1—2	·87	·01	......
2—3	1·49	·02	......
3—4	1·46	·03	......
4—5	1·40	·03	......
0—5	6·62	·09	......
5—10	6·44	·28	·01
10—15	6·15	1·59	·04
15—20	5·79	4·90	·15
20—25	4·65	9·97	·42
25—30	2·59	12·10	·70
30—35	1·14	10·40	·97
35—40	·50	6·60	·90
40—45	·31	5·26	1·34
45—50	·13	2·23	·78
50—55	·10	2·01	1·18
55—60	·03	·63	·39
60 and over	·08	1·24	1·34

CHAPTER V.

EDUCATION.

24. Details of Education will be found in Table V which also combines in one table religion and age. The age periods selected are those mostly concerned with education :— 0—10, when the child is hardly commencing schooling, 10—15 and 15—20 when he should be hard at work, and 20 and over when his primary education is presumably finished. Reference to table.

25. On the present occasion a rather important difference in the definition of literacy has affected the figures materially. In 1891 a distinction was drawn between the literate, the learners and the illiterate. In 1901 the triple division was discarded and literacy was defined as the ability to read and write any one language. In 1911 the standard of literacy was fixed and the words 'a letter' inserted after 'write'. A small difference, but it wiped out the man who could only sign his name, the man who could only read a printed book and many school children in the elementary and infant classes. Scope of the statistics.

In spite of the more stringent definition 23 per cent. (nearly) were returned as literate. This compared with the 19·06 per cent. of 1891 is quite a satisfactory result. Literate males represent 18 per cent. of the population and literate females 5 per cent., and 28 males in every hundred males and 12 females in every hundred females are literate. Some further details by age periods will be found in Subsidiary Table X.

26. The followers of the Zoroastrian religion show the highest figures of literacy with 74 per cent. There are only 13,477 Pársis who are unable to read and write a letter, of whom quite a half are still under instruction. There are still a few old conservatives who are illiterate, but the age group 20 and over should show practically no illiterates in 1921. Two Pársi females in three are literate. Education by religion.

Next to the Pársi comes the Jain. A trader by profession and hailing from Gujarát, the most literate division of the Presidency, it is natural that he should stand high on the ladder of education. Seventy per cent. of their males are literate, but only 16 per cent. of their women. Of the sexes combined 57 per cent. are educated.

Just half the Christian population can read and write a letter. The difference in education between the women and the men is small, 54 per cent. of the males and 41 per cent. of the females being literate.

The Jew shows nearly the same figure, but is weaker in respect of literate females.

The Hindu and the Musalmán are nearly side by side at the foot of the ladder, with the Musalmán slightly the worse in position on account of the backwardness of females; the proportion of literate males to the male population is the same in both races.

27. In English education the Christian with his foreign born nucleus naturally comes first with 40 per cent., closely followed by the Pársi with 39. The Jew shows 32 per cent. and then comes a wide gap before we come to the Literacy in English.

Jain with 6, the Hindu with 5 and the Musalmán with a good deal less than 3 persons in every hundred capable of reading and writing an English letter. For the City as a whole, 83 persons in a 1,000 are able both to read and write English compared with 70 *per mille* in 1901. These figures show the great progress made in education, both English and Vernacular, male and female during the past *decennium*.

Religion.	Literates per 100 co-religionists.		Literates in English per 100 co-religionists.	
	1901.	1911.	1901.	1911.
Hindu	11	17	3	5
Musalmán	13	16	2	3
Christian	53	50	46	40
Jain	53	57	2	6
Zoroastrian... ...	67	74	31	39

The progress during the decade made by the followers of the different religions both in literacy and in knowledge of English is seen at a glance in the marginal table. The Pársi and the Hindu have made most progress while the Christian has retrograded.

SUBSIDIARY TABLE X.

Showing the proportion borne by Male and Female Literate, Illiterate and Literate in English to the population at each age period.

Age period.	Sex.	Literate.	Illiterate.	Literate in English.
All ages ...	Males ...	28·23	71·77	10·52
	Females ...	12·31	87·69	4·00
0—10 ...	Males ...	8·59	91·41	1·72
	Females ...	5·25	94·75	1·28
10—15 ...	Males ...	29·64	70·36	9·63
	Females ...	18·34	81·66	5·71
15—20 ...	Males ...	31·44	68·56	12·46
	Females ...	16·23	83·77	5·56
20 and over ...	Males ...	30·50	69·50	11·63
	Females ...	12·96	87·04	4·32

CHAPTER VI.

LANGUAGE.

28. On the present occasion the language details were not compiled for each section, and the figures available are for the City as a whole and are reproduced as Subsidiary Table XI at the end of this chapter. **Principal vernaculars of the City.**

The principal language is of course Maráthi. With such a large immigrant population from Ratnágiri, Kolába, Poona and Sátára it could be nothing else. Maráthi includes the dialects of Konkani, Gomántaki and Firangi.

Next in importance is Gujaráti which is the commercial language of Bombay and is spoken by 21 per cent. of the population.

Hindustáni ranks third. With Western Hindi, of which it is a branch, the speakers number 15 per cent. It includes the dialect of Musalmáni and is spoken by the 50,000 immigrants from the United Provinces and many other Muhammadan tribes. The Konkani Musalmán of mixed Arab descent, who is numerous in Bombay, speaks Konkani, not Hindustáni. The only other language of numerical importance is Sindhi, in which is included Kachchhi, the language of the Memons, the Khojás and the Osvál Vánis. It is very difficult to place Kachchhi. Sometimes it has been classed as a Gujaráti, sometimes as a Sindhi, dialect. It is in reality a separate language, half way between Gujaráti and Sindhi and in conformity with the geographical position of its land of origin.

Speakers of Kachchhi number 25,925 males and only 14,542 females; apparently the immigants from Cutch, mostly shopkeepers, do not bring their wives with them.

29. Nearly 20,000 speak English in their homes as compared with 16,000 who have returned themselves as European and Anglo-Indian by race. The balance are probably Indian Christians of good family and Pársis. **English.**

30. Rájastháni is the language of the Márwári shop-keeper, and Portuguese of the few pure Portuguese (there are 33 who have given Portugal as their birth-place) and of the better class Indian Christian from Goa and the mainland of Thána. **Outside vernaculars.**

Támil is spoken by some 3,000 persons and Telugu by about 8,000, most of whom live in Kámátipura and hail from Hyderábád State.

Arabic spoken by 2,900 individuals is almost entirely a language of the docks and of those whose life is spent on ships, and the same is true of the 50 odd persons who talk African languages.

Subsidiary Table XI.

Languages of Bombay City.

Languages.	Persons.	Males.	Females.
Indian Languages—			
Bhil dialect	1	1	......
Gipsy languages	5	5	......
Gujaráti	205,376	131,053	74,323
Hindustáni	81,153	56,835	24,318
Kánarese	2,609	2,017	592
Maráthi	525,606	334,102	191,504
Sindhi	41,916	27,047	14,869
Sindhi (proper)	1,449	1,122	327
Kachchhi	40,467	25,925	14,542
Western Hindi	64,134	47,796	16,338
Panjábi	1,483	1,321	162
Rájasthání	9,209	8,011	1,198
Balochi	541	405	136
Pashto	2,119	1,897	222
Támil	3,061	2,180	881
Telugu	7,923	4,539	3,384
Other Indian languages ...	2,516	2,077	439
Arabic Languages—			
Arabic	2,864	2,176	688
Persian	2,746	1,856	890
Other Asiatic languages ...	1,206	850	356
European Languages—			
English	19,458	12,301	7,157
Portuguese	4,410	3,015	1,395
Other European languages ...	1,058	766	292
African Languages	51	38	13

CHAPTER VII.

INFIRMITIES.

31. The four infirmities of which the Census took cognizance were the same as on the last occasion, insanity, deaf-mutism from birth, blindness and leprosy. The figures, which were not compiled by sections or wards, are to be found in Imperial Table XI of the Provincial Census Report (Vol. VII, Part II). Details of the afflicted.

The total number of afflicted was 1,364, distributed as follows :—

Infirmity.	Persons.	Males.	Females.
Insane	225	152	73
Deaf-mute	180	130	50
Blind	453	324	129
Leper	506	352	154
Total ...	1,364	958	406

There has been a decrease of 79 infirm since 1901. Insanity has decreased 41, deaf-mutism 5 and blindness 6 per cent. On the other hand lepers with an increase of nearly 3 per cent. are now the most important infirmity.

32. The insanity figures are slightly misleading owing to the number of Europeans in the Colába Asylum. This being the only European asylum in the Presidency many of the inmates are not really Bombay residents but come from the mofussil. Insanity.

33. There are almost certainly more deaf-mutes than figure in the return. This is a congenital infirmity, which cannot be developed, except by mutilation, and the age figures should show a descending series, but the maximum is not reached until the 10—15 age group. Parents are naturally averse to returning their children as deaf and dumb so long as there is any chance of speech, but the 29 infants in the Presidency (figures were not separately abstracted for Bombay City), who, being below the age of one year, have been returned as deaf-mutes cannot have given any indications that they would eventually remain so all their lives. Presumably if they were only deaf they would come within the definition as they would hardly have got the power of speech by then and the intelligent enumerator would promptly enroll them as infirm. Deaf-mutism.

34. Blindness is largely caused by ophthalmia which itself is generally a disease of dirt. It is most prevalent in Sind, Pálanpur and Cutch where it reaches the extraordinary figure of 348 per 100,000. The prevalence in Bombay City which works out to 46 per 100,000 is therefore satisfactory. Blindness.

35. The increase in leprosy is in common with the general increase throughout the Presidency. It is not due to an increase in the number of Leprosy.

lepers detained in the Acworth Asylum at Mátunga which shows an actual decrease from 363 to 294. It is commonest in the Deccan districts of East Khándesh and Sátára, not prevalent in the Karnátak and rarely met with in Sind. As Sind and the Karnátak do not send many emigrants to our City it may account for the incidence of leprosy in the population being some 37 per cent. higher in the City than in the Presidency at large. There is, however, always a tendency for the infirm to collect in a wealthy city where private charity is largely dispensed. The Leper Act was extended to the Island of Bombay after the census was taken, so it is too early yet to secure results.

The causation of this loathsome disease is still unknown. It cannot be caused only by eating rotten fish, as Bráhmans are not immune though none of them, not even the Shenvis, eat dried fish. On the other hand the Indian Christian is exceedingly fond of sun-dried fish, often badly cured, and it is amongst this race that leprosy is most virulent, though their manner of living and habits of life may have something to do with it.

CHAPTER VIII.

CASTE, TRIBE AND RACE.

36. The principal castes, tribes and races of the Presidency which are represented in Bombay City are shown in Subsidiary Table XII appended to this Chapter. The remaining 99,000 are either castes that are numerically unimportant or immigrants from other parts of the world whose caste or race has no counterpart in this Presidency. At the present census all castes were not compiled for, only those that were either of local or general importance and amounting to at least two per mille of the district or Presidency total. Meaning of the table.

In the case of Bráhmans and Vánis the principal sub-castes only have been shown, the remainder being collected together under the heading "others." As the basis of the table is religion, castes, which occur under two religions like the Khatris and Telis who are either Hindu or Musalmán, and the Shrimáli and Osvál Vánis, who may be either Hindu or Jain, find a place under both religions.

37. In numerical supremacy no caste can touch the Marátha who with 231,000 easily heads the poll. Under this head are grouped together both the Deccani and the Konkani branches of the Marátha tribe, while the Kunbi Marátha is shown separately under Kunbi, in which latter group are also included some of the Gujarát Kunbi sub-castes. This is an increase of 17,000 on the totals of ten years ago but that total included Kunbis. Maráthas.

38. Next come the Sheikhs with 74,000. These include a variety of Muhammadans, many of whom are recent converts. One numerous and important tribe, the Konkanis or Naváyats, do not appear in the return, but must be included in this category, though their conversion to Islam dates back before the time of their peaceful entry as Arab traders into this country. They have decreased 15,000 since 1901. Sheikhs.

39. The Mahárs, Holiyas or Dheds, who represent the untouchables under names which vary according to the locality from which they come, are third on the list with 58,000. They fall into two classes, the Surati Dheds who earn a living as butlers and hamáls to the European community and those from the Deccan who work as mill-hands. Both of these classes are rising superior to the position to which they have been relegated by the Code of Manu. They have increased 11,000 or 23 per cent., and are in addition materially prosperous. Mahárs.

40. The Parsis come fourth with 51,000, an increase of 10 per cent. This increase is entirely due to a lower mortality rate and immigration; the birth rate is declining. Parsis.

41. Bráhmans of various denomination amount to nearly 54,000, of which the leading sub-caste is the Gaud Sárasvat. This term includes also the Konkani speaking Sárasvat (not to be confused with Sarsudh or Sárasvat Bráhman of Sind and the North). These two groups are again apparently coalescing after a schism, it is said, of four hundred years. The amalgamation Bráhmans.

is not yet an accomplished fact, but it is understood that the intellectual leaders of both communities desire it. The movement has been afoot for the last three years but as yet there has been no intermarriage.

Vánis.

42. There are just over 36,000 Hindu Vánis and just under 20,000 Jains of the same functional group. The difference of religion is curiously enough not a bar to marriage. This is a large increase, 24 per cent. on the figures of 1901, but it is believed that large numbers of Jains left the City in that year on account of the plague.

Bhandáris.

43. The Bhandáris, Konkan dwellers from Ratnágiri and Kolába, many of whom sail country craft coastwise, have increased 71 per cent. and show the most rapid growth of any of the important castes. They now number nearly 29,000. The Chámbhárs and Mochis, the leather workers of the City, have increased 15 per cent.

Weaving castes.

44. The local weaving community, the Bhavsars, Kshattriyas and Koshtis of 1901 have increased over 50 per cent. In view of the development of the textile trade this is not surprising. The first-named are not weavers but have been mentioned here as being calico-printers; they are closely connected with the manufacture of cotton goods. Owing to every caste not being returned this time it is a little difficult to check progress; probably the increase is even greater.

Kolis.

45. There is a decrease of nearly 25 per cent. in the Kolis. Koli is such a comprehensive term embracing the members of a ruling house, wild jungle tribes and the fishermen of the mainland and of the seven isles of Bombay itself, that it is rather difficult to say where the falling off has been. If one might hazard a guess it is probably among the Gujarát Kolis who must have migrated in numbers from the famine in their own country in 1901 whereas there was not the same inducement to leave their homes in 1911.

Lohánás.

46. The great trading caste of Lohánás has increased 35 per cent. They appear to have migrated in great numbers from Surat and Cutch, both of which areas show a heavy loss since last census. The Cutchi ones appear to have left their wives behind; there are actually 1,300 more Loháná women in Cutch than men.

Sonárs.

47. The last of the important caste is the Sonár. As their homes are mostly in Surat and the Konkan they probably fled in large numbers from the plague in 1901. They have of recent years aimed at recognition as Devadnya Bráhmans, but the voice of public opinion is against their claim.

Musalmán.

48. Of the Musalmán trading tribes the increase in number of the Bohoras and Khojas is counterbalanced by the decrease amongst the Memons.

Jews.

49. The Jews have increased 29 per cent. About three-quarters of them are Beni-Israels who are very numerous on the seacoast of Kolába and the Native State of Janjira.

Europeans and kindred races.

50. Turning to the European population the figures of which will be found in Table VIII it will be seen that Europeans have decreased slightly, a matter of 400, and Anglo-Indians have increased by 930. Armenians have fallen from 72 to 39. It is believed that the Armenian business man feels the competition of the Parsi excessively, is gradually being pushed out and is migrating to Calcutta where the game of business is not played so keenly.

Subsidiary Table XII.

Showing the Principal Castes in Bombay City.

Caste.	Persons.	Males.	Females.
Hindu—			
Bhandári	28,846	18,292	10,554
Bhangi or Halálkhor	5,645	3,415	2,230
Bharvád, Dhangar or Kurub	1,292	797	495
Bhátiá	7,780	4,554	3,226
Bhil	46	37	9
Bhoi	1,601	1,341	260
Bráhman Audich	5,092	3,896	1,196
„ Chitpávan	8,104	5,255	2,849
„ Deshasth	4,876	3,264	1,612
„ Gaud Sárasvat	9,691	6,115	3,576
„ Others	25,893	19,634	6,259
Chámbhár or Mochi	21,305	12,604	8,701
Chhatri, Khatri, Kshatri, Kiliket or Katabu .	10,406	6,430	3,976
Darji, Shimpi, Sai or Mirai	8,190	5,154	3,036
Dhobi, Parit, Agasá or Madivál ...	5,720	3,773	1,947
Dhodiá	11	11	......
Dublá or Talávia	637	502	135
Gavli	5,962	4,043	1,919
Gavandi, Uppár or Chunára	110	79	31
Gurav	1,351	871	480
Hajám, Nhávi or Nádig	4,526	3,214	1,312
Kaikádi	14	10	4
Kalál or Kalon	15	12	3
Kámáti	3,370	1,835	1,535
Kasár	1,174	757	417
Kátkari	10	1	9
Káyasth Prabhu	5,090	2,742	2,348
Khárva	716	603	113
Khárvi	4,870	3,544	1,326
Koli	12,602	8,547	4,055
Komti or Vaishya	6,578	4,378	2,200
Koshti, Hutgár, Jed or Vinkár ...	542	304	238
Kumbhár	3,798	2,419	1,379
Kunbi	14,458	10,763	3,695
Lingáyat	1,179	769	410
Loháná	14,364	10,107	4,257
Lohár or Kammár	4,935	3,454	1,481
Mahár, Holiya or Dhed	57,855	34,811	23,044
Máli	6,480	3,730	2,750
Máng or Madig	4,247	2,311	1,936
Marátha	231,924	153,045	78,879
Naikda	51	47	4
Panchál	270	185	85
Pátane Prabhu	2,359	1,348	1,011
Rájput	4,006	2,978	1,028
Rámoshi	267	181	86
Rávalia or Rával	117	74	43
Sáli or Sálvi	1,353	749	604
Sangera	4	......	4
Soni, Sonár or Aksáli	12,259	7,358	4,901
Sutár or Badig	6,950	4,567	2,383
Teli or Ghánchi	4,782	2,928	1,854
Thákur	2,822	2,497	325
Vaddar or Od	34	21	13
Vághri	802	559	243
Vaiti	196	122	74
Vani Kapol	2,594	1,739	855
„ Marátha	1,236	751	485
„ Osvál	3,169	2,520	649
„ Proper	28,342	19,067	9,275
„ Shrimáli	923	585	338
Vanjári	1,977	1,129	848
Várli	9	9	......

SUBSIDIARY TABLE XII—*continued.*

Showing the Principal Castes in Bombay City—continued.

Caste.	Persons.	Males.	Females.
JAIN—			
Vani Osvál	5,051	3,670	1,381
„ Proper	6,154	4,607	1,547
„ Shrimáli	1,008	677	331
„ Unspecified	7,316	5,794	1,522
MUSALMAN—			
Arab	1,191	967	224
Bohora	13,272	8,436	4,836
Khatri	2,358	1,350	1,008
Khoja	12,243	6,538	5,705
Memon	15,381	8,739	6,642
Pathan	11,106	8,058	3,048
Sayad	8,135	5,485	2,650
Sheikh	73,949	52,427	21,522
Teli	2,901	963	1,938
CHRISTIAN—			
European British Subjects	10,131	6,821	3,310
„ Others	1,724	1,262	462
Anglo Indians	4,188	2,323	1,865
Armenians	39	28	11
Goanese	17,315	13,819	3,496
Indian Christians	23,958	14,330	9,628
ZOROASTRIAN	50,931	26,764	24,167
JEW	5,957	3,505	3,092
ANIMISTIC	6	4	2

CHAPTER IX.

Occupation or Means of Livelihood.

51. There were some important differences in the occupational columns of the schedule compared with 1901. An attempt was then made to ascertain the home occupations of the huge immigrant population. In 1911 this attempt was given up and the schedule did not differ in the occupational columns from that in use in the mofussil. There were three columns dealing with occupation, one for the main occupation of actual workers, another for their subsidiary occupation, and lastly a column for dependant's means of subsistence. **Differences in Classification. 1901—1911.**

In addition, an industrial census was taken of all concerns which employed more than 20 hands on the 10th March. The schedules were, however, filled in by the heads of the businesses themselves though they were afterwards collected by the regular census staff.

The results of this census are to be found in Imperial Table XV-E, printed in Vol. VII, Part II.

Another important improvement on this occasion was the adoption of Dr. J. Bertillon's scheme of classification. The objection to the 1901 classification which extended to 520 groups was its extreme minuteness, which was unsuited to the economic conditions of India as well as impossible to work with the very vague information that was available from the schedules. The great obstacle to a change is that it vitiates comparison with former census figures. But the classification now adopted was similar on broad lines to the classification of ten years ago, and it was therefore possible by taking proportionate figures to subdivide fifty or so group s that did not tally accurately. There are 169 groups in the present classification divided into the four main classes, raw-material, manufacture, distribution and miscellaneous.

52. The statistics are to be found in Table VII. In the City of Bombay 596,000 persons are workers or 61 per cent. and 383,000 are dependants. Agriculture, which bulks so large in the statistics of occupation for the Presidency generally, only supports 20,000 persons, of whom 5,600 are growers of special products, such as the cocoanut-gardeners of Mahim, and 3,900 are dairy farmers. **Details of occupations. Agriculture.**

53. Fishing supports 5,000 persons, while a solitary individual lives by hunting. He must have been a stranger caught unawares in the enumeration as the days of Bombay as a game preserve are long past. **Fishing and Hunting.**

54. Of extraction of minerals there is very little; those who figure in group 16 are mostly coal-brokers, while in group 18 are the 1,300 who are dependent on quarries of lime-stone and building materials. **Extraction of Minerals.**

55. The importance of the textile industry is well shown in this table. There are 93,000 workers in textiles in the City and 174,000 are dependent on textiles for a livelihood. Twenty-two per cent. of the Hindu population is dependent on this industry, 13 per cent. of the Musalmán, 6 per cent. of the Parsi, 1½ per cent. of the Christian, and less than 1 per cent. of the Jain. The last named, however, is not a producer but a retailer, so it was not to be expected **Textiles.**

that he would have a large share in cotton manufacture. The bulk of the textile industry is centred in cotton spinning and weaving.

Leather.

56. Industries connected with hides and leather support 2,300 persons. With the exception of 260 Hindus the trade is almost entirely in the hands of the Muhammadan The leather trade of India is chiefly centred in Calcutta and Karáchi, and hides do not come along in large numbers to Bombay.

Timber, pottery, chemical products, food.

57. About 3 per cent. of the population is dependent on the timber trade, mostly in the fashioning of timber and carpentry, while 14,000 are dependent on metals.

Of potters and brickmakers there are just one thousand, nearly all Hindus.

Chemical products, chiefly the oil trade, employ only 522 persons and food industries 16,000. Of these the butchers, who are mostly Musalmán, form the largest section, followed by the sweetmeat workers, a Hindu trade.

Dress.

58. Hindus, Christians and Muhammadans take up nearly all the dress trade, the first named having by far the greatest share. It will be noticed that washing clothes is not such a female occupation as it is in Europe. There are four female barbers amongst the Muhammadans.

Building trades.

In the building trade which supports over 12,000 individuals the Hindu again asserts his numerical superiority, with a 50 per cent. advantage over the Musalmán.

Boat-building.

60. Boat-building is apparently not a flourishing trade. Whereas Parsi names are intimately connected with the building of the old Indian Navy, there is now not a single Zoroastrian engaged in ship-building or boat-building. Musalmáns with 21 workers, all males, have a virtual monopoly of this decayed industry.

Literature, Arts and Sciences.

61. Two-thirds of the printers and nine-tenths of the jewellers are Hindus, the Parsis with 1,600 coming second in the printing trade and Musalmáns second in the jewellery line.

Transport Industries.

62. Nearly 50,000 are connected with the harbour works, dockyards, and ships and all the miscellaneous marine occupations which are grouped under the head of Transport by water. 36,500 are dependent on road transport, including the upkeep of the roads, and messengers and 31,500 get a livelihood from the railways while the Post Office and its now amalgamated sister services the Telegraph and the Telephone support another 5,500. Altogether 12½ per cent. of the population are supported by Transport industries.

Banks and export trade.

63. In the Banking business which supports nearly 8,000 persons the Hindus show the way, followed by the Jains, and then the Parsis and the Musalmáns and Christians last. The Musalmán however ranks second to the Hindu in the matter of export trade and brokerage, though he is a long way behind the latter.

Trade Textiles.

64. As one would expect the principal branch of trade is in textiles which supports 19,000 persons, the Hindus being twice as numerous as the Musalmáns. Metals support twice the number who live by wood, and there is

a single individual who returns his trade as pottery. Probably there are many others who are sellers of pots and not makers as well.

65. Hotels, cookshops and the like are doing well but the successful ones are the large body of men who cater for the requirements of the Indian and not the population of the European hotels. **Hotels, Cafes, Restaurants.**

66. Of the 44,000 who exist by trade in food-stuffs it is rather curious to find that one-fourth are dependent on the sale of vegetables, fruit and spices, while another one-fourth live by grain-dealing. Twenty-three per cent. are dependent on salt, vegetable oil and similar groceries, and 11 per cent. on the sale of dairy produce. Fish dealing, it may be noticed, is a female occupation, the females engaged in it outnumbering the males by 4 to 1. **Food-stuffs.**

67. Of the other trades the most important is fuel, with 6,500 dependent on it. There are 8,000 persons who deal in articles of luxury, 5,000 of whom are jewellers. Order 41 is the order into which all those trades which are insufficiently described are placed. This would have been very much larger if it had not been for the Commercial Directory which was of use in clearing up many doubtful and ambiguous entries. **Other trades.**

68. We now come to the public administration. Of the 2,930 soldiers who constitute the Army in Bombay, 1,057 are Hindus, 482 are Musalmáns and 1,358 are Christians. The Navy is almost entirely Christian. The Police force with the exception of 103 Englishmen is largely Hindu, though there is a good contribution of Muhammadans. **Public Administration and the Liberal Arts.**

Of those dependent on administration 10,000 were in the service of the State and 10,000 in Municipal service.

It is rather a surprise to find that Religion supports nearly 8,000 where Law only protects 3,000. The number of Parsi ministers of religion is 733, which appears to be rather a large number to look after the spiritual welfare of 50,000 people. Doctors, dentists, and the like number with their dependants 6,600; many of them are women.

School-masters and professors number 2,169 and the actual workers (male) in the Letters and Sciences number 5,850, half of whom are Hindus.

20,500 persons are not obliged to work for their living.

69. Of the 264,000 classed under this sub-class, domestic service accounts for 72,000, and the balance consists almost entirely of the insufficiently described. This is rather more than should be shown in this order but it is good evidence of the difficulty the enumerator feels in recording occupation. It must be remembered also that the schedules in Bombay City were all in English and many entries were therefore written unintelligibly when they could have been quite easily shown in the vernacular. Frequently it was necessary to retranslate the English back literally into the vernacular to ascertain what the entry meant. One entry that occurred was "a seller of bad things" which with a little puzzling out resolved itself into the 'old clo' man! **Class D—Miscellaneous.**

The sweepers are nearly all Hindus.

The number of the unproductive and disreputable classes amount to 12,000, about $1\frac{1}{2}$ per cent. of the population returned.

CHAPTER X.

SPECIAL BOMBAY TABLES.

70. Tables IX to XV are special tables compiled for Bombay City with the intention of casting some light on the housing problem and showing the areas where overcrowding is most common. **Some statistics of overcrowding and size and nature of buildings.**

In the last Census Report Mr. Edwardes went into the matter of figures in great detail, section by section. The Improvement Trust had then been only recently constituted and this information was of considerable value to it. But now more than ten years have elapsed and the Improvement Trust officials are in a better position to know the details and to analyse the figures shown up by this census than any writer of a report.

Suffice it to say that Byculla and Tadwadi are *par excellence* mill areas, and Dongri and Market are rapidly approaching their figures. There are 4 chals in Mandvi with over 400 persons each, 7 in Umarkhadi, 4 in Tardeo, 6 in Byculla, 6 in Parel and 6 in Warli. Altogether there are 56 chals of this size or over in the City.

76 per cent. of the population lives in one-room tenements. There are over 166,000 of these tenements and the average number of persons per room is 4·47. Persons living in five and six room tenements average 1·43 and 1·45 persons per room.

The reader who is interested in statistics and in the question of overcrowding will find material for thought in perusing the details contained in the tables relating to buildings. To the Improvement Trust those details must be particularly valuable, but they have already carefully scrutinized them and I do not propose to discuss them any further.

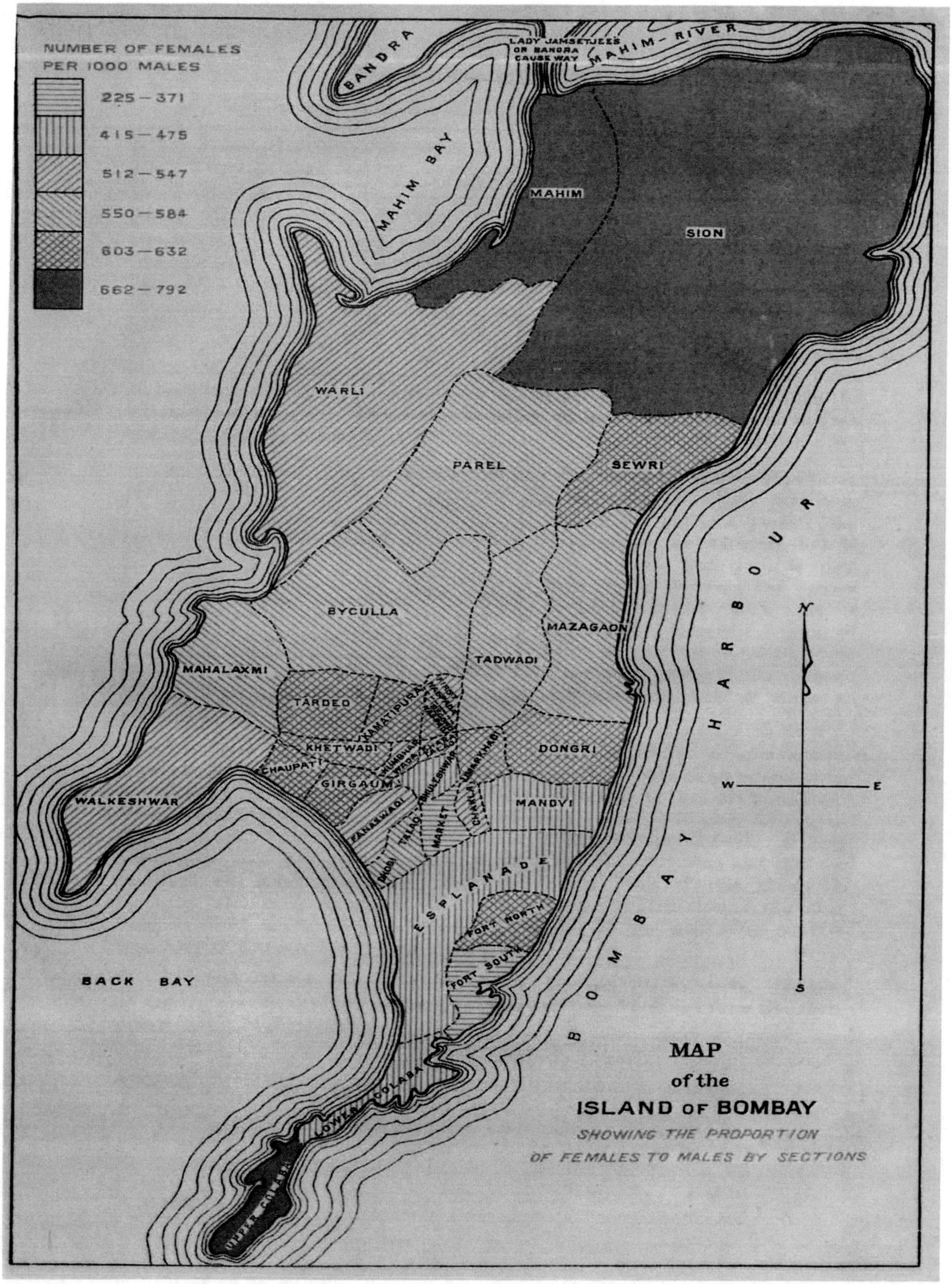

MAP
of the
ISLAND OF BOMBAY
SHOWING THE PROPORTION OF FEMALES TO MALES BY SECTIONS

PART II.

TABLES.

BOMBAY

(TOWN AND ISLAND).

TABLE I (CORRESPONDING TO IMPERIAL TABLE I).

AREA, HOUSES AND POPULATION.

B 1038—1 ←

TABLE I.

Area, Houses and Population.

Section.		Area in Acres.	Houses.			Population.		
						Persons.		
			Total.	Occupied.	Unoccupied.	Total.	Males.	Females.
1		2	3	4	5	6	7	8
Bombay City ...		14,575·51	45,716	37,932	7,784	979,445	640,288	339,157
A Ward ...	Upper Colába ...	144·19	114	76	38	1,557	869	688
	Lower Colába ...	282·46	1,082	716	366	19,679	13,514	6,165
	Fort, South ...	131·70	414	395	19	3,462	2,825	637
	Fort, North ...	161·29	1,227	1,161	66	25,400	15,564	9,836
	Esplanade ...	677·44	756	576	180	17,761	12,544	5,217
B Ward ...	Chakla ...	51·58	911	894	17	24,231	15,768	8,463
	Mándvi ...	164·66	1,130	1,101	29	33,202	23,317	9,885
	Umarkhádi ...	105·33	1,156	1,101	55	45,679	28,491	17,188
	Dongri ...	285·47	659	589	70	27,246	16,985	10,261
C Ward ...	Market ...	89·11	1,257	1,042	215	30,172	22,011	8,161
	Dhobi Taláo ...	99·69	1,382	1,259	123	38,684	24,670	14,014
	Fanaswádi ...	125·23	929	830	99	27,403	18,125	9,278
	Bhuleshwar ...	75·79	1,320	1,238	82	36,459	24,713	11,746
	Kumbhárwáda ...	46·06	712	683	29	27,703	17,908	9,795
	Khára Taláo ...	41·64	680	654	26	22,979	15,052	7,927
D Ward ...	Khetwádi ...	170·30	1,371	1,239	132	31,937	19,850	12,087
	Girgaum ...	124·60	1,197	1,115	82	30,779	19,156	11,623
	Chaupáti ...	111·77	799	731	68	11,397	7,088	4,309
	Wálkeshwar ...	545·43	1,554	1,209	345	10,640	6,883	3,757
	Mahálaxmi ...	642·01	1,767	1,478	289	26,302	16,608	9,694
E Ward ...	Tárdeo ...	228·68	934	741	193	27,758	17,241	10,517
	Kámátipura ...	66·14	1,146	1,093	53	36,751	22,523	14,228
	First Nágpada ...	29·00	111	100	11	6,414	4,182	2,232
	Second Nágpada .	34·00	542	498	44	21,700	13,321	8,379
	Byculla ...	511·52	2,661	2,338	323	75,348	47,672	27,676
	Tádwádi ...	479·68	1,743	958	785	28,424	18,141	10,283
	Mázagaon ...	728·67	2,093	1,739	354	30,075	19,398	10,677
F Ward ...	Parel ...	552·45	2,057	1,612	415	45,474	28,858	16,616
	Sewri ...	506·07	1,643	1,403	240	19,067	11,841	7,226
	Sion ...	4,261·08	3,350	2,405	945	30,680	18,463	12,217
G Ward ...	Máhim ...	1,286·23	4,085	3,057	1,028	30,492	18,271	12,221
	Warli ...	1,815·64	4,934	3,871	1,063	89,611	58,473	31,138
Harbour and Docks, Railways, Military and Homeless ...		...	...	...	...	44,979	39,963	5,016

TABLE II—(CORRESPONDING TO IMPERIAL TABLE II).

VARIATION IN POPULATION SINCE 1872.

TABLE II.

VARIATION IN POPULATION SINCE 1872.

Section.	Persons.					Males.			
	1911.	1901.	1891.	1881.	1872.	1911.	1901.	1891.	1881.
1	2	3	4	5	6	7	8	9	10
Bombay City ...	979,445	776,006	821,764	773,196	644,405	640,288	479,786	518,093	464,763
A Ward. Upper Colába ...	1,557	3,956	4,335	2,867	3,348	869	2,758	3,155	1,848
Lower Colába ...	19,679	13,023	13,622	14,266	18,253	13,514	8,109	8,759	8,855
Fort, South ...	3,462	3,309	3,951	3,515	2,363	2,825	2,660	3,064	2,633
Fort, North ...	25,400	22,956	32,847	33,828	29,732	15,564	13,588	19,340	19,793
Esplanade ...	17,761	10,358	10,064	13,080	10,464	12,544	7,264	7,145	7,942
B Ward. Chakla ...	24,231	24,384	32,197	37,048	36,748	15,768	14,672	19,633	21,875
Mándvi ...	33,202	31,402	37,295	42,351	35,100	23,317	18,413	22,981	24,877
Umarkhádi ...	45,679	48,431	52,466	54,656	49,873	28,491	28,641	31,063	31,033
Dongri ...	27,216	25,778	30,317	33,290	25,556	16,985	14,559	18,680	18,442
C Ward. Market ...	30,172	28,415	44,751	49,130	43,198	22,011	18,734	30,126	31,458
Dhobi Taláo ...	28,684	29,553	39,945	39,409	37,915	24,670	17,737	24,508	23,278
Fanaswádi ...	27,403	16,354	24,069	23,218	20,760	18,125	10,034	15,420	14,187
Bhuleshwar ...	36,459	30,229	38,363	38,106	36,029	24,713	19,135	25,101	23,734
Kumbhárwáda ..	27,703	27,544	32,209	34,290	27,594	17,908	16,384	20,142	20,071
Khára Taláo ...	22,979	23,161	27,035	28,691	23,638	15,052	14,164	16,660	16,453
D Ward. Khetwádi ...	31,937	27,160	28,814	29,436	24,317	19,850	16,287	18,069	17,418
Girgaum ...	30,779	14,866	26,909	25,319	21,234	19,156	9,151	16,503	15,030
Chaupáti ...	11,307	6,729	11,512	10,975	7,531	7,088	4,104	7,011	6,359
Walkeshwar ...	10,640	10,563	12,990	11,303	7,741	6,883	6,897	8,203	6,904
Mahálaxmi ..	26,302	18,092	17,014	6,232	4,317	16,608	10,953	10,734	3,769
E Ward. Tárdeo ...	27,758	20,958	13,980	20,231	...	17,241	12,213	11,403	11,932
Kámátipura ...	36,751	26,706	29,203	28,455	46,996	22,523	15,275	16,742	15,453
First Nágpáda ...	6,414	10,577	11,133	9,372	...	4,182	6,308	6,674	5,442
Second Nágpáda .	21,700	18,591	18,768	15,922	...	13,321	10,636	10,902	8,816
Byculla ...	75,348	57,646	47,403	26,842	28,032	47,673	34,544	29,557	15,811
Tádwádi ...	28,424	18,460	21,298	14,542	10,083	18,141	11,509	13,587	8,802
Mázagaon ...	30,075	27,933	33,640	27,904	20,973	19,398	16,590	20,413	16,099
F Ward. Parel ...	45,474	33,390	28,740	18,560	13,773	28,858	20,430	18,008	10,863
Sewri ...	19,067	9,294	6,063	5,555	4,460	11,841	5,605	3,767	3,250
Sion ...	30,680	25,443	19,601	17,237	11,572	18,463	15,139	11,983	9,932
G Ward. Mahim ...	30,492	27,386	18,505	17,309	14,310	18,271	15,927	10,838	9,873
Warli ...	89,611	45,588	25,493	14,621	10,042	58,473	27,329	15,755	8,191
Harbour and Docks, Railways, Military and Homeless ...	44,979	37,681	22,142	24,867	22,953	39,963	34,018	21,799	24,340

TABLE II—*continued.*

VARIATION IN POPULATION SINCE 1872.

	Females.					Variation—Increase (+) or Decrease (−).				Net Variation in period 1872 to 1911 Increase (+) or Decrease (−).
1872.	1911.	1901.	1891.	1881.	1872.	1901 to 1911.	1891 to 1901.	1881 to 1891.	1872 to 1881.	
11	12	13	14	15	16	17	18	19	20	21
399,716	339,157	296,220	303,671	308,433	244,689	+203,439	45,758	+48,568	+128,791	+335,040
2,068	688	1,198	1,180	1,019	1,260	−2,399	−379	+1,468	−481	−1,791
8,289	6,165	4,914	4,863	5,410	4,964	+6,650	−599	−643	+1,012	+6,428
1,893	637	629	887	882	470	+153	−642	+436	+1,152	+1,099
17,611	9,836	9,368	13,507	14,035	12,121	+2,444	−9,891	−981	+4,096	−4,332
6,905	5,217	3,134	2,919	5,138	3,559	+7,363	+334	−3,016	+2,616	+7,297
22,317	8,463	9,712	12,564	15,173	14,431	−153	−7,813	−4,851	+300	−12,517
20,751	9,885	12,989	14,314	17,474	14,349	+1,800	−5,893	−5,056	+7,251	−1,898
29,167	17,188	19,840	21,398	23,623	20,706	−2,802	−3,985	−2,190	+4,783	−4,194
14,723	10,261	11,219	11,637	14,848	10,833	+1,468	−4,539	−2,973	+7,734	+1,690
28,464	8,161	9,681	14,625	17,672	14,734	+1,757	−16,336	−4,379	+5,932	−13,026
23,074	14,014	11,816	15,437	16,131	14,841	+9,131	−10,392	+536	+1,494	+769
12,956	9,278	6,320	8,649	9,031	7,804	+11,049	−7,715	+851	+2,458	+6,643
22,784	11,746	11,094	13,262	14,372	13,245	+6,230	−8,134	+257	+2,077	+430
16,381	9,795	11,160	12,067	14,919	11,213	+159	−4,666	−2,781	+7,396	+109
14,099	7,927	8,997	10,375	12,238	9,539	−182	−3,874	−1,656	+5,053	−659
14,824	12,087	10,873	10,745	12,018	9,993	+4,777	−1,654	−622	+4,619	+7,120
12,456	11,623	5,715	10,193	10,289	8,778	+15,913	−12,133	+1,680	+4,085	+9,545
4,622	4,309	2,625	4,501	4,616	2,909	+4,068	−4,783	+537	+3,444	+3,866
5,151	3,757	3,666	4,787	4,399	2,590	+77	−2,427	+1,687	+3,562	+2,899
2,647	9,694	7,139	6,280	2,463	1,670	+8,210	+1,078	+10,782	+1,915	+21,985
...	10,517	8,745	7,577	8,349	...	+6,800	+1,978	−1,301	+20,281	+27,758
27,064	14,228	11,431	12,461	13,602	19,932	+10,045	−2,497	+748	−18,541	−10,245
...	2,232	4,269	4,459	3,930	...	−4,163	−556	+1,761	+9,372	+6,414
...	8,379	7,956	7,806	7,106	...	+3,109	−177	+2,846	+15,922	+21,700
16,793	27,676	23,102	17,846	11,031	11,239	+17,702	+10,243	+20,561	−1,130	+47,316
6,707	10,283	6,951	7,711	5,740	3,376	+9,964	−2,838	+6,756	+4,459	+18,341
12,631	10,677	11,343	13,227	11,805	8,342	+2,142	−5,707	+5,736	+6,931	+9,102
8,779	16,616	12,960	10,732	7,697	4,994	+12,084	+4,650	+10,180	+4,787	+31,701
2,803	7,226	3,689	2,206	2,305	1,658	+9,773	+3,231	+508	+1,095	+14,607
6,887	12,217	10,304	7,618	7,305	4,685	+5,237	+5,842	+2,364	+5,665	+19,108
8,382	12,221	11,459	7,667	7,436	5,928	+3,106	+8,881	+1,196	+2,999	+16,182
5,609	31,138	18,259	9,738	6,480	4,433	+44,023	+20,095	+10,872	+4,579	+79,569
22,860	5,016	3,663	343	547	93	+7,298	+15,539	−2,745	+1,934	+22,026

TABLE III—(Corresponding to Imperial Table VI.)

RELIGION.

Note.—There is 1 male in Esplanade, there are 5 males and 5 females in Mandvi, 5 males and 2 females in Dhobitalao, 3 males and 1 female in Khetwadi, 1 male and 1 female in Walkeshwar, and 3 males and 2 females in Parel, making a total of 29 persons who are classed together as others and have not been included in this table.

TABLE III.

RELIGION.

Section.	Populations.			Hindu.			Musalman.			Christian.			Jain.			Zoroastrian.			Buddhist.			Sikh.			Jew.		
	Persons.	Males.	Females.	Persons.	Males.	Females.	Persons.	Males.	Females.	Persons.	Males.	Females.	Persons.	Males.	Females.	Persons.	Males.	Females.	Persons.	Males.	Females.	Persons.	Males.	Females.	Persons.	Males	Females.
1	2	3	4	5	6	7	8	9	10	11	12	13	14	15	16	17	18	19	20	21	22	23	24	25	26	27	28
Bombay	979,445	640,288	339,157	664,043	436,521	227,521	179,346	118,984	60,362	57,356	38,583	18,772	20,450	15,385	5,065	50,931	26,764	24,167	578	425	153	107	93	14	6,597	3,505	3,092
A Ward. Upper Colaba ...	1,557	869	688	1,123	503	620	89	59	30	314	139	75	15	15	...	104	63	41	...	...	...	...	...	...	4	...	4
A Ward. Lower Colaba ...	19,679	13,514	6,165	13,024	9,112	3,912	1,190	856	334	4,020	2,697	1,323	149	131	18	1,085	587	498	24	20	4	17	16	1	170	95	75
A Ward. Fort, South ...	3,462	2,825	637	1,745	1,550	195	165	144	21	1,363	997	366	...	...	...	96	84	12	...	...	...	...	...	...	93	52	41
A Ward. Fort, North ...	25,400	15,564	9,836	11,711	7,772	3,939	1,440	1,042	398	1,700	1,095	605	800	561	239	9,692	5,045	4,647	9	9	...	36	34	2	12	6	6
A Ward. Esplanade ...	17,761	12,544	5,217	11,862	8,300	3,562	3,019	2,436	583	2,277	1,476	801	1	1	...	503	256	247	43	39	4	...	...	...	65	35	30
B Ward. Chakla	24,231	15,768	8,463	8,267	5,793	2,474	15,082	9,363	5,719	53	31	22	765	552	213	74	39	35	...	...	...	...	...	...	...	...	...
B Ward. Mandvi ...	33,202	23,317	9,885	24,616	17,780	6,836	5,217	3,449	1,768	214	115	99	2,562	1,645	917	9	9	...	33	33	...	...	...	...	541	291	250
B Ward. Umarkhadi ...	45,679	28,491	17,188	13,123	8,359	4,764	29,280	18,010	11,270	701	416	285	1,158	924	234	38	35	3	8	7	1	...	...	...	1,371	740	631
B Ward. Dongri ...	27,346	16,985	10,361	23,610	14,495	9,115	2,571	1,777	794	251	177	74	351	267	84	24	21	3	2	1	1	...	...	...	436	246	190
C Ward. Market ...	30,172	22,011	8,161	19,824	14,449	5,375	3,415	2,401	1,014	1,201	1,057	144	4,459	3,428	1,031	1,206	639	567	35	35	...	2	2	...	...	...	...
C Ward. Dhobi Talao ...	38,684	24,670	14,014	21,299	13,464	7,835	1,050	618	432	6,822	5,382	1,440	881	750	131	8,619	4,465	4,154	5	5	...	...	...	...	1	1	...
C Ward. Fanaswadi ...	27,403	18,125	9,278	22,136	14,610	7,526	502	311	101	2,229	1,806	423	520	373	147	2,006	1,016	990	9	8	1	...	...	...	2	2	...
C Ward. Bhuleshwar ...	36,459	24,713	11,746	22,386	15,582	6,804	11,377	7,352	4,025	32	25	7	1,949	1,379	570	715	375	340	...	...	...	...	...	...	...	...	...
C Ward. Kumbharwada	27,703	17,908	9,795	24,095	15,490	8,605	2,822	1,677	915	66	42	24	391	314	77	326	184	142	...	...	...	...	...	...	3	1	2
C Ward. Khara Talao ...	22,979	15,052	7,927	6,330	4,283	2,047	15,938	10,216	5,722	41	31	10	471	411	60	171	96	75	...	...	...	...	...	...	28	15	13
D Ward. Khetwadi ...	31,937	19,850	12,087	19,575	12,867	6,708	3,643	2,423	1,220	1,174	660	514	167	140	27	7,326	3,825	3,501	12	7	5	...	...	...	36	15	21
D Ward. Girgaum ...	30,779	19,156	11,623	28,379	17,654	10,725	295	207	88	1,144	717	427	378	275	103	583	303	279	...	...	...	...	...	...	1	...	1
D Ward. Chaupati ...	11,397	7,088	4,309	9,537	5,976	3,561	331	218	113	473	304	169	191	138	53	859	447	412	...	...	...	1	1	...	5	4	1
D Ward. Walkeshwar ...	10,640	6,883	3,757	7,374	4,990	2,384	677	434	243	1,129	663	466	275	168	107	1,117	581	536	27	21	6	35	26	9	14	9	5
D Ward. Mahalaxmi ...	26,302	16,608	9,694	19,855	13,163	6,793	887	601	290	1,361	781	580	34	27	7	4,049	2,033	2,016	...	...	...	...	...	...	16	4	12
E Ward. Tardeo	27,758	17,241	10,517	17,663	11,369	6,294	4,839	3,065	1,774	1,009	575	434	246	203	43	2,865	1,061	1,804	71	19	52	3	3	...	72	16	56
E Ward. Kamatipura ...	36,751	22,523	14,228	27,619	16,081	11,538	7,742	5,626	2,116	643	343	300	314	244	70	174	106	68	72	6	66	...	...	...	137	67	70
E Ward. First Nagpada	6,414	4,182	2,232	3,197	2,179	1,018	1,233	818	415	1,009	615	394	120	87	33	46	32	14	1	1	...	...	...	...	808	450	358
E Ward. Second Nagpada	21,700	13,321	8,379	6,280	3,979	2,301	14,690	8,951	5,739	204	128	76	67	57	10	82	47	35	1	...	1	2	...	2	374	156	218
E Ward. Byculla ...	75,348	47,672	27,676	51,662	32,702	18,960	16,556	10,673	5,883	4,585	2,670	1,915	783	631	152	833	451	383	3	3	...	...	...	...	906	483	424
E Ward. Tadwadi ...	28,424	18,141	10,283	20,989	13,752	7,237	3,080	1,872	1,208	2,564	1,504	1,060	200	155	45	990	531	459	1	...	1	...	...	...	600	324	276
E Ward. Mazagaon ...	30,075	19,398	10,677	20,140	13,170	6,970	4,562	2,912	1,650	3,619	2,422	1,197	237	189	48	1,243	657	586	33	24	8	7	7	...	35	17	18
F Ward. Parel	45,474	28,858	16,616	39,878	25,259	14,619	2,192	1,385	807	1,029	676	353	592	476	116	1,681	1,009	672	1	1	...	...	...	...	96	40	47
F Ward. Sewri	19,067	11,841	7,226	17,322	10,711	6,611	962	643	319	503	316	187	201	144	57	42	24	18	...	...	...	...	...	...	7	3	4
F Ward. Sion	30,680	18,463	12,217	24,661	14,989	9,672	2,412	1,488	924	2,397	1,252	1,145	459	331	128	728	389	339	...	...	...	2	2	...	21	12	9
G Ward. Mahim ...	30,492	18,271	12,221	22,740	13,577	9,163	3,909	2,236	1,673	3,141	1,839	1,302	410	318	92	550	279	271	2	1	1	...	...	...	40	21	19
G Ward. Worli	89,611	58,473	31,138	77,150	50,519	26,631	4,859	3,243	1,616	4,086	2,506	1,580	915	741	174	1,918	1,083	835	...	...	...	...	...	...	683	381	302
Harbour and Docks, Railways, Military and Homeless ..	44,979	39,963	5,016	24,741	21,883	2,858	13,560	12,257	1,303	5,912	5,156	756	319	279	40	229	190	39	186	184	2	2	2	...	39	31	8

ACCOMPANIMENT TO TABLE III.

Details of the entry under the head of Harbour and Docks, Railways, Homeless and Military.

Section.	Population.			Hindu.			Jain.			Buddhist.			Zoroastrian.			Musalman.			Christian.			Jew.			Sikh.		
	Persons.	Males.	Females.	Persons.	Males.	Females.	Persons.	Males.	Females.	Persons.	Males.	Females.	Persons.	Males.	Females.	Persons.	Males.	Females.	Persons.	Males.	Females.	Persons.	Males.	Females.	Persons.	Males.	Females.
1	2	3	4	5	6	7	8	9	10	11	12	13	14	15	16	17	18	19	20	21	22	23	24	25	26	27	28
Bombay City	44,979	39,963	5,016	24,741	21,883	2,858	319	270	49	186	184	2	229	190	39	13,560	12,257	1,303	5,912	5,156	756	30	21	9	2	2	...
A Ward—Homeless	1,133	1,083	50	690	645	45	1	1	...	...	...	...	7	7	...	362	358	4	73	72	1	...	...	...	...	...	...
B Do. do.	1,093	1,060	33	581	561	20	...	...	...	...	...	...	1	1	...	480	469	11	30	29	1	...	...	...	...	...	...
C Do. do.	1,901	1,807	94	1,391	1,315	76	1	1	...	...	...	...	3	3	...	453	437	16	53	51	2	...	...	...	...	...	...
D Do. do.	416	393	23	399	376	23	...	...	...	...	...	...	...	...	...	15	15	...	3	3	...	...	...	...	...	...	...
E Do. do.	456	435	21	333	313	20	...	...	...	...	...	...	...	...	...	99	99	...	22	21	1	2	2	...	...	...	...
F Do. do.	380	364	16	198	189	9	6	6	...	...	...	...	2	2	...	68	63	5	6	5	1	...	...	...	...	...	...
G Do. do.	56	41	15	31	19	12	...	...	...	...	...	...	...	...	...	25	23	3	...	...	...	...	...	...	...	...	...
B. B., & C. I. Railway—																											
Staff	1,884	1,184	700	1,540	974	566	...	...	...	...	...	...	43	24	19	99	76	23	202	110	92	...	...	...	...	...	...
Passengers	1,493	1,198	295	898	693	205	90	76	14	...	...	...	57	46	11	407	352	55	41	32	9	...	...	...	...	...	...
G. I. P. Railway—																											
Staff	2,672	1,760	912	2,038	1,398	640	...	...	...	...	...	...	1	1	...	99	70	29	544	201	343	...	...	...	...	...	...
Passengers	3,850	3,321	529	2,916	2,481	435	137	123	14	...	...	...	74	67	7	569	516	53	145	125	20	10	10	...	...	...	...
Harbour and Docks and Military ...	29,746	27,417	2,329	13,726	12,920	806	84	63	21	186	184	2	41	39	2	10,885	9,782	1,103	4,804	4,418	386	18	9	9	2	2	...

TABLE IV—(Corresponding to Imperial Table VII).

AGE, SEX AND CIVIL CONDITION.

TABLE IV.

Age, Sex and Civil Condition.

A.—All Religions.

Age.	Population.			Unmarried.			Married.			Widowed.		
	Persons.	Males.	Females.	Persons.	Males.	Females.	Persons.	Males.	Females.	Persons.	Males.	Females.
1	2	3	4	5	6	7	8	9	10	11	12	13
0—1	13.738	7,231	6,507	13.683	7,206	6,477	56	26	30	......	...	...
1—2	8.612	4,284	4,328	8.547	4,246	4,301	65	38	27	......	...	...
2—3	14.759	7,270	7,489	14.551	7,156	7,395	200	109	91	8	5	3
3—4	14.573	7,088	7,485	14.305	6,944	7,361	264	143	121	4	1	3
4—5	13.995	7,134	6,861	13.720	7,000	6,720	266	133	133	9	1	8
Total 0—5 ...	65.677	33.007	32.670	64.805	32.551	32.254	851	449	402	21	7	14
5—10	65.854	34,393	31,461	63.046	33,381	29,665	2.726	996	1,730	82	16	66
10—15	76.285	48,224	28,061	60.256	42,963	17,293	15.580	5,185	10,395	449	76	373
15—20	106.150	68,239	37,911	56.690	49,259	7,431	48.005	18,795	29,210	1.455	285	1,170
20—25	147.312	96,233	51,079	45.581	41,184	4,397	97.610	53,912	43,698	4.121	1,137	2,984
25—30	150.708	106,451	44,257	125.352	22,897	2,455	118.521	81,355	37,166	6.835	2,199	4,636
30—35	122.591	88,352	34,239	11.181	9,900	1,281	101.909	75,552	26,357	9.501	2,900	6,601
35—40	78.330	58,212	20,118	4.865	4,198	667	64.648	51,441	13,207	8.817	2,573	6,244
40—45	67.730	46,718	21,012	3.052	2,496	556	51.557	41,151	10,406	13.121	3,071	10,050
45—50	30.675	20,350	10,325	1.238	1,046	192	21.810	17,445	4,365	7.627	1,859	5,768
50—55	31.733	19,485	12,248	969	742	227	19.704	16,056	3,648	11.060	2,687	8,373
55—60	10.349	6,326	4,023	296	234	62	6.209	5,047	1,162	3.844	1,045	2,799
60—65	16.117	8,802	7,315	453	347	106	7.825	6,552	1,273	7.840	1,903	5,937
65—70	3.680	2,098	1,582	123	97	26	1.709	1,442	267	1.848	559	1,289
70 and over	6.254	3,298	2,956	239	194	45	2.604	2,136	468	3.411	968	2,443
Total all Religions ...	979,445	640,288	339.157	338.145	241.489	96.656	561.268	377.514	183.754	80.032	21.285	58.747

B.—Hindu.

Age.	Population.			Unmarried.			Married.			Widowed.		
	Persons.	Males.	Females.	Persons.	Males.	Females.	Persons.	Males.	Females.	Persons.	Males.	Females.
1	2	3	4	5	6	7	8	9	10	11	12	13
0—1	9.282	4,879	4,403	9.240	4,856	4,384	42	23	19	......	...	...
1—2	5.854	2,922	2,932	5.803	2,891	2,912	51	31	20	......	...	...
2—3	10.200	5,001	5,199	10.029	4,906	5,123	164	91	73	7	4	3
3—4	9.904	4,826	5,078	9.686	4,707	4,979	214	118	96	4	1	3
4—5	9.180	4,708	4,472	8.968	4,604	4,364	208	103	105	4	1	3
Total 0—5 ...	44.420	22.336	22.084	43.726	21.964	21.762	679	366	313	15	6	9
5—10	42.636	22,226	20,410	40.343	21,476	18,867	2.224	737	1,487	69	13	56
10—15	50.459	32,281	18,178	136.742	28,001	8,741	13.339	4,226	9,113	378	54	324
15—20	74.390	47,688	26,702	34.650	33,198	2,452	38.541	15,281	23,260	1.199	209	990
20—25	102.690	67,545	35,145	35.628	34,283	1,345	74.840	42,374	32,466	3.222	788	2,434
25—30	107.739	76,778	30,961	13.016	12,292	724	99.406	62,969	36,437	5.317	1,517	3,800
30—35	85.288	62,296	23,092	5.028	4,659	369	73.201	55,660	17,541	7.159	1,977	5,182
35—40	53.513	40,106	13,407	2.062	1,856	206	44.811	36,454	8,357	6.640	1,796	4,844
40—45	43.763	30,330	13,433	1.339	1,170	169	33.149	27,175	5,974	9.275	1,985	7,290
45—50	19.053	12,644	6,409	469	419	50	13.291	10,990	2,301	5.293	1,235	4,058
50—55	19.229	11,523	7,706	428	351	77	11.425	9,498	1,927	7.376	1,674	5,702
55—60	5.972	3,627	2,345	114	97	17	3.428	2,894	534	2.430	636	1,794
60—65	8.912	4,607	4,305	201	164	37	4.055	3,413	642	4.656	1,030	3,626
65—70	1.753	943	810	55	48	7	778	665	113	920	230	690
70 and over	3.125	1,591	1,534	112	99	13	1.304	1,067	238	1.708	425	1,283
Total Hindu ...	664.042	436.521	227.521	203.913	149.167	54.746	404.481	273.789	130.693	55.647	13.565	42.082

TABLE IV—*continued.*

Age, Sex and Civil Condition.

C.—Jain.

Age.	Population.			Unmarried.			Married.			Widowed.		
	Persons.	Males.	Females.	Persons.	Males.	Females.	Persons.	Males.	Females.	Persons.	Males.	Females.
1	2	3	4	5	6	7	8	9	10	11	12	13
0—1	182	85	97	181	85	96	1	...	1	......	...	...
1—2	158	74	84	158	74	84	......	...	...	......	...	...
2—3	263	134	129	262	134	128	1	...	1	......	...	...
3—4	232	111	121	225	106	119	7	5	2	......	...	...
4—5	214	107	107	209	107	102	5	...	5	......	...	...
Total 0—5 ...	1,049	511	538	1,035	506	529	14	5	9	......	...	...
5—10	1,056	633	423	1,023	616	407	32	16	16	......	...	...
10—15	1,900	1,494	406	1,619	1,370	249	274	120	154	7	4	3
15—20	2,999	2,209	790	1,705	1,655	50	1,266	549	717	28	5	23
20—25	3,993	2,983	1,010	1,279	1,253	26	2,640	1,695	945	74	35	39
25—30	3,138	2,492	646	504	494	10	2,536	1,951	585	98	47	51
30—35	2,349	1,886	463	195	190	5	2,049	1,648	401	105	48	57
35—40	1,353	1,147	206	95	92	3	1,159	1,008	151	99	47	52
40—45	1,191	942	249	59	56	3	962	823	139	170	63	107
45—50	534	429	105	16	15	1	420	374	46	98	40	58
50—55	446	349	97	30	26	4	293	263	30	123	60	63
55—60	141	110	31	9	8	1	89	81	8	43	21	22
60—65	194	129	65	5	5	...	94	82	12	95	42	53
65—70	47	34	13	3	3	...	23	23	...	21	8	13
70 and over	71	48	23	3	3	...	29	23	6	39	22	17
Total Jain ...	20,460	15,395	5,065	7,580	6,292	1,288	11,880	8,661	3,219	1,000	442	558

D.—Zoroastrian.

Age.	Population.			Unmarried.			Married.			Widowed.		
	Persons.	Males.	Females.	Persons.	Males.	Females.	Persons.	Males.	Females.	Persons.	Males.	Females.
1	2	3	4	5	6	7	8	9	10	11	12	13
0—1	934	509	425	933	509	424	1	...	1	......	...	...
1—2	522	251	271	519	249	270	3	2	1	......	...	...
2—3	664	329	335	659	326	333	5	3	2	......	...	...
3—4	804	407	397	801	405	396	3	2	1	......	...	...
4—5	872	435	437	869	434	435	2	1	1	1	...	1
Total 0—5 ...	3,796	1,931	1,865	3,781	1,923	1,858	14	8	6	1	...	1
5—10	4,485	2,279	2,206	4,438	2,256	2,182	45	23	22	2	...	2
10—15	4,824	2,506	2,318	4,710	2,456	2,254	105	46	59	9	4	5
15—20	5,093	2,710	2,383	4,661	2,605	2,056	414	101	313	18	4	14
20—25	5,526	2,863	2,663	4,069	2,488	1,581	1,407	366	1,041	50	9	41
25—30	5,180	2,757	2,423	2,709	1,805	904	2,352	936	1,416	119	16	103
30—35	4,787	2,572	2,215	1,481	1,028	453	3,093	1,494	1,599	213	50	163
35—40	3,902	2,158	1,744	813	580	233	2,772	1,501	1,271	317	77	240
40—45	3,897	2,133	1,764	474	314	160	2,909	1,725	1,184	514	94	420
45—50	2,509	1,344	1,165	200	153	47	1,854	1,090	764	455	101	354
50—55	2,460	1,287	1,173	113	70	43	1,658	1,066	592	689	151	538
55—60	1,419	743	676	37	23	14	883	598	285	499	122	377
60—65	1,516	735	781	39	25	14	792	572	220	685	138	547
65—70	700	373	327	18	11	7	318	244	74	364	118	246
70 and over	837	373	464	26	14	12	297	216	81	514	143	371
Total Zoroastrian ...	50,931	26,764	24,167	27,569	15,751	11,818	18,913	9,986	8,927	4,449	1,027	3,422

TABLE IV—*continued.*

Age, Sex and Civil Condition.

E.—Musalman.

Age.	Population.			Unmarried.			Married.			Widowed.		
	Persons.	Males.	Females.	Persons.	Males.	Females.	Persons.	Males.	Females.	Persons.	Males.	Females.
1	2	3	4	5	6	7	8	9	10	11	12	13
0—1	2,396	1,207	1,129	2,385	1,265	1,120	11	2	9	......	...	...
1—2	1,530	752	778	1,523	749	774	7	3	4	......	...	...
2—3	2,742	1,340	1,402	2,723	1,339	1,394	18	10	8	1	1	...
3—4	2,742	1,312	1,430	2,716	1,302	1,414	26	10	16	......	...	...
4—5	2,881	1,436	1,445	2,837	1,414	1,423	40	22	18	4	...	4
Total 0—5 ...	12,391	6,107	6,184	12,184	6,059	6,125	102	47	55	5	1	4
5—10	13,499	7,080	6,419	13,157	6,907	6,250	334	170	164	8	3	5
10—15	14,219	8,994	5,225	12,546	8,314	4,232	1,634	671	963	45	9	36
15—20	16,653	11,061	5,592	9,788	8,483	1,300	6,691	2,522	4,169	174	57	117
20—25	24,009	15,772	8,237	7,784	7,349	435	15,615	8,159	7,456	610	264	346
25—30	25,213	17,809	7,404	4,923	4,675	248	19,279	13,586	6,684	1,020	548	472
30—35	22,873	16,655	6,218	2,624	2,483	141	18,666	13,450	5,216	1,583	722	861
35—40	13,994	10,721	3,273	1,008	933	75	11,682	9,265	2,417	1,304	523	781
40—45	14,487	10,324	4,163	720	626	94	11,267	8,914	2,353	2,500	784	1,716
45—50	5,880	4,082	1,798	255	234	21	4,355	3,481	874	1,270	367	903
50—55	7,304	4,908	2,396	231	191	40	4,844	4,062	783	2,229	656	1,573
55—60	1,858	1,219	639	59	56	3	1,186	964	222	613	199	414
60—65	4,444	2,685	1,759	144	107	37	2,318	2,000	318	1,982	578	1,404
65—70	833	538	305	15	13	2	420	363	57	398	152	246
70 and over	1,789	1,038	751	70	57	13	791	677	114	928	304	624
Total Musalman ...	179,346	118,984	60,362	65,502	46,486	19,016	99,175	67,331	31,844	14,669	5,167	9,502

F.—Christian.

Age.	Population.			Unmarried.			Married.			Widowed.		
	Persons.	Males.	Females.	Persons.	Males.	Females.	Persons.	Males.	Females.	Persons.	Males.	Females.
1	2	3	4	5	6	7	8	9	10	11	12	13
0—1	793	407	386	792	406	386	1	1	...	......	...	...
1—2	465	246	219	462	245	217	3	1	2	......	...	...
2—3	737	377	360	728	374	354	9	3	6	......	...	...
3—4	732	365	367	721	358	363	11	7	4	......	...	...
4—5	712	383	329	706	380	326	6	3	3	......	...	...
Total 0—5 ...	3,439	1,778	1,661	3,409	1,763	1,646	30	15	15	......	...	...
5—10	3,380	1,780	1,600	3,328	1,755	1,573	49	25	24	3	...	3
10—15	4,166	2,531	1,635	3,997	2,442	1,555	163	88	75	6	1	5
15—20	6,301	4,261	2,040	5,405	4,001	1,404	871	255	616	25	5	20
20—25	9,188	6,003	2,585	6,424	5,435	989	2,648	1,142	1,506	116	26	90
25—30	8,578	6,150	2,428	3,939	3,463	476	4,416	2,632	1,784	223	55	108
30—35	6,464	4,513	1,951	1,703	1,444	259	4,388	2,983	1,405	373	86	287
35—40	5,071	3,758	1,313	839	700	139	3,824	2,944	880	408	114	294
40—45	3,889	2,694	1,195	435	317	118	2,891	2,256	635	563	121	442
45—50	2,441	1,713	728	280	214	66	1,713	1,396	317	448	103	345
50—55	2,042	1,290	752	153	97	56	1,332	1,067	265	557	126	431
55—60	850	553	207	73	47	26	533	433	97	244	70	174
60—65	905	573	332	55	43	12	504	436	68	346	94	252
65—70	305	191	114	29	19	10	146	125	21	130	47	83
70 and over	336	195	141	25	20	5	140	115	25	171	60	111
Total Christian ...	57,355	38,583	18,772	30,094	21,760	8,334	23,648	15,915	7,733	3,613	908	2,705

TABLE IV—*continued.*

Age, Sex and Civil Condition.

G.—Minor and Unspecified Religions.

Age.	Population.			Unmarried.			Married.			Widowed.		
	Persons.	Males.	Females.	Persons.	Males.	Females.	Persons.	Males.	Females.	Persons.	Males.	Females.
1	2	3	4	5	6	7	8	9	10	11	12	13
0—1	151	84	67	151	84	67	......	...	...	......	...	...
1—2	83	39	44	82	38	44	1	1	...	......	...	...
2—3	153	89	64	150	87	63	3	2	1	......	...	...
3—4	159	67	92	156	66	90	3	1	2	......	...	...
4—5	136	65	71	131	61	70	5	4	1	......	...	...
Total 0—5 ...	682	344	338	670	336	334	12	8	4	......	...	...
5—10	799	396	403	757	371	386	42	25	17	......	...	...
10—15	717	418	299	648	380	268	65	34	31	4	4	...
15—20	714	410	304	481	328	153	222	77	145	11	5	6
20—25	906	467	439	397	276	121	460	176	284	49	15	34
25—30	860	465	395	261	169	92	541	281	260	58	16	42
30—35	730	430	300	150	96	54	512	317	195	68	17	51
35—40	497	322	175	48	37	11	400	269	131	49	16	33
40—45	503	295	208	25	13	12	379	258	121	99	24	75
45—50	258	138	120	18	11	7	177	114	63	63	13	50
50—55	252	127	125	14	7	7	152	100	52	86	20	66
55—60	109	74	35	4	3	1	80	64	16	25	7	18
60—65	146	73	73	8	3	5	62	49	13	76	21	55
65—70	42	29	13	3	3	...	24	22	2	15	4	11
70 and over	96	53	43	3	1	2	42	38	4	51	14	37
Total Minor and unspecified Religions ...	7,311	4,041	3,270	3,487	2,033	1,454	3,170	1,832	1,338	654	176	478

TABLE V—(Corresponding to Imperial Table VIII).

EDUCATION BY RELIGION AND AGE.

TABLE V.

Education by Religion and Age.

Section and Age.	Population.									Literate in English.		
	Total.			Literate.			Illiterate.					
	Persons.	Males.	Females.	Persons.	Males.	Females.	Persons.	Males.	Females.	Persons.	Males.	Females
1	2	3	4	5	6	7	8	9	10	11	12	13
Bombay City ... Total ...	979.445	640.288	339,157	222.513	180.760	41.753	756.932	459.528	297.404	80.947	67.376	13,571
0–10 ...	131.531	67,400	64,131	9.157	5,792	3,365	122.374	61,608	60,766	1.982	1,161	821
10–15 ...	76.285	48,224	28,061	19.439	14,292	5,147	56.846	33,932	22,914	6.247	4,645	1,602
15–20 ...	106.150	69,339	37,811	27.637	21,489	6,138	78.523	46,860	31,673	10.617	8,514	2,103
20 and over ...	665.479	456,325	209,154	166.290	139,187	27,103	499.189	317,138	182,051	62.101	53,056	9,045
Hindu ... Total ...	664.042	436.521	227.521	112.293	98.775	13.518	551.749	337.746	214.003	30.449	28.959	1.490
0–10 ...	87.056	44,562	42,494	3.976	2,723	1,253	83.080	41,839	41,241	209	166	43
10–15 ...	50.459	32,281	18,178	9.561	7,611	1,950	40.898	24,670	16,228	2.286	1,991	295
15–20 ...	74.390	47,688	26,702	14.656	12,150	2,506	59.734	35,538	24,196	4.405	4,073	332
20 and over ...	452.137	311,990	140,147	84.100	76,291	7,809	368.037	235,699	132,338	23.549	22,729	820
Musalman ... Total ...	179.346	118.984	60.362	29.512	26.849	2.663	149.834	92,135	57.699	4.607	4,407	200
0–10 ...	25.790	13,187	12,603	1.051	793	260	24.739	12,405	12,334	49	40	9
10–15 ...	14.219	8,994	5,225	2.544	2,127	417	11.675	6,867	4,808	358	328	30
15–20 ...	16.653	11,061	5,592	3.185	2,882	303	13.468	8,239	5,229	605	565	40
20 and over ...	122.684	85,742	36,942	22.732	21,118	1,614	99.952	64,634	35,328	3.595	3,474	121
Christian ... Total ...	57.355	38.583	18.772	28.512	20.760	7.752	28.843	17.823	11.020	23.088	16.613	6.475
0–10 ...	6.819	3,558	3,261	1.540	812	728	5.279	2,746	2,533	1.290	681	609
10–15 ...	4.166	2,531	1,635	2.118	1,284	834	2.048	1,247	801	1.705	1,046	659
15–20 ...	6.301	4,261	2,040	3.255	2,203	1,052	3.046	2,058	988	2.584	1,721	863
20 and over ...	40.069	28,233	11,836	21.599	16,461	5,138	18.470	11,772	6,698	17.509	13,165	4,344
Jain ... Total ...	20.460	15.395	5.065	11.627	10.801	826	8.833	4.594	4.239	1.192	1.166	26
0–10 ...	2.104	1,143	961	271	213	58	1.833	930	903	11	6	5
10–15 ...	1.900	1,494	406	1.046	952	94	854	542	312	90	86	4
15–20 ...	2.999	2,209	790	1.836	1,651	185	1.163	558	605	194	187	7
20 and over ...	13.457	10,549	2,908	8.474	7,985	489	4.983	2,564	2,419	897	887	10
Zoroastrian ... Total ...	50.931	26.764	24.167	37.454	21.459	15.995	13.477	5.305	8.172	19.926	14.988	4.938
0–10 ...	8.281	4,210	4,071	2.112	1,150	962	6.169	3,060	3,109	327	212	115
10–15 ...	4.824	2,506	2,318	3.809	2,090	1,719	1.015	416	599	1.628	1,072	556
15–20 ...	5.093	2,710	2,383	4.332	2,422	1,910	761	288	473	2.609	1,809	800
20 and over ...	32.733	17,338	15,395	27.201	15,797	11,404	5.532	1,641	3,891	15.362	11,895	3,467
Jew ... Total ...	6.597	3.505	3.092	2.771	1.814	957	3.826	1.691	2.135	1.470	1.048	422
0–10 ...	1.446	719	727	203	110	93	1.243	609	634	95	56	39
10–15 ...	701	405	296	351	219	132	350	186	164	173	116	57
15–20 ...	671	390	281	356	238	118	315	152	163	216	156	60
20 and over ...	3.779	1,991	1,788	1.861	1,247	614	1.918	744	1,174	986	720	266
Minor and Unspecified Religions ... Total ...	714	536	178	344	302	42	370	234	136	215	195	20
0–10 ...	35	21	14	4	2	2	31	19	12	1	—	1
10–15 ...	16	13	3	10	9	1	6	4	2	7	6	1
15–20 ...	43	20	23	7	3	4	36	17	19	4	3	1
20 and over ...	620	482	138	323	288	35	297	194	103	203	186	17

TABLE V—*continued.*

EDUCATION BY RELIGION AND AGE.

Section and Age.		Population.									Literate in English.		
		Total.			Literate.			Illiterate.					
		Persons.	Males.	Females.	Persons.	Males.	Females.	Persons.	Males.	Females.	Persons.	Males.	Females.
1		2	3	4	5	6	7	8	9	10	11	12	13
Upper Colaba—													
Hindu	... **Total** ...	1,122	593	529	137	116	21	985	477	508	33	33	...
	0—10 ...	267	133	134	6	6	...	261	127	134	...	...	...
	10—15 ...	93	52	41	19	16	3	74	36	38	2	2	...
	15—20 ...	69	35	34	19	13	6	50	22	28	7	7	...
	20 and over ...	693	373	320	93	81	12	600	292	308	24	24	...
Musalman	... **Total** ...	98	59	39	19	19	...	79	40	39	4	4	...
	0—10 ...	18	9	9	......	...	...	18	9	9	...	...	...
	10—15 ...	6	4	2	1	1	...	5	3	2	...	...	...
	15—20 ...	5	5	......	2	2	...	3	3	...	1	1	...
	20 and over ...	69	41	28	16	16	...	53	35	28	3	3	...
Zoroastrian	... **Total** ...	104	63	41	81	60	21	23	3	20	33	31	2
	0—10 ...	2	......	2	......	...	...	2	...	2	...	...	...
	10—15 ...	5	1	4	1	...	1	4	1	3	1	...	1
	15—20 ...	8	7	1	7	7	...	1	...	1	1	1	...
	20 and over ...	89	55	34	73	53	20	16	2	14	31	30	1
Lower Colaba—													
Hindu	... **Total** ...	13,024	9,112	3,912	1,331	1,308	23	11,693	7,804	3,889	207	206	1
	0—10 ...	1,393	690	703	23	21	2	1,370	669	701	...	...	...
	10—15 ...	833	531	302	104	97	7	729	434	295	6	6	...
	15—20 ...	1,322	957	365	180	176	4	1,142	781	361	60	60	...
	20 and over ...	9,476	6,934	2,542	1,024	1,014	10	8,453	5,920	2,532	141	140	1
Musalman	... **Total** ...	1,190	856	334	284	255	29	906	601	305	98	87	11
	0—10 ...	141	80	61	8	6	2	133	74	59	1	1	...
	10—15 ...	66	49	17	20	17	3	46	32	14	8	6	2
	15—20 ...	104	74	30	34	30	4	70	44	26	19	16	3
	20 and over ...	879	653	226	222	202	20	657	451	206	70	64	6
Zoroastrian	... **Total** ...	1,085	587	498	895	492	403	190	95	95	653	412	240
	0—10 ...	155	80	75	46	27	19	109	53	56	17	10	7
	10—15 ...	95	54	41	88	51	37	7	3	4	62	36	26
	15—20 ...	105	56	49	101	55	46	4	1	3	87	52	35
	20 and over ...	739	397	338	660	359	301	70	38	32	486	314	172
Fort South—													
Hindu	... **Total** ...	1,745	1,550	195	213	211	2	1,532	1,339	193	17	16	1
	0—10 ...	71	34	37	3	2	1	68	32	36	3	3	...
	10—15 ...	71	66	5	3	3	...	68	63	5	...	...	...
	15—20 ...	185	163	22	28	28	...	157	135	22	4	4	...
	20 and over ...	1,418	1,287	131	179	178	1	1,239	1,109	130	11	10	1
Musalman	... **Total** ...	166	142	24	46	42	4	120	100	20	15	15	...
	0—10 ...	11	9	2	1	1	...	10	8	2	...	...	...
	10—15 ...	15	14	1	5	5	...	10	9	1	1	1	...
	15—20 ...	15	10	5	4	3	1	11	7	4	2	2	...
	20 and over ...	125	109	16	36	33	3	89	76	13	12	12	...

TABLE V—*continued.*

Education by Religion and Age.

Section and Age.	Population.									Literate in English.		
	Total.			Literate.			Illiterate.					
	Persons.	Males.	Females.	Persons.	Males.	Females.	Persons.	Males.	Females.	Persons.	Males.	Females.
1	2	3	4	5	6	7	8	9	10	11	12	13
Fort South—*continued.*												
Zoroastrian ... Total ...	96	84	12	70	58	12	26	26	...	46	38	8
0—10 ...	5	4	1	2	1	1	3	3	...	—	...	—
10—15 ...	6	2	4	5	1	4	1	1	...	3	...	3
15—20 ...	8	8	......	4	4	...	4	4	...	2	2	...
20 and over ...	77	70	7	59	52	7	18	18	...	41	36	5
Fort, North—												
Hindu ... Total ...	11,711	7,772	3,939	3,661	3,185	476	8,050	4,587	3,463	866	851	15
0—10 ...	1,459	776	683	180	125	55	1,279	651	628	4	4	—
10—15 ...	972	660	312	364	312	52	608	348	260	117	117	...
15—20 ...	1,317	832	485	498	406	92	819	426	393	135	127	8
20 and over ...	7,963	5,504	2,459	2,619	2,342	277	5,344	3,162	2,182	610	603	7
Musalman ... Total ...	1,440	1,042	398	466	418	48	974	624	350	119	115	4
0—10 ...	179	91	88	16	13	3	163	78	85	1	1	...
10—15 ...	107	71	36	34	25	9	73	46	27	4	4	...
15—20 ...	162	124	38	59	53	6	103	71	32	21	20	1
20 and over ...	992	756	236	357	327	30	635	429	206	93	90	3
Zoroastrian ... Total ...	9,692	5,045	4,647	7,693	4,315	3,378	1,999	730	1,269	3,474	2,825	649
0—10 ...	1,469	730	739	448	242	206	1,021	488	533	42	30	12
10—15 ...	874	441	433	786	410	376	88	31	57	267	186	81
15—20 ...	951	509	442	884	483	401	67	26	41	457	328	129
20 and over ...	6,398	3,365	3,033	5,575	3,180	2,395	823	185	638	2,708	2,281	427
Esplanade—												
Hindu ... Total ...	11,863	8,300	3,563	1,062	991	61	10,810	7,309	3,501	308	287	21
0—10 ...	872	490	382	34	26	8	838	464	374	...	...	...
10—15 ...	536	352	184	70	66	4	466	286	180	21	19	2
15—20 ...	1,154	702	452	129	120	9	1,025	582	443	48	47	1
20 and over ...	9,300	6,756	2,544	819	779	40	8,481	5,977	2,504	239	221	18
Musalman ... Total ...	3,019	2,436	583	594	563	31	2,425	1,873	552	90	88	2
0—10 ...	114	74	40	6	4	2	108	70	38	—	—	...
10—15 ...	105	80	25	18	15	3	87	65	22	5	5	—
15—20 ...	239	159	80	40	37	3	199	122	77	18	18	—
20 and over ...	2,561	2,123	438	530	507	23	2,031	1,616	415	67	65	2
Zoroastrian ... Total ...	503	256	247	402	205	197	101	51	50	301	180	121
0—10 ...	79	47	32	16	10	6	63	37	26	10	6	4
10—15 ...	33	15	18	30	14	16	3	1	2	20	14	6
15—20 ...	42	15	27	37	13	24	5	2	3	35	13	22
20 and over ...	349	179	170	319	168	151	30	11	19	236	147	89
Chakla—												
Hindu ... Total ...	8,267	5,793	2,474	3,954	3,656	298	4,313	2,137	2,176	407	403	4
0—10 ...	1,003	509	494	103	81	22	900	428	472	...	...	...
10—15 ...	663	455	208	313	286	27	350	169	181	27	27	—
15—20 ...	1,042	698	344	533	467	66	509	231	278	68	68	—
20 and over ...	5,559	4,131	1,428	3,005	2,822	183	2,554	1,309	1,245	312	308	4

TABLE V—*continued.*

EDUCATION BY RELIGION AND AGE.

Section and Age.	Population.									Literate in English.		
	Total.			Literate.			Illiterate.					
	Persons.	Males.	Females.	Persons.	Males.	Females.	Persons.	Males.	Females.	Persons.	Males.	Females.
1	2	3	4	5	6	7	8	9	10	11	12	13
Chakla—*continued.*												
Musalman ... Total ...	15,082	9.363	5.719	5.556	5.154	402	9.526	4.209	5.317	510	494	16
0—10 ...	2.693	1,356	1,337	167	133	34	2.526	1,223	1,303	5	5	...
10—15 ...	1.600	942	658	441	389	52	1.159	553	606	19	18	1
15—20 ...	1.697	1,086	611	631	580	51	1.066	506	560	62	56	6
20 and over ...	9.092	5,979	3,113	4.317	4,052	265	4.775	1,927	2,848	424	415	9
Zoroastrian ... Total ...	74	39	35	67	37	30	7	2	5	20	15	5
0—10 ...	10	3	7	5	2	3	5	1	4	...	...	...
10—15 ...	6	2	4	6	2	4	...	...	...	...	...	...
15—20 ...	6	1	5	6	1	5	...	...	...	...	...	...
20 and over ...	52	33	19	50	32	18	2	1	1	20	15	5
Mandvi—												
Hindu ... Total ...	24.616	17.780	6.836	7,417	7.123	294	17,199	10.657	6.542	514	511	3
0—10 ...	2.022	1,035	987	108	98	10	1.924	937	987	4	4	...
10—15 ...	1.520	1,000	520	448	413	35	1.072	587	485	51	51	...
15—20 ...	2.939	1,953	986	856	801	55	2.083	1,152	931	72	71	1
20 and over ...	18,125	13,792	4,333	6.005	5,811	194	12.120	7,981	4,139	387	385	2
Musalman ... Total ...	5.217	3.449	1.768	1.663	1.382	281	3.554	2.067	1.487	356	340	16
0—10 ...	750	371	379	76	46	30	674	325	349	1	...	1
10—15 ...	478	294	184	218	143	75	260	151	109	40	34	6
15—20 ...	542	366	176	200	171	29	342	195	147	57	55	2
20 and over ...	3.447	2,418	1,029	1.169	1,022	147	2.278	1,396	882	258	251	7
Zoroastrian ... Total ...	9	9	......	5	5	...	4	4	...	...	...	...
0—10 ...	......	......	......	......	...	...	...	...	...	...	...	...
10—15 ...	1	1	......	1	1	...	...	...	...	...	...	...
15—20 ...	......	......	......	......	...	...	...	...	...	...	...	...
20 and over ...	8	8	......	4	4	...	4	4	...	...	...	...
Umarkhadi—												
Hindu ... Total ...	13.123	8.359	4.764	1.481	1.427	54	11.642	6.932	4.710	132	127	5
0—10 ...	1.686	833	853	23	21	2	1.663	812	851	...	...	...
10—15 ...	912	548	364	98	91	7	814	457	357	2	2	...
15—20 ...	1.327	832	495	209	200	9	1.118	632	486	21	20	1
20 and over ...	9.198	6,146	3,053	1.151	1,115	36	8.047	5,031	3,016	109	105	4
Musalman ... Total ...	29.280	18.010	11.270	4.706	4.190	516	24.574	13.820	10.754	799	787	12
0—10 ...	4.844	2,474	2,370	186	140	46	4.658	2,334	2,324	13	10	3
10—15 ...	2.610	1,603	1,007	491	411	80	2.119	1,192	927	101	99	2
15—20 ...	2.901	1,810	1,091	544	471	73	2.357	1,339	1,018	118	116	2
20 and over ...	18.925	12,123	6,802	3.485	3,168	317	15.440	8,955	6,485	567	562	5
Zoroastrian ... Total ...	38	35	3	22	21	1	16	14	2	1	1	...
0—10 ...	......	......	......	......	...	...	...	...	...	...	...	...
10—15 ...	4	4	......	3	3	...	1	1	...	...	...	...
15—20 ...	5	5	......	3	3	...	2	2	...	...	...	...
20 and over ...	29	26	3	16	15	1	13	11	2	1	1	...

TABLE V—*continued.*

EDUCATION BY RELIGION AND AGE.

Section and Age.		Population.									Literate in English.		
		Total.			Literate.			Illiterate.					
		Persons.	Males.	Females.	Persons.	Males.	Females.	Persons.	Males.	Females.	Persons.	Males.	Females.
1		2	3	4	5	6	7	8	9	10	11	12	13
Dongri—													
Hindu	... Total ...	23.610	14.495	9.115	862	823	39	22.748	13.672	9.076	126	117	9
	0—10 ...	3.511	1,751	1,760	20	18	2	3.491	1,733	1,758	2	1	1
	10—15 ...	1.541	921	620	58	51	7	1.483	870	613	5	5	...
	15—20 ...	2.141	1,198	943	101	99	2	2.040	1,099	941	19	18	1
	20 and over ...	16.417	10,625	5,792	683	655	28	15.734	9,970	5,764	100	93	7
Musalman	... Total ...	2.571	1.777	794	332	287	45	2.239	1.490	749	65	64	1
	0—10 ...	331	170	161	8	3	5	323	167	156	...	...	...
	10—15 ...	213	133	80	26	18	8	187	115	72	3	3	...
	15—20 ...	319	235	84	42	35	7	277	200	77	11	11	...
	20 and over ...	1.708	1,239	469	256	231	25	1.452	1,008	444	51	50	1
Zoroastrian	... Total ...	24	21	3	7	7	...	17	14	3	...	...	...
	0—10 ...	2	......	2	......	...	...	2	...	2	...	...	...
	10—15 ...	......	......	......	......	...	...	...	...	...	...	...	...
	15—20 ...	2	2	......	2	2	...	...	...	...	...	...	...
	20 and over ...	20	19	1	5	5	...	15	14	1	...	...	...
Market—													
Hindu	... Total ...	19.824	14.449	5.375	8.323	7,674	649	11.501	6.775	4.726	1.166	1.121	45
	0—10 ...	1.810	933	877	163	117	46	1.647	816	831	8	6	2
	10—15 ...	1.319	891	428	500	425	75	819	466	353	86	79	7
	15—20 ...	2.513	1,711	802	1.139	1,005	134	1.374	706	668	197	183	14
	20 and over ...	14.182	10,914	3,268	6.521	6,127	394	7.661	4,787	2,874	875	853	22
Musalman	... Total ...	3.415	2.401	1.014	1.413	1.295	118	2.002	1.106	896	115	114	1
	0—10 ...	454	231	223	32	25	7	422	206	216	...	...	...
	10—15 ...	303	217	86	114	101	13	189	116	73	10	10	...
	15—20 ...	407	276	131	145	126	19	262	150	112	14	13	1
	20 and over ...	2.251	1,677	574	1.122	1,043	79	1.129	634	495	91	91	...
Zoroastrian	... Total ...	1.206	639	567	829	507	322	377	132	245	227	168	59
	0—10 ...	196	101	95	43	21	22	153	80	73	4	...	4
	10—15 ...	91	53	38	65	45	20	26	8	18	16	13	3
	15—20 ...	133	74	59	105	66	39	28	8	20	40	30	10
	20 and over ...	786	411	375	616	375	241	170	36	134	158	116	42
Dhobi-Talao—													
Hindu	... Total ...	21.299	13.464	7.835	4.558	3.897	661	16.741	9.567	7.174	1.390	1.312	78
	0—10 ...	2.979	1,509	1,470	168	125	43	2.811	1,384	1,427	16	16	...
	10—15 ...	1.776	1,120	656	358	281	77	1.418	839	579	86	73	13
	15—20 ...	2.446	1,492	954	538	426	112	1.908	1,066	842	183	164	19
	20 and over ...	14.698	9,343	4,755	3.494	3,065	429	10.604	6,278	4,326	1.105	1,059	46
Musalman	... Total ...	1.050	618	432	103	91	12	947	527	420	14	14	...
	0—10 ...	168	79	89	......	...	...	168	79	89	...	...	...
	10—15 ...	85	49	36	5	2	3	80	47	33	...	...	...
	15—20 ...	105	78	27	12	11	1	93	67	26	2	2	...
	20 and over ...	692	412	280	86	78	8	606	334	272	12	12	...

TABLE V—*continued.*

Education by Religion and Age.

Section and Age.	Population.									Literate in English.		
	Total.			Literate.			Illiterate.					
	Persons.	Males.	Females.	Persons.	Males.	Females.	Persons.	Males.	Females.	Persons.	Males.	Females.
1	2	3	4	5	6	7	8	9	10	11	12	13
Dhobi-Talao—*continued.*												
Zoroastrian ... Total ...	8,619	4,465	4,154	5,940	3,485	2,455	2,679	980	1,699	2,850	2,294	556
0—10 ...	1,395	686	709	275	150	125	1,120	536	584	23	16	7
10—15 ...	896	432	464	612	337	255	274	105	169	199	129	70
15—20 ...	883	468	415	709	409	300	174	59	115	381	265	96
20 and over ...	5,455	2,879	2,576	4,344	2,599	1,745	1,111	280	831	2,247	1,864	383
Fanaswadi—												
Hindu ... Total ...	22,136	14,610	7,526	6,832	5,614	1,218	15,304	8,996	6,308	2,597	2,443	154
0—10 ...	2,684	1,359	1,325	301	178	123	2,383	1,181	1,202	28	15	13
10—15 ...	1,725	1,050	675	614	446	168	1,111	602	509	194	165	29
15—20 ...	2,631	1,648	983	955	717	238	1,676	931	745	364	335	29
20 and over ...	15,096	10,553	4,543	4,962	4,271	691	10,134	6,282	3,852	2,011	1,928	83
Musalman ... Total ...	502	311	191	48	46	2	454	265	189	11	11	...
0—10 ...	75	34	41	1	1	...	74	33	41	...	...	...
10—15 ...	36	20	16	2	2	...	34	18	16	1	1	...
15—20 ...	51	31	20	4	4	...	47	27	20	1	1	...
20 and over ...	340	226	114	41	39	2	299	187	112	9	9	...
Zoroastrian ... Total ...	2,005	1,015	990	1,411	821	590	594	194	400	806	646	160
0—10 ...	315	171	144	75	48	27	240	123	117	6	6	...
10—15 ...	183	90	93	139	74	65	44	16	28	66	45	21
15—20 ...	191	91	100	160	80	80	31	11	20	104	74	30
20 and over ...	1,316	663	653	1,037	619	418	279	44	235	630	531	100
Bhuleshwar—												
Hindu ... Total ...	22,386	15,582	6,804	10,651	9,539	1,112	11,735	6,043	5,692	1,896	1,861	35
0—10 ...	2,479	1,237	1,242	324	213	111	2,155	1,024	1,131	4	4	...
10—15 ...	1,479	940	539	757	605	152	722	335	387	128	121	7
15—20 ...	2,930	1,905	1,025	1,500	1,258	242	1,430	647	783	286	276	10
20 and over ...	15,498	11,500	3,998	8,070	7,463	607	7,428	4,037	3,391	1,478	1,460	18
Musalman ... Total ...	11,377	7,352	4,025	2,089	1,902	187	9,288	5,450	3,838	279	273	6
0—10 ...	1,686	842	844	102	82	20	1,584	760	824	...	...	...
10—15 ...	989	591	398	177	143	34	812	448	364	9	8	1
15—20 ...	1,195	790	405	185	168	17	1,010	622	388	20	20	...
20 and over ...	7,507	5,129	2,378	1,625	1,509	116	5,882	3,620	2,262	250	245	5
Zoroastrian ... Total ...	715	375	340	538	315	223	177	60	117	147	131	16
0—10 ...	129	65	64	39	17	22	90	48	42	1	...	1
10—15 ...	76	40	36	68	39	29	8	1	7	11	7	4
15—20 ...	75	36	39	65	33	32	10	3	7	24	18	6
20 and over ...	435	234	201	366	226	140	69	8	61	111	106	5
Kumbharwada—												
Hindu ... Total ...	24,095	15,490	8,605	3,600	3,284	316	20,495	12,206	8,289	673	654	19
0—10 ...	3,205	1,663	1,542	133	100	33	3,073	1,563	1,510	3	3	...
10—15 ...	1,801	1,150	651	289	248	41	1,512	907	610	46	41	5
15—20 ...	2,865	1,831	1,034	502	449	53	2,363	1,382	981	110	105	5
20 and over ...	16,224	10,846	5,378	2,677	2,487	190	13,547	8,359	5,188	514	505	9

TABLE V—*continued.*

EDUCATION BY RELIGION AND AGE.

Section and Age.	POPULATION.									Literate in English.		
	Total.			Literate.			Illiterate.					
	Persons.	Males.	Females.	Persons.	Males.	Females.	Persons.	Males.	Females.	Persons.	Males.	Females.
1	2	3	4	5	6	7	8	9	10	11	12	13
Kumbharwada—*continued.*												
Musalman ... Total ...	2,822	1,877	945	477	472	5	2,345	1,405	940	60	60	...
0—10 ...	415	219	196	17	16	1	398	203	195	1	1	...
10—15 ...	185	130	55	33	33	...	152	97	55	5	5	...
15—20 ...	305	205	100	58	58	...	247	147	100	11	11	...
20 and over ...	1,917	1,323	594	369	365	4	1,548	958	590	43	43	...
Zoroastrian ... Total ...	326	184	142	196	128	68	130	56	74	69	61	8
0—10 ...	64	28	36	12	6	6	52	22	30	2	2	...
10—15 ...	26	17	9	15	12	3	11	5	6	4	4	...
15—20 ...	34	20	14	23	14	9	11	6	5	8	8	...
20 and over ...	202	119	83	146	96	50	56	23	33	55	47	8
Khara Talao—												
Hindu ... Total ...	6,330	4,283	2,047	665	624	41	5,665	3,659	2,006	57	57	...
0—10 ...	639	335	304	9	8	1	630	327	303	...	...	...
10—15 ...	446	300	146	64	52	12	382	248	134	8	8	...
15—20 ...	634	440	194	85	80	5	549	360	189	12	12	...
20 and over ...	4,611	3,208	1,403	507	484	23	4,104	2,724	1,380	37	37	...
Musalman ... Total ...	15,938	10,216	5,722	2,173	1,939	234	13,765	8,277	5,488	246	238	8
0—10 ...	2,549	1,316	1,233	119	82	37	2,430	1,234	1,196	1	1	...
10—15 ...	1,473	873	600	263	227	36	1,210	646	564	23	22	1
15—20 ...	1,470	915	555	296	267	29	1,174	648	526	28	28	...
20 and over ...	10,447	7,113	3,334	1,496	1,364	132	8,951	5,749	3,202	194	187	7
Zoroastrian ... Total ...	171	96	75	92	60	32	79	36	43	40	33	7
0—10 ...	23	13	10	3	2	1	20	11	9	...	...	...
10—15 ...	18	7	11	11	4	7	7	3	4	2	1	1
15—20 ...	20	10	10	11	6	5	9	4	5	6	4	2
20 and over ...	110	66	44	67	48	19	43	18	25	32	28	4
Khetwadi—												
Hindu ... Total ...	19,575	12,867	6,708	5,683	4,615	1,068	13,892	8,252	5,640	2,569	2,399	170
0—10 ...	2,514	1,263	1,251	244	142	102	2,270	1,121	1,149	14	14	...
10—15 ...	1,581	1,042	539	591	434	157	990	608	382	220	184	36
15—20 ...	2,307	1,485	822	857	650	207	1,450	835	615	388	347	41
20 and over ...	13,173	9,077	4,096	3,991	3,389	602	9,182	5,688	3,494	1,947	1,854	93
Musalman ... Total ...	3,643	2,423	1,220	495	462	33	3,148	1,961	1,187	131	120	11
0—10 ...	456	233	223	10	6	4	446	227	219	1	...	1
10—15 ...	340	246	94	98	90	8	242	156	86	30	27	3
15—20 ...	380	277	103	91	86	5	289	191	98	25	23	2
20 and over ...	2,467	1,667	800	296	280	16	2,171	1,387	784	75	70	5
Zoroastrian ... Total ...	7,326	3,735	3,591	5,320	2,985	2,335	2,006	750	1,256	3,041	2,279	762
0—10 ...	1,296	643	653	269	134	135	1,027	509	518	38	26	12
10—15 ...	630	309	321	493	258	235	137	51	86	201	129	72
15—20 ...	706	340	366	613	313	300	93	27	66	395	249	146
20 and over ...	4,694	2,443	2,251	3,945	2,280	1,665	749	163	586	2,407	1,875	532

TABLE V—*continued.*

EDUCATION BY RELIGION AND AGE.

Section and Age.	Population.									Literate in English.		
	Total.			Literate.			Illiterate.					
	Persons.	Males.	Females.	Persons.	Males.	Females.	Persons.	Males.	Females.	Persons.	Males.	Females.
1	2	3	4	5	6	7	8	9	10	11	12	13
Girgaum—												
Hindu ... Total ...	28.379	17.654	10.725	13.502	10.589	2.913	14.877	7,065	7.812	6.311	5.913	398
0—10 ...	4.457	2,227	2,230	661	417	244	3.796	1,810	1,986	42	32	10
10—15 ...	2.597	1,558	1,039	1.433	978	455	1.164	580	584	506	422	84
15—20 ...	3.516	2,104	1,412	1.967	1,430	537	1.549	674	875	942	844	98
20 and over ...	17.809	11,765	6,044	9.441	7,764	1,677	8,368	4,001	4,367	4.821	4,615	206
Musalman ... Total ...	295	207	88	100	86	14	195	121	74	18	18	...
0—10 ...	34	23	11	4	4	...	30	19	11	...	...	...
10—15 ...	37	25	12	12	12	...	25	13	12	1	1	...
15—20 ...	51	30	15	27	24	3	24	12	13	7	7	...
20 and over ...	173	123	50	57	46	11	116	77	39	10	10	...
Zoroastrian ... Total ...	562	303	259	484	263	221	98	40	58	308	199	109
0—10 ...	94	44	50	45	23	22	49	21	28	2	...	2
10—15 ...	52	25	27	47	24	23	5	1	4	28	16	12
15—20 ...	61	38	23	53	33	20	8	5	3	45	27	18
20 and over ...	375	196	179	339	183	156	36	13	23	233	156	77
Chaupati—												
Hindu ... Total ...	9.537	5.976	3.561	3.902	2.906	996	5.635	3.070	2.565	1.972	1.804	168
0—10 ...	1.556	775	781	220	125	95	1.336	650	686	16	12	4
10—15 ...	828	475	353	413	256	157	415	219	196	152	110	42
15—20 ...	1.116	716	400	558	393	165	558	323	235	297	264	33
20 and over ...	6.037	4,010	2,027	2.711	2,132	579	3.326	1,878	1,448	1.507	1,418	60
Musalman ... Total ...	331	218	113	115	83	32	216	135	81	52	44	8
0—10 ...	53	28	25	13	10	3	40	18	22	3	3	...
10—15 ...	23	13	10	15	9	6	8	4	4	7	5	2
15—20 ...	44	32	12	22	16	6	22	16	6	10	9	1
20 and over ...	211	145	66	65	48	17	146	97	49	32	27	5
Zoroastrian ... Total ...	859	447	412	668	359	309	191	88	103	464	302	162
0—10 ...	149	81	68	37	25	12	112	56	56	10	7	3
10—15 ...	68	40	28	51	30	21	17	10	7	33	20	13
15—20 ...	69	33	36	58	31	27	11	2	9	51	29	22
20 and over ...	573	293	280	522	273	249	51	20	31	379	246	134
Walkeshwar—												
Hindu ... Total ...	7,364	4,980	2,384	1,160	955	205	6,204	4,025	2,179	417	353	64
0—10 ...	1,139	579	560	47	22	25	1,092	557	535	7	2	5
10—15 ...	518	339	179	118	89	29	400	250	150	50	38	12
15—20 ...	741	451	290	186	146	40	555	305	250	89	79	10
20 and over ...	4,966	3,611	1,355	809	698	111	4,157	2,913	1,244	271	234	37
Musalman ... Total ...	677	434	243	213	171	42	464	263	201	74	62	12
0—10 ...	124	61	63	18	13	5	106	48	58	4	4	...
10—15 ...	50	33	17	21	17	4	29	16	13	8	8	...
15—20 ...	83	54	29	31	24	7	52	30	22	11	10	1
20 and over ...	420	286	134	143	117	26	277	169	108	51	40	11

TABLE V—*continued.*

Education by Religion and Age.

Section and Age.	Population.									Literate in English.		
	Total.			Literate.			Illiterate.					
	Persons.	Males.	Females.	Persons.	Males.	Females.	Persons.	Males.	Females.	Persons.	Males.	Females.
1	2	3	4	5	6	7	8	9	10	11	12	13
Walkeshwar—*continued.*												
Zoroastrain ... Total ...	1.117	581	536	864	466	398	253	115	138	670	379	291
0—10 ...	166	81	85	50	25	25	116	56	60	19	14	5
10—15 ...	98	54	44	83	48	35	15	6	9	63	37	25
15—20 ...	81	43	30	73	39	34	8	3	5	60	30	33
20 and over ...	772	404	368	638	354	304	114	50	64	520	292	228
Mahalaxmi—												
Hindu ... Total ...	19.955	13.162	6.793	2.862	2.353	509	17.093	10.809	6.284	957	890	67
0—10 ...	2.759	1,516	1,243	116	74	42	2.643	1,442	1,201	11	9	2
10—15 ...	1.536	930	606	266	189	77	1.270	741	529	63	50	12
15—20 ...	1.990	1,280	710	378	295	81	1.614	985	629	145	129	16
20 and over ...	13.670	9,436	4,234	2.104	1,795	309	11.566	7,641	3,925	739	702	37
Musalman ... Total ...	887	601	286	206	140	66	681	461	220	87	56	31
0—10 ...	123	70	53	8	6	2	115	64	51	2	2	...
10—15 ...	73	45	28	27	14	13	46	31	15	10	6	4
15—20 ...	89	62	27	34	23	11	55	39	16	18	12	6
20 and over ...	602	424	178	137	97	40	465	327	138	57	36	21
Zoroastrian ... Total ...	4.049	2.033	2.016	3.303	1.721	1.582	746	312	434	2.085	1.367	718
0—10 ...	674	339	335	240	125	115	434	214	220	52	33	19
10—15 ...	360	190	170	320	168	152	40	22	18	186	113	73
15—20 ...	370	172	198	346	163	183	24	9	15	234	133	72
20 and over ...	2.645	1,332	1,313	2.397	1,265	1,132	248	67	181	1.643	1,089	554
Tardeo—												
Hindu ... Total ...	17.683	11.389	6.294	1.718	1.527	191	15.965	9.862	6.103	561	543	18
0—10 ...	2.522	1,319	1,203	68	45	23	2.454	1,274	1,180	3	3	...
10—15 ...	1.058	694	364	118	89	29	970	605	365	29	25	4
15—20 ...	1.648	966	682	218	187	31	1.430	779	651	77	74	3
20 and over ...	12.425	8,410	4,015	1.314	1,206	108	11.111	7,204	3,907	452	441	11
Musalman ... Total ...	4.859	3.085	1.774	415	375	40	4.444	2.710	1.734	57	53	4
0—10 ...	802	412	390	18	13	5	784	399	385	4	2	2
10—15 ...	337	199	138	30	24	6	307	175	132	3	2	1
15—20 ...	431	262	169	40	33	7	391	229	162	4	4	...
20 and over ...	3.289	2,212	1,077	327	305	22	2.962	1,907	1,055	46	45	1
Zoroastrian ... Total ...	3.815	1.951	1.864	2.450	1.388	1.062	1.365	563	802	1.494	1.112	382
0—10 ...	649	362	287	153	84	69	496	278	218	30	19	11
10—15 ...	439	200	239	283	137	146	156	63	93	139	83	56
15—20 ...	441	239	202	297	173	124	144	66	78	223	153	70
20 and over ...	2.286	1,150	1,136	1.717	994	723	569	156	413	1.102	857	245
Kamatipura—												
Hindu ... Total ...	27.619	16.081	11.538	1.761	1.655	106	25.858	14.426	11.432	338	333	5
0—10 ...	3.981	2,001	1,980	38	31	7	3.943	1,970	1,973	3	3	...
10—15 ...	1.714	993	721	107	95	12	1.607	898	709	13	12	1
15—20 ...	2.265	1,248	1,017	170	160	10	2.095	1,088	1,007	37	37	...
20 and over ...	19.659	11,830	7,829	1.446	1,369	77	18.213	10,470	7,743	285	281	4

TABLE V—*continued.*

Education by Religion and Age.

Section and Age.	Population.									Literate in English.		
	Total.			Literate.			Illiterate.					
	Persons.	Males.	Females.	Persons.	Males.	Females.	Persons.	Males.	Females.	Persons.	Males.	Females.
1	2	3	4	5	6	7	8	9	10	11	12	13
Kamatipura—*continued.*												
Musalman ... Total ...	7.742	5.626	2.116	491	464	27	7.251	5.162	2.089	59	59	...
0—10 ...	796	431	365	5	2	3	791	429	362	...	...	...
10—15 ...	403	274	129	22	20	2	381	254	127	2	2	...
15—20 ...	523	375	148	41	39	2	482	336	146	9	9	...
20 and over ...	6.020	4,546	1,474	423	403	20	5.597	4,143	1,454	48	48	...
Zoroastrian ... Total ...	174	106	68	66	53	13	108	53	55	30	28	2
0—10 ...	31	12	19	1	1	...	30	11	19	...	...	...
10—15 ...	9	7	2	2	2	...	7	5	2	2	2	...
15—20 ...	12	6	6	8	5	3	4	1	3	2	2	...
20 and over ...	122	81	41	55	45	10	67	36	31	26	24	2
First Nagpada—												
Hindu ... Total ...	3.197	2.179	1.018	714	680	34	2.483	1.499	984	384	376	8
0—10 ...	413	193	220	13	11	2	400	182	218	1	1	...
10—15 ...	194	123	71	33	32	1	161	91	70	5	5	...
15—20 ...	361	223	138	106	96	10	255	127	128	48	46	2
20 and over ...	2.229	1,640	589	562	541	21	1.667	1,099	568	330	324	6
Musalman ... Total ...	1.233	818	415	314	306	8	919	512	407	77	74	3
0—10 ...	165	84	81	11	11	...	154	73	81	...	...	...
10—15 ...	91	57	34	13	13	...	78	44	34	1	1	...
15—20 ...	141	81	60	34	31	3	107	50	57	10	9	1
20 and over ...	836	596	240	256	251	5	580	345	235	66	64	2
Zoroastrian ... Total ...	46	32	14	33	27	6	13	5	8	9	7	2
0—10 ...	5	4	1	......	...	...	5	4	1	...	...	...
10—15 ...	2	2	......	1	1	...	1	1	...	...	...	...
15—20 ...	5	3	2	4	3	1	1	...	1	2	1	1
20 and over ...	34	23	11	28	23	5	6	...	6	7	6	1
Second Nagpada—												
Hindu ... Total ...	6.280	3.979	2.301	425	402	23	5.855	3.577	2.278	36	34	2
0—10 ...	865	441	424	17	16	1	848	425	423	1	1	...
10—15 ...	432	270	162	33	31	2	399	239	160	1	...	1
15—20 ...	592	386	206	62	59	4	530	327	202	6	5	1
20 and over ...	4.391	2,882	1,509	313	297	16	4.078	2,585	1,493	28	28	...
Musalman ... Total ...	14.690	8.954	5.736	1.938	1.825	113	12.752	7.129	5.623	354	345	9
0—10 ...	2.267	1,161	1,106	71	50	21	2.196	1,111	1,085	...	...	...
10—15 ...	1.193	761	432	131	114	17	1.062	647	415	11	9	2
15—20 ...	1.158	665	493	135	117	18	1.023	548	475	23	19	4
20 and over ...	10.072	6,367	3,705	1.601	1,544	57	8.471	4,823	3,648	320	317	3
Zoroastrian ... Total ...	82	47	35	57	40	17	25	7	18	19	19	...
0—10 ...	11	4	7	1	1	...	10	3	7	...	...	...
10—15 ...	6	5	1	6	5	1	...	...	...	2	2	...
15—20 ...	14	7	7	10	6	4	4	1	3	4	4	...
20 and over ...	51	31	20	40	28	12	11	3	8	13	13	...

TABLE V—*continued.*

EDUCATION BY RELIGION AND AGE.

Section and Age.	Population.									Literate in English.		
	Total.			Literate.			Illiterate.					
	Persons.	Males.	Females.	Persons.	Males.	Females.	Persons.	Males.	Females.	Persons.	Males.	Females.
1	2	3	4	5	6	7	8	9	10	11	12	13
Byculla—												
Hindu ... Total ...	51,683	32,762	18,920	4,192	4,054	138	47,490	28,708	18,782	965	956	9
0—10 ...	6,903	3,391	3,512	112	94	18	6,791	3,297	3,494	9	8	1
10—15 ...	3,755	2,394	1,361	314	292	22	3,441	2,102	1,339	40	40	...
15—20 ...	5,303	3,301	2,002	467	442	25	4,836	2,859	1,977	126	123	3
20 and over ...	35,721	23,676	12,045	3,299	3,226	73	32,422	20,450	11,972	790	785	5
Musalman ... Total ...	16,556	10,673	5,883	1,209	1,105	104	15,347	9,568	5,779	246	230	16
0—10 ...	2,668	1,358	1,310	47	34	13	2,621	1,324	1,297	1	...	1
10—15 ...	1,232	744	488	95	83	12	1,137	661	476	18	17	1
15—20 ...	1,251	801	450	108	95	13	1,143	706	437	22	19	3
20 and over ...	11,405	7,770	3,635	959	893	66	10,446	6,877	3,569	205	194	11
Zoroastrian ... Total ...	833	451	382	642	364	278	191	87	104	405	281	124
0—10 ...	142	68	74	50	29	21	92	39	53	22	11	11
10—15 ...	64	22	42	50	17	33	14	5	9	25	8	17
15—20 ...	61	30	31	53	27	26	8	3	5	41	25	16
20 and over ...	566	331	235	489	291	198	77	40	37	317	237	80
Tadwadi—												
Hindu ... Total ...	20,989	13,752	7,237	1,543	1,457	86	19,446	12,295	7,151	372	363	9
0—10 ...	2,637	1,370	1,267	45	39	6	2,592	1,331	1,261	3	3	...
10—15 ...	1,711	1,077	634	162	151	11	1,549	926	623	16	16	...
15—20 ...	2,284	1,457	827	184	168	16	2,100	1,289	811	47	45	2
20 and over ...	14,357	9,848	4,509	1,152	1,099	63	13,205	8,749	4,456	306	299	7
Musalman ... Total ...	3,080	1,872	1,208	445	360	85	2,635	1,512	1,123	131	115	16
0—10 ...	560	281	279	35	20	15	525	261	264	8	7	1
10—15 ...	262	162	100	44	37	7	218	125	93	12	10	2
15—20 ...	231	138	93	38	26	12	193	112	81	18	14	4
20 and over ...	2,027	1,291	736	328	277	51	1,699	1,014	685	93	84	9
Zoroastrian ... Total ...	990	534	456	759	443	316	231	91	140	494	349	145
0—10 ...	132	66	66	35	24	11	97	42	55	7	6	1
10—15 ...	72	37	35	60	31	29	12	6	6	43	25	18
15—20 ...	119	67	52	105	61	44	14	6	8	74	48	26
20 and over ...	667	364	303	559	327	232	108	37	71	370	270	100
Masagaon—												
Hindu ... Total ...	20,140	13,170	6,970	1,341	1,262	79	18,799	11,908	6,891	172	171	1
0—10 ...	2,583	1,354	1,229	43	31	12	2,540	1,323	1,217	2	2	...
10—15 ...	1,201	832	459	129	115	14	1,162	717	445	17	17	...
15—20 ...	2,064	1,244	820	150	135	15	1,914	1,109	805	21	21	...
20 and over ...	14,202	9,740	4,462	1,019	981	38	13,183	8,759	4,424	132	131	1
Musalman ... Total ...	4,562	2,912	1,650	319	300	19	4,243	2,612	1,631	35	33	2
0—10 ...	697	353	344	9	9	...	688	344	344	...	...	...
10—15 ...	325	192	133	24	20	4	301	172	129	1	1	...
15—20 ...	357	220	137	30	29	1	327	191	136	2	2	...
20 and over ...	3,183	2,147	1,036	256	242	14	2,927	1,905	1,022	32	30	2

TABLE V—*continued.*

Education by Religion and Age.

Section and Age.	Population.									Literate in English.		
	Total.			Literate.			Illiterate.					
	Persons.	Males.	Females.	Persons.	Males.	Females.	Persons.	Males.	Females.	Persons.	Males.	Females.
1	2	3	4	5	6	7	8	9	10	11	12	13
Mazagaon—*continued.*												
Zoroastrian ... Total ...	1,243	657	586	871	513	358	372	144	228	344	285	59
0—10 ...	199	94	105	42	17	25	157	77	80	5	1	4
10—15 ...	128	74	54	109	66	43	19	8	11	29	22	7
15—20 ...	134	76	58	117	67	50	17	9	8	49	38	11
20 and over ...	782	413	369	603	363	240	179	50	129	261	224	37
Parel—												
Hindu ... Total ...	39,878	25,259	14,619	2,805	2,677	128	37,073	22,582	14,491	498	497	1
0—10 ...	5,478	2,783	2,695	41	36	5	5,437	2,747	2,690	1	1	...
10—15 ...	3,657	2,358	1,299	281	262	19	3,376	2,096	1,280	26	26	...
15—20 ...	5,195	3,266	1,929	245	216	29	4,950	3,050	1,900	33	33	...
20 and over ...	25,548	16,852	8,696	2,238	2,163	75	23,310	14,689	8,621	438	437	1
Musalman ... Total ...	2,192	1,385	807	342	325	17	1,850	1,060	790	58	56	2
0—10 ...	362	177	185	6	5	1	356	172	184	...	...	...
10—15 ...	170	111	59	26	24	2	144	87	57	2	2	...
15—20 ...	198	119	79	33	30	3	165	89	76	9	8	1
20 and over ...	1,462	978	484	277	266	11	1,185	712	473	47	46	1
Zoroastrian ... Total ...	1,681	1,009	672	1,349	863	486	332	146	186	618	547	71
0—10 ...	256	152	104	66	45	21	190	107	83	5	5	...
10—15 ...	262	202	60	246	195	51	16	7	9	125	115	10
15—20 ...	252	174	78	236	169	67	16	5	11	149	136	13
20 and over ...	911	481	430	801	454	347	110	27	83	339	291	48
Sewri—												
Hindu ... Total ...	17,322	10,711	6,611	849	784	65	16,473	9,927	6,546	142	136	6
0—10 ...	2,723	1,370	1,353	49	39	10	2,674	1,331	1,343	...	...	...
10—15 ...	1,426	879	547	69	60	9	1,357	819	538	16	14	2
15—20 ...	2,019	1,276	743	98	92	6	1,921	1,184	737	25	25	...
20 and over ...	11,154	7,186	3,968	613	573	40	10,541	6,613	3,928	101	97	4
Musalman ... Total ...	992	643	349	94	81	13	898	562	336	8	8	...
0—10 ...	153	75	78	3	2	1	150	73	77	...	...	...
10—15 ...	80	63	17	6	6	...	74	57	17	2	2	...
15—20 ...	69	46	23	7	4	3	62	42	20	...	...	...
20 and over ...	690	459	231	78	69	9	612	390	222	6	6	...
Zoroastrian ... Total ...	42	24	18	35	21	14	7	3	4	19	19	...
0—10 ...	12	4	8	5	1	4	7	3	4	...	...	...
10—15 ...	1	1	......	1	1	...	...	...	...	...	...	...
15—20 ...	1	......	1	1	...	1	...	...	...	...	...	...
20 and over ...	28	19	9	28	19	9	...	...	...	19	19	...
Sion—												
Hindu ... Total ...	24,661	14,989	9,672	3,216	2,657	559	21,445	12,332	9,113	1,154	1,103	51
0—10 ...	4,292	2,244	2,048	201	128	73	4,091	2,116	1,975	7	6	1
10—15 ...	2,147	1,300	847	343	260	83	1,804	1,040	764	108	95	13
15—20 ...	2,635	1,547	1,088	422	300	122	2,213	1,247	966	137	123	14
20 and over ...	15,587	9,898	5,689	2,250	1,969	281	13,337	7,929	5,408	902	879	23

TABLE V—*continued.*

Education by Religion and Age.

Section and Age.		Population.									Literate in English.		
		Total.			Literate.			Illiterate.					
		Persons.	Males.	Females.	Persons.	Males.	Females.	Persons.	Males.	Females.	Persons.	Males.	Females.
1		2	3	4	5	6	7	8	9	10	11	12	13
Sion—*continued.*													
Musalman	... Total ...	2.412	1.488	924	263	247	16	2.149	1.241	908	31	30	1
	0—10 ...	417	186	231	3	3	...	414	183	231	...	...	...
	10—15 ...	160	98	62	16	15	1	144	83	61	6	5	1
	15—20 ...	202	118	84	23	18	5	179	100	79	3	3	...
	20 and over ...	1.633	1,086	547	221	211	10	1,412	875	537	22	22	...
Zoroastrian	... Total ...	728	389	339	510	292	218	218	97	121	315	226	89
	0—10 ...	155	83	72	26	13	13	129	70	59	10	7	3
	10—15 ...	69	38	31	59	32	27	10	6	4	31	21	10
	15—20 ...	71	43	28	66	43	23	5	...	5	41	28	13
	20 and over ...	433	225	208	359	204	155	74	21	53	233	170	63
Mahim—													
Hindu	... Total ...	22.740	13.577	9.163	3.733	3.073	660	19.007	10.504	8.503	1.342	1.255	87
	0—10 ...	4.282	2,128	2,154	201	136	65	4.081	1,992	2,089	13	10	3
	10—15 ...	1.995	1,182	813	427	314	113	1.568	868	700	127	111	16
	15—20 ...	2.179	1,297	882	469	363	106	1.710	934	776	197	181	16
	20 and over ...	14.284	8,970	5,314	2.636	2,260	376	11.648	6,710	4,938	1.005	953	52
Musalman	... Total ...	3.609	2.236	1.373	496	444	52	3.113	1.792	1.321	123	120	3
	0—10 ...	652	325	327	25	22	3	627	303	324	2	2	...
	10—15 ...	319	199	120	39	30	9	280	169	111	3	3	...
	15—20 ...	325	208	117	64	49	15	261	159	102	28	27	1
	20 and over ...	2.312	1,504	809	368	343	25	1.945	1,161	784	90	88	2
Zoroastrian	... Total ...	550	279	271	430	224	206	120	55	65	245	167	78
	0—10 ...	105	61	44	24	14	10	81	47	34	3	2	1
	10—15 ...	61	31	30	50	24	26	11	7	4	25	13	12
	15—20 ...	43	27	16	40	26	14	3	1	2	30	20	10
	20 and over ...	341	160	181	316	160	156	25	...	25	187	132	55
Warli—													
Hindu	... Total ...	77.150	50.519	26.631	4.645	4.257	388	72.505	46.262	26.243	1.152	1.128	24
	0—10 ...	10.603	5,638	4,965	223	164	59	10.380	5,474	4,906	3	3	...
	10—15 ...	6.997	4,726	2,271	525	442	83	6.472	4,284	2,188	91	84	7
	15—20 ...	10.185	6,900	3,285	592	529	63	9.593	6,371	3,222	141	138	3
	20 and over ...	49.365	33,255	16,110	2.305	2,122	183	46.060	30,133	15,927	917	903	14
Musalman	... Total ...	4.859	3.243	1.616	467	416	51	4.392	2.827	1.565	83	79	4
	0—10 ...	731	389	342	18	13	5	713	376	337	...	...	...
	10—15 ...	372	259	113	39	32	7	333	227	106	6	6	...
	15—20 ...	472	324	148	52	47	5	420	277	143	9	8	1
	20 and over ...	3.284	2,271	1,013	358	324	34	2.926	1,947	979	68	65	3
Zoroastrian	... Total ...	1.918	1.083	835	1.190	773	417	728	310	418	566	463	103
	0—10 ...	345	174	171	100	60	40	245	114	131	18	10	8
	10—15 ...	179	95	84	100	55	45	79	40	39	32	18	14
	15—20 ...	174	99	75	121	77	44	53	22	31	66	49	17
	20 and over ...	1.320	715	605	869	581	288	351	134	217	450	386	64

TABLE V—*continued.*

EDUCATION BY RELIGION AND AGE.

Section and Age.	Population.									Literate in English.		
	Total.			Literate.			Illiterate.					
	Persons.	Males.	Females.	Persons.	Males.	Females.	Persons.	Males.	Females.	Persons.	Males.	Females.
1	2	3	4	5	6	7	8	9	10	11	12	13
Harbour, Docks and Railways—												
Hindu ... Total ..	24,741	21,883	2,858	3,505	3,400	105	21,236	18,483	2,753	718	706	12
0—10 ...	1,259	683	576	40	34	6	1,219	649	570	2	1	1
10—15 ...	1,305	1,073	232	120	108	12	1,185	965	220	28	26	2
15—20 ...	2,475	2,144	331	257	245	12	2,218	1,899	319	63	62	1
20 and over ...	19,702	17,983	1,719	3,088	3,013	75	16,614	14,970	1,644	625	617	8
Musalman ... Total ...	13,560	12,257	1,303	1,621	1,604	17	11,939	10,653	1,286	202	201	1
0—10 ...	302	185	117	8	7	1	294	178	116	1	1	...
10—15 ..	482	444	38	39	36	3	443	408	35	6	5	1
15—20 ..	1,131	1,079	52	119	115	4	1,012	964	48	12	12	...
20 and over ...	11,645	10,549	1,096	1,455	1,446	9	10,190	9,103	1,087	183	183	...
Zoroastrian ... Total ...	229	190	39	175	148	27	54	42	12	134	124	10
0—10 ..	16	10	6	4	3	1	12	7	5	1	1	...
10—15 ..	20	15	5	18	13	5	2	2	...	14	13	1
15—20 ...	16	12	4	14	10	4	2	2	...	10	8	2
20 and over ...	177	153	24	139	122	17	38	31	7	109	102	7

TABLE VI.

PART I—(Corresponding to Imperial Table XI).

BIRTH-PLACE.

TABLE VI.

BIRTH-PLACE WITHIN THE PRESIDENCY.

TABLE VI.

BIRTH-PLACE.

A. I.—BORN WITHIN THE PROVINCE.

	District or State where born.	Population. Persons.	Population. Males.	Population. Females.	A Ward. Males.	A Ward. Females.	B Ward. Males.	B Ward. Females.	C Ward. Males.	C Ward. Females.	D Ward. Males.	D Ward. Females	E Ward. Males.	E Ward. Females.	F Ward. Males.	F Ward. Females.	G Ward. Males.	G Ward. Females.	Harbours and Docks, Railways and Homeless. Males.	Harbours and Docks, Railways and Homeless. Females.
	1	2	3	4	5	6	7	8	9	10	11	12	13	14	15	16	17	18	19	20
1	**Total Bombay City ...**	**979,445**	**640,288**	**339,157**	**45,316**	**22,543**	**84,561**	**45,797**	**122,479**	**60,921**	**69,585**	**41,470**	**142,478**	**83,992**	**59,162**	**36,059**	**76,744**	**43,359**	**39,963**	**5,016**
2	(a) BRITISH DISTRICTS	699,608	437,128	262,480	30,860	17,177	46,644	29,227	72,638	42,696	55,072	35,464	99,331	65,951	49,337	32,152	59,287	37,031	23,959	2,982
3	Aden	216	155	61	41	18	9	1	7	3	...	...	67	20	5	3	6	...	30	19
4	Ahmadábád	16,298	11,925	4,373	323	68	949	220	4,072	1,705	1,463	429	3,552	1,519	173	67	264	273	239	63
5	Ahmadnagar	14,611	9,079	5,532	715	370	665	457	708	407	452	296	3,460	2,669	1,003	752	1,000	684	694	97
6	Belgaum	2,356	1,430	926	70	42	30	19	186	117	217	63	401	281	70	37	390	315	64	29
7	Bijápur	1,622	1,133	489	45	7	12	4	66	28	17	14	471	282	30	18	460	134	32	2
8	Bombay City	191,581	103,367	88,214	9,511	7,161	15,935	13,263	22,061	18,516	16,512	13,473	19,627	17,544	8,071	7,405	11,807	10,170	1,783	660
9	Broach	1,660	1,088	572	239	105	56	43	310	139	301	173	65	36	20	14	34	55	67	7
10	Dhárwár	833	579	254	51	19	26	25	45	33	100	39	120	83	24	16	109	82	33	7
11	Kaira	2,576	1,547	1,029	21	13	357	198	440	370	151	66	78	59	62	41	309	219	90	36
12	Kánara	2,418	1,730	688	491	67	50	13	120	25	672	357	131	111	24	14	158	99	69	2
13	Karáchi	1,317	796	521	129	96	183	53	121	79	119	62	141	157	28	21	20	26	105	25
14	Khándesh East	916	699	217	14	17	14	7	75	19	76	33	108	127	52	20	201	16	132	10
15	Khándesh West	501	221	280	......	......	26	30	17	60	70	21	63	32	26	18	10	125	...	...
16	Kolába	37,119	23,580	13,539	1,574	866	2,784	1,079	2,672	1,496	2,030	1,008	4,976	2,914	2,869	1,643	4,179	2,719	1,571	120
17	Násik	9,863	5,821	4,042	1,191	570	213	146	413	308	439	159	2,088	1,601	570	436	384	515	493	206
18	Pánch Maháls	372	114	258	1	......	41	11	16	114	32	5	9	117	6	2	3	7	7	2
19	Poona	71,185	42,114	29,071	3,038	1,648	6,001	5,426	3,491	2,008	2,232	1,596	16,583	11,870	4,201	3,274	3,063	2,225	1,385	430
20	Ratnágiri	216,069	143,498	72,562	5,603	2,593	8,681	3,929	16,427	6,987	20,257	12,124	30,606	18,451	26,301	14,994	24,616	12,517	11,008	637
21	Sátára	56,754	39,818	16,936	2,480	1,107	4,330	1,404	6,109	2,570	3,872	1,640	10,138	4,912	2,674	1,589	6,573	3,269	1,123	245
22	Sholápur	8,528	5,381	3,147	412	197	822	474	511	295	251	152	1,958	1,050	419	280	770	646	200	41
23	Sukkur	395	334	61	4	1	280	54	31	......	2	2	11	...	6	1	3	...	7	3
24	Surat	35,072	24,331	10,741	4,300	1,443	1,680	930	6,927	4,305	3,352	1,013	1,904	822	1,648	678	1,902	833	2,716	117
25	Thána	15,705	10,112	5,593	743	454	561	286	604	653	1,441	872	1,092	844	716	528	2,383	1,846	1,647	102
26	Thar and Párkar	68	68	......	......	......	......	......	......	......	...	...	...	...	...	...	...	...	68	...
27	Unspecified	11,582	8,338	3,244	862	297	853	263	3,441	1,363	1,010	359	1,104	510	188	92	406	247	408	111

TABLE VI—*continued.*

BIRTH-PLACE.

A. I.—BORN WITHIN THE PROVINCE—*continued.*

	District or State where born.	Population.			A Ward.		B Ward.		C Ward.		D Ward.		E Ward.		F Ward.		G Ward.		Harbours and Docks, Railway and Homeless.	
		Persons.	Males.	Females.	Males.	Females.	Males.	Females.	Males.	Females.	Males.	Females.	Males.	Females.	Males.	Females.	Males.	Females.	Males.	Females.
	1	2	3	4	5	6	7	8	9	10	11	12	13	14	15	16	17	18	19	20
28	(*b*) FEUDATORY STATES	115,288	77,228	38,060	4,212	1,983	27,015	13,909	21,475	11,791	4,373	1,886	8,751	6,036	4,029	2,211	4,413	1,919	2,961	325
29	Akalkot	45	22	23	1	......	2	......	4	3	3	1	12	19	...	...	...	...	...	...
30	Aundh	137	128	9	1	......	13	1	......	...	1	...	118	7	5	1	...	...	...	...
31	Bhávnagar	7,122	4,604	2,518	137	5	1,403	851	1,658	857	460	189	657	411	10	70	131	98	134	7
32	Bhor	837	496	341	8	1	32	10	16	19	25	16	214	140	119	104	55	40	7	1
33	Cambay	18	12	6	13	1	......	......	......	5	...	...	...	...	...	...	...	...	...	...
34	Cutch	36,479	25,009	11,470	1,123	778	15,164	7,541	2,487	1,126	485	327	2,018	645	1,408	606	824	157	788	120
35	Ichalkaranji	2	2	......	......	......	......	......	......	...	2	...	...	...	...	...	...	...	...	...
36	Jamkhandi	44	29	15	......	3	......	......	3	5	7	1	7	6	...	...	2	1	10	...
37	Janjira	2,121	1,408	713	49	33	150	73	438	343	123	40	158	68	38	15	131	110	333	2
38	Jath	55	36	19	......	......	......	......	......	...	1	...	34	19	1	...	...	...	...	...
39	Jawhár	3	3	......	......	......	......	......	......	...	3	...	...	...	...	...	...	...	...	...
40	Káthiáwár	50,615	33,252	17,363	1,949	973	9,635	5,183	15,276	6,718	1,046	688	1,781	815	1,040	500	553	277	1,361	114
41	Khairpur	20	20	......	......	......	6	......	14	...	...	...	...	...	...	...	...	...	...	...
42	Kolhápur	9,309	6,456	2,853	241	86	218	117	335	231	361	194	1,747	770	1,318	634	2,120	753	193	48
43	Kurundwád	20	8	12	......	......	......	......	......	...	5	4	1	1	2	2	...	...	...	8
44	Máhi Kántha Agency ...	112	96	16	13	......	38	8	16	4	19	3	...	...	4	...	5	1	1	...
45	Miraj	474	325	149	44	30	14	4	73	20	36	32	119	32	17	8	4	3	[illegible]	...
46	Mudhol	5	4	1	......	......	4	......	......	...	...	1	...	...	...	...	...	...	[illegible]	...
47	Pálanpur Agency	2,607	1,925	682	4	......	165	24	293	127	214	1[illegible]8	1,0[illegible]3	417	3	...	10	5	24	1
48	Phaltan	233	121	112	3	3	13	8	9	10	6	7	71	61	9	11	11	12	...	...
49	Rájkot	1,038	730	308	34	23	77	40	408	168	64	24	40	36	...	...	7	3	31	6
50	Ramdurg	19	19	......	......	......	......	......	......	...	...	...	...	...	...	...	...	...	19	...
51	Rewá Kántha Agency ...	73	63	10	......	......	5	......	34	9	14	11	...	...	...	...	...	...	...	...
52	Sángli	218	160	58	6	3	21	3	14	10	19	7	88	27	7	4	11	3	4	1
53	Sávantvádi	3,630	2,302	1,328	241	73	84	30	237	75	422	232	601	487	152	62	519	360	43	20
54	Savanúr	17	15	2	......	......	......	......	......	...	11	2	...	...	...	...	4	...	...	...
55	Surat Agency	44	2	42	......	1	2	......	......	41	...	...	...	...	...	...	...	...	...	...

TABLE VI.

Birth-place in India beyond the Presidency.

TABLE VI—*continued.*

Birth-place.

A. II.—(a) BORN IN ADJACENT PROVINCES AND STATES.

	District or State where born.	Population.			A Ward.		B Ward.		C Ward.		D Ward.		E Ward.		F Ward.		G Ward.		Harbour and Docks, Railways and Homeless.	
		Persons.	Males.	Females.	Males.	Females.	Males.	Females.	Males.	Females.	Males.	Females.	Males.	Females.	Males.	Females.	Males.	Females.	Males.	Females.
	1	2	3	4	5	6	7	8	9	10	11	12	13	14	15	16	17	18	19	20
	(a) BRITISH DISTRICTS—																			
56	**Districts in Madras** .	8,378	5,981	2,397	304	275	927	444	583	203	436	107	1,319	591	127	93	1,498	491	388	93
57	Anantapur	2	1	1	1	1	...	...	...	...	...	...	...	...	...	...	...	...	...	...
58	North Arcot	11	9	2	1	...	...	...	...	...	...	...	4	...	3	...	1	2	...	...
59	South Arcot	22	18	4	2	...	...	...	...	...	...	...	...	...	...	...	16	...	...	4
60	Bellary	126	90	36	1	2	4	...	...	...	23	3	15	7	5	4	26	26	8	4
61	Coimbatore	2	2	...	...	...	...	...	...	...	...	...	...	...	...	...	...	...	2	...
62	Cuddapa	4	4	...	4	...	...	...	...	...	...	...	...	...	...	...	...	...	...	...
63	Ganjám	2	1	1	1	...	...	...	...	...	...	...	...	...	...	1	...	...	...	...
64	Godávari	8	7	1	4	...	...	...	...	...	...	...	...	1	...	...	2	...	1	...
65	Kistna	6	4	2	...	...	...	...	...	...	...	1	2	...	1	1	...	...	1	...
66	Kurnool	6	2	4	1	...	...	...	...	...	1	2	...	...	...	1	...	1	...	...
67	Madras	3,764	2,537	1,227	394	163	200	31	440	140	230	77	512	383	56	41	624	329	73	49
68	Madura	475	473	2	...	...	...	...	1	1	18	...	283	...	10	...	130	...	31	1
69	Malabar	858	605	253	21	7	232	169	33	10	29	15	40	21	7	6	77	5	166	20
70	Nellore	3	...	3	...	...	...	...	...	...	...	...	...	...	...	...	...	...	...	3
71	Nilgiris	7	1	6	1	1	...	2	...	...	...	...	...	1	...	...	...	...	...	2
72	Salem	5	5	...	...	...	...	...	...	...	5	...	...	...	...	...	...	...	...	...
73	South Kánara	2,207	1,546	661	359	101	468	236	87	41	131	7	283	172	30	30	88	70	89	4
74	Tanjore	23	15	8	3	1	...	...	5	...	...	1	5	3	...	...	...	...	2	3
75	Tinnevelly	701	637	64	3	...	23	3	6	2	...	1	67	...	1	2	528	51	9	2
76	Trichinopoly	28	22	6	4	...	...	...	1	...	...	...	5	2	4	1	3	3	5	...
77	Vizagapatam	18	12	6	4	...	...	...	...	...	...	...	...	1	1	3	4	1	3	1
78	**Districts in Central Provinces and Berar** .	3,843	2,195	1,648	99	83	212	107	189	129	262	176	667	519	139	123	426	445	212	86
79	Akola	160	100	60	...	2	8	4	9	1	4	13	32	25	9	11	10	2	28	3
80	Amraoti	184	104	80	5	13	29	22	14	2	12	8	10	3	8	13	11	18	15	1

TABLE VI—*continued.*

BIRTH-PLACE.

A. II.—(*a*) BORN IN ADJACENT PROVINCES AND STATES—*continued.*

	District or State where born.	Population.			A Ward.		B Ward.		C Ward.		D Ward.		E Ward.		F Ward.		G Ward.		Harbour and Docks, Railways and Homeless.	
		Persons.	Males.	Females.	Males.	Females.	Males.	Females.	Males.	Females.	Males.	Females.	Males.	Females.	Males.	Females.	Males.	Females.	Males.	Females.
	1	2	3	4	5	6	7	8	9	10	11	12	13	14	15	16	17	18	19	20
81	Bálághát	9	5	4	...	...	...	...	...	...	...	...	4	...	...	...	...	...	1	4
82	Betul	...	...	...	...	...	...	...	...	...	...	...	...	...	...	...	...	...	...	...
83	Bhandára	1	1	...	...	...	...	...	1	...	...	...	...	...	...	...	...	...	...	...
84	Bilāspur	2	2	1	...	...	...	...	...	...	...	...	...	...	...	...	...	...	2	1
85	Buldána	33	18	15	...	...	2	3	...	...	8	4	...	...	...	1	4	3	4	4
86	Chánda	21	9	12	...	...	2	...	2	...	...	6	2	...	...	5	...	...	2	1
87	Chindwara	3	3	...	...	...	3	...	...	...	...	...	...	...	...	...	...	...	...	...
88	Hoshangábád	86	58	28	3	3	3	...	28	1	4	3	6	11	3	2	...	7	12	1
89	Jubbulpore	628	397	231	25	6	10	...	34	6	25	12	198	138	10	9	64	39	31	21
90	Nágpur	1,846	956	893	53	44	49	32	51	48	141	80	230	261	66	68	292	363	83	19
91	Narsinghpur	20	20	...	...	...	1	...	...	...	...	...	18	...	...	...	1	...	...	...
92	Nimár	205	116	89	3	2	67	30	...	1	...	...	39	46	1	2	4	4	13	4
93	Raipur	131	66	65	...	2	7	...	1	61	...	...	46	...	...	...	5	...	8	2
94	Saugor	61	43	18	1	...	...	...	9	1	6	6	3	2	17	7	3	...	4	3
95	Seoni	1	...	1	...	...	...	1	...	...	...	...	...	...	...	...	...	...	...	...
96	Wardhá	26	20	6	...	...	1	...	...	...	...	...	9	4	...	...	4	2	6	...
97	Yeotmál	7	7	...	...	...	...	...	...	...	...	...	...	...	...	...	6	...	1	...
98	Berar Unspecified	310	207	103	6	6	24	15	12	8	40	24	81	29	13	10	20	8	2	3
99	Central Provinces Unspecified	106	63	43	5	1	6	...	28	...	13	42	10	...	...	...	1	...	...	...
100	**Districts in the Punjab.**	8,457	7,098	1,359	673	190	1,134	139	1,297	236	370	130	2,637	514	121	32	99	43	777	96
101	Ambála	28	12	16	3	...	1	...	...	...	1	1	3	13	4	3	...	...	...	1
102	Amritsar	124	84	40	16	1	5	...	37	21	9	9	...	6	9	1	4	...	4	2
103	Attock	1	...	1	...	...	...	1	...	...	...	...	...	...	...	...	...	...	...	...
104	Delhi	2,830	2,406	424	67	21	644	80	481	94	126	31	717	155	61	15	33	16	56	13
105	Dera Ghází-Khán	18	15	3	...	...	...	...	...	...	...	...	...	3	...	...	...	...	15	...
106	Ferozepore	18	14	4	3	...	...	...	10	3	1	...	...	...	...	...	...	...	...	1
107	Gujránwála	5	3	2	...	...	...	...	1	2	1	...	...	...	...	...	1	...	...	...

TABLE VI.

BIRTH-PLACE IN INDIA BEYOND THE PRESIDENCY.

TABLE VI—*continued.*

BIRTH-PLACE.

A. II.—(a) BORN IN ADJACENT PROVINCES AND STATES—*continued.*

	District or State where born.	Population.			A Ward.		B Ward.		C Ward.		D Ward.		E Ward.		F Ward.		G Ward.		Harbours and Docks, Railways and Homeless.	
		Persons.	Males.	Females.	Males.	Females.	Males.	Females.	Males.	Females.	Males.	Females.	Males.	Females.	Males.	Females.	Males.	Females.	Males.	Females.
	1	2	3	4	5	6	7	8	9	10	11	12	13	14	15	16	17	18	19	20
108	Gurdáspur	18	18	......	......	......	......	......	......	......	2	...	16	...	...	...	...	...	...	...
109	Gurgaon	17	13	5	......	......	......	......	1	......	1	5	...	...	...	...	...	...	10	...
110	Hissár	60	50	10	......	......	......	......	35	6	3	3	...	...	3	...	...	...	9	1
111	Jhelum	187	179	8	1	......	3	......	1	1	8	2	95	2	...	1	...	...	71	2
112	Jullundur	27	19	8	8	......	......	......	1	......	4	...	6	8	...	...	...	...	...	...
113	Karnál	6	6	......	......	......	1	......	2	......	1	...	...	...	1	...	...	...	1	...
114	Lahore	511	405	106	171	50	27	2	14	......	59	24	72	20	9	3	18	2	35	5
115	Ludhiána	40	27	13	......	......	......	......	1	......	25	7	...	6	...	...	...	...	1	...
116	Lyallpur	6	6	......	6	......	......	......	......	......	...	...	...	...	...	...	...	...	...	...
117	Mainwala	1	1	......	......	......	......	......	......	......	...	...	1	...	...	...	...	...	...	...
118	Montgomery	1	1	......	......	......	......	......	1	......	...	...	...	...	...	...	...	...	...	...
119	Multán	75	47	28	1	2	6	6	......	......	3	1	43	5	3	1	11	...	...	11
120	Ráwalpindi	104	96	8	8	1	8	1	2	......	1	2	47	1	1	...	1	...	30	3
121	Rohtak	126	121	5	......	......	......	......	40	1	27	3	...	...	...	...	...	...	64	1
122	Shahpur	1	1	......	......	......	......	......	......	......	...	...	...	...	...	...	...	...	1	...
123	Sialkot	34	13	23	1	......	......	......	2	2	8	1	...	2	1	...	...	2	...	18
124	Simla	34	17	17	3	8	1	......	10	5	1	1	1	...	...	...	1	3	...	...
125	Unspecified	4,185	3,546	639	385	107	230	47	658	90	91	30	1,065	204	29	9	40	30	458	42
126	Baluchistan (Quetta) ...	579	425	154	219	127	11	......	15	......	7	1	78	7	27	4	6	3	83	13
	(b) FEUDATORY STATES—																			
127	Mysore	877	645	232	63	15	34	16	149	64	59	6	217	92	30	14	41	4	43	31
128	Hydera'ba'd State ...	8,302	5,681	2,621	384	168	762	273	538	291	343	176	2,774	1,969	165	116	635	448	300	172
129	Central India Agency.	4,055	3,010	1,045	130	101	395	107	783	314	200	140	1,110	248	87	38	124	50	292	47
130	Bhopal	429	317	112	15	3	62	13	87	23	7	14	129	30	16	11	14	4	37	5
131	Bundelkhand	13	12	1	1	......	4	......	......	......	...	...	3	...	...	...	2	1	2	...
132	Dewás	6	5	1	......	......	......	......	......	......	3	...	1	1	...	...	1	...	...	...
133	Dhar	25	21	4	......	......	11	......	4	......	1	1	3	1	...	...	...	...	3	2

TABLE VI—*continued.*

BIRTH-PLACE.

A. II.—(*a*) BORN IN ADJACENT PROVINCES AND STATES—*continued.*

	District or State where born.	Population.			A Ward.		B Ward.		C Ward.		D Ward.		E Ward.		F Wards.		G Ward.		Harbours and Docks, Railways and Homeless.	
		Persons.	Males.	Females.	Males.	Females.	Males.	Females.	Males.	Females.	Males.	Females.	Males.	Females.	Males.	Females.	Males.	Females.	Males.	Females.
	1	2	3	4	5	6	7	8	9	10	11	12	13	14	15	16	17	18	19	20
134	Gwalior	931	744	187	27	3	128	35	248	77	86	36	146	15	31	4	36	7	83	10
135	Indore	1,809	1,232	577	86	40	67	53	329	105	133	77	363	206	40	32	57	38	138	27
136	Jaorá	1	......	1	......	......	......	......	......	......	...	1	...	...	...	...	...	...	...	...
137	Ratlám	175	143	32	......	......	35	5	85	9	5	8	14	9	8	1	1	...	5	...
138	Rewah	198	119	79	......	......	......	......	......	......	...	...	116	76	...	...	3	...	...	3
139	Central India Unspecified...	468	417	51	10	40	......	1	......	......	23	3	317	1	2	...	20	...	46	...
140	**Rajputana Agency** ...	12,453	10,852	1,601	210	33	288	111	6,464	948	727	97	1,251	201	275	47	655	137	273	27
141	Alwar	150	145	5	2	1	3	......	117	3	3	...	16	1	...	...	3	...	3	...
142	Bánswára	19	19	......	......	......	......	......	......	......	...	...	19	...	...	...	...	...	...	...
143	Bharatpur	20	18	2	......	......	4	......	1	1	...	...	1	...	5	...	...	...	7	1
144	Bikaner	498	434	64	......	......	2	......	363	54	13	4	2	...	2	...	21	6	11	...
145	Bundi	10	10	......	......	......	......	......	7	......	...	...	1	...	...	...	...	...	2	...
146	Dholpur	4	3	1	......	......	......	......	......	......	...	...	3	1	..	...	...	...	...	...
147	Jaipur	4,632	4,025	607	99	11	431	64	2,620	354	245	39	331	75	61	8	209	47	89	9
148	Jaisalmer	3	......	3	......	......	......	......	......	......	...	...	...	...	...	...	...	...	...	3
149	Jhálawár	15	6	9	......	......	4	......	2	9	...	...	...	...	...	...	...	...	...	...
150	Jodpur	5,481	4,636	845	81	17	257	27	2,702	374	280	30	764	86	314	35	338	77	90	9
151	Kotah	23	22	1	......	......	......	......	......	......	1	...	1	...	...	...	...	...	20	1
152	Shahpura	15	13	2	......	......	......	......	......	......	...	...	12	...	...	...	...	3	1	...
153	Sirohi	205	192	13	28	4	......	......	127	7	33	1	6	1	...	...	1	...	...	...
154	Tonk	65	53	12	1	......	25	7	......	......	1	2	4	3	..	...	...	...	22	...
155	Udaipur	297	243	54	1	......	17	7	163	14	6	2	64	24	1	3	2	3	6	1
156	Unspecified	1,016	843	173	1	......	155	6	442	133	155	19	67	10	2	1	21	2	20	8
157	**Baroda State**	4,501	3,255	1,246	135	84	342	75	1,156	417	660	327	310	132	197	79	449	103	146	30
158	**Patiala**	159	142	17	......	......	30	12	40	......	4	4	3	1	...	...	...	...	15	—

TABLE VI.

BIRTH-PLACE IN INDIA BEYOND THE PRESIDENCY.

TABLE VI—*continued.*

BIRTH-PLACE.

A. II.—(b) BORN IN OTHER PROVINCES AND STATES IN INDIA—*continued.*

	District or State where born.	Population.			A Ward.		B Ward.		C Ward.		D Ward.		E Ward.		F Ward.		G Ward.		Harbours, Docks, Railways and Homeless.	
		Persons.	Males.	Females.	Males.	Females.	Males.	Females.	Males.	Females.	Males.	Females.	Males.	Females.	Males.	Females.	Males.	Females.	Males.	Females.
	1	2	3	4	5	6	7	8	9	10	11	12	13	14	15	16	17	18	19	20
	(a) BRITISH DISTRICTS—																			
159	Districts in Eastern Bengal and Assam ...	967	875	92	5	3	41	7	72	38	7	3	33	1	32	14	35	8	661	18
160	Backergunge	38	34	4	...	3	1	...	...	...	...	1	...	...	...	...	7	...	16	...
161	Chittagong	409	401	8	...	...	2	...	45	...	...	1	...	...	14	...	...	3	340	4
162	Dacca	327	299	29	3	...	16	6	5	1	6	...	30	...	4	11	18	3	217	8
163	Faridpur	49	6	43	...	...	...	...	...	36	...	1	1	1	...	...	...	...	5	6
164	Malda	1	1	...	...	...	...	...	...	...	...	...	...	...	1	...	...	...	...	...
165	Mymensingh	19	16	3	...	...	...	...	...	...	...	...	1	...	...	...	...	3	15	...
166	Rájsháhi	34	28	6	...	...	...	1	22	2	...	...	...	...	3	3	...	...	3	...
167	Sylhet	88	88	...	...	...	22	...	...	...	1	...	...	...	...	...	...	...	65	...
168	Eastern Bengal and Assam Unspecified	2	2	...	2	...	...	...	...	...	...	...	...	...	...	...	...	...	...	...
169	Districts in Bengal ...	2,962	2,303	659	259	137	128	35	415	83	168	34	372	156	25	14	33	12	908	189
170	Bánkurá	23	23	...	...	...	...	...	22	...	...	...	...	...	...	...	...	...	...	...
171	Bhágalpur	11	10	1	...	...	...	...	...	...	...	...	...	...	...	1	...	...	10	...
172	Burdwán	14	5	9	2	...	...	...	...	...	...	...	...	9	2	...	1	...	...	...
173	Calcutta	1,096	766	330	127	79	48	19	230	72	49	21	173	89	9	8	23	10	106	33
174	Cuttack	63	63	...	1	...	2	...	...	...	1	...	35	...	...	...	6	...	17	...
175	Darbhangá	2	1	1	...	...	1	...	...	...	...	...	...	...	...	...	...	...	...	1
176	Darjeeling	5	1	4	1	...	...	...	...	...	...	...	...	1	...	...	...	...	...	3
177	Gayá	6	5	1	...	...	1	...	...	...	...	...	...	...	...	...	...	...	4	1
178	Hooghly	9	1	8	...	...	...	...	...	...	...	1	1	7	...	...	...	...	...	...
179	Jessor	19	19	...	19	...	...	...	...	...	...	...	...	...	...	...	...	...	...	...
180	Khulná	5	3	2	...	...	3	...	...	...	...	...	...	...	...	...	...	...	...	2
181	Midnapur	10	6	4	...	...	...	...	6	...	...	3	...	...	...	1	...	...	...	1
182	Murshidábád	87	83	5	...	...	30	...	...	...	...	...	53	2	...	...	4	...	6	2
183	Muzaffarpur	33	3	30	...	...	...	...	...	...	...	...	...	30	...	...	...	...	3	...

TABLE VI.—*continued.*

BIRTH-PLACE.

A. II.—(*b*) BORN IN OTHER PROVINCES AND STATES IN INDIA—*continued.*

	District or State where born.	Population.			A Ward.		B Ward.		C Ward.		D Ward.		E Ward.		F Ward.		G Ward.		Harbour, Docks, Railways and Homeless.	
		Persons.	Males.	Females.	Males.	Females.	Males.	Females.	Males.	Females.	Males.	Females.	Males.	Females.	Males.	Females.	Males.	Females.	Males.	Females.
	1	2	3	4	5	6	7	8	9	10	11	12	13	14	15	16	17	18	19	20
184	Nadiá	11	......	11	......	9	......	......	......	......	...	...	...	...	...	1	...	1	...	...
185	Patna	80	66	14	13	1	5	......	2	......	...	...	16	1	...	...	...	1	30	11
186	Purí	2	2	......	......	......	......	......	......	......	1	...	...	...	1	...	...	...	...	...
187	Sáran	3	3	......	1	......	......	......	2	......	...	...	...	...	...	...	...	...	...	...
188	Sháhábád	87	84	3	......	......	11	......	......	......	...	...	48	1	...	1	...	...	25	1
189	Singhbhum	2	......	2	......	2	......	......	......	......	...	...	...	...	...	...	...	...	...	...
190	Unspecified	1,396	1,162	234	95	46	32	10	153	10	117	10	47	16	13	3	...	...	705	134
191	**Districts in Burma**	129	86	43	8	6	9	9	5	7	5	3	30	13	2	...	1	...	26	5
192	Mandalay	2	2	......	1	......	1	......	......	......	...	...	...	...	...	...	...	...	...	...
193	Rangoon	24	11	13	......	3	......	4	......	6	...	...	11	...	...	...	...	...	...	...
194	Burma Unspecified ...	103	73	30	7	3	8	5	5	1	5	3	19	13	2	...	1	...	23	5
195	**Districts in United Provinces of Agra and Oudh**	50,542	40,198	10,341	1,382	216	2,790	549	4,339	799	3,017	352	16,900	5,866	3,454	702	6,416	1,549	1,900	311
196	Agra	1,305	1,065	240	41	23	90	14	120	67	41	15	671	104	6	2	33	8	64	17
197	Allahábád	6,629	4,949	1,680	208	23	197	37	534	140	200	58	2,519	1,221	149	38	857	133	119	21
198	Aligarh	192	166	26	......	4	7	4	45	6	9	4	80	7	4	3	2	...	10	...
199	Almorá	116	116	......	......	......	......	......	115	......	...	...	...	...	1	...	...	...	...	...
200	Azamgarh	5,147	3,557	1,590	10	1	700	160	339	22	37	4	1,937	1,293	121	38	313	68	67	12
201	Balliá	10	10	......	1	......	1	......	......	......	...	...	...	...	...	...	...	...	8	...
202	Bándá	71	58	13	......	2	......	4	2	4	2	...	...	2	6	...	18	...	30	1
203	Bára Banki	1,446	935	511	14	1	8	2	17	2	35	3	787	407	14	2	11	3	59	2
204	Bareilly	42	41	1	......	......	......	......	41	......	...	1	...	...	...	...	...	...	...	...
205	Basti	1,918	1,382	531	30	......	170	29	63	16	71	8	729	338	169	114	53	11	91	20
206	Benares	3,385	2,875	510	93	2	144	29	117	1	53	7	1,548	332	391	46	309	66	137	28
207	Bijnor	16	13	3	8	......	......	......	......	1	5	3	...	...	...	...	...	...	...	...
208	Budaun	3	......	3	......	......	......	3	......	......	...	...	...	...	...	...	...	...	...	...
209	Bulandshahr	31	31	......	......	......	5	......	10	......	3	...	...	...	...	...	...	...	13	...

TABLE VI.

BIRTH-PLACE IN INDIA BEYOND THE PRESIDENCY.

TABLE VI—*continued.*

BIRTH-PLACE.

A. II.—(*b*) BORN IN OTHER PROVINCES AND STATES OF INDIA—*continued.*

	District or State where born.	Population.			A Ward.		B Ward.		C Ward.		D Ward.		E Ward.		F Ward.		G Ward.		Harbours and Docks, Railways and Homeless.	
		Persons.	Males.	Females.	Males.	Females.	Males.	Females.	Males.	Females.	Males.	Females.	Males.	Females.	Males.	Females.	Males.	Females.	Males.	Females.
	1	2	3	4	5	6	7	8	9	10	11	12	13	14	15	16	17	18	19	20
210	Cawnpore	2,737	2,229	508	47	35	166	18	468	79	90	12	957	218	157	60	212	76	82	10
211	Dehra-Dún	14	13	3	......	......	......	......	......	......	11	2	...	...	...	...	...	...	1	...
212	Etáwah	64	58	6	......	......	......	......	......	......	...	...	50	...	3	2	4	4	1	...
213	Farrukhábád	104	83	21	16	......	4	......	3	......	1	...	35	14	1	3	1	...	23	4
214	Fatehpur	851	676	175	18	2	275	37	77	10	10	10	130	94	78	18	44	14	47	...
215	Fyzábád	2,040	1,682	353	13	3	64	8	290	112	103	13	1,024	185	68	12	72	11	48	15
216	Gházípur	49	20	29	......	......	......	......	19	10	...	...	...	1	...	...	...	...	1	18
217	Gondá	1,024	808	216	2	1	4	14	167	......	85	34	495	161	1	1	21	...	33	5
218	Gorakhpur	295	212	83	1	8	28	......	5	......	1	2	88	67	3	4	51	5	37	7
219	Hamírpur	14	11	3	......	1	......	......	6	......	...	...	...	...	4	2	...	...	1	...
220	Hardoí	6	5	1	......	......	......	......	......	......	...	...	...	...	...	...	...	1	5	...
221	Jaunpur	6,551	5,912	639	183	13	181	3	147	8	751	11	1,375	100	790	88	2,337	408	158	8
222	Jhánsi	477	331	144	6	6	22	......	28	10	40	5	38	21	144	80	14	10	32	2
223	Lucknow	4,578	3,394	1,184	108	19	430	147	581	160	267	68	1,583	706	232	34	92	23	111	38
224	Meerut	113	91	22	14	......	3	......	9	2	...	1	19	5	1	1	10	7	35	6
225	Mirzápur	1,412	1,293	119	89	......	19	4	126	10	92	6	514	60	212	8	192	27	40	4
226	Morádábád	19	12	7	2	......	8	......	......	......	...	...	1	...	...	...	1	...	...	7
227	Muttra	652	543	109	6	......	51	10	422	83	33	9	10	6	11	...	4	2	4	...
228	Muzaffarnagar	12	12	......	......	......	3	......	......	......	9	...	...	...	...	...	...	...	...	...
229	Nainítál	15	15	......	......	......	......	......	......	......	2	...	...	...	...	...	13	...	...	...
230	Partábgarh	4,077	3,250	827	105	7	47	6	161	13	272	7	1,047	144	303	33	1,068	606	218	13
231	Ráebarelí	3,283	2,847	436	244	55	97	24	242	21	594	57	984	147	300	66	210	27	156	34
232	Sáharanpur	77	39	38	1	......	......	......	14	......	5	3	9	5	8	5	...	...	2	25
233	Sháhjahánpur	34	34	......	23	......	1	......	3	......	...	...	...	...	2	...	4	...	2	...
234	Sitápur	60	50	10	2	......	......	......	2	......	2	...	14	8	...	...	11	1	19	1
235	Sultánpur	717	603	114	34	......	43	......	24	3	29	4	107	66	97	9	110	25	159	8
236	Unao	793	658	135	69	5	30	5	110	18	72	9	106	43	163	38	67	14	50	6
237	Unspecified	160	118	42	......	5	4	1	23	......	85	9	32	36	11	1	13	...	...	...
238	Districts in North-West Frontier Province	1,101	835	266	81	24	234	61	23	2	66	36	144	86	27	1	49	6	211	47
239	Dera Ismail Khan	30	10	14	......	......	......	......	......	......	...	...	16	14	...	...	...	...	...	...
240	Házara	4	2	2	2	1	......	......	......	1	...	...	...	...	1	...	...	...	...	...

TABLE VI—*continued.*

BIRTH-PLACE.

A. II.—(*b*), (*c*), & (*d*) BORN IN OTHER PROVINCES AND STATES OF INDIA AND THE FRENCH AND PORTUGUESE SETTLEMENTS.

	District or State where born.	Population.			A Ward.		B Ward.		C Ward.		D Ward.		E Ward.		F Ward.		G Ward.		Harbours and Docks, Railways and Homeless.	
		Persons.	Males.	Females.	Males.	Females.	Males.	Females.	Males.	Females.	Males.	Females.	Males.	Females.	Males.	Females.	Males.	Females.	Males.	Females.
	1	2	3	4	5	6	7	8	9	10	11	12	13	14	15	16	17	18	19	20
241	Kohat	8	8	......	8	......	......	......	......	......	...	...	...	...	...	...	...	...	...	...
242	Peshāwar	969	737	232	71	23	222	57	23	1	20	28	129	71	17	1	45	5	211	47
243	Unspecified	90	73	18	......	1	12	7	......	......	46	8	...	1	10	...	4	1	...	...
244	**Andamans and Nicobars**	3	3	......	1	......	......	......	......	......	...	...	2	...	...	...	...	...	...	...
245	AJMER MERWA'RA ...	6.937	5,853	1.084	279	54	993	75	2,844	556	518	123	670	174	126	19	258	39	170	44
246	Ajmer	811	620	191	64	32	132	12	111	34	40	10	138	67	13	4	34	5	80	37
247	Merwāra	6,126	5,233	893	215	22	801	63	2,733	532	473	113	533	107	114	15	224	34	81	7
248	(*b*) **FEUDATORY STATES**	569	405	164	32	8	26	12	23	19	12	9	211	101	24	1	14	13	63	1
249	Cochin	325	203	122	30	8	3	1	5	6	2	6	114	90	8	1	13	10	28	1
250	Kashmir	188	155	33	2	......	17	9	15	14	10	3	76	6	...	...	...	1	35	...
251	Travancore	56	47	9	......	......	6	3	3	......	...	...	31	5	16	...	1	2	...	...
252	**State in Eastern Bengal and Assam**—Manipur	9	8	1	2	1	......	......	......	......	1	...	4	...	...	...	...	...	1	...
253	**States in Bengal** ...	6	6	......	......	......	......	......	......	......	...	...	2	...	...	...	...	...	4	...
254	Cooch Behār	2	2	......	......	......	......	......	......	......	...	...	...	...	...	...	...	...	2	...
255	Orissa States	4	4	......	......	......	......	......	......	......	...	...	2	...	...	...	...	...	2	...
256	**State in United Provinces of Agra and Oudh**—Rāmpur ...	140	81	59	2	......	11	10	31	4	10	...	12	37	3	...	10	2	2	5
257	(*c*) (*a*) **FRENCH SETTLEMENTS**	42	25	17	12	5	......	5	5	2	2	5	3	...	...	...	2	...	1	...
258	Chandernagore	8	3	5	1	......	......	5	......	......	...	...	2	...	...	...	...	...	...	...
259	Pondicherry	34	22	12	11	5	......	......	5	2	2	5	1	...	...	...	2	...	1	...
260	(*c*) (*b*) **PORTUGUESE SETTLEMENTS** ...	32.064	23.207	8.857	3,343	963	459	205	8.468	2,360	2,801	2,616	3.770	1.937	732	332	1.815	930	1.819	114
261	Damān	2.206	1,498	708	380	87	63	38	306	200	47	25	430	240	119	9	22	4	112	9
262	Diu	354	337	17	......	......	64	6	47	11	...	...	...	...	11	...	1	...	214	...
263	Goa	29.504	21,372	8,132	2,963	876	313	161	8,115	2,050	2,754	1,991	3,340	1,601	602	323	1,793	926	1,493	105
264	(*d*) **INDIA UNSPECIFIED**	1.765	1.314	451	144	34	212	63	316	52	55	34	223	173	4	3	286	39	74	74

TABLE VI.

Birth-place in Other Asiatic Countries and Europe.

TABLE VI—*continued.*

Birth-place.

	Country where born.	Population.			A Ward.		B Ward.		C Ward.		D Ward.		E Ward.		F Ward.		G Ward.		Harbours and Docks, Railways and Homeless.	
		Persons.	Males.	Females.	Males.	Females.	Males.	Females.	Males.	Females.	Males.	Females.	Males.	Females.	Males.	Females.	Males.	Females.	Males.	Females.
	1	2	3	4	5	6	7	8	9	10	11	12	13	14	15	16	17	18	19	20
	(B)—BORN IN OTHER ASIATIC COUNTRIES.																			
65	**Total** ...	7.246	5.658	1.590	663	153	1.359	285	622	195	230	165	1.180	681	59	13	87	33	1.457	67
266	Afghánistán	1.167	1,039	128	36	......	409	78	173	8	10	2	133	21	22	6	33	13	183	1
267	Arabia	2,322	1,901	421	33	9	441	97	89	36	36	18	588	248	4	...	8	4	724	9
268	Bhotán	3	3	......	......	......	......	......	3	......	...	...	...	...	...	...	...	...	...	...
269	Ceylon	94	75	19	24	8	3	......	7	2	2	5	20	1	4	...	...	2	15	1
270	China	476	416	60	30	......	23	4	75	9	2	4	35	8	...	...	...	...	246	35
271	Hongkong	3	2	1	1	......	......	......	......	......	...	...	1	1	...	...	...	...	...	...
272	Japan	270	141	129	25	6	2	1	......	......	23	12	15	106	...	...	6	4	65	...
273	Nepál	45	34	11	1	3	6	......	6	......	4	4	2	3	...	...	1	...	14	1
274	Persia	2,442	1,690	752	441	111	375	104	237	131	143	112	352	272	29	6	30	11	84	5
275	Russia in Asia ...	106	102	4	......	......	......	......	54	4	...	...	5	...	...	...	3	...	40	...
276	Straits Settlements ...	18	18	......	......	......	......	......	......	......	...	...	...	...	...	...	...	...	18	...
277	Turkey in Asia ...	281	226	55	54	15	11	1	9	5	5	9	29	21	...	...	...	...	116	15
278	Unspecified	9	9	......	9	......	......	......	......	......	...	...	...	...	...	...	...	...	...	...
	C.—BORN IN EUROPE.																			
279	**Total** ...	6.938	5.405	1.533	1.348	656	34	8	21	10	193	176	476	329	88	46	111	49	3.134	259
280	**United Kingdom** ...	5.760	4.572	1.188	1.050	516	33	7	16	7	169	134	400	196	86	46	98	42	2,720	240
281	England and Wales ...	4,878	3,806	983	847	429	27	7	13	7	136	103	316	164	81	43	85	32	2,389	190
282	Scotland	539	426	113	153	48	5	......	1	......	30	22	37	17	5	4	7	8	189	14
283	Ireland	342	210	93	51	40	1	......	3	......	3	9	41	15	...	...	6	2	143	27
284	Channel Islands and Isle of Man	1	1	......	......	......	......	......	......	......	...	...	1	...	...	...	...	...	...	...
285	Austria-Hungary ...	206	136	70	29	27	......	1	......	......	...	9	9	31	1	...	...	...	97	3
286	Belgium	9	5	4	3	1	......	......	......	......	...	...	...	3	...	...	...	...	3	...
287	Denmark	8	6	......	3	......	......	......	......	......	...	...	4	...	...	...	...	...	3	...
288	France	135	55	80	33	48	......	......	......	1	9	17	3	13	1	...	...	...	10	1
289	Germany	257	202	55	96	26	......	......	......	......	5	5	29	20	...	...	8	4	65	...
290	Gibraltar	3	......	3	......	1	......	......	......	......	...	...	...	...	...	...	...	...	...	2

TABLE VI.

Birth-place in Europe and Africa.

TABLE VI—*continued.*

Birth-place.

	Country where born.	Population.			A Ward.		B Ward.		C Ward.		D Ward.		E Ward.		F Ward.		G Ward.		Harbour and Docks, Railways and Homeless.	
		Persons.	Males.	Females.	Males.	Females.	Males.	Females.	Males.	Females.	Males.	Females.	Males.	Females.	Males.	Females.	Males.	Females.	Males.	Females.
	1	2	3	4	5	6	7	8	9	10	11	12	13	14	15	16	17	18	19	20
	(C)—BORN IN EUROPE—*continued.*																			
291	Greece	75	67	8	26	7	......	......	......	......	1	1	...	...	...	...	...	...	40	...
292	Holland	10	10	......	5	......	......	......	......	......	...	...	...	...	...	...	...	...	5	...
293	Italy	175	148	27	30	10	1	......	3	......	6	6	14	9	...	...	...	...	85	3
294	Malta	21	10	11	1	......	......	......	......	2	...	...	1	5	...	...	...	...	8	4
295	Norway	43	38	5	1	1	......	......	......	......	...	...	1	1	...	...	...	...	36	3
296	Portugal	33	25	8	5	1	......	......	1	......	...	...	9	5	...	...	3	1	7	1
297	Roumania	11	8	3	5	2	......	......	1	......	1	1	...	...	...	...	...	...	1	...
298	Russia	70	21	49	3	8	......	......	......	......	...	4	1	35	...	...	...	2	17	...
299	Spain	13	7	6	2	1	......	......	......	......	...	...	5	4	...	...	...	...	...	1
300	Sweden	31	26	5	......	......	......	......	......	......	...	...	...	3	...	...	1	...	25	2
301	Switzerland	72	65	7	40	7	......	......	......	......	2	...	...	...	...	...	1	...	13	...
302	Unspecified	6	2	4	......	......	......	......	......	......	...	...	2	4	...	...	...	...	...	...
	(D)—BORN IN AFRICA.																			
303	**Total** ...	467	284	183	38	38	36	49	44	17	8	5	87	49	1	3	4	14	66	8
304	Cape Colony	3	3	......	......	......	......	......	......	......	...	...	...	...	...	...	...	...	3	...
305	East Africa (British) ...	1	1	......	......	......	......	......	1	......	...	...	...	...	...	...	...	...	...	...
306	Egypt	63	49	14	5	2	......	......	29	......	...	...	9	12	...	...	...	...	6	...
307	Mauritius	78	45	33	17	19	......	......	......	1	...	...	11	8	...	3	1	1	16	1
308	Somaliland	5	5	......	......	......	2	......	......	......	3	...	...	...	...	...	...	...	...	...
309	Transvaal	2	1	1	1	......	......	......	......	......	...	1	...	...	...	...	...	...	...	...
310	Zanzibar	56	29	27	6	1	14	13	8	6	1	...	...	7	...	...	...	...	...	...
311	Unspecified	259	151	108	9	16	20	36	6	10	4	4	67	22	1	...	3	13	41	7

TABLE VI.

BIRTH-PLACE IN AMERICA, AUSTRALASIA, OR AT SEA.

TABLE VI—*continued.*

BIRTH-PLACE.

	Country where born.	Population.			A Ward.		B Ward.		C Ward.		D Ward.		E Ward.		F Ward.		G Ward.		Harbour and Docks, Railways and Homeless.	
		Persons.	Males.	Females.	Males.	Females.	Males.	Females.	Males.	Females.	Males.	Females.	Males.	Females.	Males.	Females.	Males.	Females.	Males.	Females.
	1	2	3	4	5	6	7	8	9	10	11	12	13	14	15	16	17	18	19	20
	(E)—BORN IN AMERICA.																			
312	**Total** ...	88	61	27	29	16	...	1	2	...	3	1	11	8	1	...	2	...	13	1
313	Brazil	1	...	1	...	...	...	...	...	...	...	1	...	...	...	...	...	...	...	...
314	Canada	3	3	...	...	...	...	...	...	...	...	...	...	...	...	...	...	...	3	...
315	Chille	1	1	...	...	...	...	...	...	...	...	...	...	...	...	...	...	...	1	...
316	Jamaica	6	6	...	...	...	...	...	...	...	...	...	...	...	...	...	...	...	6	...
317	Mexico	1	1	...	...	...	...	...	...	...	...	...	...	...	...	...	...	...	1	...
318	Newfoundland ...	1	1	...	...	...	...	...	...	...	...	...	...	...	...	...	...	...	1	...
319	Unspecified	75	49	26	29	16	...	1	2	...	3	...	11	8	1	...	2	...	1	1
	(F)—BORN IN AUSTRALASIA.																			
320	**Total** ...	64	51	13	10	...	...	...	3	...	11	4	1	6	1	2	...	...	25	1
321	Australia	43	34	9	9	...	...	...	1	...	10	3	1	6	...	...	...	...	13	...
322	Java	2	2	...	...	...	...	...	2	...	...	...	...	...	...	...	...	...	...	...
323	New Zealand	15	14	1	1	...	...	...	...	...	1	1	...	...	...	...	...	...	12	...
324	Sumatra	3	1	2	...	...	...	...	...	...	...	...	...	...	1	2	...	...	...	...
325	Tasmania	1	...	1	...	...	...	...	...	...	...	...	...	...	...	...	...	...	...	1
	(G)—BORN AT SEA.																			
326	**At Sea** ...	16	2	14	1	9	...	...	...	...	...	...	...	2	...	1	...	...	1	2

TABLE VI.

PART II—(CORRESPONDING TO IMPERIAL TABLE XI—PART III).

SPECIAL STATISTICS REGARDING BIRTH-PLACE COMBINED WITH AGE, CASTE AND OCCUPATION FOR BOMBAY CITY.

TABLE VI.

Part II.—Special Statistics regarding Birth-place combined with Age, Caste and Occupation for Bombay City.

District of Birth.	Caste.	Total number of Immigrants.			Age.						Workers.		Dependants.		Mill-hands.		Clerks.	
					0—15		15—40		40 and over.									
		Persons.	Males.	Females.	Males.	Females.	Males.	Females.	Males.	Females.	Males.	Females.	Males.	Females.	Males.	Females.	Males.	Females.
1	2	3	4	5	6	7	8	9	10	11	12	13	14	15	16	17	18	19
	Total ...	16.298	11.925	4.373	1.751	1.077	8.224	2.667	1.950	629	9.734	645	2.191	3.728	336	28	848	1
AHMADA'BA'D.	Bhangi ...	960	647	313	130	77	437	310	90	26	514	194	133	119	2	...	...	...
	Bráhman, Audich.	882	730	152	84	27	448	101	198	24	534	16	195	136	...	...	127	...
	" Others .	1,152	941	211	110	49	589	133	212	79	609	15	243	106	18	...	141	...
	Dhed or Mahár ...	299	216	83	54	7	135	61	27	15	155	61	61	23	18	3	1	...
	Kunbi ...	331	283	48	29	13	224	33	30	3	254	5	29	43	4	...	14	...
	Lohár ...	1.655	1,309	346	225	47	916	289	168	10	1,070	10	239	336	5	...	...	...
	Maráthá ...	383	303	80	27	15	224	41	51	21	273	34	29	56	63	8	15	...
	Shimpi ...	496	435	31	24	3	378	24	63	4	414	5	21	26	...	...	7	...
	Sutár ...	308	245	63	33	13	178	40	34	11	221	3	24	60	...	...	3	...
	Lohánâ ...	190	166	24	18	5	138	14	10	8	143	3	23	21	...	...	15	...
	Váni, Osvál (Hindu) ...	146	131	15	18	2	83	10	31	3	115	1	16	14	2	...	12	...
	Váni, Others (Hindu) ...	1.454	1,001	453	144	100	700	231	157	72	791	21	210	432	4	...	233	...
	Bohori ...	400	311	89	60	34	190	38	55	17	225	10	83	79	...	...	10	...
	Memon ...	239	132	107	29	44	68	49	35	14	104	4	28	103	3	...	5	...
	Pathán ...	135	106	29	14	7	80	18	12	4	83	4	13	25	12	...	...	...
	Sheikh ...	991	718	273	123	72	474	158	121	43	600	19	118	255	24	2	14	...
	Sayad ...	180	162	18	22	3	95	12	45	3	127	1	35	17	7	...	4	...

District of Birth.	Caste.	Labourers.		Domestic servants.		Gavlis.		Leather workers.		Shop-keepers.		Sweepers.		Cart-drivers.		Beggars.		Lawyers, Doctors, Teachers and Engineers.		Artisans of all kinds.	
		Males.	Females.	Males.	Females.	Males.	Females.	Males.	Females.	Males.	Females.	Males.	Females.	Males.	Females.	Males.	Females.	Males.	Females.	Males.	Females.
1	2	20	21	22	23	24	25	26	27	28	29	30	31	32	33	34	35	36	37	38	39
	Total ...	505	135	1.005	65	81	6	17	13	1.800	50	565	195	493	...	134	36	119	9	2.942	48
AHMADA'BA'D	Bhangi ...	4	...	...	...	...	...	...	...	...	...	505	194	2	...	...	...	...	...	1	...
	Bráhman, Audich.	10	...	107	2	5	...	...	...	82	2	...	...	...	...	24	6	18	...	17	...
	" Others.	14	1	155	5	7	...	...	...	104	2	...	...	4	...	12	1	23	1	46	...
	Dhed or Mahár ...	56	48	14	3	...	...	...	...	2	...	38	...	...	...	11	...	...	...	5	1
	Kunbi ...	23	3	64	1	...	...	...	...	33	1	...	...	3	...	4	...	...	...	65	...
	Lohár ...	15	...	12	...	...	...	...	...	15	...	...	...	6	...	7	...	...	...	1,001	10
	Maráthá ...	27	6	41	3	4	...	...	...	39	2	...	...	35	...	4	4	2	...	27	1
	Shimpi ...	1	1	2	...	...	...	...	...	9	...	...	...	...	...	...	...	...	...	420	...
	Sutár ...	...	...	...	...	...	...	...	...	4	...	...	...	...	...	...	...	2	...	210	3
	Lohánâ ...	6	...	11	1	...	...	...	...	80	1	...	...	3	...	5	...	5	...	10	...
	Váni, Osvál (Hindu) ...	...	...	17	...	2	...	...	...	58	...	...	...	1	...	2	...	...	...	13	...
	Váni, Others (Hindu) ...	3	...	91	6	...	...	...	...	326	5	...	...	9	...	9	...	20	...	41	2
	Bohori ...	13	1	40	8	...	...	...	...	100	...	...	...	1	...	1	...	3	...	23	...
	Memon ...	5	...	10	2	...	...	...	...	25	1	...	...	34	...	...	...	1	...	7	1
	Pathán ...	10	...	1	3	...	...	...	...	12	...	...	...	1	...	2	...	2	...	45	1
	Sheikh ...	60	...	92	5	11	...	...	...	118	...	...	1	33	...	10	2	2	...	134	3
	Sayad ...	9	...	14	...	...	...	...	...	42	...	...	...	1	...	1	...	1	...	39	...

TABLE VI—*continued.*

PART II.—Special Statistics regarding Birth-place combined with Age, Caste and Occupation for Bombay City.

District of Birth.	Caste.	Total number of Immigrants.			Age. 0—15		Age. 15—40		Age. 40 and over.		Workers.		Dependants.		Mill-hands.		Clerks.	
		Persons.	Males.	Females.	Males.	Females.	Males.	Females.	Males.	Females.	Males.	Females.	Males.	Females.	Males.	Females.	Males.	Females.
1	2	3	4	5	6	7	8	9	10	11	12	13	14	15	16	17	18	19
SURAT.	Total ...	35,072	24,331	10,741	3,724	2,556	15,912	5,339	4,695	2,346	19,666	1,244	4,665	9,497	509	41	1,754	3
	Bhangi ...	296	194	102	49	32	111	62	85	8	137	38	67	64	...	...	...	...
	Bráhman, Gaud Sárasvat.	191	166	26	25	5	112	13	29	7	125	1	41	24	...	...	83	...
	" Audich ...	357	237	120	46	25	163	71	29	24	195	6	42	114	2	...	67	...
	" Others ...	1,823	1,288	535	297	133	799	279	192	123	945	21	343	514	7	...	350	...
	Chámbhár or Mochi ...	480	360	120	88	39	220	69	52	12	229	10	131	110	30	1	1	...
	Dhed or Mahár ...	2,498	2,055	443	263	100	1,460	395	832	48	1,632	97	223	346	23	7	4	...
	Kshatriya ...	534	338	136	74	43	270	76	54	16	320	15	69	121	9	...	9	...
	Koli ...	2,699	2,119	580	306	169	1,501	385	312	36	1,845	67	274	513	36	1	...	...
	Khárwa ...	1,170	1,073	97	92	27	823	61	158	9	1,015	41	58	56	2	6	5	...
	Maráthá ...	969	783	186	116	45	548	113	119	28	662	51	121	135	166	5	19	...
	Shimpi ...	525	339	186	70	70	227	98	42	18	279	21	60	165	1	...	8	...
	Sutár ...	611	420	191	63	57	273	110	85	24	331	12	89	179	1	...	1	...
	Lohána ...	245	185	60	29	12	118	40	38	8	147	6	38	55	...	...	21	...
	Váni, Osvál (Hindu) ...	210	167	43	25	10	110	25	32	8	131	5	36	40	...	...	31	...
	Váni, Others (Hindu) ...	2,990	1,632	1,158	307	291	1,045	664	280	203	1,334	69	298	1,089	18	1	336	...
	Bohori ...	1,113	753	360	190	116	376	190	187	54	507	6	246	354	4	...	26	...
	Memon ...	205	101	104	19	35	63	56	19	13	83	9	18	95	3	...	...	...
	Sheikh ...	1,378	897	481	143	113	576	256	178	112	767	65	130	416	44	1	14	...
	Váni, Osvál (Jain).	311	190	121	30	41	125	68	35	12	151	2	39	119	...	...	18	...
	" Others (Jain).	520	288	232	45	66	222	139	21	27	221	13	77	219	1	...	19	...
	Zoroastrian ...	6,674	3,837	2,837	527	455	1,978	1,312	1,332	1,070	2,715	233	1,122	2,604	69	...	580	2

District of Birth.	Caste.	Labourers.		Domestic servants.		Gavlis.		Leather workers.		Shop-keepers.		Sweepers.		Cart-drivers.		Beggars.		Lawyers, Doctors, Teachers and Engineers.		Artisans of all kinds.	
		Males.	Females.	Males.	Females.	Males.	Females.	Males.	Females.	Males.	Females.	Males.	Females.	Males.	Females.	Males.	Females.	Males.	Females.	Males.	Females.
1	2	20	21	22	23	24	25	26	27	28	29	30	31	32	33	34	35	36	37	38	39
SURAT.	Total ...	2,533	191	3,617	262	32	4	163	21	2,420	150	122	29	761	4	177	49	471	30	2,850	224
	Bhangi ...	10	1	10	7	...	...	...	...	...	...	100	28	...	...	1	1	...	...	...	...
	Bráhman, Gaud Sárasvat.	2	...	16	3	...	...	...	...	20	...	...	...	...	...	11	...	4	1	16	...
	" Audich ...	1	...	34	2	2	...	...	...	35	1	...	...	3	...	5	...	11	...	10	1
	" Others ...	5	1	104	6	...	1	...	...	112	...	...	...	...	...	25	3	63	...	165	...
	Chámbhár or Mochi ...	10	...	4	...	...	...	151	6	1	...	...	...	1	...	...	1	...	...	11	...
	Dhed or Mahár ...	489	33	1,003	42	...	...	...	...	16	1	11	1	52	...	4	1	2	...	62	6
	Kshatriya ...	9	...	6	...	...	...	...	...	21	1	...	...	2	...	...	...	1	...	258	13
	Koli ...	279	20	329	11	...	...	...	...	23	1	...	...	300	3	35	3	4	...	137	6
	Khárwa ...	309	7	38	3	...	...	...	...	10	1	...	...	47	...	2	13	60	...	...	...
	Maráthá ...	130	12	99	2	...	...	...	...	41	8	...	...	43	...	6	3	4	...	77	3
	Shimpi ...	2	...	2	...	...	...	...	...	5	...	...	...	...	...	...	...	6	...	224	21
	Sutár ...	3	...	5	...	...	...	...	...	1	...	...	...	...	...	...	...	3	...	294	9
	Lohána ...	...	...	31	2	...	...	...	...	66	3	...	...	2	...	...	...	1	...	7	...
	Váni, Osvál (Hindu) ...	1	2	12	...	...	...	...	...	34	...	...	...	4	...	2	...	1	...	17	...
	Váni, Others (Hindu) ...	20	4	184	14	3	...	...	...	377	23	...	...	22	...	13	...	27	3	109	3
	Bohori ...	1	...	68	1	...	...	...	...	201	1	...	...	3	...	2	1	9	...	43	...
	Memon ...	4	...	12	3	1	...	...	...	36	2	...	...	13	...	1	1	...	1	2	1
	Sheikh ...	59	11	84	14	12	2	...	...	143	6	6	...	13	1	14	7	12	2	201	9
	Váni, Osvál (Jain).	...	...	4	...	...	...	...	...	106	...	...	...	...	...	1	...	...	...	1	...
	" Others (Jain)	...	...	20	...	...	...	...	...	143	...	...	...	...	...	...	...	1	...	4	1
	Zoroastrian ...	...	...	234	80	...	...	...	...	446	21	...	...	...	...	...	...	264	17	816	36

TABLE VI—*continued.*

PART II.—Special Statistics regarding Birth-place combined with Age, Caste and Occupation for Bombay City.

District of Birth.	Caste.	Total number of Immigrants.			Age. 0—15		Age. 15—40		Age. 40 and over.		Workers.		Dependants.		Mill-hands.		Clerks.	
		Persons.	Males.	Females.	Males.	Females.	Males.	Females.	Males.	Females.	Males.	Females.	Males.	Females.	Males.	Females.	Males.	Females.
1	2	3	4	5	6	7	8	9	10	11	12	13	14	15	16	17	18	19
	Total ...	15.705	10.112	5.593	1.889	1.396	6.599	3.114	1.644	1.083	7.687	1.215	2.425	4.378	1.094	396	776	...
THA'NA.	A'gri	753	705	48	73	16	536	25	97	7	663	13	43	35	18	1	3	...
	Bhandári	560	407	153	100	41	210	92	97	20	286	28	121	125	57	11	10	...
	Bráhman, Chitpávan	303	200	103	54	29	122	60	24	13	110	1	90	101	...	...	63	...
	Bráhman, Deshasth	533	363	170	90	51	201	84	71	35	212	6	150	164	...	...	119	...
	Bráhman, Gaud Sárasvat ...	140	103	37	32	15	61	18	10	4	55	...	48	37	1	...	34	...
	Bráhman, Others.	356	264	92	57	30	179	42	28	20	169	3	95	59	...	...	101	...
	Chámbhár or Mochi	642	366	276	99	64	199	153	68	57	243	86	123	190	115	43	...	...
	Dhed or Mahár ...	804	574	230	49	23	431	181	104	26	532	140	42	61	45	10	1	...
	Kshatriya, Khatri or Chatri ...	530	305	225	72	58	178	104	54	63	210	6	95	219	13	...	46	...
	Koli	643	523	120	63	25	319	65	111	30	470	59	53	61	24	7	4	...
	Maráthá	2,421	1,656	765	272	141	1,192	537	172	107	1,370	379	266	406	719	278	26	...
	Sonár	523	297	226	62	52	182	108	53	66	214	5	83	221	1	...	35	...
	Váni	305	177	128	29	33	118	61	30	34	131	9	46	119	...	1	17	...
	Sheikh	992	624	368	84	86	411	194	129	88	438	49	196	319	5	8	7	...
	Zoroastrian ...	465	269	196	48	41	154	109	72	46	167	12	102	184	...	...	30	...

District of Birth.	Caste.	Labourers.		Domestic servants.		Gavlis.		Leather workers.		Shop-keepers.		Sweepers.		Cart-drivers.		Beggars.		Lawyers, Doctors, Teachers and Engineers.		Artisans of all kinds.	
		Males.	Females.	Males.	Females.	Males.	Females.	Males.	Females.	Males.	Females.	Males.	Females.	Males.	Females.	Males.	Females.	Males.	Females.	Males.	Females.
1	2	20	21	22	23	24	25	26	27	28	29	30	31	32	33	34	35	36	37	38	39
	Total ...	803	354	410	60	13	...	106	23	616	125	39	4	157	6	85	18	76	5	1.158	62
THA'NA.	A'gri	17	5	10	1	1	...	...	...	1	3	...	...	9	...	3	...	...	...	30	3
	Bhandári	3	4	3	...	...	...	...	...	57	6	...	...	...	...	...	...	1	...	60	2
	Bráhman, Chitpávan	...	...	6	...	...	...	...	...	6	...	...	...	4	...	2	...	5	...	3	...
	Bráhman, Deshasth	...	...	5	3	...	...	...	...	11	...	...	...	3	...	3	...	5	...	7	...
	Bráhman, Gaud Sárasvat ...	...	...	1	...	...	...	...	...	12	...	...	...	...	...	...	...	2	...	3	...
	Bráhman, Others.	...	...	9	1	...	...	...	...	13	1	...	...	...	...	1	...	11	...	7	...
	Chámbhár or Mochi	6	11	...	...	...	...	103	23	...	1	...	...	...	...	...	...	...	...	3	3
	Dhed or Mahár ...	333	120	60	3	...	...	1	...	13	...	34	...	2	...	2	...	...	...	9	1
	Kshatriya, Khatri or Chatri ...	2	3	8	1	...	...	...	...	6	...	...	...	10	...	...	...	4	...	39	1
	Koli	11	...	13	2	...	...	...	...	13	36	...	...	3	...	1	...	...	...	23	...
	Maráthá	103	60	77	6	2	...	...	...	55	6	...	...	39	5	39	4	2	...	110	8
	Sonár	...	2	8	3	...	...	...	...	9	...	...	...	2	...	1	...	8	...	129	...
	Váni	2	...	17	2	...	...	...	...	56	...	...	...	1	...	...	...	5	...	10	...
	Sheikh	21	6	17	2	1	...	...	...	90	12	...	...	17	...	34	2	2	...	128	14
	Zoroastrian ...	...	...	18	4	...	...	...	...	35	...	...	...	...	...	...	...	11	1	14	...

TABLE VI—*continued.*

PART II.—Special Statistics regarding Birth-place combined with Age, Caste and Occupation for Bombay City.

District of Birth.	Caste.	Total number of Immigrants.			Age. 0—15		Age. 15—40		Age. 40 and over.		Workers.		Dependants.		Mill-hands.		Clerks.	
		Persons.	Males.	Females.	Males.	Females.	Males.	Females.	Males.	Females.	Males.	Females.	Males.	Females.	Males.	Females.	Males.	Females.
1	2	3	4	5	6	7	8	9	10	11	12	13	14	15	16	17	18	19
AHMADNAGAR.	Total ...	14.611	8.979	5.632	1.596	1.183	5.939	3.351	1.432	1.099	7.456	1.729	1.523	3.903	1.330	398	204	...
	Chámbhár or Mochi	450	244	206	37	46	176	131	31	30	207	69	37	137	36	18	2	...
	Dhed or Mahár...	3.133	1,763	1,369	319	371	1,155	851	289	347	1,474	489	289	881	194	63	3	...
	Maráthá	4.006	2,669	1,337	446	276	1,837	836	383	235	2,320	497	349	840	604	240	23	...
	Pathán	188	121	67	26	16	66	37	29	14	99	12	22	55	17	2	2	...
	Sheikh	1.432	1.017	415	207	82	640	241	170	92	813	70	206	345	116	1	7	...
	Sayad	178	121	57	30	16	64	29	27	12	84	8	37	49	19	...	...	...

District of Birth.	Caste.	Labourers.		Domestic servants.		Gavlis.		Leather workers.		Shop-keepers.		Sweepers.		Cart-drivers.		Beggars.		Lawyers, Doctors, Teachers and Engineers.		Artisans of all kinds.	
		Males.	Females.	Males.	Females.	Males.	Females.	Males.	Females.	Males.	Females.	Males.	Females.	Males.	Females.	Males.	Females.	Males.	Females.	Males.	Females.
1	2	20	21	22	23	24	25	26	27	28	29	30	31	32	33	34	35	36	37	38	39
AHMADNAGAR.	Total ...	2.494	614	363	126	29	2	66	21	486	140	34	23	397	...	39	40	42	12	840	174
	Chámbhár or Mochi	90	23	2	2	...	...	59	15	1	1	...	...	2	...	1	2	...	...	10	4
	Dhed or Mahár ...	927	327	79	37	...	...	...	...	10	8	...	16	30	...	13	8	1	...	66	3
	Maráthá	838	101	66	43	1	1	...	...	111	27	...	...	205	...	22	2	8	...	138	14
	Pathán	18	...	10	2	...	...	...	1	12	4	...	...	4	...	3	...	...	...	11	3
	Sheikh	105	18	80	9	1	...	1	...	79	12	1	...	47	...	28	2	7	...	139	6
	Sayad	9	1	12	...	...	...	1	...	9	6	...	...	2	...	2	...	1	...	18	1

District of Birth.	Caste.	Total number of Immigrants.			Age. 0—15		Age. 15—40.		Age. 40 and over.		Workers.		Dependants.		Mill-hands.		Clerks.	
		Persons	Males.	Females.	Males.	Females.	Males.	Females.	Males.	Females.	Males.	Females.	Males.	Females.	Males.	Females.	Males.	Females.
1	2	3	4	5	6	7	8	9	10	11	12	13	14	15	16	17	18	19
NA'SIK.	Total ...	9.863	5.821	4.042	1.045	866	3.733	2.441	1.040	735	4.683	1.076	1.139	2.966	801	242	161	...
	Dhed or Mahár...	1.409	848	561	181	114	556	381	111	66	663	248	185	313	19	23	4	...
	Maráthá	3.508	2,122	1,386	318	288	1,397	850	407	348	1,800	350	323	1,006	468	135	22	...
	Sheikh	808	434	374	73	71	259	193	102	104	318	53	116	321	31	4	3	...

District of Birth.	Caste.	Labourers.		Domestic servants.		Gavlis.		Leather workers.		Shop-keepers.		Sweepers.		Cart-drivers.		Beggars.		Lawyers, Doctors, Teachers and Engineers.		Artisans of all kinds.	
		Males.	Females.	Males.	Females.	Males.	Females	Males	Females.	Males.	Females.	Males.	Females.	Males.	Females.	Males.	Females.	Males.	Females.	Males.	Females
1	2	20	21	22	23	24	25	26	27	28	29	30	31	32	33	34	35	36	37	38	39
NA'SIK.	Total ...	1.149	395	185	93	15	...	56	21	242	95	65	9	1.024	10	44	37	29	8	524	67
	Dhed or Mahár...	447	171	45	21	...	...	3	...	1	3	56	2	11	1	6	6	...	...	25	...
	Maráthá	361	111	43	30	...	...	...	...	66	38	...	...	852	5	15	10	1	...	78	12
	Sheikh	34	6	15	7	2	...	3	...	45	6	1	1	13	...	1	4	5	1	138	16

TABLE VI—*continued*.

PART II.—Special Statistics regarding Birth-place combined with Age, Caste and Occupation for Bombay City.

District of Birth.	Caste.	Total number of Immigrants.			Age. 0—15		Age. 15—40		Age. 40 and over.		Workers.		Dependants.		Mill-hands.		Clerks.	
		Persons.	Males.	Females.	Males.	Females.	Males.	Females.	Males.	Females.	Males.	Females.	Males.	Females.	Males.	Females.	Males.	Females.
1	2	3	4	5	6	7	8	9	10	11	12	13	14	15	16	17	18	19
POONA.	**Total** ...	71.185	42.114	29.071	7.056	6.534	28.593	17.349	6.466	5.188	34.461	8.543	7.653	20.528	5.164	1.528	990	...
	Bráhman, Chitpávan	592	388	204	76	69	241	106	71	30	242	1	146	203	...	...	129	...
	Bráhman, Deshasth	1.014	657	357	120	97	412	190	125	61	465	9	192	349	...	...	232	...
	Bráhman, Others.	698	434	264	62	65	294	153	78	47	316	16	118	248	9	3	116	...
	Chámbhár or Mochi	2.395	1,371	1,024	343	279	843	547	185	198	1,047	239	324	753	256	89	3	...
	Dhed or Mahár ...	10.108	5,304	4,8?4	800	93?	3,723	3,037	781	846	4,494	1,915	810	2,889	423	391	67	...
	Dhobi or Parit ...	572	307	265	60	65	206	144	41	86	255	103	52	102	54	13	...	...
	Gavli	269	183	86	42	22	108	42	33	22	148	37	38	49	20	3	12	...
	Gháti	2.327	1,682	745	376	197	1,024	419	184	129	1,256	243	328	502	159	64	6	...
	Kunbi	1.575	962	613	149	160	715	354	98	99	806	136	156	475	78	28	11	...
	Máli	2.559	1,408	1,151	257	263	881	649	270	239	1,197	564	211	587	423	180	1	...
	Maráthá	31.947	19,749	12,198	2,988	2,698	14,037	7,630	2,724	1,870	16,393	3,465	3,356	8,631	3,071	783	107	...
	Nhávi	701	407	294	86	91	262	107	59	36	321	36	86	259	11	10	2	...
	Shimpi	691	375	316	65	84	227	154	83	78	308	30	67	286	13	5	13	...
	Sonár	510	302	208	52	53	193	116	57	39	215	19	87	189	6	5	15	...
	Teli	782	424	358	107	85	228	197	89	76	327	112	97	346	46	20	1	...
	Váni (Hindu) ...	339	233	106	33	29	161	57	39	20	187	21	46	85	24	5	11	...
	Pathán	461	300	161	52	31	175	91	73	39	240	41	51	120	30	2	8	...
	Sheikh	2.593	2,011	582	252	122	1,267	334	452	126	1,669	138	342	444	167	3	28	...
	Sayad	431	273	158	30	32	103	94	72	32	230	20	43	138	16	2	5	...
	Zoroastrian ...	504	270	224	49	39	155	138	66	57	178	7	92	227	...	...	29	...

District of Birth.	Caste.	Labourers.		Domestic servants.		Gavlis.		Leather workers.		Shop-keepers.		Sweepers.		Cart-drivers.		Beggars.		Lawyers, Doctors, Teachers and Engineers.		Artisans of all kinds.	
		Males.	Females.	Males.	Females.	Males.	Females.	Males.	Females.	Males.	Females.	Males.	Females.	Males.	Females.	Males.	Females.	Males.	Females.	Males.	Females.
1	2	20	21	22	23	24	25	26	27	28	29	30	31	32	33	34	35	36	37	38	39
POONA.	**Total** ...	11.255	3,621	1.455	648	82	43	4:5	74	3.076	980	388	49	4.562	92	471	146	244	35	3,536	690
	Bráhman, Chitpávan	...	...	6	...	...	...	...	...	17	...	...	...	3	...	2	...	37	...	9	...
	Bráhman, Deshasth	...	...	12	5	...	...	...	...	42	...	...	...	9	...	11	...	21	1	14	...
	Bráhman, Others.	9	...	19	5	...	...	...	...	37	3	...	...	1	...	21	...	24	1	15	1
	Chámbhár or Mochi	310	50	17	1	...	...	385	45	19	14	...	...	31	...	5	2	1	...	94	58
	Dhed or Mahár ...	2,700	1,136	340	250	...	...	23	...	26	...	170	32	157	8	98	38	10	4	160	10
	Dhobi or Parit ...	11	2	2	2	...	...	...	...	9	...	...	...	...	...	...	1	...	...	173	72
	Gavli	34	1	1	4	30	20	...	...	23	4	...	...	2	...	8	2	2	...	7	3
	Gháti	372	68	14	15	2	...	...	...	60	31	...	...	476	23	3	2	...	...	62	11
	Kunbi	245	71	8	15	1	...	...	...	33	12	...	...	371	1	4	2	2	...	35	2
	Máli	255	128	29	25	...	...	...	...	208	103	...	...	143	5	5	3	2	...	70	18
	Maráthá	6,188	1,997	498	181	30	16	...	...	1,4?8	463	12	...	2,946	3	171	73	24	3	1,035	169
	Nhávi	35	16	...	3	...	...	...	...	1	3	...	...	...	...	...	...	...	...	285	3
	Shimpi	9	...	6	2	...	...	...	...	63	2	...	...	...	...	...	...	4	7	180	13
	Sonár	2	4	1	...	...	...	...	...	12	1	...	...	...	...	1	...	3	...	165	3
	Teli	51	12	4	4	...	...	...	...	144	69	...	...	43	...	3	1	...	...	15	9
	Váni (Hindu) ...	12	1	8	1	...	...	...	...	83	8	...	1	3	...	...	...	1	...	16	...
	Pathán	34	2	17	3	...	...	...	...	23	6	...	...	36	...	3	...	5	...	53	3
	Sheikh	2?8	11	1?8	24	3	...	5	...	283	17	1	...	140	...	54	5	22	...	322	22
	Sayad	20	1	23	3	...	...	...	...	29	3	...	...	14	...	5	3	3	...	60	6
	Zoroastrian ...	...	...	4	1	...	...	...	...	27	...	...	...	...	...	...	...	31	...	16	1

TABLE VI—*continued.*

PART II.—Special Statistics regarding Birth-place combined with Age, Caste and Occupation for Bombay City.

District of Birth.	Caste.	Total number of Immigrants.			Age. 0–15		Age. 15–40		Age. 40 and over.		Workers.		Dependants.		Mill-hands.		Clerks.	
		Persons.	Males.	Females.	Males.	Females.	Males.	Females.	Males.	Females.	Males.	Females.	Males.	Females.	Males.	Females.	Males.	Females.
1	2	3	4	5	6	7	8	9	10	11	12	13	14	15	16	17	18	19
SATARA.	Total ...	56.754	39.818	16.936	5.735	3.270	28.118	10.613	5.965	3.053	34.940	5.835	4.878	11.181	7.216	1.404	467	...
	Bráhman, Chitpávan	318	227	91	44	20	147	57	36	14	138	3	89	88	...	...	72	...
	Bráhman, Deshasth	361	239	122	41	38	161	64	47	20	174	1	65	121	...	...	67	...
	Bráhman, Others.	391	262	129	44	37	170	77	48	15	163	3	80	126	9	...	72	...
	Chámbhár or Mochi	3,244	2,000	1,244	454	340	1,284	670	264	225	1,701	316	299	928	301	103	...	...
	Dhed or Mahár ...	9,723	6,043	3,680	1,055	713	4,210	2,412	778	555	5,232	1,634	811	2,046	1,313	477	...	...
	Dhobi or Parit ...	317	190	127	41	30	115	63	34	34	161	40	39	78	61	14	...	...
	Ghāti	2,156	1,789	367	210	80	1,433	256	146	62	1,614	125	146	272	613	63	4	...
	Kunbi	969	744	225	66	32	571	155	107	38	681	63	63	136	93	18	7	...
	Máli	400	276	124	49	26	199	71	28	27	249	31	36	90	87	9	...	...
	Maráthá	29,369	22,028	7,341	2,689	1,280	15,922	4,781	3,437	1,300	19,824	2,716	2,204	4,626	4,313	593	91	...
	Nhávi	1,078	841	247	92	56	663	153	83	38	759	13	82	234	29	4	...	...
	Shimpi	315	178	137	31	26	119	76	28	35	137	18	41	119	2	3	2	...
	Pathán	200	128	72	17	13	86	34	25	25	109	12	19	60	6	...	5	...
	Sheikh	1,613	1,017	596	70	105	675	312	302	149	856	120	191	446	107	13	10	...
	Sayad	278	175	103	42	25	109	53	24	25	135	17	40	86	21	2	4	...

District of Birth.	Caste.	Labourers.		Domestic servants.		Gavlis.		Leather workers.		Shop-keepers.		Sweepers.		Cart-drivers.		Beggars.		Lawyers, Doctors, Teachers and Engineers.		Artisans of all kinds.	
		Males.	Females.	Males.	Females.	Males.	Females.	Males.	Females.	Males.	Females.	Males.	Females.	Males.	Females.	Males.	Females.	Males.	Females.	Males.	Females.
1	2	20	21	22	23	24	25	26	27	28	29	30	31	32	33	34	35	36	37	38	39
SATARA.	Total ...	13.828	2.426	1.732	536	70	6	1.019	76	1.912	480	461	39	2.083	8	328	101	96	4	3.423	315
	Bráhman, Chitpávan	...	1	2	...	2	...	...	...	8	...	...	...	...	...	4	...	16	...	3	...
	Bráhman, Deshasth	...	1	6	...	...	...	...	...	26	...	...	...	3	...	7	...	7	...	8	...
	Bráhman, Others.	8	...	13	1	1	...	...	...	26	...	...	...	2	...	5	...	5	1	8	...
	Chámbhár or Mochi	151	72	8	6	...	...	969	81	16	16	10	1	6	...	5	4	...	...	120	28
	Dhed or Mahár ...	2,711	964	270	46	...	...	34	1	24	11	430	29	134	1	52	12	9	1	139	47
	Dhobi or Parit ...	8	1	5	...	...	...	...	...	2	2	...	...	...	...	1	...	...	...	93	32
	Ghāti	410	34	128	8	...	...	...	...	93	11	...	...	220	4	14	...	...	...	59	...
	Kunbi	321	42	27	11	1	...	...	...	36	9	...	...	38	...	2	...	...	...	93	1
	Máli	91	9	2	1	...	...	...	...	12	7	...	...	7	...	5	2	...	...	10	1
	Maráthá	9,167	1,036	915	891	33	4	...	...	994	331	...	...	1,478	1	150	40	26	...	1,516	110
	Nhávi	7	7	...	...	...	...	...	...	1	2	...	...	3	...	...	...	...	...	898	...
	Shimpi	4	1	1	1	...	...	...	...	26	2	...	...	3	...	...	...	...	...	95	11
	Pathán	27	1	9	3	...	...	7	...	10	...	...	...	3	...	...	6	...	1	21	3
	Sheikh	196	19	85	22	3	...	3	...	103	17	6	...	34	...	24	5	2	...	148	12
	Sayad	27	5	11	8	...	...	...	...	13	1	1	...	5	...	5	...	11	...	4	1

District of Birth.	Caste.	Total number of Immigrants.			Age. 0–15		Age. 15–40		Age. 40 and over.		Workers.		Dependants.		Mill-hands.		Clerks.	
		Persons.	Males.	Females.	Males.	Females.	Males.	Females.	Males.	Females.	Males.	Females.	Males.	Females.	Males.	Females.	Males.	Females.
1	2	3	4	5	6	7	8	9	10	11	12	13	14	15	16	17	18	19
SHOLAPUR.	Total ...	8.528	5.381	3.147	821	718	3.617	1.841	943	558	4.428	1.006	953	2.141	911	321	115	...
	Chámbhár or Mochi ...	373	133	240	27	65	78	121	28	54	116	117	17	123	31	14	1	...
	Dhed or Mahár ...	952	526	426	67	76	371	278	88	72	464	186	63	241	58	34	1	...
	Maráthá	2,901	2,068	833	257	162	1,481	520	330	151	1,676	312	392	521	437	108	8	...
	Sheikh	888	502	386	96	67	298	201	108	98	410	86	92	300	44	6	3	...

District of Birth.	Caste.	Labourers.		Domestic servants.		Gavlis.		Leather workers.		Shop-keepers.		Sweepers.		Cart-drivers.		Beggars.		Lawyers, Doctors, Teachers and Engineers.		Artisans of all kinds.	
		Males.	Females.	Males.	Females.	Males.	Females.	Males.	Females.	Males.	Females.	Males.	Females.	Males.	Females.	Males.	Females.	Males.	Females.	Males.	Females.
1	2	20	21	22	23	24	25	26	27	28	29	30	31	32	33	34	35	36	37	38	39
SHOLAPUR.	Total ...	1431	386	180	89	21	1	36	36	430	49	19	9	196	3	51	13	16	8	602	133
	Chámbhár or Mochi ...	26	28	...	5	...	...	31	36	...	4	1	...	...	...	...	...	...	...	20	23
	Dhed or Mahár ...	294	118	24	9	...	...	1	...	1	2	14	4	13	2	10	5	...	...	32	4
	Maráthá	732	104	53	23	1	...	...	...	115	15	...	...	87	...	11	3	...	9	116	3
	Sheikh	51	4	28	25	...	...	...	...	69	7	...	1	19	...	15	3	3	...	130	21

TABLE VI—*continued.*

PART II.—Special Statistics regarding Birth-place combined with Age, Caste and Occupation for Bombay City.

District of Birth.	Caste.	Total number of Immigrants.			Age. 0–15		Age. 15–40.		Age. 40 and over.	
		Persons.	Males.	Females.	Males.	Females.	Males.	Females.	Males.	Females.
1	2	3	4	5	6	7	8	9	10	11
	Total ...	37.119	23,580	13,539	4.515	3,246	15,464	7,976	3,601	2,317
KOLA'BA.	A'gri	4,575	2,954	1,621	597	406	1,986	963	371	252
	Bhandári ...	1,479	883	596	180	133	579	378	124	85
	Bráhman, Chitpávan	1.385	847	538	163	161	543	285	111	92
	Bráhman, Deshasth	173	105	68	17	16	78	43	10	9
	Bráhman, Gaud Sárasvat ...	205	124	81	35	24	74	41	15	16
	Bráhman, Others.	613	401	212	76	63	269	120	56	29
	Chámbhár or Mochi	1.875	1,068	807	260	181	620	482	188	144
	Dhed or Mahár ...	3.359	2,016	1,343	336	278	1,420	856	260	209
	Maráthá	10.852	7,209	3,643	1,243	820	5,005	2,208	961	615
	Gavli	608	467	141	56	34	342	84	69	23
	Koli	874	614	260	80	65	395	145	139	50
	Kshatriya ...	464	263	201	57	57	160	109	46	35
	Kunbi	1,054	659	395	110	111	445	210	104	74
	Sonár	881	528	353	124	98	334	191	70	64
	Váni (Hindu) ...	620	395	225	94	56	254	120	47	40
	Sheikh	1,399	986	413	210	101	498	232	278	80

District of Birth.	Caste.	Workers.		Dependants.		Mill-hands.		Clerks.	
		Males.	Females.	Males.	Females.	Males.	Females.	Males.	Females.
1	2	12	13	14	15	16	17	18	19
	Total ...	19.288	4,313	4,292	9,226	5,334	2,049	1,026	...
KOLA'BA.	A'gri	2,500	722	454	899	554	358	18	...
	Bhandári ...	727	172	156	424	192	88	12	...
	Bráhman, Chitpávan	524	9	323	529	2	...	301	...
	Bráhman, Deshasth	67	1	38	67	...	...	40	...
	Bráhman, Gaud Sárasvat ...	72	1	52	80	1	...	28	...
	Bráhman, Others.	280	10	121	202	4	1	92	...
	Chámbhár or Mochi	830	237	238	570	311	112	9	...
	Dhed or Mahár ...	1,722	604	294	739	239	108	3	...
	Maráthá	6,280	1,698	929	1,945	3,218	1,117	46	...
	Gavli	418	48	49	93	70	21	1	...
	Koli	547	108	67	92	8	1	...	...
	Kshatriya ...	202	7	61	194	3	...	41	...
	Kunbi	571	177	88	218	290	132	1	...
	Sonár	408	33	120	320	6	6	32	...
	Váni (Hindu) ...	301	41	94	184	40	6	7	...
	Sheikh	759	34	227	379	100	4	8	...

District of Birth.	Caste.	Labourers.		Domestic servants.		Gavlis.		Leather workers.		Shop-keepers.	
		Males.	Females.	Males.	Females.	Males.	Females.	Males	Females	Males.	Females.
1	2	20	21	22	23	24	25	26	27	28	29
	Total ...	3,670	1.254	842	199	105	8	185	24	951	180
KOLA'BA.	A'gri	823	261	43	23	...	...	...	...	29	13
	Bhandári	81	40	32	15	...	1	...	...	111	14
	Bráhman, Chitpávan	...	...	11	6	...	...	...	...	37	3
	Bráhman, Deshasth	...	...	...	1	...	...	...	...	2	...
	Bráhman, Gaud Sárasvat ...	2	...	2	1	...	...	...	...	9	...
	Bráhman, Others.	14	2	17	3	...	...	...	...	93	...
	Chámbhár or Mochi	182	73	19	1	...	...	141	24	10	1
	Dhed or Mahár ...	566	353	86	12	2	...	15	...	35	1
	Maráthá... ...	1,049	338	370	45	8	...	...	...	211	41
	Gavli	150	8	6	5	87	3	...	...	53	10
	Koli	40	52	24	19	...	...	...	...	10	60
	Kshatriya ...	3	1	7	1	...	...	...	...	2	...
	Kunbi	109	32	54	1	1	...	...	...	39	4
	Sonár	7	4	3	15	...	...	...	...	10	1
	Váni (Hindu) ...	21	8	22	6	...	...	...	...	114	9
	Sheikh	33	8	24	4	...	...	3	...	55	9

District of Birth.	Caste.	Sweepers.		Cart-drivers.		Beggars.		Lawyers, Doctors, Teachers and Engineers.		Artisans of all kinds.	
		Males.	Females.	Males.	Females.	Males.	Females.	Males.	Females.	Males.	Females.
1	2	30	31	32	33	34	35	36	37	38	39
	Total ...	182	107	471	...	117	54	148	12	3,205	222
KOLA'BA.	A'gri	...	...	10	...	5	15	3	...	429	19
	Bhandári	7	...	15	...	4	...	13	...	143	9
	Bráhman, Chitpávan	...	...	1	...	1	...	36	...	22	...
	Bráhman, Deshasth	...	...	...	...	...	...	2	...	3	...
	Bráhman, Gaud Sárasvat ...	...	...	...	...	...	...	1	...	4	...
	Bráhman, Others.	...	...	9	...	...	...	15	...	21	...
	Chámbhár or Mochi	9	5	45	...	6	2	2	...	41	19
	Dhed or Mahár ...	144	95	109	...	15	11	5	...	40	2
	Maráthá... ...	...	...	192	...	50	19	10	1	476	56
	Gavli	...	...	3	...	7	...	...	...	6	...
	Koli	...	...	3	...	3	2	...	...	68	35
	Kshatriya ...	...	...	1	...	2	...	2	...	122	3
	Kunbi	...	...	25	...	1	...	...	...	30	6
	Sonár	...	...	...	...	...	...	5	3	337	4
	Váni (Hindu) ...	...	...	2	...	4	...	3	...	50	12
	Sheikh	...	...	18	...	5	...	12	1	177	3

TABLE VI—*continued.*

PART II.—Special Statistics regarding Birth-place combined with Age, Caste and Occupation for Bombay City.

District of Birth.	Caste.	Total number of Immigrants. Persons.	Total number of Immigrants. Males.	Total number of Immigrants. Females.	Age 0–15 Males.	Age 0–15 Females.	Age 15–40 Males.	Age 15–40 Females.	Age 40 and over. Males.	Age 40 and over. Females.	Workers. Males.	Workers. Females.	Dependants. Males.	Dependants. Females.	Mill hands. Males.	Mill hands. Females.	Clerks. Males.	Clerks. Females.
1	2	3	4	5	6	7	8	9	10	11	12	13	14	15	16	17	18	19
RATNA'GIRI.	Total ...	216,060	143,498	72,562	23,481	16,256	97,157	44,199	22,860	12,107	121,269	23,465	22,229	49,097	44,347	13,918	3,543	...
	A'gri	536	313	223	57	65	208	134	49	34	253	62	60	161	40	14	10	...
	Bhandári	20,969	13,809	7,160	2,377	1,735	9,069	4,185	2,373	1,250	11,318	1,838	2,491	5,322	3,829	924	255	...
	Bráhman, Chitpávan	3,588	2,410	1,139	357	307	1,618	623	474	209	1,741	45	708	1,094	...	...	854	...
	Bráhman, Deshasth	475	328	147	53	38	210	65	57	44	252	6	76	141	...	...	68	...
	Bráhman, Gaud Sarasvat ...	2,785	1,705	1,080	265	286	1,213	581	237	213	1,704	59	501	1,021	...	..	485	...
	Bráhman, Others.	2,999	1,971	1,038	243	270	1,162	512	366	216	1,544	106	427	923	63	5	418	...
	Chámbhár or Mochi	4,008	3,258	1,750	513	404	1,351	1,065	394	291	1,852	776	406	974	1,145	68	19	...
	Dhed or Mahár ...	11,050	6,692	4,358	1,176	883	4,587	2,870	929	605	5,066	1,167	1,026	2,371	1,010	447	9	...
	Dhobi	813	468	345	74	87	304	106	40	62	411	135	57	200	131	43	3	...
	Gavli	1,712	1,117	595	215	140	732	317	160	108	967	243	150	353	540	177	1	...
	Gháti	630	405	225	65	35	283	155	67	32	383	102	42	123	76	58	3	...
	Kshatriya ...	346	186	160	29	12	122	81	35	38	153	12	33	118	21	3	30	...
	Koli	1,046	870	176	87	18	600	135	123	23	792	48	78	124	75	1	1	...
	Kunbi	7,867	6,858	1,979	767	417	4,323	1,219	858	343	5,332	837	550	1,141	1,405	461	7	...
	Khárva	734	673	61	38	16	513	36	122	9	638	19	5	43	8	2	...	...
	Lohár	321	215	106	28	27	101	61	20	18	190	23	25	83	18	17	...	...
	Maráthá	114,159	75,337	38,822	12,721	8,344	51,515	24,278	11,101	6,100	61,314	14,371	11,023	24,451	32,892	9,882	824	...
	Nhávi	1,085	706	380	98	90	403	235	104	55	597	78	108	302	92	53	...	...
	Shimpi	494	275	219	71	56	108	118	38	45	211	35	64	184	14	3	8	...
	Sonár	3,019	1,913	1,106	383	290	1,273	636	257	190	1,408	148	415	958	31	22	71	...
	Sutár	1,910	1,207	703	161	170	869	451	174	83	1,038	82	169	631	103	50	3	...
	Teli	2,454	1,583	871	316	224	1,028	512	238	135	1,311	311	272	560	688	199	11	...
	Loháná	179	173	6	19	1	131	3	23	2	155	...	18	6	6	...	1	...
	Váni, Osvál (Hindu) ...	166	126	40	19	5	80	26	27	9	104	11	22	29	27	8	5	...
	Váni, Others (Hindu) ...	8,410	5,386	3,024	1,012	693	3,083	1,767	1,292	534	4,204	782	1,123	2,242	1,336	377	134	...
	Bohori	484	468	16	40	3	313	11	85	2	409	3	59	14	...	...	1	...
	Khoja	146	102	44	35	15	65	26	12	3	75	3	27	41	13	...	...	...
	Pathán	547	397	150	79	33	213	90	75	27	297	10	100	140	42	1	3	...
	Sheikh	9,263	7,381	1,882	782	477	5,103	1,049	1,493	356	6,652	173	720	1,700	353	23	81	...
	Sayad	545	450	95	43	18	329	61	79	16	383	6	67	80	11	1	10	...

District of Birth	Caste.	Labourers. Males.	Labourers. Females.	Domestic servants. Males	Domestic servants. Females.	Gavlis. Males.	Gavlis. Females.	Leather workers. Males.	Leather workers. Females.	Shop-keepers. Males.	Shop-keepers. Females.	Sweepers. Males.	Sweepers. Females	Cart-drivers. Males.	Cart-drivers. Females	Beggars. Males.	Beggars. Females.	Lawyers, Doctors, Teachers and Engineers. Males.	Lawyers, Doctors, Teachers and Engineers. Females.	Artisans of all kinds. Males.	Artisans of all kinds. Females
1	2	20	21	22	23	24	25	26	27	28	29	30	31	32	33	34	35	36	37	38	39
RATNA'GIRI.	Total ...	16,865	4,359	6,994	1,387	434	43	403	40	7,128	795	668	568	1,736	7	1,060	242	495	39	13,005	1,059
	A'gri	61	26	15	6	...	1	...	...	...	7	...	...	29	...	2	...	...	...	65	5
	Bhandári	995	505	406	79	2	2	...	...	1,125	103	...	...	214	...	14	20	38	4	1,401	112
	Bráhman, Chitpávan	...	...	114	23	...	...	...	...	194	2	...	...	14	...	24	3	157	2	60	1
	Bráhman, Deshasth	...	...	37	4	...	...	...	...	44	...	...	...	1	...	4	...	5	...	14	1
	Bráhman, Gaud Sarasvat.	...	...	125	45	...	...	...	...	180	1	...	...	8	...	5	...	64	7	63	...
	Bráhman, Others.	38	2	183	69	2	...	...	...	197	3	...	...	15	...	10	...	64	...	131	6
	Chámbhár or Mochi	123	45	7	8	...	...	400	24	5	9	...	1	17	...	3	3	...	...	51	3
	Dhed or Mahár ...	2,508	852	318	24	...	...	...	7	335	14	605	523	171	...	44	20	...	...	303	20
	Dhobi	17	15	18	2	14	...	...	...	3	2	...	...	...	...	...	...	...	...	165	81
	Gavli	119	31	51	5	62	14	...	...	60	6	...	...	19	...	3	3	...	...	48	2
	Gháti	68	20	97	16	1	1	...	...	19	1	...	...	23	...	...	...	...	...	25	4
	Kshatriya ...	12	2	20	3	...	...	...	...	20	...	...	...	...	...	1	3	3	...	16	...
	Koli	71	17	39	3	...	...	...	...	75	12	...	...	26	...	1	...	...	...	40	3
	Kunbi	1,638	227	447	54	12	...	...	...	148	9	...	...	86	...	23	1	...	...	249	30
	Khárva	18	5	1	1	...	...	...	...	4	10	...	...	1	...	...	...	...	...	...	...
	Lohár	8	3	...	1	...	...	...	...	1	...	...	...	1	...	5	...	...	...	117	3
	Maráthá	9,496	2,208	3,663	786	143	27	...	...	1,612	392	...	4	607	2	754	127	78	10	5,896	320
	Nhávi	20	6	2	6	...	...	...	...	1	...	...	...	3	...	...	1	...	...	388	3
	Shimpi	6	12	3	2	...	...	...	...	20	3	...	...	3	...	...	1	...	...	132	16
	Sonár	7	26	24	34	...	...	...	...	24	3	...	...	1	...	...	...	7	1	1,001	42
	Sutár	21	8	3	7	1	...	...	...	6	1	...	...	...	...	1	...	...	...	718	9
	Teli	159	50	71	14	...	...	...	...	82	16	...	...	20	...	...	3	3	...	131	14
	Loháná	53	...	15	...	1	...	...	...	35	...	...	...	12	...	...	...	1	...	30	...
	Váni, Osvál (Hindu) ...	6	2	16	...	...	...	...	...	40	1	...	...	1	...	2	...	...	...	1	...
	Váni, Others (Hindu) ...	160	41	198	54	19	...	...	...	1,543	106	...	...	29	...	23	4	3	1	339	114
	Bohori	...	...	76	...	...	...	...	...	265	...	...	...	...	...	...	...	...	...	50	...
	Khoja	4	2	8	...	...	...	...	...	28	...	...	...	4	...	1	...	...	...	3	...
	Pathán	26	4	33	2	2	...	...	...	30	...	...	...	13	...	5	...	1	1	76	...
	Sheikh	317	43	389	24	1	...	...	...	515	22	...	2	224	...	106	7	45	7	709	30
	Sayad	47	1	29	3	...	...	...	...	17	...	...	...	8	...	8	...	2	...	74	...

TABLE VI—*continued.*

PART II.—Special Statistics regarding Birth-place combined with Age, Caste and Occupation for Bombay City.

District of Birth.	Caste.	Total number of Immigrants.			Age. 0—15		15—40		40 and over.		Workers.		Dependants.		Mill-hands.		Clerks.	
		Persons.	Males.	Females.	Males.	Females.	Males.	Females.	Males.	Females.	Males.	Females.	Males.	Females.	Males.	Females.	Males.	Females.
1	2	3	4	5	6	7	8	9	10	11	12	13	14	15	16	17	18	19
CUTCH.	Total ...	36.470	25,000	11,470	3.885	2,646	16,316	6,430	4,799	2,394	20,367	1,296	4,633	10.174	200	15	886	...
	Bráhman, Gaud Sárasvat ...	497	305	192	41	38	204	109	60	45	256	31	47	161	...	...	31	...
	Bráhman, Others.	1,306	837	469	118	128	531	218	168	93	684	56	153	413	4	...	69	...
	Bhátiá ...	2,230	1,269	961	241	261	697	416	328	284	923	103	346	858	2	...	110	...
	Lohána ...	8,467	6,410	2,057	674	414	4,713	1,223	1,023	420	5,806	237	604	1,820	10	...	201	...
	Váni, Osvál (Hindu) ...	674	517	157	84	38	358	95	75	24	410	11	107	146	6	...	16	...
	Váni, Others (Hindu) ...	4,230	3,157	1,073	500	256	2,234	672	423	145	2,611	101	546	972	58	1	103	...
	Khoja ...	1,846	1,008	838	265	222	450	379	293	237	625	97	383	741	6	...	34	...
	Memon ...	1,863	1,076	787	207	170	595	384	274	233	788	149	288	638	5	...	14	...
	Sheikh ...	1,541	1,012	529	162	95	240	293	604	141	607	83	205	446	17	3	13	...
	Sayad ...	539	379	160	50	43	248	83	81	35	202	20	87	140	5	...	16	...
	Lohána (Jain) ...	138	116	22	25	6	72	12	19	5	85	1	31	21	...	...	4	...
	Váni, Osvál (Jain)	1,671	1,202	469	257	113	779	290	166	66	942	16	260	453	...	...	26	...
	Váni, Others (Jain) ...	3,476	2,507	969	460	267	1,713	603	334	109	1,955	44	552	925	4	1	33	...

District of Birth.	Caste.	Labourers.		Domestic servants.		Gavlis.		Leather workers.		Shop-keepers.		Sweepers.		Cart-drivers.		Beggars.		Lawyers, Doctors, Teachers and Engineers.		Artisans of all kinds.	
		Males.	Females.	Males.	Females.	Males.	Females.	Males.	Females.	Males.	Females.	Males.	Females.	Males.	Females.	Males.	Females.	Males.	Females.	Males.	Females.
1	2	20	21	22	23	24	25	26	27	28	29	30	31	32	33	34	35	36	37	38	39
CUTCH.	Total ...	1,771	178	1,350	326	22	1	219	...	11,884	269	19	1	97	1	117	56	53	8	2,012	189
	Bráhman, Gaud Sárasvat ...	22	1	35	6	...	...	...	...	113	2	...	...	...	...	31	17	...	...	13	...
	Bráhman, Others.	26	...	121	25	2	...	...	...	253	8	...	...	6	...	15	9	5	2	67	5
	Bhátiá ...	18	6	78	14	...	...	...	...	505	19	...	...	1	...	...	2	3	...	7	1
	Lohána ...	820	48	434	68	...	1	...	...	3,837	56	...	...	6	...	15	6	9	...	296	15
	Váni, Osvál (Hindu) ...	12	...	7	1	1	...	...	...	348	6	...	...	...	...	...	...	1	...	5	2
	Váni, Others (Hindu) ...	150	8	194	28	2	...	...	...	1,889	46	...	...	...	...	7	...	8	...	104	2
	Khoja ...	35	12	56	20	...	...	...	...	278	26	...	...	6	...	0	1	...	...	28	6
	Memon ...	78	15	75	57	...	...	...	...	458	15	...	...	15	...	2	2	2	1	78	25
	Sheikh ...	55	16	34	14	2	...	...	...	197	12	13	...	16	...	5	4	...	1	237	25
	Sayad ...	16	4	17	5	1	...	...	...	97	2	1	...	15	...	4	...	4	...	44	4
	Lohána (Jain) ...	12	...	1	...	...	...	...	...	68	...	...	...	...	...	...	...	1	...	6	...
	Váni, Osvál (Jain)	14	...	18	2	...	...	...	...	858	9	...	...	...	...	5	...	1	...	3	...
	Váni, Others (Jain) ...	21	...	80	1	...	...	...	...	1,733	38	...	...	...	...	7	...	2	...	31	...

TABLE VI—*continued.*

PART II.—Special Statistics regarding Birth-place combined with Age, Caste and Occupation for Bombay City.

District of Birth.	Caste.	Total number of Immigrants. Persons.	Males.	Females.	Age 0—15 Males.	Females.	Age 15—40 Males.	Females.	Age 40 and over. Males.	Females.	Workers. Males.	Females.	Dependants. Males.	Females.	Mill-hands. Males.	Females.	Clerks. Males	Females.
1	2	3	4	5	6	7	8	9	10	11	12	13	14	15	16	17	18	19
KATHIAWAR.	Total ...	53,775	33,586	20,189	6,365	4,875	24,997	11,475	7,224	3,839	30,839	3,026	7,747	17,163	388	138	2,675	...
	Bhangi ...	848	511	337	89	51	317	229	106	57	433	213	79	125	6	...	...	...
	Bráhman, Gaud Sárasvat ...	322	261	61	37	11	183	36	41	14	214	4	47	57	3	...	33	...
	Bráhman, Audich.	1,367	953	414	137	115	645	265	170	34	775	41	177	374	3	...	157	...
	" Others.	4,257	3,200	1,057	368	255	2,269	640	563	162	2,511	60	689	997	14	...	817	...
	Bhátiá ...	2,236	1,360	876	288	256	704	509	273	211	819	56	441	920	1	...	115	...
	Chámbhár or Mochi ...	679	430	259	87	65	279	106	74	38	361	56	59	303	22	1	...	...
	Dhed or Mahár ...	2,882	1,786	1,096	391	293	1,152	651	243	153	1,319	691	467	505	15	46	...	...
	Kshatriya ...	768	516	252	86	57	312	152	88	43	440	12	76	240	4	...	33	...
	Koli ...	440	331	109	49	15	237	75	45	10	307	76	34	63	9	2	1	...
	Khárva ...	1,566	953	613	210	149	557	343	186	111	743	174	210	439	6	4	3	...
	Lohár ...	747	494	253	89	57	340	169	65	37	408	33	86	230	1	...	3	...
	Maráthá ...	966	775	191	134	42	555	103	96	47	634	86	151	125	107	4	5	...
	Shimpi ...	1,494	1,155	339	165	66	824	225	162	28	1,094	26	151	313	...	...	6	...
	Sonár ...	989	790	199	100	45	515	125	175	29	685	15	105	184	...	...	8	...
	Sutár ...	1,400	1,091	309	120	61	559	242	312	46	803	15	130	354	3	...	4	...
	Loháná ...	3,207	2,023	1,184	349	333	1,338	563	336	288	1,592	85	431	1,099	3	2	277	...
	Váni, Osvál (Hindu) ...	267	197	70	36	21	136	37	36	12	172	7	25	64	...	...	28	...
	Váni, Others (Hindu)	9,353	6,317	3,036	900	717	4,356	1,509	1,132	513	6,071	171	1,276	2,863	16	...	663	...
	Bohori ...	2,140	1,415	725	236	185	822	378	357	162	1,072	28	343	697	19	...	19	...
	Khoja ...	2,743	1,556	1,187	393	283	925	638	239	267	1,176	137	381	1,050	15	...	44	...
	Memon ...	3,599	2,365	1,234	413	304	1,319	616	634	291	1,872	144	493	1,090	8	...	24	...
	Pathán ...	558	377	181	66	51	240	98	71	29	307	27	70	154	4	3	4	...
	Sheikh ...	2,486	1,800	686	256	145	1,143	282	401	159	1,621	116	279	570	36	4	26	...
	Sayad ...	457	320	137	67	30	191	75	62	32	232	31	88	116	3	...	9	...
	Váni, Osvál (Jain).	502	351	151	57	37	238	101	56	13	285	5	66	146	1	...	96	...
	Váni, Others (Jain) ...	1,886	1,635	251	294	59	987	160	354	33	1,390	4	349	247	2	...	260	...

District of Birth.	Caste.	Labourers. Males.	Females.	Domestic servants. Males.	Females.	Gavlis. Males.	Females.	Leather workers. Males.	Females.	Shop-keepers. Males.	Females.	Sweepers. Males.	Females	Cart-drivers. Males.	Females.	Beggars. Males.	Females.	Lawyers, Doctors, Teachers and Engineers. Males.	Females	Artisans of all kinds. Males	Females.
1	2	20	21	22	23	24	25	26	27	28	29	30	31	32	33	34	35	36	37	38	39
KATHIAWAR.	Total ...	859	541	2,716	508	82	3	178	30	10,940	323	1,255	583	463	26	266	106	256	11	5,630	226
	Bhangi ...	47	41	1	1	...	...	...	...	...	1	369	169	12	...	3	...	...	...	2	...
	Bráhman, Gaud Sárasvat ...	7	...	39	3	3	...	...	...	68	...	...	...	1	...	13	1	6	...	10	...
	Bráhman, Audich.	18	...	178	21	30	...	...	...	275	6	...	...	4	...	16	5	28	...	27	1
	" Others .	64	10	463	24	14	1	...	...	611	5	...	...	17	...	63	4	77	1	167	4
	Bhátiá ...	30	1	101	11	5	...	...	...	515	17	...	...	1	...	1	...	[illegible]	...	6	7
	Chámbhár or Mochi ...	10	6	6	8	...	...	134	29	73	...	12	3	1	...	1	...	...	...	73	8
	Dhed or Mahár ...	174	150	87	21	...	...	1	...	10	58	856	289	46	3	30	5	...	...	8	1
	Kshatriya ...	13	...	43	7	1	...	...	...	91	3	...	...	13	...	4	...	3	...	183	...
	Koli ...	153	36	6	9	...	...	...	...	3	2	...	...	15	...	7	5	...	...	34	1
	Khárva ...	236	36	15	35	...	...	...	...	139	42	...	...	2	1	3	2	...	...	[illegible]	7
	Lohár ...	4	4	3	5	...	...	...	...	19	...	...	...	...	...	...	...	1	...	317	16
	Maráthá ...	171	20	81	21	3	...	...	...	57	5	...	...	26	...	6	7	3	...	89	...
	Shimpi ...	2	1	14	...	...	...	...	...	13	...	...	...	...	...	...	...	...	...	948	29
	Sonár ...	1	1	31	5	...	...	...	...	45	...	...	...	...	...	1	...	13	1	578	5
	Sutár ...	15	3	2	1	...	...	...	...	28	...	...	...	...	...	2	...	3	...	802	10
	Loháná ...	89	18	220	22	...	2	...	...	768	13	...	...	38	...	3	...	9	...	89	5
	Váni, Osvál (Hindu) ...	...	...	29	...	...	...	...	...	75	6	...	...	1	...	...	...	3	...	23	...
	Váni, Others (Hindu) ...	106	18	587	53	...	...	...	...	2,749	43	...	...	41	...	16	...	23	2	374	14
	Bohori ...	16	...	140	9	...	...	...	...	697	13	...	...	6	...	13	3	6	...	75	...
	Khoja ...	53	13	36	32	...	...	4	...	739	23	...	...	13	...	...	...	4	...	60	19
	Memon ...	27	17	144	67	1	...	...	...	1,363	23	...	...	16	...	2	6	8	1	128	25
	Pathán ...	35	5	27	12	...	...	...	...	101	5	...	...	12	...	3	...	6	...	40	1
	Sheikh ...	162	21	132	34	2	...	1	...	416	15	4	...	50	...	18	8	36	...	302	25
	Sayad ...	19	4	9	11	...	...	...	1	98	1	3	...	10	...	3	...	11	...	36	2
	Váni, Osvál (Jain).	4	...	13	...	...	...	...	...	123	2	...	...	...	...	3	...	1	...	19	...
	Váni, Others (Jain) ...	13	...	67	3	1	...	...	...	715	1	...	...	2	...	...	...	6	...	35	...

TABLE VI—*continued.*

PART II.—Special Statistics regarding Birth-place combined with Age, Caste and Occupation for Bombay City.

District of Birth.	Caste.	Total number of Immigrants. Persons.	Total number of Immigrants. Males.	Total number of Immigrants. Females.	Age 0—15 Males.	Age 0—15 Females.	Age 15—40 Males.	Age 15—40 Females.	Age 40 and over. Males.	Age 40 and over. Females.	Workers. Males.	Workers. Females.	Dependants. Males.	Dependants. Females.	Mill-hands. Males.	Mill-hands. Females.	Clerks. Males.	Clerks. Females.
1	2	3	4	5	6	7	8	9	10	11	12	13	14	15	16	17	18	19
KOLHA'PUR.	Total ...	9,309	6,456	2,853	1,028	632	4,653	1,782	787	449	5,625	1,024	831	1,829	2,975	659	32	...
	Dhed or Mahár ...	946	607	339	74	56	461	236	69	47	555	156	52	183	115	32	...	...
	Ghâti ...	588	437	151	51	24	355	111	31	16	410	67	27	84	221	56	...	...
	Maráthá ...	5,188	3,751	1,437	647	334	2,709	902	335	201	3,280	578	471	839	2,276	491	19	...
	Sheikh ...	429	269	160	43	25	175	110	51	25	237	47	32	113	66	17	...	...

District of Birth.	Caste.	Labourers. Males.	Labourers. Females.	Domestic servants. Males.	Domestic servants. Females.	Gavlis. Males.	Gavlis. Females.	Leather workers. Males.	Leather workers. Females.	Shop-keepers. Males.	Shop-keepers. Females.	Sweepers. Males.	Sweepers. Females.	Cart-drivers. Males.	Cart-drivers. Females.	Beggars. Males.	Beggars. Females.	Lawyers, Doctors, Teachers and Engineers. Males.	Lawyers, Doctors, Teachers and Engineers. Females.	Artisans of all kinds. Males.	Artisans of all kinds. Females.
1	2	20	21	22	23	24	25	26	27	28	29	30	31	32	33	34	35	36	37	38	39
KOLHA'PUR.	Total ...	838	150	248	43	27	1	45	7	246	24	16	6	202	1	53	19	21	...	414	36
	Dhed or Mahár ...	283	74	65	6	...	...	...	...	6	...	10	6	26	...	3	10	...	...	16	1
	Ghâti ...	63	6	34	1	...	...	...	...	7	...	...	...	51	1	...	...	...	...	10	...
	Maráthá ...	389	39	93	16	12	...	...	...	64	10	...	...	92	...	20	7	3	...	140	5
	Sheikh ...	15	4	13	6	1	...	...	...	35	5	...	...	3	...	15	1	...	...	57	2

District of Birth.	Caste.	Total number of Immigrants. Persons.	Total number of Immigrants. Males.	Total number of Immigrants. Females.	Age 0—15 Males.	Age 0—15 Females.	Age 15—40 Males.	Age 15—40 Females.	Age 40 and over. Males.	Age 40 and over. Females.	Workers. Males.	Workers. Females.	Dependants. Males.	Dependants. Females.	Mill-hands. Males.	Mill-hands. Females.	Clerks. Males.	Clerks. Females.
1	2	3	4	5	6	7	8	9	10	11	12	13	14	15	16	17	18	19
JAIPUR.	Total ...	4,632	4,025	607	364	174	2,922	314	739	119	3,673	94	352	513	100	22	104	...
	Bráhman, Gaud Sárasvat ...	210	182	28	9	4	136	11	37	13	162	2	20	26	2	...	19	...
	Bráhman, Others.	320	314	6	23	4	238	2	53	...	295	1	19	5	7	...	19	...
	Váni ...	519	483	37	36	7	322	20	124	10	434	1	48	36	...	...	35	...
	Pathán ...	139	127	12	7	3	98	9	22	...	119	3	8	10	1	...	...	...
	Sheikh ...	1,088	981	107	70	24	737	74	174	9	924	13	57	94	1	3	...	...

District of Birth.	Caste.	Labourers. Males.	Labourers. Females.	Domestic servants. Males.	Domestic servants. Females.	Gavlis. Males.	Gavlis. Females.	Leather workers. Males.	Leather workers. Females.	Shop-keepers. Males.	Shop-keepers. Females.	Sweepers. Males.	Sweepers. Females.	Cart-drivers. Males.	Cart-drivers. Females.	Beggars. Males.	Beggars. Females.	Lawyers, Doctors, Teachers and Engineers. Males.	Lawyers, Doctors, Teachers and Engineers. Females.	Artisans of all kinds. Males.	Artisans of all kinds. Females.
1	2	20	21	22	23	24	25	26	27	28	29	30	31	32	33	34	35	36	37	38	39
JAIPUR.	Total ...	232	1	330	27	39	...	13	...	746	17	16	7	36	...	71	3	9	...	1,288	11
	Bráhman, Gaud Sárasvat ...	...	...	21	2	...	...	...	...	65	...	...	...	3	...	6	...	...	...	17	...
	Bráhman, Others.	2	...	49	...	...	...	...	...	76	1	...	...	1	...	26	...	...	...	38	...
	Váni ...	4	...	55	...	2	...	...	...	243	1	...	...	...	...	7	...	1	...	19	...
	Pathán ...	48	...	1	...	...	...	...	...	15	...	...	...	1	...	1	...	1	...	14	2
	Sheikh ...	111	...	30	6	...	...	...	...	61	2	...	...	1	...	22	...	...	...	605	...

TABLE VI—*continued.*

PART II.—Special Statistics regarding Birth-place combined with Age, Caste and Occupation for Bombay City.

District of Birth.	Caste.	Total number of Immigrants.			Age. 0—15.		Age. 15—40.		Age. 40 and over.		Workers.		Dependants.		Mill-hands.		Clerks.	
		Persons.	Males.	Females.	Males.	Females.	Males.	Females.	Males.	Females.	Males.	Females.	Males.	Females.	Males.	Females.	Males.	Females.
1	2	3	4	5	6	7	8	9	10	11	12	13	14	15	16	17	19	19
JODHPUR.	Total ...	5,481	4,826	655	673	149	3,477	394	676	113	4,088	62	738	593	130	7	140	...
	Bráhman, Gaud Sárasvat ...	144	142	2	30	...	88	1	34	1	107	...	35	2	10	...	11	...
	Bráhman, Others.	606	550	56	31	12	416	39	103	5	474	6	76	50	6	...	22	...
	Váni, Osvál (Hindu) ...	130	130	...	31	...	90	...	20	...	110	...	20	...	2	...	1	...
	Váni, others (Hindu) ...	799	702	97	64	17	537	65	97	15	634	4	68	93	17	...	21	...
	Váni, Osvál (Jain)	480	423	57	77	14	301	32	45	11	343	1	81	56	4	...	8	...
	Váni, Others (Jain) ...	743	640	103	120	38	449	64	71	11	546	1	94	103	...	...	20	...

District of Birth.	Caste.	Labourers.		Domestic servants.		Gavlis.		Leather workers.		Shop-keepers.		Sweepers.		Cart-drivers.		Beggars.		Lawyers, Doctors, Teachers and Engineers.		Artisans of all kinds.	
		Males.	Females.	Males.	Females.	Males.	Females.	Males.	Females.	Males.	Females.	Males.	Females.	Males.	Females.	Males.	Females.	Males.	Females.	Males.	Females.
1	2	20	21	22	23	24	25	26	27	28	29	30	31	32	33	34	35	36	37	38	39
JODHPUR.	Total ...	128	1	476	4	16	...	13	...	3,049	10	3	3	64	...	35	4	25	...	511	11
	Bráhman, Gaud Sárasvat ...	...	...	14	...	2	...	...	...	34	...	...	...	...	...	...	...	4	...	16	...
	Bráhman, Others	11	...	101	1	...	...	...	...	174	...	...	...	6	...	29	3	3	...	23	...
	Váni, Osvál (Hindu) ...	...	...	8	...	1	...	...	...	60	...	...	...	2	...	...	...	2	...	8	...
	Váni, Others (Hindu) ...	4	...	73	...	7	...	...	...	349	1	...	...	4	...	2	...	9	...	60	...
	Váni, Osvál (Jain)	3	...	2[illegible]	...	...	...	...	...	284	1	...	...	...	...	...	...	...	...	3	...
	Váni, Others (Jain) ...	7	...	60	...	...	...	...	...	391	1	...	...	...	...	...	...	...	...	25	...

District of Birth.	Caste.	Total number of Immigrants.			Age. 0—15		Age. 15—40		Age. 40 and over.		Workers.		Dependants.		Mill-hands.		Clerks.	
		Persons.	Males.	Females.	Males.	Females.	Males.	Females.	Males.	Females.	Males.	Females.	Males.	Females.	Males.	Females.	Males.	Females.
1	2	3	4	5	6	7	8	9	10	11	12	13	14	15	16	17	18	19
ALLA'HA'BA'D.	Total ..	6,619	4,919	1,680	563	363	3,536	985	858	332	4,101	457	848	1,223	1,410	174	44	...
	Maráthá ...	552	492	70	48	19	393	40	41	11	432	25	60	45	314	18	1	...
	Pathán ...	156	113	43	7	5	83	20	23	12	103	9	10	33	5	...	1	...
	Sheikh ...	1,559	1,042	517	128	98	723	318	191	101	802	116	150	402	319	40	4	...

District of Birth.	Caste.	Labourers.		Domestic servants.		Gavlis.		Leather workers.		Shop-keepers.		Sweepers.		Cart-drivers.		Beggars.		Lawyers, Doctors, Teachers and Engineers.		Artisans of all kinds.	
		Males.	Females.	Males.	Females.	Males.	Females.	Males.	Females.	Males.	Females.	Males.	Females.	Males.	Females.	Males.	Females.	Males.	Females.	Males.	Females.
1	2	20	21	22	23	24	25	26	27	28	29	30	31	32	33	34	35	36	37	38	39
ALLA'HA'BA'D.	Total ...	299	34	217	28	114	...	43	...	339	28	33	...	130	...	53	19	19	...	976	150
	Maráthá ...	41	7	12	...	2	...	...	...	6	...	...	...	3	...	2	...	...	...	25	...
	Pathán ...	16	1	12	3	...	...	...	...	7	1	...	...	11	...	2	...	...	...	26	3
	Sheikh ...	70	6	46	14	...	...	...	...	52	9	...	...	6	...	7	9	8	...	274	23

TABLE VI—*continued.*

PART II.—Special Statistics regarding Birth-place combined with Age, Caste and Occupation for Bombay City.

District of Birth.	Caste.	Total number of Immigrants.			Age. 0—15		Age. 15—40		Age. 40 and over.		Workers.		Dependants.		Mill-hands.		Clerks.	
		Persons.	Males.	Females.	Males.	Females.	Males.	Females.	Males.	Females.	Males.	Females.	Males.	Females.	Males.	Females.	Males.	Females.
1	2	3	4	5	6	7	8	9	10	11	12	13	14	15	16	17	18	19
JAUNPUR.	Total ...	6,551	5,912	639	419	112	4,645	431	848	105	5,484	240	428	399	1,876	152	92	...
	Bráhman, Others.	642	623	20	40	3	503	11	70	6	585	1	37	19	133	1	25	...
	Dhobi or Parit ...	166	150	16	8	2	112	19	30	4	146	6	4	10	...	...	...	...
	Gavli ...	340	299	41	13	6	269	28	27	7	292	14	7	27	169	12	1	...
	Kunbi ...	600	577	23	46	2	477	17	54	4	558	10	19	13	370	9	...	...
	Lohár ...	148	147	1	6	...	128	1	15	...	137	...	10	1	12	...	...	...
	Maráthá ...	862	656	206	50	37	584	139	72	30	536	115	120	91	292	76	4	...
	Váni, Others (Hindu) ...	120	100	20	9	7	77	12	14	1	93	6	7	14	19	8	1	...
	Sheikh ...	247	220	27	26	6	152	17	42	4	197	2	23	25	55	...	3	...

District of Birth.	Caste.	Labourers.		Domestic servants.		Gavlis.		Leather workers.		Shop-keepers.		Sweepers.		Cart-drivers.		Beggars.		Lawyers, Doctors, Teachers and Engineers.		Artisans of all kinds.	
		Males.	Females.	Males.	Females.	Males.	Females.	Males.	Females.	Males.	Females.	Males.	Females.	Males.	Females.	Males.	Females.	Males.	Females.	Males.	Females.
1	2	20	21	22	23	24	25	26	27	28	29	30	31	32	33	34	35	36	37	38	39
JAUNPUR.	Total ...	523	26	325	3	466	2	13	1	492	7	8	...	351	...	26	...	14	...	431	30
	Bráhman, Others.	53	...	99	...	95	...	...	...	67	...	...	...	9	...	7	...	7	...	32	...
	Dhobi or Parit ...	...	...	1	...	...	...	...	...	...	...	...	...	...	...	...	...	...	...	145	5
	Gavli ...	20	...	2	2	38	...	...	...	13	...	...	...	17	...	...	...	...	...	6	...
	Kunbi ...	33	...	14	1	82	...	...	...	16	...	...	...	30	...	...	...	...	...	8	...
	Lohár ...	...	...	...	...	...	...	...	...	...	...	...	...	1	...	...	...	...	...	117	...
	Maráthá ...	50	20	60	1	11	...	...	...	25	...	...	...	51	...	...	...	...	...	12	8
	Váni, Others (Hindu) ...	6	...	4	...	1	...	...	...	31	2	...	...	7	...	4	...	...	...	3	...
	Sheikh ...	14	...	18	...	1	...	2	...	18	...	...	...	5	...	5	...	...	...	53	2

District of Birth.	Caste.	Total number of Immigrants.			Age. 0—15		Age. 15—40		Age. 40 and over.		Workers.		Dependants.		Mill-hands.		Clerks.	
		Persons.	Males.	Females.	Males.	Females.	Males.	Females.	Males.	Females.	Males.	Females.	Males.	Females.	Males.	Females.	Males.	Females.
1	2	3	4	5	6	7	8	9	10	11	12	13	14	15	16	17	18	19
MERWA'RA.	Total ...	6,126	5,233	893	683	133	3,613	543	937	167	4,457	121	776	772	[illegible]	[illegible]	163	...
	Bráhman, Audich.	150	139	11	13	2	108	7	18	2	124	...	15	11	...	...	4	...
	" Gaud Sárasvat.	138	134	4	22	...	83	3	30	1	103	1	31	3	10	...	9	...
	" Others	740	645	95	71	17	428	53	140	25	588	14	62	81	5	...	23	...
	Maráthá ...	140	121	19	14	5	88	10	19	4	93	3	28	16	6	1	...	...
	Váni, Others (Hindu) ...	888	752	136	84	19	508	93	160	21	619	17	113	119	2	2	46	...
	Sheikh ...	180	151	29	13	7	112	17	26	5	138	3	13	26	...	...	...	...
	Váni, Osvál Jain).	376	286	90	56	23	178	44	53	28	235	4	61	88	2	...	22	...
	" Others (Jain).	635	527	108	116	19	600	79	111	19	681	4	146	164	5	...	49	...

District of Birth.	Caste.	Labourers.		Domestic servants.		Gavlis.		Leather workers.		Shop-keepers.		Sweepers.		Cart-drivers.		Beggars.		Lawyers, Doctors, Teachers and Engineers.		Artisans of all kinds.	
		Males.	Females.	Males.	Females.	Males.	Females.	Males.	Females.	Males.	Females.	Males.	Females.	Males.	Females.	Males.	Females.	Males.	Females.	Males.	Females.
1	2	20	21	22	23	24	25	26	27	28	29	30	31	32	33	34	35	36	37	38	39
MERWA'RA.	Total ...	152	8	557	20	11	1	48	4	1,970	13	2	...	50	2	43	14	83	1	488	2
	Bráhman, Audich	39	...	28	...	5	...	...	...	20	...	...	...	...	...	3	...	2	...	13	...
	" Gaud Sárasvat.	...	1	10	...	...	...	...	...	37	...	...	...	3	...	1	...	18	...	9	...
	" Others.	3	...	165	1	2	...	...	...	111	...	...	...	4	...	71	10	7	...	47	...
	Maráthá ...	24	...	14	...	1	...	...	...	28	1	...	...	4	...	2	...	1	...	3	...
	Váni, Others (Hindu) ...	13	1	71	4	...	...	...	...	378	3	...	...	2	...	5	...	6	...	47	1
	Sheikh ...	8	...	14	2	...	...	...	...	15	...	...	...	2	...	...	...	1	...	55	...
	Váni, Osvál (Jain).	5	1	19	...	...	...	...	...	135	...	...	...	...	...	...	...	...	...	28	...
	" Others (Jain).	4	...	56	1	3	...	...	...	466	1	...	...	...	...	1	1	1	...	35	...

TABLE VI—*continued.*

PART II.—Special Statistics regarding Birth-place combined with Age, Caste and Occupation for Bombay City.

District of Birth.	Caste.	Total number of Immigrants.			Age.						Workers.		Dependants.		Mill-hands.		Clerks.	
					0—15		15—40		40 and over.									
		Persons.	Males.	Females.	Males.	Females.	Males.	Females.	Males.	Females.	Males.	Females.	Males.	Females.	Males.	Females.	Males.	Females.
1	2	3	4	5	6	7	8	9	10	11	12	13	14	15	16	17	18	19
	Total ...	29.504	21,372	8.132	3,256	1,687	14.899	4.830	4,217	1,615	18,458	3.436	2,914	4,697	251	60	1,727	...
GOA.	Bhandári ...	313	234	79	26	14	172	53	36	12	203	12	31	67	27	4	2	...
	Bráhman, Gaud Sárasvat ...	463	362	101	67	24	245	60	60	37	224	7	138	94	1	...	117	...
	Maráthá ...	1 309	585	724	125	167	365	436	95	121	432	366	153	358	84	33	25	...
	Sonár ...	207	127	80	24	17	79	47	24	16	95	2	32	78	1	2	3	...
	Goanese ...	17.971	14,110	3,861	1,351	693	9,621	2,322	2,639	846	13,488	1,737	1,622	2.124	15	8	1,066	...

District of Birth.	Caste.	Labourers.		Domestic servants.		Gavlis.		Leather workers.		Shop-keepers.		Sweepers.		Cart-drivers.		Beggars.		Lawyers, Doctors, Teachers and Engineers.		Artisans of all kinds.	
		Males.	Females.	Males.	Females.	Males.	Females.	Males.	Females.	Males.	Females.	Males.	Females.	Males.	Females.	Males.	Females.	Males.	Females.	Males.	Females.
1	2	20	21	22	23	24	25	26	27	28	29	30	31	32	33	34	35	36	37	38	39
	Total ...	463	183	7.764	2.217	5	5	11	...	594	114	1	...	143	...	48	80	223	95	3.872	115
GOA.	Bhandári ...	11	...	8	2	...	...	...	...	5	...	...	...	4	...	...	1	...	...	8	4
	Bráhman, Gaud Sárasvat ...	1	...	18	3	...	...	...	...	24	...	...	...	1	...	...	1	8	...	10	...
	Maráthá ...	29	10	25	3	...	...	...	...	18	...	...	...	1	...	2	23	6	...	90	20
	Sonár ...	2	...	1	...	...	...	...	...	2	...	...	...	...	...	...	...	1	...	82	...
	Goanese ...	260	136	5,790	1,393	4	5	11	...	400	19	...	...	82	...	22	21	167	8	2,706	28

TABLE VII—(Corresponding to Imperial Table XV, Part A).

OCCUPATION OR MEANS OF LIVELIHOOD.

TABLE VII.

Occupation or Means of Livelihood.

TABLE VII.

Occupation or Means of Livelihood.

Occupation.	All Religions.						Hindu.						Musalman.					
	Total workers and dependants.	Actual Workers.				Dependants.	Total workers and dependants.	Actual Workers.				Dependants.	Total workers and dependants	Actual Workers.				Dependants.
		Total.		Partially agriculturists.				Total		Partially agriculturists.				Total.		Partially agriculturists.		
		Males.	Females.	Males.	Females.			Males.	Females.	Males.	Females.			Males.	Females.	Males.	Females.	
1	2	3	4	5	6	7	8	9	10	11	12	13	14	15	16	17	18	19
TOTAL ALL CLASSES	979,445	514.665	81.455	1.538	3	383.325	664.042	359 720	64.966	1.440	3	76.967 162.389	179.346	9.3637	8.600	92	...	25.415 51.694
CLASS A.—PRODUCTION OF RAW MATERIALS.	23.064	12.837	1.726	3	...	7.501	17.826	10.532	1,448	2	...	1,986 3,860	2.443	1.671	42	......	...	192 538
Sub-Class 1.—Exploitation of the surface of the Earth.	20.466	11.965	1,604	2	...	6.907	16.504	9.760	1.335	2	...	1.859 3.550	2.368	1.636	42	......	...	175 515
ORDER 1.—PASTURE AND AGRICULTURE.	15.413	9,470	655	2	...	5,288	12.426	7.679	574	2	...	1,240 2,833	2.276	1.593	35	......	...	179 489
(a) Ordinary Cultivation ...	5,809	3.796	266	...	...	1.747	3,371	2,286	210	...	...	310 565	1.849	1,357	18	......	...	86 388
(1) Income from rent of agricultural land.	458	160	22	...	...	290	208	106	5	...	...	23 74	54	10	5	......	...	12 27
(2) Ordinary cultivators	4.123	2,606	196	...	...	1,331	1.996	1,174	151	...	...	220 412	1.761	1,333	13	......	...	69 356
(4) Farm servants and field labourers.	1.228	1,040	58	...	...	130	1.167	1,000	54	...	...	68 49	34	24	......	......	...	5 5
(b) Growers of special products and market gardening.																		
(6) Fruit, flower, vegetable, betel vine, arecanut, etc., growers.	5.578	2,740	193	3	...	2,026	5.383	3,068	182	2	...	761 1.772	104	55	3	......	...	37 9
(c) Forestry	96	73	......	...	...	24	91	69	......	...	...	17 5	2	......	......	......	...	 2
(7) Forest officers, rangers, guards etc.	29	22	......	...	...	7	26	10	......	...	...	4 3	......	......	......	......	...	....
(8) Wood cutters, firewood, lac, catechu, rubber, etc., collectors and charcoal burners.	67	50	......	...	...	17	65	60	......	...	...	13 2	2	......	......	......	...	 2
(d) Raising of farm stock ...	3.030	2.853	196	...	...	881	3.581	2.656	182	...	...	252 491	321	181	14	......	...	34 92
(9) Cattle and buffalo breeders and keepers.	3.667	2,074	180	...	...	813	3,352	3,400	178	...	...	230 455	295	160	12	......	...	31 80
(11) Breeders of other animals (horses, mules, camels, asses, etc.)	34	25	......	...	...	9	10	9	......	...	...	1	16	9	......	......	...	2 5
(12) Herdsmen, shepherds, goat-herds, etc.	229	154	16	...	...	59	219	148	14	...	...	21 36	10	6	3	......	...	1 1
ORDER 2.—FISHING AND HUNTING.	5,052	2.485	949	...	...	1.619	4.078	2,061	761	...	...	519 717	92	43	7	......	...	16 36
(14) Fishing	5,052	2.485	949	...	...	1.618	4,078	2,061	761	...	...	519 717	91	47	7	......	...	16 25
(15) Hunting	1	......	......	...	...	1	......	......	......	...	...	......						......

TABLE VII—*continued*.

OCCUPATION OR MEANS OF LIVELIHOOD.

OCCUPATION.	CHRISTIAN. Total workers and dependants.	CHRISTIAN. Actual Workers. Total. Males.	CHRISTIAN. Actual Workers. Total. Females.	CHRISTIAN. Actual Workers. Partially agriculturists. Males.	CHRISTIAN. Actual Workers. Partially agriculturists. Females.	CHRISTIAN. Dependants.	JAIN. Total workers and dependants.	JAIN. Actual Workers. Total. Males.	JAIN. Actual Workers. Total. Females.	JAIN. Actual Workers. Partially agriculturists. Males.	JAIN. Actual Workers. Partially agriculturists. Females.	JAIN. Dependants.	ZOROASTRIAN. Total workers and dependants.	ZOROASTRIAN. Actual Workers. Total. Males.	ZOROASTRIAN. Actual Workers. Total. Females.	ZOROASTRIAN. Actual Workers. Partially agriculturists. Males.	ZOROASTRIAN. Actual Workers. Partially agriculturists. Females.	ZOROASTRIAN. Dependants.	MINOR AND UNSPECIFIED RELIGIONS. Total workers and dependants.	MINOR AND UNSPECIFIED RELIGIONS. Actual Workers. Total. Males.	MINOR AND UNSPECIFIED RELIGIONS. Actual Workers. Total. Females.	MINOR AND UNSPECIFIED RELIGIONS. Actual Workers. Partially agriculturists. Males.	MINOR AND UNSPECIFIED RELIGIONS. Actual Workers. Partially agriculturists. Females.	MINOR AND UNSPECIFIED RELIGIONS. Dependants.
1	20	21	22	23	24	25	26	27	28	29	30	31	32	33	34	35	36	37	38	39	40	41	42	43
TOTAL ALL CLASSES	57,355	30,809	5,640	3	...	7,778 13,128	20,460	13,266	221	1	...	3,133 4,840	50,931	15,678	1,606	2	...	11,097 22,550	7,311	2,555	423	...	...	1,489 2,845
CLASS A.—PRODUCTION OF RAW MATERIALS.	1,413	510	223	...	...	788 393	17	10	1	...	...	3 3	353	112	12	...	...	133 96	12	2	...	...	...	3 7
Sub-Class I.—Exploitation of the surface of the Earth.	1,321	487	214	...	...	270 350	17	10	1	...	...	3 3	244	60	12	...	...	76 96	12	2	...	...	...	3 7
ORDER 1.—PASTURE AND AGRICULTURE.	438	176	33	...	...	115 164	17	10	1	...	...	3 3	244	60	12	...	...	76 96	12	2	...	...	...	3 7
(a) Ordinary Cultivation ...	357	95	25	...	...	101 136	11	7	1	...	...	2 1	209	49	12	...	...	74 74	12	2	...	...	...	3 7
(1) Income from rent of agricultural land.	39	1	1	...	...	16 21	4	3	1	...	...	...	145	28	10	...	...	50 57	8	2	...	...	...	3 3
(2) Ordinary cultivators	303	90	20	...	...	83 111	6	3	...	...	...	2 1	53	16	2	...	...	18 17	4	...	...	...	...	4
(4) Farm servants and field labourers.	15	4	4	...	...	3 4	1	1	...	...	...	...	11	5	...	...	...	6	...	...	...	...	...	...
(b) Growers of special products and market gardening.																								
(6) Fruit, flower, vegetable, betel vine, arecanut, etc., growers.	66	21	8	...	...	10 27	6	3	...	...	...	1 2	19	3	...	...	...	2 15	...	...	...	...	...	...
(c) Forestry	3	3	...	...	...	......	...	...	...	...	...	...	...	...	...	...	...	......	...	...	...	...	...	...
(7) Forest officers, rangers, guards, etc.	3	3	...	...	...	......	...	...	...	...	...	...	...	...	...	...	...	......	...	...	...	...	...	...
(8) Wood cutters, firewood, lac, catechu, rubber, etc., collectors and charcoal burners.	......	...	...	...	...	......	...	...	...	...	...	...	...	...	...	...	...	......	...	...	...	...	...	...
(d) Raising of farm stock ...	12	7	...	...	...	4 1	...	...	...	...	...	...	16	9	...	...	...	7	...	...	...	...	...	...
(9) Cattle and buffalo breeders and keepers.	4	...	...	...	...	3 1	...	...	...	...	...	...	16	9	...	...	...	7	...	...	...	...	...	...
(11) Breeders of other animals (horses, mules, camels, asses, etc.).	8	7	...	...	...	1	...	...	...	...	...	...	...	...	...	...	...	......	...	...	...	...	...	...
(12) Herdsmen, shepherds, goatherds, etc.	......	...	...	...	...	......	...	...	...	...	...	...	...	...	...	...	...	......	...	...	...	...	...	...
ORDER 2.—FISHING AND HUNTING.	883	361	181	...	...	155 186	...	...	...	...	...	...	...	...	...	...	...	......	...	...	...	...	...	...
(14) Fishing	883	361	151	...	...	135 186	...	...	...	...	...	...	...	...	...	...	...	......	...	...	...	...	...	...
(15) Hunting	......	...	...	...	...	......	...	...	...	...	...	...	...	...	...	...	...	......	...	...	...	...	...	...

TABLE VII.

Occupation or Means of Livelihood.

TABLE VII—*continued.*

Occupation or Means of Livelihood.

OCCUPATION.	ALL RELIGIONS. Total workers and dependants.	ALL RELIGIONS. Actual Workers. Total. Males.	ALL RELIGIONS. Actual Workers. Total. Females.	ALL RELIGIONS. Actual Workers. Partially agriculturists. Males.	ALL RELIGIONS. Actual Workers. Partially agriculturists. Females.	ALL RELIGIONS. Dependants.	HINDU. Total workers and dependants.	HINDU. Actual Workers. Total. Males.	HINDU. Actual Workers. Total. Females.	HINDU. Actual Workers. Partially agriculturists. Males.	HINDU. Actual Workers. Partially agriculturists. Females.	HINDU. Dependants.	MUSALMAN. Total workers and dependants.	MUSALMAN. Actual Workers. Total. Males.	MUSALMAN. Actual Workers. Total. Females.	MUSALMAN. Actual Workers. Partially agriculturists. Males.	MUSALMAN. Actual Workers. Partially agriculturists. Females.	MUSALMAN. Dependants
1	2	3	4	5	6	7	8	9	10	11	12	13	14	15	16	17	18	19
CLASS A.—PRODUCTION OF RAW MATERIALS—*continued.*																		
Sub-Class II.—Extraction of minerals.	1,508	882	123	...	...	594	1,322	772	113	...	...	127 / 310	75	35	......	......	...	17 / 23
ORDER 3.—MINES	109	52	......	...	...	57	......	......	......	...	...	......	......	......	......	......	...	......
(16) Coal mines and petroleum wells.																		
ORDER 4.—QUARRIES OF HARD ROCKS	1,312	730	109	...	...	473	1,337	695	1·9	...	...	127 / 303	75	35	......	......	...	17 / 23
(18) Other minerals (jade, diamonds, limestone, etc.).																		
ORDER 5.—SALT, ETC.	177	100	13	...	...	64	85	77	4	...	...	...... / 4	......	......	......	......	...	......
(19) Rock, sea and marsh salt ..																		
CLASS B.—PREPARATION AND SUPPLY OF MATERIAL SUBSTANCES.	606,039	321,429	47,916	1,514	1	236,694	415,553	224,968	42,114	1,424	1	46,314 / 102,157	126,416	65,777	4,580	88	...	18,421 / 37,038
Sub-Class III.—Industry ...	323,070	169,729	36,721	37	...	116,630	252,652	134,260	33,060	33	...	26,300 / 59,032	51,968	36,811	3,125	4	...	6,875 / 15,157
ORDER 6.—TEXTILES	174,338	92,965	27,514	22	...	53,839	147,038	79,857	25,200	21	...	13,021 / 28,960	22,962	11,631	2,068	1	...	3,125 / 6,138
(21) Cotton, ginning, cleaning and pressing.	332	94	54	...	...	184	170	20	32	...	...	2 / 116	142	64	22	......	...	20 / 81
(22) Cotton, spinning, sizing and weaving.	171,175	91,544	26,968	13	...	52,653	145,959	79,478	24,922	12	...	12,932 / 28,027	21,226	10,613	1,962	1	...	3,949 / 5,703
(23) Jute spinning, pressing and weaving.	35	21	1	...	...	13	19	9	1	...	...	1 / 8	12	12	......	......	...	......
(24) Rope, twine, and string ...	145	67	28	9	...	50	124	50	26	9	...	11 / 28	11	5	......	......	...	2 / 4
(26) Woolcarders and spinners, weavers of woollen blankets, carpets, etc.	183	11	135	...	...	37	179	11	134	...	...	6 / 28	4	......	1	......	...	...... / 3
(27) Silk spinners and weavers ...	77	42	9	...	...	26	46	23	8	...	...	4 / 11	28	19	1	......	...	2 / 6
(28) Hair, camel, and horsehair, bristles work, brush makers, etc.	14	7	1	...	...	6	14	7	1	...	...	1 / 5	......	......	......	......	...	......
(29) Persons occupied with feathers...	3	3	......	...	...	......	2	2	......	...	...	......	......	......	......	......	...	......
(30) Dyeing, bleaching, printing, preparation and sponging of textiles.	29	17	......	...	...	12	17	13	......	..	...	2 / 2	11	4	......	......	...	7
(31) Other (lace, crape, embroideries fringes, etc.) and insufficiently described textile industries.	2,346	1,180	318	...	...	848	508	235	76	...	...	62 / 135	1,548	914	102	......	...	146 / 386

TABLE VII—*continued*.

OCCUPATION OR MEANS OF LIVELIHOOD.

OCCUPATION.	CHRISTIAN. Total workers and dependants.	CHRISTIAN. Actual Workers. Total. Males.	CHRISTIAN. Actual Workers. Total. Females.	CHRISTIAN. Actual Workers. Partially agriculturists. Males.	CHRISTIAN. Actual Workers. Partially agriculturists. Females.	CHRISTIAN. Dependants.	JAIN. Total workers and dependants.	JAIN. Actual Workers. Total. Males.	JAIN. Actual Workers. Total. Females.	JAIN. Actual Workers. Partially agriculturists. Males.	JAIN. Actual Workers. Partially agriculturists. Females.	JAIN. Dependants.	ZOROASTRIAN. Total workers and dependants.	ZOROASTRIAN. Actual Workers. Total. Males.	ZOROASTRIAN. Actual Workers. Total. Females.	ZOROASTRIAN. Actual Workers. Partially agriculturists. Males.	ZOROASTRIAN. Actual Workers. Partially agriculturists. Females.	ZOROASTRIAN. Dependants.	MINOR AND UNSPECIFIED RELIGIONS. Total workers and dependants.	MINOR AND UNSPECIFIED RELIGIONS. Actual Workers. Total. Males.	MINOR AND UNSPECIFIED RELIGIONS. Actual Workers. Total. Females.	MINOR AND UNSPECIFIED RELIGIONS. Actual Workers. Partially agriculturists. Males.	MINOR AND UNSPECIFIED RELIGIONS. Actual Workers. Partially agriculturists. Females.	MINOR AND UNSPECIFIED RELIGIONS. Dependants.
1	20	21	22	23	24	25	26	27	28	29	30	31	32	33	34	35	36	37	38	39	40	41	42	43
CLASS A.—PRODUCTION OF RAW MATERIALS—*continued*.																								
Sub-Class II.—Extraction of minerals.	92	23	9	...	...	18 / 43	...	...	...	...	...	...	109	53	...	...	...	57	...	...	...	...	...	...
ORDER 3.—MINES																								
(16) Coal mines and petroleum wells.	......	...	...	...	...	......	...	...	...	...	...	...	109	53	...	...	...	57	...	...	...	...	...	...
ORDER 4.—QUARRIES OF HARD ROCKS.																								
(18) Other minerals (jade, diamonds, limestone, etc.).	......	...	...	...	...	......	...	...	...	...	...	...	...	...	...	...	...	......	...	...	...	...	...	...
ORDER 5.—SALT, ETC.																								
(19) Rock, sea, and marsh salt ..	93	21	9	...	...	18 / 43	...	...	...	...	...	...	...	...	...	...	...	......	...	...	...	...	...	...
CLASS B.—PREPARATION AND SUPPLY OF MATERIAL SUBSTANCES.	20,765	12,425	647	...	...	2,659 / 5,024	15,858	9,387	116	1	...	2,541 / 3,814	23,026	7,169	370	1	...	5,165 / 10,323	4,421	1,703	80	...	...	861 / 1,767
Sub-Class III.—Industry ...	8,082	4,066	228	...	...	1,066 / 1,812	812	541	20	...	...	67 / 164	6,759	2,187	213	...	...	1,435 / 2,974	2,797	1,014	65	...	...	556 / 1,162
ORDER 6.—TEXTILES	802	318	73	...	...	96 / 315	145	86	10	...	...	19 / 20	2,953	961	116	...	...	622 / 1,254	418	132	27	...	...	98 / 161
(21) Cotton ginning, cleaning, and pressing.	12	9	...	...	...	1 / 2	1	1	...	...	...	...	7	...	...	...	...	7	...	...	...	...	...	...
(22) Cotton spinning, sizing and weaving.	700	301	35	...	...	93 / 271	107	67	6	...	...	11 / 23	2,792	956	25	...	...	597 / 1,215	381	130	18	...	...	94 / 149
(23) Jute spinning, pressing and weaving.	4	...	...	...	...	4	...	...	...	...	...	...	...	...	...	...	...	...	...	...	...	...	...	...
(24) Rope, twine and string ..	2	2	...	...	...	......	...	...	...	...	...	...	5	...	2	...	...	3	3	1	...	...	...	2
(26) Woolcarders and spinners, weavers of woollen blankets, carpets, etc.	......	...	...	...	...	......	...	...	...	...	...	...	...	...	...	...	...	......	...	...	...	...	...	...
(27) Silk spinners and weavers ..	......	...	...	...	...	......	3	...	...	...	...	3	...	...	...	...	...	......	...	...	...	...	...	...
(28) Hair, camel and horsehair, bristles work, brush makers, etc.	......	...	...	...	...	......	...	...	...	...	...	...	...	...	...	...	...	......	...	...	...	...	...	...
(29) Persons occupied with feathers...	......	...	...	...	...	......	...	...	...	...	...	...	...	...	...	...	...	......	...	...	...	...	...	...
(30) Dyeing, bleaching, printing, preparation and sponging of textiles.	1	...	...	...	...	1	...	...	...	...	...	...	...	...	...	...	...	......	...	...	...	...	...	...
(31) Other (lace, crape, embroideries, fringes, etc.) and insufficiently described textile industries.	53	6	38	...	...	2 / 37	34	16	4	...	...	8 / 4	149	6	80	...	...	25 / 29	34	1	9	...	...	2 / 12

TABLE VII.

OCCUPATION OR MEANS OF LIVELIHOOD.

TABLE VII.

Occupation or Means of Livelihood.

TABLE VII—*continued.*

Occupation or Means of Livelihood.

Occupation.	All Religions. Total workers and dependants.	All Religions. Actual Workers. Total. Males.	All Religions. Actual Workers. Total. Females.	All Religions. Actual Workers. Partially agriculturists. Males.	All Religions. Actual Workers. Partially agriculturists. Females.	All Religions. Dependants.	Hindu. Total workers and dependants.	Hindu. Actual Workers. Total. Males.	Hindu. Actual Workers. Total. Females.	Hindu. Actual Workers. Partially agriculturists. Males.	Hindu. Actual Workers. Partially agriculturists. Females.	Hindu. Dependants.	Musalman. Total workers and dependants.	Musalman. Actual Workers. Total. Males.	Musalman. Actual Workers. Total. Females.	Musalman. Actual Workers. Partially agriculturists. Males.	Musalman. Actual Workers. Partially agriculturists. Females.	Musalman. Dependants.
1	2	3	4	5	6	7	8	9	10	11	12	13	14	15	16	17	18	19
CLASS B.—PREPARATION AND SUPPLY OF MATERIAL SUBSTANCES—*continued.*																		
Sub-class III.—Industry.—*contd.*																		
ORDER 7.—HIDES, SKINS AND HARD MATERIALS FROM THE ANIMAL KINGDOM.	2,303	1,329	227	...	...	747	2,007	1,155	207	...	...	215 433	365	160	20	......	......	11 74
(32) Tanners, curriers, leather dressers and dyers, etc.	2,265	1,339	223	...	...	738	2,007	1,155	207	...	...	215 430	228	160	16	......	......	11 41
(33) Makers of leather articles, such as trunks, water bags, etc.	14	......	1	...	...	13	......	......	......	...	...	......	3	......	1	......	......	 2
(35) Bone, ivory, horn, shell, etc., workers.	34	......	3	...	...	31	......	......	......	...	...	......	34	......	3	......	......	 31
ORDER 8.—WOOD	24,923	12,496	573	4	...	11,854	17,745	8,964	513	4	...	2,250 6,028	3,037	1,825	27	......	......	283 1,008
(36) Sawyers, carpenters, turners and joiners, etc.	23,095	11,631	129	4	...	11,335	16,342	8,408	94	4	...	2,095 5,747	2,670	1,329	18	......	......	252 971
(37) Basket makers and other industries of woody material, including leaves.	1,827	864	444	...	...	519	1,423	548	419	...	...	155 291	367	296	9	......	......	31 31
ORDER 9.—METALS	14,120	7,381	186	...	...	6,558	9,163	5,071	151	...	...	1,192 2,749	4,845	2,141	33	......	......	853 1,818
(38) Forging and rolling of iron and other metals.	24	10	......	...	...	14	10	5	......	...	...	3 2	......	......	......	......	......	......
(39) Plough and agricultural implement makers.	125	120	......	...	...	5	......	......	......	...	...	......	125	130	......	......	......	6 ......
(40) Makers of arms, guns, etc. ...	4	1	......	...	...	3	3	......	......	...	...	3	......	......	......	......	......	......
(41) Other workers in iron and makers of implements and tools principally or exclusively of iron.	8,974	4,817	72	...	...	4,085	6,483	3,750	55	...	...	...... 903 1,854	2,360	984	17	......	......	286 1,073
(42) Workers in brass, copper and bell metal.	2,305	1,100	79	...	...	1,126	2,091	1,000	73	...	...	291 737	179	83	4	......	......	30 63
(43) Workers in other metals (tin, zinc, lead, quicksilver, etc.)	2,451	1,300	29	...	...	1,222	446	233	17	...	...	72 135	1,960	916	12	......	......	331 671
(44) Workers in mints, die-sinkers, etc.	237	133	6	...	...	98	151	94	6	...	...	20 41	21	9	......	......	......	1 11
ORDER 10.—CERAMICS	1,046	434	191	...	...	421	913	385	166	...	...	132 230	122	48	25	......	......	14 35
(46) Makers of glass and crystal ware.	37	13	2	...	...	23	4	1	2	...	...	 1	27	13	......	......	......	4 11
(47) Potters and earthen pipe and bowlmakers.	809	331	161	...	...	317	709	924	136	...	...	97 183	95	38	25	......	......	10 34
(48) Brick and tile makers ...	200	90	28	...	...	83	200	90	29	...	...	35 47	......	......	......	......	......	....

TABLE VII—*continued.*

OCCUPATION OR MEANS OF LIVELIHOOD.

OCCUPATION.	CHRISTIAN.						JAIN.						ZOROASTRIAN.						MINOR AND UNSPECIFIED RELIGIONS.					
	Total workers and dependants.	ACTUAL WORKERS.				Dependants.	Total workers and dependants.	ACTUAL WORKERS.				Dependants.	Total workers and dependants.	ACTUAL WORKERS.				Dependants.	Total workers and dependants.	ACTUAL WORKERS.				Dependants.
		Total.		Partially agriculturists.				Total.		Partially agriculturists.				Total.		Partially agriculturists.				Total.		Partially agriculturists.		
		Males.	Females.	Males.	Females.			Males.	Females.	Males.	Females.			Males.	Females.	Males.	Females.			Males.	Females.	Males.	Females.	
1	20	21	22	23	24	25	26	27	28	29	30	31	32	33	34	35	36	37	38	39	40	41	42	43
CLASS B.—PREPARATION AND SUPPLY OF MATERIAL SUBSTANCES—*continued.*																								
Sub-class III.—Industry—*contd.*																								
ORDER 7.—HIDES, SKINS AND HARD MATERIALS FROM THE ANIMAL KINGDOM.	26	14	...	...	...	4 8	...	...	...	...	...	...	5	...	...	...	...	 5	...	...	...	...	...	...
(32) Tanners, curriers, leather dressers and dyers, etc.	20	14	...	...	...	4 2	...	...	...	...	...	...	...	...	...	...	...	......	...	...	...	...	...	...
(33) Makers of leather articles such as trunks, water-bags, etc.	6	...	...	...	...	 6	...	...	...	...	...	...	5	...	...	...	...	 5	...	...	...	...	...	...
(35) Bone, ivory, horn, shell, etc., workers.	......	...	...	...	...	...	...	...	...	...	...	...	...	...	...	...	...	......	...	...	...	...	...	...
ORDER 8.—WOOD	1,227	826	33	...	...	132 246	43	26	...	...	...	4 13	1,012	358	1	...	...	182 471	1,858	706	9	...	...	358 785
(36) Sawyers, carpenters, turners, and joiners, etc.	1,138	815	8	...	...	127 238	42	25	...	...	...	4 13	1,003	353	1	...	...	179 470	1,851	704	8	...	...	356 783
(37) Basket makers and other industries of woody materials including leaves.	89	11	15	...	...	5 6	1	1	...	...	...	...	10	6	...	...	...	3 1	7	2	1	...	...	2 2
ORDER 9.—METALS	117	71	...	...	...	11 35	45	24	2	...	...	7 12	114	65	...	...	...	33 17	36	9	...	...	...	9 18
(38) Forging and rolling of iron and other metals.	9	2	...	...	...	1 6	...	...	...	...	...	...	5	3	...	...	...	2	...	...	...	...	...	...
(39) Plough and agricultural implement makers.	......	...	...	...	...	......	...	...	...	...	...	...	...	...	...	...	...	......	...	...	...	...	...	...
(40) Makers of arms, guns, etc. ...	......	...	...	...	...	......	...	...	...	...	...	...	1	1	...	...	...	......	...	...	...	...	...	...
(41) Other workers in iron and makers of implements and tools principally or exclusively of iron.	90	59	...	...	...	8 23	18	7	...	...	...	7 4	28	12	...	...	...	1 15	16	5	...	...	...	6 5
(42) Workers in brass, copper and bell metal.	4	...	...	...	...	 4	27	17	2	...	...	... 8	...	...	...	...	...	......	4	1	...	...	...	2 1
(43) Workers in other metals (tin, zinc, lead, quicksilver, etc.)	11	6	...	...	...	3 1	...	...	...	...	...	...	23	13	...	...	...	9 2	11	2	...	...	...	1 8
(44) Workers in mints, die-sinkers, etc.	3	2	...	...	...	 1	...	...	...	...	...	...	57	37	...	...	...	20	5	1	...	...	...	... 4
ORDER 10.—CERAMICS	2	...	...	...	...	 2	3	1	...	...	...	1 1	5	...	...	...	...	5	1	...	...	...	...	1
(45) Makers of glass and crystal ware.	......	...	...	...	...	......	...	...	...	...	...	...	5	...	...	...	...	5	1	...	...	...	...	1
(47) Potters and earthen pipe and bowlmakers.	2	...	...	...	...	 2	3	1	...	...	...	1 1	...	...	...	...	...	......	...	...	...	...	...	...
(48) Brick and tile makers ...	......	...	...	...	...	......	...	...	...	...	...	...	...	...	...	...	...	......	...	...	...	...	...	...

TABLE VII—*continued.*

OCCUPATION OR MEANS OF LIVELIHOOD.

OCCUPATION.	ALL RELIGIONS.						HINDU.						MUSALMAN.					
	Total workers and dependants.	ACTUAL WORKERS. Total		ACTUAL WORKERS. Partially agriculturists.		Dependants.	Total workers and dependants.	ACTUAL WORKERS. Total.		ACTUAL WORKERS. Partially agriculturists.		Dependants	Total workers and dependants.	ACTUAL WORKERS. Total.		ACTUAL WORKERS. Partially agriculturists.		Dependants.
		Males.	Females.	Males.	Females.			Males.	Females.	Males.	Females.			Males.	Females.	Males.	Females.	
1	2	3	4	5	6	7	8	9	10	11	12	13	14	15	16	17	18	19
CLASS B.—PREPARATION AND SUPPLY OF MATERIAL SUBSTANCES—*continued.*																		
Sub-Class III.—Industry—*contd.*																		
ORDER 11.—CHEMICAL PRODUCTS PROPERLY SO CALLED, AND ANALOGOUS.	523	258	32	...	...	232	270	135	26	...	...	47 62	173	95	5	......	...	28 45
(60) Manufacture of matches and explosive materials.	80	24	25	...	...	31	78	24	23	...	...	15 14	......	......	......	......	...	......
(61) Manufacture of ærated and mineral waters.	82	33	1	...	...	48	45	21	......	...	...	5 19	3	1	......	......	...	2 ......
(62) Manufacture of dyes, paint and ink.	38	26	1	...	...	11	16	12	1	...	...	2 1	3	1	......	......	...	2 ......
(63) Manufacture and refining of vegetable and mineral oils.	275	151	5	...	...	119	108	61	......	...	...	22 25	160	88	5	......	...	22 45
(64) Manufacture of paper, cardboard and papier maché.	11	6	......	...	...	5	2	2	......	...	...	......	5	3	......	......	...	2 ......
(65) Others (soap, candles, lac, cutch, perfumes and miscellaneous drugs).	36	18	......	...	...	18	21	15	......	...	...	3 3	2	2	......	......	...	......
ORDER 12.—FOOD INDUSTRIES ...	16,208	7,101	2,836	...	...	6,271	9,535	4,045	2,371	...	...	1,105 2,014	5,363	2,185	427	......	...	799 1,853
(56) Rice pounders and huskers and flour grinders.	677	191	319	...	...	167	534	173	232	...	...	62 67	124	9	87	......	...	7 21
(57) Bakers and biscuit makers ...	1,836	1,131	81	...	...	624	395	238	21	...	...	57 79	932	548	40	......	...	127 210
(58) Grain parchers, etc.	66	55	1	...	...	10	57	53	......	...	...	 4	9	3	1	......	...	6 ......
(59) Butchers	3,009	1,195	77	...	...	1,737	478	223	18	...	...	67 170	2,490	919	58	......	...	381 1,093
(62) Makers of sugar, molasses and gur.	83	76	......	...	...	7	20	20	......	...	...	......	7	......	......	......	...	2 5
(63) Sweetmeat makers, preparers of jams and condiments, etc.	3,245	1,948	158	...	...	1,139	2,498	1,684	133	...	...	241 478	548	232	10	......	...	83 214
(64) Brewers and distillers	6	2	......	...	...	4	......	......	......	...	...	......	......	......	......	......	...	......
(65) Toddy drawers	1,722	863	30	...	...	829	1,276	519	21	...	...	298 438	45	36	2	......	...	5 2
(66) Manufacture of tobacco, opium and ganja.	5,564	1,640	2,170	...	...	1,754	4,379	1,205	1,043	...	...	450 778	1,106	411	311	......	...	178 308

TABLE VII—*continued.*

OCCUPATION OR MEANS OF LIVELIHOOD.

OCCUPATION.	CHRISTIAN. Total workers and dependants.	CHRISTIAN. Actual Workers. Total. Males.	CHRISTIAN. Actual Workers. Total. Females.	CHRISTIAN. Actual Workers. Partially agriculturists. Males.	CHRISTIAN. Actual Workers. Partially agriculturists. Females.	CHRISTIAN. Dependants.	JAIN. Total workers and dependants.	JAIN. Actual Workers. Total. Males.	JAIN. Actual Workers. Total. Females.	JAIN. Actual Workers. Partially agriculturists. Males.	JAIN. Actual Workers. Partially agriculturists. Females.	JAIN. Dependants.	ZOROASTRIAN. Total workers and dependants.	ZOROASTRIAN. Actual Workers. Total. Males.	ZOROASTRIAN. Actual Workers. Total. Females.	ZOROASTRIAN. Actual Workers. Partially agriculturists. Males.	ZOROASTRIAN. Actual Workers. Partially agriculturists. Females.	ZOROASTRIAN. Dependants.	MINOR AND UNSPECIFIED RELIGIONS. Total workers and dependants.	MINOR AND UNSPECIFIED RELIGIONS. Actual Workers. Total. Males.	MINOR AND UNSPECIFIED RELIGIONS. Actual Workers. Total. Females.	MINOR AND UNSPECIFIED RELIGIONS. Actual Workers. Partially agriculturists. Males.	MINOR AND UNSPECIFIED RELIGIONS. Actual Workers. Partially agriculturists. Females.	MINOR AND UNSPECIFIED RELIGIONS. Dependants.
1	20	21	22	23	24	25	26	27	28	29	30	31	32	33	34	35	36	37	38	39	40	41	42	43
CLASS B.—PREPARATION AND SUPPLY OF MATERIAL SUBSTANCES—*continued.*																								
Sub-Class III.—Industry—*contd.*																								
ORDER 11.—CHEMICAL PRODUCTS PROPERLY SO CALLED, AND ANALOGOUS.	10	1	1	...	...	...... / 8	7	6	...	...	...	... / 1	62	21	...	...	...	22 / 19	...	...	...	...	...	...
(50) Manufacture of matches and explosive materials.	2	...	...	...	...	2 /	...	..	...	...	...	...	...	...	...	...	...	......	...	...	...	...	...	...
(51) Manufacture of ærated and mineral waters.	2	1	1	...	...	......	1	...	...	...	...	1 / ...	31	10	...	...	...	14 / 7	...	...	...	...	...	...
(52) Manufacture of dyes, paint and ink.	......	...	...	...	...	......	4	4	...	...	...	...	15	9	...	...	...	4 / 3	...	...	...	...	...	...
(53) Manufacture and refining of vegetable and mineral oil.	......	...	...	...	...	......	2	2	...	...	...	...	5	...	...	...	...	5 /	...	...	...	...	...	...
(54) Manufacture of paper, cardboard and papier maché.	2	...	...	...	...	2 /	...	...	...	...	...	...	2	1	...	...	...	1 /	...	...	...	...	...	...
(55) Others (soap, candles, lac, cutch, perfumes and miscellaneous drugs).	4	...	...	...	...	4 /	...	...	...	...	...	...	9	1	...	...	...	3 / 6	...	...	...	...	...	...
ORDER 12.—FOOD INDUSTRIES ...	974	635	23	...	...	129 / 168	198	157	4	...	...	14 / 23	173	63	7	...	...	32 / 71	65	16	5	...	...	12 / 32
(56) Rice pounders and huskers and flour grinders.	7	1	...	...	...	6 /	10	8	...	...	...	1 / 1	3	...	...	...	...	3 /	...	...	...	...	...	...
(57) Bakers and biscuit makers ...	437	316	8	...	...	50 / 54	2	3	...	...	...	...	54	20	3	...	...	9 / 16	16	3	...	...	...	6 / 7
(58) Grain parchers, etc.	......	...	...	...	...	......	...	...	...	...	...	...	...	...	...	...	...	......	...	...	...	...	...	...
(59) Butchers	17	16	...	...	...	2 /	...	...	...	...	...	...	8	2	...	...	...	1 / 5	18	6	1	...	...	1 / 8
(62) Makers of sugar, molasses and gur.	......	...	...	...	...	......	56	56	...	...	...	...	...	...	...	...	...	......	...	...	...	...	...	...
(63) Sweetmeat makers, preparers of jams and condiments, etc.	33	15	...	...	...	7 / 11	114	84	1	...	...	11 / 18	90	28	4	...	...	14 / 44	34	5	1	...	...	4 / 14
(64) Brewers and distillers	5	1	...	...	...	4 /	...	...	...	...	...	...	1	1	...	...	...	......	...	...	...	...	...	..
(65) Toddy drawers	441	278	7	...	...	50 / 97	...	...	...	...	...	...	...	...	...	...	...	......	...	...	...	...	...	...
(66) Manufacture of tobacco, opium and ganja.	34	9	7	...	...	4 / 14	16	7	3	...	...	2 / 4	18	6	...	...	...	8 / 4	9	2	3	...	...	1 / 3

TABLE VII.

OCCUPATION OR MEANS OF LIVELIHOOD.

TABLE VII—*continued.*

OCCUPATION OR MEANS OF LIVELIHOOD.

OCCUPATION.	ALL RELIGIONS.						HINDU.						MUSALMAN.					
	Total workers and dependants.	Actual Workers. Total.		Actual Workers. Partially agriculturists.		Dependants.	Total workers and dependants.	Actual Workers. Total.		Actual Workers. Partially agriculturists.		Dependants.	Total workers and dependants.	Actual Workers. Total.		Actual Workers. Partially agriculturists.		Dependants.
		Males.	Females.	Males.	Females.			Males.	Females.	Males.	Females.			Males.	Females.	Males.	Females.	
1	2	3	4	5	6	7	8	9	10	11	12	13	14	15	16	17	18	19
CLASS B.—PREPARATION AND SUPPLY OF MATERIAL SUBSTANCES—*continued.*																		
Sub-Class III.—Industry—*contd.*																		
ORDER 13.—INDUSTRIES OF DRESS AND THE TOILET.	40.209	22.744	2.454	1	...	15.011	28.513	15.997	1.837	1	...	3,041 7,727	7.994	4.453	402	......	...	858 2.276
(67) Hat, cap and turban makers ...	307	147	10	...	...	150	184	100	7	...	...	22 55	48	27	2	......	...	10 9
(68) Tailors, milliners, dress makers and darners, embroiderers on linen.	14.067	8.219	731	...	...	5.087	7,926	4,629	341	...	...	878 2,118	2.696	1,301	178	......	...	335 823
(69) Shoe, boot and sandal makers ...	8.538	4.295	593	...	...	3.650	8.201	4,138	557	...	...	940 2,506	278	131	34	......	...	22 91
(70) Other industries pertaining to dress, gloves, socks, gaiters, belts, buttons, umbrellas, canes, etc.	159	86	8	...	...	65	32	28	......	...	...	3 1	127	68	8	......	...	13 48
(71) Washing, cleaning and dyeing ...	10.479	5.597	1.108	...	...	3.774	6.910	3,657	932	...	...	810 1,511	3.512	1,911	170	......	...	398 1,037
(72) Barbers, hairdressers and wig-makers.	6.658	4.369	4	1	...	2.285	5,259	3,355	......	1	...	428 1,470	1.333	970	4	......	...	90 269
(73) Other industries connected with the toilet (tattooers, shampooers, bath houses, etc.)	1	1	......	...	...	......	......	......	......	...	...	......	......	......	......	......	...	......
ORDER 14.—FURNITURE INDUSTRIES.	841	465	9	...	...	367	566	327	7	...	...	232	186	88	......	......	...	98 ......
(74) Cabinet makers, carriage painters, etc.	838	462	9	...	...	367	565	327	7	...	...	232	184	86	......	......	...	98 ......
(75) Upholsterers, tent makers, etc. ...	3	3	......	...	...	......	......	......	......	...	...	......	2	2	......	......	...	......
ORDER 15.—BUILDING INDUSTRIES.	12.235	7.410	243	8	...	4.632	7,207	4.265	190	6	...	747 2.005	4.637	3.010	51	2	...	443 1.133
(76) Lime burners and cement workers.	59	38	8	...	...	13	48	34	8	...	...	6 1	11	4	......	......	...	3 4
(77) Excavators, plinth builders and well sinkers.	91	45	8	...	...	38	89	43	8	...	...	10 28	2	2	......	......	...	......
(78) Stone and marble workers, masons, bricklayers	10.113	6.466	216	8	...	3.431	6.273	3,745	109	6	...	678 1,742	3.763	3,650	40	2	...	287 750
(79) Others (thatchers, building contractors, house painters, tilers, plumbers, locksmiths, etc.)	2.022	851	11	...	...	1.160	797	443	6	...	...	114 231	861	324	5	......	...	153 379
ORDER 16.—CONSTRUCTION OF MEANS OF TRANSPORT.	594	205	3	...	...	385	221	88	......	...	...	44 89	146	47	2	......	...	41 56
(80) Cart, carriage, palki, etc., makers and wheel wrights.	289	105	......	...	...	184	73	34	......	...	...	11 28	21	10	......	......	...	3 8
(81) Saddlers, harness makers, whip and lash makers.	241	73	2	...	...	166	146	52	......	...	...	33 61	74	16	2	......	...	29 27

TABLE VII—*continued*.

OCCUPATION OR MEANS OF LIVELIHOOD.

Occupation.	Christian. Total workers and dependants.	Christian. Actual Workers. Total. Males.	Christian. Actual Workers. Total. Females.	Christian. Actual Workers. Partially agriculturists. Males.	Christian. Actual Workers. Partially agriculturists. Females.	Christian. Dependants.	Jain. Total workers and dependants.	Jain. Actual Workers. Total. Males.	Jain. Actual Workers. Total. Females.	Jain. Actual Workers. Partially agriculturists. Males.	Jain. Actual Workers. Partially agriculturists. Females.	Jain. Dependants.	Zoroastrian. Total workers and dependants.	Zoroastrian. Actual Workers. Total. Males.	Zoroastrian. Actual Workers. Total. Females.	Zoroastrian. Actual Workers. Partially agriculturists. Males.	Zoroastrian. Actual Workers. Partially agriculturists. Females.	Zoroastrian. Dependants.	Minor and Unspecified Religions. Total workers and dependants.	Minor and Unspecified Religions. Actual Workers. Total. Males.	Minor and Unspecified Religions. Actual Workers. Total. Females.	Minor and Unspecified Religions. Actual Workers. Partially agriculturists. Males.	Minor and Unspecified Religions. Actual Workers. Partially agriculturists. Females.	Minor and Unspecified Religions. Dependants.
1	20	21	22	23	24	25	26	27	28	29	30	31	32	33	34	35	36	37	38	39	40	41	42	43
CLASS B.—PREPARATION AND SUPPLY OF MATERIAL SUBSTANCES—*continued*.																								
Sub-Class III.—Industry—*contd*.																								
ORDER 13.—INDUSTRIES OF DRESS AND THE TOILET.	3,231	2,233	105	...	...	333 / 495	125	81	2	...	...	7 / 32	242	37	84	...	...	33 / 88	105	25	21	...	...	15 / 41
(67) Hat, cap and turban makers ...	......	...	...	...	...	......	1	...	...	...	...	... / 1	63	17	1	...	...	21 / 21	6	3	...	...	...	1 / 2
(68) Tailors, milliners, dress makers and darners, embroiderers on linen.	3,126	2,161	104	...	...	381 / 475	97	69	1	...	...	4 / 23	150	15	81	...	...	7 / 45	72	14	21	...	...	9 / 25
(69) Shoe, boot and sandal makers ...	23	14	1	...	...	3 / 5	18	8	1	...	...	3 / 0	...	...	...	...	...	......	18	4	...	...	...	4 / 10
(70) Other industries pertaining to dress, gloves, socks, gaiters, belts, buttons, umbrellas, canes, etc.	......	...	...	...	...	......	...	...	...	...	...	...	...	...	...	...	...	......	...	...	...	...	...	...
(71) Washing, cleaning and dyeing ...	30	30	...	...	...	3 / 7	1	1	...	...	...	...	19	4	...	...	...	2 / 13	7	4	...	...	...	1 / 2
(72) Barbers, hairdressers and wig makers.	51	37	...	...	...	6 / 8	8	6	...	...	...	... / 2	5	1	...	...	...	... / 4	2	...	...	...	...	... / 2
(73) Other industries connected with the toilet (tattooers, shampooers, bath houses, etc.).	1	1	...	...	...	......	...	...	...	...	...	...	...	...	...	...	...	......	...	...	...	...	...	...
ORDER 14.—FURNITURE INDUSTRIES.	46	33	2	...	...	11	...	...	...	...	...	...	27	11	...	...	...	16 /	16	6	...	...	...	10 / ...
(74) Cabinet makers, carriage painters, etc.	46	33	2	...	...	11	...	...	...	...	...	...	26	10	...	...	...	16 /	10	6	...	...	...	10 / ...
(75) Upholsterers, tent makers, etc. ...	......	...	...	...	...	......	...	...	...	...	...	...	1	1	...	...	...	......	...	...	...	...	...	...
ORDER 15.—BUILDING INDUSTRIES.	82	36	2	...	...	21 / 23	28	23	...	...	...	4 / 1	278	62	...	...	...	84 / 132	53	14	...	...	...	14 / 25
(76) Lime burners and cement workers.	......	...	...	...	...	......	...	...	...	...	...	...	...	...	...	...	...	......	...	...	...	...	...	...
(77) Excavators, plinth builders and well sinkers.	......	...	...	...	...	......	...	...	...	...	...	...	...	...	...	...	...	......	...	...	...	...	...	...
(78) Stone and marble workers, masons, bricklayers.	40	16	2	...	...	12 / 10	26	23	...	...	...	... / 4	...	...	...	...	...	......	11	3	...	...	...	3 / 6
(79) Others (thatchers, building contractors, house painters, tilers, plumbers, lock-smiths, etc.)	42	20	...	...	...	9 / 13	2	1	...	...	...	... / 1	278	62	...	...	...	84 / 132	42	11	...	...	...	11 / 20
ORDER 16.—CONSTRUCTION OF MEANS OF TRANSPORT.	72	34	1	...	...	19 / 18	3	2	...	...	...	1 / ...	148	33	...	...	...	27 / 88	4	1	...	...	...	3 / ...
(80) Cart, carriage, palki, etc., makers and wheel wrights.	46	27	...	...	...	9 / 10	...	...	...	...	...	...	145	33	...	...	...	27 / 85	4	1	...	...	...	3 / ...
(81) Saddlers, harness makers, whip and lash makers.	15	3	...	...	...	9 / 3	3	2	...	...	...	1 / ...	3	...	...	...	...	... / 3	...	...	...	...	...	...

TABLE VII—*continued.*

OCCUPATION OR MEANS OF LIVELIHOOD.

OCCUPATION.	ALL RELIGIONS.						HINDU.						MUSALMAN.					
	Total workers and dependants.	ACTUAL WORKERS.				Dependants.	Total workers and dependants.	ACTUAL WORKERS.				Dependants.	Total workers and dependants.	ACTUAL WORKERS.				Dependants.
		Total.		Partially agriculturists.				Total.		Partially agriculturists.				Total.		Partially agriculturists.		
		Males.	Females.	Males.	Females.			Males.	Females.	Males.	Females.			Males.	Females.	Males.	Females.	
1	2	3	4	5	6	7	8	9	10	11	12	13	14	15	16	17	18	19
CLASS B.—PREPARATION AND SUPPLY OF MATERIAL SUBSTANCES—*continued.*																		
Sub-Class III.—Industry—*contd.*																		
ORDER 16.—CONSTRUCTION OF MEANS OF TRANSPORT—*continued.*																		
(82) Ship and boat builders	64	27	1	...	...	36	2	2	......	...	...	......	51	21	......	......	...	9 21
ORDER 17.—PRODUCTION AND TRANSMISSION OF PHYSICAL FORCES (HEAT, LIGHT, ELECTRICITY, MOTIVE POWER, ETC.) (83) Gas works, electric light and ice factories.	1,780	853	6	...	...	920	1,122	507	8	...	...	144 403	330	131	......	......	...	51 148
ORDER 18.—INDUSTRIES OF LUXURY AND THOSE PERTAINING TO LITERATURE AND THE ARTS AND SCIENCES.	22,885	11,445	198	2	...	11,243	17,489	8,952	157	1	...	2,380 6,000	2,063	1,133	28	1	...	340 562
(84) Printers, lithographers, engravers, etc.	9,751	4,815	33	...	...	4,903	6,838	3,538	20	...	...	(35) 2,240	779	413	4	......	...	133 23
(85) Newspaper and magazine managers, editors, journalists, etc.	148	40	1	1	...	98	19	9	......	...	...	6 4	2	2	......	1	...	......
(86) Book-binders and stitchers and envelope makers, etc.	961	518	10	...	...	433	584	330	7	...	...	60 187	216	119	3	......	...	44 50
(87) Makers of musical instruments ...	155	98	9	...	...	48	139	93	9	...	...	17 20	10	4	......	......	...	2 4
(88) Makers of watches and clocks and optical, photographic and surgical instruments.	800	331	......	...	...	469	189	80	......	...	...	17 83	274	130	......	......	...	47 97
(89) Workers in precious stones and metals, enamellers, imitation jewellery makers, gilders, etc.	10,129	5,185	129	1	...	4,615	9,352	4,713	111	1	...	1,398 3,225	548	331	18	......	...	81 118
(90) Makers of bangles, rosaries, bead and other necklaces, spangles, lingams and sacred threads.	237	160	5	...	...	72	115	77	4	...	...	15 19	93	70	1	......	...	10 12
(91) Toy, kite, cage and fishing tackle, etc., makers, taxidermists, etc.	112	47	4	...	...	61	29	13	2	...	...	2 12	60	30	2	......	...	4 23
(92) Others including managers, persons other than performers employed in theatres and other places of public entertainment, employés of public societies, race course service, huntsmen, etc.	593	243	7	...	...	343	229	90	4	...	...	25 110	81	38	......	......	...	17 29
ORDER 19.—INDUSTRIES CONCERNED WITH REFUSE MATTER. (93) Sweepers, scavengers, dust and sweeping contractors.	11,017	4,655	2,247	...	...	4,115	10,604	4,532	2,2 7	...	...	1,750 2,335	125	59	17	......	...	31 18

TABLE VII—*continued.*

OCCUPATION OR MEANS OF LIVELIHOOD.

OCCUPATION.	CHRISTIAN.						JAIN.						ZOROASTRIAN.						MINOR AND UNSPECIFIED RELIGIONS.					
	Total workers and dependants.	ACTUAL WORKERS. Total.		Partially agriculturists.		Dependants.	Total workers and dependants.	ACTUAL WORKERS. Total.		Partially agriculturists.		Dependants.	Total workers and dependants.	ACTUAL WORKERS. Total.		Partially agriculturists.		Dependants.	Total workers and dependants.	ACTUAL WORKERS. Total.		Partially agriculturists.		Dependants.
		Males.	Females.	Males.	Females.			Males.	Females.	Males.	Females.			Males.	Females.	Males.	Females.			Males.	Females.	Males.	Females.	
1	20	21	22	23	24	25	26	27	28	29	30	31	32	33	34	35	36	37	38	39	40	41	42	43
CLASS B.—PREPARATION AND SUPPLY OF MATERIAL SUBSTANCES—*continued.*																								
Sub-Class III.—Industry—*contd.*																								
ORDER 16.—CONSTRUCTION OF MEANS OF TRANSPORT—*continued.*																								
(82) Ship and boat builders	11	4	1	...	...	1 5	...	...	...	...	...	...	...	...	...	...	...	......	...	...	...	...	...	...
ORDER 17.—PRODUCTION AND TRANSMISSION OF PHYSICAL FORCES (HEAT, LIGHT, ELECTRICITY, MOTIVE POWER, ETC.).																								
(83) Gas works, electric light and ice factories.	204	102	...	...	...	43 59	...	...	...	...	...	...	99	40	...	...	...	29 30	25	12	...	...	...	2 11
ORDER 18.—INDUSTRIES OF LUXURY AND THOSE PERTAINING TO LITERATURE AND THE ARTS AND SCIENCES.	1,261	649	6	...	...	200 406	215	132	2	...	...	30 51	1,641	486	5	...	...	356 794	216	93	...	...	...	35 88
(84) Printers, lithographers, engravers, etc.	876	459	4	...	...	152 261	22	5	2	...	...	6 9	1,056	323	3	...	...	218 512	185	78	...	...	...	32 75
(85) Newspaper and magazine managers, editors, journalists, etc.	38	18	...	...	...	10 10	3	1	...	...	...	0 2	86	19	1	...	...	17 40	...	...	...	...	...	...
(86) Book-binders and stitchers and envelope makers, etc.	136	50	...	...	...	14 66	...	...	...	...	...	...	12	6	...	...	...	0 6	13	7	...	...	...	1 5
(87) Makers of musical instruments ..	4	1	...	...	...	1 2	...	...	...	...	...	...	2	...	...	...	...	0 2	...	...	...	...	...	...
(88) Makers of watches and clocks and optical, photographic and surgical instruments.	61	27	...	...	...	7 27	1	1	...	...	...	...	262	80	...	...	...	63 119	13	4	...	...	...	2 7
(89) Workers in precious stones and metals, enamellers, imitation jewellery makers, gilders, etc.	21	9	...	...	...	5 7	182	125	...	...	...	19 38	22	3	...	...	...	1 18	4	4	...	...	...	...
(90) Makers of bangles, rosaries, bead and other necklaces, spangles, lingams and sacred threads.	......	...	...	...	...	......	7	...	...	...	...	5 2	22	13	...	...	...	4 5	...	...	...	...	...	...
(91) Toy, kite, cage and fishing tackle, etc., makers, taxidermists, etc.	6	1	...	...	...	1 4	...	...	...	...	...	...	17	3	...	...	...	5 9	...	...	...	...	...	...
(92) Others including managers, persons other than performers employed in theatres and other places of public entertainment, employés of public societies race course service, huntsmen, etc.	119	78	2	...	...	10 29	...	...	...	...	...	...	162	39	1	...	...	48 74	1	...	...	...	...	0 1
ORDER 19.—INDUSTRIES CONCERNED WITH REFUSE MATTER																								
(93) Sweepers, scavengers, dust and sweeping contractors.	25	11	3	...	...	2 9	...	...	...	...	...	...	...	...	...	...	...	...	...	...	...	...	...	...

TABLE VII—*continued.*

OCCUPATION OR MEANS OF LIVELIHOOD.

OCCUPATION.	ALL RELIGIONS. Total workers and dependants.	ALL RELIGIONS. Actual Workers. Total. Males.	ALL RELIGIONS. Actual Workers. Total. Females.	ALL RELIGIONS. Actual Workers. Partially agriculturists. Males.	ALL RELIGIONS. Actual Workers. Partially agriculturists. Females.	ALL RELIGIONS. Dependants.	HINDU. Total workers and dependants.	HINDU. Actual Workers. Total. Males.	HINDU. Actual Workers. Total. Females.	HINDU. Actual Workers. Partially agriculturists. Males.	HINDU. Actual Workers. Partially agriculturists. Females.	HINDU. Dependants.	MUSALMAN. Total workers and dependants.	MUSALMAN. Actual Workers. Total. Males.	MUSALMAN. Actual Workers. Total. Females.	MUSALMAN. Actual Workers. Partially agriculturists. Males.	MUSALMAN. Actual Workers. Partially agriculturists. Females.	MUSALMAN. Dependants.
1	2	3	4	5	6	7	8	9	10	11	12	13	14	15	16	17	18	19
CLASS B.—PREPARATION AND SUPPLY OF MATERIAL SUBSTANCES—*continued.*																		
Sub-Class IV.—Transport... ...	122,230	74,500	4,070	1,370	1	43,660	80,308	48,728	3,661	1,293	1	8,148 19,771	37,129	18,167	295	83	...	2,502 6,165
ORDER 20.—TRANSPORT BY WATER.	48,801	36,293	2,932	1,326	...	9,571	27,687	20,306	2,656	1,243	...	1,527 3,198	15,503	12,111	254	83	...	920 2,218
(94) Harbour works, dockyards and pilots.	23,309	13,764	2,793	9	...	6,752	16,436	10,025	2,343	9	...	1,100 [illegible]	5,244	3,067	213	......	...	863 1,373
(95) Ship owners and their employés, ship brokers, ships' officers, engineers, mariners and firemen.	21,451	18,848	133	953	...	2,470	8,910	8,036	108	800	...	300 376	8,681	7,678	9	60	...	287 707
(96) persons employed on the maintenance of streams, rivers, canals (including construction).	4	1	......	...	...	3	......	......	......	...	...	......	4	1	......	......	...	 3
(97) Boat owners, boatmen, and tow-men.	4,037	3,685	6	361	...	346	2,341	2,245	3	344	...	31 62	1,574	1,365	2	17	...	71 136
ORDER 21.—TRANSPORT BY ROAD...	36,551	20,060	598	50	1	15,893	28,025	15,810	555	50	1	8,232 3,428	7,707	3,863	40	......	...	1,041 2,764
(98) Persons employed on the construction and maintenance of roads and bridges.	356	111	109	...	...	136	340	107	107	...	...	20 106	5	1	2	......	...	 2
(99) Cart owners and drivers, coachmen, stable boys, tramway, mail carriage, etc., managers and employés, (excluding private servants).	28,575	15,173	138	48	1	13,359	20,862	11,270	107	48	1	2,523 6,956	7,107	3,666	31	......	...	1,004 2,467
(100) Palki, etc., bearers and owners ...	3	3	......	...	...	......	3	3	......	...	...	......	......	......	......	......	...	......
(102) Porters and messengers	7,517	4,768	351	2	...	2,398	6,820	4,424	341	2	...	659 1,386	595	270	7	......	...	37 275
ORDER 22.—TRANSPORT BY RAIL ...	31,318	15,454	497	...	...	15,367	20,542	10,028	449	...	...	2,735 6,730	3,583	2,013	1	......	...	494 1,070
(103) Railway employés of all kinds other than construction coolies.	26,315	12,675	114	...	...	13,526	15,917	8,029	67	...	...	2,315 5,506	3,182	1,839	......	......	...	409 935
(104) Labourers employed on railway construction.	5,003	2,779	383	...	...	1,841	4,595	2,599	382	...	...	390 1,224	401	174	1	......	...	85 141
ORDER 23.—POST OFFICE, TELEGRAPH AND TELEPHONE SERVICES. (105) Post Office, Telegraph and Telephone services.	5,500	2,688	43	...	...	2,529	4,054	1,984	1	...	...	654 1,415	336	183	......	......	...	47 107
Sub Class V.—Trade	160,739	77,200	7,125	101	...	76,414	82,593	41,080	5,393	98	...	11,603 23,351	47,319	20,799	1,160	1	...	9,044 16,316
ORDER 24.—BANKS, ESTABLISHMENTS OF CREDIT, EXCHANGE AND INSURANCE. (106) Bank managers, money-lenders, exchange and insurance agents, money changers and brokers and their employés.	7,802	4,186	193	3	...	3,423	3,322	1,727	117	3	...	583 875	592	[illegible]	29	......	...	93 162
ORDER 25.—BROKERAGE, COMMISSION AND EXPORT. (107) Brokers, commission agents, commercial travellers, warehouse owners and employés	12,615	6,096	47	1	...	6,473	7,078	3,651	25	...	...	1,107 [illegible]	2,042	834	6	......	...	410 731

TABLE VII—*continued.*

OCCUPATION OR MEANS OF LIVELIHOOD.

OCCUPATION.	CHRISTIAN. Total workers and dependants.	CHRISTIAN. Actual Workers. Total. Males.	CHRISTIAN. Actual Workers. Total. Females.	CHRISTIAN. Actual Workers. Partially agriculturists. Males.	CHRISTIAN. Actual Workers. Partially agriculturists. Females.	CHRISTIAN. Dependants.	JAIN. Total workers and dependants.	JAIN. Actual Workers. Total. Males.	JAIN. Actual Workers. Total. Females.	JAIN. Actual Workers. Partially agriculturists. Males.	JAIN. Actual Workers. Partially agriculturists. Females.	JAIN. Dependants.	ZOROASTRIAN. Total workers and dependants.	ZOROASTRIAN. Actual Workers. Total. Males.	ZOROASTRIAN. Actual Workers. Total. Females.	ZOROASTRIAN. Actual Workers. Partially agriculturists. Males.	ZOROASTRIAN. Actual Workers. Partially agriculturists. Females.	ZOROASTRIAN. Dependants.	MINOR AND UNSPECIFIED RELIGIONS. Total workers and dependants.	MINOR AND UNSPECIFIED RELIGIONS. Actual Workers. Total. Males.	MINOR AND UNSPECIFIED RELIGIONS. Actual Workers. Total. Females.	MINOR AND UNSPECIFIED RELIGIONS. Actual Workers. Partially agriculturists. Males.	MINOR AND UNSPECIFIED RELIGIONS. Actual Workers. Partially agriculturists. Females.	MINOR AND UNSPECIFIED RELIGIONS. Dependants.
1	20	21	22	23	24	25	26	27	28	29	30	31	32	33	34	35	36	37	38	39	40	41	42	43
CLASS B.—PREPARATION AND SUPPLY OF MATERIAL SUBSTANCES—*continued.*																								
Sub-Class IV.—Transport ...	9,383	5,695	100	...	...	1,178 / 2,409	107	71	...	...	...	8 / 28	4,553	1,483	10	...	...	981 / 2,079	751	356	4	...	...	122 / 269
ORDER 20.—TRANSPORT BY WATER.	4,033	3,250	18	...	...	225 / 549	56	44	...	...	...	3 / 9	1,162	356	1	...	...	248 / 557	300	231	3	...	...	33 / 93
(94) Harbour works, dockyards and pilots.	717	350	1	...	...	120 / 240	34	30	...	...	...	... / 4	697	225	1	...	...	154 / 317	181	61	3	...	...	33 / 84
(95) Ship owners and their employés, ship brokers, ships' officers, engineers, mariners and firemen.	3,218	2,831	16	...	...	96 / 275	17	9	...	...	...	3 / 5	449	127	...	...	...	91 / 231	176	167	...	...	...	... / 9
(96) Persons employed on the maintenance of streams, rivers, canals (including construction).	......	...	...	...	...	......	...	...	...	...	...	...	...	...	...	...	...	......	...	...	...	...	...	...
(97) Boat owners, boatmen, and tow-men.	98	63	1	...	...	9 / 25	6	5	...	...	...	...	16	4	...	...	...	3 / 9	3	3	...	...	...	...
ORDER 21.—TRANSPORT BY ROAD ...	539	267	3	...	...	96 / 178	22	15	...	...	...	3 / 4	216	101	...	...	...	44 / 101	12	5	...	...	...	1 / 6
(98) Persons employed on the construction and maintenance of roads and bridges.	7	1	...	...	...	3 / 3	...	...	...	...	...	...	4	2	...	...	...	2	...	...	...	...	...	...
(99) Cart owners and drivers, coachmen, stable boys, tramway, mail carriage, etc. managers and employés (excluding private servants).	446	210	...	...	...	82 / 154	8	3	...	...	...	2 / 3	241	99	...	...	...	42 / 100	11	5	...	...	...	1 / 5
(100) Palki etc. bearers and owners ...	......	...	...	...	...	......	...	...	...	...	...	...	...	...	...	...	...	......	...	...	...	...	...	...
(102) Porters and messengers ...	86	56	3	...	...	11 / 16	14	12	...	...	...	1 / 1	1	...	...	...	...	... / 1	1	...	...	...	...	... / 1
ORDER 22.—TRANSPORT BY RAIL ...	3,975	1,778	38	...	...	717 / 1,442	23	9	...	...	...	2 / 12	2,851	923	8	...	...	632 / 1,369	344	105	1	...	...	79 / 159
(103) Railway employés of all kinds other than construction coolies.	3,968	1,773	38	...	...	717 / 1,441	23	9	...	...	...	2 / 12	2,851	932	8	...	...	632 / 1,289	344	106	1	...	...	79 / 159
(104) Labourers employed on railway construction.	7	6	...	...	...	...... / 1	...	...	...	...	...	...	...	...	...	...	...	......	...	...	...	...	...	...
ORDER 23.—POST OFFICE, TELEGRAPH AND TELEPHONE SERVICES. (105) Post Office, Telegraph and Telephone services.	835	400	41	...	...	140 / 254	6	3	...	...	...	... / 3	294	104	1	...	...	57 / 132	35	15	...	...	...	9 / 11
Sub-Class V.—Trade	3,301	1,764	309	...	...	425 / 803	14,939	8,775	96	1	...	2,440 / 3,622	11,714	3,549	146	1	...	3,749 / 5,270	373	333	21	...	...	183 / 336
ORDER 24.—BANKS, ESTABLISHMENTS OF CREDIT, EXCHANGE AND INSURANCE. (106) Bank managers, money lenders, exchange and insurance agents, money changers and brokers and their employés.	326	190	6	...	...	38 / 92	2,860	1,599	11	...	...	427 / 333	1,155	336	29	...	...	238 / 552	67	36	1	...	...	11 / 29
ORDER 25.—BROKERAGE, COMMISSION AND EXPORT. (107) Brokers, commission agents, commercial travellers, warehouse owners and employés.	282	137	3	...	...	32 / 110	1,671	982	1	...	...	250 / 436	1,433	404	8	1	...	325 / 696	109	28	1	...	...	31 / 49

TABLE VII.

OCCUPATION OR MEANS OF LIVELIHOOD.

TABLE VII—*continued*.

OCCUPATION OR MEANS OF LIVELIHOOD.

OCCUPATION.	ALL RELIGIONS.						HINDU.						MUSALMAN.					
	Total workers and dependants.	ACTUAL WORKERS.				Dependants.	Total workers and dependants.	ACTUAL WORKERS.				Dependants.	Total workers and dependants.	ACTUAL WORKERS.				Dependants.
		Total.		Partially agriculturists.				Total.		Partially agriculturists				Total		Partially agriculturists.		
		Males.	Females.	Males.	Females.			Males.	Females.	Males.	Females.			Males.	Females.	Males.	Females.	
1	2	3	4	5	6	7	8	9	10	11	12	13	14	15	16	17	18	19
CLASS B.—PREPARATION AND SUPPLY OF MATERIAL SUBSTANCES—*continued*.																		
Sub-Class V.—Trade—*continued*.																		
ORDER 23.—TRADE IN TEXTILES.																		
(108) Trade in piece-goods, wool, cotton, silk, hair and other textiles.	19,161	9,262	134	...	...	9,765	11,396	5,730	63	...	...	1,602 3,911	5,148	2,720	46	......	...	1,607 1,675
ORDER 27.—TRADE IN SKINS, LEATHER AND FURS. (109) Trade in skins, leather, furs, feathers, horn, etc.	684	263	16	...	...	406	238	92	15	...	...	30 92	403	140	1	......	...	103 150
ORDER 28.—TRADE IN WOOD. (110) Trade in wood (not firewood), cork, bark, etc.	1,607	526	4	...	...	1,077	167	57	......	...	...	30 80	1,256	429	2	......	...	335 492
ORDER 29.—TRADE IN METALS. (111) Trade in metals, machinery, knife, tool, etc. sellers.	3,075	1,581	24	5	...	1,471	616	320	11	5	...	93 192	2,177	1,091	9	......	...	509 50
ORDER 30.—TRADE IN POTTERY. (112) Trade in pottery	1	......	......	...	...	1	......	......	......	...	...	......	1	......	......	......	...	1
ORDER 31.—TRADE IN CHEMICAL PRODUCTS. (113) Trade in chemical products (drugs, dyes, paints, petroleum, explosives, etc.)	1,304	522	26	...	...	756	613	243	23	...	...	110 238	403	164	4	......	...	107 128
ORDER 33.—HOTELS, CAFÉS, RESTAURANTS, ETC.	13,498	6,874	900	1	...	5,724	6,373	3,159	793	1	...	912 1,515	3,268	2,080	55	......	...	491 642
(114) Vendors of wine, liquors, aerated waters, etc.	4,621	1,862	78	...	...	2,681	2,410	1,230	64	...	...	408 708	348	180	5	......	...	72 83
(115) Owners and managers of hotels, cookshops, sarais, etc., and their employés.	8,877	5,012	822	1	...	3,043	3,963	1,929	728	1	...	504 807	2,920	1,891	50	......	...	419 560
ORDER 33.—OTHER TRADE IN FOOD STUFFS.	43,799	21,321	3,955	5	...	18,623	27,805	13,696	3,148	5	...	3,771 7,190	9,674	4,137	540	......	...	1,717 3,280
(116) Fish dealers	2,101	468	935	...	...	698	1,395	240	762	...	...	167 207	368	126	63	......	...	47 150
(117) Grocers and sellers of vegetable oil, salt and other condiments.	9,868	4,938	353	1	...	4,577	4,738	2,564	190	1	...	627 1,357	2,738	1,029	149	......	...	686 1,324
(118) Sellers of milk, butter, ghee, poultry, eggs, etc.	4,809	2,412	349	...	...	2,048	3,103	1,730	225	...	...	318 830	1,440	564	117	......	...	308 451
(119) Sellers of sweetmeats, sugar, gur, molasses.	643	308	16	...	...	319	291	145	8	...	...	75 63	253	105	3	......	...	54 92
(120) Cardamom, betel-leaf, vegetables, fruit and areca nut sellers.	10,997	4,362	1,917	...	...	4,718	8,054	3,100	1,663	...	...	1,036 2,306	2,630	1,186	178	......	...	413 823
(121) Grain and pulse dealers	1,1203	6,737	188	4	...	4,278	6,784	4,238	132	4	...	922 1,492	628	293	21	......	...	105 204

TABLE VII.

Occupation or Means of Livelihood.

TABLE VII—*continued.*

Occupation or Means of Livelihood.

Occupation.	Christian.						Jain.						Zoroastrian.						Minor and Unspecified Religions.					
	Total workers and dependants	Actual Workers. Total.		Partially agriculturists.		Dependants.	Total workers and dependants.	Actual Workers. Total.		Partially agriculturists.		Dependants.	Total workers and dependants.	Actual Workers. Total.		Partially agriculturists.		Dependants.	Total workers and dependants.	Actual Workers. Total.		Partially agriculturists.		Dependants.
		Males.	Females.	Males.	Females.			Males.	Females.	Males.	Females.			Males	Females.	Males.	Females.			Males.	Females.	Males.	Females.	
1	20	21	22	23	24	25	26	27	28	29	30	31	32	33	34	35	36	37	38	39	40	41	42	43
CLASS B.—PREPARATION AND SUPPLY OF MATERIAL SUBSTANCES—*continued.*																								
Sub-Class V.—Trade—*continued.*																								
ORDER 26.—TRADE IN TEXTILES. (108) Trade in piece-goods, wool, cotton, silk, hair and other textiles.	88	63	4	...	...	8 13	1,668	856	6	...	...	361 443	686	316	14	...	...	151 305	175	77	1	...	...	35 62
ORDER 27.—TRADE IN SKINS, LEATHER AND FURS. (109) Trade in skins, leather, furs, feathers, horn, etc.	1	1	...	...	...	......	...	...	...	...	...	...	31	15	...	...	...	6 10	11	5	...	...	...	3 3
ORDER 28.—TRADE IN WOOD. (110) Trade in wood (not firewood), cork, bark, etc.	27	11	...	...	...	9 7	4	1	...	...	...	1 2	153	29	2	...	...	44 78	...	...	...	...	...	...
ORDER 29.—TRADE IN METALS. (111) Trade in metals, machinery, knife, tool, etc. sellers.	17	7	3	...	...	4 3	214	151	1	...	...	33 20	45	10	...	...	...	16 20	7	3	...	...	...	4 1
ORDER 30.—TRADE IN POTTERY. (112) Trade in pottery	......	...	...	...	...	......	...	...	...	...	...	...	...	...	...	...	...	......	...	...	...	...	...	...
ORDER 31.—TRADE IN CHEMICAL PRODUCTS. (113) Trade in chemical products (drugs, dyes, paints, petroleum, explosives, etc.)	96	54	...	...	...	6 36	40	14	...	...	...	16 10	150	47	...	...	...	33 70	3	...	...	...	...	... 3
ORDER 32.—HOTELS, CAFÉS, RESTAURANTS, ETC.	848	679	27	...	...	74 108	58	43	2	...	...	8 6	2,904	942	23	...	...	755 1,184	42	12	1	...	...	15 14
(114) Vendors of wine, liquors, aerated waters, etc.	75	35	3	...	...	7 31	8	6	...	...	...	2 1	1,773	390	6	...	...	515 853	5	4	...	...	...	... 2
(115) Owners and managers of hotels, cookshops, sarais, etc., and their employés.	772	604	24	...	...	67 77	50	37	2	...	...	6 5	1,131	543	17	...	...	240 331	30	8	1	...	...	15 12
ORDER 33.—OTHER TRADE IN FOOD STUFFS.	551	131	204	...	...	90 126	4,917	2,919	39	...	...	801 1,128	773	276	15	...	...	181 301	79	33	9	...	...	8 30
(116) Fish dealers	230	34	130	...	...	28 24	...	...	...	...	...	...	130	50	...	...	...	40 22	...	...	...	...	...	...
(117) Grocers and sellers of vegetable oil, salt, and other condiments.	79	30	3	.	...	10 27	939	584	6	...	...	129 211	331	115	3	...	...	75 138	12	7	2	...	...	... 3
(118) Sellers of milk, butter, ghee, poultry, eggs, etc.	23	8	4	...	...	4 7	134	86	...	...	...	22 26	106	24	2	...	...	26 55	1	...	...	...	...	... 1
(119) Sellers of sweetmeats, sugar, gur, molasses.	......	...	...	...	...	......	65	47	3	...	...	5 11	13	5	...	...	...	6 2	21	6	4	...	...	3 8
(120) Cardamom, betel-leaf, vegetables, fruit and areca nut sellers.	165	20	67	...	...	31 37	27	17	...	...	...	2 8	81	81	7	...	...	13 40	30	8	2	...	...	4 15
(121) Grain and pulse dealers	27	9	...	...	...	5 13	3,687	3,162	30	...	...	638 857	70	26	2	...	...	13 30	9	9	...	...	...	...

TABLE VII—*continued.*

OCCUPATION OR MEANS OF LIVELIHOOD.

OCCUPATION.	ALL RELIGIONS. Total workers and dependants.	ALL RELIGIONS. Actual Workers. Total. Males.	ALL RELIGIONS. Actual Workers. Total. Females.	ALL RELIGIONS. Actual Workers. Partially agriculturists. Males.	ALL RELIGIONS. Actual Workers. Partially agriculturists. Females.	ALL RELIGIONS. Dependants.	HINDU. Total workers and dependants.	HINDU. Actual Workers. Total. Males.	HINDU. Actual Workers. Total. Females.	HINDU. Actual Workers. Partially agriculturists. Males.	HINDU. Actual Workers. Partially agriculturists. Females.	HINDU. Dependants.	MUSALMAN. Total workers and dependants.	MUSALMAN. Actual Workers. Total. Males.	MUSALMAN. Actual Workers. Total. Females.	MUSALMAN. Actual Workers. Partially agriculturists. Males.	MUSALMAN. Actual Workers. Partially agriculturists. Females.	MUSALMAN. Dependants.
1	2	3	4	5	6	7	8	9	10	11	12	13	14	15	16	17	18	19
CLASS B.—PREPARATION AND SUPPLY OF MATERIAL SUBSTANCES—*continued.*																		
Sub-Class V.—Trade—*continued.*																		
ORDER 33.—OTHER TRADE IN FOOD STUFFS—*continued.*																		
(122) Tobacco, opium, gānja, etc., sellers.	2,817	1,378	149	...	...	1,236	2,315	1,138	134	...	...	472 601	408	169	25	......	...	79 115
(123) Dealers in sheep, goats and pigs.	31	11	2	...	...	18	23	8	1	...	...	5 9	8	3	1	......	...	1 3
(124) Dealers in hay, grass and fodder.	1,330	612	46	...	...	671	1,102	534	44	...	...	169 365	155	43	1	......	...	34 78
ORDER 34.—TRADE IN CLOTHING AND TOILET ARTICLES—																		
(125) Trade in ready-made clothing and other articles of dress and the toilet (hats, umbrellas, socks, ready-made shoes, perfumes), etc.	2,779	1,186	42	...	...	1,551	365	445	20	...	...	131 260	1,608	632	7	......	...	312 653
ORDER 35.—TRADE IN FURNITURE—	3,046	1,125	107	1	...	1,814	433	153	93	1	...	50 134	2,455	913	12	......	...	400 1,070
(126) Trade in furniture, carpets, curtains and bedding.	878	329	84	...	...	465	217	81	79	...	...	25 83	549	235	5	......	...	92 227
(127) Hardware, cooking utensils, porcelain, crockery, glassware, bottles, articles for gardening, the cellar, etc.	2,168	796	23	1	...	1,349	166	71	14	1	...	25 56	1,906	699	7	......	...	363 843
ORDER 36.—TRADE IN BUILDING MATERIALS—																		
(128) Trade in building materials (stone, bricks, plaster, cement, sand, tiles, thatch, etc).	613	265	161	83	...	187	184	124	13	83	...	3 44	378	131	147	......	...	80 30
ORDER 37.—TRADE IN MEANS OF TRANSPORT—																		
(129) Dealers in and hirers of elephants, camels, horses, cattle, asses, mules, etc., sellers, (not makers) of carriages, saddlery, etc.	461	324	......	...	...	137	13	6	......	...	...	1 6	426	290	......	......	...	58 71
ORDER 38.—TRADE IN FUEL—																		
(130) Dealers in firewood, charcoal, coal, cowdung, etc.	6,494	3,420	434	1	...	2,630	4,355	2,604	390	...	...	307 964	1,978	762	40	1	...	418 758

TABLE VII—*continued*.

OCCUPATION OR MEANS OF LIVELIHOOD.

OCCUPATION.	CHRISTIAN.						JAIN.						ZOROASTRIAN.						MINOR AND UNSPECIFIED RELIGIONS.					
	Total workers and dependants.	ACTUAL WORKERS. Total.		Partially agriculturists.		Dependants.	Total workers and dependants.	ACTUAL WORKERS. Total.		Partially agriculturists.		Dependants.	Total workers and dependants.	ACTUAL WORKERS. Total.		Partially agriculturists.		Dependants.	Total workers and dependants.	ACTUAL WORKERS. Total.		Partially agriculturists.		Dependants.
		Males.	Females.	Males.	Females.			Males.	Females.	Males.	Females.			Males.	Females.	Males.	Females.			Males.	Females.	Males.	Females.	
1	20	21	22	23	24	25	26	27	28	29	30	31	32	33	34	35	36	37	38	39	40	41	42	43
CLASS B.—PREPARATION AND SUPPLY OF MATERIAL SUBSTANCES—*continued*.																								
Sub-Class V.—Trade—*continued*.																								
ORDER 33.—OTHER TRADE IN FOOD STUFFS—*continued*.																								
(122) Tobacco, opium, ganja, etc., seller.	37	11	...	...	...	12 14	28	20	...	...	...	1 7	26	14	...	...	...	6 5	4	1	...	...	...	1 2
(123) Dealers in sheep, goats and pigs.	......	...	...	...	...	......	...	...	...	...	...	...	...	...	...	...	...	......	...	...	...	...	...	...
(124) Dealers in hay, grass and fodder.	......	...	...	...	...	......	46	33	1	...	...	4 8	25	13	...	...	...	4 9	2	1	...	...	...	... 1
ORDER 34.—TRADE IN CLOTHING AND TOILET ARTICLES—																								
(125) Trade in ready-made clothing and other articles of dress and the toilet (hats, umbrellas, socks, ready-made shoes, perfumes), etc.	40	15	3	...	...	10 13	61	42	...	...	...	6 13	157	43	9	...	...	42 63	53	9	3	...	...	7 34
ORDER 35.—TRADE IN FURNITURE—	16	7	2	...	...	 7	51	31	...	...	...	3 17	77	18	...	...	...	15 44	14	4	...	...	...	6 4
(126) Trade in furniture, carpets, curtains and bedding.	4	1	...	...	...	 3	13	7	...	...	...	... 6	33	13	...	...	...	11 14	7	2	...	...	...	3 2
(127) Hardware, cooking utensils, porcelain, crockery, glassware, bottles, articles for gardening, the cellar, etc.	12	6	2	...	...	 4	33	31	...	...	...	3 11	39	5	...	...	...	4 30	7	2	...	...	...	3 3
ORDER 36.—TRADE IN BUILDING MATERIALS— (128) Trade in building materials (stone, bricks, plaster, cement, sand, tiles, thatch, etc.)	10	3	1	...	...	3 4	1	...	...	...	...	... 1	40	18	...	...	...	17 5	...	...	...	...	...	...
ORDER 37.—TRADE IN MEANS OF TRANSPORT— (129) Dealers in and hirers of elephants, camels, horses, cattle, asses, mules, etc., sellers (not makers) of carriages, saddlery, etc.	15	9	...	...	...	 6	2	1	...	...	...	... 1	20	9	...	...	...	2 9	5	...	...	...	...	... 5
ORDER 38.—TRADE IN FUEL— (130) Dealers in firewood, charcoal, coal, cowdung, etc.	18	8	...	...	...	4 6	15	7	2	...	...	1 5	118	39	2	...	...	31 46	...	...	...	...	...	...

TABLE VII.

OCCUPATION OR MEANS OF LIVELIHOOD.

TABLE VII—*continued.*

OCCUPATION OR MEANS OF LIVELIHOOD.

OCCUPATION.	ALL RELIGIONS.						HINDU.						MUSALMAN.					
	Total workers and dependants.	ACTUAL WORKERS. Total.		ACTUAL WORKERS. Partially agriculturists.		Dependants.	Total workers and dependants.	ACTUAL WORKERS. Total.		ACTUAL WORKERS. Partially agriculturists.		Dependants.	Total workers and dependants.	ACTUAL WORKERS. Total		ACTUAL WORKERS. Partially agriculturists.		Dependants.
		Males.	Females.	Males.	Females.			Males.	Females.	Males.	Females.			Males.	Females.	Males.	Females.	
1	2	3	4	5	6	7	8	9	10	11	12	13	14	15	16	17	18	19
CLASS B.—PREPARATION AND SUPPLY OF MATERIAL SUBSTANCES—*continued.*																		
Sub-Class V.—Trade—*continued.*																		
ORDER 39.—TRADE IN ARTICLES OF LUXURY AND THOSE PERTAINING TO LETTERS, AND THE ARTS, AND SCIENCES.	7,882	3,564	171	...	...	3,847	3,174	1,507	101	...	...	580 936	2,451	1,250	49	......	...	452 700
(131) Dealers in precious stones, jewellery (real and immitation), clocks, optical instruments, etc.	4,928	2,496	23	...	...	2,409	1,877	139	18	...	...	392 528	1,115	593	1	......	...	234 297
(132) Dealers in common bangles, beads, necklaces, fans, small articles, toys, hunting and fishing tackle, flowers, etc.	1,080	487	109	...	...	484	687	319	66	...	...	95 207	291	116	32	......	...	49 94
(133) Publishers, booksellers, stationers, dealers in music, pictures, musical instruments and curiosities.	1,874	831	39	...	...	954	619	210	17	...	...	93 251	1,045	541	16	......	...	170 309
ORDER 40.—TRADE IN REFUSE MATTER— (134) Dealers in rags, stable refuse, etc.	51	32	16	...	..	3	35	19	16	...	...	......	16	13	......	......	3	3
ORDER 41.—TRADE OF OTHER SORTS.	35,856	16,454	895	1	...	18,507	15,941	8,448	564	...	...	2,367 4,562	13,048	5,338	318	......	...	2,492 5,005
(135) Shopkeepers otherwise unspecified.	31,425	14,450	755	1	...	16,220	14,533	7,731	470	...	...	2,213 4,166	10,114	4,110	100	......	...	1,934 3,901
(136) Itinerant traders, pedlars, hawkers, etc.	3,791	1,625	113	...	...	1,983	879	475	69	...	...	69 266	2,858	1,187	43	......	...	545 1,063
(137) Conjurors, acrobats, fortunetellers, reciters, exhibitors of curiosities and wild animals.	371	191	22	...	...	158	307	157	31	...	...	58 71	52	36	1	......	...	9 16
(138) Other trade (including farmers of pounds, tolls and markets	263	118	5	...	...	146	172	82	4	...	...	27 59	24	15	......	......	...	4 5
CLASS C.—PUBLIC ADMINISTRATION AND LIBERAL ARTS.	87,228	36,317	4,701	11	1	46,210	46,244	20,624	2,051	6	1	8,856 11,313	14,240	6,347	665	3	...	2,655 4,573
Sub-Class VI.—Public Force.	11,055	6,865	18	1	...	4,172	6,206	3,575	18	1	...	703 1,910	2,318	1,433	......	......	...	229 657
ORDER 42.—ARMY— (139) Army (Imperial)	3,773	2,930	......	...	...	843	1,331	1,057	......	...	...	75 210	682	481	......	......	...	27 73
ORDER 43.—NAVY— (141) Navy	363	349	......	...	...	13	......	......	......	...	...	....	12	11	......	......	...	1 ......

TABLE VII.

Occupation or Means of Livelihood.

TABLE VII—*continued.*

Occupation or Means of Livelihood.

OCCUPATION.	CHRISTIAN. Total workers and dependants.	Christian Actual Workers Total Males.	Christian Actual Workers Total Females.	Christian Partially agriculturists Males.	Christian Partially agriculturists Females	Christian Dependants	JAIN. Total workers and dependants.	Jain Actual Workers Total Males.	Jain Actual Workers Total Females.	Jain Partially agriculturists Males.	Jain Partially agriculturists Females.	Jain Dependants.	ZOROASTRIAN. Total workers and dependants.	Zoroastrian Actual Workers Total Males.	Zoroastrian Actual Workers Total Females	Zoroastrian Partially agriculturists Males.	Zoroastrian Partially agriculturists Females	Zoroastrian Dependants.	MINOR AND UNSPECIFIED RELIGIONS. Total workers and dependants	Minor Actual Workers Total Males.	Minor Actual Workers Total Females.	Minor Partially agriculturists Males.	Minor Partially agriculturists Females.	Minor Dependants.
1	20	21	22	23	24	25	26	27	28	29	30	31	32	33	34	35	36	37	38	39	40	41	42	43
CLASS B.—PREPARATION AND SUPPLY OF MATERIAL SUBSTANCES—*continued.*																								
Sub-Class V.—Trade—*continued.*																								
ORDER 39.—TRADE IN ARTICLES OF LUXURY AND THOSE PERTAINING TO LETTERS, AND THE ARTS, AND SCIENCES.	149	69	15	...	...	21 64	1,762	947	5	...	...	260 550	313	81	1	...	...	53 173	33	10	...	...	...	12 11
(131) Dealers in precious stones, jewellery (real and imitation), clocks, optical instruments, etc.	37	16	...	...	...	3 6	1,675	891	4	...	...	319 511	209	48	...	...	...	36 125	25	9	...	...	...	6 10
(132) Dealers in common bangles, beads, necklaces, fans, small articles, toys, hunting and fishing tackle, flowers, etc.	13	3	10	...	...	 6	70	48	1	...	...	11 10	12	1	...	...	...	4 7	1	...	...	...	...	1
(133) Publishers, booksellers, stationers, dealers in music, pictures, musical instruments and curiosities.	103	60	5		...	18 30	17	8	...	...	...	... 9	92	33	1	...	...	18 41	7	1	...	...	...	5 1
ORDER 40.—TRADE IN REFUSE MATTERS—																								
(134) Dealers in rags, stable refuse, etc.	...	...	...	...	...	......	...	...	...	...	...	...	...	...	...	...	...	......	...	...	...	...	...	...
ORDER 41.—TRADE OF OTHER SORTS.	817	421	41	...	...	126 229	2,115	1,053	29	1	...	376 657	3,659	1,066	43	...	...	836 1,714	276	128	5	...	...	51 93
(135) Shopkeepers otherwise unspecified.	788	406	41	...	...	119 223	2,073	1,029	28	1	...	309 046	3,615	1,054	43	...	...	828 1,600	253	117	4	...	...	47 66
(136) Itinerant traders, pedlars, hawkers, etc.	7	4	...	...	...	3	34	18	...	...	...	3 3	2	2	...	...	...	......	21	9	1	...	...	4 7
(137) Conjurors, acrobats fortune tellers, reciters, exhibitors of curiosities and wild animals.	6	4	...	...	...	2	...	...	...	...	...	...	6	4	...	...	...	 3	...	...	...	...	...	...
(138) Other trade (including farmers of pounds, tolls and markets).	16	7	...	...	...	2 7	19	6	1	...	...	4 8	36	6	...	...	...	8 22	2	2	...	...	...	...
CLASS C.—PUBLIC ADMINISTRATION AND LIBERAL ARTS.	11,29[illegible]	4,896	1,088	1	...	2,091 3,217	660	222	26	...	...	234 187	13,725	4,028	305	1	...	2,951 5,941	1,058	300	66	...	...	265 427
Sub-Class VI.—Public Force	2,419	1,799	...	...	...	165 455	4	3	...	...	...	1 ...	38	20	...	...	...	11 7	70	36	...	...	...	12 23
ORDER 42.—ARMY—																								
(139) Army (Imperial)	1,798	1,359	...	...	...	111 329	...	...	...	...	...	...	2	2	...	...	...	......	60	31	...	...	...	13 17
ORDER 43.—NAVY—																								
(141) Navy	350	333	...	...	...	3 9	...	...	...	...	...	...	...	...	...	...	...	......	...	...	...	...	...	...

TABLE VII.

Occupation or Means of Livelihood.

TABLE VII—*continued.*

Occupation or Means of Livelihood.

OCCUPATION.	ALL RELIGIONS.						HINDU.						MUSALMAN.					
	Total workers and dependants.	Actual Workers.				Dependants.	Total workers and dependants.	Actual Workers.				Dependants.	Total workers and dependants.	Actual Workers.				Dependants.
		Total.		Partially agriculturists.				Total.		Partially agriculturists.				Total.		Partially agriculturists.		
		Males.	Females.	Males.	Females.			Males.	Females.	Males.	Females.			Males.	Females.	Males.	Females.	
1	2	3	4	5	6	7	8	9	10	11	12	13	14	15	16	17	18	19
CLASS C.—PUBLIC ADMINISTRATION AND LIBERAL ARTS—*continued.*																		
Sub-Class VI.—Public Force—*continued.*																		
ORDER 44.—POLICE	6,920	3,586	18	1	...	3,316	4,875	2,518	18	1	...	548 1,691	1,724	939	......	......	...	201 584
(142) Police	6,817	3,510	......	1	...	3,307	4,801	2,460	......	1	...	546 1,083	1,696	916	......	......	...	196 584
(143) Village watchmen	103	76	18	...	...	9	74	53	18	...	...	2 3	28	23	......	......	...	5 ......
Sub-Class VII.—Public Administration. / ORDER 45.—PUBLIC ADMINISTRATION	20,034	8,979	613	1	...	10,442	14,772	6,807	592	...	...	2,536 4,837	1,323	651	5	......	...	204 460
(144) Service of the State ...	10,001	4,146	6	...	...	5,849	6,613	2,707	......	...	...	1,398 2,518	636	297	2	......	...	114 223
(145) Service of Native and foreign States.	91	18	......	1	...	73	65	10	......	...	...	13 42	5	2	......	......	...	2 1
(146) Municipal and other local (not village) service.	9,911	4,787	607	...	...	4,517	8,069	3,978	592	...	...	1,224 2,275	683	352	6	......	...	88 231
(147) Village officials and servants other than watchmen.	31	28	......	...	...	3	25	23	......	...	...	1 2	......	......	......	......	...	......
Sub-Class VIII.—Professions and Liberal Arts.	35,607	15,789	2,038	9	1	17,780	16,780	7,849	726	5	1	2,963 5,243	6,074	3,326	266	3	...	833 1,649
ORDER 46.—RELIGION	7,783	4,310	324	...	...	3,149	3,595	2,194	123	...	...	487 791	1,772	1,151	136	......	...	153 332
(148) Priests, ministers, etc.	5,129	2,706	63	...	...	2,360	2,309	1,433	21	...	...	355 507	685	402	5	......	...	68 210
(149) Religious mendicants, inmates of monasteries, etc.	1,196	804	211	...	...	181	455	274	79	...	...	28 74	705	526	113	......	...	29 38
(150) Catechists, readers, church and mission service.	123	36	3	...	...	84	18	9	......	...	...	3 6	3	1	......	......	...	2 ......
(151) Temple, burial or burning ground service, pilgrim conductors, circumcisers.	1,335	764	47	...	...	524	813	485	23	...	...	101 204	379	222	18	......	...	55 84
ORDER 47.—LAW	3,070	1,037	2	5	...	2,031	1,634	601	......	1	...	427 606	164	63	......	3	...	30 65
(152) Lawyers of all kinds including kazis, law agents and mukhtiárs.	2,643	872	......	5	...	1,771	1,426	473	......	1	...	387 561	153	58	......	3	...	34 61
(153) Lawyers' clerks, petition-writers, etc.	427	165	2	...	...	260	208	88	......	...	...	40 80	11	5	......	......	...	2 4

TABLE VII—*continued*.

OCCUPATION OR MEANS OF LIVELIHOOD.

OCCUPATION.	CHRISTIAN. Total workers and dependants	CHRISTIAN. Actual Workers. Total. Males.	CHRISTIAN. Actual Workers. Total. Females.	CHRISTIAN. Actual Workers. Partially agriculturists. Males.	CHRISTIAN. Actual Workers. Partially agriculturists. Females.	CHRISTIAN. Dependants	JAIN. Total workers and dependants.	JAIN. Actual Workers. Total. Males.	JAIN. Actual Workers. Total. Females.	JAIN. Actual Workers. Partially agriculturists. Males.	JAIN. Actual Workers. Partially agriculturists. Females.	JAIN. Dependants.	ZOROASTRIAN. Total workers and dependants.	ZOROASTRIAN. Actual Workers. Total. Males.	ZOROASTRIAN. Actual Workers. Total. Females.	ZOROASTRIAN. Actual Workers. Partially agriculturists. Males.	ZOROASTRIAN. Actual Workers. Partially agriculturists. Females.	ZOROASTRIAN. Dependants	MINOR AND UNSPECIFIED RELIGIONS. Total workers and dependants.	MINOR. Actual Workers. Total. Males.	MINOR. Actual Workers. Total. Females.	MINOR. Actual Workers. Partially agriculturists. Males.	MINOR. Actual Workers. Partially agriculturists. Females.	MINOR. Dependants.
1	20	21	22	23	24	25	26	27	28	29	30	31	32	33	34	35	36	37	38	39	40	41	42	43
CLASS C.—PUBLIC ADMINISTRATION AND LIBERAL ARTS—*continued*.																								
Sub-Class VI—Public Force—*continued*.																								
ORDER 44.—POLICE	271	103	...	...	...	51 / 117	4	3	...	...	...	... / 1	36	18	...	...	...	11 / 7	10	5	...	...	...	... / 5
(142) Police	271	103	...	...	...	51 / 117	4	3	...	...	...	... / 1	36	18	...	...	...	11 / 7	9	4	...	...	...	... / 5
(143) Village watchmen	......	...	...	...	...	......	...	...	...	...	...	...	...	...	...	...	...	......	1	1	...	...	...	...
Sub-Class VII—Public Administration. ORDER 45.—PUBLIC ADMINISTRATION :—	1,341	633	9	1	...	227 / 472	82	42	...	...	...	21 / 19	2,300	766	2	...	...	494 / 1,038	226	80	2	...	...	52 / 92
(144) Service of the State	909	440	3	...	...	140 / 326	70	31	...	...	...	20 / 19	1,681	542	1	...	...	355 / 783	92	39	...	...	...	22 / 31
(145) Service of Native and foreign States.	8	5	...	1	...	... / 3	1	...	...	...	...	... / 1	8	...	...	...	...	... / 8	4	1	...	...	...	1 / 2
(146) Municipal and other local (not village) service.	424	188	6	...	...	87 / 143	5	5	...	...	...	...	611	224	1	...	...	139 / 247	130	40	2	...	...	29 / 59
(147) Village officials and servants other than watchmen.	......	...	...	...	...	......	6	6	...	...	...	...	...	...	...	...	...	......	...	...	...	...	...	...
Sub-Class VIII—Professions and Liberal Arts.	4,998	2,152	813	...	...	667 / 1,361	304	143	7	...	...	68 / 86	6,982	2,213	177	1	...	1,547 / 3,045	469	106	44	...	...	100 / 219
ORDER 46.—RELIGION	352	148	55	...	...	37 / 112	64	43	3	...	...	4 / 14	1,963	764	6	...	...	391 / 802	37	10	1	...	...	4 / 22
(148) Priests, ministers, etc.	188	104	28	...	...	23 / 33	49	37	3	...	...	3 / 6	1,887	733	6	...	...	378 / 770	11	4	...	...	...	1 / 6
(149) Religious mendicants, inmates of monasteries, etc.	22	...	19	...	...	... / 3	11	2	...	...	...	1 / 8	2	1	...	...	...	... / 1	1	1	...	...	...	...
(150) Catechists, readers, church and mission service.	98	25	3	...	...	8 / 62	...	...	...	...	...	...	...	...	...	...	...	...	4	1	...	...	...	1 / 2
(151) Temple or burial or burning ground service, pilgrim conductors, circumcisors.	44	19	5	...	...	6 / 14	4	4	...	...	...	...	74	30	...	...	...	12 / 32	21	4	1	...	...	2 / 14
ORDER 47.—Law	177	90	1	...	...	21 / 65	51	13	1	...	...	17 / 20	1,019	385	...	1	...	226 / 458	25	5	...	...	...	4 / 15
(152) Lawyers of all kinds including kazis, law agents and mukhtiars.	126	74	...	...	...	15 / 37	45	12	...	...	...	15 / 18	868	350	...	1	...	199 / 419	25	5	...	...	...	4 / 16
(153) Lawyers, clerks, petition writers, etc.	51	16	1	...	...	6 / 28	6	1	1	...	...	2 / 2	151	55	...	...	...	27 / 69	...	...	...	...	...	...

TABLE VII—*continued.*

OCCUPATION OR MEANS OF LIVELIHOOD.

OCCUPATION.	ALL RELIGIONS.						HINDU.						MUSALMAN.					
	Total workers and dependants.	Actual Workers. Total.		Actual Workers. Partially agriculturists.		Dependants.	Total workers and dependants.	Actual Workers. Total.		Actual Workers. Partially agriculturists.		Dependants.	Total workers and dependants.	Actual Workers. Total.		Actual Workers. Partially agriculturists.		Dependants.
		Males.	Females.	Males.	Females.			Males.	Females.	Males.	Females.			Males.	Females.	Males.	Females.	
1	2	3	4	5	6	7	8	9	10	11	12	13	14	15	16	17	18	19
CLASS C.—PUBLIC ADMINISTRATION AND LIBERAL ARTS—*continued.*																		
Sub-Class VIII.—Professions and Liberal Arts—*continued.*																		
ORDER 48.—MEDICINE	6,636	2,428	779	4	1	3,434	3,161	1,171	270	4	1	534 1,086	835	362	33	......	...	169 272
(154) Medical practitioners of all kinds, including dentists, oculists and veterinary surgeons.	4,158	1,524	129	...	...	2,505	1,913	714	30	...	...	476 693	684	308	1	......	...	139 236
(155) Midwives, vaccinators, compounders, nurses, masseurs, etc.	2,478	899	650	4	1	929	1,248	457	340	4	1	158 283	151	54	31	......	...	30 36
ORDER 49.—INSTRUCTION—																		
(156) Professors and teachers of all kinds, except law, medicine, music, dancing and drawing, and clerks and servants connected with education.	5,456	2,169	518	...	...	2,763	2,483	1,132	58	...	...	485 818	1,104	522	37	......	...	173 372
ORDER 50.—LETTERS AND ARTS AND SCIENCES.	12,668	5,850	415	...	...	6,403	5,907	2,801	275	...	...	939 1,902	2,199	1,228	61	......	...	372 508
(157) Public scribes, stenographers, etc.	302	111	43	...	...	148	129	57	......	...	...	31 43	...	......	......	......	...	......
(158) Architects, surveyors, engineers, and their employés.	4,546	1,596	8	...	...	2,942	1,348	442	...	...	...	322 584	454	194	......	......	...	88 172
(159) Others (authors, photographers, artists, sculptors, astronomers, meteorologists, botanists, astrologers, etc.).	5,308	2,707	26	...	...	2,575	3,137	1,635	16	...	...	465 1,051	1,013	558	6	......	...	151 298
(160) Music composers and masters, players on all kinds of musical instruments (not military), singers, actors and dancers.	2,512	1,436	338	...	...	738	1,298	697	260	...	...	113 225	732	476	55	......	...	63 138
Sub-Class IX.—Persons living on their income— ORDER 51.—PERSONS LIVING PRINCIPALLY ON THEIR INCOME— (161) Proprietors (other than of agricultural land), fund and scholarship holders and pensioners.	20,532	4,684	3,033	...	...	12,816	8,486	2,203	716	...	...	2,065 3,823	4,526	938	301	......	...	1,389 1,807
CLASS D.—MISCELLANEOUS ...	264,114	144,062	27,112	11	1	93,920	184,419	103,696	19,353	8	1	19,811 41,559	36,247	19,842	3,313	1	...	4,147 8,945
Sub-Class X.—Domestic service ORDER 52.—DOMESTIC SERVICE—	71,956	45,130	9,736	9	1	17,090	41,103	37,524	4,242	7	1	3,215 6,822	12,633	7,259	1,733	1	...	1,290 2,351
(162) Cooks, water-carriers, door-keepers, watchmen and other indoor servants.	62,440	38,756	9,734	7	1	13,950	33,264	21,087	4,243	6	1	3,449 5,186	11,215	6,511	1,733	......	...	1,120 1,853

TABLE VII—*continued*.

OCCUPATION OR MEANS OF LIVELIHOOD.

OCCUPATION.	CHRISTIAN.						JAIN.						ZOROASTRIAN.						MINOR AND UNSPECIFIED RELIGIONS.					
	Total workers and dependants	ACTUAL WORKERS. Total.		Partially agriculturists.		Dependants.	Total workers and dependants.	ACTUAL WORKERS. Total.		Partially agriculturists.		Dependants.	Total workers and dependants.	ACTUAL WORKERS. Total.		Partially agriculturists.		Dependants.	Total workers and dependants.	ACTUAL WORKERS. Total.		Partially agriculturists.		Dependants.
		Males.	Females.	Males.	Females.			Males.	Females.	Males.	Females.			Males.	Females.	Males.	Females.			Males.	Females.	Males.	Females.	
1	30	31	32	33	34	35	26	27	28	29	30	31	32	33	34	35	36	37	38	39	40	41	42	43
CLASS C.—PUBLIC ADMINISTRATION AND LIBERAL ARTS—*continued*.																								
Sub-Class VIII.—Professions and Liberal Arts—*continued*.																								
ORDER 48.—MEDICINE	1,515	560	398	...	...	183 / 365	49	10	...	...	...	4 / 35	1,012	305	57	...	...	231 / 419	84	6	23	...	...	9 / 27
(154) Medical practitioners of all kinds, including dentists, oculists and veterinary surgeons.	581	199	65	...	...	119 / 198	20	9	...	...	...	3 / 8	938	290	82	...	...	227 / 367	34	4	1	...	...	6 / 13
(155) Midwives, vaccinators, compounders, nurses, masseurs, etc.	934	370	330	...	...	64 / 167	29	1	...	...	...	1 / 27	76	16	25	...	...	4 / 32	40	2	21	...	...	2 / 14
ORDER 49.—INSTRUCTION—																								
(156) Professors and teachers of all kinds, except law, medicine, music, dancing and drawing, and clerks and servants connected with education.	781	208	288	...	...	116 / 150	50	35	3	...	...	5 / 7	908	257	107	...	...	191 / 363	124	25	15	...	...	34 / 50
ORDER 50.—LETTERS AND ARTS AND SCIENCES.	2,173	1,137	66	...	...	319 / 660	90	42	...	...	...	38 / 10	2,020	582	7	...	...	518 / 973	219	60	6	...	...	49 / 104
(157) Public scribes, stenographers, etc.	101	25	41	...	...	14 / 21	...	...	...	...	...	...	57	25	2	...	...	8 / 22	15	4	...	...	...	3 / 8
(158) Architects, surveyors, engineers and their employés.	1,058	615	4	...	...	163 / 376	...	...	...	...	...	...	1,549	4 3	4	...	...	393 / 740	137	42	...	...	...	25 / 70
(159) Others (authors, photographers, artists, sculptors, astronomers, meteorologists, botanists, astrologers, etc.).	718	404	4	...	...	103 / 104	73	20	...	...	...	38 / 6	322	95	...	...	...	81 / 143	45	13	...	...	...	12 / 20
(160) Music composers and masters, players on all kinds of musical instruments (not military), singers, actors and dancers.	396	193	17	...	...	31 / 55	17	13	...	...	...	... / 4	152	53	1	...	...	36 / 59	22	1	6	...	...	9 / 6
Sub-Class IX.—Persons living on their income— ORDER 51.—PERSONS LIVING PRINCIPALLY ON THEIR INCOME— (161) Proprietors (other than of agricultural lands), fund and scholarship holders and pensioners.	2,534	313	261	...	...	1,032 / 929	279	34	19	...	...	144 / 62	4,465	1,029	626	...	...	899 / 1,851	303	79	20	...	...	101 / 104
CLASS D.—MISCELLANEOUS ...	23,885	12,978	3,682	2	...	2,730 / 4,495	3,916	2,647	78	...	...	355 / 836	13,827	4,369	420	...	...	2,848 / 6,190	1,820	550	266	...	...	360 / 644
Sub-Class X.—Domestic Service ORDER 52.—DOMESTIC SERVICE—	14,452	8,744	3,331	1	...	903 / 1,474	961	756	46	...	...	63 / 86	1,860	772	317	...	...	226 / 545	257	75	167	...	...	39 / 76
(162) Cooks, water-carriers, door-keepers, watchmen and other indoor servants.	14,393	8,711	3,330	1	...	877 / 1,465	909	716	46	...	...	63 / 84	1,808	775	317	...	...	218 / 510	251	74	67	...	...	36 / 74

TABLE VII—*continued*.

OCCUPATION OR MEANS OF LIVELIHOOD.

OCCUPATION.	ALL RELIGIONS. Total workers and dependants.	ALL RELIGIONS. Actual Workers. Total. Males.	ALL RELIGIONS. Actual Workers. Total. Females.	ALL RELIGIONS. Actual Workers. Partially agriculturists. Males.	ALL RELIGIONS. Actual Workers. Partially agriculturists. Females.	ALL RELIGIONS. Dependants.	HINDU. Total workers and dependants.	HINDU. Actual Workers. Total. Males.	HINDU. Actual Workers. Total. Females.	HINDU. Actual Workers. Partially agriculturists. Males.	HINDU. Actual Workers. Partially agriculturists. Females.	HINDU. Dependants.	MUSALMA'N. Total workers and dependants.	MUSALMA'N. Actual Workers. Total. Males.	MUSALMA'N. Actual Workers. Total. Females.	MUSALMA'N. Actual Workers. Partially agriculturists. Males.	MUSALMA'N. Actual Workers. Partially agriculturists. Females.	MUSALMA'N. Dependants.
1	2	3	4	5	6	7	8	9	10	11	12	13	14	15	16	17	18	19
CLASS D.—MISCELLANEOUS— *continued.*																		
Sub-Class X.—Domestic Service —*continued.*																		
ORDER 52.—DOMESTIC SERVICE—*continued.*																		
(163) Private grooms, coachmen, dog boys, etc.	9.516	6.374	2	2	...	3.140	7.939	5,637	......	1	...	765 1.536	1,418	748	1	1	...	170 499
Sub-Class XI.—Insufficiently described occupations.	180.198	92.903	13.651	1	...	73.644	134.831	72.268	12,665	...	...	15,997 33,881	20,288	10,658	654	......	...	3,461 6,335
ORDER 53.—GENERAL TERMS WHICH DO NOT INDICATE A DEFINITE OCCUPATION—																		
(164) Manufacturers, business men and contractors otherwise unspecified.	3.262	1.145	44	...	...	2.163	1.623	585	14	...	...	315 708	794	290	3	......	...	194 301
(165) Cashiers, accountants, book-keepers, clerks and other employés in unspecified offices, warehouses, and shops.	74.486	35.297	786	1	...	38.403	47.736	24,170	554	...	...	8,110 14,902	7.613	3,578	53	......	...	1,134 2,815
(166) Mechanics otherwise unspecified.	12.873	5.773	11	...	...	7,090	5.244	2,476	......	...	...	798 1,970	3.499	1,570	......	......	...	480 1,440
(167) Labourers and workmen otherwise unspecified.	89.487	50.689	12.810	...	...	25.988	80.229	45,067	12,' 97	...	...	6,774 16,301	8.382	5.214	595	......	...	834 1,749
Sub-Class XII.—Unproductive.	11.960	6.049	2.725	1	...	3.186	7,785	3.884	2.446	1	...	599 556	3.326	1.925	936	......	...	216 259
ORDER 54.—INMATES OF JAILS, ASYLUMS AND HOSPITALS. (168) Inmates of jails, asylums and hospitals.	801	322	61	...	...	508	359	129	......	...	...	141 90	231	73	1	......	...	47 10
ORDER 55.—BEGGARS, VAGRANTS AND PROSTITUTES—																		
(169) Beggars, vagrants, procurers, prostitutes, receivers of stolen goods, cattle poisoners.	11.069	6.727	3.684	1	...	1.678	7.429	3,786	2,446	1	...	458 766	2.195	1,852	925	......	...	160 319

TABLE VII—*continued.*

Occupation or Means of Livelihood.

Occupation.	Christian. Total workers and dependants.	Christian. Actual Workers. Total. Males.	Christian. Actual Workers. Total. Females.	Christian. Partially agriculturists. Males.	Christian. Partially agriculturists. Females.	Christian. Dependants.	Jain. Total workers and dependants.	Jain. Actual Workers. Total. Males.	Jain. Actual Workers. Total. Females.	Jain. Partially agriculturists. Males.	Jain. Partially agriculturists. Females.	Jain. Dependants.	Zoroastrian. Total workers and dependants.	Zoroastrian. Actual Workers. Total. Males.	Zoroastrian. Actual Workers. Total. Females.	Zoroastrian. Partially agriculturists. Males.	Zoroastrian. Partially agriculturists. Females.	Zoroastrian. Dependants.	Minor and Unspecified Religions. Total workers and dependants.	Minor and Unspecified Religions. Actual Workers. Total. Males.	Minor and Unspecified Religions. Actual Workers. Total. Females.	Minor and Unspecified Religions. Partially agriculturists. Males.	Minor and Unspecified Religions. Partially agriculturists. Females.	Minor and Unspecified Religions. Dependants.
1	20	21	22	23	24	25	26	27	28	29	30	31	32	33	34	35	36	37	38	39	40	41	42	43
CLASS D.—MISCELLANEOUS— *continued.*																								
Sub-Class X.—Domestic service —*continued.*																								
ORDER 52.—DOMESTIC SERVICE—*continued.*																								
(163) Private grooms, coachmen, dog boys, etc.	59	33	1	...	...	6 / 19	42	40	...	...	...	... / 2	52	15	...	...	...	8 / 29	6	1	...	...	...	3 / 3
Sub-Class XI.—Insufficiently described occupations.	8,930	4,090	228	1	...	1,705 / 2,817	2,924	1,864	20	...	...	291 / 749	11,873	3,541	69	...	...	2,621 / 5,643	1,352	462	15	...	...	379 / 566
ORDER 53.—GENERAL TERMS WHICH DO NOT INDICATE A DEFINITE OCCUPATION—																								
(164) Manufacturers, business men and contractors otherwise unspecified.	124	39	10	...	...	31 / 51	72	27	6	...	...	21 / 18	671	163	11	...	...	163 / 314	69	15	...	...	...	18 / 30
(165) Cashiers, accountants, book-keepers, clerks and other employés in unspecified offices, warehouses, and shops.	5,794	2,627	109	1	...	1,211 / 1,814	2,702	1,721	8	...	...	261 / 709	9,755	2,893	53	...	...	2,078 / 4,731	866	305	6	...	...	210 / 375
(166) Mechanics otherwise unspecified.	2,434	1,164	11	...	...	475 / 791	18	7	...	...	...	5 / 6	1,352	443	...	...	...	348 / 563	326	122	...	...	...	75 / 129
(167) Labourers and workmen otherwise unspecified.	578	270	98	...	...	82 / 125	133	100	6	...	...	4 / 16	95	23	5	...	...	38 / 35	71	20	9	...	...	16 / 36
Sub-Class XII.—Unproductive.	503	144	123	...	...	32 / 204	41	27	12	...	...	1 / 1	94	56	34	...	...	2 / 2	211	13	184	...	...	12 / 2
ORDER 54.—INMATES OF JAILS, ASYLUMS AND HOSPITALS. (168) Inmates of jails, asylums and hospitals.	313	65	27	...	...	23 / 191	...	...	...	...	...	...	81	52	29	...	...	... / ...	7	3	4	...	...	... / ...
ORDER 55.—BEGGARS, VAGRANTS, PROSTITUTES. (169) Beggars, vagrants, procurers, prostitutes, receivers of stolen goods, cattle poisoners.	190	78	96	...	...	4 / 12	41	27	12	...	...	1 / 1	13	4	5	...	...	2 / 3	204	10	180	...	...	12 / 3

TABLE VIII—(Corresponding to Imperial Table XVIII).

EUROPEANS AND ANGLO-INDIANS BY RACE AND AGE.

TABLE VIII.

EUROPEANS AND ANGLO-INDIANS BY RACE AND AGE.

TABLE VIII.

EUROPEANS AND ANGLO INDIANS BY RACE AND AGE.

Bombay City.

Wards.	TOTAL.			EUROPEAN AND ALLIED RACES.																									
				British Subjects.													Others.												
				All ages.			0–12.		12–15.		15–30.		30–50.		50 and over.		All ages.			0–12.		12–15.		15–30.		30–50.		50 and over.	
	Total.	Males.	Females.	Total.	Males.	Females.	Males.	Females.	Males.	Females.	Males.	Females.	Males.	Females.	Males.	Females.	Total.	Males.	Females.	Males.	Females.	Males.	Females.	Males.	Females.	Males.	Females.	Males.	Females.
1	2	3	4	5	6	7	8	9	10	11	12	13	14	15	16	17	18	19	20	21	22	23	24	25	26	27	28	29	30
Bombay City ...	16.082	10.434	5.648	10.131	6.821	3.310	793	712	155	107	2.903	1.038	2.522	1.079	448	379	1.724	1,262	462	80	77	31	17	560	176	505	156	86	37
Ward A ...	4.584	2,622	1,912	3.210	1,873	1,338	206	259	41	23	532	431	831	481	202	141	567	373	194	27	30	4	5	140	72	108	68	34	19
,, B	183	118	65	88	51	37	13	6	1	...	12	15	23	9	2	7	35	35	...	2	...	2	...	20	...	11	...	...	...
,, C	505	330	175	93	62	31	17	7	1	2	27	15	16	4	1	3	240	178	62	17	19	10	0	92	20	44	16	15	1
,, D	681	367	314	456	238	218	30	32	...	3	43	62	131	93	34	28	92	57	35	4	4	1	1	20	19	30	10	2	1
,, E	4.566	2,575	1,991	2.015	1,085	930	255	201	79	47	308	210	332	276	111	116	240	133	104	10	12	8	1	40	44	54	36	9	11
,, F	486	270	216	251	143	108	23	20	5	2	24	37	75	39	16	10	36	18	18	2	6	...	1	7	5	9	4	...	2
,, G	921	540	381	413	261	152	56	31	19	19	72	30	90	47	18	16	111	81	30	8	6	5	3	31	11	28	9	9	1
Railway, Harbour Docks, &c.	4,206	3,612	594	3.605	3,100	490	133	153	9	11	1,865	141	1,018	130	64	68	403	384	19	1	...	1	...	204	5	161	12	17	2

Wards.	Armenians.													Anglo-Indians.												
	All ages.			0–12.		12–15.		15–30.		30–50.		50 and over.		All ages.			0–12.		12–15.		15–30.		30–50.		50 and over.	
	Total.	Males.	Females.	Males.	Females.	Males.	Females.	Males.	Females.	Males.	Females.	Males.	Females.	Total.	Males.	Females.	Males.	Females.	Males.	Females.	Males.	Females.	Males.	Females.	Males.	Females.
1	31	32	33	34	35	36	37	38	39	40	41	42	43	44	45	46	47	48	49	50	51	52	53	54	55	56
Bombay City ...	39	28	11	1	4	1	...	14	1	11	4	1	2	4.188	2 323	1.865	512	435	146	101	953	747	509	425	144	157
Ward A	31	23	8	1	3	1	...	10	...	10	3	1	2	726	354	372	71	88	31	14	117	170	108	85	27	15
,, B	...	...	...	...	...	...	...	...	...	...	...	...	...	60	32	28	10	5	2	...	6	10	8	12	6	1
,, C	2	1	1	...	1	...	...	1	...	...	...	...	...	170	89	81	17	19	6	5	30	33	18	10	9	5
,, D	1	1	...	...	...	...	...	1	...	...	...	...	...	132	71	61	18	15	4	2	21	22	22	17	6	5
,, E	5	3	2	...	...	...	...	2	1	1	1	...	...	2.306	1,351	955	206	208	82	54	600	380	300	217	73	96
,, F	...	...	...	...	...	...	...	...	...	...	...	...	...	199	100	99	20	31	7	4	47	32	30	20	5	8
,, G	...	...	...	...	...	...	...	...	...	...	...	...	...	397	198	199	63	49	10	20	69	74	65	40	12	10
Railway, Harbour Docks, &c.	...	...	...	...	...	...	...	...	...	...	...	...	...	198	119	79	27	23	4	2	54	26	28	16	0	11

TABLE IX.

CLASSIFICATION OF BUILDINGS.

NOTE.—135 houses under construction and 39 unfit for human habitation have been including in this table.

TABLE IX.

Classification of Buildings.

Ward.	Charge No.	Section.	Circle No.	Bungalows and Dwelling houses.	Shops.	Temples and Churches.	Schools.	Dispensaries, Hospitals and sanitaria.	Theatres.	Stables.	Godowns.	Residence and shop combined.	Dharamshalas.	Mills.	Workshops and factories.	Barracks.	Offices.	Chowkies.	Tents.	Total.	Remarks.
		Grand Total, Bombay City ...	...	28,467	1,120	810	232	160	30	3,400	3,742	4,714	109	206	837	19	879	959	12	45,716	
A		Grand Total for A Ward ...	...	1,700	108	47	31	51	18	366	363	426	2	6	133	1	367	74	...	3,593	Total for A Ward ... { Buildings under construction ... 13; Buildings declared unfit for human habitation ... 4; Total ... 17 }
	1	Upper Colaba Total ...	1	81	3	7	3	...	...	10	5	...	...	...	...	...	3	2	...	114	
	2	Lower Colaba Total ...	...	598	22	13	3	4	...	104	149	96	...	4	30	...	48	11	...	1,082	
			1	115	3	1	...	3	...	43	6	6	...	...	3	...	2	1	...	184	
			2	127	2	3	...	1	...	27	38	3	...	4	10	...	7	6	...	234	
			3	47	7	1	1	...	...	2	...	30	...	...	1	...	...	...	...	95	
			4	47	3	...	...	...	...	1	...	6	...	...	...	...	...	...	...	57	
			5	31	1	3	...	...	...	1	4	19	...	...	...	...	...	...	...	59	
			6	90	1	3	2	...	...	23	63	7	...	...	3	...	28	4	...	224	
			7	65	1	...	...	...	...	2	30	4	...	...	5	...	6	...	...	113	
			8	76	4	2	...	...	...	5	6	15	...	...	3	...	5	...	...	116	
	3	Fort. South Total ...	...	93	27	4	1	...	...	19	39	29	...	...	20	...	167	15	...	414	
			1	5	4	...	...	...	...	1	6	15	...	...	...	...	32	...	...	63	
			2	63	7	3	...	...	...	12	11	5	...	...	8	...	53	4	...	166	
			3	6	8	1	...	...	...	2	13	6	...	...	6	...	43	2	...	87	
			4	2	4	...	...	...	...	...	5	2	...	...	4	...	33	2	...	52	
			5	17	4	...	1	...	...	4	4	1	...	...	2	...	6	7	..	46	
	4	Fort. North Total ...	...	508	21	17	9	37	15	62	108	288	1	1	53	1	81	16	..	1,227	
			1	102	...	5	...	3	...	3	8	32	...	...	4	...	30	...	...	182	
			2	60	4	...	1	1	...	6	9	33	...	...	10	...	8	...	...	133	
			3	115	...	3	2	4	...	3	13	18	...	...	5	1	8	...	...	172	
			4	67	2	5	2	2	...	11	9	28	...	...	...	...	5	...	...	131	
			5	48	7	1	1	4	...	2	17	51	...	...	7	...	15	...	...	153	
			6	36	4	2	3	12	15	...	22	73	1	...	12	...	1	1	...	182	
			7	17	2	1	...	7	...	23	17	29	...	1	6	...	2	1	...	106	
			8	63	2	...	...	4	...	14	18	21	...	...	18	...	11	11	...	105	
	5	Esplanade Total ...	...	420	35	6	15	10	3	71	62	13	1	1	21	...	68	30	..	756	
			1	144	4	1	2	...	...	40	10	1	...	...	2	...	13	8	...	234	
			2	66	5	1	5	3	2	12	14	2	...	1	7	...	25	4	...	131	
			3	167	22	3	7	3	1	7	22	10	...	...	8	...	12	5	...	257	
			4	61	4	1	1	4	...	3	16	...	1	...	4	...	18	13	...	123	
B		Grand Total for B Ward ...	...	1,038	167	102	34	8	...	188	893	1,149	14	22	54	1	103	73	...	3,856	Total for B Ward, { Buildings under construction ... 7; Buildings declared unfit for human habitation ... 11; Total ... 18 }
	7	Chakla Total ...	...	116	53	24	8	2	...	22	70	591	5	1	13	...	6	1	...	911	
			1	2	13	3	1	...	...	...	...	87	1	...	...	...	...	...	...	107	
			2	2	3	2	1	...	...	...	5	118	1	...	...	...	1	...	...	133	
			3	9	3	3	2	...	...	1	2	85	...	...	...	...	2	...	...	107	
			4	19	6	2	1	1	...	4	3	97	...	...	...	...	2	1	..	133	
			5	50	3	4	1	...	...	7	4	32	...	...	1	...	1	...	...	103	
			6	8	...	7	2	...	...	...	3	19	2	...	...	...	...	...	...	41	
			7	10	5	...	...	1	...	1	7	42	...	1	9	...	...	...	...	76	
			8	7	10	1	...	...	...	3	15	44	...	...	3	...	...	...	...	83	
			9	8	9	2	...	...	...	6	31	67	1	...	...	...	...	...	...	126	

SPECIAL TABLE IX—*continued.*

CLASSIFICATION OF BUILDINGS.

Ward.	Charge No.	Section.	Circle No.	Bungalows and Dwelling houses.	Shops.	Temples and Churches.	Schools.	Dispensaries, Hospitals and Sanitaria.	Theatres.	Stables.	Godowns.	Residence and shop combined.	Dharamshalas.	Mills.	Workshops and factories.	Barracks.	Offices.	Chowkies.	Tents.	Total.	Remarks.
	6	Mandvi Total ...	...	156	84	27	5	1	...	39	579	117	2	3	9	...	78	20	...	1,130	
			1	26	25	6	...	...	...	15	23	32	...	1	4	...	...	1	...	132	
			2							Demolished.											
			3	2	11	2	1	...	...	...	47	3	1	...	...	...	...	1	...	68	
			4	10	12	1	...	...	...	2	17	33	...	...	...	...	...	...	...	75	
			5	2	4	3	...	...	...	...	22	18	...	...	...	...	...	...	...	49	
			6	4	2	1	...	...	...	...	36	3	...	...	...	...	...	...	...	40	
			7	8	8	3	...	...	...	3	72	...	...	...	...	...	...	...	...	94	
			8	2	7	1	...	...	...	...	73	...	...	...	1	...	...	...	...	84	
			9	47	6	4	3	1	...	4	62	4	1	1	2	...	32	...	...	167	
			10	9	3	2	...	...	...	1	68	12	...	...	...	...	33	1	...	122	
			11	13	1	1	...	...	...	9	65	8	...	1	...	...	4	3	...	135	
			12	43	5	3	1	...	...	5	75	4	...	...	2	...	6	14	...	158	
	8	Umarkhadi Total ...	...	491	15	37	20	...	...	95	131	319	6	3	30	1	13	6	...	1,156	
			1	29	2	4	1	...	...	4	3	46	...	...	2	...	...	...	...	86	
			2	19	...	1	...	...	...	...	...	27	...	...	1	...	...	...	...	48	
			3	51	...	1	...	...	...	11	7	27	...	...	1	...	...	...	...	98	
			4	21	...	9	1	...	...	2	10	7	...	...	...	...	1	2	...	53	
			5	44	2	3	...	...	...	3	3	14	...	...	2	...	...	...	...	71	
			6	35	...	4	1	...	...	5	5	13	...	1	1	...	...	...	...	65	
			7	61	...	2	...	...	...	20	20	32	...	...	3	...	1	...	...	139	
			8	41	5	6	3	...	...	14	53	60	...	1	2	...	4	...	...	195	
			9	100	4	5	3	...	...	25	12	32	...	1	10	...	4	4	...	200	
			10	93	2	2	11	...	...	11	8	55	6	...	8	1	2	...	...	199	
	9	Dongri Total ...	...	265	16	14	1	5	...	32	123	122	1	15	2	...	12	51	...	659	
			1	55	1	2	1	1	...	4	5	44	...	1	...	...	1	1	...	116	
			2	126	4	9	...	1	...	...	8	57	...	1	...	...	...	1	...	207	
			3	58	2	2	...	...	...	22	35	14	...	10	...	...	1	5	...	149	
			4	26	9	1	...	3	...	9	75	7	1	3	2	...	10	44	...	187	
C		Grand Total for C Ward ..	...	3,329	390	176	41	33	4	298	476	1,552	27	23	61	2	37	*31	...	6,280	
	10	Market Total ...	...	593	69	31	7	2	2	36	106	391	1	...	4	1	10	4	...	1,257	
			1	56	11	3	1	...	...	2	8	46	...	...	1	...	5	3	...	133	
			2	29	2	1	...	2	1	5	3	18	...	...	3	...	1	...	...	65	
			3	31	12	3	...	...	1	...	30	47	...	...	...	...	3	...	...	136	
			4	60	5	1	...	...	...	9	10	8	...	...	...	...	...	...	...	93	
			5	147	1	3	...	...	...	12	29	32	...	...	...	...	...	...	...	224	
			6	104	11	5	3	...	...	6	5	63	1	...	...	...	...	1	...	199	
			7	57	15	10	2	...	...	1	3	60	...	...	...	1	1	...	...	156	
			8	109	12	5	1	...	...	1	9	111	...	...	...	...	...	...	...	248	
	11	Dhobi Talao Total ..	...	1,032	64	12	9	1	1	81	100	45	8	5	9	...	11	4	...	1,382	
			1	254	8	3	1	...	...	5	16	2	...	...	...	...	1	1	...	301	
			2	73	3	2	1	1	...	...	5	1	...	...	...	...	...	2	...	88	
			3	140	2	...	...	...	...	16	11	...	8	...	...	...	1	...	...	178	
			4	114	12	3	5	...	...	6	11	14	...	1	1	...	7	1	...	175	
			5	78	4	1	...	...	1	11	13	16	...	2	4	...	1	...	...	132	
			6	137	15	1	2	...	...	16	17	4	...	...	3	...	1	...	...	196	
			7	223	20	2	...	...	...	27	28	6	...	2	1	...	...	...	...	313	
	12	Fanaswadi Total ...	...	645	35	30	7	1	1	68	33	73	2	7	22	...	4	1	...	929	
			1	250	14	9	4	1	...	29	10	26	1	3	12	...	2	...	...	330	
			2	216	11	7	1	...	1	25	14	39	...	4	9	...	...	1	...	321	
			3	179	10	14	2	...	...	15	9	15	1	...	1	...	2	...	...	248	

Remarks: * Total for C Ward ... { Buildings under construction ... 43; Buildings declared unfit for human habitation ... 10 } Total ... 53

SPECIAL TABLE IX—*continued.*

Classification of Buildings.

Ward.	Charge No.	Section.	Circle No.	Bungalows and Dwelling houses.	Shops.	Temples and Churches.	Schools.	Dispensaries, Hospitals and Sanitaria.	Theatres.	Stables.	Godowns.	Residence and shops combined.	Dharamshalas.	Mills.	Workshops and factories.	Barracks.	Offices.	Chowkies.	Tents.	Total.	Remarks.
	13	Bhuleshwar Total ...	...	295	41	65	15	25	...	74	162	593	15	2	14	1	8	7	...	1,320	
			1	83	4	10	1	3	...	10	18	45	2	...	...	...	...	...	...	104	
			2	44	8	11	2	2	...	26	13	60	3	...	6	...	1	2	...	107	
			3	38	11	6	2	1	...	13	21	37	10	...	3	...	1	4	...	149	
			4	79	8	10	6	7	...	10	50	176	...	...	3	...	1	1	...	349	
			5	30	9	3	2	3	...	5	30	193	1	1	1	...	1	...	...	287	
			6	21	7	16	2	9	...	2	18	93	...	1	2	1	4	...	...	176	
	14	Kumbharwada Total ...	...	552	9	16	2	1	...	25	21	65	1	5	10	...	1	4	...	712	
			1	222	4	2	2	1	...	19	11	10	...	1	4	...	...	2	...	278	
			2	19[illegible]	4	9	...	...	...	3	7	21	1	1	...	...	...	...	...	236	
			3	8[illegible]	...	4	...	...	...	1	2	9	...	1	6	...	...	2	...	104	
			4	6[illegible]	1	1	...	...	...	2	1	25	...	2	1	...	1	...	...	94	
	15	Khara Talao Total ...	...	112	69	22	1	3	...	14	54	385	...	4	2	...	3	11	...	680	
			1	8	22	6	...	...	...	1	11	62	...	1	...	...	...	7	...	118	
			2	13	17	5	...	...	...	...	3	41	...	...	...	...	...	...	...	79	
			3	22	16	4	...	1	...	6	12	106	...	...	...	...	3	...	...	169	
			4	40	6	5	1	...	...	1	15	88	...	3	...	...	...	4	...	163	
			5	29	8	2	...	2	...	7	13	88	...	...	2	...	...	...	...	151	
D		Total for D Ward	...	4,326	136	117	39	14	5	855	273	123	18	6	107	5	45	119	...	6,668	Total for D Ward ... { Buildings under construction ... 29; Buildings declared unfit for human habitation ... 3 } Total ... 32
	16	Khetwadi Total ...	...	1,016	38	20	20	2	4	79	52	61	6	2	52	...	6	13	...	1,371	
			1	137	2	3	8	...	...	17	2	3	2	...	7	...	...	3	...	184	
			2	160	7	1	...	...	...	15	8	14	...	...	8	...	1	1	...	215	
			3	146	1	1	2	2	...	4	7	3	1	...	1	...	...	2	...	173	
			4	15[illegible]	7	2	5	...	...	16	9	8	...	...	8	...	2	2	...	218	
			5	105	1	4	1	...	...	6	3	7	...	1	1	...	1	...	...	130	
			6	87	7	3	3	...	...	5	3	1	3	...	5	...	1	...	...	118	
			7	100	3	3	...	...	2	6	4	16	...	...	4	...	1	...	...	141	
			8	12[illegible]	10	3	1	...	2	8	16	9	...	1	18	...	...	5	...	198	
	31	Girgaum Total ...	...	1,003	39	24	3	1	...	64	35	...	...	...	14	...	3	12	...	1,197	
			1	195	5	8	2	1	...	23	10	...	...	...	10	...	2	7	...	2[illegible]3	
			2	100	12	3	...	...	...	3	...	...	...	...	...	...	...	...	...	118	
			3	129	9	4	...	...	...	8	11	...	...	...	...	...	...	...	...	161	
			4	52	1	1	...	...	...	3	2	...	...	...	...	...	...	...	...	59	
			5	154	3	...	...	...	...	4	5	...	...	...	...	...	...	...	...	166	
			6	2[illegible]8	4	6	...	...	...	15	5	...	...	...	2	...	...	3	...	293	
			7	115	5	2	1	...	...	8	2	...	...	...	2	...	...	2	...	137	
	30	Chaupati Total ...	...	598	16	6	8	1	1	81	35	31	...	...	13	...	4	15	...	799	
			1	66	...	...	2	...	...	10	3	6	...	...	...	...	1	2	...	89	
			2	116	8	1	1	...	...	23	8	4	...	...	1	...	...	6	...	168	
			3	67	1	...	...	...	...	9	2	1	...	...	1	...	...	2	...	83	
			4	82	...	1	...	...	...	12	8	2	...	...	1	...	...	...	...	106	
			5	18[illegible]	2	4	4	1	...	18	6	3	...	...	3	...	1	1	...	233	
			6	87	5	...	1	...	1	9	9	5	...	...	7	...	2	4	...	130	
	29	Walkeshwar Total ...	...	1,010	13	45	6	7	...	362	24	27	11	...	3	5	8	33	...	1,554	
			1	78	3	3	5	...	...	11	3	9	3	...	...	4	4	5	...	128	
			2	165	2	13	...	2	...	42	6	7	2	...	2	1	...	4	...	246	
			3	194	3	2	...	...	...	86	3	...	...	...	...	...	2	4	...	294	
			4	52	1	...	...	...	...	27	...	...	...	...	...	...	...	3	...	83	
			5	104	...	1	...	...	...	58	3	...	...	...	...	...	...	2	...	166	
			6	223	3	31	1	5	...	60	4	6	6	...	...	...	1	6	...	340	
			7	195	1	2	...	...	...	80	5	3	...	...	1	...	1	9	...	297	

SPECIAL TABLE IX—*continued.*

CLASSIFICATION OF BUILDINGS.

Ward.	Charge No.	Section.	Circle No.	Bungalows and Dwelling houses.	Shops.	Temples and Churches.	Schools.	Dispensaries, Hospitals and Sanitaria.	Theatres.	Stables.	Godowns.	Residence and shops combined.	Dharmsalas.	Mills.	Workshops and factories.	Barracks.	Offices.	Chowkies.	Tents.	Total.	Remarks.
D	17	Mahalaxmi Total ...	...	1,199	30	22	2	3	...	269	127	14	1	4	25	...	25	46	...	1,767	
			1	244	2	3	...	2	...	99	9	2	...	...	...	...	...	14	...	375	
			2	70	...	11	...	...	...	10	...	...	...	...	...	...	...	1	...	93	
			3	91	2	...	...	...	...	43	4	...	...	1	1	...	...	5	...	148	
			4	159	12	2	1	1	...	43	26	2	...	...	10	...	11	8	...	273	
			5	69	7	5	1	...	...	17	11	4	1	...	4	...	6	...	...	125	
			6	129	4	...	...	...	...	14	9	1	...	1	2	...	...	4	...	164	
			7	103	...	1	...	...	...	13	16	...	...	2	3	...	3	...	...	141	
			8	97	2	...	...	...	...	10	19	...	...	...	2	...	3	3	...	136	
			9	236	1	...	...	...	...	23	33	5	...	...	3	...	2	11	...	315	
E		Total for E Ward ...	...	5,930	133	142	52	46	3	779	679	752	17	76	273	9	136	202	1	9,230	Total for E Ward ... { Buildings under construction ... 26; Buildings declared unfit for human habitation ... 11; Total ... 37 }
	20	Tardeo Total ...	...	510	23	10	7	1	3	138	77	95	2	4	36	...	11	17	...	934	
			1	138	4	2	3	1	...	27	12	10	...	...	5	...	1	1	...	203	
			2	121	3	1	...	...	...	20	18	34	1	...	12	...	1	5	...	216	
			3	1[illegible]4	12	5	1	...	3	45	19	34	1	2	8	...	5	5	...	294	
			4	67	4	2	4	...	...	46	28	17	...	2	11	...	4	6	...	221	
	21	Kamatipura Total ...	...	850	20	33	4	1	...	35	47	127	6	2	13	...	3	5	...	1,146	
			1	171	2	11	2	1	...	16	7	46	...	1	2	...	1	4	...	267	
			2	539	9	10	1	...	...	11	14	41	4	...	3	...	...	...	...	63[illegible]	
			3	140	9	9	1	...	...	8	26	37	2	1	8	...	2	1	...	244	
	18	First Nagpada Total ...	...	85	...	7	1	2	...	12	2	...	...	...	1	...	1	...	...	111	
			1	62	...	5	1	2	...	11	2	...	...	...	1	...	1	...	...	85	
			2	2[illegible]	...	2	...	...	...	1	...	...	...	...	...	...	...	...	...	26	
	19	Second Nagpada Total ...	...	417	1	15	1	1	...	11	41	36	...	6	12	...	...	1	...	542	
			1	45	...	4	...	...	...	6	10	24	...	4	9	...	...	...	...	102	
			2	133	...	5	1	1	...	2	16	8	...	1	1	...	...	1	...	168	
			3	151	...	5	...	...	...	1	9	1	...	1	1	...	...	...	...	169	
			4	88	1	1	...	...	...	2	7	3	...	...	1	...	...	...	...	103	
	32	Byculla Total ...	...	1,442	61	27	17	19	...	320	233	271	3	32	123	6	51	66	...	2,661	
			1	414	34	8	2	6	...	101	96	71	1	17	47	2	22	38	...	851	
			2	13[illegible]	3	5	6	3	...	30	31	27	1	2	11	...	7	5	...	255	
			3	338	6	5	2	...	...	61	43	39	...	6	3[illegible]	4	8	11	...	613	
			4	169	6	6	2	1	...	47	25	40	...	2	8	...	4	4	...	320	
			5	56	1	2	...	...	...	4	4	30	...	...	...	...	1	1	...	99	
			6	115	5	...	1	9	...	5[illegible]	15	21	...	5	2	...	7	6	...	244	
			7	62	1	2	...	...	...	8	2	19	...	...	...	...	...	...	...	90	
			8	104	5	2	4	...	...	9	17	19	1	...	15	...	2	1	...	179	
	22	Tadwadi Total ...	...	1,331	1	16	11	17	...	84	134	52	2	24	32	...	33	5	1	1,743	
			1	261	...	4	7	10	...	29	37	12	...	3	8	...	9	...	...	380	
			2	373	1	6	2	...	...	12	14	6	2	...	11	...	7	2	1	437	
			3	697	...	6	2	7	...	43	83	34	...	21	13	...	17	3	...	926	
	23	Mazagaon Total ...	...	1,295	27	34	11	5	...	179	145	171	4	8	66	3	37	108	...	2,093	
			1	168	1	6	3	1	...	30	16	11	...	...	12	...	3	8	...	264	
			2	214	14	2	2	1	...	14	23	23	...	1	11	2	8	18	...	337	
			3	150	1	4	2	2	...	9	10	23	...	...	13	1	4	10	...	210	
			4	231	2	11	2	1	...	19	21	5[illegible]	3	1	3	...	5	5	...	384	
			5	512	9	11	2	...	...	54	75	64	1	6	37	...	17	67	...	865	

SPECIAL TABLE IX—*continued.*

Classification of Buildings.

Ward.	Charge No.	Section.	Circle No.	Bungalows and Dwelling houses.	Shops.	Temples and Churches.	Schools.	Dispensaries, Hospitals and Sanitaria.	Theatres.	Stables.	Godowns.	Residence and shops combined.	Dharamshalas.	Mills.	Workshops and factories.	Barracks.	Offices.	Chowkies.	Tents.	Total.	Remarks.
F		Total for Ward F ...	...	5,025	154	101	13	2	...	583	396	249	8	26	153	...	106	224	11	7,050	Total for F Ward ... {Buildings under construction ... 10; Buildings declared unfit for human habitation ... —; 10}
	24	Parel ... Total ...	...	1,149	76	28	4	2	...	274	154	179	...	9	70	...	56	56	...	2,057	
			1	43	2	1	...	...	...	2	...	3	...	...	1	...	...	...	...	52	
			2	131	25	4	...	...	...	27	30	25	...	1	14	...	8	13	...	278	
			3	178	15	5	1	...	...	30	41	5	...	...	23	...	18	11	...	328	
			4	68	5	...	...	...	...	2	...	17	...	1	...	...	1	...	...	94	
			5	67	9	2	...	...	...	14	17	11	...	...	2	...	7	2	...	131	
			6	234	4	7	...	...	...	41	17	23	...	4	...	...	1	7	...	338	
			7	42	6	2	...	...	...	4	13	44	...	2	9	...	6	6	...	134	
			8	254	6	5	3	2	...	146	31	33	...	1	20	...	15	17	...	536	
			9	132	2	1	...	...	...	9	5	16	...	...	1	...	...	...	...	166	
	25	Sewri ... Total ...	...	1,297	26	17	...	...	...	86	97	8	2	9	13	...	20	63	...	1,643	
			1	435	10	3	...	...	...	20	45	3	2	6	3	...	6	10	...	553	
			2	224	6	4	...	...	...	19	7	...	...	2	2	...	2	5	...	271	
			3	235	4	5	...	...	...	6	17	4	...	...	8	...	5	15	...	299	
			4	328	5	5	...	...	...	41	13	...	...	...	...	...	2	2	...	396	
			5	75	1	...	...	...	...	...	15	1	...	1	5	...	5	22	...	125	
	26	Sion ... Total ...	...	2,579	52	56	9	...	...	222	145	62	6	8	65	...	30	105	11	3,350	
			1	189	10	6	...	...	...	21	17	6	...	1	7	...	9	5	...	281	
			2	74	4	1	1	...	...	20	10	9	1	...	1	...	2	5	...	129	
			3	235	9	5	2	...	...	27	35	13	...	...	13	...	1	5	4	349	
			4	312	4	5	2	...	...	33	25	11	...	1	24	...	1	13	...	431	
			5	219	2	2	...	...	...	31	11	10	...	2	5	...	4	15	...	321	
			6	346	5	9	3	...	...	26	15	9	1	4	7	...	1	12	...	438	
			7	300	...	8	1	...	...	26	10	...	2	...	2	...	11	41	6	416	
			8	238	5	3	...	...	...	14	15	3	...	...	2	...	...	4	1	275	
			9	169	6	4	...	...	...	13	1	...	...	...	...	...	...	1	...	193	
			10	184	4	8	...	...	...	3	2	1	...	...	1	...	1	...	...	204	
			11	275	3	5	...	...	...	18	4	...	2	...	4	...	...	4	...	316	
G		Total for G Ward ...	...	6,719	132	125	22	6	...	432	662	463	23	47	46	1	80	261	...	9,019	Total for G Ward ... {Buildings under construction ... 6; Buildings declared unfit for human habitation ... —; 6}
	27	Mahim ... Total.	...	3,014	37	59	10	3	...	216	422	202	12	4	38	1	24	43	...	4,085	
			1	264	5	1	...	...	...	19	44	6	4	1	12	...	5	15	...	376	
			2	459	5	1	1	...	...	27	57	22	...	...	...	...	...	3	...	575	
			3	319	7	6	4	...	...	29	64	11	1	2	17	...	3	9	...	472	
			4	320	3	6	...	1	...	27	19	18	2	...	1	...	4	3	...	404	
			5	483	8	32	3	1	...	36	47	95	3	1	1	...	...	1	...	699	
			6	639	5	6	...	1	...	23	101	22	...	...	1	1	1	5	...	805	
			7	168	...	6	...	...	...	20	32	11	1	...	5	...	6	3	...	252	
			8	363	4	11	2	...	...	30	66	17	1	...	1	...	6	4	...	502	
	28	Warli ... Total ...	...	3,705	95	66	12	3	...	216	240	261	11	43	8	...	56	218	...	4,934	
			1	317	1	19	...	...	...	22	12	3	5	...	...	...	2	8	...	389	
			2	247	8	2	...	1	...	21	29	34	...	6	1	...	10	23	...	384	
			3	116	3	1	...	...	...	8	3	15	...	1	2	...	1	1	...	150	
			4	53	1	1	1	...	...	3	1	...	...	...	...	...	...	...	...	60	
			5	336	12	3	...	...	...	10	37	29	...	10	...	...	9	41	...	487	
			6	764	4	10	2	1	...	27	7	25	2	...	...	...	1	3	...	846	
			7	746	38	13	2	1	...	49	64	63	1	18	2	...	27	113	...	1,136	
			8	1,126	29	17	7	...	...	76	87	92	3	8	3	...	6	29	...	1,483	

TABLE X.

CLASSIFICATION OF BUILDINGS BY FLOORS.

TABLE X.

Classification of Buildings by Floors.

Ward.	Charge.	Section.	Circle No.	Number of Buildings with: Ground floor only.	One upper floor.	Two upper floors.	Three upper floors.	Four upper floors.	Five upper floors and over.	Total number of Buildings.
		Grand Total, Bombay City ...	...	**26,512**	**7,596**	**5,238**	**3,431**	**2,020**	**869**	**45,716**
A		**Grand Total for A Ward ...**	...	**1,566**	**480**	**397**	**438**	**387**	**325**	**3,593**
	1	**Upper Colaba ... Total ...**	...	**107**	**6**	...	**1**	...	...	**114**
	2	**Lower Colaba ... Total ...**	...	**651**	**165**	**139**	**83**	**17**	**27**	**1,082**
			1	103	35	27	18	...	1	184
			2	184	28	13	9	...	...	234
			3	23	20	32	19	1	...	95
			4	27	14	13	3	...	...	57
			5	17	17	14	10	1	...	59
			6	155	32	30	5	1	1	224
			7	91	9	4	4	4	1	113
			8	51	10	6	15	10	24	116
	3	**Fort South ... ... Total ...**	...	**152**	**85**	**91**	**60**	**25**	**1**	**414**
			1	8	13	17	17	7	1	63
			2	74	38	32	20	2	...	166
			3	28	20	23	13	3	...	87
			4	9	8	17	7	11	...	52
			5	33	6	2	3	2	...	46
	4	**Fort North ... ... Total ...**	...	**169**	**118**	**102**	**237**	**317**	**284**	**1,227**
			1	8	8	7	55	66	38	182
			2	16	21	22	29	30	18	136
			3	8	9	16	37	54	48	172
			4	11	13	2	22	37	46	131
			5	16	26	18	34	26	33	153
			6	9	15	16	28	57	57	182
			7	11	5	7	17	32	34	106
			8	90	21	14	15	15	10	165
	5	**Esplanade ... ... Total ..**	...	**487**	**106**	**65**	**57**	**28**	**13**	**756**
			1	131	52	26	10	6	9	234
			2	66	17	15	23	15	3	139
			3	204	23	15	12	3	...	257
			4	86	14	9	12	4	1	126
B		**Grand Total for B Ward ...**	...	**1,027**	**649**	**687**	**713**	**560**	**220**	**3,856**
	7	**Chakla ... ... Total ...**	..	**92**	**133**	**147**	**218**	**227**	**94**	**911**
			1	14	14	9	11	42	14	107
			2	9	17	19	36	35	17	133
			3	11	8	18	33	30	7	107
			4	6	10	27	36	29	28	136
			5	16	12	9	28	30	9	103
			6	4	2	6	8	19	2	41
			7	7	18	16	19	12	4	76
			8	11	25	24	14	3	6	83
			9	15	27	19	30	27	7	125
	6	**Mandvi ... ... Total ...**	...	**338**	**204**	**153**	**164**	**175**	**96**	**1,120**
			1	55	10	19	28	16	4	132
			2			Demolished.				
			3	25	12	7	11	12	1	68
			4	5	9	23	12	15	11	75
			5	2	10	7	5	8	17	49
			6	4	8	4	7	12	11	46
			7	20	30	14	8	14	8	94
			8	17	23	11	14	11	8	84
			0	29	35	20	39	31	13	167
			10	8	17	32	21	30	14	122
			11	53	25	12	16	23	6	185
			12	120	25	4	3	3	3	158
	8	**Umarkhadi .. ... Total ...**	...	**311**	**216**	**215**	**251**	**136**	**27**	**1,156**
			1	6	20	16	21	24	1	88
			2	10	9	15	10	4	...	48
			3	4	9	25	31	22	7	98
			4	20	11	8	12	2	...	53
			5	10	10	4	20	22	5	71
			6	13	8	17	22	5	...	65
			7	22	21	35	39	20	2	139
			8	83	36	36	51	28	11	195
			9	123	33	17	20	6	1	200
			10	70	59	42	25	3	...	199

TABLE X—*continued.*

CLASSIFICATION OF BUILDINGS BY FLOORS.

Ward.	Charge.	Section.	Circle No.	Number of Buildings with: Ground floors only.	One upper floor.	Two upper floors.	Three upper floors.	Four upper floors.	Five upper floors and over.	Total number of Buildings.
B	9	**Dongri ... ... Total ...**	...	**286**	**93**	**172**	**80**	**23**	**3**	**659**
			1	8	20	46	25	14	3	116
			2	29	45	80	48	5	...	207
			3	105	14	27	2	1	...	149
			4	144	17	19	5	2	...	187
C		**Grand Total for C Ward ...**	...	**1,403**	**1,069**	**1,405**	**1,262**	**838**	**303**	**6,280**
	10	**Market ... ... Total ...**	...	**283**	**192**	**178**	**208**	**266**	**150**	**1,257**
			1	50	18	20	29	13	6	136
			2	24	15	9	7	4	6	65
			3	50	35	22	9	12	8	136
			4	21	23	10	11	21	7	93
			5	27	25	27	89	56	50	224
			6	35	18	38	47	44	17	199
			7	37	34	22	22	26	15	156
			8	19	24	30	44	90	41	248
	11	**Dhobi Talao ... Total ...**	...	**276**	**281**	**327**	**276**	**162**	**60**	**1,682**
			1	39	36	68	86	63	9	301
			2	21	13	6	35	8	5	88
			3	48	42	52	25	8	3	178
			4	27	39	56	28	14	11	175
			5	30	29	26	28	16	12	132
			6	35	44	51	33	27	6	196
			7	76	87	68	41	26	14	312
	12	**Fanaswadi ... Total ...**	...	**313**	**200**	**237**	**124**	**39**	**16**	**929**
			1	147	61	70	56	14	12	360
			2	105	73	97	33	11	2	321
			3	61	66	70	35	14	2	248
	13	**Bhuleshwar ... Total ...**	...	**233**	**181**	**278**	**365**	**225**	**38**	**1,320**
			1	31	36	40	36	40	11	194
			2	42	39	36	31	18	1	167
			3	45	42	34	24	3	...	148
			4	46	38	85	105	64	10	348
			5	50	17	64	102	52	12	297
			6	19	9	29	67	48	4	176
	14	**Khumbharwada ... Total ...**	...	**144**	**128**	**259**	**151**	**27**	**3**	**712**
			1	67	65	89	50	7	...	278
			2	25	34	98	65	14	...	236
			3	24	18	40	21	1	...	104
			4	28	11	32	15	5	3	94
	15	**Khara Talao ... Total ...**	...	**174**	**87**	**126**	**138**	**119**	**36**	**680**
			1	35	20	28	25	7	3	118
			2	34	4	8	18	13	2	79
			3	30	22	38	36	34	9	169
			4	49	23	21	31	29	10	163
			5	26	18	31	28	36	12	151
D		**Grand Total for D Ward ...**	...	**3,592**	**1,523**	**1,005**	**442**	**113**	**13**	**6,688**
	16	**Khetwadi ... ... Total ...**	...	**622**	**301**	**210**	**165**	**69**	**4**	**1,371**
			1	125	39	10	5	5	...	184
			2	117	20	28	28	11	1	215
			3	57	34	33	38	10	...	172
			4	122	66	15	8	7	...	218
			5	84	43	20	21	11	1	130
			6	25	18	24	29	20	2	118
			7	50	26	42	20	3	...	141
			8	92	45	38	16	2	...	193
	31	**Girgaum ... ... Total ...**	...	**384**	**305**	**368**	**118**	**19**	**3**	**1,197**
			1	140	61	45	14	8	...	263
			2	25	31	47	13	1	1	118
			3	51	33	58	19	...	...	161
			4	17	10	18	7	7	...	59
			5	21	33	84	26	1	1	166
			6	83	111	70	24	4	1	293
			7	47	26	46	15	3	...	137

TABLE X—*continued.*

Classification of Buildings by Floors.

Ward.	Charge.	Section.	Circle No.	Number of Buildings with: Ground floor only.	One upper floor.	Two upper floors.	Three upper floors.	Four upper floors.	Five upper floors and over.	Total Number of buildings.
D	30	Chaupati ... ... Total ..	...	371	209	154	58	5	2	799
			1	55	13	12	9	...	...	89
			2	90	42	31	4	1	...	168
			3	30	28	18	6	1	...	83
			4	49	32	18	7	...	...	106
			5	66	68	66	21	2	...	223
			6	81	26	9	11	1	2	130
	29	Walkeshwar ... Total ...	...	949	378	166	53	7	1	1.554
			1	61	38	19	8	2	...	128
			2	154	61	28	3	...	...	246
			3	178	83	26	7	...	...	294
			4	66	12	5	...	...	...	83
			5	131	25	6	4	...	...	166
			6	156	87	67	24	5	1	340
			7	203	72	15	7	...	...	297
	17	Mahalaxmi ... ... Total ...	...	1,266	330	107	48	13	3	1.767
			1	249	95	24	4	3	...	375
			2	50	30	8	4	...	...	92
			3	103	29	10	4	...	..	146
			4	210	43	14	6	...	...	273
			5	90	24	10	...	1	..	125
			6	66	40	20	28	9	1	164
			7	90	39	10	...	...	2	141
			8	113	15	8	...	...	...	136
			9	295	15	3	2	...	...	315
E		Grand Total for E Ward ..	...	5,740	1.644	1.196	528	114	8	9.230
	20	Tardeo ... ... Total ...	...	595	204	80	32	23	...	934
			1	116	62	16	7	2	...	203
			2	113	42	29	16	16	...	216
			3	199	70	19	4	2	...	294
			4	167	30	16	5	3	...	221
	21	Kamatipura ... Total ...	...	295	248	424	163	15	1	1,146
			1	98	68	78	22	1	...	267
			2	92	129	289	115	9	1	635
			3	105	51	67	26	5	...	244
	18	First Nagpada ... Total ...	...	49	18	31	13	...	...	111
			1	44	15	16	10	...	...	85
			2	5	3	15	3	...	...	26
	19	Second Nagpada .. Total ...	...	66	110	132	161	48	5	542
			1	29	45	20	7	1	...	102
			2	32	34	52	40	10	...	168
			3	14	14	45	72	21	3	169
			4	11	17	15	42	16	2	103
	32	Byculla ... ... Total ...	...	1.798	459	299	95	10	...	2,661
			1	598	170	61	31	1	...	861
			2	156	51	34	11	3	...	255
			3	409	108	73	20	3	...	613
			4	221	42	38	16	3	...	320
			5	43	19	31	6	...	...	99
			6	211	21	11	1	...	...	244
			7	35	27	25	3	...	...	90
			8	125	21	26	7	...	...	179
	22	Tadwadi ... ... Total ...	...	1,381	251	80	18	11	2	1743
			1	279	70	16	7	8	...	380
			2	347	66	23	1	...	...	437
			3	755	115	41	10	3	2	926
	23	Mazagaon ... ... Total ...	...	1,536	354	150	46	7	...	2,093
			1	189	59	16	2	2	...	268
			2	193	76	48	17	3	...	337
			3	137	39	28	13	2	...	219
			4	256	91	26	11	...	...	381
			5	761	89	32	3	...	...	885

TABLE X—*continued.*

Classification of Buildings by Floors.

Ward.	Charge.	Section.	Circle No.	Number of Buildings with						Total Number of buildings.
				Ground floor only.	One upper floor.	Two upper floors.	Three upper floors.	Four upper floors.	Five upper floors and over.	
F		**Grand Total for F Ward** ...	...	**5.906**	**855**	**217**	**68**	**4**	...	**7.050**
	24	**Parel ... ... Total** ...	...	**1.563**	**314**	**127**	**51**	**2**	...	**2.057**
			1	18	11	12	11	...	...	52
			2	242	25	10	...	1	...	278
			3	257	42	17	11	1	...	328
			4	35	25	19	15	...	...	94
			5	109	18	3	1	...	...	131
			6	263	59	15	1	...	...	338
			7	92	29	9	4	...	...	134
			8	482	33	14	7	...	...	536
			9	65	72	28	1	...	...	166
	25	**Sewri ... ... Total** ...	...	**1.473**	**135**	**29**	**5**	**1**	...	**1,643**
			1	519	23	7	3	...	...	552
			2	258	11	...	1	1	...	271
			3	272	23	4	...	...	...	299
			4	302	75	18	1	...	...	396
			5	122	3	...	...	...	...	125
	26	**Sion ... ... Total** ...	...	**2,570**	**406**	**61**	**12**	**1**	...	**3 350**
			1	230	34	14	3	...	...	281
			2	96	21	11	...	...	...	128
			3	280	51	12	4	1	...	348
			4	394	30	6	1	...	...	431
			5	262	52	6	1	...	...	321
			6	391	42	4	1	...	...	438
			7	390	24	1	1	...	...	416
			8	231	41	2	1	...	...	275
			9	146	44	3	...	...	...	193
			10	175	27	2	...	...	...	204
			11	275	40	...	...	...	...	315
G		**Grand Total for G Ward** ...	...	**7.278**	**1.376**	**331**	**30**	**4**	...	**9,019**
	27	**Máhim ... ... Total** ...	...	**3.398**	**665**	**103**	**8**	**1**	...	**4.035**
			1	321	48	5	1	1	...	376
			2	447	114	14	...	...	...	575
			3	416	47	9	...	...	...	472
			4	294	90	18	2	...	...	404
			5	452	192	50	5	...	...	699
			6	665	133	7	...	...	...	805
			7	233	19	...	...	...	...	252
			8	480	22	...	...	...	...	502
	28	**Warli ... ... Total** ...	...	**3.970**	**711**	**228**	**22**	**3**	...	**4.934**
			1	365	22	2	...	...	...	389
			2	275	79	26	3	1	...	384
			3	94	20	33	3	...	...	150
			4	23	31	6	...	...	...	60
			5	387	33	61	5	1	...	487
			6	724	116	6	...	...	...	846
			7	961	133	35	6	...	...	1,135
			8	1,141	277	59	5	1	...	1,483

TABLE XI.

CLASSIFICATION OF BUILDINGS BY THE NUMBER OF TENEMENTS.

NOTE.—The difference between the total of this table and the total shown in tables IX and X is due to the fact that the buildings under construction and those declared unfit for human habitation have been omitted and detached buildings such as servants' quarters, and stables which are rented jointly with a main building are not separately accounted for.

TABLE XI.

Classification of buildings by the number of tenements.

Ward.	Charge.	Section.	Circle Number.	Number of buildings containing: Ten tenements and under.	Eleven to twenty tenements.	Twenty-one to thirty tenements.	Thirty-one to forty tenements.	Forty-one to fifty tenements.	Over fifty-one tenements.	Total No. of buildings.
		Grand Total, Bombay City ...	...	32,247	3,285	1,293	560	268	279	37,932
A		Grand Total for A Ward ...	...	2,610	213	51	24	11	15	2,924
	1	Upper Colaba ... Total ...	...	69	6	...	1	...	...	76
	2	Lower Colaba ... Total ...	...	600	83	19	6	4	4	716
			1	109	16	3	...	...	...	128
			2	152	3	...	...	1	2	158
			3	74	12	5	1	...	...	92
			4	47	3	3	...	...	...	53
			5	47	7	3	1	...	1	59
			6	104	7	...	1	3	1	116
			7	27	5	2	...	...	...	34
			8	40	30	3	3	...	...	76
	3	Fort South ... ... Total ...	...	376	13	5	1	...	...	395
			1	58	3	1	...	...	...	62
			2	164	2	...	...	...	...	166
			3	81	5	1	...	...	...	87
			4	44	3	1	...	...	...	48
			5	29	...	2	1	...	...	32
	4	Fort North ... ... Total ...	...	1,020	88	27	14	6	6	1,161
			1	172	2	1	...	...	...	175
			2	125	...	...	...	...	...	125
			3	159	7	1	1	...	...	168
			4	111	11	7	1	...	1	131
			5	132	5	1	...	...	...	138
			6	138	26	3	1	1	...	169
			7	57	28	8	4	3	3	103
			8	126	9	6	7	2	2	152
	5	Esplanade ... ... Total ...	...	545	23	...	2	1	5	576
			1	179	6	...	1	...	...	186
			2	100	2	...	...	...	...	102
			3	174	12	...	1	1	4	192
			4	92	3	...	...	...	1	96
B		Grand Total for B Ward ...	...	2,567	648	270	103	54	43	3,685
	7	Chakla ... ... Total ...	...	650	162	56	15	7	4	894
			1	80	20	4	2	...	...	106
			2	99	22	9	...	...	...	130
			3	79	15	6	2	2	...	104
			4	79	33	15	2	1	3	133
			5	70	21	8	1	...	...	100
			6	30	8	2	...	...	...	40
			7	56	9	6	3	1	...	75
			8	64	11	1	3	2	1	82
			9	93	23	5	2	1	...	124
	6	Mandvi ... ... Total ...	...	819	148	80	27	19	8	1,101
			1	88	21	15	2	1	...	127
			2	...	...	...	...	...	...	...
			3	63	2	2	...	...	2	68
			4	24	22	13	4	3	...	66
			5	31	14	3	...	1	...	49
			6	24	9	7	2	2	...	44
			7	73	12	7	1	1	...	94
			8	62	10	5	3	...	...	80
			9	139	21	7	1	...	...	168
			10	75	26	5	4	2	1	112
			11	90	12	13	8	8	1	132
			12	151	...	3	2	1	4	161
	8	Umarkhadi ... ... Total ...	...	723	221	76	41	12	28	1,101
			1	50	14	9	8	1	6	88
			2	25	13	9	1	...	...	48
			3	46	39	7	2	1	3	98
			4	35	5	3	1	1	8	53
			5	38	20	5	3	1	...	67
			6	42	18	3	1	...	...	64
			7	86	32	9	3	...	3	133
			8	135	87	14	6	1	2	135
			9	156	14	5	5	...	5	185
			10	110	29	12	11	7	1	170

TABLE XI—*continued.*

Classification of buildings by the number of tenements.

Ward.	Charge.	Section.	Circle Number.	Number of buildings containing						
				Ten tenements and under.	Eleven to twenty tenements.	Twenty-one to thirty tenements.	Thirty-one to forty tenements.	Forty-one to fifty tenements.	Over fifty-one tenements.	Total Number of buildings.
B	9	Dongri ... ... Total ...	...	375	117	58	20	16	3	589
			1	63	32	15	2	3	...	115
			2	83	58	31	9	9	1	191
			3	90	18	4	7	4	2	125
			4	139	9	8	2	...	...	158
C		Grand Total for C Ward ...	...	4,350	879	283	113	47	35	5,706
	10	Market ... ... Total ...	...	845	140	31	17	5	4	1,042
			1	76	14	2	4	...	...	95
			2	33	3	1	2	...	3	41
			3	105	3	1	1	...	...	110
			4	50	16	5	...	...	...	71
			5	144	37	7	3	2	1	194
			6	138	26	6	3	1	...	174
			7	105	12	6	4	2	...	129
			8	196	29	3	...	...	...	228
	11	Dhobitalao ... ... Total ...	...	1,044	148	38	17	3	9	1,259
			1	260	11	2	1	1	1	276
			2	70	7	1	...	...	6	84
			3	138	14	4	7	...	...	163
			4	98	24	8	3	...	1	144
			5	89	20	6	1	...	...	116
			6	144	27	8	2	1	...	180
			7	245	35	11	3	1	1	296
	12	Fanaswadi ... ... Total ...	...	666	97	37	16	8	6	830
			1	280	20	5	6	1	2	314
			2	218	43	19	5	2	4	291
			3	168	34	13	5	5	...	225
	13	Bhuleshwar... ... Total ...	...	944	185	69	23	11	6	1,238
			1	152	26	8	4	1	1	192
			2	117	23	13	5	5	4	167
			3	106	18	7	3	2	...	136
			4	249	58	17	8	2	...	334
			5	192	32	12	1	1	...	238
			6	128	28	12	2	...	1	171
	14	Khumbharwada ... Total ...	...	437	149	59	20	12	6	683
			1	203	43	11	4	1	...	262
			2	131	67	22	7	7	2	236
			3	51	22	15	3	1	3	95
			4	52	17	11	6	3	1	90
	15	Khara Talao ... Total ...	...	414	160	48	20	8	4	654
			1	73	23	10	5	4	2	117
			2	48	17	4	4	...	1	74
			3	98	46	14	5	2	...	165
			4	109	36	9	2	1	...	157
			5	86	38	11	4	1	1	141
D		Grand Total for D Ward ...	...	5,210	318	155	56	17	16	5,772
	16	Khetwadi ... ... Total ...	...	1,052	100	56	22	2	7	1,239
			1	128	10	2	1	...	...	141
			2	181	10	8	7	...	1	207
			3	134	7	9	3	...	1	154
			4	179	4	1	...	...	...	184
			5	109	11	4	2	1	1	128
			6	108	1	...	1	...	1	111
			7	89	27	14	3	1	...	134
			8	124	30	18	5	...	3	180
	21	Girgaum ... ... Total ...	...	924	97	59	20	10	5	1,115
			1	211	17	14	4	4	...	250
			2	87	18	6	3	...	...	114
			3	109	17	14	5	3	...	148
			4	52	4	1	...	...	...	57
			5	124	21	11	3	1	1	161
			6	237	15	12	2	1	2	269
			7	104	5	1	3	1	2	116

TABLE XI—*continued.*

CLASSIFICATION OF BUILDINGS BY THE NUMBER OF TENEMENTS.

Ward.	Charge.	Section.	Circle Number.	Number of buildings containing: Ten tenements and under.	Eleven to twenty tenements.	Twenty-one to thirty tenements.	Thirty-one to forty tenements.	Forty-one to fifty tenements.	Over-fifty one tenements.	Total No. of buildings.
D	30	**Chaupati ... ... Total ...**	...	**683**	**39**	**5**	**3**	**1**	...	**731**
			1	75	4	...	2	...	...	81
			2	144	5	...	1	...	...	150
			3	69	11	...	...	...	...	80
			4	99	5	1	...	1	...	106
			5	198	13	4	...	...	...	215
			6	98	1	...	...	...	...	99
	29	**Walkeshwar ... Total ...**	...	**1,190**	**14**	**5**	...	...	...	**1,209**
			1	109	1	...	...	...	...	110
			2	187	4	4	...	...	...	195
			3	229	3	...	...	...	...	232
			4	57	...	...	...	...	...	57
			5	127	...	...	...	...	...	127
			6	249	5	1	...	...	...	255
			7	232	1	...	...	...	...	233
	17	**Mahalaxmi ... Total ...**	...	**1,361**	**68**	**30**	**11**	**4**	**4**	**1,478**
			1	325	2	...	...	...	...	327
			2	87	...	1	...	...	...	88
			3	131	4	...	...	...	...	135
			4	182	7	2	...	...	...	191
			5	98	8	4	1	...	...	111
			6	111	11	4	...	...	1	127
			7	68	10	6	8	3	3	98
			8	86	17	7	1	1	...	112
			9	273	9	6	1	...	...	289
E		**Grand Total for E Ward ...**	...	**6,002**	**779**	**329**	**153**	**91**	**113**	**7,467**
	20	**Tardeo ... ... Total ...**	...	**594**	**64**	**37**	**18**	**11**	**17**	**741**
			1	129	12	5	4	2	2	154
			2	139	19	13	4	2	2	179
			3	224	22	12	7	3	8	276
			4	102	11	7	3	4	5	132
	21	**Kamatipura ... Total ...**	...	**802**	**194**	**63**	**16**	**9**	**9**	**1,093**
			1	194	43	13	5	2	1	258
			2	469	98	27	4	1	...	599
			3	139	53	23	7	6	8	236
	19	**First Nagpada ... Total ...**	...	**57**	**16**	**7**	**7**	**7**	**6**	**100**
			1	51	11	4	4	2	4	76
			2	6	5	3	3	5	2	24
	20	**Second Nagpada ... Total ...**	...	**342**	**94**	**35**	**11**	**10**	**6**	**498**
			1	47	13	15	7	5	2	89
			2	108	26	8	2	2	3	149
			3	127	24	8	...	2	1	162
			4	60	31	4	2	1	...	98
	32	**Byculla ... ... Total ...**	...	**1,831**	**231**	**124**	**63**	**43**	**46**	**2,338**
			1	698	48	23	13	11	26	819
			2	155	17	10	4	1	...	187
			3	390	61	33	15	9	5	513
			4	224	36	15	10	9	5	299
			5	62	17	10	4	2	1	96
			6	151	17	8	3	1	3	183
			7	39	21	8	6	7	4	80
			8	112	14	22	8	3	2	161
	22	**Tadwadi ... ... Total ...**	...	**819**	**55**	**35**	**23**	**9**	**17**	**958**
			1	176	17	10	9	1	6	219
			2	264	4	3	...	...	...	271
			3	379	34	22	14	8	11	468
	23	**Mazagaon ... ... Total ...**	...	**1,557**	**125**	**28**	**15**	**2**	**12**	**1,739**
			1	185	16	4	4	1	3	213
			2	277	13	3	...	...	1	294
			3	168	22	2	2	...	4	198
			4	266	20	7	1	1	2	297
			5	661	54	12	8	0	2	737

TABLE XI—*continued.*

Classification of buildings by the number of tenements.

Ward.	Charge.	Section.	Circle Number.	Number of buildings containing: Ten tenements and under.	Eleven to twenty tenements.	Twenty-one to thirty tenements.	Thirty-one to forty tenements.	Forty-one to fifty tenements.	Over fifty-one tenements.	Total No. of buildings.
F		**Grand Total for F Ward ...**	...	**5,050**	**201**	**93**	**57**	**17**	**32**	**5,450**
	24	**Parel ... ... Total ...**	...	**1,389**	**100**	**67**	**43**	**14**	**29**	**1,642**
			1	17	11	6	7	1	4	46
			2	189	10	10	3	...	7	219
			3	156	22	8	5	...	7	198
			4	43	16	15	9	3	5	91
			5	103	4	...	...	...	...	107
			6	262	12	10	3	4	2	293
			7	70	12	6	8	2	2	100
			8	420	2	8	8	4	2	444
			9	129	11	4	...	...	...	144
	25	**Sewri ... ... Total ...**	...	**1,338**	**43**	**15**	**5**	**1**	**1**	**1,403**
			1	477	7	4	4	1	...	493
			2	218	17	4	...	...	1	240
			3	257	1	...	...	...	...	258
			4	292	17	7	1	...	...	317
			5	94	1	...	...	...	...	95
	26	**Sion ... ... Total ..**	...	**2,323**	**58**	**11**	**9**	**2**	**2**	**2,405**
			1	182	11	4	5	1	...	208
			2	82	5	...	1	...	...	88
			3	230	16	5	1	1	2	255
			4	312	10	1	1	...	...	324
			5	250	3	...	1	...	...	254
			6	295	2	...	...	...	...	297
			7	259	...	...	...	...	...	259
			8	203	6	1	...	...	...	210
			9	144	1	...	...	...	...	145
			10	138	2	...	...	...	...	140
			11	228	2	...	...	...	...	230
G		**Grand Total for G Ward ...**	...	**6,458**	**247**	**113**	**54**	**31**	**25**	**6,928**
	27	**Mahim ... ... Total ...**	...	**3,014**	**40**	**3**	...	...	...	**3,057**
			1	335	7	...	...	...	...	342
			2	413	1	...	...	...	...	414
			3	339	5	2	...	...	...	346
			4	278	3	...	...	...	...	281
			5	507	7	...	...	...	...	514
			6	600	2	...	...	...	...	602
			7	172	2	...	...	...	...	174
			8	370	13	1	...	...	...	384
	28	**Warli ... ... Total ...**	...	**3,444**	**207**	**110**	**54**	**31**	**25**	**3,871**
			1	326	7	1	...	...	...	334
			2	255	29	16	8	6	2	316
			3	86	18	19	5	1	6	135
			4	23	13	6	8	3	1	54
			5	276	28	14	9	13	8	348
			6	646	2	2	...	...	...	650
			7	717	42	27	10	2	6	804
			8	1,115	68	25	14	6	2	1,230

TABLE XII.

CLASSIFICATION OF BUILDINGS BY THE NUMBER OF OCCUPANTS.

NOTE.—The total number of buildings shown in this table does not include temples, churches, schools, dispensaries, theatres, offices, shops, workshops, factories and unoccupied buildings generally.

TABLE XII.

Classification of buildings by the number of occupants.

Ward.	Charge.	Section.	Circle No.	Number of Buildings containing: 20 persons and under.	21 to 40 persons.	41 to 60 persons.	61 to 80 persons.	81 to 100 persons.	101 to 150 persons.	151 to 200 persons.	201 to 250 persons.	251 to 300 persons.	301 to 350 persons.	351 to 400 persons.	401 persons and over.	Total No. of Buildings.
		Grand Total ... Bombay City ...	...	21,096	5,440	2,458	1,240	803	1,066	382	194	85	50	35	53	32,902
A		Grand Total for A Ward.	...	1,570	472	203	69	36	61	9	10	3	4	2	6	2,445
	1	Upper Colaba ...	1	58	10	5	3	...	2	...	1	...	...	...	...	79
	2	Lower Colaba ... Total ...	...	424	96	75	25	13	26	5	5	1	...	1	3	674
			1	88	31	9	2	1	2	1	...	...	...	...	...	134
			2	98	12	3	1	1	4	...	1	...	...	1	1	122
			3	35	15	19	11	2	5	1	...	...	...	...	...	88
			4	29	6	11	1	1	1	1	1	...	...	...	...	51
			5	27	8	5	3	2	2	2	...	1	...	...	1	51
			6	95	8	5	2	2	3	...	2	...	...	...	...	117
			7	25	5	1	...	1	6	...	...	...	...	...	...	38
			8	27	11	22	5	3	3	...	1	...	...	...	1	73
	3	Fort, South ... Total ...	...	208	37	5	2	5	1	...	...	...	...	...	...	258
			1	39	6	1	...	...	...	...	...	...	...	...	...	46
			2	81	16	2	1	...	...	...	...	...	...	...	...	100
			3	46	6	1	...	...	...	...	...	...	...	...	...	53
			4	25	5	1	...	2	...	...	...	...	...	...	...	33
			5	17	4	...	1	3	1	...	...	...	...	...	...	26
	4	Fort, North ... Total ...	...	577	277	87	23	11	21	3	2	2	2	...	...	1,005
			1	114	33	11	1	1	...	...	...	...	...	...	...	160
			2	75	27	4	1	...	...	...	...	...	...	...	...	107
			3	112	35	5	1	1	...	...	...	...	...	...	...	154
			4	68	36	9	4	2	2	...	1	...	...	...	...	122
			5	56	40	12	...	...	...	...	...	...	...	...	...	108
			6	82	56	19	3	1	3	...	...	...	...	...	...	164
			7	26	32	16	10	3	8	1	1	...	...	...	...	97
			8	44	18	11	3	3	8	2	...	2	2	...	...	93
	5	Esplanade ... Total ...	...	303	52	31	16	7	11	1	2	...	2	1	3	429
			1	110	11	4	6	...	4	...	...	...	...	...	...	135
			2	62	11	4	1	1	1	...	...	...	...	...	...	80
			3	97	22	18	8	6	6	1	1	...	2	1	...	162
			4	34	8	5	1	...	...	...	1	...	...	...	3	52
B		Grand Total for B Ward.	...	1,288	668	418	222	138	177	51	23	5	5	2	12	3,009
	7	Chakla ... Total ...	...	314	231	115	46	22	21	3	1	...	...	...	...	753
			1	38	30	13	4	2	2	...	...	...	...	...	...	89
			2	51	35	18	5	1	...	...	...	...	...	...	...	110
			3	51	21	12	5	2	2	...	...	...	...	...	...	93
			4	44	36	27	5	7	7	2	...	...	...	...	...	128
			5	31	33	14	5	2	1	...	...	...	...	...	...	86
			6	14	13	6	4	2	...	...	...	...	...	...	...	39
			7	21	20	6	6	3	3	1	...	...	...	...	...	60
			8	30	15	6	4	...	5	...	1	...	...	...	...	61
			9	34	28	13	8	3	1	...	...	...	...	...	...	87
	6	Mandvi ... Total ...	...	381	154	86	51	38	36	13	4	...	...	...	4	767
			1	41	19	13	6	6	7	1	...	...	...	...	...	93
			2					Demolished.								
			3	28	6	1	1	...	1	1	...	...	...	...	1	39
			4	13	14	14	6	4	5	1	...	...	...	...	...	57
			5	15	13	8	1	2	...	...	...	...	...	...	...	39
			6	12	3	8	4	5	2	...	...	...	...	...	1	35
			7	34	12	8	2	2	...	1	1	...	...	...	...	60
			8	46	7	4	5	1	...	...	...	...	...	...	...	63
			9	64	35	13	9	2	3	...	...	...	...	...	...	126
			10	48	29	10	5	6	4	2	...	...	...	...	...	104
			11	33	10	7	10	9	9	6	3	...	...	...	...	87
			12	47	6	...	2	1	5	1	...	...	...	...	2	64
	8	Umarkhadi ... Total ...	...	385	212	147	80	42	67	18	7	3	4	2	7	974
			1	20	22	14	7	5	8	6	2	...	1	1	...	86
			2	13	10	8	5	1	6	...	1	...	...	...	...	44
			3	21	29	24	8	3	9	1	...	...	...	...	...	95
			4	16	4	2	2	2	3	1	1	...	...	1	5	37
			5	13	17	18	6	3	4	...	...	...	...	...	...	61
			6	29	8	9	5	5	1	1	...	...	...	...	...	58
			7	44	34	21	7	7	7	1	...	...	...	...	...	121
			8	69	38	27	15	8	7	3	...	...	1	...	...	168
			9	103	25	8	9	2	4	...	1	3	1	...	1	157
			10	57	25	16	16	6	18	5	2	...	1	...	1	147

TABLE XII—*continued.*

Classification of buildings by the number of occupants.

Ward.	Charge.	Section.	Circle No.	Number of Buildings containing 20 persons and under.	21 to 40 persons.	41 to 60 persons.	61 to 80 persons.	81 to 100 persons.	101 to 150 persons.	151 to 200 persons.	201 to 250 persons.	251 to 300 persons.	301 to 350 persons.	351 to 400 persons.	401 persons and over.	Total No. of Buildings.
B	9	Dongri ... Total ...	...	208	71	70	45	36	53	17	11	2	1	...	1	515
			1	25	21	22	10	10	11	5	1	1	...	...	...	106
			2	44	26	32	22	20	28	9	4	...	1	...	...	186
			3	68	18	10	5	4	8	2	6	1	...	...	1	123
			4	71	6	6	8	2	6	1	...	...	...	...	...	100
C		Grand Total for C Ward.	...	2,309	1,330	659	346	191	197	49	26	11	4	6	5	5,133
	10	Market ... Total ...	...	443	228	127	58	24	30	7	5	...	1	...	1	929
			1	36	13	9	8	3	6	3	3	...	1	...	...	82
			2	18	9	2	2	1	3	2	1	...	...	...	...	38
			3	41	9	4	3	3	2	1	...	...	...	...	...	66
			4	37	12	14	6	3	3	...	...	...	...	...	...	75
			5	66	51	31	16	4	8	...	...	...	...	...	1	177
			6	81	40	31	8	3	3	...	...	...	...	...	...	166
			7	63	27	11	8	3	4	1	1	...	...	...	...	118
			8	103	67	25	7	4	1	...	...	...	...	...	...	207
	11	Dhobi Talao ... Total ...	...	535	331	131	63	31	31	10	2	2	...	3	3	1,145
			1	161	76	15	10	3	6	2	...	...	...	...	...	273
			2	34	23	6	2	1	2	...	...	...	...	3	3	74
			3	73	43	15	5	3	6	2	...	1	...	...	...	150
			4	54	33	24	18	9	6	2	1	...	...	...	...	147
			5	34	35	16	8	2	4	2	...	...	...	...	...	101
			6	62	54	21	10	4	4	2	1	1	...	...	...	159
			7	117	65	34	13	9	3	...	...	...	...	...	...	241
	12	Fanaswadi ... Total ...	...	383	175	64	43	30	37	12	9	3	...	1	...	769
			1	173	72	20	14	6	9	4	4	...	...	1	...	303
			2	125	55	28	11	14	18	4	4	1	...	...	...	260
			3	88	48	16	18	10	10	4	1	2	...	...	...	197
	13	Bhuleshwar ... Total ...	...	507	297	151	71	42	33	8	4	...	1	...	...	1,114
			1	81	38	27	5	8	7	1	1	...	...	...	...	168
			2	57	22	17	10	6	9	5	1	...	1	...	...	128
			3	62	14	12	10	2	3	1	...	...	...	...	...	104
			4	114	99	42	25	13	9	...	1	...	...	...	...	303
			5	120	75	31	13	7	4	1	...	...	...	...	...	251
			6	73	40	22	8	6	1	...	1	...	...	...	...	160
	14	Kumbharwada - Total ...	...	228	152	92	55	34	40	8	6	3	2	1	..	621
			1	109	76	24	17	4	8	2	...	...	...	...	...	240
			2	69	49	44	23	14	11	1	3	1	2	...	...	217
			3	25	19	15	9	9	8	2	...	1	...	1	...	89
			4	25	8	9	6	7	13	3	3	1	...	...	...	75
	15	Khara Talao .. Total ...	...	205	147	94	53	30	26	4	...	3	...	1	1	564
			1	47	16	10	11	4	6	2	...	...	...	1	...	97
			2	28	14	11	3	5	2	...	...	1	...	...	...	64
			3	47	37	26	15	9	10	2	...	...	...	...	...	146
			4	42	40	23	9	7	4	...	...	1	...	...	...	126
			5	41	40	24	15	5	4	...	...	1	...	...	1	131
D		Grand Total for D Ward.	...	3,373	800	285	130	82	145	39	14	5	4	1	1	4,879
	16	Khetwadi ... Total ...	...	622	248	89	46	33	46	12	3	1	2	...	...	1,102
			1	88	18	10	7	1	1	1	1	...	...	...	...	125
			2	85	55	10	5	3	9	4	1	...	...	...	...	172
			3	77	33	12	6	5	8	1	...	...	...	...	...	142
			4	113	23	11	3	1	1	...	...	...	...	...	...	152
			5	66	31	10	2	4	6	2	...	...	...	...	...	121
			6	54	39	6	1	...	1	...	...	1	...	...	..	102
			7	58	23	18	7	10	10	1	...	...	...	...	...	127
			8	81	28	12	15	9	10	3	1	...	2	...	...	161
	31	Girgaum ... Total ...	...	533	291	82	38	28	53	10	9	...	2	...	...	961
			1	98	30	17	6	6	15	2	3	...	...	...	...	177
			2	42	18	15	11	11	1	...	1	...	...	...	...	99
			3	63	42	10	8	4	12	5	2	...	...	...	...	146
			4	32	10	4	...	1	2	...	...	...	...	...	...	49
			5	81	37	10	7	5	9	1	1	...	...	...	...	151
			6	158	43	20	3	1	10	1	1	...	1	...	...	238
			7	64	21	6	3	...	4	1	1	...	1	...	...	101

TABLE XII—*continued.*

Classification of buildings by the number of occupants.

Ward.	Charge.	Section.	Circle No.	Number of Buildings containing: 20 persons and under.	21 to 40 persons.	41 to 60 persons.	61 to 80 persons.	81 to 100 persons.	101 to 150 persons.	151 to 200 persons.	201 to 250 persons.	251 to 300 persons.	301 to 350 persons.	351 to 400 persons.	401 persons and over.	Total No. of buildings.
D	30	Chaupati ... Total ...	...	423	101	37	11	6	13	...	1	...	...	...	...	592
			1	57	4	5	3	2	1	...	...	...	...	...	...	72
			2	94	14	6	...	1	2	...	...	...	...	...	...	117
			3	39	20	5	1	2	3	...	...	...	...	...	...	70
			4	62	12	4	2	...	2	...	1	...	...	...	...	83
			5	123	30	15	5	1	4	...	...	...	...	...	...	187
			6	48	12	2	...	...	1	...	...	...	...	...	...	63
	32	Walkeshwar . Total ...	...	872	83	14	5	5	1	...	1	...	...	...	1	982
			1	64	21	6	1	1	...	...	...	...	...	...	...	93
			2	138	14	2	3	1	1	...	1	...	...	...	...	160
			3	167	21	2	...	...	...	...	...	...	...	...	...	190
			4	53	...	...	...	...	...	...	...	...	...	...	...	53
			5	110	5	...	...	...	...	...	...	...	...	...	...	115
			6	180	17	4	...	2	...	...	...	...	...	...	1	204
			7	160	5	...	1	1	...	...	...	...	...	...	...	167
	17	Mahalaxmi ... Total ...	...	918	167	63	30	10	32	17	...	4	...	1	...	1,242
			1	207	26	1	...	...	...	1	...	...	...	...	...	235
			2	53	9	...	1	...	...	...	...	...	...	...	...	63
			3	93	13	1	...	...	...	...	...	...	...	...	...	107
			4	127	26	7	4	...	2	1	...	...	...	...	...	167
			5	55	18	5	4	...	6	1	...	...	...	...	...	89
			6	71	32	12	4	3	5	2	...	1	...	...	...	130
			7	47	9	9	7	3	7	9	...	2	...	1	...	94
			8	49	11	11	6	2	6	2	...	1	...	...	...	88
			9	216	23	17	4	2	6	1	...	...	...	...	...	269
E		Grand Total for E Ward.	...	3,855	1,020	536	289	219	283	137	63	32	18	15	17	6,484
	20	Tardeo ... Total ..	...	363	100	54	26	22	34	16	11	6	3	4	4	643
			1	84	40	8	3	5	5	3	...	1	...	...	...	149
			2	84	27	26	10	6	11	3	3	...	...	...	1	171
			3	123	22	9	9	6	10	7	5	3	3	2	2	201
			4	72	11	11	4	5	8	3	3	2	...	2	1	122
	21	Kamatipura ... Total ...	...	508	238	96	66	40	41	15	4	4	2	...	3	1,017
			1	120	49	26	14	11	12	3	...	...	1	...	...	236
			2	312	147	56	32	13	10	...	1	...	..	...	...	576
			3	76	42	14	20	11	19	12	3	4	1	...	3	205
	18	First Nagpada. Total ...	...	39	8	3	9	6	7	10	2	1	...	2	1	88
			1	36	6	3	4	4	4	4	2	1	...	...	1	65
			2	3	2	...	5	2	3	6	...	...	...	2	...	23
	19	Second Nagpada . Total.	...	143	151	82	22	23	38	12	3	...	2	...	1	477
			1	26	8	4	3	7	21	6	1	...	2	...	1	79
			2	51	46	23	5	8	8	3	1	...	...	...	...	145
			3	44	61	34	7	6	4	2	...	...	...	...	...	158
			4	22	36	21	7	2	5	1	1	...	...	...	...	95
	32	Byculla ... Total ...	...	1,148	250	157	93	82	104	49	22	15	8	7	6	1,941
			1	397	64	22	19	21	25	15	10	5	2	4	4	588
			2	106	23	16	11	9	7	...	1	...	...	...	...	172
			3	280	69	48	26	15	25	7	3	3	1	...	...	471
			4	154	35	30	6	7	19	6	3	3	1	1	1	266
			5	36	13	7	9	9	4	3	...	...	1	1	...	83
			6	104	22	11	6	9	6	4	1	1	1	1	...	166
			7	20	14	13	8	3	5	9	6	1	2	...	...	80
			8	51	10	16	8	9	13	5	...	2	...	...	1	115
	22	Tadwadi ... Total ...	...	662	94	51	29	19	30	24	13	2	3	2	2	931
			1	184	28	16	9	5	7	13	4	...	1	1	1	219
			2	224	25	11	2	2	1	...	...	1	...	...	...	266
			3	304	41	24	18	12	22	11	9	1	2	1	1	446
	23	Mazagaon ... Total ...	...	992	179	93	44	27	29	11	8	4	...	...	...	1,387
			1	138	30	15	3	4	6	2	...	2	...	...	...	200
			2	135	38	13	9	4	1	...	1	...	...	...	...	201
			3	91	26	11	8	4	3	1	4	...	...	...	...	148
			4	199	34	10	2	2	8	1	1	...	...	...	...	257
			5	429	51	44	22	13	11	7	3	2	...	...	...	581

TABLE XII—*continued.*

Classification of buildings by the number of occupants.

Ward.	Charge.	Section.	Circle No.	Number of Buildings containing: 20 persons and under.	21 to 40 persons.	41 to 60 persons.	61 to 80 persons.	81 to 100 persons.	101 to 150 persons.	151 to 200 persons.	201 to 250 persons.	251 to 300 persons.	301 to 350 persons.	351 to 400 persons.	401 persons and over.	Total No. of buildings.
F		**Grand Total for F Ward.**	...	**3,830**	**545**	**186**	**87**	**57**	**94**	**43**	**18**	**9**	**5**	**6**	**6**	**4,886**
	24	**Parel ... Total**	...	**901**	**165**	**68**	**32**	**38**	**67**	**35**	**15**	**7**	**5**	**4**	**6**	**1,343**
			1	8	7	3	3	7	6	8	4	1	1	...	...	43
			2	108	11	3	2	2	14	2	2	1	...	2	2	149
			3	96	23	18	6	8	3	6	1	...	2	...	3	166
			4	21	11	13	3	8	14	9	3	...	...	1	...	83
			5	59	6	1	3	1	...	...	...	1	...	...	...	71
			6	173	37	14	7	4	7	4	2	1	1	1	...	251
			7	44	7	3	3	3	9	8	1	...	...	...	1	79
			8	302	35	6	4	1	12	3	2	3	1	...	...	369
			9	90	28	7	1	4	2	...	...	...	...	...	...	132
	25	**Sewri ... Total**	...	**995**	**163**	**54**	**18**	**7**	**14**	**2**	**2**	...	...	**1**	...	**1,256**
			1	331	54	17	4	2	5	1	2	...	...	...	...	416
			2	157	30	11	6	3	2	...	...	...	...	1	...	210
			3	222	11	2	1	..	...	...	...	...	...	...	...	236
			4	213	55	18	6	1	7	1	...	...	...	...	...	301
			5	72	13	6	1	1	...	...	...	...	...	...	...	93
	26	**Sion ... Total**	..	**1,934**	**217**	**64**	**37**	**12**	**13**	**6**	**1**	**2**	...	**1**	...	**2,287**
			1	145	23	8	5	6	5	1	1	...	...	1	...	194
			2	66	7	8	1	...	1	...	...	...	...	...	...	83
			3	178	38	9	8	3	4	3	...	2	...	...	...	245
			4	247	39	13	6	3	1	...	...	...	...	...	...	309
			5	215	12	3	5	...	...	1	...	...	...	...	...	236
			6	271	23	3	2	...	1	...	...	...	...	...	...	300
			7	202	16	8	4	...	1	...	...	...	...	...	...	231
			8	154	32	6	5	1	...	1	...	...	...	...	...	199
			9	125	10	1	...	...	...	...	...	...	...	...	...	136
			10	120	9	2	1	...	...	...	...	...	...	...	...	132
			11	211	8	3	...	...	...	...	...	...	...	...	...	222
G		**Grand Total for G Ward.**	...	**4,871**	**605**	**171**	**97**	**80**	**109**	**54**	**40**	**20**	**10**	**3**	**6**	**6,066**
	27	**Mahim ... Total**	...	**2,451**	**265**	**53**	**13**	**6**	**1**	**1**	...	...	...	...	...	**2,790**
			1	229	23	7	1	...	...	...	...	...	...	...	...	260
			2	348	22	4	...	...	...	...	...	...	...	...	...	374
			3	242	32	6	...	1	1	...	...	...	...	...	...	282
			4	256	15	1	2	...	...	...	...	...	...	...	...	274
			5	448	46	7	...	...	...	...	...	...	...	...	...	501
			6	527	51	7	...	...	...	...	...	...	...	...	...	585
			7	143	17	3	3	1	...	...	...	...	...	...	...	167
			8	258	59	18	7	4	...	1	...	...	...	...	...	347
	28	**Warli ... Total**	...	**2,420**	**340**	**118**	**84**	**74**	**108**	**53**	**40**	**20**	**10**	**3**	**6**	**3,276**
			1	232	14	8	2	2	...	1	...	...	...	...	...	259
			2	152	26	14	17	5	18	13	1	5	...	1	1	253
			3	64	14	8	4	8	16	5	8	3	1	...	2	133
			4	13	4	7	3	6	6	6	4	2	...	...	1	52
			5	163	25	16	9	14	18	10	8	5	3	1	1	273
			6	583	39	1	1	1	3	...	...	...	...	...	...	628
			7	425	73	22	19	17	25	6	11	2	3	...	...	603
			8	788	145	42	29	21	22	12	8	3	3	1	1	1,075

TABLE XIII.

DISTRIBUTION OF PERSONS BY ROOMS.

TABLE XIII.

Distribution of persons by rooms.

Ward.	Charge.	Section	Circle No.	Total number of persons living in rooms each occupied by				Total population	Number of occupied buildings.	Average population per inhabited building.
				5 persons and under.	6 to 9 persons.	10 to 19 persons.	20 persons and over.			
		Grand Total, Bombay City ...	...	627,387	189,782	81,650	30,263	929,082	32,992	28·24
A		Grand Total, for A Ward ...	...	40,919	11,138	5,416	10,103	67,576	2,445	27·64
	1	Upper Colaba	1	552	543	261	137	1,493	79	18·89
	2	Lower Colaba ... Total ...	...	12,248	4,154	1,934	1,341	19,677	674	29·19
			1	2,044	287	144	49	2,524	134	18·84
			2	1,241	783	373	371	2,768	122	22·69
			3	2,214	916	351	23	3,504	88	39·82
			4	772	434	379	22	1,607	51	31·51
			5	1,362	722	356	...	2,440	51	47·84
			6	1,495	346	101	221	2,163	117	18·49
			7	594	323	150	98	1,165	38	30·66
			8	2,526	343	80	557	3,506	73	46·66
	3	Fort South ... Total ...	...	2,293	652	381	134	3,460	258	13·41
			1	365	66	95	...	526	46	11·43
			2	691	195	150	84	1,120	100	11·20
			3	313	122	37	24	526	53	9·92
			4	449	42	45	26	562	33	17·03
			5	445	227	54	...	726	26	27·92
	4	Fort North ... Total ...	...	21,568	2,775	905	152	25,400	1,005	25·27
			1	2,487	156	36	...	2,679	160	16·74
			2	1,700	63	24	...	1,787	107	16·70
			3	2,487	127	50	...	2,664	154	17·29
			4	2,799	316	61	...	3,176	122	26·03
			5	2,130	84	22	30	2,266	108	20·98
			6	3,447	382	155	122	4,106	164	25·04
			7	3,870	432	66	...	4,368	97	45·03
			8	2,648	1,215	491	...	4,354	93	46·82
	5	Esplanade ... ... Total ...	...	4,258	3,014	1,935	8,339	17,546	429	40·89
			1	858	710	486	116	2,170	135	16·07
			2	386	277	318	112	1,093	80	13·66
			3	2,520	1,683	933	153	5,298	162	32·70
			4	485	344	198	7,958	8,985	52	17·28
B		Grand Total, for B Ward ...	...	87,238	26,854	9,891	2,683	126,666	3,009	42·15
	6	Chakla ... ... Total ...	...	16,074	5,491	2,392	274	24,231	753	32·22
			1	1,542	740	341	65	2,688	89	30·20
			2	2,180	457	176	35	2,848	110	25·89
			3	1,980	442	147	...	2,569	93	27·92
			4	3,602	961	310	21	4,894	128	38·23
			5	1,378	741	475	25	2,619	86	30·45
			6	780	320	117	45	1,268	39	32·51
			7	1,510	621	262	...	2,393	60	39·88
			8	1,665	423	124	...	2,212	61	36·26
			9	1,437	780	440	83	2,740	87	31·49
	7	Mandvi ... ... Total ...	...	22,729	4,770	2,337	632	30,468	767	39·72
			1	2,474	733	265	45	3,517	93	37·82
			2			Demolished.				
			3	1,024	194	25	25	1,268	39	32·51
			4	2,221	412	191	21	2,845	57	49·91
			5	981	104	69	...	1,154	39	29·59
			6	3,621	1,119	452	98	5,290	35	151·14
			7	1,195	206	268	25	1,694	60	28·23
			8	898	183	52	22	1,155	63	18·33
			9	2,301	659	383	22	3,365	126	26·71
			10	2,899	367	232	...	3,498	104	33·63
			11	4,127	689	358	23	5,197	87	59·74
			12	988	104	42	351	1,485	64	23·05
	8	Umarkhadi ... ... Total ...	...	30,724	9,885	3,583	1,487	45,679	974	46·89
			1	3,800	1,419	276	159	5,654	[illegible]	[illegible]5·74
			2	1,138	488	497	92	2,215	[illegible]	[illegible]0·34
			3	2,932	1,031	368	27	4,358	[illegible]	[illegible]5·87
			4	3,633	530	75	81	4,319	37	116·74
			5	1,789	636	252	24	2,701	61	44·28
			6	1,352	[illegible]04	229	22	2,107	58	[illegible]6·33
			7	3,371	973	194	83	4,621	17[illegible]	[illegible]8·19
			8	4,224	1,536	493	264	6,517	[illegible]	38·79
			9	3,350	1,036	542	216	5,144	157	32·76
			10	5,135	1,732	657	519	8,043	147	54·71

TABLE XIII—*continued.*

Distribution of persons by rooms.

Ward.	Charge.	Section.	Circle No.	Total number of persons living in rooms each occupied by 5 persons and under.	6 to 9 persons.	10 to 19 persons.	20 persons and over.	Total population.	Number of occupied buildings.	Average population per inhabited building.
B	9	**Dongri ... ... Total ...**	...	**17.711**	**6.708**	**1.579**	**290**	**26.288**	**515**	**51·04**
			1	4,483	1,513	226	21	6,243	106	58 89
			2	8,894	2,778	436	23	12,131	186	65·22
			3	3,058	1,795	540	146	5,539	123	45·03
			4	1,276	622	377	100	2,375	100	23·75
C		**Grand Total, for C Ward ...**	...	**136,186**	**27.838**	**14.070**	**4.950**	**183.044**	**5.133**	**35·66**
	10	**Market .. ... Total ...**	...	**23,706**	**3,468**	**1,987**	**788**	**29.949**	**929**	**32·24**
			1	2,792	441	432	302	3,967	82	48·38
			2	1,432	196	180	...	1,808	38	47·[illegible]8
			3	998	307	71	221	1,597	66	24·19
			4	1,986	265	122	22	2,395	75	31·93
			5	5,689	676	246	22	6,633	177	38·04
			6	3,638	530	353	68	4,589	166	27·54
			7	2,921	382	221	87	3,611	118	30 60
			8	4,250	671	362	66	5,349	207	25·84
	11	**Dhobi Talao ... ... Total ...**	...	**29,051**	**5.419**	**3.076**	**1.138**	**38.684**	**1.145**	**33·79**
			1	4,903	1,028	865	143	6,939	273	19·59
			2	3,696	594	209	...	4,499	74	60 79
			3	3,657	907	346	22	4,932	150	32·88
			4	4,493	949	469	230	6,141	147	41·78
			5	2,517	744	383	61	3,705	101	36·68
			6	4,290	611	311	521	5,733	159	36·06
			7	5,495	586	493	161	6,735	241	27·95
	12	**Fanaswadi ... ... Total ...**	...	**18.460**	**5,048**	**3,250**	**645**	**27.403**	**760**	**36·06**
			1	5,820	1,637	1,384	483	9,324	303	30·77
			2	7,521	1,754	953	106	10,334	260	39·75
			3	5,119	1,657	913	56	7,745	197	39·32
	13	**Bhuleshwar ... Total ...**	...	**27.846**	**5.254**	**2.178**	**1.179**	**36,457**	**1.114**	**32·73**
			1	4,620	417	223	289	5,549	168	33·03
			2	4,555	655	256	...	5,466	128	196·21
			3	2,281	506	338	46	3,171	104	30·49
			4	6,893	2,059	833	637	10,422	303	34·39
			5	5,428	1,217	372	207	7,224	251	28·78
			6	4,069	400	156	...	4,625	160	28·91
	14	**Kumbharwada ... Total ..**	...	**20.316**	**4.650**	**2.315**	**334**	**27.615**	**821**	**34 81**
			1	6.642	1,102	471	49	7,264	240	30·27
			2	7,048	2,128	975	123	10,274	217	47·35
			3	4,043	491	322	58	4.914	89	55·21
			4	3,583	929	547	104	5,163	75	68·84
	15	**Khara Talao ... Total ...**	...	**16,897**	**3.999**	**1.264**	**866**	**22.936**	**564**	**40·67**
			1	3.141	621	143	53	3,958	97	40·80
			2	1,766	464	136	22	2,388	64	37·31
			3	4.352	1,160	434	351	6,297	146	43·13
			4	3.205	920	281	142	4,548	126	36 09
			5	4,343	834	270	298	5,745	131	43·85
D		**Grand Total, for D Ward ...**	...	**77.794**	**21.909**	**8.413**	**2.831**	**110.947**	**4.879**	**22·74**
	16	**Khetwadi ... ... Total ...**	...	**23.149**	**5.657**	**2.344**	**784**	**31.934**	**1.102**	**28·98**
			1	1,917	452	151	217	2,737	125	21·89
			2	4,869	864	215	20	5,468	172	31·79
			3	2,728	624	580	386	4,318	142	30·41
			4	2,332	214	10	78	2,634	152	17·33
			5	2,623	676	275	...	3,574	121	29·54
			6	1,795	388	184	...	2,367	102	23·21
			7	3,284	878	367	38	4,567	127	35·96
			8	4,101	1,561	562	45	6,269	161	38·94
	31	**Girgaum ... Total ...**	...	**21.962**	**6 294**	**1.986**	**489**	**30,711**	**961**	**31·96**
			1	3,779	1,646	659	42	6,126	177	34·61
			2	2.767	791	211	...	3,769	99	38·7
			3	3,482	1,765	453	289	5,929	146	40·61
			4	755	191	124	53	1,123	49	22·92
			5	4.263	467	30	62	4,822	151	31·[illegible]7
			6	4,760	1,001	319	...	6,080	238	22·55
			7	2,206	443	170	43	2,862	101	28·34

TABLE XIII—*continued.*

Distribution of persons by rooms.

Ward.	Charge.	Section.	Circle No.	Total number of persons living in rooms each occupied by: 5 persons and under.	6 to 9 persons.	10 to 19 persons.	20 persons and over.	Total population.	Number of occupied buildings.	Average population per inhabited building.
D.	30	**Chaupati ... Total ...**	...	**9.060**	**1.650**	**570**	**89**	**11.369**	**592**	**19·20**
			1	988	220	20	44	1,272	72	17·67
			2	1,454	255	49	...	1,758	117	15·03
			3	1,268	386	173	20	1,847	70	26·39
			4	1,212	251	155	...	1,618	83	19·49
			5	3,386	458	86	...	3,930	187	21·02
			6	752	80	87	25	944	63	14·98
	29	**Walkeshwar ... Total ...**	...	**6,357**	**2.306**	**1,266**	**702**	**10.631**	**982**	**10·83**
			1	616	442	347	186	1,591	93	17·11
			2	1,330	493	216	93	2,132	160	13·32
			3	1,035	353	317	118	1,873	190	9·86
			4	188	70	14	...	272	53	5·17
			5	706	114	15	...	835	115	7·26
			6	1,579	652	290	173	2,694	204	13·20
			7	853	182	67	132	1,234	167	7·39
	17	**Mahalaxmi ... ... Total ...**	...	**17.286**	**6.002**	**2,267**	**767**	**26.302**	**1.242**	**21·18**
			1	1,881	406	222	86	2,595	235	11·04
			2	616	92	36	...	744	63	11·81
			3	881	153	22	...	1,056	107	9·87
			4	1,904	706	207	...	2,817	167	16·87
			5	1,561	499	236	69	2,365	89	26·57
			6	1,935	1,003	502	416	3,856	130	29·66
			7	3,477	1,485	208	70	5,240	94	55·74
			8	2,096	712	323	97	3,228	88	36·68
			9	2,915	946	511	29	4,401	269	16·36
E.		**Grand Total for Ward E. ...**	...	**1,44,694**	**52.297**	**22.981**	**6.260**	**2,26,232**	**6.484**	**34·89**
	20	**Tardeo ... ... Total ...**	...	**15,352**	**7,254**	**4,403**	**714**	**27,723**	**643**	**43·12**
			1	2,623	1,035	510	138	4,306	149	28·89
			2	3,289	2,487	1,057	198	7,031	171	41·19
			3	5,328	2,779	2,070	209	10,386	201	51·67
			4	4,112	953	766	169	6,000	122	49·18
	21	**Kamatipura ... Total ...**	...	**24.694**	**7,585**	**3,687**	**645**	**36.611**	**1,017**	**35·99**
			1	5,883	1,619	663	194	7,859	236	33·30
			2	11,812	2,958	853	119	15,742	576	27·33
			3	7,499	3,008	2,171	332	13,010	205	63·46
	18	**First Nagpada ... Total ...**	...	**5,090**	**820**	**483**	**21**	**6,414**	**88**	**72·89**
			1	3,042	361	208	21	3,632	65	55·88
			2	2,048	459	275	...	2,782	23	120·96
	19	**Second Nagpada ... Total ...**	...	**14.573**	**4.502**	**1,884**	**741**	**21.700**	**477**	**45·49**
			1	3,973	1,306	579	309	6,167	79	78·06
			2	3,950	1,045	453	340	5,788	145	39·92
			3	4,206	1,084	485	20	5,795	158	36·68
			4	2,444	1,067	367	72	3,950	95	41·58
	33	**Byculla ... Total ...**	...	**49.597**	**18.140**	**6.355**	**1.215**	**75.307**	**1.941**	**7·89**
			1	6,921	2,703	827	271	10,722	206	83·09
			2	2,949	830	844	224	4,847	172	28·18
			3	11,119	2,905	1,063	194	15,281	471	32·44
			4	13,961	5,667	21,89	287	22,104	588	18·23
			5	2,830	1,079	237	...	4,146	83	49·95
			6	3,518	1,778	418	126	5,835	166	35·15
			7	4,026	1,787	415	52	6,280	80	78·50
			8	4,278	1,391	362	61	6,092	115	52·97

TABLE XIII—*continued.*

Distribution of persons by rooms.

Ward.	Charge.	Section.	Circle No.	Total number of persons living in rooms each occupied by: 5 persons and under.	5 to 9 persons.	10 to 19 persons.	20 persons and over.	Total population.	Number of occupied buildings.	Average population per inhabited building.
	22	**Tadwadi ... Total ...**	...	**16,298**	**7,989**	**3,417**	**709**	**28,413**	**931**	**31·12**
			1	5,003	2,942	1,087	381	9,413	219	42·98
			2	2,075	786	587	28	3,476	266	13·07
			3	9,220	4,261	1,743	300	15,524	446	34·81
	23	**Mazagaon ... Total ...**	...	**19,090**	**6,007**	**2,752**	**2,215**	**30,064**	**1,387**	**21·68**
			1	3,286	789	435	268	4,780	200	23·90
			2	2,569	668	532	288	4,057	201	20·81
			3	2,626	791	413	366	4,196	148	28 35
			4	3,042	1,051	377	73	4,543	257	17·68
			5	7,565	2,708	995	1,220	12,488	581	21·49
F.		**Grant Total for Ward F. ...**	...	**66,069**	**19,843**	**7,218**	**1,768**	**94,898**	**4,886**	**19·42**
	24	**Parel ... ... Total ...**	...	**32,845**	**9,226**	**2,762**	**383**	**45,216**	**1,343**	**33·67**
			1	2,841	960	209	...	4,010	43	93·26
			2	3,807	1,549	357	67	5,780	149	38·79
			3	4,958	1,455	457	46	6,916	166	41·66
			4	4,890	1,528	115	...	6,533	83	78·71
			5	663	109	58	...	830	71	11·69
			6	5,198	1,209	378	22	6,807	251	27·12
			7	3,334	640	325	...	4,299	79	*54·42
			8	4,961	1,313	800	248	7,322	369	19·84
			9	2,193	463	63	...	2,719	132	20·59
	25	**Sewri .. ... Total ...**	...	**12,063**	**4,460**	**2,050**	**459**	**19,032**	**1,256**	**15·15**
			1	3,636	1,716	866	235	6,453	416	15·51
			2	2,872	764	236	...	3,872	210	18·44
			3	1,206	537	126	...	1,869	236	7·92
			4	3,981	1,176	518	...	5,675	301	18·85
			5	368	267	304	224	1,163	93	12·51
	26	**Sion ... ... Total ...**	...	**21,161**	**6,157**	**2,406**	**926**	**30,650**	**2,287**	**13·40**
			1	2,907	823	299	111	4,140	194	21·34
			2	1,105	185	...	...	1,290	83	15·54
			3	3,415	1,218	491	...	5,124	245	20·91
			4	3,229	786	353	58	4,426	309	14·52
			5	1,936	282	90	112	2,420	236	10·25
			6	2,136	628	228	...	2,992	300	9·97
			7	1,277	469	326	559	2,631	231	11·39
			8	1,848	855	431	86	3,215	199	16·31
			9	927	192	29	...	1,148	136	8·41
			10	1,047	197	68	...	1,312	132	9·94
			11	1,339	523	91	...	1,952	222	8·79
G.		**Grand Total for Ward G. ...**	...	**74,487**	**29,903**	**13,661**	**1,668**	**119,719**	**6,056**	**19·73**
	27	**Mahim ... Total ...**	...	**21,798**	**6,214**	**2,098**	**143**	**30,253**	**2,790**	**10·84**
			1	1,907	606	112	...	2,625	260	10·09
			2	2,926	587	202	...	3,715	374	9·93
			3	2,423	729	266	22	3,440	282	12·19
			4	1,637	562	114	...	2,313	274	8·44
			5	4,021	689	300	58	5,068	501	10·12
			6	4,155	1,155	515	...	5,825	585	9·95
			7	1,279	480	127	...	1,886	167	11·29
			8	3,450	1,406	462	63	5,381	347	15·51
	28	**Warli ... ... Total ...**	...	**52,689**	**23,689**	**11,563**	**1,525**	**89,466**	**3,276**	**27,31**
			1	1,368	916	233	168	2,685	259	10·37
			2	7,170	2,306	1,003	285	10,764	253	42·55
			3	4,193	3,160	1,805	32	9,190	133	69·09
			4	2,793	1,594	404	21	4,812	52	92·54
			5	8,779	3,034	1,333	181	13,327	273	48·82
			6	3,836	1,266	617	147	5,866	628	9·34
			7	9,536	5,320	2,244	312	17,412	603	28,88
			8	15,014	6,093	3,924	379	25,410	1,075	23·64

TABLE XIV.

TABLE SHOWING THE NUMBER OF TENEMENTS PER INHABITED HOUSE.

TABLE XIV.

Table showing the number of tenements per inhabited house.

Ward.	Charge.	Section.	Circle Number.	Tenements with	Total Number of occupied tenements of each class.	Percentage of each class of tenements to total tenements.	Total Number of occupants of each class of tenements.	Percentage borne by population in each class of tenements to total population.	Average Number of occupants per room in each class of tenements.
				Total ...	200,308	...	*929,082	...	...
	...	Grand Total for Bombay City ...	...	1 Room ...	166,337	83·04	743,247	79·99	4·47
				2 Rooms ...	19,412	9·19	92,109	9·90	2·38
				3 Rooms ...	6,122	3·06	33,055	3·56	1·80
				4 Rooms ...	3,799	1·89	23,375	2·50	1·54
				5 Rooms ...	1,964	·98	14,014	1·51	1·43
				6 Rooms and over.	2,674	1·33	23,282	2·51	1·45
				Total ...	13,308	...	67,576	...	...
A.	...	Total for A Ward.	...	1 Room ...	9,197	69·14	47,716	70·61	5·19
				2 Rooms ...	1,761	13·23	7,164	10·60	2·03
				3 Rooms ...	894	6·72	4,221	6·25	1·57
				4 Rooms ...	598	4·49	2,974	4·40	1·24
				5 Rooms ...	333	2·50	1,829	2·71	1·10
				6 Rooms and over.	525	3·94	3,672	5·43	1·17
				Total ...	316	...	1,493	...	...
	1	Upper Colaba ...	1	1 Room ...	260	82·28	1,194	79·97	4·59
				2 Rooms ...	19	6·01	171	11·45	4·50
				3 Rooms ...	10	3·16	45	3·01	1·50
				4 Rooms ...	12	3·80	40	2·68	·83
				5 Rooms ...	7	2·22	14	·94	·40
				6 Rooms and over.	8	2·53	29	1·94	·60
				Total ...	4,655	...	19,677	...	...
		Total for Lower Colaba ...	...	1 Room ...	3,194	78·77	15,920	80·91	4·98
				2 Rooms ...	163	4·02	761	3·87	2·33
				3 Rooms ...	148	3·65	507	2·53	1·14
				4 Rooms ...	178	4·39	696	3·54	·98
				5 Rooms ...	152	3·75	670	3·40	·89
				6 Rooms and over.	220	5·43	1,123	5·71	·85
				Total ...	655	...	2,524	...	...
	2	Lower Colaba ...	1	1 Room ...	439	65·50	1,206	47·78	2·74
				2 Rooms ...	30	4·58	119	4·75	1·98
				3 Rooms ...	24	3·66	64	2·54	·89
				4 Rooms ...	34	5·19	175	6·93	1·29
				5 Rooms ...	51	7·78	220	8·72	·86
				6 Rooms and over.	77	11·76	740	29·32	1·60
				Total ...	505	...	2,768	...	...
		" ...	2	1 Room ...	439	84·95	2,405	86·89	5·48
				2 Rooms ...	11	2·18	46	1·66	2·09
				3 Rooms ...	5	·99	24	·87	1·60
				4 Rooms ...	14	2·77	62	2·24	1·11
				5 Rooms ...	7	1·39	33	1·19	·94
				6 Rooms and over.	29	5·74	198	7·15	1·14
				Total ...	629	...	3,504	...	...
		" ...	3	1 Room ...	555	88·24	3,145	89·44	5·67
				2 Rooms ...	45	7·15	199	5·65	2·21
				3 Rooms ...	11	1·75	44	1·40	1·33
				4 Rooms ...	12	1·91	42	1·20	·87
				5 Rooms ...	2	·32	46	1·31	4·60
				6 Rooms and over.	4	·64	28	·80	1·17
				Total ...	278	...	1,607	...	...
		" ...	4	1 Room ...	255	91·73	1,430	88·98	5·61
				2 Rooms ...	11	3·96	102	6·35	4·64
				3 Rooms ...	10	3·60	63	3·92	2·10
				4 Rooms ...	2	·72	12	·75	1·50
				5 Rooms ...	...	...	...	...	...
				6 Rooms and over.	...	...	...	...	...

* This figure is exclusive of the population enumerated as homeless, docks and harbour, railways and camps.

TABLE XIV—*continued.*

Table showing the number of tenements per inhabited house.

Ward.	Charge.	Section.	Circle Number.	Tenements with	Total Number of occupied tenements of each class.	Percentage of each class of tenements to total tenements.	Total Number of occupants of each class of tenements.	Percentage borne by population in each class of tenements to total population.	Average Number of occupants per room in each class of tenements.
				Total ...	401	...	2,440	...	...
A	2	Lower Colaba ...	5	1 Room ...	385	96·01	2,304	94·43	5·98
				2 Rooms ...	10	2·49	69	2·83	3·45
				3 Rooms ...	2	·50	28	1·15	4·67
				4 Rooms ...	2	·50	26	1·07	3·25
				5 Rooms ...	1	·25	8	·33	1·60
				6 Rooms and over.	1	·25	5	·20	·83
				Total ...	655	...	2,163	...	...
		" ...	6	1 Room ...	509	77·71	1,865	86·22	3·66
				2 Rooms ...	21	3·21	87	4·02	2·07
				3 Rooms ...	13	1·97	47	2·13	1·21
				4 Rooms ...	9	1·37	34	1·57	·94
				5 Rooms ...	11	1·68	34	1·57	·62
				6 Rooms and over.	92	14·05	96	4·44	·17
				Total ...	209	...	1,165	...	...
		" ...	7	1 Room ...	177	84·69	966	82·92	5·46
				2 Rooms ...	25	11·96	129	11·07	2·58
				3 Rooms ...	3	1·44	26	2·23	2·89
				4 Rooms ...	2	·96	J9	1·63	2·37
				5 Rooms ...	1	·47	18	1·54	3·60
				6 Rooms and over.	1	·47	7	·60	1·17
				Total ...	723	...	3,506	...	...
		" ...	8	1 Room ...	435	60·17	2,599	74·13	5·97
				2 Rooms ...	10	1·38	10	·29	·50
				3 Rooms ...	80	11·07	211	6·02	·88
				4 Rooms ...	103	14·25	326	9·30	·79
				5 Rooms ...	79	10·93	311	8·87	·79
				6 Rooms and over.	16	2·21	49	1·40	·51
				Total ...	772	...	3,460	...	...
		Total for Fort South ...	...	1 Room ...	707	91·58	3,007	86·91	4·25
				2 Rooms ...	38	4·92	125	3·61	1·64
				3 Rooms ...	7	·91	92	2·66	4·38
				4 Rooms ...	9	1·17	80	2·31	2·22
				5 Rooms ...	4	·52	25	·72	1·25
				6 Rooms and over.	7	·91	131	3·79	3·12
				Total ...	136	...	526	...	...
	3	Fort South ...	1	1 Room ...	120	88·24	460	87·45	3·83
				2 Rooms ...	14	10·29	40	7·60	1·43
				3 Rooms ...	1	·74	25	4·75	8·33
				4 Rooms ...	...	...	...	...	...
				5 Rooms ...	1	·74	1	19	·20
				6 Rooms and over.	...	...	...	...	...
				Total ...	169	...	1,120	...	...
		" ...	2	1 Room ...	149	88·17	961	85·80	6·45
				2 Rooms ...	12	7·10	55	4·91	2·29
				3 Rooms ...	4	2·37	60	5·36	5·00
				4 Rooms ...	2	1·18	2	·18	·25
				5 Rooms ...	1	·59	18	1·61	3·60
				6 Rooms and over.	1	·59	24	2·14	4·00
				!Total ...	210	...	526	...	...
		" ...	3	1 Room ...	192	91·43	376	71·48	1·96
				2 Rooms ...	6	2·86	20	3·80	1·67
				3 Rooms ...	2	·95	7	1·33	1·17
				4 Rooms ...	3	1·43	19	3·61	1·58
				5 Rooms ...	2	·95	6	1·14	·60
				6 Rooms and over.	5	2·38	98	18·63	3·27

TABLE XIV—*continued.*

Table showing the number of tenements per inhabited house.

Ward.	Charge.	Section.	Circle Number.	Tenements with	Total Number of occupied tenements of each class.	Percentage of each class of tenements to total tenements.	Total Number of occupants of each class of tenements	Percentage borne by population in each class of tenements to total population.	Average Number of occupants per room in each class of tenements.
				Total ...	126	...	562	...	...
A	3	Fort South ...	4	1 Room ...	120	95·24	546	97·15	4·55
				2 Rooms ...	4	3·17	6	1·07	75
				3 Rooms ...	...	...	...	...	...
				4 Rooms ...	1	·79	1	·18	·25
				5 Rooms ...	...	...	...	...	...
				6 Rooms and over.	1	·79	9	1·60	1·50
				Total ...	131	...	726	...	...
		„ ...	5	1 Room ...	126	96·18	664	91·46	5·27
				2 Rooms ...	2	1·53	4	·55	1·00
				3 Rooms ...	...	...	...	...	...
				4 Rooms ...	3	2·29	58	7·99	4·83
				5 Rooms ...	...	...	...	...	...
				6 Rooms and over.	...	...	...	...	...
				Total ...	6,330	...	25,400	...	...
		Total for Fort North ...	...	1 Room ...	3,460	54·66	12,143	47·80	3·51
				2 Rooms ...	1,458	23·03	5,590	22·01	1·77
				3 Rooms ...	682	10·77	3,219	12·67	1·57
				4 Rooms ...	370	5·85	1,944	7·65	1·31
				5 Rooms ...	158	3·19	1,063	4·19	1·35
				6 Rooms and over.	202	2·50	1,441	5·67	1·19
				Total ...	556	...	2,679	...	...
..	4	Fort North ...	1	1 Room ...	170	30·58	654	24·41	3·85
				2 Rooms ...	207	37·23	879	32·81	2·12
				3 Rooms ...	90	16·19	504	18·81	1·87
				4 Rooms ...	38	6·83	229	8·55	1·51
				5 Rooms ...	23	4·14	215	8·03	1·87
				6 Rooms and over.	28	5·04	198	7·01	1·12
				Total ...	496	...	1,787	...	...
		„ ...	2	1 Room ...	145	29·23	318	17·74	2·19
				2 Rooms ...	123	24·80	356	19·92	1·04
				3 Rooms ...	94	18·95	414	23·17	1·43
				4 Rooms ...	71	14·31	297	16·62	1·05
				5 Rooms ...	28	5·65	143	8·00	1·02
				6 Rooms and over.	35	7·06	259	14·49	1·23
				Total ...	712	...	2,664	...	...
		„ ...	3	1 Room ...	304	42·70	954	35·81	3·14
				2 Rooms ...	266	37·36	1,035	38·85	1·95
				3 Rooms ...	74	10·39	287	10·77	1·29
				4 Rooms ...	53	7·44	271	10·14	1·28
				5 Rooms ...	6	·84	36	1·35	1·20
				6 Rooms and over.	9	1·26	81	3·04	1·50
				Total ...	804	...	3,176	...	...
		„ ...	4	1 Room ...	459	57·09	1,594	50·19	3·47
				2 Rooms ...	204	25·37	800	25·19	3·85
				3 Rooms ...	86	10·70	420	13·23	1·63
				4 Rooms ...	28	3·48	151	4·75	1·35
				5 Rooms ...	13	1·62	87	2·74	1·34
				6 Rooms and over.	14	1·74	124	3·90	1·48
				Total ...	535	...	2,266	...	...
		„ ...	5	1 Room ...	158	29·53	548	24·18	3·47
				2 Rooms ...	112	20·93	397	17·52	1·77
				3 Rooms ...	142	26·54	655	28·91	1·54
				4 Rooms ...	58	10·84	293	12·49	1·26
				5 Rooms ...	28	5·23	163	7·29	1·16
				6 Rooms and over.	37	6·92	210	9·27	·95

TABLE XIV—*continued.*

Table showing the number of tenements per inhabited house.

Ward.	Charge.	Section.	Circle Number.	Tenements with	Total Number of occupied tenements of each class.	Percentage of each class of tenements to total tenements.	Total Number of occupants of each class of tenements.	Percentage borne by population in each class of tenements to total population.	Average Number of occupants per room in each class of tenements.
				Total ...	985	...	4,106	...	...
A	4	Fort North	6	1 Room ...	592	60·10	2,157	52·53	3·64
				2 Rooms ...	221	22·44	987	24·04	2·23
				3 Rooms ...	79	5·02	377	9·18	1·59
				4 Rooms ...	47	4·77	247	6·01	1·31
				5 Rooms ...	19	1·93	166	4·04	1·75
				6 Rooms and over.	27	2·74	172	4·19	1·06
				Total ...	1,404	...	4,368	...	...
		"	7	1 Room ...	921	65·60	2,348	53·64	2·54
				2 Rooms ...	268	11·97	879	20·12	1·64
				3 Rooms ...	95	6·77	420	9·62	1·47
				4 Rooms ...	50	3·56	277	6·34	1·38
				5 Rooms ..	32	2·28	180	4·12	1·12
				6 Rooms and over.	38	2·71	269	6·16	1·18
				Total ...	838	...	4,354	...	...
		"	8	1 Room ...	711	84·84	3,575	82·11	5·03
				2 Rooms ...	57	6·80	257	5·90	2·25
				3 Rooms ...	22	2·63	142	3·26	2·15
				4 Rooms ...	25	2·98	179	4·12	1·79
				5 Rooms ...	9	1·07	73	1·22	1·62
				6 Rooms and over.	14	1·67	128	2·94	1·52
				Total ..	1,835	...	17,546	...	...
		Total for Esplanade	...	1 Room ...	1,576	85·89	15,452	88·17	9·80
				2 Rooms ...	83	4·52	517	2·95	3·11
				3 Rooms ...	47	2·56	358	2·04	2·54
				4 Rooms ...	29	1·58	214	1·22	1·84
				5 Rooms ...	12	·65	57	·32	·95
				6 Rooms and over.	88	4·80	948	2·55	1·80
				Total ...	333	...	2,170	—	...
	5	Esplanade	1	1 Room ...	170	51·05	1,085	47·70	6·08
				2 Rooms ...	44	13·21	296	13·69	3·36
				3 Rooms ...	24	7·20	140	6·45	1·88
				4 Rooms ...	11	3·30	46	2·12	1·05
				5 Rooms ...	7	2·10	27	1·24	·77
				6 Rooms and over	77	23·12	626	28·85	1·36
				Total ...	146	...	1,093	...	...
		"	2	1 Room ...	134	91·78	783	71·64	5·84
				2 Rooms ...	...	...	...	...	...
				3 Rooms ...	4	2·74	78	7·14	6·50
				4 Rooms ...	3	2·05	77	7·05	6·42
				5 Rooms ...	...	...	...	...	...
				6 Rooms and over.	5	3·42	155	14·18	5·17
				Total ...	1,121	...	5,298	...	...
		"	3	1 Room ...	1,079	96·25	4,893	90·47	4·53
				2 Rooms ...	28	2·50	203	3·83	4·41
				3 Rooms ...	8	·71	45	·85	1·87
				4 Rooms ...	3	·27	10	·19	·83
				5 Rooms ...	1	·9	3	·6	·60
				6 Rooms and over.	2	·10	144	2·74	12·
				Total ...	235	...	8,985	...	...
		"	4	1 Room ...	193	82·13	8,741	97·40	45·90
				2 Rooms ...	11	4·68	18	·20	·82
				3 Rooms ...	11	4·68	95	1·6	2·88
				4 Rooms ...	12	5·11	81	·90	1·69
				5 Rooms ...	4	1·70	27	·30	1·35
				6 Rooms and over.	4	1·70	23	·26	·96

TABLE XIV—*continued.*

Table showing the number of tenements per inhabited house.

Ward.	Charge.	Section.	Circle Number.	Tenements with	Total Number of occupied tenements of each class	Percentage of each class of tenements to total tenements.	Total Number of occupants of each class of tenements.	Percentage borne by population in each class of tenements to total population.	Average Number of occupants per room in each class of tenements.
				Total ...	30,122	...	126,666	...	...
B	...	Total for B Ward .	...	1 Room ...	27,565	91·51	114,966	90·84	4·17
				2 Rooms ...	1,718	5·70	6,842	5·40	1·99
				3 Rooms ...	441	1·46	2,120	1·67	1·60
				4 Rooms ...	220	·73	1,293	1·02	1·47
				5 Rooms ...	71	·24	530	·42	1·49
				6 Rooms and over.	107	·36	915	·72	1·43
				Total ..	5,655	...	24,231	...	...
		Total for Chakla ...	...	1 Room ...	5,054	89·37	21,496	88·76	4·28
				2 Rooms ...	372	6·58	1,476	6·06	1·98
				3 Rooms ...	115	2·03	454	1·87	1·32
				4 Rooms ...	73	1·29	422	1·73	1·45
				5 Rooms ...	17	·30	101	·41	1·19
				6 Rooms and over.	24	·42	282	1·16	1·96
				Total ...	565	...	2,688	...	...
	7	Chakla	1	1 Room ...	520	93·81	2,491	9·27	4·79
				2 Rooms ...	28	4·97	143	5·32	2·55
				3 Rooms ...	11	1·96	36	1·34	1·09
				4 Rooms ...	4	·71	12	·45	·75
				5 Rooms ...	2	·35	6	·22	·60
				6 Rooms and over.	...	...	...	...	...
				Total ...	644	...	2,848	...	...
		"	2	1 Room ...	522	81·06	2,159	75·81	4·14
				2 Rooms ...	66	10·25	284	9·97	2·15
				3 Rooms ...	23	3·57	139	4·88	2·01
				4 Rooms ...	16	2·48	140	4·92	2·19
				5 Rooms ...	7	1·09	29	1·02	·83
				6 Rooms ond over.	10	1·55	97	3·41	1·60
				Total ...	654	...	2,569	...	...
		"	3	1 Room ...	563	86·09	2,269	88·33	4·03
				2 Rooms ...	51	7·80	161	6·27	1·58
				2 Rooms ...	32	4·89	66	2·57	·69
				4 Rooms ...	4	·61	21	·82	1·31
				5 Rooms ...	1	·15	12	·47	2·40
				6 Rooms and over.	3	·46	40	1·56	2·22
				Total ...	1,107	...	4,894	...	...
		"	4	1 Room ...	908	82·02	4,067	83·10	4·48
				2 Rooms ...	146	13·19	523	10·69	1·79
				3 Rooms ...	30	2·71	133	2·72	1·48
				4 Rooms ...	17	1·54	134	2·74	1·97
				5 Rooms ...	2	·18	14	·29	1·40
				6 Rooms and over.	4	·36	23	·47	·96
				Total ...	654	...	2,619	...	...
		"	5	1 Room ...	606	92·66	2,401	91·68	3·96
				2 Rooms ...	28	4·28	94	3·59	1·68
				3 Rooms ...	4	·61	40	1·53	3·33
				4 Rooms ...	13	1·99	48	1·83	·92
				5 Rooms ...	1	·15	10	·38	2·00
				6 Rooms and over.	2	·31	26	·99	2·17
				Total ...	289	...	1,268	...	...
		"	6	1 Room ...	276	95·50	1,115	88·11	4·04
				2 Rooms ...	...	...	...	...	...
				3 Rooms ..	1	·35	8	·63	2·67
				4 Rooms ...	4	1·38	23	1·82	1·44
				5 Rooms ...	4	1·38	30	2·37	1·50
				6 Rooms and over.	4	1·38	92	7·26	3·83

TABLE XIV—*continued.*

Table showing the number of tenements per inhabited house.

Ward.	Charge.	Section.	Circle Number.	Tenements with	Total Number of occupied tenements of each class.	Percentage of each class of tenements to total tenements.	Total Number of occupants of each class of tenements.	Percentage borne by population in each class of tenements to total population.	Average Number of occupants per room in each class of tenements.
				Total ...	466	...	2,393	...	...
B	7	Chakla	7	1 Room ...	440	93·99	2,278	95·19	5·18
				2 Rooms ...	21	4·51	89	3·72	2·12
				3 Rooms ...	2	·43	9	·38	1·50
				4 Rooms ...	3	·64	17	·71	1·42
				5 Rooms ...	...	...	...	...	...
				6 Rooms and over.	...	...	...	...	...
				Total ...	647	...	2,212	...	...
		,, ...	8	1 Room ...	626	96·60	2,124	96·03	3·39
				2 Rooms ...	9	1·39	48	2·17	2 67
				3 Rooms ...	1	·15	16	·72	5·33
				4 Rooms ...	11	1·70	24	1·08	·55
				5 Rooms ...	...	..	...	...	...
				6 Rooms and over.	...	...	...	...	...
				Total ...	629	...	2,740	...	...
		,, ...	9	1 Room ...	593	94·28	2,592	94·60	4·37
				2 Rooms ...	23	3·66	134	4·89	2 39
				3 Rooms ...	11	1·75	7	·26	·21
				4 Rooms ...	1	·16	3	·11	·75
				5 Rooms ...	...	...	...	...	...
				6 Rooms and over.	1	·16	4	·15	·67
				Total ...	7,411	...	30,468	..	...
		Total for Mandvi ...	...	1 Room ...	6,564	88·57	26,523	87·07	4·04
				2 Rooms ..	562	7·58	2,339	7·68	2·08
				3 Rooms ...	147	1·98	704	2·31	1·60
				4 Rooms ..	58	·78	337	1·11	1·45
				5 Rooms ...	27	·36	177	·58	1·31
				6 Rooms and over.	53	·72	383	1·26	1·20
				Total ...	930	...	3,517	...	...
	6	Mandvi	1	1 Room ...	855	91·94	3,053	£6·81	3·57
				2 Rooms ...	49	5·27	287	8·16	2·93
				3 Rooms ...	13	1·40	68	1·93	1·74
				4 Rooms ...	6	·65	37	1·05	1·54
				5 Rooms ...	2	·22	12	·34	1·20
				6 Rooms and over .	5	·54	60	1·70	2·00
				Total ...	326	...	1,268	...	...
		,, ...	3	1 Room ...	299	91·72	1,113	87·78	3·72
				2 Rooms ...	18	5·52	113	8·90	3·14
				3 Rooms ..	5	1·53	19	1·50	1·27
				4 Rooms ...	2	·61	6	4·7	·75
				5 Rooms ...	2	·61	17	1·35	1·70
				6 Rooms and over .	...	...	...	...	...
				Total ...	861	...	2,845	...	...
		,, ...	4	1 Room ...	809	93·96	2,607	91·63	3·22
				2 Rooms ...	37	4·30	167	5·87	2·26
				3 Rooms ...	8	·93	41	1·44	1·71
				4 Rooms ...	3	·35	19	·67	1·58
				5 Rooms ...	...	...	...	...	...
				6 Rooms and over.	4	4·6	11	·39	·46
				Total ...	392	...	1,154	...	...
		,, ...	5	1 Room ...	348	88·78	1,077	93·33	3·12
				2 Rooms ..	30	7·65	49	4·25	1·32
				3 Rooms ...	11	2·81	16	1·39	·48
				4 Rooms ..	1	·26	2	·17	·50
				5 Rooms ...	...	...	...	...	...
				6 Rooms and over .	2	·51	10	·88	·83

B 1038—33

TABLE XIV—*continued.*

Table showing the number of tenements per inhabited house.

Ward.	Charge.	Section.	Circle Number.	Tenements with.	Total Number of occupied tenements of each class.	Percentage of each class of tenements to total tenements.	Total Number of occupants of each class of tenements.	Percentage borne by population in each class of tenements to total population.	Average Number of occupants per room in each class of tenements.
				Total ...	421	...	5,290	...	...
B	6	Mandvi ...	6	1 Room ...	327	77·67	4,927	93 14	15·07
				2 Rooms ...	61	14·49	198	3·47	1·62
				3 Rooms ...	19	4·51	97	1·64	1·70
				4 Rooms ...	7	1·66	25	·47	·89
				5 Rooms ..	2	·47	13	·22	1·30
				6 Rooms and over .	5	1·19	30	·57	1·00
				Total ...	471	...	1,694	...	...
		"	7	1 Room ...	361	76·65	1,253	73 97	3·49
				2 Rooms ...	66	14·01	203	11·39	1·53
				3 Rooms ...	19	4·04	84	4·96	1·47
				4 Rooms ...	8	1·70	50	2·95	1·56
				5 Rooms ...	3	·64	9	·53	·60
				6 Rooms and over .	14	2·97	95	5·61	1·13
				Total ...	327	...	1,155	...	...
		"	8	1 Room ...	217	66·36	663	57·40	3·06
				2 Rooms ...	65	19·85	314	27·19	2·42
				3 Rooms ...	22	6·73	55	4·77	·83
				4 Rooms ...	9	2·75	28	2·43	·78
				5 Rooms ...	4	1·22	29	2·51	1·45
				6 Rooms and over .	10	3·06	66	5·71	1·10
				Total ...	890	...	3,365	...	...
		"	9	1 Room ...	852	95·73	3,144	93·43	3·69
				2 Rooms ...	19	2·13	81	2·41	2·13
				3 Rooms ...	10	1·12	63	1·87	2·10
				4 Rooms ...	4	·45	36	1·07	2·25
				5 Rooms ...	2	·22	7	·21	·70
				6 Rooms and over .	3	·34	34	1·01	1·89
				Total ...	1,069	...	3,498	...	...
		"	10	1 Room ...	936	87·56	2,824	80·73	3·02
				2 Rooms ..	103	9·63	488	13·95	2·37
				3 Rooms ...	19	1·78	112	3·20	1·96
				4 Rooms ...	4	·37	41	1·17	2·56
				5 Rooms ...	3	·28	19	·54	1·27
				6 Rooms and over .	4	·37	14	·40	·58
				Total ...	1,372	...	5,197	...	...
		"	11	1 Room ...	1,239	90·31	4,512	86·82	3·64
				2 Rooms ...	92	6·71	360	6·93	1·96
				3 Rooms ...	19	1·38	142	2·73	2·49
				4 Rooms ...	10	·73	76	1·44	1·90
				5 Rooms ...	9	·66	71	1·37	1·58
				6 Rooms and over .	3	·22	36	·69	2·00
				Total ...	352	...	1,485	...	...
		"	12	1 Room ...	321	91·48	1,356	91·38	4·22
				2 Rooms ...	22	6·25	79	5·32	1·80
				3 Rooms ...	2	·57	7	·47	1·17
				4 Rooms ...	4	1·14	17	1·14	1·06
				5 Rooms ...	...	...	...	...	...
				6 Rooms and over .	3	·85	27	1·82	1·50
				Total ...	11,401	...	45 679	...	...
		Total for Umarkhadi ...	...	1 Room ...	10,503	92·12	41,523	90·91	3·95
				2 Rooms ...	652	5·72	2,454	5·17	1·89
				3 Rooms ..	139	1·22	787	1·72	1·89
				4 Rooms ...	64	·56	470	1·03	1·84
				5 Rooms ...	19	·17	215	·47	2·26
				6 Rooms and over .	24	·21	230	·50	1·60

TABLE XIV—*continued.*

Table showing the number of tenements per inhabited house.

Ward.	Charge.	Section.	Circle Number.	Tenements with.	Total Number of occupied tenements of each class.	Percentage of each class of tenements to total tenements.	Total Number of occupants of each class of tenements.	Percentage borne by population in each class of tenements to total population.	Average Number of occupants per room in each class of tenements.
				Total ...	**1,750**	...	**5,654**	...	...
B	8	Umarkhadi	1	1 Room ...	1,695	96·86	5,437	96·16	3·21
				2 Rooms ...	35	2·00	135	2·39	1·93
				3 Rooms ...	11	·63	34	·60	1·03
				4 Rooms ...	5	·29	11	·19	·55
				5 Rooms ...	2	·11	7	·12	·70
				6 Rooms and over.	2	·11	30	·53	2·50
				Total ...	**459**	...	**2,215**	...	...
		"	2	1 Room ...	457	99·56	2,207	99·64	4·83
				2 Rooms ...	2	·44	8	·36	2·00
				3 Rooms ...	...	...	...	...	...
				4 Rooms ...	...	...	...	...	...
				5 Rooms ...	...	...	...	...	...
				6 Rooms and over .	...	...	...	...	...
				Total ...	**1,006**	...	**4,358**	...	...
		"	3	1 Room ...	880	87·48	3,795	87·08	4·31
				2 Rooms ...	97	9·64	326	7·48	1·68
				3 Rooms ...	16	1·59	105	2·41	2·19
				4 Rooms ...	9	·89	84	1·93	2·33
				5 Rooms ...	2	·20	24	·55	2·40
				6 Rooms and over .	2	·20	24	·55	2·00
				Total ...	**1,207**	...	**4,319**	...	...
		"	4	1 Room ...	1,196	99·09	4,270	99·07	3·57
				2 Rooms ...	10	·83	40	·93	2·40
				3 Rooms ...	...	...	...	...	...
				4 Rooms ...	1	·8	9	·21	2·25
				5 Rooms ...	...	...	...	...	...
				6 Rooms and over .	...	...	...	...	...
				Total ...	**762**	...	**2,701**	...	...
		"	5	1 Room ...	740	97·11	2,620	97·00	3·54
				2 Rooms ...	19	2·49	57	2·11	1·50
				3 Rooms ...	2	·26	16	·59	2·67
				4 Rooms ...	1	·13	8	·30	2·00
				5 Rooms ...	...	...	...	...	...
				6 Rooms and over .	...	...	...	...	...
				Total ...	**507**	...	**2,107**	...	...
		"	6	1 Room ...	488	96·25	1,995	94·68	4·09
				2 Rooms ...	12	2·37	73	3·46	3·04
				3 Rooms ...	2	·39	7	·33	1·17
				4 Rooms ...	2	·39	10	·47	1·25
				5 Rooms ...	3	·59	22	1·04	1·47
				6 Rooms and over .	...	...	...	...	...
				Total ...	**1,162**	...	**4,621**	...	...
		"	7	1 Room ...	1,069	92·00	4,018	86·95	3·76
				2 Rooms ...	65	5·59	350	7·57	2·62
				3 Rooms ...	19	1·64	139	3·01	2·44
				4 Rooms ...	3	·26	25	·54	2·08
				5 Rooms ...	2	·17	51	1·10	5·10
				6 Rooms and over .	4	·34	38	·82	1·58
				Total ...	**1,542**	...	**6,517**	...	...
		"	8	1 Room ...	1,384	89·75	5,737	88·03	4·15
				2 Rooms ...	99	6·42	440	6·75	2·22
				3 Rooms ...	35	2·27	188	2·88	1·79
				4 Rooms ...	13	·84	96	1·47	1·85
				5 Rooms ...	3	·19	4	·6	·27
				6 Rooms and over .	8	·52	52	·80	1·04

TABLE XIV—*continued.*

Table showing the number of tenements per inhabited house.

Ward.	Charge.	Section.	Circle Number.	Tenements with	Total Number of occupied tenements of each class.	Percentage of each class of tenements to total tenements.	Total Number of occupants of each class of tenements.	Percentage born by population in each class of tenements to total population.	Average Number of occupants per room in each class of tenements.
				Total ..	**1,277**	...	**5,144**	...	...
B	8	Umarkhadi ...	9	1 Room ...	1,017	79·64	4,257	82·76	4·19
				2 Rooms ...	201	15·74	488	9·49	1·21
				3 Rooms ...	35	2·74	176	3·42	1·68
				4 Rooms ...	16	1·25	109	2·12	1·70
				5 Rooms ...	3	·23	66	1·28	4·40
				6 Rooms and over .	5	·39	48	·93	1·60
				Total ...	**1,729**	...	**8,043**	...	...
		"	10	1 Room ...	1,577	91·21	7,167	89·36	4·56
				2 Rooms ...	112	6·48	537	6·68	2·40
				3 Rooms ...	19	1·10	122	1·52	2·14
				4 Rooms ...	14	·81	118	1·34	2·11
				5 Rooms ...	4	·23	41	·51	2·05
				6 Rooms and over.	3	·17	38	·47	2·11
				Total ...	**5,655**	...	**26,288**	...	...
		Total for Dongri ...	...	1 Room ...	5,444	96·27	25,419	96·70	4·67
				2 Rooms ...	132	2·33	573	2·18	2·13
				3 Rooms ...	40	·71	175	·67	1·46
				4 Rooms ...	25	·44	64	·24	·64
				5 Rooms ..	8	·14	37	·14	·92
				6 Rooms and over	6	·11	20	·8	·56
				Total ...	**1,258**	...	**6,243**	...	...
	9	Dongri ...	1	1 Room ...	1,180	93·00	6,035	96·67	5·11
				2 Rooms ...	59	4·69	184	2·95	1·56
				3 Rooms ...	13	1·03	18	·29	·46
				4 Rooms ...	5	·40	5	·8	·25
				5 Rooms ...	...	...	...	...	...
				6 Rooms and over .	1	·78	1	·2	·17
				Total ...	**2,867**	...	**12,131**	...	...
		"	2	1 Room ...	2,783	97·07	11,726	96·66	4·21
				2 Rooms ...	51	1·78	258	2·13	2·53
				3 Rooms ...	18	·63	87	·72	1·61
				4 Rooms ...	11	·36	34	·28	·77
				5 Rooms ...	3	·10	20	·16	1·33
				6 Rooms and over .	1	·3	6	·5	1.00
				Total ...	**1,074**	...	**5,539**	...	...
		"	3	1 Room ..	1,070	99·63	5,515	99·57	5·15
				2 Rooms ...	3	·28	19	·34	3·17
				3 Rooms ...	1	·1	5	·9	1·67
				4 Rooms ...	...	...	...	...	...
				5 Rooms ...	...	...	...	...	...
				6 Rooms and over .	...	...	...	...	...
				Total ...	**456**	...	**2,375**	...	...
		"	4	1 Room ...	411	90·13	2,143	90·23	5·21
				2 Rooms ...	19	4·17	112	4·72	2·95
				3 Rooms ...	8	1·75	65	2·74	2·71
				4 Rooms ..	9	1·97	25	1·05	·69
				5 Rooms ...	5	1·10	17	·72	·68
				6 Rooms and over.	4	·88	13	·55	·54
				Total ...	**38,727**	...	**183,044**	...	...
C		**Total for C Ward** .	...	1 Room ...	31,050	80·19	135,613	74·09	4·36
				2 Rooms ...	4,285	11·07	20,640	11·28	2·41
				3 Rooms ...	1,404	3·63	9,758	5·33	2·32
				4 Rooms ...	990	2·61	7,420	4·05	1·98
				5 Rooms ...	497	1·28	4,475	2·66	1·80
				6 Rooms and over.	501	1·29	5,138	2·81	1·71

TABLE XIV—*continued.*

Table showing the number of tenements per inhabited house.

Ward.	Charge.	Section.	Circle Number.	Tenements with	Total Number of occupied tenements of each class.	Percentage of each class of tenements to total tenements.	Total Number of occupants of each class of tenements.	Percentage borne by population in each class of tenements to total population.	Average Number of occupants per room in each class of tenements.
				Total ...	**6,989**	...	**29,949**	...	...
C	...	**Total for Market...**	...	1 Room ...	5,196	74·35	19,537	65·23	3·76
				2 Rooms ...	936	13·39	4,545	15·18	2·43
				3 Rooms ...	324	4·64	1,983	66·21	2·04
				4 Rooms ...	245	3·51	1,356	4·56	1·38
				5 Rooms ...	131	1·87	967	3·23	1·47
				6 Rooms and over .	157	2·25	1,561	5·21	1·66
				Total ...	**621**	...	**3,967**	...	...
	10	Market ...	1	1 Room ...	475	76·49	2,782	70·13	5·86
				2 Rooms ...	60	9·66	500	12·60	4·17
				3 Rooms ..	36	5·80	312	7·86	2·89
				4 Rooms ...	24	3·86	146	3·68	1·52
				5 Rooms ...	15	2·42	112	2·82	1·49
				6 Rooms and over .	11	1·79	115	2·90	1·74
				Total ...	**398**	...	**1,808**	...	...
		„ ...	2	1 Room ...	336	84·42	1,360	75·22	4·05
				2 Rooms ...	29	7·29	141	7·80	2·43
				3 Rooms ...	11	2·77	77	4·26	2·33
				4 Rooms ...	10	2·51	72	3·98	1·80
				5 Rooms ...	4	1·01	38	2·10	1·40
				6 Rooms and over .	8	2·02	120	6·64	2·50
				Total ...	**326**	...	**1,597**	...	...
		„ ...	3	1 Room ...	265	81·[illegible]0	1,209	75·70	4·56
				2 Rooms ...	20	6·13	81	5·07	2·02
				3 Rooms ...	26	7·98	196	12·28	2·51
				4 Rooms ...	7	2·15	39	2·44	1·39
				5 Rooms ...	3	·92	14	·81	·93
				6 Rooms and over	5	1·55	58	3·63	1·93
				Total ...	**602**	...	**2,395**	...	...
		„ ...	4	1 Room ...	491	81·56	1,70[illegible]	71·06	3·47
				2 Rooms ...	49	8·14	243	10·15	2·48
				3 Rooms ...	17	2·82	137	5·72	2·69
				4 Rooms ...	14	2·33	85	3·55	1·52
				5 Rooms ...	21	3·49	102	4·26	·97
				6 Rooms and over .	10	1·66	126	5·26	2·10
				Total ...	**1,790**	...	**6,633**	...	...
		„ ...	5	1 Room ...	1,325	74·02	4,145	62·49	3·13
				2 Rooms ...	229	12·79	989	14·91	2·15
				3 Rooms ..	78	4·36	444	6·69	1·90
				4 Rooms ..	69	3·85	315	4·75	1·14
				5 Rooms ...	31	1·73	223	3·36	1·44
				6 Rooms and over .	58	3·24	517	7·79	1·49
				Total ...	**1,150**	...	**4,589**	...	...
		„ ...	6	1 Room ...	938	81·57	3,556	77·49	3·79
				2 Rooms ...	122	10·61	504	10·98	2·02
				3 Rooms ...	31	2·70	124	2·70	1·33
				4 Rooms ...	33	2·87	190	4·14	1·44
				5 Rooms ...	12	1·04	108	2·35	1·80
				6 Rooms and over .	14	1·22	107	2·33	1·27
				Total ...	**927**	...	**3,611**	...	...
		„ ...	7	1 Room ...	698	75·30	2,330	64·53	3·34
				2 Rooms ...	131	14·13	593	16·42	2·26
				3 Rooms ..	43	4·64	227	6·29	1·76
				4 Rooms ...	22	2·37	129	3·57	1·47
				5 Rooms ...	11	1·19	74	2·05	1·35
				6 Rooms and over .	22	2·38	258	7·14	1·95

TABLE XIV—*continued.*

Table showing the number of tenements per inhabited house.

Ward.	Charge	Section.	Circle Number.	Tenements with	Total Number of occupied tenements of each class.	Percentage of each class of tenements to total tenements.	Total Number of occupants of each class of tenements.	Percentage borne by population in each class of tenements to total population.	Average Number of occupants per room in each class of tenements.
				Total ...	**1,175**	...	**5,349**	...	...
C	10	Market ...	8	1 Room ...	668	56·86	2,453	45·86	3·67
				2 Rooms ...	296	25·19	1,404	27·93	2·69
				3 Rooms ...	82	6·98	466	8·71	1·89
				4 Rooms ...	66	5·32	380	7·10	1·44
				5 Rooms ...	34	2·89	296	5·53	1·74
				6 Rooms and over.	29	2·47	260	4·86	1·59
				Total ...	**7,960**	...	**38,684**	...	...
	...	**Total for Dhobi Talao ...**	...	1 Room ...	5,383	67·63	22,135	57·22	4·11
				2 Rooms ...	1,198	15·65	5,734	14·82	2·39
				3 Rooms ...	544	6·83	3,712	9·60	2·27
				4 Rooms ...	433	5·44	3,287	8·50	1·90
				5 Rooms ...	209	2·63	1,779	4·60	1·70
				6 Rooms and over.	193	2·43	2,037	5·27	1·69
				Total ...	**1,428**	...	**6,939**	...	...
	11	Dhobi Talao ...	1	1 Room ...	793	55·53	3,557	51·26	4·49
				2 Rooms ...	358	25·07	1,707	24·60	2·38
				3 Rooms ...	170	11·90	980	14·13	1·92
				4 Rooms ..	81	5·67	459	6·61	1·42
				5 Rooms ...	12	·84	99	1·43	1·65
				6 Rooms and over.	14	·98	137	1·98	1·63
				Total ...	**1,014**	...	**4,499**	...	...
		" ...	2	1 Room ...	810	79·88	3,168	70·42	3·91
				2 Rooms ...	63	6·21	393	8·74	3·12
				3 Rooms ...	49	4·83	291	6·47	1·98
				4 Rooms ...	57	5·62	345	7·67	1·51
				5 Rooms ...	27	2·66	254	5·65	1·88
				6 Rooms and over.	8	·79	48	1·07	1·00
				Total ...	**678**	...	**4,932**	...	...
		" ...	3	1 Room ...	367	54·13	2,961	60·04	8·07
				2 Rooms ...	103	24·04	828	16·79	2·54
				3 Rooms ...	57	8·41	412	8·35	2·41
				4 Rooms ...	51	7·52	347	7·04	1·70
				5 Rooms ...	15	2·21	129	2·62	1·72
				6 Rooms and over.	25	3·65	255	5·17	1·70
				Total ...	**1,443**	...	**6,141**	...	...
		" ...	4	1 Room ...	1,132	78·45	3,853	62·74	3·40
				2 Rooms ...	114	7·90	713	11·61	3·13
				3 Rooms ...	68	4·37	407	6·63	2·15
				4 Rooms ...	59	4·09	544	8·86	2·31
				5 Rooms ...	42	2·91	294	4·79	1·40
				6 Rooms and over.	33	2·29	330	5·37	1·67
				Total ...	**775**	...	**3,705**	...	...
		" ...	5	1 Room ...	526	67·87	2,201	59·41	4·18
				2 Rooms ...	114	14·71	560	15·11	2·45
				3 Rooms ...	39	5·03	270	1·51	2·31
				4 Rooms ...	41	5·29	300	8·10	1·83
				5 Rooms ...	25	3·23	177	4·78	1·42
				6 Rooms and over.	30	3·85	197	5·32	1·09
				Total ...	**1,100**	...	**5,733**	...	...
		" ...	6	1 Room ...	865	78·64	3,606	62·90	4·17
				2 Rooms ...	117	10·64	612	10·68	2·61
				3 Rooms ...	44	4·00	604	10·54	4·58
				4 Rooms ...	42	3·82	420	7·48	2·4[illegible]
				5 Rooms ...	16	1·45	165	2·88	2·06
				6 Rooms and over.	16	1·45	317	5·53	3·30

TABLE XIV—*continued.*

Table showing the number of tenements per inhabited house.

Ward.	Charge.	Section.	Circle Number.	Tenements with	Total Number of occupied tenements of each class.	Percentage of each class of tenements to total tenements.	Total Number of occupants of each class of tenements.	Percentage borne by population in each class of tenements to total population.	Average Number of occupants per room in each class of tenements.
				Total ...	1,522	...	6,735	...	...
C	11	Dhobi Talao ...	7	1 Room ...	890	58·48	2,789	41·41	3·13
				2 Rooms ...	269	17·67	921	13·67	1·71
				3 Rooms ...	122	8·02	748	11·11	2·04
				4 Rooms ...	102	6·70	863	12·81	2·12
				5 Rooms ...	72	4·73	661	9·84	1·84
				6 Rooms and over .	67	4·40	753	11·18	1·87
				Total ...	4,379	...	27,403	...	...
	...	Total for Fanaswadi ...	...	1 Room ...	3,549	81·05	20,450	74·62	5·76
				2 Rooms ...	361	8·24	2,235	8·16	3·10
				3 Rooms ...	176	4·02	1,635	5·97	3·10
				4 Rooms ...	141	3·29	1,433	5·23	2·49
				5 Rooms ...	70	1·70	1,067	3·89	3·05
				6 Rooms and over .	79	1·80	583	2·13	1·23
				Total ...	1,290	...	9,324	...	...
	12	Fanaswadi ...	1	1 Room ...	883	68·60	6,398	68·62	7·25
				2 Rooms ...	173	13·41	639	7·39	1·99
				3 Rooms ...	81	6·28	628	6·73	2·61
				4 Rooms ...	72	5·58	551	5·91	1·91
				5 Rooms ...	43	3·33	735	7·89	3·42
				6 Rooms and over .	38	2·95	323	3·46	1·42
				Total ...	2,008	...	10,334	...	...
		" ...	2	1 Room ...	1,755	87·40	7,670	74·22	4·37
				2 Rooms ...	128	6·37	1,145	11·08	4·45
				3 Rooms ..	45	2·24	628	6·08	4·65
				4 Rooms ...	43	2·14	611	5·91	3·55
				5 Rooms ...	15	·75	164	1·59	2·15
				6 Rooms and over .	22	1·10	116	1·12	·088
				Total ...	1,081	...	7,745	...	...
		" ...	3	1 Room ...	911	84·27	6,382	82·39	7·01
				2 Rooms ...	60	5·55	401	5·17	3·34
				3 Rooms ...	50	4·63	379	4·89	2·53
				4 Rooms ...	29	2·68	271	3·50	2·34
				5 Rooms ...	12	1·11	168	2·17	2·80
				6 Rooms and over	19	1·76	144	1·81	1·27
				Total ..	7,951	...	36,457	...	...
	...	Total for Bhuleshwar ...	...	1 Room ...	6,387	80·20	28,875	78·20	4·52
				2 Rooms ...	1,126	14·16	4,638	12·72	2·06
				3 Rooms ...	226	2·84	1,427	3·91	2·11
				4 Rooms ...	102	1·28	758	2·08	1·86
				5 Rooms ...	61	·77	414	1·13	1·36
				6 Rooms and over .	49	·62	345	·95	1·17
				Total ...	1,090	...	5,549	...	...
	13	Bhuleshwar ...	1	1 Room ...	644	59·08	3,724	67·11	5·78
				2 Rooms ...	361	33·12	1,102	19·86	1·53
				3 Rooms ...	35	3·21	297	5·35	2·83
				4 Rooms ...	19	1·74	196	3·53	2·58
				5 Rooms ...	14	1·28	107	1·93	1·54
				6 Rooms and over.	17	1·56	123	2·22	1·21
				Total ...	1,283	...	5,466	...	...
		" ...	2	1 Room ...	1,161	90·49	4,842	88·57	4·17
				2 Rooms ...	93	7·25	458	8·38	2·41
				3 Rooms ...	15	1·17	70	1·28	1·56
				4 Rooms ...	4	·31	30	·55	1·87
				5 Rooms ...	4	·31	26	·48	1·30
				6 Rooms and over	6	·47	40	·73	1·11

TABLE XIV—*continued.*

Table showing the number of tenements per inhabited house.

Ward.	Charge.	Section.	Circle Number.	Tenements with	Total Number of occupied tenements of each class.	Percentage of each class of tenements to total tenements.	Total Number of occupants of each class of tenements.	Percentage borne by population in each class of tenements to total population.	Average Number of occupants per room in each class of tenements.
				Total ...	851	...	3.171	...	...
C	13	Bhuleshwar ...	3	1 Room ...	770	90·48	2,595	81·83	3·37
				2 Rooms ...	41	4·82	350	11·04	4·27
				3 Rooms ...	21	2·47	121	3·82	1·92
				4 Rooms ...	10	1·18	56	1·77	1·40
				5 Rooms ...	6	·71	35	1·10	1·17
				6 Rooms and over .	3	·35	14	·44	7·78
				Total ...	2.269	...	10.422	...	...
		„ ...	4	1 Room ...	1,985	87·48	8,745	83·91	4·41
				2 Rooms ...	180	7·93	950	9·11	2·64
				3 Rooms ...	61	2·69	413	3·96	2·26
				4 Rooms ...	22	·97	147	1·41	1·67
				5 Rooms ...	8	·35	68	·65	1·70
				6 Rooms and over .	13	·57	99	·95	1·27
				Total ...	1.314	...	7,224	...	...
		„ ...	5	1 Room ...	1,066	81·13	6,116	84·66	5·74
				2 Rooms ..	185	14·08	706	9·77	1·91
				3 Rooms ...	35	2·66	196	2·71	1·87
				4 Rooms ...	17	1·29	125	1·73	1·84
				5 Rooms ...	9	·68	66	·91	1·47
				6 Rooms and over.	2	·15	15	·21	1·25
				Total ...	1,144	...	4.625	...	...
		„ ...	6	1 Room ...	761	66·52	2,853	61·69	3·75
				2 Rooms ...	266	23·25	1,072	23·18	2·02
				3 Rooms ...	59	5·16	330	7·14	1·19
				4 Rooms ..	30	2·62	204	4·41	1·70
				5 Rooms ...	20	1·75	112	2·42	1·12
				6 Rooms and over.	8	·70	54	1·17	1·12
				Total ...	6.246	...	27,615	...	...
...	...	Total for Kumbharwada ...	...	1 Room ...	5,805	92·94	24,572	88·98	4·23
				2 Rooms ...	313	50·12	1,895	68·62	3·03
				3 Rooms ...	62	·99	488	1·59	2·36
				4 Rooms ...	34	·54	322	1·17	2·37
				5 Rooms ...	14	·22	136	·49	1·99
				6 Rooms and over .	18	·29	252	·84	2·33
				Total ...	1.665	...	7,264	...	...
	14	Kumbharwada ...	1	1 Room ...	1,474	88·53	5,802	79·87	3·94
				2 Rooms ...	113	6·79	736	10·13	3·26
				3 Rooms ...	39	2·34	267	3·68	2·28
				4 Rooms ...	19	1·14	162	2·23	2·13
				5 Rooms ...	8	·48	87	1·20	2·17
				6 Rooms and over .	12	·73	210	2·89	2·92
				Total ...	2.491	...	10.374	...	...
		„ ...	2	1 Room ..	2,381	95·58	9,592	93·65	4·03
				2 Rooms ...	90	3·61	537	5·23	2·98
				3 Rooms ...	8	·33	51	·20	2·12
				4 Rooms ...	6	·24	40	·39	1·67
				5 Rooms ...	3	·12	25	·24	1·67
				6 Rooms and over.	3	·12	29	·28	1·61
				Total ...	1.049	...	4,914	...	...
		„ ...	3	1 Room ...	965	91·99	4,450	90·56	4·61
				2 Rooms ...	68	6·48	351	7·14	2·58
				3 Rooms ...	10	·95	80	1·63	2·67
				4 Rooms ...	1	·10	4	·8	1·00
				5 Rooms ...	2	·20	16	·33	1·60
				6 Rooms and over .	3	·31	13	·26	·72

TABLE XIV—*continued.*

Table showing the number of tenements per inhabited house.

Ward.	Charge.	Section.	Circle Number.	Tenements with	Total Number of occupied tenements of each class.	Percentage of each class of tenements to total tenements.	Total Number of occupants of each class of tenements.	Percentage borne by population in each class of tenements to total population.	Average Number of occupants per room in each class of tenements.
				Total ...	1,041	...	5,163	...	...
C	14	Kumbharwada ...	4	1 Room ...	985	94·62	4,728	91·57	4·80
				2 Rooms ...	42	4·03	271	5·25	3·23
				3 Rooms ...	5	·48	40	·77	2·67
				4 Rooms ...	8	·77	116	2·25	3·62
				5 Rooms ...	1	·10	8	·15	1·60
				6 Room and over .	...	...	...	...	...
				Total ...	5,202	...	22,936	...	...
	...	Total for Khara Talao ...	...	1 Room ...	4,730	90·93	20,044	87·39	4·24
				2 Rooms ...	351	6·75	1,593	6·95	2·27
				3 Rooms ...	72	1·38	563	2·46	2·61
				4 Rooms ...	32	6·15	264	1·15	2·06
				5 Rooms ...	12	·23	112	·49	1·87
				6 Rooms and over .	5	·10	360	1·57	12·00
				Total ...	951	...	3,958	...	...
	15	Khara Talao ...	1	1 Room ...	927	97·48	3,759	94·97	4·06
				2 Rooms ...	18	1·88	147	3·71	4·08
				3 Rooms ...	3	·32	25	·63	2·78
				4 Rooms ...	2	·21	14	·35	1·75
				5 Rooms ...	1	·11	13	·33	2·60
				6 Rooms and over.	...	...	...	...	...
				Total ...	564	...	2,388	...	...
		" ...	2	1 Room ...	499	90·25	2,003	83·88	4·01
				2 Rooms ...	41	7·27	164	6·87	2·00
				3 Rooms ...	12	2·13	117	4·90	3·25
				4 Rooms ...	6	1·07	47	1·97	1·96
				5 Rooms ...	3	·53	32	1·34	2·15
				6 Rooms and over .	3	·53	25	1·05	1·30
				Total ...	1,341	...	6,297	...	...
		" ...	3	1 Room ...	1,246	92·92	5,722	90·87	4·59
				2 Rooms ...	77	5·74	390	6·19	2·53
				3 Rooms ...	11	·82	127	2·02	3·85
				4 Rooms ...	5	·37	39	·62	1·95
				5 Rooms ...	2	·15	19	·30	1·90
				6 Rooms and over .	...	...	...	...	...
				Total ...	1,126	...	4,548	...	...
		" ...	4	1 Room ...	994	88·28	38·74	85·18	3·88
				2 Rooms ...	108	9·59	475	10·44	2·20
				3 Rooms ...	19	1·69	137	3·01	2·40
				4 Rooms ...	3	·27	51	1·12	4·25
				5 Rooms ...	1	·9	6	·13	1·20
				6 Rooms and over .	1	·9	5	·11	·83
				Total ...	1,220	...	5,745	...	...
		" ...	5	1 Room ...	1,064	87·21	4,686	81·57	4·40
				2 Rooms ...	107	8·77	417	7·26	1·95
				3 Rooms ...	27	2·21	157	2·73	1·94
				4 Rooms ...	16	1·31	113	1·97	1·77
				5 Rooms ...	5	·41	42	·73	1·68
				6 Rooms and over .	1	·8	330	5·74	55·00
				Total ...	23,134	...	110,947	...	...
D		Total for D Ward		1 Room ...	17,338	74·95	78,671	70·91	4·54
				2 Rooms ...	2,796	12·09	12,089	10·89	2·17
				3 Rooms ...	859	3·72	4,895	4·41	1·82
				4 Rooms ...	743	3·21	4,386	3·95	1·48
				5 Rooms ...	544	2·35	3,671	3·31	1·35
				6 Rooms and over.	854	3·69	7,235	6·52	1·41

TABLE XIV—*continued.*

Table showing the number of tenements per inhabited house.

Ward.	Charge.	Section.	Circle Number.	Tenements with	Total Number of occupied tenements of each class.	Percentage of each class of tenements to total tenements.	Total Number of occupants of each class of tenements.	Percentage borne by population in each class of tenements to total population.	Average Number of occupants per room in each class of tenements.
				Total ...	7.758	...	31.934	...	...
D	...	Total for Khetwadi ...	...	1 Room ...	6,280	80·95	22.864	71·60	3·64
				2 Rooms ...	520	6·70	2,321	7·27	2·23
				3 Rooms ...	266	3·43	1,494	4·68	1·87
				4 Rooms ...	225	2·90	1,369	4·29	1·52
				5 Rooms ...	198	2·55	1,329	4·16	1·34
				6 Rooms and over .	269	3·47	2,557	8·01	1·58
				Total ...	496	...	2.737	...	...
	16	Khetwadi ...	1	1 Room ...	348	70·16	1,411	51·55	4·05
				2 Rooms ...	38	7·66	160	5·85	2·11
				3 Rooms ...	26	5·24	136	4 97	1·75
				4 Rooms ...	34	6·85	215	7·86	1·58
				5 Rooms ...	17	3·43	143	5·22	1·68
				6 Rooms and over .	33	6 65	672	24 55	3·39
				Total ...	1.427	...	5.468	...	...
		" ...	2	1 Room ...	1,151	80·66	3,678	67·26	3·20
				2 Rooms ...	71	4·98	337	6·16	2·37
				3 Rooms ...	26	1·82	195	3·57	2·50
				4 Rooms ...	37	2 59	249	4·55	1·68
				5 Rooms ...	64	4·48	375	6·86	1·17
				6 Rooms and over .	78	5·47	634	11·59	1·35
				Total ...	947	...	4.318	...	...
		" ...	3	1 Room ...	762	80·46	3,243	75·10	4·26
				2 Rooms ...	72	7·60	366	8·48	2·54
				3 Rooms ...	26	2·75	143	3·31	1·80
				4 Rooms ...	26	2·75	169	3·91	1·62
				5 Rooms ...	22	2·32	158	3·66	1·44
				6 Rooms and over .	39	4·12	239	5·53	1·02
				Total ...	508	...	2.634	...	...
		" ...	4	1 Room ...	251	49·41	925	35·12	3·69
				2 Rooms ...	19	3·74	66	2·50	1·74
				3 Rooms ...	54	10·63	274	10·40	1·69
				4 Rooms ...	53	10·43	331	12·57	1·56
				5 Rooms ...	52	10 24	368	13 97	1·42
				6 Rooms and over .	79	15·55	670	25·43	1·41
				Total ...	858	...	3,574	...	...
		" ...	5	1 Room ...	580	67 60	2,302	64·41	3·97
				2 Rooms ...	121	14·10	417	11·67	1·72
				3 Rooms ...	63	7·34	339	9·49	1·79
				4 Rooms ...	50	5·83	267	7·47	1·33
				5 Rooms ...	27	3·15	152	4 25	1·13
				6 Rooms and over .	17	1·98	97	2·71	·95
				Total ...	565	...	2.367	...	...
		" ...	6	1 Room ...	418	73·98	1,555	65·69	3·72
				2 Rooms ...	97	13·63	457	19·31	2·36
				3 Rooms ...	23	4·07	144	6·08	2·09
				4 Rooms ...	13	2 30	76	3·21	1·46
				5 Rooms ...	3	·53	24	1·01	1·60
				6 Rooms and over .	11	1·95	111	4·69	1·68
				Total ...	1.210	...	4.567	...	...
		" ...	7	1 Room ...	1,101	90 99	3,894	85·26	3·55
				2 Rooms ...	59	4·88	267	5·85	2·26
				3 Rooms ...	28	2·31	175	3·83	2·08
				4 Rooms ...	7	·58	52	1·14	1·86
				5 Rooms ...	7	·58	86	1·88	2·46
				6 Rooms and over.	8	·66	93	2·04	1·94

TABLE XIV—continued.

Table showing the number of tenements per inhabited house.

Ward.	Charge.	Section.	Circle Number.	Tenements with	Total Number of occupied tenements of each class.	Percentage of each class of tenements to total tenements.	Total Number of occupants of each class of tenements.	Percentage borne by population in each class of tenements to total population.	Average Number of occupants per room in each class of tenements.
				Total ...	**1,747**	...	**6,269**	...	...
D.	16	Khetwadi ...	8	1 Room ...	1,669	95·54	5,856	93·43	3·51
				2 Rooms ...	43	2·46	251	4·00	2·92
				3 Rooms ...	20	1·14	88	1·40	1·47
				4 Rooms ...	5	·29	10	·16	·50
				5 Rooms ...	6	·34	23	·37	·77
				6 Rooms and over .	4	·23	41	·66	1·71
				Total ...	**6,279**	...	**30,711**	...	...
		Total for Girgaum ...	...	1 Room ...	4,455	70·95	20,738	67·52	4·66
				2 Rooms ...	1,100	17·52	5,066	16·49	2·30
				3 Rooms ...	245	3·90	1,457	4·42	1·98
				4 Rooms ...	176	2·80	1,048	3·41	1·49
				5 Rooms ...	108	1·72	733	2·39	1·36
				6 Rooms and over .	195	3·11	1,669	5·40	1·43
				Total ...	**1,213**	...	**6,126**	...	...
	31	Girgaum ...	1	1 Room ...	1,053	86·81	5,120	83·58	4·86
				2 Rooms ...	84	6·92	372	6·07	2·21
				3 Rooms ...	16	1·32	119	1·94	2·48
				4 Rooms ...	25	2·06	178	2·91	1·78
				5 Rooms ...	5	·41	40	·65	1·60
				6 Rooms and over .	30	2·47	297	4·85	1·65
				Total ...	**800**	...	**3,769**	...	...
		" ...	2	1 Room ...	567	70·87	2,494	66·17	4·40
				2 Rooms ...	152	19·00	635	16·83	2·09
				3 Rooms ...	11	1·37	86	2·28	2·61
				4 Rooms ...	23	2·87	138	3·66	1·50
				5 Rooms ...	21	2·62	138	3·66	1·31
				6 Rooms and over .	26	3·25	278	7·38	1·78
				Total ...	**1,076**	...	**5,929**	...	...
		" ...	3	1 Room ...	915	85·04	5,010	84·50	5·48
				2 Rooms ...	138	12·82	747	12·60	2·71
				3 Rooms ...	18	1·67	136	2·29	2·52
				4 Rooms ...	2	·19	14	·24	1·75
				5 Rooms ...	2	·19	16	·27	1·60
				6 Rooms and over .	1	·9	6	·11	1·00
				Total ...	**163**	...	**1,123**	...	..
		" ...	4	1 Room ...	112	68·71	769	68·48	6·87
				2 Rooms ...	25	15·34	152	13·53	3·04
				3 Rooms ...	7	4·29	42	3·74	2·
				4 Rooms ...	8	4·85	53	4·72	1·66
				5 Rooms ...	8	4·85	44	3·93	1·10
				6 Rooms and over .	3	1·84	63	5·61	3·50
				Total ...	**983**	...	**4,822**	...	...
		" ...	5	1 Room ...	373	37·95	1,671	34·65	4·48
				2 Rooms ...	401	40·79	1,961	40·67	2·45
				3 Rooms ...	144	14·65	802	16·63	1·58
				4 Rooms ...	31	3·15	176	3·65	1·42
				5 Rooms ...	24	2·44	151	3·13	1·26
				6 Rooms and over .	10	1·02	61	1·27	1·02
				Total ...	**1,287**	...	**6,080**	...	...
		" ...	6	1 Room ...	922	71·64	3,895	64.06	4·22
				2 Rooms ...	172	13·36	792	13·02	2·30
				3 Rooms ...	41	3·19	197	3·24	1·60
				4 Rooms ...	44	3·43	287	4·72	1·63
				5 Rooms ...	34	2·64	278	4·57	1·64
				6 Rooms and over .	74	5·75	631	10·38	1·42

TABLE XIV—*continued.*

Table showing the number of tenements per inhabited house.

Ward.	Charge.	Section.	Circle Number.	Tenements with	Total Number of occupied tenements of each class.	Percentage of each class of tenements to total tenements.	Total Number of occupants of each class of tenements.	Percentage borne by population in each class of tenements to total population.	Average Number of occupants per room in each class of tenements.
				Total ...	757	...	2,862	...	...
D.	31	Girgaum ...	7	1 Room ...	513	67·77	1,779	62·16	3·47
				2 Rooms ...	128	16·91	407	14·22	1·59
				3 Rooms ...	8	1·06	75	2·62	3·12
				4 Rooms ...	43	5·68	202	7·06	1·17
				5 Rooms ...	14	1·85	66	2·31	·94
				6 Rooms and over .	51	6·74	333	11·64	1·09
				Total ...	2,272	...	11,369	...	...
		Total for Chaupati ...	...	1 Room ...	1,523	67·03	6,189	54·44	4·06
				2 Rooms ...	197	8·67	961	8·45	2·44
				3 Rooms ...	192	8·45	1,073	9·44	1·86
				4 Rooms ...	150	6·60	994	8·74	1·16
				5 Rooms ...	101	4·44	789	6·85	1·56
				6 Rooms and over .	109	4·80	1,363	11·99	2·08
				Total ...	291	...	1,272	...	...
	30	Chaupati ...	1	1 Room ...	222	76·29	788	61·95	3·55
				2 Rooms ...	14	4·81	61	4·80	2·18
				3 Rooms ...	17	5·84	72	5·66	1·41
				4 Rooms ...	11	3·78	32	2·52	·73
				5 Rooms ...	8	2·75	57	4·48	1·62
				6 Rooms and over .	19	6·53	263	20·56	2·30
				Total ...	409	...	1,758	...	...
		" ...	2	1 Room ...	280	68·46	948	53·92	3·08
				2 Rooms ...	30	7·33	94	5·34	1·57
				3 Rooms ...	34	8·31	171	9·72	1·06
				4 Rooms ...	27	6·60	197	11·21	1·82
				5 Rooms ...	19	4·65	134	7·62	1·41
				6 Rooms and over .	19	4·65	214	12·12	1·88
				Total ...	364	...	1,847	...	...
		" ...	3	1 Room ...	286	78·60	1,251	67·19	4·72
				2 Rooms ...	12	3·30	83	4·49	3·46
				3 Rooms ...	21	5·77	120	6·49	1·9
				4 Rooms ...	19	5·22	140	7·58	1·84
				5 Rooms ...	14	3·85	74	4·01	1·6
				6 Rooms and over .	12	3·30	179	4·49	2·49
				Total ...	295	...	1,618	...	...
		" ...	4	1 Room ...	200	67·80	970	59·95	4·85
				2 Rooms ...	24	8·14	117	7·28	2·44
				3 Rooms ...	23	7·80	110	6·80	1·59
				4 Rooms ...	20	6·78	141	8·71	1·76
				5 Rooms ...	14	4·75	80	4·94	1·14
				6 Rooms and over .	14	4·76	200	12·36	2·38
				Total ...	767	...	3,930	...	...
		" ...	5	1 Room ...	474	61·80	1,923	48·91	4·05
				2 Rooms ...	109	14·21	578	14·71	2·65
				3 Rooms ...	80	10·43	498	12·67	2·07
				4 Rooms ...	50	6·5	325	8·27	1·62
				5 Rooms ...	31	4·04	295	7·51	1·90
				6 Rooms and over .	23	2·99	312	7·9	2·26
				Total ...	146	...	944	...	...
		" ...	6	1 Room ...	61	41·78	310	32·84	5·08
				2 Rooms ...	8	5·48	28	2·97	1·75
				3 Rooms ...	17	11·64	102	10·80	2·
				4 Rooms ...	23	15·75	159	16·84	1·73
				5 Rooms ...	15	10·27	149	15·78	1·99
				6 Rooms and over .	22	15·07	196	20·76	1·43

TABLE XIV—*continued.*

Table showing the number of tenements per inhabited house.

Ward.	Charge.	Section.	Circle Number.	Tenements with	Total Number of occupied tenements of each class.	Percentage of each class of tenements to total tenements.	Total Number of occupants of each class of tenements.	Percentage borne by population in each class of tenements to total population.	Average Number of occupants per room in each class of tenements.
				Total ...	2,259	...	10,631	...	...
D.		Total for Walkeshwar ...	...	1 Room ...	1,487	65·83	7,862	73·95	5·29
				2 Rooms ...	430	19·08	834	7·84	·96
				3 Rooms ...	66	2·48	335	3·15	1·69
				4 Rooms ...	68	3·01	364	3·42	1·34
				5 Rooms ...	38	1·68	255	2·39	1·34
				6 Rooms and over .	170	7·53	981	9·22	·96
				Total ...	187	...	1,591	...	...
	29	Walkeshwar ...	1	1 Room ...	75	40·11	1,031	64·80	13·75
				2 Rooms ...	18	9·63	51	3·21	1·42
				3 Rooms ...	9	4·81	51	3·21	1·89
				4 Rooms ...	13	6·95	64	4·02	1·23
				5 Rooms ...	11	5·88	96	6·03	1·75
				6 Rooms and over .	61	32·62	298	18·73	·81
				Total ...	480	...	2,132	...	...
		„ ...	2	1 Room ...	272	56·67	1,817	80·53	6·68
				2 Rooms ...	156	32·50	162	7·60	·52
				3 Rooms ...	16	3·33	52	2·44	1·08
				4 Rooms ...	15	3·12	66	3·19	1·10
				5 Rooms ...	6	1·[illegible]5	23	1·08	·77
				6 Rooms and over.	15	3·12	12	·56	·13
				Total ...	361	...	1,873	...	...
		„ ...	3	1 Room ...	224	62·05	1,041	55·58	4·65
				2 Rooms ...	21	5·82	138	7·37	3·29
				3 Rooms ...	16	4·43	37	1·98	7·77
				4 Rooms ...	23	6·[illegible]7	64	3·42	·70
				5 Rooms ...	10	2·77	67	3·58	1·34
				6 Rooms and over.	67	18·56	526	2·81	1·31
				Total ...	102	...	272	...	...
		„ ...	4	1 Room ...	94	92·16	247	90·81	1·46
				2 Rooms ...	5	4·90	17	6·21	1·70
				3 Rooms ...	1	·98	4	1·46	1·33
				4 Rooms ...	...	...	...	...	...
				5 Rooms ...	2	1·96	4	1·46	·40
				6 Rooms and over .	...	...	...	...	...
				Total ...	246	...	835	...	...
		„ ...	5	1 Room ...	216	87·80	631	75·57	2·92
				2 Rooms ...	9	3·66	64	7·66	3·56
				3 Rooms ...	6	2·44	50	5·99	2·78
				4 Rooms ...	6	2·44	46	5·51	1·92
				5 Rooms ...	2	·81	16	1·92	1·60
				6 Rooms and over .	7	2·85	28	3·35	·67
				Total ...	661	...	2,694	...	...
		„ ...	6	1 Room ...	492	74·43	2,063	76·58	4·19
				2 Rooms ...	127	19·21	296	10·99	1·17
				3 Rooms ...	15	2·27	127	4·71	2·82
				4 Rooms ...	9	1·36	114	4·23	3·17
				5 Rooms ...	6	·91	37	1·37	1·23
				6 Rooms and over .	12	1·83	57	2·12	.79
				Total ...	222	...	1,234	...	...
		„ ...	7	1 Room ...	114	51·35	1,032	83·68	9·05
				2 Rooms ...	94	42·34	106	8·59	·56
				3 Rooms ...	3	1·35	14	1·13	1·56
				4 Rooms ...	2	·90	10	·81	1·28
				5 Rooms ...	1	·45	12	·97	2·40
				6 Rooms and over .	8	3·60	60	4·86	1·25

TABLE XIV—*continued.*

Table showing the number of tenements per inhabited house.

Ward.	Charge.	Section.	Circle Number.	Tenements with	Total Number of occupied tenements of each class.	Percentage of each class of tenements to total tenements.	Total Number of occupants of each class of tenements.	Percentage borne by population in each class of tenements to total population.	Average Number of occupants per room in each class of tenements.
				Total ...	**4 566**	...	**26,302**	...	...
D		**Total for Mahalaxmi**	...	1 Room ...	3,593	78·69	21,018	79·91	5·85
				2 Rooms ...	549	12·02	2,907	11·05	2·65
				3 Rooms ...	90	1·98	536	2·04	1·99
				4 Rooms ...	124	2·72	611	2·32	1·23
				5 Rooms ...	99	2·17	565	2·14	1·14
				6 Rooms and over.	111	2·43	665	2·52	1·00
				Total ...	**307**	...	**2,595**	...	...
	17	Mahalaxmi ...	1	1 Room ...	195	63·52	1,633	62·93	3·37
				2 Rooms ...	74	24·10	628	24·20	4·18
				3 Rooms ...	8	2·61	70	2·70	2·92
				4 Rooms ...	14	4·56	116	4·47	2·07
				5 Rooms ...	6	1·95	63	2·43	2·10
				6 Rooms and over.	10	3·26	85	3·28	1·42
				Total ...	**156**	...	**744**	...	...
		" ...	2	1 Room ...	84	53·85	363	48·79	4·32
				2 Rooms ...	66	42·31	351	47·18	2·66
				3 Rooms ...	6	3·85	30	4·03	1·67
				4 Rooms ...	...	...	...	...	...
				5 Rooms ...	...	...	...	..	...
				6 Rooms and over.	...	...	...	...	...
				Total ...	**213**	...	**1,056**	...	...
		" ..	3	1 Room ...	166	77·93	768	72·73	4·62
				2 Rooms ...	6	2·82	20	1·09	1·67
				3 Rooms ...	5	2·35	10	·95	·67
				4 Rooms ...	4	1·88	24	2·27	1·50
				5 Rooms ...	7	3·29	29	2·75	·83
				6 Rooms and over.	25	11·74	205	19·41	1·37
				Total ...	**497**	...	**2,817**	...	...
		" ...	4	1 Room ...	346	69·62	2,219	78·45	6·41
				2 Rooms ...	83	16·70	230	7·21	1·39
				3 Rooms ...	...	...	...	...	...
				4 Rooms ...	14	2·82	80	2·84	1·43
				5 Rooms ...	22	4·43	160	5·68	1·45
				6 Rooms and over.	32	6·44	128	4·54	·67
				Total ...	**440**	...	**2,335**	...	...
		" ...	5	1 Room ...	264	60·00	1,730	73·15	6·55
				2 Rooms ...	63	14·32	165	6·98	1·31
				3 Rooms ...	22	5·00	90	3·81	1·36
				4 Rooms ...	43	9·77	170	7·19	·99
				5 Rooms ...	36	8·11	150	6·34	·83
				6 Rooms and over.	12	2·73	60	2·54	·83
				Total ...	**501**	...	**3,856**	...	...
		" ...	6	1 Room ...	245	48·90	2,296	59·54	9·37
				2 Rooms ...	138	27·54	898	23·29	3·25
				3 Rooms ...	37	7·39	202	6·79	2·36
				4 Rooms ...	39	7·75	160	4·15	1·03
				5 Rooms ...	22	4·39	135	3·50	1·32
				6 Rooms and over	20	3·99	105	2·72	·87
				Total ...	**1,026**	...	**5,240**	...	...
		" ...	7	1 Room ...	994	96·88	4,997	95·36	5·03
				2 Rooms ...	22	2·14	152	2·90	3·45
				3 Rooms ...	4	·39	37	·71	3·08
				4 Rooms ...	3	·29	28	·53	2·33
				5 Rooms ...	1	·10	5	·10	5·00
				6 Rooms and over.	2	·19	21	·40	1·75

TABLE XIV—*continued.*

Table showing the number of tenements per inhabited house.

Ward.	Charge.	Section.	Circle Number.	Tenements with	Total Number of occupied tenements of each class.	Percentage of each class of tenements to total tenements.	Total Number of occupants of each class of tenements.	Percentage borne by population in each class of tenements to total population.	Average Number of occupants per room in each class of tenements.
				Total ...	**665**	...	**3,228**	...	...
D	17	Mahalaxmi ...	8	1 Room ...	582	87·52	2,885	89·37	4·96
				2 Rooms ...	83	12·48	343	10·63	2·07
				3 Rooms ...	...	...	...	...	...
				4 Rooms ...	...	...	...	...	...
				5 Rooms ...	...	...	...	...	...
				6 Rooms and over.	...	...	...	...	...
				Total ...	**761**	...	**4.401**	...	...
		" ...	9	1 Room ...	717	94·22	4,127	93·77	5·76
				2 Rooms ...	14	1·84	120	2·73	4·29
				3 Rooms ...	8	1·05	87	·84	1·54
				4 Rooms ...	7	·92	33	·75	1·18
				5 Rooms ...	5	·66	23	·52	·93
				6 Rooms and over.	10	1·31	61	1·39	1·02
				Total ...	**50.543**	...	**226.232**	...	...
E	...	**Total for E Ward.**	...	1 Room ...	45,675	90·37	202,993	89·73	4·45
				2 Rooms ...	2,997	5·93	14,060	62·15	2·51
				3 Rooms ...	1,103	2·18	3,780	1·67	1·14
				4 Rooms ...	444	·88	2,093	·93	1·18
				5 Rooms ...	136	·27	948	·42	1·39
				6 Rooms and over.	188	·37	2,358	1·05	2·20
				Total ...	**5.555**	...	**27,723**	...	...
		Total for Tardeo	...	1 Room ...	5,329	95·93	26,361	95·09	4·95
				2 Rooms ...	134	2·41	790	2·85	2·95
				3 Rooms ...	36	·64	196	·71	1·81
				4 Rooms ...	23	·41	109	·39	1·18
				5 Rooms ...	7	·13	65	·23	1·86
				6 Rooms and over.	26	·47	202	·73	1·28
				Total ...	**1.172**	...	**4.306**	...	...
	20	Tardeo ...	1	1 Room ...	1,079	92·06	3,551	82·47	3·29
				2 Rooms ...	47	4·01	368	8·55	3·91
				3 Rooms ...	14	1·19	105	2·44	2·50
				4 Rooms ...	15	1·28	84	1·95	1·40
				5 Rooms ...	3	·25	54	1·25	3·60
				6 Rooms and over.	14	1·19	144	3·34	1·71
				Total ...	**1.250**	...	**7,031**	...	...
		" ...	2	1 Room ...	1,169	93·52	6,726	95·65	5·75
				2 Rooms ...	49	3·92	202	2·87	2·06
				3 Rooms ...	14	1·12	57	·81	1·35
				4 Rooms ...	7	·56	24	·34	·86
				5 Rooms ...	4	·32	11	·16	·55
				6 Rooms and over.	7	·56	11	·16	26
				Total ...	**2,207**	...	**10,386**	...	...
		" ...	3	1 Room ...	2,194	94·88	10,308	99·25	4·70
				2 Rooms ...	9	·41	64	·62	8·56
				3 Rooms ...	1	·41	4	·4	1·33
				4 Rooms ...	1	·41	1	·1	·25
				5 Rooms ...	...	...	...	...	...
				6 Rooms and over.	2	9	9	9	·75
				Total ...	**926**	...	**6,000**	...	...
		" ...	4	1 Room ...	887	95·79	5,776	96·27	6·51
				2 Rooms ...	29	3·13	156	2·60	2·69
				3 Rooms ...	7	·76	30	·50	1·48
				4 Rooms ...	...	...	...	...	...
				5 Rooms ...	...	...	...	...	...
				6 Rooms and over.	3	·32	38	·63	2·11

TABLE XIV—*continued.*

Table showing the number of tenements per inhabited house.

Ward.	Charge.	Section.	Circle Number.	Tenements with	Total Number of occupied tenements of each class.	Percentage of each class of tenements to total tenements.	Total Number of occupants of each class of tenements.	Percentage borne by population in each class of tenements to total population.	Average Number of occupants per room in each class of tenements.
				Total ...	9.079	...	36.611	...	...
E	21	Total for Kamatipura ...	...	1 Room ...	6,153	66·77	25,181	69·05	4·09
				2 Rooms ...	1,793	19·75	8,165	22·30	2·28
				3 Rooms ...	796	8·77	2,117	5·78	·89
				4 Rooms ...	253	2·79	672	1·84	·66
				5 Rooms ...	51	·56	287	·78	1·13
				6 Rooms and over.	33	·36	189	·52	·95
				Total ...	1,833	...	7,859	...	...
	21	Kamatipura ...	1	1 Room ...	1,253	68·36	5,012	63·77	4·00
				2 Rooms ...	456	24·88	2,061	26·22	2·26
				3 Rooms ...	105	5·73	682	8·68	2·17
				4 Rooms ...	19	1·04	104	1·32	1·37
				5 Rooms ...	...	...	...	...	...
				6 Rooms and over.	...	...	...	...	...
				Total ...	4,197	...	15.742	...	...
		" ...	2	1 Room ...	1.988	47·37	8,158	51·82	4·10
				2 Rooms ...	1,236	29·45	5,511	35·01	2·23
				3 Rooms ...	674	16·06	1,210	7·81	·59
				4 Rooms ...	228	5·43	524	3·33	·57
				5 Rooms ...	47	1·12	217	1·38	·92
				6 Rooms and over.	24	·60	122	·79	·85
				Total ...	3,049	...	13,010	...	...
		" ...	3	1 Room ...	2.912	95·51	12,011	92·32	4·12
				2 Rooms ...	101	3·31	593	4·56	2·94
				3 Rooms ...	17	·56	225	1 73	4·41
				4 Rooms ...	6	·20	44	·34	1·83
				5 Rooms ...	4	·13	70	·54	3·50
				6 Rooms and over.	9	·30	67	·51	1·24
				Total ...	1.526	...	6.414	...	...
		Total for First-Nagpada ...	...	1 Room ...	1,305	85·51	5,364	86·75	4·11
				2 Rooms ...	116	7·60	476	7·42	2·05
				3 Rooms ...	41	2·69	222	3·46	1·80
				4 Rooms ...	31	2·03	116	1·81	·94
				5 Rooms ...	18	1·18	107	1·67	1·19
				6 Rooms and over.	15	·98	129	2 01	1·43
				Total ...	659	...	3.632	...	...
	18	First Nagpada ...	1	1 Room ...	609	92·41	2,864	78·85	4·70
				2 Rooms ...	32	4·86	273	7·52	4·27
				3 Rooms ...	4	·61	198	5·47	16·50
				4 Rooms ...	3	·46	108	2·70	9·
				5 Rooms ...	6	·91	103	2 84	3·43
				6 Rooms and over.	5	·76	86	2·37	2·87
				Total ...	867	...	2.782	...	...
		" ...	2	1 Room ...	696	80·28	2,590	89·86	3 59
				2 Rooms ...	84	9·69	203	7·66	1·21
				3 Rooms ...	37	4·27	24	·86	·22
				4 Rooms ...	28	3·23	8	·29	·7
				5 Rooms ...	12	1·38	4	·14	·7
				6 Rooms and over.	10	1·15	43	1·55	·72
				Total ...	6.153	...	21.700	...	...
		Total for Second Nagpada ...	...	1 Room ...	5,761	93·63	19,881	91·62	3·45
				2 Rooms ...	308	5·01	1,434	6·61	2·33
				3 Rooms ...	47	·76	190	·88	1·35
				4 Rooms ...	12	·20	67	·31	1 40
				5 Rooms ...	15	·24	87	·41	1·16
				6 Rooms and over.	10	·16	41	·19	·68

TABLE XIV—*continued.*

Table showing the number of tenements per inhabited house.

Ward.	Charge.	Section.	Circle Number.	Tenements with	Total Number of occupied tenements of each class.	Percentage of each class of tenements to total tenements.	Total Number of occupants of each class of tenements.	Percentage borne by population in each class of tenements to total population.	Average Number of occupants per room in each class of tenements.
				Total ...	**1,706**	...	**6,167**	...	...
E	19	Second Nagpada ...	1	1 Room ...	1,664	97·53	5,919	95·98	3·55
				2 Rooms ...	30	1·17	159	2·58	2·65
				3 Rooms ...	4	·23	33	·54	2·75
				4 Rooms ...	4	·23	17	·28	1·06
				5 Rooms ...	3	·18	32	·52	2·13
				6 Rooms and over .	1	·6	7	·11	1·17
				Total ...	**1,653**	...	**5,788**	...	...
		" ..	2	1 Room ...	1,455	88·02	4,936	81·82	3·39
				2 Rooms ...	163	9·86	705	12·18	2·16
				3 Rooms ...	18	1·09	82	1·42	1·52
				4 Rooms ...	2	·12	7	·12	·87
				5 Rooms ...	9	·54	44	·76	·98
				6 Rooms and over .	6	·36	14	·24	·37
				Total ...	**1,617**	...	**5,795**	...	...
		" ...	3	1 Room ...	1,480	91·53	5,145	88·78	3·48
				2 Rooms ...	101	6·25	504	8·70	2·50
				3 Rooms ...	24	1·48	72	1·24	1·00
				4 Rooms ..	6	·37	43	·74	1·79
				5 Rooms ...	3	·19	11	·19	·73
				6 Rooms and over .	3	·19	20	·35	1·11
				Total ...	**1,177**	...	**3.950**	...	...
		" ..	4	1 Room ..	1,162	98·73	3,881	98·25	3·34
				2 Rooms ...	14	1·20	66	1·67	2·36
				3 Rooms ...	1	·8	3	·8	1·00
				4 Rooms ..	...	–	...	...	...
				5 Rooms ...	...	...	...	...	...
				6 Rooms and over .	...	...	...	...	...
				Total ...	**16,622**	...	**75,307**	...	...
		Total for Byculla	...	1 Room ...	15,998	98·25	70,970	94·24	4·44
				2 Rooms ..	347	2·09	1,760	2·34	2·54
				3 Rooms ...	118	·71	658	·87	1·86
				4 Rooms ...	79	·48	872	1·16	2·44
				5 Rooms ..	25	·15	232	·31	1·86
				6 Rooms and over .	55	·33	815	1·08	2·47
				Total ...	**4,512**	...	**22,104**	...	...
	32	Byculla ...	1	1 Room ...	4,361	96·65	21,234	96·06	4·87
				2 Rooms ..	88	1·95	241	1·09	1·35
				3 Rooms ..	33	·73	146	·36	1·47
				4 Rooms ...	14	·31	237	1·07	4·23
				5 Rooms ...	6	·13	123	·56	4·10
				6 Rooms and over .	10	·22	123	·56	2·05
				Total ...	**895**	...	**4.847**	...	...
		" ...	2	1 Room ...	756	84·47	3.407	70·29	4·51
				2 Rooms ..	41	4·58	249	5·14	3·04
				3 Rooms ...	40	4·47	204	4·21	1·70
				4 Rooms ...	37	4·13	471	9·72	3·18
				5 Rooms ...	4	·45	8	·17	·40
				6 Rooms and over .	17	1·90	508	10·48	4·98
				Total ..	**3,849**	...	**15,281**	...	...
		" ...	3	1 Room ...	3,733	96·98	14,632	95·75	3·92
				2 Rooms ...	75	1·95	395	2·38	2·63
				3 Rooms ...	18	·47	119	·78	2·20
				4 Rooms ...	9	·23	28	·18	·78
				5 Rooms ...	5	·13	46	·30	1·84
				6 Rooms and over .	9	·23	61	·40	1·13

TABLE XIV—*continued.*

Table showing the number of tenements per inhabited house.

Ward.	Charge.	Section.	Circle Number.	Tenements with	Total Number of occupied tenements of each class.	Percentage of each class of tenements to total tenements.	Total Number of occupants of each class of tenements.	Percentage borne by population in each class of tenements to total population.	Average Number of occupants per room in each class of tenements.
				Total ...	**2,239**	...	**10,722**	...	...
E	32	Byculla ...	4	1 Room ...	2,163	96·61	10,197	95·10	4·71
				2 Rooms ..	53	2·37	335	3·12	3·16
				3 Rooms ..	7	·31	65	·61	3·10
				4 Rooms ...	8	·36	70	·65	2·19
				5 Rooms ...	4	·18	26	·24	1·30
				6 Rooms and over.	4	·18	29	·27	1·21
				Total ...	**937**	...	**4.146**	...	...
		" ...	5	1 Room ..	893	95·30	3,905	94·19	4·37
				2 Rooms ...	33	3·73	171	4·12	2·59
				3 Rooms ...	8	·85	49	1·18	2·04
				4 Rooms ...	2	·22	16	·38	2·00
				5 Rooms ...	1	·11	5	·12	1·00
				6 Rooms and over.	...	...	...	...	...
				Total ...	**1,216**	...	**5,835**	...	...
		" ...	6	1 Room ...	1,181	97·12	5,599	95·96	4·74
				2 Rooms ...	17	1·40	116	1·99	3·41
				3 Rooms ...	8	·66	47	·81	1·96
				4 Rooms ...	5	·41	34	·58	1·70
				5 Rooms ...	3	·25	10	·17	·67
				6 Rooms and over.	2	·16	29	·50	2·42
				Total ...	**1,457**	...	**6,280**	...	...
		" ...	7	1 Room ...	1,430	98·15	6,153	97·98	4·30
				2 Rooms ...	17	1·17	101	1·61	2·97
				3 Rooms ...	1	·7	4	·6	1·33
				4 Rooms ...	2	·14	8	·5	·87
				5 Rooms ...	...	...	...	...	...
				6 Rooms and over.	7	·48	19	·30	·45
				Total ...	**1,517**	...	**6,092**	...	...
		" ...	8	1 Room ...	1,481	97·63	5,843	95·91	3·95
				2 Rooms ...	23	1·52	153	2·49	3·30
				3 Rooms ...	3	·20	24	·39	2·67
				4 Rooms ...	2	·13	13	·21	1·62
				5 Rooms ...	2	·13	14	·23	1·4)
				6 Rooms and over.	6	·40	46	·76	1·28
				Total ...	**5,070**	...	**23,413**	...	...
		Total for Tadwadi.	...	1 Room ...	4,807	94·81	26,196	92·16	5·45
				2 Rooms ...	129	2·54	673	2·37	2·61
				3 Rooms ...	39	·77	275	·97	2·35
				4 Rooms ...	35	·69	198	·7)	1·41
				5 Rooms ...	15	·30	129	·42	1·72
				6 Rooms and over.	45	·89	952	3·35	3·53
				Total ...	**2,094**	...	**9 413**	...	...
	22	Tadwadi ...	1	1 Room ...	2,038	97·33	8,808	93·58	4·32
				2 Rooms ...	33	1·58	157	1·67	2·32
				3 Rooms ...	8	·33	130	1·38	5·42
				4 Rooms ...	6	·29	30	·32	1·25
				5 Rooms ...	3	·14	20	·21	1·33
				6 Rooms and over.	6	·29	268	2·85	7·44
				Total ...	**818**	...	**3.476**	...	...
		" ...	2	1 Room ...	740	90·46	2,718	78·10	3·67
				2 Rooms ...	38	4·65	147	4·23	1·93
				3 Rooms ...	17	2·08	77	2·22	1·51
				4 Rooms ...	1	·12	9	·26	2·25
				5 Rooms ...	7	·86	72	2·07	2·06
				6 Rooms and over.	15	·83	453	13·03	5·03

TABLE XIV—*continued.*

Table showing the number of tenements per inhabited house.

Ward.	Charge.	Section.	Circle Number.	Tenements with	Total Number of occupied tenements of each class.	Percentage of each class of tenements to total tenements.	Total Number of occupants of each class of tenements.	Percentage borne by population in each class of tenements to total population.	Average Number of occupants per room in each class of tenements.
...				**Total ...**	**2,158**	...	**15,524**	...	...
E	22	Tadwadi ...	3	1 Room ...	2,029	94·02	14,660	94·43	7·22
				2 Rooms ...	58	2·69	369	2·38	3·18
				3 Rooms ...	14	·65	68	·44	1·62
				4 Rooms ..	28	1·30	159	1·02	1·33
				5 Rooms ...	5	·23	37	·24	1·48
				6 Rooms and over .	24	1·11	231	·49	1·60
				Total ...	**6,538**	...	**30,064**	...	...
		Total for Mazagaon ...	...	1 Room ...	6,322	95·17	29,050	96·63	4·60
				2 Rooms ...	170	2·60	762	2·53	2·24
				3 Rooms ...	26	·40	122	·41	1·56
				4 Rooms ...	11	·17	59	·20	1·34
				5 Rooms ...	5	·8	41	·14	1·64
				6 Rooms and over .	4	·6	30	·10	1·25
				Total ...	**1,081**	...	**4,780**	...	...
	23	Mazagaon ...	1	1 Room ...	1,079	99·81	4,768	99·75	4·42
				2 Rooms ...	1	·9	5	·10	2·50
				3 Rooms ...	...	...	...	...	...
				4 Rooms ...	1	·9	7	·15	1·75
				5 Rooms ...	...	...	...	...	...
				6 Rooms and over .	...	...	...	...	...
				Total ...	**740**	...	**4,057**	...	...
		" ...	2	1 Room ...	732	5·49	4,017	98·92	99·01
				2 Rooms ...	6	2·08	25	·81	·62
				3 Rooms ...	2	2·50	15	·27	·37
				4 Rooms ...	...	...	...	...	...
				5 Rooms ..	...	...	...	...	...
				6 Rooms and over .	...	...	...	...	...
				Total ...	**970**	...	**4,196**	...	...
		" ...	3	1 Room ...	943	97·22	4,089	97·45	4·34
				2 Rooms ..	24	2·47	91	2·17	1·90
				3 Rooms ...	2	·21	10	·24	1·67
				4 Rooms ...	...	...	...	...	...
				5 Rooms ...	...	...	...	...	...
				6 Rooms and over .	1	·10	6	·14	1·00
				Total ...	**1,129**	...	**4,543**	...	...
		" ...	4	1 Room ...	1,050	92·93	4,209	92·65	4·01
				2 Rooms ...	60	5·40	238	5·24	1·98
				3 Rooms ...	12	1·06	42	·92	1·17
				4 Rooms ...	3	1·27	20	·44	1·67
				5 Rooms ..	4	·35	34	·75	1·70
				6 Rooms and over .	...	...	...	...	...
				Total ...	**2,618**	...	**12,488**	...	...
		" ...	5	1 Room ...	2,518	96·18	11,967	95·83	4·75
				2 Rooms ...	70	3·02	403	3·23	2·55
				3 Rooms ...	10	·38	55	·44	1·83
				4 Rooms ...	7	·27	82	·26	1·14
				5 Rooms ...	1	·4	7	·6	1·40
				6 Rooms and over .	3	·11	24	·19	1·33
				Total ...	**21,571**	...	**94,898**	...	...
F	...	**Total for F Ward...**	...	1 Room ...	17,948	83·20	73,836	77·81	4·16
				2 Rooms ...	2,374	10·96	12,659	13·27	2·67
				3 Rooms ...	515	2·39	2,971	3·13	1·92
				4 Rooms ...	304	1·41	2,329	2·45	1·93
				5 Rooms ...	131	·61	929	·97	1·42
				6 Rooms and over .	299	1·39	2,144	2·26	1·19

TABLE XIV—*continued.*

Table showing the number of tenements per inhabited house.

Ward.	Charge.	Section.	Circle Number.	Tenements with	Total Number of occupied tenements of each class.	Percentage of each class of tenements to total tenements.	Total Number of occupants of each class of tenements.	Percentage borne by population in each class of tenements to total population.	Average Number of occupants per room in each class of tenements.
				Total ...	**11,361**	...	**45,216**	...	...
F		**Total for Parel** ...	...	1 Room ...	9,779	86·07	37,136	82·13	3·80
				2 Rooms ...	1,053	9·27	4,908	10·85	2·33
				3 Rooms ...	212	1·87	1,175	2·60	1·85
				4 Rooms ...	129	1·05	818	1·81	1·59
				5 Rooms ...	50	·44	308	·68	1·23
				6 Rooms and over .	138	1·21	871	1·71	1·05
				Total ...	**1,183**	...	**4,010**	...	...
	24	Parel ...	1	1 Room ...	1,069	90·36	3,474	86·63	3·25
				2 Rooms ...	76	6·42	332	8·28	2·18
				3 Rooms ...	10	·85	54	1·35	1·80
				4 Rooms ...	9	·76	38	·95	1·06
				5 Rooms ...	3	·25	15	·37	1·00
				6 Rooms and over .	16	1·35	97	2·42	1·01
				Total ...	**1,198**	...	**5,780**	...	...
		" ...	2	1 Room ...	1,018	84·98	4,903	84·83	4·55
				2 Rooms ...	97	8·10	491	8·49	2·53
				3 Rooms ...	46	3·84	209	3·62	1·51
				4 Rooms ...	14	1·17	71	1·23	1·27
				5 Rooms ...	8	·61	13	·22	·32
				6 Rooms and over .	15	1·25	93	1·61	1·03
				Total ...	**1,640**	...	**6,916**	...	...
		" ...	3	1 Room ...	1,377	83·96	5,672	82·16	4·12
				2 Rooms ...	210	12·80	927	13·40	2·21
				3 Rooms ...	15	·91	100	1·45	2·22
				4 Rooms ...	27	1·65	150	2·17	1·39
				5 Rooms ...	6	·37	37	·53	1·23
				6 Rooms and over .	5	·30	30	·43	1·00
				Total ...	**1,821**	...	**6,533**	...	...
		" ...	4	1 Room ...	1,693	92·92	5,854	89·61	3·46
				2 Rooms ...	99	6·43	490	7·50	2·47
				3 Rooms ...	9	·49	81	1·24	3·00
				4 Rooms ...	5	·27	18	·28	·90
				5 Rooms ...	4	·22	28	·43	1·40
				6 Rooms and over .	11	·60	62	·95	·94
				Total ...	**220**	...	**830**	...	...
		" ...	5	1 Room ...	140	63·64	438	52·77	3·18
				2 Rooms ...	52	23·64	214	25·78	2·06
				3 Rooms ...	12	5·45	87	10·48	2·42
				4 Rooms ...	7	3·18	46	5·54	1·64
				5 Rooms ...	2	·91	7	·84	·70
				6 Rooms and over .	7	3·18	38	4·58	·90
				Total ...	**1,659**	...	**6,807**	...	...
		" ...	6	1 Room ...	1,330	80·17	4,984	77·22	3·75
				2 Rooms ...	174	10·49	837	12·29	2·41
				3 Rooms ...	60	3·62	321	4·72	1·78
				4 Rooms ...	37	2·23	255	3·75	1·11
				5 Rooms ...	10	·60	105	1·54	2·10
				6 Rooms and over .	48	2·89	295	4·33	1·03
				Total ...	**1,177**	...	**4,299**	...	...
		" ...	7	1 Room ...	1,097	9·32	3,789	88·13	3·45
				2 Rooms ...	59	5·01	329	7·65	2·79
				3 Rooms ...	10	·85	89	2·07	2·97
				4 Rooms ...	4	·34	41	·95	12·56
				5 Rooms ...	2	·17	23	·51	12·20
				6 Rooms and over .	5	·42	29	·67	1·97

TABLE XIV—*continued.*

Table showing the number of tenements per inhabited house.

Ward.	Charge.	Section.	Circle Number.	Tenements with	Total Number of occupied tenements of each class.	Percentage of each class of tenements to total tenements.	Total Number of occupants of each class of tenements.	Percentage borne by population in each class of tenements to total population.	Average Number of occupants per room in each class of tenements.
				Total ...	**1,761**	...	**7,322**	...	...
F	24	Parel ..	8	1 Room ...	1,568	89·04	6,302	86·07	4·02
				2 Rooms ...	140	7·95	708	19·67	2·53
				3 Rooms ...	24	1·36	119	1·63	1·65
				4 Rooms ...	7	·40	51	1·70	1·82
				5 Rooms ...	11	1·62	58	1·80	1·05
				6 Rooms and over.	11	·62	84	1·15	1·27
				Total ...	**702**	...	**2,719**	...	...
		„ ...	9	1 Room ...	487	69·37	1,720	63·26	3·53
				2 Rooms ...	146	20·80	580	21·33	1·99
				3 Rooms ...	26	3·70	115	4·23	1·48
				4 Rooms ...	19	2·71	138	5·08	1·82
				5 Rooms ...	4	·57	23	·85	1·15
				6 Rooms and over.	20	2·85	143	5·26	1·19
				Total ...	**4,149**	...	**19,032**	...	...
		Total for Sewri ...	...	1 Room ...	3,813	91·90	16,959	89·11	4·19
				2 Rooms ...	250	6·02	1,530	8·04	3·06
				3 Rooms ...	45	1·08	311	1·63	2·30
				4 Rooms ...	24	·58	155	·82	1·61
				5 Rooms ...	7	·17	33	·17	·94
				6 Rooms and over.	10	·24	44	·23	·73
				Total ...	**1,424**	...	**6,453**	...	...
	25	Sewri ...	1	1 Room ...	1,386	97·33	6,281	97·33	4·53
				2 Rooms ...	32	2·25	129	1·84	2·02
				3 Rooms ...	4	·28	31	·48	2·58
				4 Rooms ...	1	·7	5	·8	1·25
				5 Rooms ...	1	·7	7	·2	1·40
				6 Rooms and over.	...	...	...	...	...
				Total ...	**952**	...	**3,872**	...	...
		„ ...	2	1 Room ...	933	98·00	3,765	97·24	4·04
				2 Rooms ..	18	1·89	103	2·66	2·86
				3 Rooms ...	1	·10	4	·10	1·33
				4 Rooms ...	...	...	...	...	...
				5 Rooms ...	...	...	...	...	...
				6 Rooms and over.	...	...	...	...	...
				Total ...	**472**	...	**1,869**	...	...
		„ ...	3	1 Room ...	434	91·93	1,743	93·26	4·02
				2 Rooms ...	25	5·30	89	4·67	1·78
				3 Rooms ..	10	2·12	30	1·61	1·00
				4 Rooms ...	3	·64	7	·37	·58
				5 Rooms ...	...	...	...	...	...
				6 Rooms and over.	...	...	...	...	...
				Total ...	**1,134**	...	**5,675**	...	...
		„ ..	4	1 Room ...	894	78·84	4,022	7·09	4·72
				2 Rooms ...	174	15·34	1,194	21·04	4·77
				3 Rooms ...	30	2·65	246	4·33	2·73
				4 Rooms ...	20	1·76	143	2·52	1·79
				5 Rooms ...	6	·53	26	·46	·87
				6 Rooms and over.	10	·88	44	·78	·73
				Total ...	**167**	...	**1,163**	...	...
		„ ...	5	1 Room ...	166	99·40	1,148	98·71	6·92
				2 Rooms ...	1	·60	15	1·29	7·50
				3 Rooms ...	...	...	...	...	...
				4 Rooms ...	...	...	...	...	...
				5 Rooms ...	...	...	...	...	...
				6 Rooms and over.	...	...	...	...	...

TABLE XIV—*continued.*

Table showing the number of tenements per inhabited house.

Ward.	Charge.	Section.	Circle Number.	Tenements with	Total Number of occupied tenements of each class.	Percentage of each class of tenements to total tenements.	Total Number of occupants in each class of tenements.	Percentage borne by population in each class of tenements to total population.	Average Number of occupants per room in each class of tenements.
				Total ...	**6,061**	...	**30,650**	...	...
F		**Total for Sion** ...	...	1 Room ...	4,356	71·87	19,741	64·41	4·53
				2 Rooms ...	1,071	17·67	6,251	20·36	2·92
				3 Rooms ...	258	4·26	1,485	4·84	1·92
				4 Rooms ...	161	2·49	1,356	4·43	2·24
				5 Rooms ...	74	1·22	588	1·45	1·59
				6 Rooms and over .	161	2·49	1,229	4·01	1·35
				Total ...	**816**	...	**4,140**	...	...
	26	Sion ...	1	1 Room ...	588	72·06	2,747	66·35	4·33
				2 Rooms ...	138	16·91	763	18·43	2·40
				3 Rooms ...	26	3·18	144	3·48	1·85
				4 Rooms ...	19	2·33	153	3·70	2·01
				5 Rooms ...	10	1·22	45	1·09	·90
				6 Rooms and over .	35	4·29	288	6·96	1·37
				Total ...	**285**	...	**1,299**	...	...
		" ...	2	1 Room ...	185	64·91	692	53·64	3·74
				2 Rooms ...	52	18·25	245	18·99	2·36
				3 Rooms ...	18	6·32	58	4·49	1·07
				4 Rooms ...	10	3·51	121	9·38	3·02
				5 Rooms ...	7	2·46	49	3·72	1·40
				6 Rooms and over .	13	4·56	125	9·69	1·60
				Total ...	**1,132**	...	**5,124**	...	...
		" ...	3	1 Room ...	881	77·83	3,337	65·12	3·79
				2 Rooms ...	192	16·96	1,538	30·01	4·01
				3 Rooms ...	32	2·83	108	2·17	1·12
				4 Rooms ...	7	·62	30	·55	1·07
				5 Rooms ...	5	·44	46	·89	1·84
				6 Rooms and over .	15	1·32	65	1·27	·72
				Total ...	**951**	...	**4,426**	...	...
		" ...	4	1 Room ...	684	71·92	2,875	64·96	4·20
				2 Rooms ...	207	21·77	1,085	24·51	2·62
				3 Rooms ...	24	12·52	125	2·82	1·73
				4 Rooms ...	21	2·21	194	4·38	2·31
				5 Rooms ...	7	·74	64	1·44	1·83
				6 Rooms and over .	8	·84	83	1·88	1·73
				Total ...	**475**	...	**2,420**	...	...
		" ...	5	1 Room ...	273	57·47	1,279	52·85	4·69
				2 Rooms ...	109	20·84	513	21·19	2·35
				3 Rooms ...	44	9·27	217	8·96	1·64
				4 Rooms ...	20	4·21	209	8·63	2·61
				5 Rooms ...	12	2·53	75	3·10	1·25
				6 Rooms and over .	17	3·58	127	5·25	1·25
				Total ...	**525**	...	**2,992**	...	...
		" ...	6	1 Room ...	372	70·85	1,987	66·42	5·34
				2 Rooms ...	94	17·90	484	16·18	2·58
				3 Rooms ...	28	5·33	210	7·02	2·50
				4 Rooms ...	12	2·28	163	5·45	3·40
				5 Rooms ...	5	·95	38	1·27	1·52
				6 Rooms and over .	14	2·67	110	3·68	1·31
				Total ...	**403**	...	**2,631**	...	...
		" ...	7	1 Room ...	315	78·16	2,025	76·97	6·43
				2 Rooms ..	50	12·41	232	88·18	2·32
				3 Rooms ...	23	5·71	136	5·18	1·97
				4 Rooms ..	8	1·98	63	2·39	1·97
				5 Rooms ..	5	1·24	146	5·55	5·76
				6 Rooms and over .	2	1·50	29	1·10	2·42

TABLE XIV—*continued.*

Table showing the number of tenements per inhabited house.

Ward.	Charge.	Section.	Circle Number.	Tenements with	Total Number of occupied tenements of each class.	Percentage of each class of tenements to total tenements.	Total Number of occupants of each class of tenements.	Percentage borne by population in each class of tenements to total population.	Average Number of occupants per room in each class of tenements.
				Total ...	**561**	...	**3,215**	...	...
F	26	Soin ...	8	1 Room	469	83·24	2,368	73·65	5·05
				2 Rooms ...	53	9·45	526	16·36	4·52
				3 Rooms ...	11	1·96	115	3·58	3·49
				4 Rooms ...	13	2·32	87	2·71	1·67
				5 Rooms ..	7	1·25	43	1·34	1·23
				6 Rooms and over .	8	1·43	76	2·36	1·59
				Total ...	**262**	...	**1,148**	...	...
		" ...	9	1 Room ...	149	56·87	533	46·43	3·58
				2 Rooms ...	64	24·43	273	23·78	2·13
				3 Rooms ...	19	7·25	148	12·89	2·60
				4 Rooms ..	15	5·73	100	8·71	1·67
				5 Rooms ...	8	3·05	38	3·31	·95
				6 Rooms and over .	7	2·67	56	4·88	1·33
				Total ..	**270**	...	**1,312**	...	...
		" ...	10	1 Room ...	170	62·93	652	49·69	3·84
				2 Rooms ...	55	20·37	281	21·42	2·55
				3 Rooms ...	10	3·70	82	6·25	2·73
				4 Rooms ...	7	2·22	63	4·80	2·25
				5 Rooms ..	4	1·48	24	1·83	1·20
				6 Rooms and over.	24	8·89	210	1·60	1·46
				Total ...	**381**	...	**1,952**	...	...
		" ...	11	1 Room ...	270	70·87	1,246	63·83	4·62
				2 Rooms ...	57	14·97	311	15·93	2·73
				3 Rooms ..	23	6·04	142	7·28	2·06
				4 Rooms ...	19	4·99	173	8·86	2·28
				5 Rooms ...	4	1·05	20	1·02	1·00
				6 Rooms and over .	8	2·10	60	3·07	1·25
				Total ...	**22,903**	...	**1,19,719**	...	...
G	...	**Total for G Ward** .	...	1 Room ...	17,564	76·69	89,452	74·64	5·09
				2 Rooms ...	3,481	15·20	18,625	15·56	2·68
				3 Rooms ...	906	3·96	5,310	4·44	2·95
				4 Rooms ...	500	2·18	2,880	2·41	1·44
				5 Rooms ...	252	2·10	1,632	1·36	1·30
				6 Rooms and over .	200	·87	1,820	1·52	1·52
				Total ...	**5,715**	...	**30,253**	...	...
		Total for Mahim ..	...	1 Room ...	3,410	59·68	17,692	58·48	5·19
				2 Rooms ...	1,147	20·07	5,956	19·69	2·40
				3 Rooms ...	548	9·61	3,178	10·50	1·93
				4 Rooms ...	334	5·85	1,630	5·39	1·22
				5 Rooms ...	184	3·22	1,125	3·39	1·22
				6 Rooms and over .	92	1·61	672	2·22	1·22
				Total ...	**592**	...	**2,625**	...	...
	27	Mahim ...	1	1 Room ...	456	77·03	1,878	71·55	4·12
				2 Rooms ...	66	11·15	320	12·19	2·42
				3 Rooms .	40	6·76	218	8·30	1·82
				4 Rooms	24	4·05	149	5·68	1·55
				5 Rooms ...	3	·51	48	1·83	3·20
				6 Rooms and over.	3	·51	12	·46	·67
				Total ...	**658**	...	**3,715**	...	...
		" ...	2	1 Room ...	298	45·29	1,720	46·30	5·77
				2 Rooms ...	136	20·67	848	22·08	3·12
				3 Rooms ...	77	11·70	392	10·55	1·70
				4 Rooms ...	80	12·16	422	11·36	1·32
				5 Rooms ...	36	5·47	185	4·98	1·08
				6 Rooms and over .	31	4·71	148	3·98	·80

TABLE XIV—*continued.*

Table showing the number of tenements per inhabited house.

Ward.	Charge.	Section.	Circle Number.	Tenements with	Total Number of occupied tenements of each class.	Percentage of each class of tenements to total tenements.	Total Number of occupants of each class of tenements.	Percentage borne by population in each class of tenements to total population.	Average Number of occupants per room in each class of tenements.
				Total ...	652	...	3.440	...	...
G	27	Mahim ...	3	1 Room ...	446	68·40	2,240	65·12	5·02
				2 Rooms ...	181	20·09	605	17·59	2·31
				3 Rooms ...	32	4·91	245	7·12	2·55
				4 Rooms ...	26	3·99	185	5·38	1·78
				5 Rooms ...	6	·92	52	1·51	1·73
				6 Rooms and over .	11	1·69	113	3·28	1·71
				Total ...	413	...	2,313	...	...
		" ...	4	1 Room ...	192	46·49	1,086	46·95	5·66
				2 Rooms ...	95	23·00	485	20·97	3·55
				3 Rooms ...	51	12·35	364	15·74	2·38
				4 Rooms ...	43	10·41	178	7·74	1·03
				5 Rooms ...	26	6·30	150	6·48	1·15
				6 Rooms and over.	6	1·45	50	2·16	1·39
				Total ...	1,057	...	5,068	...	...
		" ...	5	1 Room ...	694	65·66	2,981	58·82	4·30
				2 Rooms ...	195	18·45	986	19·46	2·53
				3 Rooms ...	84	7·95	484	9·55	1·92
				4 Rooms ...	47	4·45	232	4·58	1·23
				5 Rooms ...	20	1·89	235	4·64	2·35
				6 Rooms and over .	17	1·61	150	·33	1·47
				Total ...	1.055	...	5.825	...	...
		" ...	6	1 Room ...	552	52·32	3,261	55·98	5·91
				2 Rooms ...	250	23·70	1,225	21·03	2·45
				3 Rooms ...	138	13·08	737	12·65	1·78
				4 Rooms ...	56	5·31	233	4·00	1·04
				5 Rooms ...	42	3·98	256	4·39	1·27
				6 Rooms and oyer .	17	1·61	113	1·94	1·11
				Total ...	346	...	1.886.	...	...
		" ...	7	1 Room ...	247	71·39	1,268	67·23	5·13
				2 Rooms ...	69	19·94	440	23·33	3·19
				3 Rooms ...	23	6·65	127	6·73	1·84
				4 Rooms ...	5	1·45	36	1·91	1·80
				5 Rooms ...	1	·29	9	·48	1·80
				6 Rooms and over.	1	·29	6	·32	1·00
				Total ...	942	...	5.381	...	...
		" ...	8	1 Room ...	525	55·73	3,258	60·55	6·21
				2 Rooms ...	205	21·76	1,047	19·45	2·55
				3 Rooms ...	103	10·93	611	11·36	1·98
				4 Rooms ...	53	5·63	195	3·62	·92
				5 Rooms ...	50	5·31	190	3·54	·76
				6 Rooms and over.	6	·64	80	1·49	2·22
				Total ...	17.188	...	89.468	...	...
		Total for Warli ...	...	1 Room ...	14,154	82·35	71,760	80·32	5·07
				2 Rooms ...	2,334	18·58	12,669	14·16	2·70
				3 Rooms ..	358	2·08	2,132	2·38	1·91
				4 Rooms ...	166	·97	1,250	1·40	1·88
				5 Rooms ...	68	·40	507	·58	1·49
				6 Rooms and over.	108	·63	1,148	1·28	1·77
				Total ...	594	...	2.685	...	...
	28	Warli ...	1	1 Room ...	576	96·97	2,594	96·61	4·50
				2 Rooms ...	12	2·02	64	2·38	2·67
				3 Rooms ...	3	·51	19	·71	2·11
				4 Rooms ...	2	·34	2	·7	·25
				5 Rooms ...	...	...	...	...	...
				6 Rooms and over .	1	·17	6	·22	1·00

TABLE XIV—*continued.*

Table showing the number of tenements per inhabited house.

Ward.	Charge.	Section.	Circle Number.	Tenements with	Total Number of occupied tenements of each class.	Percentage of each class of tenements to total tenements.	Total Number of occupants of each class of tenements.	Percentage borne by population in each class of tenements to total population.	Average Number of occupants per room in each class of tenements.
				Total ...	2,077	...	10,764	...	...
G	28	Warli ...	2	1 Room ...	1,805	86·90	9,270	86·12	5·10
				2 Rooms ...	233	11·22	1,287	11·96	2·76
				3 Rooms ...	14	·67	71	·66	1·69
				4 Rooms ...	12	·58	58	·54	1·21
				5 Rooms ...	5	·24	9	·8	·36
				6 Rooms and over .	8	·39	69	·64	1·44
				Total ...	1,649	...	9.190	...	...
		" ...	3	1 Room ...	1,426	86·48	8,020	87·27	5·62
				2 Rooms ...	130	7·88	682	7·42	2·62
				3 Rooms ...	52	3·15	202	2·20	1·29
				4 Rooms ...	22	1·33	152	1·65	1·73
				5 Rooms ...	3	·18	32	·35	2·13
				6 Rooms and over .	16	·97	102	1·11	1·06
				Total ...	910	...	4,812	...	...
		" ...	4	1 Room ...	787	86·48	4,056	84·29	5·15
				2 Rooms ...	120	13·19	737	15·32	3·07
				3 Rooms ...	3	·33	19	·39	2·11
				4 Rooms ...	...	...	...	...	...
				5 Rooms ...	...	...	...	...	...
				6 Rooms and over .	...	...	...	...	...
				Total ...	2,727	...	13,327	...	...
		" ...	5	1 Room ...	2,260	82·87	10,487	75·69	4·64
				2 Rooms ...	359	13·16	2,107	15·81	2·93
				3 Rooms ...	59	2·16	359	2·69	2·03
				4 Rooms ...	23	·84	171	1·28	1·86
				5 Rooms ...	11	·40	62	·47	1·13
				6 Rooms and over.	15	·55	141	1·06	1·57
				Total ...	991	...	5,866	...	...
		" ...	6	1 Room ...	726	73·26	4,074	69·45	5·61
				2 Rooms ...	203	20·48	1,196	2·04	2·94
				3 Rooms ...	30	3·03	241	4·11	2·68
				4 Rooms ...	17	1·72	170	2·90	2·50
				5 Rooms ...	8	·81	96	1·69	2·40
				6 Rooms and over .	7	·71	89	1·5	2·12
				Total ...	3.591	...	17,412	...	...
		" ...	7	1 Room ...	3,200	89·11	14,949	85·85	4·67
				2 Rooms ...	230	6·40	1,317	7·56	2·86
				3 Rooms ...	96	2·67	507	2·91	1·76
				4 Rooms ...	24	·67	155	·89	1·61
				5 Rooms ...	16	·45	127	·73	1·59
				6 Rooms and over .	25	·70	357	2·05	2·38
				Total ...	4,649	...	25,410	...	...
		" ...	8	1 Room ...	3,374	72·57	18,310	72·06	5·48
				2 Rooms ...	1,047	22·52	5,279	20·78	2·52
				3 Rooms ...	101	2·17	714	2·81	2·36
				4 Rooms ...	66	1·42	542	2·13	2·05
				5 Rooms ...	25	·54	181	·71	1·45
				6 Rooms and over .	36	·77	384	1·61	1·76

TABLE XV.

TABLE SHOWING TOTAL POPULATION OF EACH RELIGION IN EACH CIRCLE AND ITS RELATION TO HOUSES.

TABLE XV.

TOTAL POPULATION OF EACH RELIGION, ETC.

TABLE XV.

TABLE SHOWING TOTAL POPULATION OF EACH RELIGION IN EACH CIRCLE AND ITS RELATION TO HOUSES AND TENEMENTS.

Ward.	Charge.	Section.	Circle No.	Total number of buildings.	Total number of persons.	Religion.	Total number of separate tenements occupied by persons of each religion with One room.	Two rooms.	Three rooms.	Four rooms.	Five rooms.	Six rooms and over.	Total number of tenements of all kinds occupied by members of each religion.	Total number of members of each religion occupying tenements with One room.	Two rooms.	Three rooms.	Four rooms.	Five rooms.	Six rooms and over.	Total number of members of each religion occupying tenements of all kinds.	Percentage of total population of each religion occupying each class of tenements with One room.	Two rooms.	Three rooms.	Four rooms.	Five rooms.	Six rooms and over.
		1	2	3	4	5	6	7	8	9	10	11	12	13	14	15	16	17	18	19	20	21	22	23	24	25
						Grand Total ...	166,337	19,412	6,122	3,799	1,964	3,674	200,308	743,247	92,109	33,055	23,375	14,014	23,282	929,682	80·00	9·91	3·56	3·52	1·51	2·50
	...	Total, Bombay City.	...	30,909	929,062	Christians ...	6,694	1,073	650	698	398	402	9,705	28,751	5,682	4,197	4,150	2,581	3,911	49,272	58·38	11·53	8·52	8·42	5·24	7·94
						Parsis ...	4,878	2,034	1,234	678	479	631	10,100	21,401	9,508	6,611	4,837	3,133	4,836	50,326	42·27	18·78	13·06	9·56	6·79	9·55
						Mahomedans ...	37,781	2,973	707	347	169	249	42,326	145,055	13,371	4,217	2,702	1,207	2,025	172,507	85·84	7·75	2·44	1·57	·70	1·70
						Hindus ...	111,825	12,408	3,149	1,760	877	1,258	131,343	527,401	59,937	16,922	10,836	6,408	10,911	632,503	83·30	9·48	2·68	1·71	1·02	1·72
						Jains ...	3,801	727	203	147	44	99	5,021	12,570	2,980	958	720	287	550	18,054	69·63	16·14	5·31	3·99	1·59	3·05
						Jews and others ...	1,368	137	59	33	8	32	1,637	4,940	632	150	130	40	149	6,060	81·67	10·59	2·48	2·14	·66	2·46
						Total ...	9,197	1,761	894	598	333	535	13,318	47,718	7,164	4,221	2,974	1,829	3,672	67,576	70·61	10·60	6·25	4·40	2·71	5·43
A.	...	Total, A Ward ...	...	2,656	67,576	Christians ...	1,305	171	124	154	134	112	2,000	6,182	819	580	664	598	931	9,785	63·18	8·30	6·02	6·79	6·11	9·54
						Parsis ...	767	790	497	251	117	159	2,621	2,729	3,085	2,347	1,446	738	1,145	11,492	23·75	26·85	20·42	12·60	6·42	9·96
						Mahomedans ...	910	129	40	23	12	28	1,156	5,222	488	191	188	61	228	6,378	81·88	7·65	2·99	2·95	·96	3·57
						Hindus ...	5,908	550	209	104	61	201	7,062	32,847	2,482	1,007	578	394	1,301	38,609	85·08	6·43	2·61	1·50	1·02	3·36
						Jains ...	219	51	17	15	4	15	322	524	218	71	70	10	37	930	56·34	23·41	7·63	7·53	1·08	3·98
						Jews and others ...	79	21	7	6	5	9	127	212	73	16	26	28	27	382	55·50	19·11	4·19	6·80	7·33	7·07
						Total ...	260	19	10	12	7	8	316	1,194	171	45	40	14	29	1,493	79·97	11·45	3·01	2·68	·94	1·95
	1	Upper Colaba ...	1	79	1,493	Christians ...	28	4	1	2	2	3	40	143	38	6	6	4	10	213	69·96	16·90	2·82	3·75	1·88	4·69
						Parsis ...	6	3	1	1	2	4	17	59	20	10	4	1	10	104	56·73	19·23	9·62	3·85	·96	9·61
						Mahomedans ...	32	4	2	1	...	...	39	81	15	8	10	0	...	94	64·89	15·96	8·51	10·64	...	...
						Hindus ...	187	8	6	9	3	1	213	907	100	21	16	9	9	1,064	85·24	9·40	1·97	1·60	·85	·85
						Jains ...	5	...	...	...	...	...	5	14	...	...	...	...	...	14	100·	...	...	...	...	...
						Jews and others ...	2	...	...	...	...	...	2	4	...	...	...	...	...	4	100·	...	...	...	...	...
						Total ...	3,194	163	148	178	153	220	4,056	15,920	761	507	696	670	1,123	19,677	80·91	3·87	2·57	3·54	3·40	5·71
	...	Total for Lower Colaba	...	688	19,677	Christians ...	592	39	76	115	117	44	983	2,552	135	204	410	472	285	4,058	62·89	3·33	5·03	10·10	11·63	7·02
						Parsis ...	131	12	33	35	19	33	262	460	52	102	133	90	213	1,008	45·15	4·73	9·29	12·11	9·02	10·40
						Mahomedans ...	370	12	9	11	2	8	412	957	42	31	56	21	48	1,155	83·86	3·64	2·94	4·35	1·91	3·90
						Hindus ...	2,018	89	26	12	12	132	3,240	11,725	402	159	72	63	571	13,081	89·63	3·76	1·21	·55	·48	4·37
						Jains ...	37	7	...	...	...	...	44	103	26	...	...	...	...	128	70·60	20·31	...	...	...	...
						Jews and others ...	46	4	4	5	3	3	65	95	14	9	25	15	9	157	54·15	8·93	5·73	15·92	9·55	5·73
						Total ...	439	30	24	34	51	77	655	1,206	119	64	175	220	740	2,524	47·78	4·71	2·54	6·93	8·72	29·32
	2	Lower Colaba ...	1	134	2,524	Christians ...	168	10	13	17	33	20	200	530	39	31	84	119	162	965	54·92	4·05	3·21	8·70	12·33	16·79
						Parsis ...	90	7	10	12	13	12	134	208	44	23	53	57	93	508	52·46	7·75	4·05	9·33	10·04	16·37
						Mahomedans ...	39	1	1	3	2	5	51	101	6	6	20	21	35	195	51·79	3·08	3·08	13·33	10·77	17·95
						Hindus ...	119	9	1	2	3	40	174	224	24	4	12	23	450	741	30·77	3·24	·54	1·62	3·10	60·73
						Jains ...	3	...	...	...	...	...	3	10	...	...	...	...	...	10	100·	...	...	...	...	...
						Jews and others ...	30	3	...	...	...	...	33	39	6	...	...	...	...	45	86·67	13·33	...	...	...	...
						Total ...	439	11	6	14	7	29	505	2,405	46	24	62	83	198	2,768	86·89	1·66	·87	2·24	1·19	7·15
	...	,,	2	123	2,768	Christians ...	32	4	2	7	6	17	68	63	14	7	30	26	100	269	30·86	5·20	2·60	14·50	9·67	37·17
						Parsis ...	7	...	1	5	...	8	21	36	...	6	12	...	53	107	33·64	...	5·61	11·21	...	49·51
						Mahomedans ...	24	3	1	1	...	1	30	85	12	5	7	...	1	110	77·27	10·91	4·55	6·36	...	·91
						Hindus ...	376	4	1	1	1	3	385	2,100	12	6	4	7	44	2,273	96·79	·53	·26	·17	·31	1·94
						Jains ...	1	...	...	...	...	...	1	2	...	...	...	...	...	2	100·	...	...	...	...	...
						Jews and others ...	...	1	...	...	...	...	1	...	8	...	...	...	...	8	100·	...	...	...	...	...

TABLE XV—*continued.*

TABLE SHOWING TOTAL POPULATION OF EACH RELIGION IN EACH CIRCLE AND ITS RELATION TO HOUSES AND TENEMENTS.

Ward.	Charge.	Section.	Circle No.	Total number of buildings.	Total number of persons.	Religion.	Total number of separate tenements occupied by persons of each religion with: One room.	Two rooms.	Three rooms.	Four rooms.	Five rooms.	Six rooms and over.	Total number of tenements of all kinds occupied by members of each religion.	Total number of members of each religion occupying tenements with: One room.	Two rooms.	Three rooms.	Four rooms.	Five rooms.	Six rooms and over.	Total number of members of each religion occupying tenements of all kinds.	Percentage of total population of each religion occupying each class of tenements with: One room.	Two rooms.	Three rooms.	Four rooms.	Five rooms.	Six rooms and over.
		1	2	3	4	5	6	7	8	9	10	11	12	13	14	15	16	17	18	19	20	21	22	23	24	25
						Total ...	555	45	11	12	2	4	629	3,145	199	44	42	46	28	3,504	89·75	5·68	1·26	1·20	1·31	·80
A.	2	Lower Colaba ...	3	88	3,504	Christians ...	33	4	1	3	1	...	42	161	19	6	11	23	...	220	73·18	8·64	2·73	5·	10·45	...
						Parsis ...	10	...	1	3	1	1	16	54	...	3	4	23	5	89	60·67	...	3·38	4·49	25·84	5·62
						Mahomedans ...	77	2	...	1	...	...	80	143	5	...	7	...	...	154	92·21	3·25	...	4·54	...	...
						Hindus ...	413	37	9	5	...	3	468	2,730	166	35	20	...	23	2,974	91·80	5·58	1·18	·67	...	·77
						Jains ...	22	2	...	...	...	...	24	55	9	...	...	...	...	64	85·94	14·06	...	...	...	...
						Jews and others ...	1	...	...	...	...	...	1	3	...	...	...	...	...	3	100·	...	...	...	...	...
						Total ...	255	11	10	2	...	...	278	1,430	102	63	12	...	...	1,607	88·98	6·35	3·92	·75	...	...
		" ...	4	51	1,607	Christians ...	12	...	...	...	...	...	12	48	...	...	...	...	...	48	100·	...	...	...	...	...
						Parsis ...	1	...	1	1	...	...	3	8	...	5	3	...	...	16	50·	...	31·25	18·75	...	...
						Mahomedans ...	23	1	...	1	...	...	25	69	9	...	9	...	...	87	79·32	10·34	...	10·34	...	...
						Hindus ...	218	10	9	...	...	...	237	1,302	93	58	...	...	...	1,453	89·61	6·40	3·99	...	...	...
						Jains ...	...	...	...	...	...	...	...	...	...	...	...	...	...	...	...	...	...	...	...	...
						Jews and others ...	1	...	...	...	...	...	1	3	...	...	...	...	...	3	100·	...	...	...	...	...
						Total ...	385	10	2	2	1	1	401	2,304	69	28	26	8	5	2,440	94·43	2·83	1·15	1·06	·33	·20
		" ...	5	51	2,440	Christians ...	5	2	1	...	...	...	8	30	7	7	...	...	...	44	68·18	15·91	15·91	...	...	...
						Parsis ...	...	...	...	...	...	1	1	...	...	...	...	...	5	5	...	...	...	...	...	100·
						Mahomedans ...	28	1	...	...	...	...	29	77	1	...	...	...	...	78	98·72	1·28	...	...	...	...
						Hindus ...	319	7	1	2	1	...	300	2,186	61	21	26	8	...	2,302	94·96	2·65	·91	1·13	·35	...
						Jains ...	3	...	...	...	...	...	3	11	...	...	...	...	...	11	100·	...	...	...	...	...
						Jews and others ...	...	...	...	...	...	...	...	...	...	...	...	...	...	...	...	...	...	...	...	...
						Total ...	509	21	13	9	11	92	655	1,865	87	47	34	34	96	2,163	86·22	4·02	2·17	1·58	1·57	4·44
		" ...	6	117	2,163	Christians ...	112	7	7	4	3	1	134	344	20	13	14	7	3	401	85·79	4·98	3·24	3·49	1·75	·75
						Parsis ...	18	2	5	3	1	6	35	25	3	32	14	2	46	122	20·49	2·46	26·23	11·48	1·64	37·70
						Mahomedans ...	98	...	...	1	...	1	100	207	...	...	1	...	2	270	76·66	...	...	·37	...	·74
						Hindus ...	273	13	1	1	7	84	378	1,209	64	2	5	25	45	1,350	89·56	4·74	·15	·37	1·85	3·33
						Jains ...	3	...	...	...	...	...	3	7	...	...	...	...	...	7	100·	...	...	...	...	...
						Jews and others ...	5	...	...	...	...	...	5	13	...	...	...	...	...	13	100·	...	...	...	...	...
						Total ...	177	25	3	2	1	1	209	923	129	26	19	18	7	1,165	82·92	11·07	2·23	1·63	1·55	·60
		" ...	7	31	1,165	Christians ...	36	6	...	1	1	...	44	171	30	...	17	18	...	236	72·46	12·71	...	7·20	7·63	...
						Parsis ...	1	1	...	1	...	...	3	1	3	...	2	...	...	6	16·67	50·	...	33·33	...	...
						Mahomedans ...	33	3	...	...	...	...	36	114	7	...	...	...	...	121	94·21	5·79	...	...	...	...
						Hindus ...	103	10	3	...	...	1	117	671	72	26	...	...	7	776	86·47	9·28	3·35	...	...	·90
						Jains ...	4	5	...	...	...	...	9	9	17	...	...	...	...	26	34·62	65·38	...	...	...	...
						Jews and others ...	...	...	...	...	...	...	...	...	...	...	...	...	...	...	...	...	...	...	...	...
						Total ...	435	10	80	103	79	16	723	2,599	10	211	326	311	49	3,506	74·13	·28	6·02	9·30	8·87	1·40
		" ...	8	73	3,506	Christians ...	194	6	53	83	73	6	415	1,185	6	140	245	279	20	1,875	63·20	·32	7·47	13·07	14·88	1·06
						Parsis ...	14	2	15	10	3	5	49	77	2	33	45	17	11	185	41·62	1·08	17·84	24·32	9·19	5·95
						Mahomedans ...	48	2	7	4	...	1	62	102	2	23	6	...	7	140	72·86	1·43	16·43	4·28	...	5·
						Hindus ...	169	...	1	1	...	1	172	1,200	...	6	5	...	2	1,213	98·93	...	·49	·42	...	·16
						Jains ...	1	...	...	...	...	...	1	8	...	...	...	...	...	8	100·	...	...	...	...	...
						Jews and others ...	9	...	4	5	3	3	24	27	...	9	25	15	9	85	31·76	...	10·59	29·41	17·65	10·59

TABLE XV.

TOTAL POPULATION OF EACH RELIGION, ETC.

TABLE XV—*continued.*

TABLE SHOWING TOTAL POPULATION OF EACH RELIGION IN EACH CIRCLE AND ITS RELATION TO HOUSES AND TENEMENTS.

Ward.	Charge.	Section.	Circle Nos.	Total No. of buildings.	Total No. of persons.	Religion.	Total No. of separate tenements occupied by persons of each religion with						Total No. of tenements of all kinds occupied by members of each religion.	Total No. of members of each religion occupying tenements with						Total No. of members of each religion occupying tenements of all kinds.	Percentage of total population of each religion occupying each class of tenements with					
							One room.	Two rooms.	Three rooms.	Four Rooms.	Five rooms.	Six rooms and over.		One room.	Two rooms.	Three rooms.	Four rooms.	Five rooms.	Six rooms and over.		One room.	Two rooms.	Three rooms.	Four rooms.	Five rooms.	Six rooms and over.
		1	2	3	4	5	6	7	8	9	10	11	12	13	14	15	16	17	18	19	20	21	22	23	24	25
						Total ...	707	33	7	9	4	7	773	3,007	125	92	80	25	131	3,460	86·90	3·64	3·65	2·31	·72	3·78
A.		Total for Fort South.		255	3,460	Christians ...	232	12	2	6	2	2	246	1,153	63	60	40	19	33	1,307	94·35	4·61	3·68	3·53	1·39	2·41
						Parsis ...	34	...	...	...	...	...	34	102	...	...	...	...	...	102	100·	...	...	...	...	...
						Mahomedans ...	46	6	2	2	...	3	59	164	18	7	10	...	50	239	64·44	7·53	3·13	4·18	...	20·92
						Hindus ...	356	19	3	1	2	2	412	1,632	40	33	21	6	48	1,682	91·04	2·38	2·08	1·25	·35	2·85
						Jains ...	...	...	...	...	...	...	...	...	...	...	...	...	...	...	...	...	...	...	...	...
						Jews and others ...	20	1	...	...	...	...	21	66	4	...	...	...	...	70	94·29	5·71	...	...	...	...
						Total ...	120	14	1	...	1	...	136	460	40	25	...	1	...	526	87·45	7·60	4·75	...	·20	...
	5	Fort South	1	48	526	Christians ...	30	4	...	...	1	...	35	192	21	...	...	1	...	214	89·72	9·81	...	...	·47	...
						Parsis ...	4	...	...	...	...	...	4	9	...	...	...	...	...	9	100·	...	...	...	...	...
						Mahomedans ...	9	2	...	...	...	...	11	21	4	...	...	...	...	25	84·	16·	...	...	...	...
						Hindus ...	70	7	1	...	...	...	78	213	11	25	...	...	...	249	85·54	4·42	10·04	...	...	...
						Jains ...	...	...	...	...	...	...	...	...	...	...	...	...	...	...	...	...	...	...	...	...
						Jews and others ...	7	1	...	...	...	...	8	25	4	...	...	...	...	29	86·21	13·79	...	...	...	...
						Total ...	149	13	4	2	1	1	169	961	55	60	2	18	24	1,120	85·80	4·91	5·36	·18	1·61	2·14
		,, ...	2	100	1,120	Christians ...	60	8	2	2	1	1	74	362	43	50	2	18	24	498	72·69	8·63	10·04	·40	3·62	4·82
						Parsis ...	7	...	...	...	...	...	7	12	...	...	...	...	...	12	100·	...	...	...	...	...
						Mahomedans ...	14	...	...	...	...	...	14	40	...	...	...	...	...	40	100·	...	...	...	...	...
						Hindus ...	60	4	2	...	...	...	66	510	13	10	...	...	...	533	95·68	2·44	1·88	...	...	...
						Jains ...	...	...	...	...	...	...	...	...	...	...	...	...	...	...	...	...	...	...	...	...
						Jews and others ...	8	...	...	...	...	...	8	28	...	...	...	...	...	28	100·	...	...	...	...	...
						Total ...	192	6	2	3	2	5	210	376	20	7	19	6	98	526	71·48	3·80	1·33	3·61	1·15	18·63
		,, ...	3	53	526	Christians ...	22	...	...	2	...	...	24	85	...	...	10	...	...	95	89·47	...	...	10·53	...	...
						Parsis ...	9	...	...	...	...	...	9	27	...	...	...	...	...	27	100·	...	...	...	...	...
						Mahomedans ...	3	2	2	1	...	3	11	8	10	7	9	...	50	84	9·53	11·91	8·33	10·72	...	59·52
						Hindus .	157	4	...	...	2	2	165	255	10	...	...	6	48	319	79·94	3·13	...	...	1·88	15·04
						Jains ...	...	...	...	...	...	...	...	...	...	...	...	...	...	...	...	...	...	...	...	...
						Jews and others ...	1	...	...	...	...	...	1	1	...	...	...	...	...	1	100·	...	...	...	...	...
						Total ...	120	4	...	1	...	1	126	546	6	...	1	...	9	562	97·15	1·07	...	·18	...	1·60
		,, ...	4	33	562	Christians ...	41	...	...	...	...	1	42	197	...	...	...	...	9	206	95·63	...	...	...	...	4·37
						Parsis ...	11	...	...	...	...	...	11	33	...	...	...	...	...	33	100·	...	...	...	...	...
						Mahomedans ...	12	2	...	1	...	...	15	36	4	...	1	...	...	41	87·80	9·76	...	2·44	...	...
						Hindus ...	56	2	...	...	...	...	58	280	2	...	...	...	...	282	99·29	·71	...	...	...	...
						Jains ...	...	...	...	...	...	...	...	...	...	...	...	...	...	...	...	...	...	...	...	...
						Jews and others ...	...	...	...	...	...	...	...	...	...	...	...	...	...	...	...	...	...	...	...	...
						Total ...	126	2	...	3	...	...	131	664	4	...	58	...	...	726	91·46	·55	...	7·99	...	...
		,, ...	5	23	726	Christians ...	60	...	...	3	...	...	71	317	...	...	37	...	...	354	89·55	...	...	10·45	...	...
						Parsis ...	3	...	...	...	...	...	3	21	...	...	...	...	...	21	100·	...	...	...	...	...
						Mahomedans ...	8	...	...	...	...	...	8	40	...	...	...	...	...	40	100·	...	...	...	...	...
						Hindus ...	42	2	...	1	...	...	45	274	4	...	21	...	...	299	91·64	1·34	...	7·02	...	...
						Jains ...	...	...	...	...	...	...	...	...	...	...	...	...	...	...	...	...	...	...	...	...
						Jews and others ...	4	...	...	...	...	...	4	12	...	...	...	...	...	12	100·	...	...	...	...	...

TABLE XV—*continued.*

TABLE SHOWING TOTAL POPULATION OF EACH RELIGION IN EACH CIRCLE AND ITS RELATION TO HOUSES AND TENEMENTS.

Ward.	Charge.	Section.	Circle No.	Total No. of buildings.	Total No. of persons.	Religion.	TOTAL NO. OF SEPARATE TENEMENTS OCCUPIED BY PERSONS OF EACH RELIGION WITH						Total No. of tenements of all kinds occupied by members of each religion	TOTAL NO. OF MEMBERS OF EACH RELIGION OCCUPYING TENEMENTS WITH						Total No. of members of each religion occupying tenements of all kinds	PERCENTAGE OF TOTAL POPULATION OF EACH RELIGION OCCUPYING EACH CLASS OF TENEMENTS WITH					
							One room.	Two rooms.	Three rooms.	Four rooms.	Five rooms.	Six rooms and over.		One room.	Two rooms.	Three rooms.	Four rooms.	Five rooms.	Six rooms and over.		One room.	Two rooms.	Three rooms.	Four rooms.	Five rooms.	Six rooms and over.
		1	2	3	4	5	6	7	8	9	10	11	12	13	14	15	16	17	18	19	20	21	22	23	24	25
						Total ...	3,460	1,458	682	270	158	202	6,330	12,143	5,590	3,219	1,944	1,063	1,441	25,400	47·81	22·01	12·67	7·65	4·19	5·67
A.		Total for Fort North	...	541	25,400	Christians ...	239	85	33	30	12	5	392	929	375	164	164	96	48	1,758	52·84	21·33	9·33	9·00	4·80	2·61
						Parsis ...	538	772	456	240	93	114	2,220	1,742	3,004	2,185	1,237	632	832	9,623	18·10	31·22	22·70	12·86	6·47	8·65
						Mahomedans ...	282	96	14	11	6	12	404	1,065	355	78	90	32	75	1,695	62·84	20·94	4·60	5·31	1·89	4·42
						Hindus ...	2,346	440	158	75	42	64	3,020	7,994	1,610	719	359	300	444	11,456	69·78	14·05	6·28	3·40	2·61	3·88
						Jains ...	175	44	17	15	4	15	270	398	192	71	70	10	36	777	51·22	24·71	9·14	9·01	1·29	4·63
						Jews and others ...	4	15	1	...	2	2	24	16	54	2	...	13	8	92	10·30	58·70	2·17	...	14·13	8·70
						Total ...	170	207	96	38	23	28	556	654	879	501	229	315	196	2,679	24·41	32·81	18·81	8·55	8·03	7·39
	4	Fort North	1	161	2,679	Christians ..	30	19	3	1	1	...	54	155	99	15	10	12	...	291	53·26	34·04	5·15	3·43	4·12	...
						Parsis ...	65	167	83	34	20	24	393	251	693	443	191	190	173	1,941	12·93	35·70	22·83	9·84	9·79	8·91
						Mahomedans ...	4	3	...	...	...	...	7	18	11	...	...	...	...	29	62·07	37·93	...	...	...	...
						Hindus ...	71	18	4	3	2	4	102	230	76	46	28	13	25	418	55·02	18·18	11·01	6·70	3·11	5·98
						Jains ...	...	...	...	...	...	...	...	...	...	...	...	...	...	...	...	...	...	...	...	...
						Jews and Others ...	...	...	...	...	...	...	...	...	...	...	...	...	...	...	...	...	...	...	...	...
						Total ...	145	122	94	71	28	35	496	318	356	414	297	143	259	1,787	17·80	19·92	23·17	16·62	8·	14·49
		.. ..	2	107	1,787	Christians ..	8	12	6	3	4	...	33	33	23	22	13	24	...	114	28·07	20·18	19·30	11·40	21·05	...
						Parsis ...	73	103	83	65	24	35	383	164	314	382	266	119	259	1,504	10·90	20·88	25·40	17·69	7·91	17·22
						Mahomedans ...	3	3	1	...	...	...	7	7	1	3	...	...	...	11	63·64	9·09	27·27	...	...	...
						Hindus ...	61	6	4	3	...	...	74	115	18	7	18	...	...	158	72·79	11·39	4·43	11·39	...	...
						Jains ...	...	...	...	...	...	...	...	...	...	...	...	...	...	...	...	...	...	...	...	...
						Jews and others ...	...	...	...	...	...	...	...	...	...	...	...	...	...	...	...	...	...	...	...	...
						Total ...	304	266	74	53	6	9	712	954	1,035	287	271	36	81	2,664	35·81	38·85	10·78	10·17	1·35	3·04
		.. ..	3	161	2,664	Christians ...	4	3	1	2	...	...	10	17	8	9	9	...	...	43	30·64	18·60	20·93	20·93	...	...
						Parsis ...	77	215	60	50	5	8	415	182	841	230	254	31	65	1,603	11·35	53·44	14·35	15·85	1·93	4·06
						Mahomedans ...	11	6	2	...	...	...	19	17	18	6	...	...	...	41	41·46	43·90	14·64	...	...	...
						Hindus ...	212	42	11	1	1	1	268	738	168	43	8	5	16	977	75·54	17·19	4·30	·82	·61	1·64
						Jains ...	...	...	...	...	...	...	...	...	...	...	...	...	...	...	...	...	...	...	...	...
						Jews and others ...	...	...	...	...	...	...	...	...	...	...	...	...	...	...	...	...	...	...	...	...
						Total ...	459	204	85	28	13	14	804	1,594	800	420	151	87	124	3,176	50·19	25·19	13·22	4·75	2·74	3·91
		.. ..	4	122	3,176	Christians ...	2	1	1	1	2	1	8	5	4	6	8	15	8	46	10·87	8·70	13·04	17·39	32·61	17·39
						Parsis ...	43	100	54	15	4	3	218	193	422	253	63	33	40	1,003	19·14	42·07	25·22	6·29	3·29	3·99
						Mahomedans ...	3	2	1	...	...	...	6	8	5	3	...	...	...	16	50·00	31·25	18·75	...	...	...
						Hindus ...	412	101	30	12	7	8	570	1,369	369	163	80	30	68	2,103	66·05	17·55	7·61	3·90	1·66	3·23
						Jains ...	...	...	...	...	...	...	...	...	...	...	...	...	...	...	...	...	...	...	...	...
						Jews and others ...	...	...	...	...	...	2	2	...	...	...	...	...	8	8	...	...	...	...	...	100·
						Total ...	158	112	142	58	28	37	535	548	397	655	293	163	210	2,266	24·18	17·52	28·91	12·93	7·19	9·27
		.. ..	5	109	2,266	Christians ...	20	10	3	3	1	2	39	87	91	16	23	4	11	232	37·50	39·22	6·90	9·91	1·73	4·74
						Parsis ...	70	73	137	50	24	25	309	260	184	591	243	143	135	1,556	17·30	11·83	37·98	15·63	9·20	8·18
						Mahomedans ...	18	6	4	2	2	4	36	36	16	20	6	12	23	113	31·86	14·16	17·70	5·31	10·62	20·35
						Hindus ...	49	22	8	3	1	6	89	154	100	30	31	4	41	358	43·02	27·93	10·61	5·87	1·12	11·45
						Jains ...	...	1	...	...	...	...	1	...	6	...	...	...	...	6	...	100·	...	...	...	...
						Jews and others ...	1	...	...	...	...	...	1	2	...	...	...	...	...	3	100·	...	...	...	...	...

TABLE XV.

TOTAL POPULATION OF EACH RELIGION, ETC.

TABLE XV—*continued.*

TABLE SHOWING TOTAL POPULATION OF EACH RELIGION IN EACH CIRCLE AND ITS RELATION TO HOUSES AND TENEMENTS.

Ward.	Charge.	Section.	Circle number.	Total number of buildings.	Total number of persons.	Religion.	Total number of separate tenements occupied by persons of each religion with — One room.	Two rooms.	Three rooms.	Four rooms.	Five rooms.	Six rooms and over.	Total number of tenements of all kinds occupied by members of each religion.	Total number of members of each religion occupying tenements with — One room.	Two rooms.	Three rooms.	Four rooms.	Five rooms.	Six rooms and over.	Total number of members of each religion occupying tenements of all kinds.	Percentage of total population of each religion occupying each class of tenements with — One room.	Two rooms.	Three rooms.	Four rooms.	Five rooms.	Six rooms and over.
		1	2	3	4	5	6	7	8	9	10	11	12	13	14	15	16	17	18	19	20	21	22	23	24	25
						Total ...	589	221	79	47	19	27	985	2,157	987	377	247	166	172	4,106	52·53	24·04	9·18	6·02	4·04	4·19
A.	4	Fort North ...	6	164	4,106	Christians ...	20	1	2	...	...	1	24	112	9	7	...	...	15	143	78·32	6·29	4·90	...	...	10·49
						Parsis ...	42	68	17	6	7	3	143	176	360	106	42	44	35	763	23·07	47·18	13·89	5·50	5·77	4·59
						Mahomedans ...	77	15	2	3	1	2	100	458	90	12	24	11	20	615	74·47	14·64	1·95	3·90	1·79	3·25
						Hindus ...	393	114	47	28	9	10	601	1,222	441	208	136	106	91	2,204	55·44	20·01	9·44	6·17	4·81	4·13
						Jains ...	60	23	11	10	2	11	117	189	87	44	45	5	11	381	49·61	22·83	11·55	11·81	1·31	2·89
						Jews and others ...	...	...	...	...	...	...	...	...	...	...	...	...	...	...	...	...	...	...	...	...
						Total ...	931	268	95	50	32	38	1,404	2,343	879	420	277	180	269	4,368	53·64	20·12	9·62	6·34	4·12	6·16
		" ...	7	97	4,368	Christians ...	80	25	12	8	4	...	120	210	93	54	70	31	...	502	40·60	18·33	10·76	15·14	6·17	...
						Parsis ...	77	28	20	12	5	10	160	123	98	112	40	12	70	455	27·03	21·54	24·61	8·79	2·64	15·38
						Mahomedans ...	81	53	6	4	...	5	151	211	168	24	51	...	24	468	45·05	35·89	4·49	10·90	...	4·48
						Hindus ...	595	127	50	22	19	20	833	1,580	344	201	89	119	157	2,590	61·03	13·80	7·94	3·62	4·70	6·21
						Jains ...	88	20	6	4	2	3	123	110	99	27	18	5	18	277	39·71	35·71	9·75	6·50	1·80	6·50
						Jews and others ...	...	15	1	...	2	...	18	...	54	2	...	13	...	69	...	78·26	2·90	...	18·84	...
						Total ...	711	57	22	25	9	14	808	3,575	257	142	179	73	128	4,354	82·11	5·90	3·26	4·11	1·68	2·94
		" ...	8	83	4,354	Christians ...	74	14	4	2	...	1	95	272	40	35	19	...	12	387	70·21	12·06	9·04	4·91	...	3·10
						Parsis ...	90	21	12	17	4	6	150	385	92	78	134	50	55	798	48·25	11·53	9·77	16·79	6·27	6·89
						Mahomedans ...	65	8	2	2	2	1	78	280	22	10	6	9	8	335	83·58	6·57	2·98	1·79	2·69	2·39
						Hindus ...	453	16	4	3	3	6	483	2,526	94	10	9	14	46	2,708	93·28	3·47	·37	·33	·52	1·70
						Jains ...	27	...	...	1	...	1	29	99	...	...	7	...	7	113	87·61	...	...	6·20	...	6·19
						Jews and others ...	3	...	...	...	...	...	3	13	...	...	...	...	...	13	100·	...	...	...	...	...
						Total ...	1,576	83	47	29	12	88	1,835	15,452	517	338	214	57	949	17,546	88·07	2·95	2·04	1·22	·32	5·40
		Total for Esplanade.	...	498	17,546	Christians ...	225	31	13	11	1	59	340	1,399	203	165	30	17	560	2,389	58·56	8·50	6·91	1·63	·71	23·44
						Parsis ...	60	3	7	6	4	8	88	327	9	50	74	10	90	566	57·77	1·59	8·83	13·07	2·83	15·90
						Mahomedans ...	200	11	9	3	5	5	212	3,095	58	61	22	8	59	3,313	93·43	1·82	2·00	·66	·24	1·82
						Hindus ...	1,073	37	10	8	2	12	1,142	10,531	240	74	78	16	221	11,526	91·37	2·12	·65	·68	·14	2·02
						Jains ...	2	...	...	...	...	1	3	10	...	...	...	...	1	11	90·91	...	...	...	...	9·09
						Jews and others ...	7	1	2	1	...	4	15	42	1	5	1	...	10	59	71·19	1·70	8·47	1·69	...	16·95
						Total ..	170	44	24	11	7	77	333	1,035	393	140	46	27	628	2,170	47·70	18·64	6·45	2·12	1·24	28·86
	5	Esplanade ...	1	135	2,170	Christians ...	70	27	8	8	...	55	168	509	200	60	31	...	532	1,352	37·65	14·79	5·02	2·29	...	39·35
						Parsis ...	4	2	4	...	3	5	18	20	8	5	...	8	14	64	31·25	12·50	7·81	...	12·50	21·88
						Mahomedans ...	16	1	2	1	2	3	25	55	2	10	5	3	10	85	64·71	2·35	11·77	5·88	3·53	11·76
						Hindus ...	70	13	8	2	2	9	110	408	85	40	10	16	59	618	66·02	13·75	6·47	1·62	2·59	9·54
						Jains ...	...	...	...	...	...	1	1	...	...	...	...	...	1	1	100·	...	...	...	...	...
						Jews and others ...	4	1	2	...	...	4	11	34	1	5	...	...	10	50	68·	2·	10·	...	...	20·
						Total ...	134	...	4	3	...	5	145	783	...	78	77	...	155	1,093	71·64	...	7·14	7·04	...	14·18
		"	2	80	1,093	Christians ...	43	...	1	...	...	1	45	265	...	18	...	...	24	307	86·32	...	5·86	...	...	7·82
						Parsis ...	30	...	1	1	...	2	34	192	...	39	17	...	65	313	61·34	...	12·46	5·43	...	20·77
						Mahomedans ...	8	...	2	...	...	...	10	40	...	21	...	...	...	61	65·57	...	34·43	...	...	...
						Hindus ...	50	...	...	1	...	1	54	276	...	...	60	...	66	402	68·66	...	...	14·93	...	16·42
						Jains ...	1	...	...	...	...	...	1	9	...	...	...	...	...	9	100·	...	...	...	...	...
						Jews and others ...	1	...	...	...	...	...	2	1	...	...	...	...	...	1	100·	...	...	...	...	...

TABLE XV—*continued.*

TABLE SHOWING TOTAL POPULATION OF EACH RELIGION IN EACH CIRCLE AND ITS RELATION TO HOUSES AND TENEMENTS.

Ward.	Charge.	Section.	Circle No.	Total number of buildings.	Total number of persons.	Religion.	Total number of separate tenements occupied by persons of each religion with One room.	Two rooms.	Three rooms.	Four rooms.	Five rooms.	Six rooms and over.	Total number of tenements of all kinds occupied by members of each religion.	Total number of members of each religion occupying tenements with One room.	Two rooms.	Three rooms.	Four rooms.	Five rooms.	Six rooms and over.	Total number of members of each religion occupying tenements of all kinds.	Percentage of total population of each religion occupying each class of tenements with One room.	Two rooms.	Three rooms.	Four rooms.	Five rooms.	Six rooms and over.
		1	2	3	4	5	6	7	8	9	10	11	12	13	14	15	16	17	18	19	20	21	22	23	24	25
						Total ...	1,079	28	8	3	1	2	1,121	4,893	203	45	10	3	144	5,298	92·35	3·83	·85	·19	·06	2·73
A.	6	Esplanade	3	162	5,298	Christians ...	74	1	...	...	...	...	75	368	6	...	...	...	...	374	98·40	1·60	...	...	...	...
						Parsis ...	11	...	...	...	...	...	11	28	...	...	...	...	...	28	100·	...	...	...	...	...
						Mahomedans ...	157	6	2	1	1	1	168	863	50	15	4	3	40	975	88·51	5·13	1·54	·41	·31	4·10
						Hindus ...	835	21	6	1	...	1	864	3,626	147	30	5	...	104	3,912	92 69	3 76	·76	·13	...	2·66
						Jains ...	1	...	...	...	...	...	1	1	...	...	...	...	...	1	100·	...	...	...	...	...
						Jews and others ...	1	...	...	1	...	...	2	7	...	...	1	...	...	8	87 50	...	...	12 50	...	...
						Total ...	193	11	11	12	4	4	235	8,741	18	95	81	27	23	8,985	97·28	·20	1·06	·90	·30	·26
		... ...	4	82	8,985	Christians ...	38	3	4	3	1	2	51	257	3	67	8	17	4	356	72·19	·84	18·82	2·25	4·78	1·12
						Parsis ...	15	1	2	6	1	1	26	78	1	6	57	8	11	161	48·45	·62	3·73	35·40	4·97	0·83
						Mahomedans ...	29	4	3	1	2	1	39	2,027	6	18	13	2	8	3,074	97·73	·29	·87	·63	·10	·38
						Hindus ...	112	3	2	3	...	...	120	6,379	8	4	3	...	...	6,394	99·76	·13	·06	·05	...	...
						Jains ...	...	...	...	...	...	...	...	...	...	...	...	...	...	...	...	...	...	...	...	...
						Jews and others ...	...	...	...	...	...	...	...	...	...	...	...	...	...	...	...	...	...	...	...	...
						Total ...	27,565	1,718	441	220	71	107	30,122	1,14,966	6,842	3,120	1,293	530	915	1,26,666	90·76	5·40	1·68	1·02	·42	·72
B.		Total for B Ward ...	...	2,102	126,663	Christians ...	206	30	9	10	1	5	260	823	100	51	60	9	19	1,161	70·89	10·37	4·39	5·04	·77	1·64
						Parsis ...	29	4	4	1	...	...	37	103	13	15	5	...	...	136	75·73	9·56	11·03	3·68	...	...
						Mahomedans ...	11,194	852	224	100	35	41	12,446	46,290	3,221	1,120	704	275	474	52,066	88·46	6·10	2·16	1·35	·53	·91
						Hindus ...	14,644	641	167	94	33	54	15,673	62,654	2,705	768	454	215	375	67,285	93·12	4·15	1·17	·68	·32	·56
						Jains ...	1,036	90	34	11	2	4	1,176	3,308	375	118	40	31	14	3,886	85·12	9·65	3·04	1·03	·80	·36
						Jews and others ...	455	46	13	4	...	3	521	1,788	242	22	17	...	33	2,102	85·01	11·51	1·05	·81	...	1·57
						Total ...	5,054	372	115	73	17	24	5,655	21,496	1,476	454	422	101	282	24,231	88·71	6 09	1·87	1·74	·42	1·17
		Total for Chakla ...	...	793	24,231	Christians ...	5	...	...	2	...	4	11	25	...	...	5	...	18	48	52 08	...	...	10·42	...	37·50
						Parsis ...	13	2	2	1	...	...	18	61	7	7	5	...	...	80	76 25	8·75	8·75	6·25	...	...
						Mahomedans ...	2,825	240	77	44	13	14	3,219	12,885	1,039	303	319	77	207	14,830	86 88	7 01	2·04	2·15	·52	1·40
						Hindus ...	2,014	106	33	22	4	6	2,185	7,999	368	135	77	24	57	8,630	92 34	4 26	1·57	·90	·28	·65
						Jains ...	197	18	3	4	...	...	222	550	62	9	16	...	...	643	60 47	9 64	1.40	2·49	...	...
						Jews and others ...	...	...	...	...	...	...	...	...	...	...	...	...	...	...	...	...	...	...	...	...
						Total ...	520	28	11	4	2	...	565	2,491	143	36	12	6	...	2,688	92·67	5·32	1·34	·45	·22	...
	7	Chakla	1	69	2,688	Christians ...	...	...	...	...	...	...	...	...	...	...	...	...	...	...	...	...	...	...	...	...
						Parsis ...	...	1	...	...	...	...	1	...	3	...	...	...	...	2	...	100·	...	...	...	...
						Mahomedans ...	488	27	10	4	2	...	531	2,353	140	30	12	6	...	2,541	92 60	5·51	1·18	·47	·24	...
						Hindus ...	30	...	1	...	...	...	31	124	...	6	...	...	...	130	95 38	...	4 62	...	...	...
						Jains ...	3	...	...	...	...	...	2	14	...	...	...	...	...	14	100·	...	...	...	...	...
						Jews and others ...	...	...	...	...	...	...	...	...	...	...	...	...	...	...	...	...	...	...	...	...
						Total ...	532	66	23	16	7	10	644	2,159	284	139	140	29	97	2,848	75 81	9·97	4·88	4·91	1·02	3·41
		,, ...	2	110	2,848	Christians ...	...	...	...	...	...	...	...	...	...	...	...	...	...	...	...	...	...	...	...	...
						Parsis ...	...	...	...	...	...	...	...	...	...	...	...	...	...	...	...	...	...	...	...	...
						Mahomedans ...	321	44	16	13	5	7	406	1,267	104	99	121	22	74	1,777	71·30	10 02	5·57	6 81	1·24	4·16
						Hindus ...	198	23	7	3	2	3	235	877	90	40	19	7	23	1,056	83 03	8·52	3 79	1·83	·66	3·18
						Jains ...	3	...	...	...	...	...	3	15	...	...	...	...	...	16	100·	...	...	...	...	...
						Jews and others ...	...	...	...	...	...	...	...	...	...	...	...	...	...	...	...	...	...	...	...	...

TABLE XV.

TOTAL POPULATION OF EACH RELIGION, ETC.

TABLE XV—*continued.*

TABLE SHOWING TOTAL POPULATION OF EACH RELIGION IN EACH CIRCLE AND ITS RELATION TO HOUSES AND TENEMENTS.

Ward.	Charge.	Section.	Circle No.	Total number of buildings.	Total number of persons.	Religion.	Total number of separate tenements occupied by persons of each religion with: One room.	Two rooms.	Three rooms.	Four rooms.	Five rooms.	Six rooms and over.	Total No. of tenements of all kinds occupied by members of each religion.	Total number of members of each religion occupying tenements with: One room.	Two rooms.	Three rooms.	Four rooms.	Five rooms.	Six rooms and over.	Total number of members of each religion occupying tenements of all kinds.	Percentage of total population of each religion occupying each class of tenements with: One room.	Two rooms.	Three rooms.	Four rooms.	Five rooms.	Six rooms and over.
		1	2	3	4	5	6	7	8	9	10	11	12	13	14	15	16	17	18	19	20	21	22	23	24	25
						Total ...	563	51	32	4	1	3	654	2,269	161	66	21	12	40	2,569	88·32	6·26	2·57	·83	·47	1·56
B.	7	Chakla	3	92	2,569	Christians ...	...	...	...	...	...	1	1	...	...	...	...	...	10	10	...	...	...	...	...	100·
						Parsis ...	8	1	2	1	...	...	12	34	4	7	5	...	...	50	68·	8·	14·	10·	...	...
						Mahomedans ...	31	6	7	...	...	...	44	120	31	25	...	...	...	185	69·73	16·76	13·51	...	...	...
						Hindus ...	490	39	20	3	1	2	564	2,042	110	25	16	12	30	2,235	91·36	4·92	1·12	·72	·54	1·34
						Jains ...	25	5	3	...	...	...	33	64	16	9	...	...	...	89	71·91	17·98	10·11	...	...	...
						Jews and others ...	...	...	...	...	...	...	...	...	...	...	...	...	...	...	...	...	...	...	...	...
						Total ...	908	146	30	17	2	4	1,107	4,067	533	133	134	14	23	4,894	83·10	10·69	2·73	2·74	·28	·47
		" ...	4	129	4,894	Christians ...	1	...	...	1	...	2	4	11	...	...	3	...	7	21	52·38	...	...	14·29	...	33·33
						Parsis ...	4	...	...	...	...	...	4	26	...	...	...	...	...	26	100·	...	...	...	...	...
						Mahomedans ...	490	114	26	8	1	1	640	2,530	410	76	95	8	12	3,132	80·78	13·09	2·42	3·01	·29	·38
						Hindus ...	330	20	4	4	1	1	360	1,320	70	57	20	5	4	1,476	89·43	4·74	3·86	1·36	·34	·27
						Jains ...	68	12	...	4	...	...	84	180	43	...	16	...	...	239	75·31	17·99	...	6·28	...	·42
						Jews and others ...	...	...	...	...	...	...	...	...	...	...	...	...	...	...	...	...	...	...	...	...
						Total ...	606	28	4	13	1	2	654	2,401	94	40	48	10	26	2,619	91·68	3·59	1·53	1·83	·38	·99
		" ...	5	86	2,619	Christians ...	...	...	...	...	...	...	...	...	...	...	...	...	...	...	...	...	...	...	...	...
						Parsis ...	...	...	...	...	...	...	...	...	...	...	...	...	...	...	...	...	...	...	...	...
						Mahomedans ...	541	25	4	13	1	2	586	2,154	84	40	48	10	26	2,362	91·20	3·56	1·69	2·03	·42	1·10
						Hindus ...	58	3	...	...	...	...	61	229	10	...	...	...	...	230	95·82	4·18	...	...	...	...
						Jains ...	7	...	...	...	...	...	7	18	...	...	...	...	...	18	100·	...	...	...	...	...
						Jews and others ...	...	...	...	...	...	...	...	...	...	...	...	...	...	...	...	...	...	...	...	...
						Total ...	276	...	1	4	4	4	289	1,115	...	8	23	30	92	1,268	87·93	...	·62	1·82	2·37	7·26
		" ...	6	39	1,268	Christians ...	1	...	...	1	...	1	3	1	...	...	2	...	1	4	25·	...	...	50·	...	25·
						Parsis ...	...	...	...	...	...	...	...	...	...	...	...	...	...	...	...	...	...	...	...	...
						Mahomedans ...	272	...	1	3	4	3	283	1,105	...	8	21	30	91	1,255	88·05	...	·64	1·67	2·39	7·25
						Hindus ...	2	...	...	...	...	...	2	8	...	...	...	...	...	8	100·	...	...	...	...	...
						Jains ...	1	...	...	...	...	...	1	1	...	...	...	...	...	1	100·	...	...	...	...	...
						Jews and others ...	...	...	...	...	...	...	...	...	...	...	...	...	...	...	...	...	...	...	...	...
						Total ...	440	21	2	3	...	...	466	2,278	89	9	17	...	...	2,393	95·19	3·72	·38	·71	...	...
		" ...	7	60	2,393	Christians ...	2	...	...	...	...	...	2	9	...	...	...	...	...	9	100·	...	...	...	...	...
						Parsis ...	...	...	...	...	...	...	...	...	...	...	...	...	...	...	...	...	...	...	...	...
						Mahomedans ...	86	4	1	1	...	...	92	541	20	2	7	...	...	570	94·91	3·51	·35	1·23	...	...
						Hindus ...	302	17	1	2	...	...	322	1,560	69	7	10	...	...	1,646	94·77	4·19	·43	·61	...	...
						Jains ...	50	...	...	...	...	...	50	168	...	...	...	...	...	168	100·	...	...	...	...	...
						Jews and others ...	...	...	...	...	...	...	...	...	...	...	...	...	...	...	...	...	...	...	...	...
						Total ...	626	9	1	11	...	...	647	2,124	48	16	24	...	...	2,212	96·02	2·17	·72	1·09	...	...
		" ...	8	61	2,212	Christians ...	...	...	...	...	...	...	...	...	...	...	...	...	...	...	...	...	...	...	...	...
						Parsis ...	...	...	...	...	...	...	...	...	...	...	...	...	...	...	...	...	...	...	...	...
						Mahomedans ...	100	5	1	1	...	...	107	557	30	16	12	...	...	615	90·57	4·88	2·60	1·95	...	...
						Hindus ...	486	3	...	10	...	...	499	1,476	15	...	12	...	...	1,503	98·20	1·00	...	·80	...	...
						Jains ...	40	1	...	...	...	...	41	91	3	...	...	...	...	94	96·81	3·19	...	...	...	...
						Jews and others ...	...	...	...	...	...	...	...	...	...	...	...	...	...	...	...	...	...	...	...	...

TABLE XV—*continued.*

TABLE SHOWING TOTAL POPULATION OF EACH RELIGION IN EACH CIRCLE AND ITS RELATION TO HOUSES AND TENEMENTS.

Ward.	Charge.	Section.	Circle No.	Total number of buildings.	Total number of persons.	Religion.	Total Number of separate tenements occupied by persons of each religion with						Total No. of tenements of all kinds occupied by members of each religion.	Total Number of members of each religion occupying tenements with						Total number of members of each religion occupying tenements of all kinds.	Percentage of total population of each religion occupying each class of tenements with					
							One room.	Two rooms.	Three rooms.	Four rooms.	Five rooms.	Six rooms and over.		One room.	Two rooms.	Three rooms.	Four rooms.	Five rooms.	Six rooms and over.		One room.	Two rooms.	Three rooms.	Four rooms.	Five rooms.	Six rooms and over.
		1	2	3	4	5	6	7	8	9	10	11	12	13	14	15	16	17	18	19	20	21	22	23	24	25
						Total ...	573	33	11	1	...	1	629	2,592	134	7	3	...	4	2,740	94·60	4·89	·26	·11	...	·14
B.		Chakla ...	9	87	2,740	Christians ...	1	...	...	...	...	...	1	4	...	...	...	...	...	4	100·	...	...	...	...	...
						Parsis ...	1	...	...	...	...	...	1	1	...	...	...	...	...	1	100·	...	...	...	...	...
						Mahomedans ...	467	31	11	1	...	1	521	2,249	130	7	3	...	4	2,393	93·98	5·43	·29	·13	...	·17
						Hindus ...	103	2	...	...	...	...	105	333	4	...	...	...	...	337	98·81	1·19	...	...	...	...
						Jains ...	1	...	...	...	...	...	1	5	...	...	...	...	...	5	100·	...	...	...	...	...
						Jews and others ...	...	...	...	...	...	...	...	...	...	...	...	...	...	...	...	...	...	...	...	...
						Total ...	6,564	563	147	58	27	53	7,411	26,528	2,339	704	337	177	383	30,468	87·07	7·68	2·31	1·10	·58	1·26
		Total for Mandvi ...	...	779	30,468	Christians ...	43	9	...	...	...	...	52	130	35	...	...	...	...	165	78·79	21·21	...	...	...	...
						Parsis ...	3	1	...	...	...	...	4	7	1	...	...	...	...	8	87·50	12·50	...	...	...	...
						Mahomedans ...	1,095	65	23	9	3	10	1,205	4,390	332	122	105	14	104	5,037	86·56	6·59	2·42	2·08	·28	2·07
						Hindus ...	4,813	411	109	46	24	39	5,442	19,934	1,708	500	216	163	265	22,816	87·50	7·49	2·10	·95	·71	1·16
						Jains ...	496	74	15	3	...	4	592	1,542	249	82	16	...	14	1,903	81·03	13·08	4·31	·84	...	·74
						Jews and others ...	114	2	...	...	...	...	116	525	14	...	...	...	...	539	97·40	2·60	...	...	...	...
						Total ...	855	49	13	6	2	5	930	3,053	287	68	37	12	60	3,517	86·81	8·16	1·93	1·05	·34	1·71
	6	Mandvi ...	1	93	3,517	Christians ...	...	...	...	...	...	...	...	...	...	...	...	...	...	...	...	...	...	...	...	...
						Parsis ...	2	...	...	...	...	...	2	6	...	...	...	...	...	6	100·	...	...	...	...	...
						Mahomedans ...	284	21	10	2	2	5	304	975	125	48	19	12	60	1,239	78·69	10·09	3·89	1·53	·97	4·84
						Hindus ...	563	28	3	4	...	...	618	2,042	162	20	18	...	...	2,242	91·08	7·23	·89	·80	...	...
						Jains ...	6	...	...	...	...	...	6	30	...	...	...	...	...	30	100·	...	...	...	...	...
						Jews and others ...	...	...	...	...	...	...	...	...	...	...	...	...	...	...	...	...	...	...	...	...
						Total ...	299	18	5	2	2	...	326	1,113	113	19	6	17	...	1,268	87·78	8·91	1·50	·47	1·34	...
		" ...	3	3.	1,268	Christians ...	28	5	...	...	...	...	33	83	25	...	...	...	...	108	76·85	23·15	...	...	...	...
						Parsis ...	...	...	...	...	...	...	...	...	...	...	...	...	...	...	...	...	...	...	...	...
						Mahomedans ...	55	4	...	...	...	...	59	229	23	...	...	...	...	252	90·87	9·13	...	...	...	...
						Hindus ...	203	5	3	1	2	...	214	768	54	10	5	17	...	854	89·93	6·32	1·17	·59	1·99	...
						Jains ...	12	4	2	1	...	...	19	31	11	9	1	...	...	52	59·62	21·15	17·31	1·92	...	...
						Jews and others ...	1	...	...	...	...	...	1	2	...	...	...	...	...	2	100·	...	...	...	...	...
						Total ...	809	37	9	2	...	4	861	2,607	167	41	19	...	11	2,845	91·63	5·87	1·44	·67	...	·39
		" ...	4	87	2,845	Christians ...	...	...	...	...	...	...	...	...	...	...	...	...	...	...	...	...	...	...	...	...
						Parsis ...	...	...	...	...	...	...	...	...	...	...	...	...	...	...	...	...	...	...	...	...
						Mahomedans ...	108	2	...	...	...	...	110	453	10	...	...	...	...	463	97·84	2·16	...	...	...	...
						Hindus ...	662	35	9	2	...	4	712	2,037	157	41	19	...	11	2,265	89·93	6·93	1·81	·84	...	·49
						Jains ...	39	...	...	...	...	...	39	117	...	...	...	...	...	117	100·	...	...	...	...	...
						Jews and others ...	...	...	...	...	...	...	...	...	...	...	...	...	...	...	...	...	...	...	...	...
						Total ...	348	30	11	1	...	2	393	1,077	49	16	2	...	10	1,154	93·33	4·24	1·39	·17	...	·87
		" ...	5	39	1,154	Christians ...	1	...	...	...	...	...	1	2	...	...	...	...	...	2	100·	...	...	...	...	...
						Parsis ...	...	...	...	...	...	...	...	...	...	...	...	...	...	...	...	...	...	...	...	...
						Mahomedans ...	3	...	...	...	...	...	3	13	...	...	...	...	...	13	100·	...	...	...	...	...
						Hindus ...	339	30	11	1	...	2	383	1,044	49	16	2	...	10	1,121	93·13	4·37	1·43	·18	...	·89
						Jains ...	5	...	...	...	...	...	6	18	...	...	...	...	...	18	100·	...	...	...	...	...
						Jews and others ...	...	...	...	...	...	...	...	...	...	...	...	...	...	...	...	...	...	...	...	...

TABLE XV.

TOTAL POPULATION OF EACH RELIGION, ETC.

TABLE XV—*continued.*

TABLE SHOWING TOTAL POPULATION OF EACH RELIGION IN EACH CIRCLE AND ITS RELATION TO HOUSES AND TENEMENTS.

Ward.	Charge.	Section.	Circle No.	Total number of buildings.	Total number of persons.	Religion.	Total Number of separate tenements occupied by persons of each religion with — One room.	Two rooms.	Three rooms.	Four rooms.	Five rooms.	Six rooms and over.	Total number of tenements of all kinds occupied by members of each religion.	Total Number of members of each religion occupying tenements with — One room.	Two rooms.	Three rooms.	Four rooms.	Five rooms.	Six rooms and over.	Total number of members of each religion occupying tenements of all kinds.	Percentage of total population of each religion occupying each class of tenements with — One room.	Two rooms.	Three rooms.	Four rooms.	Five rooms.	Six rooms and over.
		1	2	3	4	5	6	7	8	9	10	11	13	13	14	15	16	17	18	19	20	21	22	23	24	25
						Total ...	337	61	19	7	2	5	421	4.927	198	97	25	13	30	5,290	93·14	3·74	1·83	·47	·25	·57
B.	6	Mandvi	6	35	5,290	Christians ...	...	...	...	...	...	...	...	...	...	...	...	...	...	...	...	...	...	...	...	...
						Parsis ...	...	...	...	...	...	...	...	...	...	...	...	...	...	...	...	...	...	...	...	...
						Mahomedans ...	3	...	...	...	...	...	3	12	...	...	...	...	...	12	100·	...	...	...	...	...
						Hindus ...	323	61	19	7	2	5	416	4,834	198	97	25	13	30	5,197	93·01	3·81	1·87	·49	·25	·58
						Jains ...	1	...	...	...	...	...	1	77	...	...	...	...	...	77	100·	...	...	...	...	...
						Jews and others ...	1	...	...	...	...	...	1	4	...	...	...	...	...	4	100·	...	...	...	...	...
						Total ...	361	66	19	8	3	14	471	1.253	203	84	50	9	95	1,694	78·97	11·98	4·96	2·95	·53	5·61
		„ ...	7	60	1,694	Christians ...	...	...	...	...	...	...	...	...	...	...	...	...	...	...	...	...	...	...	...	...
						Parsis ...	...	...	...	...	...	...	...	...	...	...	...	...	...	...	...	...	...	...	...	...
						Mahomedans ...	17	...	...	3	...	3	23	68	...	...	23	...	35	106	51·72	...	...	21·70	...	33·59
						Hindus ...	339	66	19	5	3	11	443	1,187	203	84	27	9	70	1,580	75·13	12·85	5·31	1·71	·57	4·43
						Jains ...	5	...	...	...	...	...	5	8	...	...	...	...	...	8	100·	...	...	...	...	...
						Jews and others ...	...	...	...	...	...	...	...	...	...	...	...	...	...	...	...	...	...	...	...	...
						Total ...	317	65	22	9	4	10	327	663	314	55	28	29	66	1.155	57·40	27·19	4·76	2·42	2·51	5·73
		„ ...	8	63	1,155	Christians ...	...	...	...	...	...	...	...	...	...	...	...	...	...	...	...	...	...	...	...	...
						Parsis ...	...	...	...	...	...	...	...	...	...	...	...	...	...	...	...	...	...	...	...	...
						Mahomedans ...	23	...	...	...	...	...	23	101	...	...	...	...	...	104	100·	...	...	...	...	...
						Hindus ...	116	65	23	9	4	10	226	306	314	55	28	29	66	798	38·35	39·35	6·89	3·51	3·63	8·27
						Jains ...	78	...	...	...	...	...	78	253	...	...	...	...	...	253	100·	...	...	...	...	...
						Jews and others ...	...	...	...	...	...	...	...	...	...	...	...	...	...	...	...	...	...	...	...	...
						Total ...	852	19	10	4	2	3	890	3.144	81	63	36	7	34	3.365	93·43	2·41	1·87	1·07	·21	1·01
		„ ...	9	126	3,365	Christians ...	1	...	...	...	...	...	1	3	...	...	...	...	...	3	100·	...	...	...	...	...
						Parsis ...	...	...	...	...	...	...	...	...	...	...	...	...	...	...	...	...	...	...	...	...
						Mahomedans ...	536	17	9	3	1	2	568	2,030	60	53	34	2	10	2,216	92·01	3·11	2·39	1·54	·09	·86
						Hindus ...	202	2	1	1	1	1	208	577	12	10	2	5	15	621	92·91	1·93	1·61	·33	·81	2·42
						Jains ...	2	...	...	...	...	...	2	8	...	...	...	...	...	8	100·	...	...	...	...	...
						Jews and others ...	111	...	...	...	...	...	111	517	...	...	...	...	...	517	100·	...	...	...	...	...
						Total ...	936	103	19	4	3	4	1.069	2.824	488	113	41	19	14	3.498	80·73	13·95	3·20	1·17	·55	·40
		„ ...	10	104	3,498	Christians ...	1	1	...	...	...	...	2	1	2	...	...	...	...	3	33·33	66·67	...	...	...	...
						Parsis ...	...	...	...	...	...	...	...	...	...	...	...	...	...	...	...	...	...	...	...	...
						Mahomedans ...	63	21	4	1	...	...	89	269	105	21	29	...	...	424	63·44	24·77	4·95	0·84	...	...
						Hindus ...	727	50	8	3	3	...	791	2,145	209	57	12	19	...	2,502	85·73	10·75	2·28	·48	·76	...
						Jains ...	146	29	7	...	...	4	186	409	98	34	...	...	14	555	73·69	17·66	6·13	...	...	2·52
						Jews and others ...	...	2	...	...	...	...	2	...	14	...	...	...	...	14	...	100·	...	...	...	...
						Total ...	1.239	92	19	10	9	3	1.372	4.512	380	142	76	71	36	5.197	86·82	6·93	2·73	1·46	1·37	·69
		„ ...	11	67	5,197	Christians ...	1	...	...	...	...	...	1	1	...	...	...	...	...	1	100·	...	...	...	...	...
						Parsis ...	...	...	...	...	...	...	...	...	...	...	...	...	...	...	...	...	...	...	...	...
						Mahomedans ...	8	...	...	...	...	...	8	34	...	...	...	...	...	34	100·	...	...	...	...	...
						Hindus ...	1,033	53	13	8	9	3	1,119	3,011	225	103	61	71	36	4,407	68·74	5·11	2·34	1·38	1·61	·82
						Jains ...	197	39	6	2	...	...	244	576	135	39	15	...	...	765	75·29	17·65	5·10	1·96	...	...
						Jews and others ...	...	...	...	...	...	...	...	...	...	...	...	...	...	...	...	...	...	...	...	...

TABLE XV—*continued.*

TABLE SHOWING TOTAL POPULATION OF EACH RELIGION IN EACH CIRCLE AND ITS RELATION TO HOUSES AND TENEMENTS.

Ward.	Charge.	Section.	Circle number.	Total number of buildings.	Total number of persons.	Religion.	Total number of separate tenements occupied by persons of each religion with: One room.	Two rooms.	Three rooms.	Four rooms.	Five rooms.	Six rooms and over.	Total number of tenements of all kinds occupied by members of each religion.	Total number of members of each religion occupying tenements with: One room.	Two rooms.	Three rooms.	Four rooms.	Five rooms.	Six rooms and over.	Total number of members of each religion occupying tenements of all kinds.	Percentage of total population of each religion occupying each class of tenements with: One room.	Two rooms.	Three rooms.	Four rooms.	Five rooms.	Six rooms and over.
		1	2	3	4	5	6	7	8	9	10	11	12	13	14	15	16	17	18	19	20	21	22	23	24	25
						Total ...	321	22	2	4	...	3	352	1,356	79	7	17	...	27	1,485	91·25	5·32	·47	1·14	...	1·82
B.	6	Mandvi	12	64	1,485	Christians ...	11	3	...	...	...	...	14	40	8	...	...	...	...	48	83·33	16·67	...	...	...	...
						Parsis ...	1	1	...	...	...	...	2	1	1	...	...	...	...	2	50·	50·	...	...	...	...
						Mahomedans ...	16	...	...	...	...	...	16	184	...	...	...	...	...	184	100·	...	...	...	...	...
						Hindus ...	287	16	2	4	...	3	312	1,113	65	7	17	...	27	1,229	90·56	5·29	·57	1·38	...	2·20
						Jains ...	5	2	...	...	...	...	7	15	5	...	...	...	...	20	75·	25·	...	...	...	...
						Jews and others ...	1	...	...	...	...	...	1	2	...	...	...	...	...	2	100·	...	...	...	...	...
						Total ...	10,503	652	139	64	19	24	11,401	41,523	2,454	787	470	215	230	45,679	90·90	5·37	1·72	1·03	·47	·51
		Total for Umarkhadi.	...	1,018	45,679	Christians ...	116	25	7	6	1	...	155	492	147	43	64	9	...	745	66·04	19·73	5·77	7·35	1·21	...
						Parsis ...	11	...	...	...	...	...	11	34	...	...	...	...	...	34	100·	...	...	...	...	...
						Mahomedans ...	6,760	501	109	34	16	10	7,430	26,306	1,724	637	252	170	157	29,330	89·69	5·88	2·17	·86	·58	·53
						Hindus ...	3,058	78	8	18	1	6	3,169	12,546	311	72	150	10	42	13,161	95·33	2·50	·55	1·14	·07	·32
						Jains ...	274	5	3	...	1	...	283	997	32	13	...	26	...	1,068	93·35	3·	1·22	...	2·43	...
						Jews and others ...	284	43	13	2	...	3	344	1,038	210	22	14	...	31	1,315	78·94	15·97	1·67	1·06	...	2·36
						Total ...	1,696	35	11	5	2	3	1,750	5,437	135	34	11	7	30	5,654	96·16	2·39	·60	·20	·12	·53
	8	Umarkhadi ...	1	80	5,654	Christians ...	1	...	...	...	...	...	1	1	...	...	...	...	...	1	100·	...	...	...	...	...
						Parsis ...	...	...	...	...	...	...	...	...	...	...	...	...	...	...	...	...	...	...	...	...
						Mahomedans ...	1,142	30	10	5	2	2	1,191	3,390	115	30	11	7	30	3,583	94·61	3·21	·84	·31	·19	·84
						Hindus ...	420	5	...	...	...	...	425	1,029	20	...	...	...	...	1,049	98·09	1·91	...	...	...	...
						Jains ...	132	...	1	...	...	...	133	417	...	4	...	...	...	421	99·05	...	·95	...	...	...
						Jews and others ...	...	...	...	...	...	...	...	...	...	...	...	...	...	...	...	...	...	...	...	...
						Total ...	457	2	...	...	...	...	459	2,207	8	...	...	...	...	2,215	99·64	·36	...	...	...	...
		" ...	2	44	2,215	Christians ...	...	...	...	...	...	...	...	...	...	...	...	...	...	...	...	...	...	...	...	...
						Parsis ...	2	...	...	...	...	...	2	2	...	...	...	...	...	2	100·	...	...	...	...	...
						Mahomedans ...	396	2	...	...	...	...	398	2,014	8	...	...	...	...	2,022	99·60	·40	...	...	...	...
						Hindus ...	55	...	...	...	...	...	55	176	...	...	...	...	...	176	100·	...	...	...	...	...
						Jains ...	4	...	...	...	...	...	4	15	...	...	...	...	...	15	100·	...	...	...	...	...
						Jews and others ...	...	...	...	...	...	...	...	...	...	...	...	...	...	...	...	...	...	...	...	...
						Total ...	820	97	16	9	2	2	1,036	3,795	326	105	84	24	24	4,358	87·08	7·48	2·41	1·93	·55	·55
		" ...	3	95	4,358	Christians ...	1	...	...	...	...	...	1	2	...	...	...	...	...	3	100·	...	...	...	...	...
						Parsis ...	...	...	...	...	...	...	...	...	...	...	...	...	...	...	...	...	...	...	...	...
						Mahomedans ...	812	97	16	9	2	2	938	3,606	326	105	84	24	24	4,168	86·49	7·82	2·52	2·01	·58	·58
						Hindus ...	57	...	...	...	...	...	57	157	...	...	...	...	...	157	100·	...	...	...	...	...
						Jains ...	10	...	...	...	...	...	10	30	...	...	...	...	...	30	100·	...	...	...	...	...
						Jews and others ...	...	...	...	...	...	...	...	...	...	...	...	...	...	...	...	...	...	...	...	...
						Total ...	1,196	10	...	1	...	...	1,207	4,270	40	...	9	...	...	4,319	98·87	·93	...	·21	...	...
		" ...	4	37	4,319	Christians ...	...	...	...	...	...	...	...	...	...	...	...	...	...	...	...	...	...	...	...	...
						Parsis ...	...	...	...	...	...	...	...	...	...	...	...	...	...	...	...	...	...	...	...	...
						Mahomedans ...	653	6	...	1	...	...	660	2,401	20	...	9	...	...	2,430	98·81	·82	...	·37	...	...
						Hindus ...	534	2	...	...	...	...	536	1,846	6	...	...	...	...	1,852	99·68	·32	...	...	...	...
						Jains ...	9	2	...	...	...	...	11	23	14	...	...	...	...	37	62·16	37·84	...	...	...	...
						Jews and others ...	...	...	...	...	...	...	...	...	...	...	...	...	...	...	...	...	...	...	...	...

TABLE XV—*continued.*

TABLE SHOWING TOTAL POPULATION OF EACH RELIGION IN EACH CIRCLE AND ITS RELATION TO HOUSES AND TENEMENTS.

Ward.	Charge.	Section.	Circle number.	Total number of buildings.	Total number of persons.	Religion.	Total number of separate tenements occupied by persons of each religion with						Total number of tenements of all kinds occupied by members of each religion.	Total number of members of each religion occupying tenements with						Total number of members of each religion occupying tenements of all kinds.	Percentage of total population of each religion occupying each class of tenements with					
							One room.	Two rooms.	Three rooms.	Four rooms.	Five rooms.	Six rooms and over.		One room.	Two rooms.	Three rooms.	Four rooms.	Five rooms.	Six rooms and over.		One room.	Two rooms.	Three rooms.	Four rooms.	Five rooms.	Six rooms and over.
		1	2	3	4	5	6	7	8	9	10	11	12	13	14	15	16	17	18	19	20	21	22	23	24	25
						Total ...	740	19	2	1	...	...	762	2,620	57	16	8	...	...	2,701	97·	2·11	·59	·30	...	...
D.	6	Umarkhadi ...	5	61	2,701	Christians ...	1	...	...	...	...	...	1	3	...	...	...	...	...	3	100·	...	...	...	...	...
						Parsis ...	...	...	...	...	...	...	...	...	...	...	...	...	...	...	...	...	...	...	...	...
						Mahomedans ...	697	17	2	1	...	...	717	2,521	51	16	8	...	...	2,596	97·11	1·96	·62	·31	...	...
						Hindus ...	37	2	...	...	...	...	39	82	6	...	...	...	...	88	93·18	6·82	...	...	...	...
						Jains ...	5	...	...	...	...	...	5	14	...	...	...	...	...	14	100·	...	...	...	...	...
						Jews and others ...	...	...	...	...	...	...	...	...	...	...	...	...	...	...	...	...	...	...	...	...
						Total ...	488	12	2	2	3	...	507	1,995	73	7	10	22	...	2,107	94·68	3·47	·33	·48	1·04	...
		" ...	6	58	2,107	Christians ...	2	...	...	...	...	...	2	6	...	...	...	...	...	6	100·	...	...	...	...	...
						Parsis ...	1	...	...	...	...	...	1	2	...	...	...	...	...	2	100·	...	...	...	...	...
						Mahomedans ...	417	12	2	2	3	...	436	1,727	73	7	10	22	...	1,839	93·91	3·97	·38	·54	1·20	...
						Hindus ...	65	...	...	...	...	...	65	242	...	...	...	...	...	242	100·	...	...	...	...	...
						Jains ...	2	...	...	...	...	...	2	13	...	...	...	...	...	13	100·	...	...	...	...	...
						Jews and others ...	1	...	...	...	...	...	1	3	...	...	...	...	...	3	100·	...	...	...	...	...
						Total ...	1,069	65	19	3	2	4	1,163	4,018	350	139	25	51	38	4,621	86·95	7·58	3·01	·54	1·10	·82
		" ...	7	121	4,621	Christians ...	1	...	...	1	...	...	2	20	...	...	8	...	...	28	71·43	...	...	28·57	...	...
						Parsis ...	1	...	...	...	...	...	1	3	...	...	...	...	...	3	100·	...	...	...	...	...
						Mahomedans ...	861	55	16	2	1	4	939	3,350	293	124	17	25	38	3,847	87·08	7·62	3·23	·44	·65	·99
						Hindus ...	174	6	1	...	...	...	181	540	38	6	...	...	...	584	92·47	6·51	1·03	...	...	...
						Jains ...	32	2	2	...	1	...	37	105	8	9	...	26	...	148	70·95	5·40	6·08	...	17·57	...
						Jews and others ...	...	2	...	...	...	...	3	...	11	...	...	...	...	11	...	100·	...	...	...	...
						Total ...	1,384	99	35	13	3	8	1,542	5,737	440	188	96	4	52	6,517	88·03	6·75	2·89	1·47	·06	·80
		" ...	8	168	6,517	Christians ...	13	...	1	...	...	...	14	49	...	14	...	...	...	63	77·78	...	22·22	...	...	...
						Parsis ...	4	...	...	...	...	...	4	18	...	...	...	...	...	18	100·	...	...	...	...	...
						Mahomedans ...	914	85	30	3	3	2	1,037	3,935	391	132	31	4	10	4,502	87·41	8·68	2·93	·69	·09	·22
						Hindus ...	366	13	4	10	...	6	399	1,382	30	42	65	...	42	1,561	88·53	1·92	2·69	4·17	...	2·69
						Jains ...	54	1	...	...	...	...	55	207	10	...	...	...	...	217	95·39	4·61	...	...	...	...
						Jews and others ...	33	1	...	...	...	...	34	140	10	...	...	...	...	150	93·33	6·67	...	...	...	...
						Total ...	1,017	201	35	16	3	5	1,277	4,257	488	176	109	66	48	5,144	82·76	9·49	3·42	2·12	1·28	·93
		" ...	9	157	5,144	Christians ...	12	...	3	...	...	...	15	42	...	13	...	...	...	55	76·36	...	23·64	...	...	...
						Parsis ...	1	...	...	...	...	...	1	1	...	...	...	...	...	1	100·	...	...	...	...	...
						Mahomedans ...	648	188	23	10	3	5	877	2,748	394	154	44	66	48	3,454	79·56	11·41	4·46	1·27	1·91	1·39
						Hindus ...	313	9	...	5	...	...	327	1,333	76	...	61	...	...	1,470	90·68	5·17	...	4·15	...	...
						Jains ...	9	...	...	...	...	...	9	18	...	...	...	...	...	18	100·	...	...	...	...	...
						Jews and others ...	34	4	9	1	...	...	48	115	18	9	4	...	...	146	78·77	12·33	6·16	2·74	...	...
						Total ...	1,577	112	19	14	4	3	1,729	7,187	537	122	118	41	38	8,043	89·36	6·67	1·52	1·47	·51	·47
		" ...	10	117	8,043	Christians ...	85	25	3	5	1	...	119	367	147	16	46	9	...	585	62·73	25·13	2·74	7·86	1·54	...
						Parsis ...	3	...	...	...	...	...	3	8	...	...	...	...	...	8	100·	...	...	...	...	...
						Mahomedans ...	220	9	9	5	2	1	246	704	54	69	38	22	7	894	78·75	6·04	7·72	4·25	2·46	·78
						Hindus ...	1,037	43	3	3	1	...	1,086	5,179	165	24	24	10	...	5,402	95·87	3·05	·44	·44	·19	...
						Jains ...	17	...	...	...	...	...	17	155	...	...	...	...	...	155	100·	...	...	...	...	...
						Jews and others ...	216	36	4	1	...	2	259	774	171	13	10	...	31	999	77·48	17·12	1·30	1·00	...	3·10

TABLE XV—*continued*.

TABLE SHOWING TOTAL POPULATION OF EACH RELIGION IN EACH CIRCLE AND ITS RELATION TO HOUSES AND TENEMENTS.

Ward.	Charge.	Section.	Circle number.	Total number of buildings.	Total number of persons.	Religion.	Total number of separate tenements occupied by persons of each religion with						Total number of tenements of all kinds occupied by members of each religion.	Total number of members of each religion occupying tenements with						Total number of members of each religion occupying tenements of all kinds.	Percentage of total population of each religion occupying each class of tenements with					
							One room.	Two rooms.	Three rooms.	Four rooms.	Five rooms.	Six rooms and over.		One room.	Two rooms.	Three rooms.	Four rooms.	Five rooms.	Six rooms and over.		One room.	Two rooms.	Three rooms.	Four rooms.	Five rooms.	Six rooms and over.
		1	2	3	4	5	6	7	8	9	10	11	12	13	14	15	16	17	18	19	20	21	22	23	24	25
						Total ...	5,444	132	40	25	8	6	5,655	25,419	573	175	64	37	20	26,288	96·69	2·18	·67	·24	·14	·8
B.		Total for Dongri ...	...	512	26,288	Christians ...	44	2	2	2	...	1	61	176	8	8	10	...	1	203	86·70	3·94	3·94	4·93	...	·49
						Parsis ...	1	1	2	...	...	...	4	1	5	8	...	...	...	14	7·14	35·72	57·14	...	...	...
						Mahomedans ...	514	40	16	9	3	1	583	2,040	132	64	29	14	6	2,808	91·57	4·56	2·21	·97	·46	·21
						Hindus ...	4,760	66	17	8	4	3	4,877	22,156	378	81	15	18	11	22,658	97·79	1·67	·36	·06	·08	·05
						Jains ...	60	2	3	4	1	...	70	213	32	14	8	5	...	272	78·31	11·76	5·15	2·94	1·84	...
						Jews and others ...	57	1	...	2	...	1	61	225	18	...	3	...	2	248	90·73	7·26	...	1·21	...	·81
						Total ...	1,180	59	13	5	...	1	1,258	6,035	184	13	5	...	1	6,243	96·67	2·94	·29	·08	...	·02
	9	Dongri ...	1	...	6,243	Christians ...	5	...	...	...	...	...	5	26	...	...	...	...	...	26	100·	...	...	...	...	...
						Parsis ...	...	...	...	...	...	...	...	...	...	...	...	...	...	...	...	...	...	...	...	...
						Mahomedans ...	196	21	4	1	...	...	222	772	50	4	1	...	...	827	93·35	6·05	·48	·12	...	...
						Hindus ...	923	38	9	4	...	1	9.5	5,020	134	14	4	...	1	5,182	97·05	2·58	·27	·08	...	·02
						Jains ...	36	...	...	...	...	...	36	122	...	...	...	...	...	122	100·	...	...	...	...	...
						Jews and others ...	20	...	...	...	...	...	20	66	...	...	...	...	...	66	100·	...	...	...	...	...
						Total ...	2,783	61	18	11	3	1	2,867	11,726	258	87	34	20	6	12,131	96·66	2·18	·72	·28	·16	·05
		" ...	2	...	12,131	Christians ...	...	...	...	...	...	...	...	...	...	...	...	...	...	...	...	...	...	...	...	...
						Parsis ...	...	...	...	...	...	...	...	...	...	...	...	...	...	...	...	...	...	...	...	...
						Mahomedans ...	176	11	9	5	1	...	202	957	52	41	21	7	...	1,078	88·78	4·82	3·80	1·96	·65	...
						Hindus ...	2,581	38	6	2	1	1	2,629	10,623	174	33	5	8	6	10,847	97·93	1·60	·29	·05	·07	·06
						Jains ...	9	2	3	4	1	...	19	52	32	14	8	5	...	111	46·85	28·83	12·61	7·21	4·50	...
						Jews and others ...	17	...	...	...	...	...	17	95	...	...	...	...	...	95	100·	...	...	...	...	...
						Total ...	1,070	3	1	...	...	...	1,074	5,515	19	5	...	...	...	5,539	99·57	·34	·09	...	...	...
		" ...	3	...	5,539	Christians ...	12	...	...	...	...	...	12	13	...	...	...	...	...	13	100·	...	...	...	...	...
						Parsis ...	1	...	...	...	...	...	1	1	...	...	...	...	...	1	100·	...	...	...	...	...
						Mahomedans ...	118	2	1	...	...	...	121	625	1	5	...	...	...	631	98·87	·19	·94	...	...	...
						Hindus ...	915	...	...	...	...	...	915	4,004	...	...	...	...	...	4,004	100·	...	...	...	...	...
						Jains ...	4	...	...	...	...	...	4	28	...	...	...	...	...	28	100·	...	...	...	...	...
						Jews and others ...	20	1	...	...	...	...	21	44	18	...	...	...	...	62	70·97	29·03	...	...	...	...
						Total ...	411	19	8	9	5	4	456	2,143	112	65	35	17	13	2,375	90·23	4·72	2·71	1·05	·72	·54
		" ...	4	...	2,375	Christians ...	27	2	2	2	...	1	34	137	8	8	10	...	1	164	83·53	4·88	4·88	6·10	...	·61
						Parsis ...	...	1	2	...	...	...	3	...	5	8	...	...	...	13	...	38·46	61·54	...	...	...
						Mahomedans ...	24	6	2	3	2	1	38	396	29	14	6	7	6	467	86·43	6·35	3·07	1·31	1·53	1·31
						Hindus ...	340	10	2	2	3	1	358	1,600	70	35	6	10	4	1,725	92·76	4·06	2·03	·35	·58	·23
						Jains ...	20	...	...	...	...	...	20	11	...	...	...	...	...	11	100·	...	...	...	...	...
						Jews and others ...	...	...	...	2	...	1	3	...	...	...	3	...	2	5	...	...	...	60·	...	40·
						Total ...	31,050	4,285	1,404	990	497	501	38,727	135,613	20,640	9,758	7,420	4,475	5,128	183,044	74·09	11·28	5·33	4·05	2·44	2·81
C.		Total for C Ward ...	...	5,306	183,044	Christians ...	784	150	131	137	84	60	1,346	4,370	1,343	1,448	1,365	926	764	10,216	42·78	13·15	14·17	13·36	9·06	7·48
						Parsis ...	1,250	502	320	223	109	46	2,548	4,839	3,354	1,910	1,375	977	438	12,897	37·53	26·04	14·81	10·66	7·57	3·40
						Mahomedans ...	6,740	751	210	103	45	61	7,903	29,498	4,006	1,388	971	346	890	37,100	79·49	10·79	3·74	2·62	·96	2·40
						Hindus ...	20,579	2,489	603	449	230	298	24,710	90,903	10,063	4,513	3,364	2,012	2,090	114,116	79·66	9·34	3·98	2·90	1·76	2·36
						Jains ...	1,654	252	81	76	28	44	2,175	5,534	1,266	409	405	198	340	6,500	88·61	14·78	6·52	4·76	2·33	4·
						Jews and others ...	34	2	...	...	1	2	39	171	14	...	...	5	16	206	83·01	6·79	...	...	2·43	7·77

TABLE XV.

TOTAL POPULATION OF EACH RELIGION, ETC.

TABLE XV—*continued.*

TABLE SHOWING TOTAL POPULATION OF EACH RELIGION IN EACH CIRCLE AND ITS RELATION TO HOUSES AND TENEMENTS.

Ward.	Charge.	Section.	Circle number.	Total number of buildings.	Total number of persons.	Religion.	TOTAL NUMBER OF SEPARATE TENEMENTS OCCUPIED BY PERSONS OF EACH RELIGION WITH — One room.	Two rooms.	Three rooms.	Four rooms.	Five rooms.	Six rooms and over.	Total number of tenements of all kinds occupied by members of each religion.	TOTAL NUMBER OF MEMBERS OF EACH RELIGION OCCUPYING TENEMENTS WITH — One room.	Two rooms.	Three rooms.	Four rooms.	Five rooms.	Six rooms and over.	Total number of members of each religion occupying tenements of all kinds.	PERCENTAGE OF TOTAL POPULATION OF EACH RELIGION OCCUPYING EACH CLASS OF TENEMENTS WITH — One room.	Two rooms.	Three rooms.	Four rooms.	Five rooms.	Six rooms and over.
		1	2	3	4	5	6	7	8	9	10	11	12	13	14	15	16	17	18	19	20	21	22	23	24	25
						Total ...	5,196	936	324	245	131	157	6,969	19,537	4,545	1,983	1,356	967	1,561	29,949	65·23	15·18	6·62	4·63	3·23	5·21
C.		Total for Market ...	...	964	29,949	Christians ...	122	15	7	1	4	...	140	774	191	58	14	53	...	1,000	71·01	17·52	5·33	1·29	4·86	...
						Parsis ...	107	107	30	14	3	3	[illegible]	437	507	173	57	8	31	1,218	35·88	41·63	14·20	4·68	·66	2·95
						Mahomedans ...	476	113	47	21	15	13	685	1,866	822	258	138	73	225	[illegible]	55·29	24·35	7·50	4·03	2·16	6·67
						Hindus ...	3,731	520	152	155	59	108	4,785	14,066	2,268	1,170	684	640	1,015	20,102	69·97	11·28	5·87	4·40	3·43	5·05
						Jains ...	757	160	49	54	20	33	1,063	2,317	746	320	[illegible]	143	[illegible]	4,126	57·37	[illegible]	7·75	6·42	3·47	0·91
						Jews and others ...	3	1	...	...	...	...	4	27	11	...	...	...	...	38	71·05	28·95	...	...	...	...
						Total ...	475	60	36	24	15	11	621	2,782	500	312	146	113	115	3,967	70·13	12·61	7·86	3·68	2·82	2·90
	10	Market ...	1	...	3,967	Christians ...	104	14	6	1	4	...	129	642	100	67	14	53	...	956	67·16	10·88	5·98	1·46	5·54	...
						Parsis ...	5	3	2	...	...	...	10	28	15	6	...	...	...	49	57·14	30·61	12·25	...	...	...
						Mahomedans ...	7	2	...	...	2	...	11	84	17	...	...	...	...	101	83·17	16·83	...	...	...	...
						Hindus ...	334	40	28	21	9	11	443	1,621	267	240	131	59	110	2,027	[illegible]	10·10	9·88	4·61	2·24	4·19
						Jains ...	23	...	...	3	...	...	24	180	...	...	11	...	5	196	91·84	...	...	5·61	...	2·55
						Jews and others ...	3	1	...	...	...	...	4	27	11	...	...	...	...	38	71·05	28·95	...	...	...	...
						Total ...	336	29	11	10	4	8	398	1,380	141	77	72	38	120	1,868	75·22	7·80	4·28	3·98	2·10	6·64
		,, ...	2	...	1,809	Christians ...	1	...	...	...	...	...	1	4	...	...	...	...	...	4	100·	...	...	...	...	...
						Parsis ...	1	...	...	...	...	...	1	2	...	...	...	...	...	2	100·	...	...	...	...	...
						Mahomedans ...	2	...	...	...	...	...	2	6	...	...	...	...	...	6	100·	...	...	...	...	...
						Hindus ...	323	27	11	10	4	7	385	1,334	130	77	72	38	89	1,730	76·53	7·51	4·45	4·16	2·20	5·15
						Jains ...	6	2	...	...	...	1	9	24	11	...	...	...	31	66	36·36	16·67	...	...	...	46·97
						Jews and others ...	...	...	...	...	...	...	...	...	...	...	...	...	...	...	...	...	...	...	...	...
						Total ...	265	20	36	7	3	5	326	1,209	81	196	39	14	58	1,597	75·71	5·07	12·27	2·44	·88	3·63
		,, ...	3	...	1,597	Christians ...	9	...	...	...	...	...	9	104	...	...	...	...	...	104	100·	...	...	...	...	...
						Parsis ...	1	...	...	...	...	...	1	2	...	...	...	...	...	2	100·	...	...	...	...	...
						Mahomedans ...	117	7	23	1	2	4	153	474	67	143	10	8	55	759	62·45	8·83	19·50	1·32	·06	7·24
						Hindus ...	116	12	4	6	1	1	140	547	12	43	20	9	3	634	84·41	1·85	7·41	4·48	1·39	·48
						Jains ...	22	1	...	...	...	...	23	82	3	...	...	...	...	84	97·62	2·34	...	...	...	...
						Jews and others ...	...	...	...	...	...	...	...	...	...	...	...	...	...	...	...	...	...	...	...	...
						Total ...	491	49	17	14	21	10	602	1,702	243	137	85	102	126	2,395	71·06	10·15	5·72	3·55	4·26	5·26
		,, ...	4	...	2,395	Christians ...	...	...	...	...	...	...	...	...	...	...	...	...	...	...	...	...	...	...	...	...
						Parsis ...	...	...	...	...	...	...	...	...	...	...	...	...	...	...	...	...	...	...	...	...
						Mahomedans ...	...	2	1	...	6	2	11	...	11	10	...	10	62	93	...	11·83	10·75	...	10·75	66·67
						Hindus ...	487	47	15	14	15	8	586	1,086	232	118	85	93	64	3,277	74·05	10·19	5·18	3·73	4·04	2·81
						Jains ...	4	...	1	...	...	...	5	16	...	9	...	...	...	25	64·	...	35·	...	...	...
						Jews and others ...	...	...	...	...	...	...	...	...	...	...	...	...	...	...	...	...	...	...	...	...
						Total ...	1,325	229	78	69	31	58	1,790	4,145	989	444	315	223	517	6,633	62·49	14·91	6·69	4·75	3·36	7·80
		,, ...	5	...	6,633	Christians ...	1	...	...	...	...	...	1	2	...	...	...	...	...	2	100·	...	...	...	...	...
						Parsis ...	...	...	...	...	...	...	...	...	...	...	...	...	...	...	...	...	...	...	...	...
						Mahomedans ...	136	9	14	4	...	1	164	386	82	23	13	...	10	511	75·54	16·05	4·50	2·35	...	1·96
						Hindus ...	1,110	191	44	47	25	44	1,471	3,104	772	330	227	193	423	5,423	64·50	14·05	5·90	4·19	3·50	7·80
						Jains ...	78	29	20	18	6	13	164	[illegible]	145	102	70	30	64	697	37·30	[illegible]	14·64	10·01	4·30	12·66
						Jews and others ...	...	...	...	...	...	...	...	...	...	...	...	...	...	...	...	...	...	...	...	...

TABLE XV—*continued.*

TABLE SHOWING TOTAL POPULATION OF EACH RELIGION IN EACH CIRCLE AND ITS RELATION TO HOUSES AND TENEMENTS.

Ward.	Charge.	Section.	Circle Number.	Total number of buildings.	Total number of persons.	Religion.	Total number of separate tenements occupied by persons of each religion with — One room.	Two rooms.	Three rooms.	Four rooms.	Five rooms.	Six rooms and over.	Total number of tenements of all kinds occupied by members of each religion.	Total number of members of each religion occupying tenements with — One room.	Two rooms.	Three rooms.	Four rooms.	Five rooms.	Six rooms and over.	Total number of members of each religion occupying tenements of all kinds.	Percentage of total population of each religion occupying each class of tenements with — One room.	Two rooms.	Three rooms.	Four rooms.	Five rooms.	Six rooms and over.
		1	2	3	4	5	6	7	8	9	10	11	12	13	14	15	16	17	18	19	20	21	22	23	24	25
						Total ...	933	123	81	33	12	14	1.150	3.556	504	124	190	108	107	4.589	77·49	10·98	3·70	4·14	2·36	3·33
C.	10	Market ...	6	...	4,589	Christians ...	2	...	...	...	...	...	2	3	...	...	...	...	...	3	100·	...	...	...	...	...
						Parsis ...	...	1	...	...	...	...	1	...	9	...	...	...	...	9	...	100·	...	...	...	...
						Mahomedans ...	11	5	...	...	...	1	17	35	23	...	...	...	6	64	54·69	35·94	...	...	...	9·37
						Hindus ...	734	74	21	19	8	8	871	2,932	347	78	120	83	78	3,634	80·59	9·54	2·14	3·30	2·28	3·15
						Jains ...	187	42	7	14	4	5	259	586	125	46	70	25	23	875	66·97	14·28	5·26	8·	2·56	2·63
						Jews and others ...	...	...	...	...	...	...	...	...	...	...	...	...	...	...	...	...	...	...	...	...
						Total ...	698	131	43	23	11	22	927	2.330	593	227	129	74	268	3,611	64·53	16·42	6·29	3·57	2·05	7·14
		" ...	7	...	3,611	Christians ...	1	...	1	...	...	...	2	4	...	1	...	...	...	5	80·	...	20·	...	...	...
						Parsis ...	37	32	13	1	...	1	83	228	106	68	5	...	24	401	40·43	33·81	13·95	1·68	...	4·89
						Mahomedans ...	17	2	1	2	...	1	23	39	10	3	11	...	7	70	55·71	14·29	4·29	15·71	...	10·
						Hindus ...	302	39	17	6	4	11	370	1,071	184	91	39	16	99	1,502	71·30	12·33	6·06	2·60	1·07	6·59
						Jains ...	341	60	12	13	7	9	440	984	231	64	74	58	134	1,543	64·03	14·97	4·15	4·50	3·75	8·30
						Jews and others ...	...	...	...	...	...	...	...	...	...	...	...	...	...	...	...	...	...	...	...	...
						Total ...	668	298	82	66	34	29	1.175	2.453	1.494	466	380	296	260	5,349	45·86	27·93	8·71	7·11	5·53	4·86
		" ...	8	...	5,349	Christians ...	4	1	...	...	...	...	5	15	1	...	...	...	...	16	93·75	6·25	...	...	...	...
						Parsis ...	63	71	25	13	3	2	177	177	317	90	52	8	12	665	26·62	47·67	14·89	7·82	1·20	1·80
						Mahomedans ...	186	46	9	14	5	4	304	843	612	70	103	84	85	1,771	47·60	34·56	3·95	5·83	3·27	4·80
						Hindus ...	318	60	39	32	23	18	520	1,187	332	198	191	200	140	2,257	52·59	14·71	8·77	8·47	8·86	6·60
						Jains ...	97	44	9	7	3	5	169	231	232	98	34	30	14	640	36·09	36·25	15·47	5·31	4·69	2·19
						Jews and others ...	...	...	...	...	...	...	...	...	...	...	...	...	...	...	...	...	...	...	...	...
						Total ...	5.383	1.198	544	433	209	193	7.960	22.185	5.734	3.712	3.287	1.779	2.087	33.664	57·22	14·83	9·60	8·50	4·60	5·26
		Total for Dhobi Talao ...	...	1,200	33,664	Christians ...	534	103	93	113	59	44	942	2,310	1,011	1,135	1,063	574	643	6,700	34·40	14·80	16·73	15·95	8·51	9·47
						Parsis ...	847	307	209	153	86	32	1,634	2,168	2,154	1,261	970	623	332	6,212	34·90	36·23	15·36	11·88	7·54	4·04
						Mahomedans ...	237	30	13	22	3	14	319	1,180	92	89	123	17	146	1,047	71·65	5·50	5·40	7·47	1·03	8·88
						Hindus ...	3,663	726	206	130	56	97	4,978	15,283	2,342	1,138	1,013	535	874	21,185	72·14	11·05	5·37	4·78	2·53	4·13
						Jains ...	169	29	20	15	5	4	172	441	135	89	92	26	23	800	54·51	16·69	11·	11·37	3·31	3·23
						Jews and others ...	13	...	...	...	...	2	15	25	...	...	...	...	16	41	60·98	...	...	...	...	39·02
						Total ...	793	358	170	81	12	14	1.428	3.557	1.797	980	459	99	137	6.939	51·26	24·60	14·12	8·62	1·43	1·97
	11	Dhobi Talao ...	1	...	6,939	Christians ...	116	37	24	13	...	2	193	783	266	283	112	...	10	1,434	54·60	18·55	18·34	7·81	...	·70
						Parsis ...	227	142	88	64	10	9	540	740	1,006	644	319	79	106	2,983	24·82	36·75	21·60	10·66	2·63	3·55
						Mahomedans ...	66	14	2	2	1	1	86	232	28	5	17	14	13	308	75·32	9·09	1·62	5·52	4·55	3·90
						Hindus ...	364	161	53	2	1	2	583	1,748	308	60	12	7	9	2,143	81·51	14·38	2·80	·56	·33	·42
						Jains ...	19	4	3	...	...	...	26	51	9	8	...	...	...	71	70·06	12·67	11·27	...	...	...
						Jews and others ...	1	...	...	...	...	...	1	2	...	...	...	...	...	2	100·	...	...	...	...	...
						Total ...	810	63	49	57	27	8	1.014	3.168	393	291	345	254	48	4.499	70·41	8·74	6·47	7·67	5·64	1·97
		" ...	2	...	4,499	Christians ...	208	7	9	10	9	2	245	590	48	54	24	42	6	764	77·22	6·28	7·07	3·14	5·50	·79
						Parsis ...	31	50	39	37	16	5	178	137	317	236	306	206	40	1,242	11·03	25·52	19·	24·64	16·59	3·22
						Mahomedans ...	68	3	...	3	1	...	75	208	11	...	2	2	...	223	93·27	4·93	...	·90	·90	...
						Hindus ...	502	3	1	7	1	1	515	2,231	17	1	13	4	2	2,268	98·37	·75	·04	·57	·18	·09
						Jains ...	1	...	...	...	...	...	1	2	...	...	...	...	...	2	100·	...	...	...	...	...
						Jews and others ...	...	...	...	...	...	...	...	...	...	...	...	...	...	...	...	...	...	...	...	...

TABLE XV—*continued*.

TABLE SHOWING TOTAL POPULATION OF EACH RELIGION IN EACH CIRCLE AND ITS RELATION TO HOUSES AND TENEMENTS.

Ward.	Charge.	Section.	Circle No.	Total Number of buildings.	Total Number of persons.	Religion.	Total Number of separate tenements occupied by persons of each religion with						Total No. of tenements of all kinds occupied by members of each religion.	Total Number of members of each religion occupying tenements with						Total Number of members of each religion occupying tenements of all kinds.	Percentage of total population of each religion occupying each class of tenements with					
							One room.	Two rooms.	Three rooms.	Four rooms.	Five rooms.	Six rooms and over.		One room.	Two rooms.	Three rooms.	Four rooms.	Five rooms.	Six rooms and over.		One room.	Two rooms.	Three rooms.	Four rooms.	Five rooms.	Six rooms and over.
		1	2	3	4	5	6	7	8	9	10	11	12	13	14	15	16	17	18	19	20	21	22	23	24	25
						Total ...	367	163	57	51	15	25	678	2,961	828	412	347	129	255	4,932	60·04	16·79	8·35	7·04	2·61	5·17
C.	11	Dhobi Talao ...	3	...	4,932	Christians ...	51	11	12	5	6	12	97	293	15	92	42	45	121	608	48·19	2·47	15·13	6·91	7·40	19·90
						Parsis ...	114	60	30	19	6	...	229	505	460	112	106	57	...	1,240	40·72	37·10	9·03	8·55	4·60	...
						Mahomedans ...	68	9	10	5	...	13	105	633	34	76	69	...	134	966	65·53	3·52	7·87	9·21	...	13·87
						Hindus ...	133	74	15	22	3	...	236	1,507	319	132	110	27	...	2,095	71·93	15·23	6·30	5·25	1·29	...
						Jains ...	...	...	...	...	...	...	...	...	...	...	...	...	...	...	...	...	...	...	...	...
						Jews and others ...	12	...	...	...	...	...	12	33	...	...	...	...	...	23	100	...	...	...	...	...
						Total...	1,132	114	63	59	42	33	1,443	3,853	718	407	564	294	330	6,141	62·74	11·61	6·63	8·86	4·79	5·37
„	...	„ ...	4	...	6,141	Christians ..	58	12	11	13	2	...	93	200	271	137	184	30	...	831	25·15	32·61	16·49	22·14	3·61	...
						Parsis ...	236	18	33	16	35	9	347	433	118	104	141	100	68	1,018	42·53	11·59	10·23	13·75	15·71	6·19
						Mahomedans ...	13	...	...	12	...	...	25	72	...	...	15	...	...	87	83·76	...	...	17·24	...	...
						Hindu ...	617	83	10	10	3	24	947	3,101	303	129	181	93	267	4,073	76·13	7·44	3·17	4·44	2·26	6·56
						Jains ...	6	1	9	8	2	...	28	38	21	37	24	12	...	132	28·79	15·91	28·03	18·18	9·09	...
						Jews and others ...	...	...	...	...	...	...	...	...	...	...	...	...	...	...	...	...	...	...	...	...
						Total ...	526	114	39	41	25	30	775	2,201	560	270	300	177	197	3,705	59·41	15·11	7·29	8·10	4·78	5·31
„	...	„ ...	5	...	3,705	Christians ...	25	...	...	4	...	...	29	218	...	...	32	...	...	250	87·20	...	...	12·80	...	...
						Parsis ...	104	7	7	13	12	3	145	423	44	45	70	96	81	705	60·	6·24	6·38	10·78	12·20	4·40
						Mahomedans ...	3	2	...	...	...	...	5	12	16	...	...	...	...	28	42·86	57·14	...	...	...	...
						Hindu ...	383	98	32	25	13	27	577	1,534	472	225	112	91	106	2,690	57·03	17·68	8·42	7·19	3·41	6·22
						Jains ...	12	7	...	...	...	...	19	24	28	...	...	...	...	52	46·15	53·85	...	...	...	...
						Jews and others ...	...	...	...	...	...	...	...	...	...	...	...	...	...	...	...	...	...	...	...	...
						Total ...	865	117	44	43	16	16	1,100	3,606	612	604	429	165	317	5,733	62·90	10·67	10·54	7·48	2·88	5·53
„	...	„ ...	6	...	5,733	Christians ...	87	12	21	25	8	5	108	102	202	408	340	118	231	1,525	10·12	13·34	30·19	22·60	7·61	15·15
						Parsis ...	131	20	11	1	2	1	166	630	118	73	10	10	38	869	71·36	13·58	8·40	1·15	1·15	4·37
						Mahomedans ...	7	2	1	...	1	...	11	11	3	8	...	1	...	23	47·83	13·04	34·78	...	4·35	...
						Hindus ...	640	81	11	16	5	10	803	2,708	283	55	73	38	48	3,265	84·78	8·67	1·68	2·24	1·16	1·47
						Jains ..	10	2	...	...	...	...	12	45	6	...	...	...	...	51	88·23	11·77	...	...	...	...
						Jews and others ...	...	...	...	...	...	...	...	...	...	...	...	...	...	...	...	...	...	...	...	...
						Total ...	800	269	122	103	73	67	1,522	2,759	921	748	863	661	753	6,735	41·41	13·68	11·11	12·81	9·81	11·18
„	...	„ ...	7	...	6,735	Christians ...	29	27	19	43	34	23	175	85	209	121	341	315	275	1,378	6·17	15·17	8·78	24·69	25·03	19·96
						Parsis ...	4	1	11	4	5	5	30	8	1	47	20	20	51	156	5·13	·64	30·13	12·82	16·67	34·61
						Mahomedans ...	12	...	...	...	...	...	12	12	...	...	...	...	...	12	100	...	...	...	...	...
						Hindus ...	796	228	81	46	70	33	1,217	2,476	640	536	432	276	382	4,672	51·50	13·70	11·47	9·26	5·01	8·17
						Jains ...	49	15	8	7	3	4	86	278	71	44	69	14	26	501	55·49	14·17	8·78	13·57	2·60	5·19
						Jews and others ...	...	...	...	...	...	2	2	...	...	...	...	...	10	10	...	...	...	...	...	100
						Total ...	2,549	361	176	144	70	79	4,370	20,450	2,235	1,635	1,433	1,067	583	27,403	74·63	8·15	5·97	5·23	3·89	2·13
		Total for Panaswadi	...	782	27,403	Christians ...	173	25	37	23	20	16	212	1,139	127	254	266	294	121	2,200	51·73	5·77	11·55	12·09	13·36	5·50
						Parsis ...	162	120	42	45	13	8	300	905	362	307	268	295	47	2,202	41·10	16·44	13·94	12·09	13·40	2·13
						Mahomedans ..	109	66	25	16	10	8	324	1,077	560	199	200	134	47	2,273	47·38	24·64	8·75	11·71	5·46	2·07
						Hindus ...	2,966	142	81	59	26	46	3,332	16,905	1,123	868	603	349	303	20,310	83·65	5·56	4·29	2·98	1·73	1·80
						Jains ...	108	8	1	2	...	1	120	343	64	7	12	...	5	431	79·58	14·85	1·62	2·79	...	1·10
						Jews and others ...	10	...	...	...	1	...	11	83	...	...	...	5	...	87	94·25	...	...	...	5·75	...

TABLE XV—*continued.*

TABLE SHOWING TOTAL POPULATION OF EACH RELIGION IN EACH CIRCLE AND ITS RELATION TO HOUSES AND TENEMENTS.

Ward.	Charge.	Section.	Circle No.	Total number of buildings.	Total number of persons.	Religion.	Total number of separate tenements occupied by persons of each religion with — One room.	Two rooms.	Three rooms.	Four rooms.	Five rooms.	Six rooms and over.	Total number of tenements of all kinds occupied by members of each religion.	Total number of members of each religion occupying tenements with — One room.	Two rooms.	Three rooms.	Four rooms.	Five rooms.	Six rooms and over.	Total number of members of each religion occupying tenements of all kinds.	Percentage of total population of each religion occupying each class of tenements with — One room.	Two rooms.	Three rooms.	Four rooms.	Five rooms.	Six rooms and over.
1	2	1	2	3	4	5	6	7	8	9	10	11	12	13	14	15	16	17	18	19	20	2	22	23	24	25
						Total ...	883	173	81	72	43	38	1.290	6.898	689	628	551	735	323	9.324	65·62	7·39	6·74	5·91	7·88	3·45
C.	12	Fanaswadi ...	1	...	9,324	Christians ...	93	22	20	19	18	16	188	1,000	110	163	218	278	121	1,060	55·18	5·54	8·21	10·98	14·	6·09
						Parsis ...	66	88	40	39	10	4	267	647	344	193	253	270	17	1,633	39·80	15·03	11·89	15·58	16·64	1·05
						Mahomedans ...	11	14	4	...	1	...	30	200	37	37	...	9	...	349	76·22	10·00	10·00	...	2·58	...
						Hindus ...	690	40	17	14	14	18	902	4,304	298	235	61	178	165	5,341	61·71	5·58	4·40	1·52	3·33	3·40
						Jains ...	3	...	...	...	...	...	3	25	...	...	...	...	...	25	100·	...	...	...	...	...
						Jews and others ...	...	...	...	...	...	...	...	...	...	...	...	...	...	...	...	...	...	...	...	...
						Total ...	1.755	128	45	43	15	22	2.008	7.670	1.145	628	611	164	116	10.334	74·23	11·8	6·06	5·91	1·59	1·12
		" ...	2	...	10,334	Christians ...	3	...	5	3	2	...	13	14	...	60	48	16	...	158	8·86	...	50·63	30·38	10·13	...
						Parsis ...	71	33	2	6	3	4	119	233	118	114	34	25	30	554	42·06	21·30	20·58	6·14	4·51	5·41
						Mahomedans ...	44	32	3	5	4	2	90	31	380	38	187	48	10	694	4·47	54·75	5·62	26·80	6·92	1·44
						Hindus ...	1,548	62	34	27	5	15	1,001	7,196	623	389	330	70	71	8,679	82·91	7·18	4·48	3·80	·81	·82
						Jains ...	89	2	1	2	...	1	95	106	24	7	12	...	5	244	60·33	9·83	2·87	4·92	...	2·05
						Jews and others ...	...	...	...	...	1	...	1	...	...	...	...	5	...	5	...	...	...	...	100·	...
						Total ...	911	60	50	39	12	19	1.081	6.383	401	379	271	168	144	7.745	82·40	5·18	4·80	3·50	2·17	1·86
		" ...	3	...	7,745	Christians ...	6	3	2	...	...	...	11	28	17	11	...	...	...	56	50·	30·36	19·64	...	...	...
						Parsis ...	5	...	...	...	...	...	5	25	...	...	...	...	...	25	100·	...	...	...	...	...
						Mahomedans ...	144	20	18	11	5	6	204	780	143	131	79	67	37	1,230	63·41	11·63	10·08	6·42	5·45	3·01
						Hindus ...	730	31	30	18	7	13	829	5,346	201	244	192	101	107	6,190	86·35	3·25	3·94	3·10	1·63	1·73
						Jains ...	16	6	...	...	...	...	23	123	40	...	...	...	...	163	75·31	24·69	...	...	...	...
						Jews and others ...	10	...	...	...	...	...	10	82	...	...	...	...	...	82	100	...	...	...	...	...
						Total ...	6.387	1.126	226	102	61	49	7.951	28.875	4.638	1.427	758	414	345	36.457	79·20	12·72	3·91	2·08	1·14	·95
		Total for Bhuleshwar ...	...	1,143	36,457	Christians ...	5	1	1	1	...	...	8	20	1	1	2	...	...	24	83·33	4·17	4·17	8·33	...	...
						Parsis ...	73	32	25	7	1	3	141	331	103	134	30	8	23	723	45·78	20·60	19·09	4·15	1·11	3·18
						Mahomedans ...	2,042	236	68	17	9	10	2,371	9,496	1,153	308	165	71	55	11,308	84·18	10·23	2·73	1·47	·63	·76
						Hindus ...	3,762	792	133	73	48	30	4,837	17,050	3,012	936	524	306	218	22,071	77·25	13·78	4·24	2·37	1·39	·97
						Jains ...	505	66	9	5	3	6	594	1,980	340	44	30	29	24	2,371	83·50	10·53	1·66	1·53	1·22	1·01
						Jews and others ...	...	...	...	...	...	...	...	...	...	...	...	...	...	...	...	...	...	...	...	...
						Total ...	644	361	35	19	14	17	1.090	3.724	1.102	297	198	107	123	5.549	67·11	19·86	5·35	3·53	1·93	2·22
	13	Bhuleshwar ...	1	..	5,510	Christians ...	1	...	1	...	...	...	3	2	...	1	...	...	...	3	66·67	...	33·33	...	...	...
						Parsis ...	...	...	...	...	...	...	...	...	...	...	...	...	...	...	...	...	...	...	...	...
						Mahomedans ...	7	4	...	...	...	1	12	27	21	...	...	...	1	49	55·10	42·86	...	...	...	2·04
						Hindus ...	608	345	30	10	13	12	1,024	3,527	1,063	279	176	92	104	5,241	67·30	20·28	5·33	3·36	1·76	1·98
						Jains ...	28	12	4	3	1	4	52	168	18	17	20	15	16	250	65·43	7·03	6·64	7·81	5·86	7·03
						Jews and others ...	...	...	...	...	...	...	...	...	...	...	...	...	...	...	...	...	...	...	...	...
						Total ...	1.161	93	15	4	4	6	1.283	4.842	458	70	30	26	40	5.466	88·58	8·38	1·28	·55	·48	·73
		" ...	2	...	5,466	Christians ...	...	...	...	...	...	...	...	...	...	...	...	...	...	...	...	...	...	...	...	...
						Parsis ...	...	...	...	...	...	...	...	...	...	...	...	...	...	...	...	...	...	...	...	...
						Mahomedans ...	4	5	...	...	...	...	9	9	1	...	...	...	...	10	90·	10·	...	...	...	...
						Hindus ...	1,005	80	15	3	4	5	1,113	4,270	402	70	24	26	36	4,834	88·46	8·31	1·45	·50	·54	·74
						Jains ...	152	8	...	1	...	1	162	557	55	...	6	...	4	622	89·55	8·84	...	·97	...	·64
						Jews and others ...	...	...	...	...	...	...	...	...	...	...	...	...	...	...	...	...	...	...	...	...

TABLE XV—*continued*.

TABLE SHOWING TOTAL POPULATION OF EACH RELIGION IN EACH CIRCLE AND ITS RELATION TO HOUSES AND TENEMENTS.

Ward.	Charge.	Section.	Circle No.	Total number of buildings.	Total number of persons.	Religion.	Total number of separate tenements occupied by persons of each religion with — One room.	Two rooms.	Three rooms.	Four rooms.	Five rooms.	Six rooms and over.	Total number of tenement of all kinds occupied by members of each religion.	Total number of members of each religion occupying tenements with — One room.	Two rooms.	Three rooms.	Four rooms.	Five rooms.	Six rooms and over.	Total number of members of each religion occupying tenements of all kinds.	Percentage of total population of each religion occupying each class of tenements with — One room.	Two rooms.	Three rooms.	Four rooms.	Five rooms.	Six rooms and over.
		1	2	3	4	5	6	7	8	9	10	11	12	13	14	15	16	17	18	19	20	21	22	23	24	25
						Total ...	770	41	21	10	6	3	851	2,595	350	121	56	35	14	3,171	81·83	11·04	3·82	1·77	1·10	·44
C.	13	Bhuleshwar ...	3	...	3,171	Christians ...	2	...	...	...	...	...	2	11	...	...	...	...	...	11	100·	...	...	...	...	...
						Parsis ...	4	...	...	...	...	...	4	20	...	...	...	...	...	20	100	...	...	...	...	...
						Mahomedans ...	7	1	1	...	...	...	9	37	1	3	...	...	...	41	90·21	2·44	7·32	...	...	...
						Hindus ...	737	38	20	10	5	3	813	2,462	346	118	56	30	14	3,026	81·36	11·44	3·90	1·85	·99	·46
						Jains ...	10	2	...	...	1	...	23	65	3	...	...	5	...	73	89·04	4·11	...	...	6·85	...
						Jews and others ...	...	...	...	...	...	...	...	...	...	...	...	...	...	...	...	...	...	...	...	...
						Total ...	1,965	180	61	22	8	13	2,269	8,745	950	413	147	68	99	10,422	83·91	9·12	3·96	1·41	·65	·95
		" ...	4	...	10,423	Christians ...	1	1	...	...	...	...	2	2	1	...	...	...	...	3	66·67	33·33	...	...	...	...
						Parsis ...	67	32	25	7	1	3	135	305	193	138	30	8	23	697	43·76	27·69	19·80	4·30	1·15	3·30
						Mahomedans ...	1,089	104	34	9	5	8	1,249	4,835	536	193	66	39	74	5,742	84·20	9·33	3·36	1·15	·68	1·29
						Hindus ...	709	37	3	6	2	3	759	2,884	190	82	61	21	2	3,240	89·29	5·86	2·54	1·88	·65	·06
						Jains ...	119	6	...	...	...	...	125	719	31	...	...	...	...	750	95·87	4·13	...	...	...	...
						Jews and others ...	...	...	...	...	...	...	...	...	...	...	...	...	...	...	...	...	...	...	...	...
						Total ...	1,066	185	35	17	9	2	1,314	6,116	706	196	125	66	15	7,224	84·66	9·77	2·71	1·73	·92	·21
		" ...	5	...	7,224	Christians ...	1	...	...	...	...	...	1	5	...	...	...	...	...	5	100·	...	...	...	...	...
						Parsis ...	1	...	...	...	...	...	1	3	...	...	...	...	...	3	100·	...	...	...	...	...
						Mahomedans ...	902	116	22	8	4	1	1,053	4,419	578	104	100	32	10	5,243	84·29	11·03	1·98	1·91	·61	·19
						Hindus ...	100	60	12	9	5	1	187	1,510	91	87	25	34	5	1,755	86·04	5·18	4·96	1·42	1·94	·28
						Jains ...	63	9	1	...	...	...	72	179	34	5	...	...	...	218	82·11	15·60	2·29	...	...	...
						Jews and others ...	...	...	...	...	...	...	...	...	...	...	...	...	...	...	...	...	...	...	...	...
						Total ...	761	266	59	30	20	8	1,144	2,853	1,072	330	204	112	54	4,625	61·69	23·18	7·13	4·41	2·42	1·17
		" ...	6	...	4,625	Christians ...	...	...	...	1	...	...	1	...	...	...	2	...	...	2	...	...	...	100·	...	...
						Parsis ...	1	...	...	...	...	...	1	3	...	...	...	...	...	3	100·	...	...	...	...	...
						Mahomedans ...	33	5	1	...	...	...	39	158	17	8	...	...	...	183	86·34	9·29	4·37	...	...	...
						Hindus ...	608	232	54	28	19	7	943	2,391	947	200	192	103	52	3,985	60	23·76	7·23	4·82	2·58	1·31
						Jains ...	124	29	4	1	1	1	160	301	103	21	10	9	2	452	66·59	22·79	4·87	2·21	1·99	·44
						Jews and others ...	...	...	...	...	...	...	...	...	...	...	...	...	...	...	...	...	...	...	...	...
						Total ...	5,805	313	62	34	14	18	6,246	24,572	1,595	438	322	136	252	27,615	88·98	6·86	1·59	1·17	·49	·91
		Total for Kumbharwada	...	649	27,615	Christians ...	20	1	...	...	1	...	22	66	2	...	...	1	...	69	95·65	2·90	...	...	1·45	...
						Parsis ...	48	13	1	...	2	...	64	207	94	14	...	10	...	325	63·69	28·92	4·31	...	3·06	...
						Mahomedans ...	655	21	3	3	1	1	686	2,529	123	15	56	5	27	2,755	91·80	4·47	·54	2·03	·18	·98
						Hindus ...	5,018	264	57	31	10	17	5,397	21,603	1,614	400	266	120	225	24,128	89·12	6·69	1·66	1·10	·50	·93
						Jains ...	61	9	2	...	...	...	72	259	62	9	...	...	...	330	78·48	18·79	2·73	...	...	...
						Jews and others ...	3	...	...	...	...	...	3	8	...	...	...	...	...	8	100·	...	...	...	...	...
						Total ...	1,474	113	39	19	8	12	1,665	5,802	736	267	162	87	210	7,264	79·87	10·13	3·68	2·23	1·20	2·89
	14	Kumbharwada ...	1	...	7,264	Christians ...	11	1	...	...	1	...	13	39	2	...	...	1	...	42	92·86	4·76	...	...	2·38	...
						Parsis ...	45	13	1	...	2	...	61	202	94	14	...	10	...	320	63·13	29·38	4·37	...	3·12	...
						Mahomedans ...	329	7	...	1	...	1	338	1,253	53	...	2	...	27	1,335	93·86	3·97	...	·15	...	2·02
						Hindus ...	1,073	68	38	18	8	11	1,233	6,240	661	253	160	76	183	8,476	77·43	10·30	4·62	2·94	1·39	3·34
						Jains ...	15	4	...	...	...	...	19	66	23	...	...	...	...	89	74·16	25·84	...	...	...	...
						Jews and others ...	1	...	...	...	...	...	1	2	...	...	...	...	...	2	100·	...	...	...	...	...

TABLE XV—*continued.*

TABLE SHOWING TOTAL POPULATION OF EACH RELIGION IN EACH CIRCLE AND ITS RELATION TO HOUSES AND TENEMENTS.

Ward.	Charge.	Section.	Circle No.	Total number of buildings.	Total number of persons.	Religion.	Total number of separate tenements occupied by persons of each religion with One room.	Two rooms.	Three rooms.	Four Rooms.	Five rooms.	Six rooms and over.	Total number of tenements of all kinds occupied by members of each religion.	Total number of members of each religion occupying tenements with One room.	Two rooms.	Three rooms.	Four rooms.	Five rooms.	Six rooms and over.	Total number of members of each religion occupying tenements of all kinds.	Percentage of total population of each religion occupying each class of tenements with One room.	Two rooms.	Three rooms.	Four rooms.	Five rooms.	Six rooms and over.
		1	2	3	4	5	6	7	8	9	10	11	12	13	14	15	16	17	18	19	20	21	22	23	24	25
						Total ...	2,381	90	8	6	3	3	2,491	9,592	537	51	40	25	29	10,274	93·36	5·23	·50	·39	·24	·28
C.		Kumbharwada ...	2	...	10,274	Christians ...	2	...	...	...	...	...	3	7	...	...	...	...	...	7	100·	...	...	...	...	...
						Parsis ...	2	...	...	...	...	...	2	4	...	...	...	...	...	4	100·	...	...	...	...	...
						Mahomedans ...	153	8	1	...	1	...	163	610	30	13	...	5	...	654	93·70	4·56	1·98	...	·76	...
						Hindus ...	2,189	81	6	6	2	3	2,287	8,814	504	35	40	20	29	9,442	93·35	5·34	·37	·42	·21	·31
						Jains ...	34	1	1	...	...	...	36	153	3	3	...	...	...	159	96·23	1·89	1·90	...	...	...
						Jews and others ...	1	...	...	...	...	...	1	4	...	...	...	...	...	4	100·	...	...	...	...	...
						Total ...	965	68	10	1	2	3	1,049	4,450	351	80	4	16	13	4,914	90·56	7·14	1·63	·08	·33	·26
		" ...	3	...	4,914	Christians ...	...	...	...	...	...	...	...	...	...	...	...	...	...	...	...	...	...	...	...	...
						Parsis ...	...	...	...	...	...	...	...	...	...	...	...	...	...	...	...	...	...	...	...	...
						Mahomedans ...	56	1	...	...	...	...	57	191	11	...	...	...	...	202	94·55	5·45	...	...	...	...
						Hindus ...	899	63	9	1	2	3	977	4,230	304	74	4	16	13	4,641	91·14	6·55	1·59	·09	·35	·28
						Jains ...	10	4	1	...	...	...	15	29	36	6	...	...	...	71	40·85	50·70	8·45	...	...	...
						Jews and others ...	...	...	...	...	...	...	...	...	...	...	...	...	...	...	...	...	...	...	...	...
						Total ...	965	42	5	8	1	...	1,041	4,728	271	40	116	8	...	5,163	91·57	5·25	·77	2·25	·16	...
		" ...	4	...	5,163	Christians ...	6	...	...	...	...	...	6	20	...	...	...	...	...	20	100·	...	...	...	...	...
						Parsis ...	1	...	...	...	...	...	1	1	...	...	...	...	...	1	100·	...	...	...	...	...
						Mahomedans ...	118	10	1	2	...	...	131	475	29	2	54	...	...	560	84·82	5·18	·36	9·64	...	...
						Hindus ...	857	32	4	6	1	...	900	4,219	242	38	62	8	...	4,569	92·34	5·30	·83	1·36	·17	...
						Jains ...	2	...	...	...	...	...	2	11	...	...	...	...	...	11	100·	...	...	...	...	...
						Jews and others ...	1	...	...	...	...	...	1	2	...	...	...	...	...	2	100·	...	...	...	...	...
						Total ...	4,730	351	72	32	12	5	5,202	20,044	1,593	563	264	112	360	22,936	87·39	6·95	2·45	1·15	·49	1·57
		Total for Khara Talao ...	...	629	22,936	Christians ...	11	2	...	...	...	...	13	32	11	...	...	...	...	43	74·42	25·58	...	...	...	...
						Parsis ...	23	13	4	3	4	...	46	93	46	17	26	33	...	217	42·86	21·12	7·83	11·98	15·21	...
						Mahomedans ...	3,131	281	65	27	7	5	3,516	13,361	1,256	624	224	66	360	15,701	84·61	7·95	3·32	1·43	·42	2·29
						Hindus ...	1,437	54	3	2	1	...	1,497	6,006	275	22	14	13	...	6,420	94·95	4·29	·34	·22	·20	...
						Jains ...	124	...	...	...	...	...	124	433	...	...	...	...	...	433	100·	...	...	...	...	...
						Jews and others ...	5	1	...	...	...	...	6	29	3	...	...	...	...	32	90·63	9·37	...	...	...	...
						Total ...	927	18	3	2	1	...	951	3,759	147	25	14	13	...	3,958	94·97	3·72	·63	·35	·33	...
	15	Khara Talao ...	1	...	3,958	Christians ...	3	...	...	...	...	...	3	4	...	...	...	...	...	4	100·	...	...	...	...	...
						Parsis ...	3	...	...	...	...	...	3	5	...	...	...	...	...	5	100·	...	...	...	...	...
						Mahomedans ...	284	4	1	...	...	...	289	950	45	10	...	...	...	1,005	94·53	4·48	·99	...	...	...
						Hindus ...	625	14	2	2	1	...	644	2,751	102	15	14	13	...	2,895	95·03	3·52	·52	·48	·45	...
						Jains ...	12	...	...	...	...	...	12	49	...	...	...	...	...	49	100·	...	...	...	...	...
						Jews and others ...	...	...	...	...	...	...	...	...	...	...	...	...	...	...	...	...	...	...	...	...
						Total ...	499	41	12	6	3	3	564	2,003	164	117	47	32	25	2,388	83·88	6·87	4·90	1·97	1·34	1·04
		" ...	2	...	2,388	Christians ...	...	...	...	...	...	...	...	...	...	...	...	...	...	...	...	...	...	...	...	...
						Parsis ...	...	...	...	...	...	...	...	...	...	...	...	...	...	...	...	...	...	...	...	...
						Mahomedans ...	382	37	12	6	3	3	413	1,551	150	117	47	32	25	1,922	80·70	7·80	6·09	2·45	1·66	1·30
						Hindus ...	99	4	...	...	...	...	103	375	14	...	...	...	...	389	96·40	3·60	...	...	...	...
						Jains ...	18	...	...	...	...	...	18	77	...	...	...	...	...	77	100·	...	...	...	...	...
						Jews and others ...	...	...	...	...	...	...	...	...	...	...	...	...	...	...	...	...	...	...	...	...

TABLE XV.

TOTAL POPULATION OF EACH RELIGION, ETC.

TABLE XV—*continued.*

TABLE SHOWING TOTAL POPULATION OF EACH RELIGION IN EACH CIRCLE AND ITS RELATION TO HOUSES AND TENEMENTS.

Ward.	Charge.	Section.	Circle number.	Total number of buildings.	Total number of persons.	Religion.	Total No. of separate tenements occupied by persons of each religion with: One room.	Two rooms.	Three rooms.	Four rooms.	Five rooms.	Six rooms and over.	Total number of tenements of all kinds occupied by members of each religion.	Total No. of members of each religion occupying tenements with: One room.	Two rooms.	Three rooms.	Four rooms.	Five rooms.	Six rooms and over.	Total number of members of each religion occupying tenements of all kinds.	Percentage of total population of each religion occupying each class of tenements with: One room.	Two rooms.	Three rooms.	Four rooms.	Five rooms.	Six rooms and over.
		1	2	3	4	5	6	7	8	9	10	11	12	13	14	15	16	17	18	19	20	21	22	23	24	25
						Total ...	1.246	77	11	5	2	...	1.341	5.722	390	127	39	19	...	6.297	90·87	6·19	2·02	·62	·30	...
C.	15	Khara Talao ...	3	...	6,297	Christians ...	1	2	...	...	...	...	3	3	11	...	...	...	...	14	21·43	78·57	...	...	...	...
						Parsis ...	3	7	3	1	...	...	14	9	33	13	7	...	...	62	14·52	53·22	20·97	11·29	...	...
						Mahomedans ...	783	41	8	4	2	...	837	3,932	233	114	32	19	...	4,330	90·81	5·38	2·63	·74	·44	...
						Hindus ...	437	27	...	...	...	...	464	1,703	113	...	...	...	...	1,816	93·78	6·22	...	...	...	...
						Jains ...	23	...	...	...	...	...	23	75	...	...	...	...	...	75	100·	...	...	...	...	...
						Jews and others ...	...	...	...	...	...	...	...	...	...	...	...	...	...	...	...	...	...	...	...	...
						Total ...	994	106	19	3	1	1	1.126	3.874	475	137	51	6	5	4.548	85·18	10·45	3·01	1·12	·13	·11
	...	" ...	4	...	4,548	Christians ...	2	...	...	...	...	...	2	2	...	...	...	...	...	2	100·	...	...	...	...	...
						Parsis ...	7	3	1	...	...	...	11	14	6	4	...	...	...	24	58·33	25·	16·67	...	...	...
						Mahomedans ...	813	101	17	3	1	1	936	3,138	461	126	51	6	5	3,777	83·08	11·94	3·34	1·35	·16	·13
						Hindus ...	154	3	1	...	...	...	158	662	15	7	...	...	...	684	96·79	2·19	1·03	...	...	...
						Jains ...	17	...	...	...	...	...	17	53	...	...	...	...	...	53	100·	...	...	...	...	...
						Jews and others ...	1	1	...	...	...	...	2	5	3	...	...	...	...	8	62·50	37·50	...	...	...	...
						Total ...	1.064	107	27	16	5	1	1.220	4.686	417	157	113	42	330	5.745	81·57	7·26	2·73	1·97	·73	5·74
	...	" ...	5	...	5,745	Christians ...	5	...	...	...	...	...	5	23	...	...	...	...	...	23	100·	...	...	...	...	...
						Parsis ...	9	3	...	2	4	...	18	65	9	...	10	33	...	126	51·59	7·14	...	15·08	26·19	...
						Mahomedans ...	870	98	27	14	1	1	1,011	3,790	377	157	94	9	330	4,757	79·67	7·92	3·30	1·98	·19	6·94
						Hindus ...	122	6	...	...	...	...	128	605	31	...	...	...	...	636	95,13	4·87	...	...	...	...
						Jains ...	54	...	...	...	...	...	54	179	...	...	...	...	...	179	100·	...	...	...	...	...
						Jews and others ...	4	...	...	...	...	...	4	24	...	...	...	...	...	24	100·	...	...	...	...	...
						Total ...	17.336	2.796	859	743	544	854	23.134	78,671	12.089	4.895	4.386	3,671	7.235	110.947	70·91	10·90	4·41	3·95	3·31	6·52
D.	...	Total for D Ward ...	...	5,350	110,947	Christians ...	658	132	56	74	50	99	1,078	2,632	557	223	353	373	727	4,865	54·10	11·45	4·58	7·26	7·64	14·97
						Parsis ...	1,033	341	241	241	201	333	2,390	5,116	1,846	1,306	1,418	1,340	2,402	13,439	38·06	13·76	9·72	10·55	10·04	17·87
						Mahomedans ...	1,343	83	36	42	24	44	1,471	4,771	400	190	170	112	319	5,962	80·02	6·71	3·19	2·85	1·88	5·35
						Hindus ...	14,203	2,206	512	380	254	302	17,919	65,504	9,154	3,078	2,435	1,608	3,725	85,724	70·41	10·68	3·62	2·84	2·11	4·34
						Jains ...	168	28	12	4	6	8	224	567	118	68	8	39	31	822	68·98	14·36	8·30	·97	3·53	3·77
						Jews and others ...	36	4	2	2	...	8	52	82	11	9	2	...	31	135	60·74	8·15	6·67	1·48	...	22·96
						Total ...	6.280	520	266	225	198	269	7,758	22.864	2.331	1,494	1.369	1,329	2,557	31.934	71·60	7·27	4·68	4·28	4·16	8·01
	...	Total for Khetwadi ...	...	1,220	31,934	Christians ...	150	12	19	13	14	23	240	677	39	41	54	72	233	1,116	60·66	3·50	3·07	4·84	6·45	20·88
						Parsis ...	563	172	198	134	116	140	1,319	2,502	781	944	865	807	1,270	7,105	34·77	10·86	13·12	12·30	11·22	17·73
						Mahomedans ...	825	42	14	12	12	13	918	3,112	211	101	23	36	100	3,592	86·64	5·88	2·00	·60	1·	2·78
						Hindus ...	4,006	292	63	65	56	64	5,226	16,428	1,283	386	400	414	933	19,844	82·79	6·49	1·95	2·01	2·09	4·70
						Jains ...	42	2	1	...	...	2	47	138	7	11	...	...	9	165	83·64	4·24	6·67	...	...	5·45
						Jews and others ...	5	...	1	1	...	1	8	7	...	8	1	...	6	22	31·82	...	36·36	4·55	...	27·27
						Total ...	348	38	26	34	17	33	496	1,411	160	136	215	143	672	2,737	51·55	5·85	4·97	7·86	5·22	24·55
	16	Khetwadi ...	1	...	2,737	Christians ...	68	8	8	10	5	10	109	206	21	12	21	6	68	344	60·07	6·47	3·12	6·47	1·56	17·71
						Parsis ...	44	20	16	11	8	11	100	497	62	104	152	116	204	1,150	42·89	7·06	6·97	13·11	10·01	17·95
						Mahomedans ...	30	2	2	5	2	5	55	136	6	6	15	8	23	194	70·10	3·09	3·00	7·73	4·13	11·86
						Hindus ...	194	8	1	7	2	6	218	519	51	14	26	13	367	990	52·43	5·15	1·41	2·63	1·31	37·07
						Jains ...	1	...	...	...	...	...	1	1	...	...	...	...	...	1	100·	...	...	...	...	...
						Jews and others ...	2	...	...	1	...	1	4	2	...	...	1	...	6	9	22·22	...	...	11·11	...	66·67

TABLE XV—continued.

TABLE SHOWING TOTAL POPULATION OF EACH RELIGION IN EACH CIRCLE AND ITS RELATION TO HOUSES AND TENEMENTS.

Ward.	Charge.	Section	Circle number.	Total number of buildings.	Total number of persons.	Religion.	Total No. of separate tenements occupied by persons of each religion with One room.	Two rooms.	Three rooms.	Four rooms.	Five rooms.	Six rooms and over.	Total number of tenements of all kinds occupied by members of each religion.	Total No. of members of each religion occupying tenements with One room.	Two rooms.	Three rooms.	Four rooms.	Five rooms.	Six rooms and over.	Total number of members of each religion occupying tenements of all kinds.	Percentage of total population of each religion occupying each class of tenements with One room.	Two rooms.	Three rooms.	Four rooms.	Five rooms.	Six rooms and over.
		1	2	3	4	5	6	7	8	9	10	11	12	13	14	15	16	17	18	19	20	21	22	23	24	25
						Total ...	1,151	71	26	37	64	78	1,427	3,678	337	196	249	375	684	5,468	67·26	6·16	3·57	4·55	6·87	11·59
D.	16	Khetwadi ...	2	...	5,468	Christians ...	20	...	...	...	2	2	24	94	...	...	...	19	46	159	59·12	...	...	...	11·95	28·93
						Parsis ...	39	2	3	6	20	35	114	180	7	20	32	125	261	625	28·80	1·12	3·20	5·12	20·	41·76
						Mahomedans ...	38	1	...	1	3	1	44	140	5	...	4	16	7	171	81·87	2·93		2·34	8·77	4·09
						Hindus ...	1,046	67	23	30	30	40	1,236	3,238	323	175	213	216	320	4,485	72·20	7·20	3·90	4·75	4·82	7·13
						Jains ...	8	1	...	...	...	...	9	20	2	...	...	...	...	28	92·80	7·14	...	...	...	...
						Jews and others ...	...	...	...	...	...	...	...	...	...	...	...	...	...	...	...	...	...	...	...	...
						Total ...	762	72	26	26	22	39	947	3,248	366	143	169	158	239	4,318	75·10	8·48	3·31	3·91	3·66	5·54
"	"	"	3	...	4,318	Christians ...	3	1	2	1	1	6	14	17	2	5	7	1	60	92	20·73	2·14	6·10	8·53	1·22	60·08
						Parsis ...	8	1	4	6	3	7	24	13	8	30	61	20	63	185	7·03	4·32	16·22	37·57	10·81	34·05
						Mahomedans ...	...	...	...	1	1	1	3	...	...	...	1	1	1	3	...	...	...	33·33	33·33	33·34
						Hindus ...	744	70	20	18	17	23	892	3,171	356	108	110	136	116	3,997	79·31	8·91	2·70	2·75	3·40	2·10
						Jains ...	11	...	...	...	...	2	13	40	...	...	...	...	9	49	81·63	...	...	...	...	18·37
						Jews and others ...	1	...	...	...	...	...	1	2	...	...	...	...	...	2	100·	...	...	...	...	...
						Total ...	251	19	54	53	52	79	508	926	66	274	331	368	670	2,634	35·12	2·51	10·40	12·57	13·97	25·43
"	"	"	4	...	2,634	Christians ...	16	1	8	2	4	5	36	87	3	16	26	24	60	225	38·67	1·33	7·11	11·56	10·67	30·66
						Parsis ...	28	9	38	47	42	64	228	70	29	207	264	301	505	1,376	5·74	2·11	15·06	19·18	21·87	36·05
						Mahomedans ...	19	3	3	...	3	4	32	73	11	19	...	10	46	159	45·91	6·92	11·95	...	6·29	28·93
						Hindus ...	188	6	3	4	3	6	210	686	23	13	41	33	59	855	80·23	2·69	1·52	4·80	3·86	6·90
						Jains ...	...	...	1	...	...	...	1	...	...	11	...	...	...	11	...	...	100·	...	...	...
						Jews and others ...	...	...	1	...	...	...	1	...	...	8	...	...	...	8	...	...	100·	...	...	...
						Total ...	580	121	63	50	27	17	858	2,302	417	339	267	152	97	3,574	64·41	11·67	9·49	7·47	4·25	2·71
"	"	"	5	...	3,574	Christians ...	17	1	...	...	1	...	19	70	4	...	...	2	...	76	92·11	5·26	...	...	2·63	...
						Parsis ...	102	27	59	46	26	14	274	466	105	288	264	150	82	1,365	35·31	7·64	20·95	19·20	10·91	5·96
						Mahomedans ...	13	1	1	1	...	...	16	57	13	30	1	...	...	101	56·44	12·87	29·70	·99	...	...
						Hindus ...	447	92	3	3	...	3	548	1,679	295	21	2	...	15	2,012	83·45	14·66	1·04	·10	...	·75
						Jains ...	1	...	...	...	...	...	1	10	...	...	...	...	...	10	100·	...	...	...	...	...
						Jews and others ...	...	...	...	...	...	...	...	...	...	...	...	...	...	...	...	...	...	...	...	...
						Total ...	418	97	23	13	3	11	565	1,555	457	144	76	24	111	2,367	65·69	19·31	6·08	3·21	1·02	4·69
"	"	"	6	...	2,367	Christians ...	14	...	...	...	...	...	14	77	...	...	...	...	...	77	100·	...	...	...	...	...
						Parsis ...	258	95	23	13	3	8	400	913	454	144	76	24	81	1,692	53·96	26·83	8·51	4·49	1·42	4·79
						Mahomedans ...	8	1	...	...	...	...	9	31	1	...	...	...	...	32	96·88	3·12	...	...	...	...
						Hindus ...	137	1	...	...	...	3	141	530	2	...	...	...	30	562	94·31	·36	...	...	...	5·33
						Jains ...	1	...	...	...	...	...	1	4	...	...	...	...	...	4	100·	...	...	...	...	...
						Jews and others ...	...	...	...	...	...	...	...	...	...	...	...	...	...	...	...	...	...	...	...	...
						Total ...	1,101	59	28	7	7	8	1,210	3,894	267	175	52	86	93	4,567	85·26	5·85	3·83	1·14	1·88	2·04
"	"	"	7	...	4,567	Christians ...	10	1	...	...	...	...	11	27	9	...	...	...	...	36	75·	25·	...	...	...	...
						Parsis ...	64	14	23	5	5	7	118	237	81	148	46	71	85	668	35·48	12·13	22·15	6·89	10·63	12·72
						Mahomedans ...	137	10	2	...	...	1	150	513	34	16	...	...	8	571	89·84	5·96	2·80	...	...	1·40
						Hindus ...	875	34	3	2	2	...	916	3,077	143	11	6	15	...	3,252	94·62	4·40	·34	·18	·46	...
						Jains ...	14	...	...	...	...	...	14	38	...	...	...	...	...	38	100·	...	...	...	...	...
						Jews and others ...	1	...	...	...	...	...	1	2	...	...	...	...	...	2	100·	...	...	...	...	...

TABLE XV.

Total Population of each Religion, etc.

TABLE XV—*continued.*

Table showing Total Population of each Religion in each Circle and its Relation to Houses and Tenements.

Ward.	Charge.	Section.	Circle No.	Total number of buildings.	Total number of persons.	Religion.	Total number of separate tenements occupied by persons of each religion with: One room.	Two rooms.	Three rooms.	Four rooms.	Five rooms.	Six rooms and over.	Total number of tenements of all kinds occupied by members of each religion.	Total number of members of each religion occupying tenements with: One room.	Two rooms.	Three rooms.	Four rooms.	Five rooms.	Six rooms and over.	Total number of members of each religion occupying tenements of all kinds.	Percentage of total population of each religion occupying each class of tenements with: One room.	Two rooms.	Three rooms.	Four rooms.	Five rooms.	Six rooms and over.
		1	2	3	4	5	6	7	8	9	10	11	12	13	14	15	16	17	18	19	20	21	22	23	24	25
						Total ...	1,669	43	20	5	6	4	1,747	5,856	251	88	10	23	41	6,269	93·41	4·	1·40	·16	·37	·66
D.	16	Khetwadi ...	8	...	6,269	Christians ...	11	...	1	...	1	...	13	49	...	8	...	20	...	77	63·64	...	10·39	...	25·97	...
						Parsis ...	45	4	3	...	...	...	53	97	16	3	...	...	...	115	84·35	13·04	2·61	...	...	...
						Mahomedans ...	571	24	6	4	3	1	609	2,162	141	33	8	2	15	2,361	91·57	5·97	1·40	·34	·08	·64
						Hindus ...	1,036	14	10	1	2	3	1,065	3,526	90	44	2	1	26	3,691	95·58	2·44	1·19	·05	·03	·71
						Jains ...	6	1	...	...	...	...	7	19	5	...	...	...	...	24	79·17	20·83	...	...	...	...
						Jews and others ...	1	...	...	...	...	...	1	1	...	...	...	...	...	1	100·	...	...	...	...	...
						Total ...	4,455	1,100	245	178	108	195	6,379	20,738	5,066	1,457	1,048	733	1,669	30,711	67·55	16·49	4·74	3·41	2·38	5·43
		Total for Girgaum .	...	974	30,711	Christians ...	55	29	13	28	15	36	176	378	157	70	180	87	243	1,115	33·90	14·08	6·28	16·14	7·80	21·79
						Parsis ...	23	10	9	14	9	18	83	165	39	31	96	86	139	556	29·68	7·01	5·57	17·27	15·47	25·00
						Mahomedans ...	45	15	1	3	...	7	71	162	68	8	21	...	26	284	57·04	23·94	2·83	7·40	...	8·80
						Hindus ...	4,280	1,023	217	130	84	134	5,968	19,846	4,705	1,318	748	560	1,262	28,439	69·78	16·54	4·61	2·63	1·97	4·44
						Jains ...	53	23	5	1	...	...	81	187	97	30	3	...	...	317	58·99	30·60	9·46	·95	...	...
						Jews and others ...	...	...	...	...	...	...	...	...	...	...	...	...	...	...	...	...	...	...	...	...
						Total ...	1,053	84	16	25	5	30	1,213	5,120	372	119	178	40	297	6,126	83·58	6·07	1·94	2·91	·65	4·85
	31	Girgaum ...	1	...	6,126	Christians ...	23	5	1	4	1	3	37	223	26	2	49	1	16	317	70·35	8·20	·63	15·46	·31	5·05
						Parsis ...	5	6	3	10	3	12	39	39	23	25	61	24	103	274	14·23	8·03	9·13	22·26	8·76	37·59
						Mahomedans ...	37	10	1	3	...	1	52	133	50	8	21	...	8	220	60·45	22·73	3·64	9·55	...	3·64
						Hindus ...	981	61	11	8	1	14	1,076	4,690	355	84	47	15	170	5,261	89·15	4·85	1·60	·90	·28	3·23
						Jains ...	7	2	...	...	...	...	9	35	19	...	...	...	...	54	64·81	35·19	...	...	...	...
						Jews and others ...	...	...	...	...	...	...	...	...	...	...	...	...	...	...	...	...	...	...	...	...
						Total ...	567	152	11	23	21	26	800	2,494	635	86	138	138	278	3,769	66·17	16·85	2·28	3·66	3·66	7·38
		" ...	2	...	3,769	Christians ...	1	...	...	1	1	1	4	1	...	...	1	2	8	12	8·33	...	...	8·33	16·67	66·67
						Parsis ...	10	1	...	2	1	3	17	62	5	...	22	46	23	158	39·24	3·16	...	13·92	29·12	14·56
						Mahomedans ...	...	...	...	...	...	...	...	...	...	...	...	...	...	...	...	...	...	...	...	...
						Hindus ...	555	150	11	20	19	22	777	2,422	627	86	115	90	247	3,587	67·53	17·48	2·40	3·21	2·51	6·88
						Jains ...	1	1	...	...	...	...	2	9	3	...	...	...	...	12	75·	25·	...	...	...	...
						Jews and others ...	...	...	...	...	...	...	...	...	...	...	...	...	...	...	...	...	...	...	...	...
						Total ...	915	138	18	2	2	1	1,076	5,010	747	136	14	16	6	5,929	84·50	12·60	2·29	·24	·27	·10
		" ...	3	...	5,929	Christians ...	...	...	...	...	...	...	...	...	...	...	...	...	...	...	...	...	...	...	...	...
						Parsis ...	...	...	...	...	...	...	...	...	...	...	...	...	...	...	...	...	...	...	...	...
						Mahomedans ...	4	...	...	...	...	...	4	22	...	...	...	...	...	22	100·	...	...	...	...	...
						Hindus ...	894	138	18	2	2	1	1,055	4,913	747	136	14	16	6	5,832	84·24	12·81	2·33	·24	·28	·10
						Jains ...	17	...	...	...	...	...	17	75	...	...	...	...	...	75	100·	...	...	...	...	...
						Jews and others ...	...	...	...	...	...	...	...	...	...	...	...	...	...	...	...	...	...	...	...	...
						Total ...	112	25	7	8	8	3	163	769	152	42	53	44	63	1,123	68·48	13·54	3·74	4·71	3·92	5·61
		" ...	4	...	1,123	Christians ...	1	6	...	...	...	...	7	3	16	...	...	...	...	18	11·11	88·89	...	...	...	...
						Parsis ...	1	...	4	...	3	...	8	1	...	2	...	2	...	5	20·	...	40·	...	40·	...
						Mahomedans ...	...	...	...	...	...	...	...	...	...	...	...	...	...	...	...	...	...	...	...	...
						Hindus ...	100	14	2	8	5	3	132	750	117	23	53	42	63	1,048	71·57	11·16	2·19	5·06	4·01	6·01
						Jains ...	10	5	1	...	...	...	16	16	19	17	...	...	...	52	30·77	36·54	32·69	...	...	...
						Jews and others ...	...	...	...	...	...	...	...	...	...	...	...	...	...	...	...	...	...	...	...	...

TABLE XV—*continued.*

TABLE SHOWING TOTAL POPULATION OF EACH RELIGION IN EACH CIRCLE AND ITS RELATION TO HOUSES AND TENEMENTS.

Ward.	Charge.	Section.	Circle No.	Total number of buildings.	Total number of persons.	Religion.	Total number of separate tenements occupied by persons of each religion with: One room.	Two rooms.	Three rooms.	Four rooms.	Five rooms.	Six rooms and over.	Total number of tenements of all kinds occupied by members of each religion.	Total number of members of each religion occupying tenements with: One room.	Two rooms.	Three rooms.	Four rooms.	Five rooms.	Six rooms and over.	Total number of members of each religion occupying tenements of all kinds.	Percentage of total population of each religion occupying each class of tenements with: One room.	Two rooms.	Three rooms.	Four rooms.	Five rooms.	Six rooms and over.
		1	2	3	4	5	6	7	8	9	10	11	12	13	14	15	16	17	18	19	20	21	22	23	24	25
						Total ...	373	401	144	31	24	10	983	1,671	1,961	802	176	151	61	4,822	34·65	40·67	16·63	3·65	3·13	1·27
D	31	Girgaum ...	5	...	4,822	Christians ...	9	13	7	1	...	...	30	37	79	37	15	...	...	108	22·02	47·02	22·03	8·93	...	...
						Parsis ...	1	2	2	...	1	...	7	1	13	4	...	6	...	23	4·35	52·17	17·39	...	26·09	...
						Mahomedans ...	2	2	...	...	...	...	4	4	14	...	...	...	...	18	22·23	77·78	...	...	...	...
						Hindus ...	349	309	131	30	23	10	912	1,593	1,801	748	161	145	61	4,612	35·81	39·98	16·58	3·57	3·21	1·33
						Jains ...	12	14	4	...	...	...	30	36	52	13	...	...	...	101	35·64	51·48	12·88	...	...	...
						Jews and others ...	...	...	...	...	...	...	...	...	...	...	...	...	...	...	...	...	...	...	...	...
						Total ...	922	172	41	44	34	74	1,287	3,805	792	197	287	278	631	6,080	64·06	13·03	3·24	4·74	4·57	10·37
		" ...	6	...	6,090	Christians ...	18	5	5	22	13	32	95	103	36	31	115	81	219	588	17·52	6·12	5·27	19·56	14·29	37·24
						Parsis ...	5	...	...	2	1	3	11	45	...	...	13	8	13	79	56·96	...	...	16·46	10·13	16·46
						Mahomedans ...	1	3	...	...	...	6	10	1	4	...	...	...	17	22	4·55	18·18	...	...	...	77·27
						Hindus ...	896	163	36	20	20	33	1,168	3,741	718	166	159	186	383	5,383	69·52	13·34	3·08	2·96	3·46	7·09
						Jains ...	2	1	...	...	...	...	3	5	4	...	...	...	...	9	55·56	44·44	...	...	...	...
						Jews and others ...	...	...	...	...	...	...	...	...	...	...	...	...	...	...	...	...	...	...	...	...
						Total ...	513	128	8	43	14	51	757	1,779	407	75	203	66	333	2,863	62·16	14·23	2·62	7·06	2·31	11·63
		" ...	7	...	2,961	Christians ...	3	...	...	...	...	...	3	12	...	...	...	...	...	12	100	...	...	...	...	...
						Parsis ...	1	...	...	...	...	...	1	17	...	...	...	...	...	17	100·	...	...	...	...	...
						Mahomedans ...	1	...	...	...	...	...	1	2	...	...	...	...	...	2	100·	...	...	...	...	...
						Hindus ...	505	128	8	42	14	51	748	1,737	407	75	190	66	333	2,817	61·66	14·45	2·66	7·07	2·34	11·82
						Jains ...	3	...	...	1	...	...	4	11	...	...	3	...	...	14	78·57	...	...	21·43	...	...
						Jews and others ...	...	...	...	...	...	...	...	...	...	...	...	...	...	...	...	...	...	...	...	...
						Total ...	1,523	197	192	150	101	109	2,272	6,189	961	1,073	994	789	1,363	11,369	54·44	8·45	9·44	8·74	6·94	11·99
		Total for Chaupati.	...	714	11,369	Christians ...	27	10	8	12	5	6	68	144	76	26	32	49	107	434	33·18	17·51	5·99	7·37	11·29	24·66
						Parsis ...	32	15	22	33	23	16	140	120	41	110	173	133	172	747	16·06	5·49	15·03	23·16	16·33	23·03
						Mahomedans ...	40	8	6	2	6	9	70	159	23	28	14	40	124	388	40·98	5·93	7·22	3·61	10·31	31·96
						Hindus ...	1,410	164	153	103	66	75	1,971	5,721	821	870	773	560	957	9,710	58·92	8·46	9·05	7·96	5·77	9·86
						Jains ...	14	...	4	1	1	2	22	45	...	21	3	18	2	89	50·56	...	23·60	3·37	20·23	2·25
						Jews and others ...	...	...	...	...	...	1	1	...	...	...	...	...	1	1	...	...	...	...	...	100·
						Total ...	222	14	17	11	8	19	291	788	61	72	32	57	263	1,273	61·95	4·80	5·66	2·52	4·48	20·59
	30	Chaupati ...	1	72	1,273	Christians ...	6	...	2	4	...	2	14	19	...	2	6	...	40	67	28·36	...	2·98	8·96	...	59·70
						Parsis ...	6	4	8	4	1	5	28	17	2	29	7	6	51	112	15·18	1·79	25·89	6·25	5·36	45·54
						Mahomedans ...	16	2	1	1	5	6	31	75	9	10	12	36	96	238	31·51	3·78	4·20	5·04	15·13	40·34
						Hindus ...	193	8	3	1	2	6	213	675	50	24	4	15	75	843	80·07	5·93	2·85	·47	1·78	8·90
						Jains ...	1	...	3	1	...	...	5	2	...	7	3	...	...	12	16·67	...	58·33	25·	...	...
						Jews and other ...	...	...	...	...	...	...	...	...	...	...	...	...	...	...	...	...	...	...	...	...
						Total ...	280	30	34	27	19	19	409	948	94	171	197	134	214	1,758	53·92	5·35	9·73	11·21	7·62	12·17
		" ...	2	117	1,758	Christians ...	1	...	...	...	1	1	3	5	...	...	...	7	5	17	29·41	...	...	...	41·18	29·41
						Paris ...	3	5	...	5	1	1	15	25	4	...	25	9	24	88	28·41	4·55	...	29·55	10·23	27·27
						Mahomedans ...	3	2	...	1	...	...	6	10	5	...	2	...	...	17	58·82	29·41	...	11·77	...	...
						Hindus ...	273	23	34	21	17	17	385	908	85	171	169	118	185	1,636	55·50	5·20	10·45	10·33	7·21	11·31
						Jains ...	...	...	...	...	...	...	...	...	...	...	...	...	...	...	...	...	...	...	...	...
						Jews and others ...	...	...	...	...	...	...	...	...	...	...	...	...	...	...	...	...	...	...	...	...

TABLE XV—*continued.*

TABLE SHOWING TOTAL POPULATION OF EACH RELIGION IN EACH CIRCLE AND ITS RELATION TO HOUSES AND TENEMENTS.

Ward	Charge	Section	Circle	Total No. of buildings	Total No. of persons	Religion	Total No. of separate tenements occupied by persons of each religion with: One room	Two rooms	Three rooms	Four rooms	Five rooms	Six rooms and over	Total No. of tenements of all kinds occupied by members of each religion	Total No. of members of each religion occupying tenements with: One room	Two rooms	Three rooms	Four rooms	Five rooms	Six rooms and over	Total No. of members of each religion occupying tenements of all kinds	Percentage of total population of each religion occupying each class of tenements with: One room	Two rooms	Three rooms	Four rooms	Five rooms	Six rooms and over
		1	2	3	4	5	6	7	8	9	10	11	12	13	14	15	16	17	18	19	20	21	22	23	24	25
						Total ...	272	156	16	15	6	15	480	1,817	162	52	66	23	12	2,132	85·23	7·60	2·44	3·09	1·08	·56
D.	29	Walkeshwar ...	2	...	2,132	Christians ...	58	1	3	1	1	4	68	93	2	4	2	6	2	102	84·31	1·96	3·92	1·96	5·89	1·96
						Parsis	41	1	2	3	1	3	51	80	2	2	28	5	3	129	68·99	1·55	1·55	21·70	3·88	2·31
						Mahomedans ...	29	3	4	2	...	1	30	104	15	8	4	...	1	132	78·81	11·36	6·06	3·03	...	·75
						Hindus	139	151	5	6	4	6	311	1,494	143	34	29	12	5	1,717	87·01	8·33	1·98	1·69	·70	·29
						Jains	5	...	1	2	...	1	9	44	...	3	2	...	1	50	88·	...	6·	4·	...	2·
						Jews and others ...	...	...	1	1	...	...	2	...	...	1	1	...	...	2	...	...	50·	50·	...	...
						Total ...	224	31	16	23	10	67	361	1,041	138	37	64	67	526	1,873	55·58	7·37	1·97	3·42	3·58	28·08
		" ...	3	...	1,873	Christians	37	6	2	3	3	6	56	169	40	9	12	13	38	281	60·14	14·24	3·20	4·27	4·63	13·52
						Parsis	20	5	2	3	3	43	76	140	34	3	8	19	296	500	28·	6·80	·60	1·60	3·80	59·20
						Mahomedans ...	14	1	6	6	1	2	30	84	6	8	13	8	6	125	67·20	4·80	6·40	10·40	6·40	4·80
						Hindus	140	9	6	11	3	14	192	640	58	17	31	27	173	946	67·65	6·13	1·60	3·28	2·85	18·29
						Jains	1	...	...	...	...	...	1	2	...	...	...	...	...	2	100·	...	...	...	...	...
						Jews and others ...	3	...	...	...	...	3	6	6	...	...	...	...	13	19	31·58	...	...	...	...	68·42
						Total ...	94	5	1	...	2	...	102	247	17	4	...	4	...	272	90·81	6·25	1·47	...	1·47	...
		" ...	4	...	272	Christians	16	1	1	...	1	...	19	64	6	4	...	3	...	77	83·12	7·79	5·19	...	3·90	...
						Parsis	...	1	...	...	...	...	1	...	3	...	...	...	...	3	...	100·	...	...	...	...
						Mahomedans ...	8	...	...	...	1	...	9	10	...	...	...	1	...	11	90·91	...	...	...	9·09	...
						Hindus	69	3	...	...	...	...	72	167	8	...	...	...	...	175	95·43	4·57	...	...	...	...
						Jains	...	...	...	...	...	...	...	...	...	...	...	...	...	...	...	...	...	...	...	...
						Jews and others ...	1	...	...	...	...	...	1	6	...	...	...	...	...	6	100·	...	...	...	...	...
						Total ...	216	9	6	6	2	7	246	631	64	50	46	16	28	835	75·57	7·66	5·99	5·51	1·92	3·35
		" ...	5	...	835	Christians	27	1	...	2	...	1	31	55	11	...	21	...	4	91	60·44	12·09	...	23·08	...	4·39
						Parsis	30	2	1	1	1	1	36	81	10	15	7	5	2	123	65·29	8·13	12·20	5·69	4·03	1·63
						Mahomedans ...	21	2	1	3	...	2	29	103	16	6	18	...	8	153	64·63	10·40	3·92	11·76	...	5·23
						Hindus	102	3	4	...	1	2	112	316	25	29	...	11	12	393	80·41	6·36	7·38	...	2·80	3·05
						Jains	20	...	...	...	...	...	20	42	...	...	...	...	...	42	100·	...	...	...	...	...
						Jews and others ...	16	1	...	...	...	1	18	29	2	...	...	...	2	33	87·88	6·06	...	...	...	6·06
						Total ...	492	127	15	9	6	12	661	2,063	296	127	114	37	57	2,694	76·58	10·99	4·71	4·23	1·37	2·12
		" ...	6	...	2,694	Christians	56	3	...	...	...	1	60	122	12	...	...	...	4	138	88·41	8·69	...	...	...	2·90
						Parsis	...	...	...	...	...	...	...	...	...	...	...	...	...	...	...	...	...	...	...	...
						Mahomedans ...	41	4	...	1	...	1	47	129	16	...	16	...	3	164	78·66	9·76	...	9·76	...	1·82
						Hindus	391	119	15	8	6	8	547	1,804	262	127	98	37	41	2,369	76·15	11·06	5·36	4·14	1·56	1·73
						Jains	4	1	...	...	...	...	5	8	6	...	...	...	...	14	57·14	42·86	...	...	...	...
						Jews and others ...	...	...	...	...	...	2	2	...	...	...	...	...	9	9	...	...	...	...	...	100·
						Total ...	114	94	3	2	1	8	222	1,032	106	14	10	12	60	1,234	83·63	8·59	1·13	·81	·98	4·86
		" ...	7	...	1,234	Christians	43	53	...	...	...	...	96	109	61	...	...	...	...	170	64·12	35·88	...	...	...	...
						Parsis	9	...	...	...	...	1	10	35	...	...	...	...	2	37	94·59	...	...	...	...	5·41
						Mahomedans ...	29	...	...	2	1	...	32	137	...	...	10	12	...	140	85·24	...	...	0·71	8·05	...
						Hindus	25	41	3	...	...	5	74	698	45	14	...	...	44	801	87·14	5·62	1·75	...	...	5·49
						Jains	5	...	...	...	...	2	7	60	...	...	...	...	14	74	81·08	...	...	...	...	18·92
						Jews and others ...	3	...	...	...	...	...	3	3	...	...	...	...	...	3	100·	...	...	...	...	...

TABLE XV—*continued.*

TABLE SHOWING TOTAL POPULATION OF EACH RELIGION IN EACH CIRCLE AND ITS RELATION TO HOUSES AND TENEMENTS.

Ward.	Charge.	Section.	Circle No.	Total No. of buildings.	Total No. of persons.	Religion.	Total No. of separate tenements occupied by persons of each religion with						Total No. of tenements of all kinds occupied by members of each religion.	Total number of members of each religion occupying tenements with						Total No. of members of each religion occupying tenements of all kinds.	Percentage of total population of each religion occupying each class of tenements with					
							One room.	Two rooms.	Three rooms.	Four rooms.	Five rooms.	Six rooms and over.		One room.	Two rooms.	Three rooms.	Four rooms.	Five rooms.	Six rooms and over.		One room.	Two rooms.	Three rooms.	Four rooms.	Five rooms.	Six rooms and over.
		1	2	3	4	5	6	7	8	9	10	11	12	13	14	15	16	17	18	19	20	21	22	23	24	25
						Total ...	**286**	**12**	**21**	**19**	**14**	**13**	**361**	**1,251**	**83**	**120**	**160**	**74**	**179**	**1,847**	**67·73**	**4·49**	**6·50**	**7·58**	**4·00**	**9·70**
D.	30	Chaupati ...	3	70	1,847	Christians ...	6	3	1	...	...	1	11	46	31	4	...	...	29	115	40·00	31·70	3·48	...	...	25·22
						Parsis ...	16	2	1	4	...	...	23	48	13	6	49	...	...	116	41·38	11·21	5·17	42·24	...	...
						Mahomedans ...	11	...	...	...	...	...	11	42	...	...	...	...	...	42	100·	...	...	...	...	...
						Hindus ...	249	7	10	15	14	11	315	1,101	34	110	91	74	150	1,560	70·58	2·18	7·05	5·83	4·74	9·62
						Jains ...	4	...	...	...	...	...	4	14	...	...	...	...	...	14	100·	...	...	...	...	...
						Jews and others ...	...	...	...	...	...	...	...	...	...	...	...	...	...	...	...	...	...	...	...	...
						Total ...	**200**	**24**	**23**	**20**	**16**	**14**	**295**	**970**	**117**	**110**	**141**	**80**	**200**	**1,618**	**59·95**	**7·23**	**6·80**	**8·72**	**4·94**	**12·36**
		„ ...	4	83	1,618	Christians ...	10	5	2	4	3	...	24	40	80	18	16	20	...	134	32·29	24·19	14·52	12·90	15·13	...
						Parsis ...	2	3	3	7	5	...	20	7	13	10	20	42	...	98	7·14	13·27	10·33	20·41	42·86	...
						Mahomedans ...	1	...	2	...	1	...	4	2	...	9	...	4	...	15	13·33	...	60·00	...	26·67	...
						Hindus ...	183	16	16	9	5	14	243	906	74	67	105	14	200	1,368	66·87	5·41	4·90	7·68	1·03	14·62
						Jains ...	4	...	...	...	...	...	4	13	...	...	...	...	...	13	100·	...	...	...	...	...
						Jews and others ...	...	...	...	...	...	...	...	...	...	...	...	...	...	...	...	...	...	...	...	...
						Total ...	**474**	**109**	**80**	**50**	**31**	**23**	**767**	**1,022**	**578**	**498**	**325**	**295**	**312**	**3,930**	**48·90**	**14·71**	**12·67**	**8·27**	**7·51**	**7·94**
		„ ...	5	187	3,030	Christians ...	1	...	...	...	...	1	2	3	...	...	...	...	17	19	10·53	...	...	...	...	89·47
						Parsis ...	4	1	7	5	6	4	27	11	9	48	10	13	44	144	7·64	6·25	33·33	13·19	9·03	30·56
						Mahomedans ...	6	...	...	...	...	...	6	11	...	...	...	...	...	11	100·	...	...	...	...	...
						Hindus ...	458	103	73	45	25	18	727	1,882	569	450	303	282	251	3,740	50·32	15·22	12·03	8·16	7·54	6·71
						Jains ...	5	...	...	...	...	...	5	16	...	...	...	...	...	16	100·	...	...	...	...	...
						Jews and others ...	...	...	...	...	...	...	...	...	...	...	...	...	...	...	...	...	...	...	...	...
						Total ...	**61**	**8**	**17**	**23**	**15**	**22**	**146**	**310**	**28**	**102**	**159**	**149**	**195**	**944**	**32·84**	**2·97**	**10·81**	**16·84**	**15·78**	**20·76**
		„ ...	6	63	944	Christians ...	3	2	3	4	1	1	14	32	10	2	10	22	16	92	34·78	10·87	2·18	10·87	23·91	17·39
						Parsis ...	1	...	3	7	10	6	27	13	...	20	53	52	53	180	6·35	...	10·58	27·51	27·52	28·04
						Mahomedans ...	3	4	2	...	...	3	13	19	9	9	...	...	28	65	29·23	13·84	13·85	...	...	43·08
						Hindus ...	54	2	8	12	3	9	88	247	9	57	97	57	96	563	43·87	1·60	10·12	17·23	10·12	17·01
						Jains ...	...	...	1	...	1	2	4	...	...	14	...	18	2	34	...	...	41·18	...	52·94	5·88
						Jews and others ...	...	...	...	...	...	1	1	...	...	...	...	...	1	1	100·	...	...	...	...	...
						Total ...	**1,487**	**430**	**66**	**68**	**38**	**170**	**2,259**	**7,862**	**834**	**335**	**364**	**255**	**981**	**10,631**	**73·95**	**7·85**	**3·15**	**3·42**	**2·40**	**9·23**
		Total for Walkeshwar ...	...	1,084	10,631	Christians ...	255	71	7	8	9	24	374	730	154	19	42	55	63	1,063	67·41	14·22	1·75	3·68	5·08	7·63
						Parsis ...	108	12	6	9	10	84	229	540	54	25	47	70	476	1,211	44·51	4·43	2·03	3·80	5·78	39·31
						Mahomedans ...	153	12	14	17	3	9	208	680	57	41	81	21	30	910	74·73	6·24	4·50	8·90	2·31	3·30
						Hindus ...	904	330	36	31	16	43	1,360	5,690	553	242	102	100	378	7,133	79·80	7·73	3·39	2·09	1·52	4·87
						Jains ...	41	1	2	2	...	4	50	174	6	7	2	...	20	209	83·25	2·87	3·35	·96	...	9·57
						Jews and others ...	23	4	1	1	...	6	35	48	11	1	1	...	24	85	56·47	12·94	1·18	1·18	...	28·23
						Total ...	**75**	**18**	**9**	**13**	**11**	**61**	**187**	**1,031**	**51**	**51**	**64**	**96**	**298**	**1,591**	**64·80**	**3·21**	**3·21**	**4·02**	**6·03**	**18·73**
	20	Walkeshwar ...	1	...	1,591	Christians ...	18	6	1	2	4	13	44	125	23	2	7	33	35	224	55·80	9·82	·89	3·13	14·73	15·73
						Parsis ...	8	3	1	2	5	36	55	192	5	5	3	41	173	419	45·83	1·19	1·19	·72	9·79	41·29
						Mahomedans ...	11	2	3	3	...	3	22	121	4	19	20	...	12	176	68·75	2·27	10·80	11·36	...	6·82
						Hindus ...	29	4	3	6	2	8	53	571	11	21	34	22	73	732	78·01	1·50	2·87	4·65	3·00	9·97
						Jains ...	6	...	1	...	...	1	8	18	...	4	...	...	5	27	66·67	...	14·81	...	...	18·52
						Jews and others ...	3	3	...	...	...	...	6	4	9	...	...	...	...	13	30·77	69·23	...	...	...	—

TABLE XV.

TOTAL POPULATION OF EACH RELIGION, ETC.

TABLE XV—*continued.*

TABLE SHOWING TOTAL POPULATION OF EACH RELIGION IN EACH CIRCLE AND ITS RELATION TO HOUSES AND TENEMENTS.

Ward.	Charge.	Section.	Circle Number.	Total Number of buildings.	Total Number of persons	Religion.	Total Number of separate tenements occupied by persons of each religion with: One room.	Two rooms.	Three rooms.	Four rooms.	Five rooms.	Six rooms and over.	Total Number of tenements of all kinds occupied by members of each religion.	Total Number of members of each religion occupying tenements with: One room.	Two rooms.	Three rooms.	Four rooms.	Five rooms.	Six rooms and over.	Total Number of members of each religion occupying tenements of all kinds.	Percentage of total population of each religion occupying each class of tenements with: One room.	Two rooms.	Three rooms.	Four rooms.	Five rooms.	Six rooms and over.
		1	2	3	4	5	6	7	8	9	10	11	12	13	14	15	16	17	18	19	20	21	22	23	24	25
						Total ...	3,593	549	90	124	99	111	4,566	21,018	2,907	536	611	565	665	26,302	79·91	11·05	2·04	2·32	2·15	2·53
D.		Total for Mahalaxmi ...	...	1,367	23,303	Christians ...	163	10	9	13	16	10	221	703	131	67	45	110	61	1,117	62·94	11·73	6·	4·03	9·85	5·46
						Parsis ...	387	132	36	62	43	69	610	1,788	934	187	218	204	339	3,730	47·93	25·03	5·01	5·84	7·07	9·09
						Mahomedans ...	179	6	2	8	3	6	204	659	41	9	25	116	40	788	83·70	5·20	1·14	3·17	1·91	5·08
						Hindus ...	2,943	399	43	61	32	26	3,494	17,919	1,793	273	323	165	225	20,508	86·50	8·71	1·33	1·57	·80	1·09
						Jains ...	17	2	...	...	5	...	24	23	8	...	...	11	...	42	54·76	19·05	...	...	26·19	...
						Jews and others ...	5	...	...	...	...	...	5	27	...	...	...	...	...	27	100·	...	...	...	...	...
						Total ...	195	74	8	14	6	10	307	1,633	628	70	116	63	85	2,595	62·93	24·20	2·70	4·47	2·43	3·27
	17	Mahalaxmi ...	1	...	2,595	Christians ...	35	1	3	6	1	1	47	101	20	24	7	2	16	170	59·41	11·76	14·12	4·12	1·18	9·41
						Parsis ...	40	7	1	2	1	7	58	100	67	5	12	5	2	191	52·36	35·07	2·62	6·28	2·62	1·05
						Mahomedans ...	35	1	1	4	2	1	44	80	21	6	14	10	15	146	54·80	14·38	4·11	9·59	6·85	10·27
						Hindus ...	74	65	3	2	2	1	147	1,343	520	35	83	46	52	2,079	64·60	25·01	1·68	3·99	2·21	2·50
						Jains ...	10	...	...	...	...	...	10	8	...	...	...	...	...	8	100·	...	...	...	...	...
						Jews and others ...	1	...	...	...	...	...	1	1	...	...	...	...	...	1	100·	...	...	...	...	...
						Total ...	84	66	6	...	...	...	156	383	351	30	...	...	...	744	48·79	47·18	4·03	...	...	...
		" ...	2	...	746	Christians ...	3	...	...	...	...	...	3	9	...	...	...	...	...	9	100·	...	...	...	...	...
						Parsis ...	...	1	...	...	...	...	1	...	7	...	...	...	...	7	...	100·	...	...	...	...
						Mahomedans ...	1	...	...	...	...	...	1	8	...	...	...	...	...	8	100·	...	...	...	...	...
						Hindus ...	80	63	6	...	...	...	161	346	344	30	...	...	...	720	48·05	47·78	4·17	...	...	...
						Jains ...	...	...	...	...	...	...	...	...	...	...	...	...	...	...	...	...	...	...	...	...
						Jews and others ...	...	...	...	...	...	...	...	...	...	...	...	...	...	...	...	...	...	...	...	...
						Total ...	166	5	5	4	7	25	218	768	20	10	24	29	205	1,056	72·73	1·89	·95	2·27	2·75	19·41
		" ...	3	...	1,066	Christians ...	1	...	1	2	2	2	8	3	...	5	9	24	10	51	5·88	...	9·80	17·65	47·06	19·61
						Parsis ...	31	4	4	...	3	12	54	90	10	5	...	4	98	207	43·48	4·83	2·42	...	1·93	47·34
						Mahomedans ...	16	...	...	...	...	3	18	67	...	...	...	...	15	82	81·71	...	...	...	...	18·29
						Hindus ...	116	2	...	2	2	9	131	596	10	...	15	1	82	704	84·66	1·42	...	2·13	·14	11·65
						Jains ...	...	...	...	...	...	...	...	...	...	...	...	...	...	...	...	...	...	...	...	...
						Jews and others ...	2	...	...	...	...	...	2	12	...	...	...	...	...	12	100·	...	...	...	...	...
						Total ...	345	83	...	14	22	33	497	2,219	230	...	80	150	128	2,817	78·77	8·17	...	2·84	5·68	4·54
		" ...	4	...	2,817	Christians ...	22	4	...	3	6	3	38	69	16	...	12	34	8	139	49·64	11·51	...	8·63	24·46	5·76
						Parsis ...	39	25	...	10	11	23	108	116	97	...	65	94	95	407	24·94	20·77	...	13·92	20·13	20·34
						Mahomedans ...	17	4	...	...	...	2	23	74	12	...	...	...	9	96	77·09	12·63	...	...	...	9·47
						Hindus ...	268	50	...	1	5	4	328	1,900	106	...	3	32	16	2,110	93·63	4·96	...	·14	1·51	·76
						Jains ...	...	...	...	...	...	...	...	...	...	...	...	...	...	...	...	...	...	...	...	...
						Jews and others ...	...	...	...	...	...	...	...	...	...	...	...	...	...	...	...	...	...	...	...	...
						Total ...	264	68	22	43	36	12	440	1,730	165	90	170	150	60	2,365	73·15	6·98	3·80	7·19	6·34	2·54
		" ...	5	...	2,365	Christians ...	50	...	...	...	3	...	53	108	...	...	...	16	...	314	92·52	...	...	...	7·48	...
						Parsis ...	30	1	...	3	8	5	46	99	40	...	6	48	36	219	45·21	18·26	...	2·74	21·92	11·87
						Mahomedans ...	22	...	...	2	...	...	34	100	...	...	9	...	...	109	91·74	...	...	8·26	...	...
						Hindus ...	162	62	22	39	20	7	312	1,333	135	90	165	75	34	1,812	73·50	6·90	4·97	9·55	4·14	1·88
						Jains ...	...	...	...	...	5	...	5	...	...	...	...	11	...	11	...	...	...	...	100·	...
						Jews and others ...	...	...	...	...	...	...	...	...	...	...	...	...	...	...	...	...	...	...	...	...

TABLE XV—*continued*.

TABLE SHOWING TOTAL POPULATION OF EACH RELIGION IN EACH CIRCLE AND ITS RELATION TO HOUSES AND TENEMENTS.

Ward.	Charge.	Section.	Circle number.	Total number of buildings.	Total number of persons.	Religion.	Total number of separate tenements occupied by persons of each religion with One room.	Two rooms.	Three rooms.	Four rooms.	Five rooms.	Six rooms and over.	Total number of tenements of all kinds occupied by members of each religion.	Total number of members of each religion occupying tenements with One room.	Two rooms.	Three rooms.	Four rooms.	Five rooms.	Six rooms and over.	Total number of members of each religion occupying tenements of all kinds.	Percentage of total population of each religion occupying each class of tenements with One room.	Two rooms.	Three rooms.	Four rooms.	Five rooms.	Six rooms and over.
		1	2	3	4	5	6	7	8	9	10	11	12	13	14	15	16	17	18	19	20	21	22	23	24	25
						Total ...	245	138	87	39	22	20	601	2,293	898	262	160	135	105	3,856	59·54	23·29	6·80	4·15	3·50	2·72
D.	17	Mahalaxmi ...	6	...	3,856	Christians ...	31	3	2	1	2	2	44	217	86	13	13	20	25	415	50·52	20·72	3·13	3·62	6·30	6·02
						Parsis ...	100	65	26	31	18	10	251	1,580	690	101	126	100	74	3,210	49·18	30·15	7·0	6·6	4·31	3·33
						Mahomedans ...	2	...	1	2	...	1	6	17	...	3	2	...	1	23	73·91	...	13·04	8·70	...	4·35
						Hindus ...	109	50	6	2	2	1	170	943	143	85	17	6	5	1,199	78·65	11·93	7·09	1·42	·50	·41
						Jains ...	...	...	...	...	...	...	...	...	...	...	...	...	...	...	...	...	...	...	...	...
						Jews and others ...	...	...	...	...	...	...	...	...	...	...	...	...	...	...	...	...	...	...	...	...
						Total ...	994	22	4	3	1	2	1,026	4,997	152	37	28	5	21	5,240	95·36	2·90	·71	·53	·10	·40
		" ...	7	...	5,240	Christians ...	4	...	2	...	...	...	6	25	...	22	...	...	...	47	53·19	...	46·81	...	...	...
						Parsis ...	17	6	...	...	...	2	25	103	14	...	...	...	21	138	82·32	7·07	...	...	...	10·61
						Mahomedans ...	10	...	...	...	1	...	11	49	...	...	...	5	...	54	90·74	...	...	...	9·26	...
						Hindus ...	956	14	2	3	...	...	975	4,745	130	15	28	...	...	4,918	96·47	2·65	·31	·57	...	...
						Jains ...	7	2	...	...	...	...	9	15	8	...	...	...	...	23	65·22	34·78	...	...	...	...
						Jews and others ...	...	...	...	...	...	...	...	...	...	...	...	...	...	...	...	...	...	...	...	...
						Total ...	582	83	...	...	...	...	665	2,885	343	...	...	...	...	3,228	89·37	10·63	...	...	...	...
		" ...	8	...	3,228	Christians ...	8	...	...	...	...	...	8	16	...	...	...	...	...	16	100·	...	...	...	...	...
						Parsis ...	9	...	...	...	...	...	9	8	...	...	...	...	...	8	100·	...	...	...	...	...
						Mahomedans ...	54	...	...	...	...	...	54	187	...	...	...	...	...	187	100·	...	...	...	...	...
						Hindus ...	510	83	...	...	...	...	593	2,071	343	...	...	...	...	3,014	88·62	11·38	...	...	...	...
						Jains ...	...	...	...	...	...	...	...	...	...	...	...	...	...	...	...	...	...	...	...	...
						Jews and others ...	1	...	...	...	...	...	1	3	...	...	...	...	...	3	100·	...	...	...	...	...
						Total ...	717	14	8	7	5	10	761	4,127	120	37	33	23	61	4,401	93·77	2·73	·84	·75	·52	1·39
		" ...	9	...	4,401	Christians ...	5	2	1	1	2	2	13	35	9	3	2	5	2	56	62·50	16·07	5·36	3·57	8·93	3·57
						Parsis ...	21	3	3	4	2	4	37	123	30	16	9	13	23	214	57·48	14·02	7·48	4·20	6·07	10·75
						Mahomedans ...	22	1	...	...	...	...	23	76	8	...	...	...	...	84	90·48	9·52	...	...	...	...
						Hindus ...	608	8	4	2	1	4	627	3,882	73	18	22	5	36	4,036	96·18	1·81	·45	·55	·12	·89
						Jains ...	...	...	...	...	...	...	...	...	...	...	...	...	...	...	...	...	...	...	...	...
						Jews and others ...	1	...	...	...	...	...	1	11	...	...	...	...	...	11	100·	...	...	...	...	...
						Total ...	45,675	2,997	1,103	444	136	188	50,543	2,02,993	14,000	3,780	2,093	928	2,358	2,28,232	89·73	6·21	1·67	·93	·42	1·04
E.	...	Total for E Ward ...	...	6,122	2,28,232	Christians ...	2,572	125	69	58	20	41	2,911	10,232	431	605	607	195	891	13,221	77·38	4·77	4·58	5·7	1·47	6·51
						Parsis ...	1,309	165	31	36	14	27	1,521	6,419	434	123	290	145	328	7,861	81·20	5·52	1·60	2·06	1·85	4·17
						Mahomedans ...	14,101	587	104	31	19	23	15,153	49,108	2,377	471	256	133	500	53,098	92·01	4·39	·91	·48	·25	1·13
						Hindus ...	20,238	2,181	827	260	81	72	20,098	1,33,129	10,383	2,152	813	406	490	1,47,652	90·10	7·02	1·67	·57	·31	·34
						Jains ...	437	55	21	2	3	10	512	1,191	168	61	19	9	17	1,650	91·03	9·3	3·8	·00	·74	2·3
						Jews and others ...	653	44	31	15	...	6	749	2,451	217	61	78	...	21	2,828	86·67	7·67	2·16	2·76	...	·74
						Total ...	5,329	134	36	23	7	26	5,555	26,361	790	126	109	65	202	27,723	95·09	2·85	·71	·39	·23	·73
		Total for Tardeo ...	...	7,0	27,723	Christians ...	215	4	1	1	...	1	222	970	41	4	4	...	10	1,041	93·05	3·23	·38	·38	...	·96
						Parsis ...	618	10	8	3	4	13	657	3,037	68	34	7	18	134	3,098	92·82	3·31	·85	·18	·45	3·30
						Mahomedans ...	1,235	23	12	1	1	7	1,279	4,506	78	65	1	2	41	4,783	96·00	1·63	1·31	·02	·01	·86
						Hindus ...	3,151	80	15	18	2	5	3,280	10,614	545	93	97	45	17	17,011	95·1	3·09	·51	·55	·25	·10
						Jains ...	47	2	...	...	...	...	49	176	30	...	...	...	...	206	85·44	14·56	...	...	...	...
						Jews and others ...	38	...	...	...	...	...	38	99	...	...	...	...	...	99	100·	...	...	...	...	...

TABLE XV.

TOTAL POPULATION OF EACH RELIGION, ETC.

TABLE XV—*continued.*

TABLE SHOWING TOTAL POPULATION OF EACH RELIGION IN EACH CIRCLE AND ITS RELATION TO HOUSES AND TENEMENTS.

Ward.	Charge.	Section.	Circle.	Total No. of buildings.	Total No. of persons.	Religion.	Total No. of separate tenements occupied by persons of each religion with: One room.	Two rooms.	Three rooms.	Four rooms.	Five rooms.	Six rooms and over.	Total No. of tenements of all kinds occupied by members of each religion.	Total No. of members of each religion occupying tenements with: One room.	Two rooms.	Three rooms.	Four rooms.	Five rooms.	Six rooms and over.	Total No. of members of each religion occupying tenements of all kinds.	Percentage of total population of each religion occupying each class of tenements with: One room.	Two rooms.	Three rooms.	Four rooms.	Five rooms.	Six rooms and over.
		1	2	3	4	5	6	7	8	9	10	11	12	13	14	15	16	17	18	19	20	21	22	23	24	25
						Total ...	1,079	47	14	15	3	14	1,172	3,551	368	105	84	54	144	4,306	82·47	8·55	2·44	1·95	1·25	3·34
E.	30	Tardeo ...	1	...	4,306	Christians ...	41	...	...	...	...	1	42	192	...	...	...	...	10	202	95·05	...	...	...	...	4·95
						Parsis ...	264	2	2	...	2	13	283	1,203	3	10	...	12	134	1,368	87·94	·22	1·17	...	·88	9·79
						Mahomedans ...	54	1	1	...	...	...	56	157	1	1	...	...	...	159	98·74	·63	·63	...	...	...
						Hindus ...	709	44	11	15	1	...	780	1,959	364	88	84	42	...	2,537	77·22	14·34	3·47	3·31	1·66	...
						Jains ...	8	...	...	...	...	...	8	20	...	...	...	...	...	20	100·	...	...	...	...	...
						Jews and others ...	3	...	...	...	...	...	3	11	...	...	...	...	...	11	100·	...	...	...	...	...
						Total ...	1,169	49	14	7	4	7	1,250	6,726	202	87	24	11	11	7,061	95·66	2·87	·81	·34	·16	·16
		„ ...	2	...	7,061	Christians ...	30	...	...	1	...	...	31	251	...	...	4	...	...	255	98·40	...	...	1·51	...	...
						Parsis ...	300	11	6	2	2	...	321	2,234	73	18	6	6	...	2,337	95·59	3·12	·77	·26	·26	...
						Mahomedans ...	125	14	8	1	1	3	152	413	45	36	1	3	8	508	81·30	8·86	7·08	·20	·59	1·57
						Hindus ...	700	23	...	3	1	4	731	3,755	60	...	13	3	3	3,834	97·94	1·56	...	·34	·08	·08
						Jains ...	10	1	...	...	...	...	11	46	24	...	...	...	...	70	65·71	34·29	...	...	...	...
						Jews and others ...	4	...	...	...	...	...	4	17	...	...	...	...	...	17	100·	...	...	...	...	...
						Total ...	2,194	9	1	1	...	2	2,207	10,308	64	4	1	...	9	10,386	99·25	·61	·04	·01	...	·09
		„ ...	3	...	10,386	Christians ...	69	...	1	...	...	...	70	279	...	4	...	...	...	283	98·59	...	1·41	...	...	...
						Parsis ...	64	2	...	1	...	...	67	223	15	...	1	...	...	239	93·31	6·27	...	·42	...	...
						Mahomedans ...	813	2	...	...	...	2	817	2,055	7	...	...	...	9	2,071	99·23	·34	...	...	...	·43
						Hindus ...	1,196	5	...	...	...	...	1,201	6,704	42	...	...	...	...	6,746	99·38	·62	...	...	...	...
						Jains ...	23	...	...	...	...	...	23	78	...	...	...	...	...	78	100·	...	...	...	...	...
						Jews and others ...	30	...	...	...	...	...	30	60	...	...	...	...	...	60	100·	...	...	...	...	...
						Total ...	857	29	7	...	...	3	896	5,776	156	30	...	...	38	6,000	96·27	2·60	·50	...	...	·63
		„ ...	4	...	6,000	Christians ...	75	4	...	...	...	...	79	247	44	...	...	...	...	291	84·88	15·12	...	...	...	...
						Parsis ...	15	1	...	...	...	...	16	37	2	...	...	...	...	39	94·87	5·13	...	...	...	...
						Mahomedans ...	243	6	3	...	...	2	254	1,071	25	25	...	...	24	1,145	93·54	2·18	2·18	...	...	2·10
						Hindus ...	547	17	4	...	...	1	569	4,300	70	6	...	...	14	4,390	97·95	1·60	·14	...	...	·31
						Jains ...	6	1	...	...	...	...	7	23	6	...	...	...	...	29	79·31	20·69	...	...	...	...
						Jews and others ...	1	...	...	...	...	...	1	2	...	...	...	...	...	2	100·	...	...	...	...	...
						Total ...	6,153	1,793	796	253	51	33	9,079	25,161	8,165	2,117	672	287	189	36,611	68·78	22·32	5·78	1·83	·78	·51
		Total for Kamatipura.	...	1,023	36,611	Christians ...	160	10	8	8	1	...	187	489	53	60	52	1	...	663	73·76	7·99	10·41	7·84	·15	...
						Parsis ...	40	9	6	2	1	...	58	109	45	14	10	6	...	184	58·80	25·	7·78	5·55	2·78	...
						Mahomedans ...	1,902	105	33	12	1	4	2,057	6,613	463	145	59	16	34	7,330	90·22	6·32	1·98	·80	·22	·46
						Hindus ...	3,911	1,657	736	225	49	29	6,607	17,619	7,557	1,837	523	265	155	27,956	63·02	27·03	6·57	1·87	·95	·56
						Jains ...	95	9	9	2	...	...	115	263	38	29	10	...	...	340	77·35	11·18	8·53	2·94	...	...
						Jews and others ...	33	3	4	4	...	...	44	91	10	23	18	...	...	142	64·08	7·04	16·20	12·68	...	...
						Total ...	1,253	456	105	19	...	...	1,833	5,012	2,061	682	104	...	...	7,859	63·77	26·23	8·68	1·32	...	...
	31	Kamatipura ...	1	...	7,859	Christians ...	70	6	6	3	...	...	85	180	13	20	27	...	...	240	75·01	5·42	8·33	10·54	...	...
						Parsis ...	23	4	2	...	...	...	29	60	17	3	...	...	...	80	74·08	21·53	3·80	...	...	...
						Mahomedans ...	465	40	15	8	...	...	557	1,386	210	46	42	...	...	1,693	81·87	12·03	2·72	2·48	...	...
						Hindus ...	634	304	79	5	...	...	1,112	3,268	1,802	600	23	...	...	5,693	57·40	31·65	10·54	·41	...	...
						Jains ...	26	...	2	2	...	...	30	70	...	6	10	...	...	86	81·39	...	6·98	11·63	...	...
						Jews and others ...	15	3	1	1	...	...	20	40	10	7	2	...	...	59	67·80	16·95	11·86	3·39	...	...

TABLE XV—*continued*.

TABLE SHOWING TOTAL POPULATION OF EACH RELIGION IN EACH CIRCLE AND ITS RELATION TO HOUSES AND TENEMENTS.

Ward.	Charge.	Section.	Circle.	Total No. of buildings.	Total No. of persons.	Religion.	Total number of separate tenements occupied by persons of each religion with						Total Number of tenements of all kinds occupied by members of each religion.	Total number of members of each religion occupying tenements with						Total number of members of each religion occupying tenements of all kinds.	Percentage of total population of each religion occupying each class of tenements with					
							One room.	Two rooms.	Three rooms.	Four rooms.	Five rooms.	Six rooms and over.		One room.	Two rooms.	Three rooms.	Four rooms.	Five rooms.	Six rooms and over.		One room.	Two rooms.	Three rooms.	Four rooms.	Five rooms.	Six rooms and over.
		1	2	3	4	5	6	7	8	9	10	11	12	13	14	15	16	17	18	19	20	21	22	23	24	25
						Total ...	**1,988**	**1,236**	**674**	**228**	**47**	**34**	**4,197**	**8,158**	**5,511**	**1,310**	**524**	**317**	**122**	**15,742**	**51·82**	**35·01**	**7·69**	**3·33**	**1·38**	**·77**
E.	21	Kamatipura ...	2	...	15,742	Christians ...	41	4	2	4	...	...	51	143	30	40	19	...	...	250	57·20	15·60	19·00	7·60	...	...
						Parsis ...	9	5	4	1	1	...	20	27	28	11	1	5	...	72	37·50	38·89	15·28	1·39	6·04	...
						Mahomedans ...	429	32	12	4	...	...	477	1,164	131	60	17	...	...	1,371	81·90	9·56	4·30	1·24	...	...
						Hindus ...	1,405	1,100	647	216	40	24	3,588	6,706	5,203	1,055	471	212	122	13,859	48·39	38·10	7·61	3·40	1·53	·88
						Jains ...	38	5	6	...	...	...	49	106	20	20	...	...	...	146	72·60	13·70	13·70	...	...	...
						Jews and others ...	6	...	3	3	...	...	12	12	...	16	16	...	...	44	27·28	...	36·36	36·36	...	...
						Total ...	**2,912**	**101**	**17**	**6**	**4**	**9**	**3,049**	**12,011**	**593**	**225**	**44**	**70**	**67**	**13,010**	**92·32**	**4·56**	**1·73**	**·34**	**·54**	**·51**
		" ...	3	...	13,010	Christians ...	58	...	...	1	1	...	60	157	...	...	5	1	...	164	95·73	...	...	3·66	·61	...
						Parsis ...	8	...	...	1	...	...	9	20	...	...	9	...	...	29	68·97	...	...	31·03	...	...
						Mahomedans ...	988	24	6	...	1	4	1,023	4,063	113	40	...	16	34	4,266	95·24	2·65	·94	...	·37	·80
						Hindus ...	1,812	73	10	4	2	5	1,906	7,045	462	153	29	53	33	8,404	93·97	5·50	2·17	·34	·63	·30
						Jains ...	31	4	1	...	...	...	36	87	18	3	...	...	...	108	80·55	16·67	2·78	...	...	...
						Jews and others ...	15	...	...	...	...	...	15	30	...	...	...	...	...	30	100·	...	...	...	...	...
						Total ...	**1,305**	**116**	**41**	**31**	**18**	**15**	**1,526**	**5,364**	**476**	**222**	**116**	**107**	**129**	**6,414**	**83·63**	**7·42**	**3·46**	**1·81**	**1·67**	**2·01**
		Total for First Nagpada.	...	83	6,414	Christians ...	172	23	1	1	2	1	200	650	132	97	40	30	14	962	67·21	13·44	9·88	4·07	3·07	1·43
						Parsis ...	14	11	...	...	...	...	15	20	1	...	...	...	...	30	66·67	3·33	...	...	...	...
						Mahomedans ...	350	23	1	...	2	1	377	1,029	65	57	...	29	40	1,220	84·34	5·33	4·67	...	2·38	3·28
						Hindus ...	504	37	2	30	14	9	656	2,844	189	44	76	39	62	3,256	87·41	5·81	1·35	2·33	1·20	1·90
						Jains ...	31	7	14	...	...	...	52	90	21	10	...	...	...	121	74·38	17·36	8·26	...	...	...
						Jews and others ...	174	25	23	...	...	4	226	710	68	14	...	...	13	805	88·20	8·45	1·74	...	...	1·61
						Total ...	**609**	**32**	**4**	**3**	**6**	**5**	**659**	**2,604**	**273**	**198**	**108**	**103**	**86**	**3,632**	**78·85**	**7·62**	**5·45**	**2·97**	**2·84**	**2·37**
	18	First Nagpada ...	1	65	3,632	Christians ...	58	11	1	1	2	1	74	346	120	97	40	30	14	656	52·74	18·29	14·79	6·10	5·05	2·13
						Parsis ...	6	...	...	...	...	...	6	15	...	...	...	...	...	15	100·	...	...	...	...	...
						Mahomedans ...	230	2	1	...	2	1	236	691	35	57	...	29	40	852	81·10	4·11	6·69	...	3·40	4·70
						Hindus ...	256	12	2	2	2	3	277	1,508	60	44	68	35	32	1,770	84·91	5·01	2·48	3·83	1·97	1·80
						Jains ...	19	2	...	...	...	...	21	64	10	...	...	...	...	74	86·49	13·51	...	...	...	...
						Jews and others ...	40	5	...	...	...	...	45	240	10	...	...	...	...	250	92·06	7·34	...	...	...	...
						Total ...	**696**	**84**	**37**	**28**	**13**	**10**	**867**	**2,500**	**203**	**24**	**8**	**4**	**43**	**2,782**	**89·86**	**7·30**	**·86**	**·29**	**·14**	**1·55**
		" ...	3	238	2,762	Christians ...	114	12	...	...	...	...	126	314	12	...	...	...	...	326	96·32	3·68	...	...	...	...
						Parsis ...	8	1	...	...	...	...	9	14	1	...	...	...	...	15	93·33	6·67	...	...	...	...
						Mahomedans ...	120	21	...	...	...	...	141	338	30	...	...	...	...	368	91·85	8·15	...	...	...	...
						Hindus ...	308	25	...	28	12	6	379	1,338	100	...	8	4	30	1,480	90·40	6·76	...	·54	·27	2·03
						Jains ...	12	5	14	...	...	...	31	26	11	10	...	...	...	47	55·32	23·40	21·28	...	...	...
						Jews and others ...	134	20	23	...	...	4	161	470	49	14	...	...	13	546	86·08	8·98	2·56	...	...	2·38
						Total ...	**5,761**	**308**	**47**	**12**	**15**	**10**	**6,153**	**19,881**	**1,434**	**190**	**67**	**87**	**41**	**21,700**	**91·62**	**6·61**	**·87**	**·31**	**·40**	**·19**
		Total for Second Nagpada.	...	474	21,700	Christians ...	53	1	1	2	1	...	57	162	7	7	13	11	...	109	81·40	3·52	3·52	6·03	5·53	...
						Parsis ...	14	3	1	...	1	1	20	24	22	14	...	7	7	74	32·43	29·73	18·92	...	9·46	9·46
						Mahomedans ...	3,948	238	24	9	6	4	4,229	13,350	1,147	72	52	31	25	14,687	90·97	7·81	·49	·35	·21	·17
						Hindus ...	1,639	62	21	1	7	5	1,735	5,975	136	97	3	38	9	6,358	93·97	3·71	1·53	·05	·60	·14
						Jains ...	9	...	...	...	...	...	9	18	...	...	...	...	...	18	100	...	...	...	...	...
						Jews and others ...	99	4	...	...	...	...	103	342	22	...	...	...	...	364	93·96	6·04	...	...	...	...

TABLE XV—*continued*.

TABLE SHOWING TOTAL POPULATION OF EACH RELIGION IN EACH CIRCLE AND ITS RELATION TO HOUSES AND TENEMENTS.

Ward.	Charge.	Section.	Circle number.	Total number of buildings.	Total number of persons.	Religion.	Total number of separate tenements occupied by persons of each religion with: One room.	Two rooms.	Three rooms.	Four rooms.	Five rooms.	Six rooms and over.	Total number of tenements of all kinds occupied by members of each religion.	Total number of members of each religion occupying tenements with: One room.	Two rooms.	Three rooms.	Four rooms.	Five rooms.	Six rooms and over.	Total number of members of each religion occupying tenements of all kinds.	Percentage of total population of each religion occupying each class of tenements with: One room.	Two rooms.	Three rooms.	Four rooms.	Five rooms.	Six rooms and over.
		1	2	3	4	5	6	7	8	9	10	11	12	13	14	15	16	17	18	19	20	21	22	23	24	25
						Total ...	1,664	30	4	4	3	1	1,706	5,919	159	33	17	32	7	6,167	95·98	2·58	·53	·28	·52	·11
E.	10	2nd Nagpada ...	1	...	6,167	Christians ...	25	...	1	2	1	...	29	63	...	7	13	11	...	113	73·46	...	6·19	10·03	9·74	...
						Parsis ...	9	3	1	...	1	1	15	14	22	14	...	7	7	64	21·87	34·38	21·87	...	10·94	10·94
						Mahomedans ...	661	21	1	2	1	...	686	2,666	104	11	5	14	...	2,191	93·08	4·75	·50	·23	·64	...
						Hindus ...	956	6	1	...	...	...	963	3,740	33	1	...	...	...	3,774	99·10	·87	·13	...	...	...
						Jains ...	6	...	...	...	...	...	6	13	...	...	...	...	...	12	100·	...	...	...	...	...
						Jews and others ...	7	...	...	...	...	...	7	14	...	...	...	...	...	14	100·	...	...	...	...	...
						Total ...	1,455	163	13	2	3	6	1,659	4,936	705	82	7	44	14	5,788	85·28	12·18	1·42	·12	·76	·24
		" ...	2	...	5,788	Christians ...	5	1	...	...	...	...	6	14	7	...	...	...	...	21	66·67	33·33	...	...	...	...
						Parsis ...	1	...	...	...	...	...	1	1	...	...	...	...	...	1	100·	...	...	...	...	...
						Mahomedans ...	1,093	118	2	1	2	1	1,217	3,627	374	7	4	6	5	4,223	85·89	13·59	·17	·19	·14	·12
						Hindus ...	328	40	10	1	7	5	397	1,201	102	75	3	38	9	1,428	84·10	7·14	5·25	·21	2·67	·63
						Jains ...	...	...	...	...	...	...	...	...	...	...	...	...	...	...	...	...	...	...	...	...
						Jews and others ...	28	4	...	...	...	...	32	93	22	...	...	...	...	115	80·87	19·13	...	...	...	...
						Total ...	1,480	101	24	6	3	3	1,617	5,165	504	73	43	11	20	5,796	88·78	8·70	1·24	·74	·19	·35
		" ...	3	...	5,796	Christians ...	1	...	...	...	...	...	1	1	...	...	...	...	...	1	100·	...	...	...	...	...
						Parsis ...	...	...	...	...	...	...	...	...	...	...	...	...	...	...	...	...	...	...	...	...
						Mahomedans ...	1,276	87	21	8	3	8	1,306	4,476	410	54	43	11	20	5,023	89·11	8·34	1·07	·58	·22	·40
						Hindus ...	155	14	3	...	...	...	172	496	85	19	...	...	...	601	82·86	14·14	3·00	...	...	...
						Jains ...	...	...	...	...	...	...	...	...	...	...	...	...	...	...	...	...	...	...	...	...
						Jews and others ...	48	...	...	...	...	...	48	170	...	...	...	...	...	170	100·	...	...	...	...	...
						Total ...	1,162	14	1	...	...	...	1,177	3,881	66	3	...	...	...	3,950	98·25	1·67	·08	...	...	...
		" ...	4	...	3,950	Christians ...	21	...	...	...	...	...	21	61	...	...	...	...	...	61	100·	...	...	...	...	...
						Parsis ...	4	...	...	...	...	...	4	9	...	...	...	...	...	9	100·	...	...	...	...	...
						Mahomedans ...	918	12	...	...	...	...	930	3,201	50	...	...	...	...	3,251	98·46	1·54	...	...	...	...
						Hindus ...	201	2	1	...	...	...	203	533	16	3	...	...	...	555	96·58	2·88	·54	...	...	...
						Jains ...	3	...	...	...	...	...	3	6	...	...	...	...	...	6	100·	...	...	...	...	...
						Jews and others ...	10	...	...	...	...	...	10	65	...	...	...	...	...	65	100·	...	...	...	...	...
						Total ...	15,936	347	113	79	35	55	16,623	70,970	1,780	658	873	232	815	75,307	94·24	2·34	·87	1·16	·31	1·08
		Total for Byculla ...	...	2,127	75,307	Christians ...	973	60	61	30	10	33	1,096	2,503	202	273	603	70	551	4,617	62·25	6·24	6·65	13·12	1·61	11·16
						Parsis ...	103	12	6	8	1	4	104	534	33	25	44	65	55	703	70·51	4·72	3·28	5·77	8·52	7·20
						Mahomedans ...	4,733	75	17	9	0	9	4,867	15,426	278	80	121	39	105	16,049	96·11	1·73	·50	·75	·21	·07
						Hindus ...	9,807	181	31	15	7	10	10,057	50,851	1,071	253	65	51	84	52,349	97·04	2·04	·48	·18	·10	·17
						Jains ...	165	11	1	...	1	3	181	549	30	8	...	1	10	599	92·02	5·00	1·42	...	·17	1·70
						Jews and others ...	177	8	3	9	...	1	197	720	53	23	40	...	6	850	84·71	6·23	2·50	5·76	...	·71
						Total ...	4,383	88	33	14	8	10	4,612	21,234	241	166	237	128	123	22,104	96·06	1·09	·66	1·07	·58	·56
	33	Byculla	1	...	22,104	Christians ...	376	12	10	8	3	3	419	1,247	40	73	113	44	11	1,528	81·61	2·61	4·78	7·39	2·88	·72
						Parsis ...	41	1	4	4	1	3	54	147	5	12	27	65	36	291	50·52	1·72	4·12	9·24	22·31	12·02
						Mahomedans ...	2,114	16	4	3	3	3	2,141	7,071	79	21	76	14	71	7,333	96·44	1·08	·28	1·04	·19	·97
						Hindus ...	1,719	54	6	2	...	...	1,781	12,346	90	40	21	...	...	12,497	98·79	·72	·32	·17	...	...
						Jains ...	44	3	...	...	...	...	47	116	9	...	...	...	...	125	92·80	7·20	...	...	...	...
						Jews and others ...	67	3	...	...	...	1	70	307	18	...	...	...	6	331	92·75	5·44	...	...	...	1·81

TABLE XV—*continued.*

TABLE SHOWING TOTAL POPULATION OF EACH RELIGION IN EACH CIRCLE AND ITS RELATION TO HOUSES AND TENEMENTS.

Ward.	Charge.	Section.	Circle number.	Total number of buildings.	Total number of persons.	Religion.	Total number of separate tenements occupied by persons of each religion with: One room.	Two rooms.	Three rooms.	Four rooms.	Five rooms.	Six rooms and over.	Total number of tenements of all kinds occupied by members of each religion.	Total number of members of each religion occupying tenements with: One room.	Two rooms.	Three rooms.	Four rooms.	Five rooms.	Six rooms and over.	Total number of members of each religion occupying tenements of all kinds.	Percentage of total population of each religion occupying each class of tenements with: One room.	Two rooms.	Three rooms.	Four rooms.	Five rooms.	Six rooms and over.
		1	2	3	4	5	6	7	8	9	10	11	12	13	14	15	16	17	18	19	20	21	22	23	24	25
						Total ...	756	41	40	37	4	17	896	3,407	249	204	471	8	508	4,847	70·29	5·14	4·21	9·73	·16	10·48
E.	33	Byculla	2	...	4,847	Christians ...	59	34	32	20	4	16	171	281	197	158	414	8	488	1,546	18·18	12·74	10·22	26·78	·52	31·56
						Parsis ...	51	...	...	...	...	1	52	142	...	...	...	...	20	162	87·65	...	...	...	...	12·35
						Mahomedans ...	380	3	4	1	...	...	388	1,788	16	4	3	...	...	1,813	98·63	·99	·22	·17	...	...
						Hindus ...	250	3	4	3	...	...	260	1,007	24	42	10	...	...	1,173	93·62	2·05	3·58	·85	...	...
						Jains ...	...	...	...	...	...	...	...	...	...	...	...	...	...	...	...	...	...	...	...	...
						Jews and others ...	10	1	...	7	...	...	24	90	10	...	44	...	...	153	64·70	6·54	...	28·70	...	...
						Total ...	3,733	75	18	9	5	9	3,849	14,632	395	119	28	46	61	15,281	95·75	2·59	·78	·18	·30	·40
		" ...	3	...	15,281	Christians ...	162	6	1	1	1	2	173	491	22	3	2	15	23	656	88·31	3·96	·51	·36	2·70	4·13
						Parsis ...	6	1	1	1	...	...	9	8	5	7	3	...	...	22	36·36	22·73	31·82	9·09	...	...
						Mahomedans ...	1,681	32	5	2	3	3	1,726	4,416	86	25	14	18	19	4,648	96·44	1·89	·55	·31	·39	·42
						Hindus ...	1,840	33	11	3	1	2	1,890	9,639	270	84	5	13	13	10,024	96·10	2·60	·84	·05	·13	·13
						Jains ...	11	1	...	...	...	2	14	25	3	...	...	...	6	34	73·53	8·82	...	...	...	17·65
						Jews and others ...	33	2	...	2	...	...	37	53	9	...	5	...	...	97	85·57	9·28	...	5·15	...	...
						Total ...	2,163	53	7	8	4	4	2,239	10,197	335	65	70	26	29	10,722	95·10	3·13	·61	·65	·24	·27
		" ...	4	...	10,722	Christians ...	173	3	1	1	...	...	178	430	16	7	6	...	...	470	93·40	3·83	1·49	1·28	...	...
						Parsis ...	4	1	...	2	...	...	7	13	5	...	13	...	...	31	41·94	16·13	...	41·94	...	...
						Mahomedans ...	219	6	1	1	1	1	229	948	33	8	12	7	6	1,014	93·40	3·26	·79	1·18	·69	·60
						Hindus ...	1,684	40	3	4	3	3	1,737	8,443	271	28	39	19	23	8,563	95·71	3·06	·32	·44	·21	·26
						Jains ...	54	2	...	...	...	...	56	209	4	...	...	...	...	212	98·11	1·89	...	...	...	...
						Jews and others ...	29	1	2	...	...	...	32	106	4	22	...	...	...	132	80·30	3·03	16·67	...	...	...
						Total ...	893	33	8	2	1	...	937	3,905	171	49	16	5	...	4,146	94·19	4·12	1·18	·39	·12	...
		" ...	5	...	4,146	Christians ...	82	3	4	1	...	...	90	250	10	13	9	...	...	282	88·65	3·55	4·61	3·19	...	...
						Parsis ...	51	8	...	...	...	...	59	205	18	...	...	...	...	223	91·93	8·07	...	...	...	...
						Mahomedans ...	220	12	3	...	...	...	235	672	23	22	...	...	...	717	93·72	3·21	3·07	...	...	...
						Hindus ...	512	6	1	1	1	...	521	2,673	101	14	7	5	...	2,799	95·46	3·61	·50	·25	·18	...
						Jains ...	27	2	...	...	...	...	29	87	7	...	...	...	...	94	92·55	7·45	...	...	...	...
						Jews and others ...	1	2	...	...	...	...	3	19	12	...	...	...	...	31	61·29	38·71	...	...	...	...
						Total ...	1,181	17	8	5	3	3	1,216	5,599	116	47	24	10	29	5,835	95·95	1·99	·81	·58	·17	·50
		" ...	6	...	5,835	Christians ...	25	2	4	3	2	2	38	96	5	18	18	9	29	175	54·86	2·86	10·29	10·28	5·14	16·57
						Parsis ...	1	1	1	...	...	...	3	1	3	6	...	...	...	10	10·	30·	60·	...	...	...
						Mahomedans ...	57	1	...	2	...	...	60	156	6	...	16	...	...	177	87·57	3·39	...	9·04	...	...
						Hindus ...	1,068	10	2	...	1	...	1,081	5,251	95	17	...	1	...	5,364	97·81	1·77	·32	...	·02	...
						Jains ...	5	3	1	...	...	...	9	17	7	6	...	...	...	30	56·67	23·23	20·	...	...	...
						Jews and others ...	25	...	...	...	...	...	25	79	...	...	...	...	...	79	100·	...	...	...	...	...
						Total ...	1,430	17	1	2	...	7	1,457	6,153	101	4	3	...	19	6,280	97·98	1·61	·06	·05	...	·30
		" ...	7	...	6,280	Christians ...	13	...	...	1	...	...	14	38	...	...	1	...	...	39	97·44	...	...	2·56	...	...
						Parsis ...	2	...	...	1	...	...	3	13	...	...	2	...	...	15	86·67	...	...	13·33	...	...
						Mahomedans ...	24	1	...	...	...	...	25	63	12	...	...	...	...	75	84·	16·	...	...	...	...
						Hindus ...	1,374	16	1	...	...	6	1,397	6,078	89	4	...	...	15	6,086	98·22	1·46	·07	...	...	·25
						Jains ...	11	...	...	...	...	1	12	34	...	...	...	...	4	38	89·47	...	...	...	...	10·53
						Jews and others ...	6	...	...	...	...	...	6	27	...	...	...	...	...	27	100·	...	...	...	...	...

TABLE XV.

Total Population of each Religion, etc.

TABLE XV—*continued.*

Table showing Total Population of each Religion in each Circle and its Relation to Houses and Tenements.

Ward.	Charge.	Section.	Circle number.	Total number of buildings.	Total number of persons.	Religion.	Total number of separate tenements occupied by persons of each religion with						Total number of tenements of all kinds occupied by members of each religion.	Total number of members of each religion occupying tenements with						Total number of members of each religion occupying tenements of all kinds.	Percentage of total population of each religion occupying each class of tenements with					
							One room.	Two rooms.	Three rooms.	Four rooms.	Five rooms.	Six rooms and over.		One room.	Two rooms.	Three rooms.	Four rooms.	Five rooms.	Six rooms and over.		One room.	Two rooms.	Three rooms.	Four rooms.	Five rooms.	Six rooms and over.
		1	2	3	4	5	6	7	8	9	10	11	12	13	14	15	16	17	18	19	20	21	22	23	24	25
						Total ...	1,481	23	3	2	2	6	1,517	5,843	153	24	13	14	46	6,092	95·91	2·50	·39	·21	·23	·76
E.	32	Byculla ...	8	...	6,093	Christians ...	13	...	...	...	...	...	13	51	...	...	...	...	...	51	100·	...	...	...	...	...
						Parsis ...	7	...	...	...	...	...	7	9	...	...	...	...	...	9	100·	...	...	...	...	...
						Mahomedans ...	88	4	...	...	...	1	93	343	21	...	...	...	9	373	91·96	5·63	...	...	...	2·41
						Hindus ...	1,360	10	3	3	1	5	1,380	5,385	131	24	13	13	37	5,603	96·11	2·34	·43	·23	·23	·66
						Jains ...	13	...	...	...	1	...	14	55	...	...	...	1	...	56	98·21	...	...	...	1·79	...
						Jews and others ...	...	...	...	...	...	...	...	...	...	...	...	...	...	...	...	...	...	...	...	...
						Total ...	4,807	129	39	35	15	45	5,070	26,186	673	275	198	129	952	28,413	92·16	2·37	·97	·70	·45	3·35
		Total for Tadwadi...	...	133	28,413	Christians ...	410	24	14	6	6	15	475	1,748	93	140	25	68	289	2,363	73·97	3·94	5·92	1·06	2·88	12·23
						Parsis ...	191	37	6	22	5	9	270	1,212	193	27	143	43	132	1,750	69·26	11·03	1·54	8·17	2·46	7·54
						Mahomedans ...	568	32	11	3	2	9	624	2,370	192	48	15	8	354	2,987	79·34	6·43	1·61	·50	·23	11·86
						Hindus ...	3,467	29	5	3	1	4	3,509	20,241	115	42	4	2	135	20,550	98·51	·56	·20	·02	·01	·67
						Jains ...	51	3	2	...	1	7	64	140	16	16	...	6	37	217	64·52	7·37	7·37	...	3·69	17·05
						Jews and others ...	120	4	1	2	...	1	128	467	64	2	11	...	2	540	86·53	11·72	·37	2·01	...	·37
						Total ...	2,038	33	8	6	3	6	2,094	8,898	157	130	30	20	268	9,413	93·57	1·67	1·38	·32	·21	2·85
	23	Tadwadi ...	1	...	9,413	Christians ...	190	5	3	3	1	3	105	824	14	83	20	13	201	1,155	71·34	1·21	7·19	1·73	1·13	17·40
						Parsis ...	47	...	...	...	1	...	48	159	...	...	...	6	...	165	96·36	...	...	...	3·64	...
						Mahomedans ...	63	6	1	...	1	1	74	707	26	12	...	1	6	752	94·02	3·46	1·59	...	·13	·80
						Hindus ...	1,633	17	2	2	...	1	1,655	6,451	40	26	2	...	59	6,568	98·16	·58	·38	·03	...	·86
						Jains ...	18	3	1	...	...	...	22	42	16	7	...	...	...	65	64·61	24·61	10·78	...	...	...
						Jews and others ...	96	2	1	1	...	1	100	315	61	3	8	...	2	368	81·19	16·72	·81	2·03	...	·52
						Total ...	749	38	17	1	7	15	818	2,718	147	77	9	72	453	3,476	78·19	4·23	2·22	·26	2·07	13·03
		" ...	2	...	3,476	Christians ...	83	9	10	...	4	5	109	396	38	47	...	49	72	602	65·78	6·31	7·81	...	8·14	11·96
						Parsis ...	9	7	2	...	3	3	24	34	33	13	...	23	33	134	25·37	24·63	9·72	...	17·10	20·12
						Mahomedans ...	112	16	4	1	...	5	135	471	60	16	9	...	332	887	53·10	6·76	1·80	1·03	...	37·43
						Hindus ...	524	6	1	...	...	1	532	1,713	14	6	...	...	4	1,737	98·66	·78	·34	...	...	·22
						Jains ...	9	...	...	...	...	1	10	35	...	...	...	...	10	45	77·78	...	...	...	...	22·22
						Jews and Others ...	4	1	...	...	...	...	5	19	2	...	...	...	...	21	90·48	9·52	...	...	...	...
						Total ...	2,029	58	14	28	5	24	2,158	14,660	369	68	159	37	231	15,524	94·43	2·38	·44	1·03	·24	1·49
		" ...	3	...	15,524	Christians ...	148	11	1	3	1	7	171	528	41	10	5	6	16	606	87·13	6·77	1·65	·82	·99	2·64
						Parsis ...	135	30	4	22	1	6	198	1,019	160	18	143	14	97	1,451	70·23	11·03	1·24	9·86	·96	6·68
						Mahomedans ...	391	10	6	1	1	3	412	1,102	106	21	6	7	16	1,319	83·43	7·80	1·50	·44	·52	1·19
						Hindus ...	1,310	6	2	1	1	2	1,322	11,725	61	10	3	2	75	11,876	98·74	·51	·08	·03	·02	·63
						Jains ...	24	...	1	...	1	6	32	63	...	9	...	8	27	107	58·88	...	8·41	...	7·48	25·23
						Jews and others ...	21	1	...	1	...	...	23	133	1	...	3	...	...	137	97·08	·73	...	2·19	...	...
						Total ...	6,322	170	26	11	5	4	6,538	29,050	762	122	59	41	30	30,064	96·63	2·53	·41	·19	·14	·10
		Total for Mazagaon. ...	...	1,564	30,084	Christians ...	658	3	3	1	...	...	665	3,301	11	16	1	...	...	3,329	99·16	·33	·43	·03	...	...
						Parsis ...	243	27	4	1	2	...	277	1,013	44	12	5	7	...	1,081	93·71	4·07	1·11	·46	·65	...
						Mahomedans ...	1,074	11	2	2	1	...	1,090	5,874	54	8	8	8	...	5,952	98·69	·91	·14	·13	·13	...
						Hindus ...	3,690	126	17	7	2	4	3,855	18,675	650	86	45	26	30	19,512	95·71	3·33	·44	·23	·13	·16
						Jains ...	39	3	...	...	...	...	42	165	3	...	...	...	...	168	98·21	1·79	...	...	...	...
						Jews and others ...	9	...	...	...	...	...	9	22	...	...	...	...	...	22	100·	...	...	...	...	...

TABLE XV—*continued.*

TABLE SHOWING TOTAL POPULATION OF EACH RELIGION IN EACH CIRCLE AND ITS RELATION TO HOUSES AND TENEMENTS.

Ward.	Charge.	Section.	Circle Number.	Total number of buildings.	Total number of persons.	Religion.	Total number of separate tenements occupied by persons of each religion with: One room.	Two rooms.	Three rooms.	Four rooms.	Five rooms.	Six rooms and over.	Total number of tenements of all kinds occupied by members of each religion.	Total number of members of each religion occupying tenements with: One room.	Two rooms.	Three rooms.	Four rooms.	Five rooms.	Six rooms and over.	Total number of members of each religion occupying tenements of all kinds.	Percentage of total population of each religion occupying each class of tenements with: One room.	Two rooms.	Three rooms.	Four rooms.	Five rooms.	Six rooms and over.
1			2	3	4	5	6	7	8	9	10	11	12	13	14	15	16	17	18	19	20	21	22	23	24	25
						Total ...	1,079	1	...	1	...	...	1,031	4,768	5	...	7	...	...	4,780	99·75	·10	...	·15	...	...
E.	33	Mazagaon ...	1	...	4,780	Christians ...	188	...	...	...	...	...	188	885	...	...	...	...	...	885	100·	...	...	...	...	...
						Parsis ...	15	...	...	...	...	...	15	55	...	...	...	...	...	55	100·	...	...	...	...	...
						Mahomedans ...	658	...	...	...	...	...	658	2,042	...	...	...	...	...	2,042	100·	...	...	...	...	...
						Hindus ...	214	1	...	1	...	...	216	1,777	5	...	7	...	...	1,789	99·33	·28	...	·39	...	...
						Jains ...	...	...	...	...	...	...	...	...	...	...	...	...	...	...	...	...	...	...	...	...
						Jews and others ...	4	...	...	...	...	...	4	9	...	...	...	...	...	9	100·	...	...	...	...	...
						Total ...	732	6	2	...	...	...	740	4,017	25	15	...	...	...	4,057	99·01	·62	·37	...	...	...
		" ...	2	...	4,057	Christians ..	123	...	...	...	...	...	123	828	...	...	...	...	...	828	100·	...	...	...	...	...
						Parsis ...	15	...	...	...	...	...	15	65	...	...	...	...	...	65	100·	...	...	...	...	...
						Mahomedans ...	293	...	...	...	...	...	293	1,323	...	...	...	...	...	1,323	100·	...	...	...	...	...
						Hindus ...	302	6	2	...	...	...	310	1,801	25	15	...	...	...	1,841	97·83	1·36	·81	...	...	...
						Jains ...	...	...	...	...	...	...	...	...	...	...	...	...	...	...	...	...	...	...	...	...
						Jews and others ...	...	...	...	...	...	...	...	...	...	...	...	...	...	...	...	...	...	...	...	...
						Total ...	943	24	2	...	...	1	970	4,069	91	10	...	...	6	4,196	97·45	2·17	·24	...	...	·14
		" ...	3	...	4,196	Christians ...	158	...	...	...	...	...	158	488	...	...	...	...	...	488	100·	...	...	...	...	...
						Parsis ...	68	...	...	...	...	...	68	240	...	...	...	...	...	240	100·	...	...	...	...	...
						Mahomedans ..	161	...	...	...	...	...	161	563	...	...	...	...	...	563	100·	...	...	...	...	...
						Hindus ...	545	21	2	...	...	1	572	2,765	91	10	...	...	6	2,872	96·27	3·16	·35	...	...	·21
						Jains ..	8	...	...	...	...	...	8	29	...	...	...	...	...	29	100·	...	...	...	...	...
						Jews and others ...	3	...	...	...	...	...	3	5	...	...	...	...	...	5	100·	...	...	...	...	...
						Total ...	1,050	60	12	3	4	...	1,129	4,209	238	42	20	34	...	4,543	92·65	5·24	·92	·44	·75	...
		" ...	4	...	4,543	Christians ...	148	...	2	1	...	...	151	921	...	10	1	...	...	932	98·82	...	1·07	·11	...	...
						Parsis ...	139	27	4	1	2	...	173	605	44	12	5	7	...	678	89·69	6·51	1·79	·74	1·04	...
						Mahomedans ...	93	10	...	...	1	...	103	201	40	...	...	8	...	249	80·72	16·06	...	...	3·22	...
						Hindus ...	665	23	6	1	1	...	696	2,458	154	20	14	19	...	2,665	92·23	5·78	·75	·53	·71	...
						Jains ...	6	...	...	...	...	...	6	24	...	...	...	...	...	24	100·	...	...	...	...	...
						Jews and others ...	...	...	...	...	...	...	...	...	...	...	...	...	...	...	...	...	...	...	...	...
						Total ...	2,518	79	10	7	1	3	2,618	11,967	403	55	32	7	24	12,488	95·83	3·23	·44	·25	·06	·19
		" ...	5	...	12,488	Christians ...	43	3	1	...	...	...	47	179	11	6	...	...	...	196	91·33	5·61	3·06	...	...	...
						Parsis ...	6	...	...	...	...	...	6	39	...	...	...	...	...	39	100·	...	...	...	...	...
						Mahomedans ...	470	1	3	2	...	...	476	1,746	14	8	8	...	...	1,776	98·31	·79	·45	·45	...	...
						Hindus ...	1,973	72	7	5	1	3	2,061	9,894	376	41	24	7	24	10,366	95·45	3·62	·40	·23	·07	·23
						Jains ...	25	3	...	...	...	...	28	112	3	...	...	...	...	115	97·39	2·61	...	...	...	...
						Jews and others ...	2	...	...	...	...	...	2	8	...	...	...	...	...	8	100·	...	...	...	...	...
						Total, F Ward.	17,948	2,374	515	304	131	299	21,571	73,836	12,689	2,971	2,329	929	2,144	94,898	77·81	13·37	3·13	2·45	·98	2·26
F.	...	Total for F Ward ...	...	3,797	94,898	Christians ...	619	175	86	42	28	23	672	1,610	719	504	393	122	137	3,492	46·37	20·58	14·43	11·23	3·49	3·92
						Parsis ...	209	98	60	43	23	40	502	891	285	397	205	131	390	2,299	38·76	13·40	17·27	8·91	5·70	16·96
						Mahomedans ...	1,434	210	55	22	9	24	1,784	4,179	894	236	122	29	146	5,606	74·55	15·95	4·21	2·17	·53	2·60
						Hindus ...	15,613	1,740	281	179	68	188	18,069	66,635	10,316	1,770	1,517	633	1,409	82,279	80·99	12·53	2·15	1·85	·77	1·71
						Jains ...	141	120	13	18	2	14	308	414	471	60	93	10	57	1,105	37·47	42·62	5·43	8·42	·90	5·10
						Jews and others ...	33	1	1	...	1	1	80	99	6	4	...	4	5	117	53·76	5·13	3·42	...	3·42	4·27

TABLE XV.

TOTAL POPULATON OF EACH RELIGION, ETC.

TABLE XV—*continued.*

TABLE SHOWING TOTAL POPULATION OF EACH RELIGION IN EACH CIRCLE AND ITS RELATION TO HOUSES AND TENEMENTS.

Ward.	Charge.	ection.	Circle Number.	Total number of buildings.	Total number of persons.	Religion.	Total number of separate tenements occupied by persons of each religion with						Total number of tenements of all kinds occupied by members of each religion.	Total number of members of each religion occupying tenements with						Total number of members of each religion occupying tenements of all kinds.	Percentage of total population of each religion occupying each class of tenements with					
							One room.	Two rooms.	Three rooms.	Four rooms.	Five rooms.	Six rooms and over.		One room.	Two rooms.	Three rooms.	Four rooms.	Five rooms.	Six rooms and over.		One room.	Two rooms.	Three rooms.	Four rooms.	Five rooms.	Six rooms and over.
		1	2	3	4	5	6	7	8	9	10	11	12	13	14	15	16	17	18	19	20	21	22	23	24	25
						Total ...	9,779	1,053	212	139	50	138	11,361	37,136	4,908	1,175	818	308	371	45,316	82·13	10·85	2·60	1·81	·68	1·93
P.		Total for Parel ...	...	1,454	45,316	Christians ...	273	39	16	9	8	6	351	675	138	76	39	13	47	998	68·32	13·97	7·69	3·95	1·31	4·70
						Parsis ...	170	82	64	25	14	20	375	696	231	344	118	51	143	1,563	43·07	14·80	21·73	7·46	3·23	9·03
						Mahomedans ...	635	81	17	12	2	4	651	1,500	319	73	70	9	14	1,984	75·60	16·08	3·61	3·53	·45	·71
						Hindus ...	8,690	784	114	70	25	99	9,791	33,935	3,993	676	574	231	129	40,038	84·76	9·97	1·69	1·43	·58	1·57
						Jains ...	84	66	1	4	...	9	164	216	221	7	17	...	38	529	40·50	41·78	1·32	3·22	...	7·18
						Jews and others ...	27	1	...	...	1	...	29	84	6	...	...	4	...	94	89·36	6·38	...	...	4·26	...
						Total ...	1,069	76	10	9	3	16	1,163	3,474	332	54	38	15	97	4,010	86·63	8·28	1·35	·95	·37	2·42
	24	Parel ...	1	...	4,010	Christians ...	...	...	...	...	...	...	...	...	...	...	...	...	...	...	...	...	...	...	...	...
						Parsis ...	1	...	...	...	...	...	1	2	...	...	...	...	...	2	100·	...	...	...	...	...
						Mahomedans ...	80	14	5	...	...	...	99	205	50	1	...	...	...	256	80·08	19·53	·39	...	...	...
						Hindus ...	950	35	5	9	3	16	1,024	3,161	202	53	38	15	97	3,566	88·64	5·66	1·49	1·07	·42	2·72
						Jains ...	21	27	...	...	...	...	48	71	80	...	...	...	...	151	47·02	52·98	...	...	...	...
						Jews and others ...	11	...	...	...	...	...	11	35	...	...	...	...	...	35	100·	...	...	...	...	...
						Total ...	1,018	97	46	14	8	15	1,198	4,903	491	309	71	13	93	5,780	84·83	8·49	3·82	1·23	·23	1·61
		" ...	2	...	5,780	Christians ...	14	11	4	1	3	...	33	16	30	16	12	10	...	84	19·05	35·71	19·05	14·29	11·90	...
						Parsis ...	8	6	29	4	5	...	52	17	10	131	19	3	...	180	9·44	5·56	72·78	10·56	1·67	...
						Mahomedans ...	61	6	3	...	...	...	70	198	24	7	...	...	...	229	86·46	10·48	3·06	...	...	...
						Hindus ...	920	57	10	5	...	11	1,003	4,647	360	55	23	...	72	5,157	90·11	6·98	1·07	·45	...	1·39
						Jains ...	14	17	...	4	...	4	39	17	67	...	17	...	21	122	13·93	54·92	...	13·94	...	17·21
						Jews and others ...	1	...	...	...	...	...	1	8	...	...	...	...	...	8	100·	...	...	...	...	...
						Total ...	1,377	210	15	27	6	5	1,640	5,672	927	100	150	37	30	6,916	82·01	13·40	1·45	2·17	·53	·44
		" ...	3	...	6,916	Christians ...	153	15	2	1	...	...	171	417	59	10	4	...	...	490	85·10	12·04	2·04	·82	...	...
						Parsis ...	16	34	7	14	2	2	77	52	139	44	57	7	13	312	16·67	44·55	14·10	18·27	2·24	4·17
						Mahomedans ...	109	16	3	5	...	...	132	275	60	29	35	...	...	399	68·92	15·04	7·27	8·77	...	...
						Hindus ...	1,086	145	3	7	4	3	1,318	4,896	660	17	51	30	17	5,683	86·15	11·77	·30	·95	·53	·30
						Jains ...	10	...	...	...	...	...	10	26	...	...	...	...	...	26	100·	...	...	...	...	...
						Jews and others ...	2	...	...	...	...	...	2	6	...	...	...	...	...	6	100·	...	...	...	...	...
						Total ...	1,693	99	9	5	4	11	1,821	5,854	490	81	18	28	62	6,533	89·61	7·50	1·24	·27	·43	·95
		" ...	4	...	6,533	Christians ...	1	...	...	...	...	...	1	3	...	...	...	...	...	3	100·	...	...	...	...	...
						Parsis ...	1	...	1	...	1	...	3	1	...	4	...	12	...	17	5·88	...	23·53	...	70·59	...
						Mahomedans ...	68	3	2	...	1	1	65	150	18	17	...	7	2	194	77·32	9·28	8·76	...	3·61	1·03
						Hindus ...	1,610	94	5	5	2	10	1,720	5,637	401	53	18	9	60	6,238	90·37	7·30	·85	·29	·14	·96
						Jains ...	17	2	1	...	...	...	20	47	11	7	...	...	...	65	72·31	16·92	10·77	...	...	...
						Jews and others ...	6	...	...	...	...	...	6	16	...	...	...	...	...	16	100·	...	...	...	...	...
						Total ...	140	52	12	7	2	7	220	438	214	87	46	7	38	830	52·77	25·78	10·48	5·54	·85	4·58
		" ...	5	...	830	Christians ...	7	3	3	3	...	1	17	4	19	7	8	...	5	43	9·30	44·19	16·28	18·60	...	11·63
						Parsis ...	6	4	5	2	2	6	25	14	11	43	15	7	33	123	11·38	8·94	34·96	12·20	5·69	26·83
						Mahomedans ...	16	5	...	...	...	...	21	1	17	...	...	...	...	18	5·56	94·44	...	...	...	...
						Hindus ...	109	33	4	2	...	...	148	407	147	37	23	...	...	614	66·29	23·94	6·03	3·74	...	...
						Jains ...	1	7	...	...	...	...	8	11	30	...	...	...	...	31	35·48	64·52	...	...	...	...
						Jews and others ...	1	...	...	...	...	...	1	1	...	...	...	...	...	1	100·	...	...	...	...	...

TABLE XV—*continued.*

Table showing Total Population of each Religion in each Circle and its Relation to Houses and Tenements.

Ward.	Charge.	Section.	Circle.	Total number of buildings.	Total number of persons.	Religion.	Total number of separate tenements occupied by persons of each religion with: One room.	Two rooms.	Three rooms.	Four rooms.	Five rooms.	Six rooms and over.	Total number of tenements of all kinds occupied by members of each religion.	Total number of members of each religion occupying tenements with: One room.	Two rooms.	Three rooms.	Four rooms.	Five rooms.	Six rooms and over.	Total number of members of each religion occupying tenements of all kinds.	Percentage of total population of each religion occupying each class of tenements with: One room.	Two rooms.	Three rooms.	Four rooms.	Five rooms.	Six rooms and over.
		1	2	3	4	5	6	7	8	9	10	11	12	13	14	15	16	17	18	19	20	21	22	23	24	25
						Total ...	1,330	174	60	37	10	48	1,659	4,984	837	321	265	105	295	6,807	73·22	12·30	4·72	3·89	1·54	4·33
P.	24	Parel ...	6	...	6,807	Christians ...	72	8	6	3	1	3	93	105	20	30	13	1	31	359	67·47	6·92	13·40	4·50	·35	7·27
						Parsis ...	13	21	11	4	...	6	55	58	23	53	25	...	53	212	27·36	10·85	25	11·79	...	·25
						Mahomedans ...	66	22	3	5	...	2	98	210	102	12	28	...	11	363	57·85	28·10	3·31	7·71	...	3·03
						Hindus ...	1,119	118	40	25	8	32	1,392	4,480	671	217	190	100	103	5,869	76·49	11·43	3·70	3·39	1·70	3·29
						Jains ...	10	4	...	...	...	5	19	32	15	...	...	...	17	64	50·	23·44	...	...	...	26·56
						Jews and others ...	...	1	...	...	1	...	2	...	6	...	...	4	...	10	...	60·	...	...	40·	...
						Total ...	1,097	59	10	4	2	5	1,177	3,789	329	89	41	22	29	4,399	88·14	7·65	2·07	·95	·51	·68
		" ...	7	...	4,200	Christians ...	9	...	...	...	...	...	9	6	...	...	...	...	...	6	100·	...	...	...	...	...
						Parsis ...	21	2	2	...	1	2	28	12	2	30	...	1	1	46	26·09	4·35	65·22	...	2·17	2·17
						Mahomedans ...	34	3	...	1	...	...	38	97	16	...	1	...	...	114	85·09	14·04	...	·87	...	...
						Hindus ...	1,024	63	8	3	1	3	1,091	3,037	306	59	40	21	23	4,001	83·02	7·49	1·44	·97	·51	·08
						Jains ...	8	2	...	...	...	...	10	33	5	...	...	...	...	38	86·84	13·16	...	...	...	...
						Jews and others ...	1	...	...	...	...	...	1	4	...	...	...	...	...	4	100·	...	...	...	...	...
						Total ...	1,368	140	24	7	11	11	1,761	6,302	708	119	51	58	84	7,322	86·07	9·67	1·63	·69	·79	1·15
		" ...	8	...	7,322	Christians ...	17	2	1	1	4	2	27	34	10	4	2	2	21	73	46·58	13·70	5·48	2·74	2·74	28·76
						Parsis ...	102	9	9	1	2	3	125	540	27	39	2	13	36	657	82·19	4·11	5·94	·30	1·98	5·48
						Mahomedans ...	101	8	1	1	1	1	113	320	23	6	6	2	1	358	89·38	6·42	1·68	1·68	·56	·28
						Hindus ...	1,313	122	13	4	4	5	1,401	5,394	648	70	41	41	26	6,220	86·72	10·42	1·13	·66	·66	·41
						Jains ...	...	...	...	...	...	...	...	...	...	...	...	...	...	...	...	...	...	...	...	...
						Jews and others ...	5	...	...	...	...	...	5	14	...	...	...	...	...	14	100·	...	...	...	...	...
						Total ...	487	146	26	19	4	20	702	1,720	580	115	138	23	143	2,719	63·26	21·33	4·23	5·07	·85	5·26
		" ...	9	...	2,719	Christians ...	...	...	...	...	...	...	...	...	...	...	...	...	...	...	...	...	...	...	...	...
						Parsis ...	...	7	...	...	1	1	9	...	19	...	...	8	7	34	...	55·88	...	...	23·53	20·59
						Mahomedans ...	11	4	...	...	...	...	15	44	9	...	...	...	...	53	83·02	16·98	...	...	...	...
						Hindus ...	473	128	26	10	3	19	659	1,667	529	115	138	15	136	2,600	64·11	20·35	4·42	5·31	·58	5·23
						Jains ...	3	7	...	...	...	...	10	9	23	...	...	...	...	32	28·12	71·88	...	...	...	...
						Jews and others ...	...	...	...	...	...	...	...	...	...	...	...	...	...	...	...	...	...	...	...	...
						Total ...	3,812	250	45	24	7	10	4,149	16,969	1,530	311	155	33	44	19,082	89·11	8·04	1·63	·82	·17	·23
		Total for Sewri ...	...	1,267	10,032	Christians ...	90	15	3	4	1	...	113	213	66	74	19	5	...	379	56·20	17·04	19·53	5·01	1·32	...
						Parsis ...	10	1	1	3	...	2	17	28	2	3	8	...	1	42	66·67	4·76	7·14	19·05	...	2·38
						Mahomedans ...	318	40	11	1	...	1	371	833	86	61	1	...	5	989	84·23	8·69	6·17	·10	...	·51
						Hindus ...	3,308	174	20	10	5	7	3,590	15,820	1,277	168	127	21	38	17,451	90·65	7·32	·96	·73	·12	·22
						Jains ...	26	20	1	...	1	...	48	59	97	2	...	7	...	165	35·76	58·79	1·21	...	4·24	...
						Jews and others ...	1	...	...	...	...	...	1	6	...	...	...	...	...	6	100·	...	...	...	...	...
						Total ...	1,386	32	4	1	1	...	1,424	6,281	129	31	5	7	...	6,453	97·33	2·	·48	·8	·11	...
	25	Sewri ...	1	...	6,453	Christians ...	21	1	...	...	...	...	22	62	2	...	...	...	...	64	96·88	3·12	...	...	...	...
						Parsis ...	3	...	...	...	...	...	3	4	...	...	...	...	...	4	100·	...	...	...	...	...
						Mahomedans ...	47	1	4	...	...	...	52	156	4	31	...	...	...	191	81·68	2·09	16·23	...	...	...
						Hindus ...	1,312	16	...	1	...	...	1,330	6,051	82	...	5	...	...	6,138	98·58	1·34	...	·8	...	...
						Jains ...	3	14	...	...	1	...	17	8	41	...	...	7	...	56	14·29	73·21	...	...	12·50	...
						Jews and others ...	...	...	...	...	...	...	...	...	...	...	...	...	...	...	...	...	...	...	...	...

TABLE XV.

Total Population of each Religion, etc.

TABLE XV—*continued.*

Table showing Total Population of each Religion in each Circle and its Relation to Houses and Tenements.

Ward.	Charge.	Section.	Circle No.	Total number of buildings.	Total number of persons.	Religion.	Total number of separate tenements occupied by persons of each religion with: One room.	Two rooms.	Three rooms.	Four rooms.	Five rooms.	Six rooms and over.	Total number of tenements of all kinds occupied by members of each religion.	Total number of members of each religion occupying tenements with: One room.	Two rooms.	Three rooms.	Four rooms.	Five rooms.	Six rooms and over.	Total number of members of each religion occupying tenements of all kinds.	Percentage of total population of each religion occupying each class of tenements with: One room.	Two rooms.	Three rooms.	Four rooms.	Five rooms.	Six rooms and over.
		1	2	3	4	5	6	7	8	9	10	11	12	13	14	15	16	17	18	19	20	21	22	23	24	25
						Total ...	933	18	1	...	...	...	952	3,765	103	4	...	...	...	3,872	97·24	2·66	·10	...	...	...
F.	25	Sewri ...	2	...	3,872	Christians ...	1	...	...	...	...	...	1	6	...	...	...	...	...	6	100·	...	...	...	...	...
						Parsis ...	4	...	...	...	...	...	4	9	...	...	...	...	...	9	100·	...	...	...	...	...
						Mahomedans ...	139	5	...	...	...	...	144	285	21	...	...	...	...	300	93·14	6·86	...	...	...	...
						Hindus ...	771	12	1	...	...	...	784	3,434	75	4	...	...	...	3,513	97·75	2·14	·11	...	...	...
						Jains ...	18	1	...	...	...	...	19	31	7	...	...	...	...	38	81·58	18·42	...	...	...	...
						Jews and others ...	...	...	...	...	...	...	...	...	...	...	...	...	...	...	...	...	...	...	...	...
						Total ...	434	25	10	3	...	...	472	1,743	89	30	7	...	...	1,869	93·26	4·76	1·61	·37	...	...
		" ...	3	...	1,869	Christians ...	35	3	...	...	...	...	38	113	9	...	...	...	...	122	92·62	7·38	...	...	...	...
						Parsis ...	3	...	...	...	...	...	3	15	...	...	...	...	...	15	100·	...	...	...	...	...
						Mahomedans ...	43	10	3	...	...	...	56	106	37	14	...	...	...	157	67·51	23·57	8·92	...	...	...
						Hindus ...	353	12	7	3	...	...	375	1,509	43	16	7	...	...	1,575	95·81	2·73	1·02	·44	...	...
						Jains ...	...	...	...	...	...	...	...	...	...	...	...	...	...	...	...	...	...	...	...	...
						Jews and others ...	...	...	...	...	...	...	...	...	...	...	...	...	...	...	...	...	...	...	...	...
						Total ...	894	174	30	20	6	10	1,134	4,023	1,194	246	143	26	44	5,675	70·87	21·04	4·33	2·52	·46	·78
		" ...	4	...	5,675	Christians ...	26	11	3	4	1	...	45	11	57	74	19	5	...	166	6·63	34·33	44·58	11·45	3·01	...
						Parsis ...	...	1	1	3	...	2	7	...	2	3	8	...	1	14	...	14·29	21·43	57·14	...	7·14
						Mahomedans ...	62	24	4	1	...	1	92	204	24	19	1	...	5	253	80·63	9·49	7·51	·40	...	1·97
						Hindus ...	801	133	21	12	5	7	979	3,788	1,063	148	115	21	38	5,173	73·24	20·53	2·86	2·23	·41	·74
						Jains ...	5	5	1	...	...	...	11	19	49	2	...	...	...	70	27·14	70·	2·86	...	...	...
						Jews and others ...	...	...	...	...	...	...	...	...	...	...	...	...	...	...	...	...	...	...	...	...
						Total ...	166	1	...	...	...	...	167	1,148	15	...	...	...	...	1,163	98·71	1·29	...	...	...	...
		" ...	5	...	1,163	Christians ...	7	...	...	...	...	...	7	21	...	...	...	...	...	21	100·	...	...	...	...	...
						Parsis ...	...	...	...	...	...	...	...	...	...	...	...	...	...	...	...	...	...	...	...	...
						Mahomedans ...	27	...	...	...	...	...	27	82	...	...	...	...	...	82	100·	...	...	...	...	...
						Hindus ...	130	1	...	...	...	...	131	1,038	15	...	...	...	...	1,053	98·58	1·42	...	...	...	...
						Jains ...	1	...	...	...	...	...	1	1	...	...	...	...	...	1	100·	...	...	...	...	...
						Jews and others ...	1	...	...	...	...	...	1	6	...	...	...	...	...	6	100·	...	...	...	...	...
						Total ...	4,356	1,071	258	151	74	151	6,061	19,741	6,251	1,485	1,356	588	1,229	30,650	64·40	20·40	4·85	4·42	1·92	4·01
		Total for Sion ...	...	1,076	30,650	Christians ...	156	121	86	29	19	17	408	731	612	354	334	104	90	2,125	34·40	28·80	16·66	15·72	4·89	4·24
						Parsis ...	29	15	15	16	9	27	110	167	52	50	79	60	216	674	24·78	7·71	7·42	11·72	11·87	36·50
						Mahomedans ...	581	119	27	9	7	19	762	1,846	469	100	51	20	127	2,633	70·11	18·67	3·80	1·94	·76	4·82
						Hindus ...	3,555	782	138	84	38	82	4,670	16,880	5,045	926	816	381	742	24,790	68·09	20·35	3·74	3·29	1·53	3·00
						Jains ...	31	34	11	14	1	5	96	100	153	51	76	8	19	411	26·52	37·23	12·41	18·50	·73	4·62
						Jews and others ...	4	...	1	...	...	1	6	8	...	4	...	...	5	17	47·06	...	23·53	...	...	29·41
						Total ...	588	138	26	19	10	35	816	2,747	762	144	153	45	288	4,140	66·35	18·43	3·48	3·69	1·09	6·96
	26	Sion ...	1	107	4,140	Christians ...	29	4	8	2	2	4	49	85	12	36	13	7	24	176	48·29	6·82	20·45	6·82	3·92	13·64
						Parsis ...	3	5	2	3	2	12	27	9	9	13	10	10	128	179	5·03	5·03	7·26	5·59	5·59	71·50
						Mahomedans ...	185	43	4	4	...	7	243	579	184	11	14	...	25	813	71·22	22·63	1·35	1·72	...	3·08
						Hindus ...	304	65	11	7	6	11	404	2,060	553	82	104	28	106	2,933	70·24	18·85	2·80	3·55	·95	3·61
						Jains ...	4	1	1	3	...	...	9	8	5	2	13	...	...	28	28·57	17·86	7·14	46·43	...	...
						Jews and others ...	3	...	...	...	...	1	4	6	...	...	...	...	5	11	54·55	...	...	...	...	45·45

TABLE XV—*continued.*

TABLE SHOWING TOTAL POPULATION OF EACH RELIGION IN EACH CIRCLE AND ITS RELATION TO HOUSES AND TENEMENTS.

Ward.	Charge.	Section.	Circle No.	Total number of buildings.	Total number of persons.	Religion.	Total number of separate tenements occupied by persons of each religion with: One room.	Two rooms.	Three rooms.	Four rooms.	Five rooms.	Six rooms and over.	Total number of tenements of all kinds occupied by members of each religion.	Total number of members of each religion occupying tenements with: One room.	Two rooms.	Three rooms.	Four rooms.	Five rooms.	Six rooms and over.	Total number of members of each religion occupying tenements of all kinds	Percentage of total population of each religion occupying each class of tenements with: One room.	Two rooms.	Three rooms.	Four rooms.	Five rooms.	Six rooms and over.
		1	2	3	4	5	6	7	8	9	10	11	12	13	14	15	16	17	18	19	20	21	22	23	24	25
						Total ...	185	53	18	10	7	13	285	692	245	58	121	49	125	1,290	53·64	18·99	4·50	9·38	3·80	9·69
F.	36	Sion ...	2	79	1,200	Christians ...	...	1	...	1	...	3	5	...	6	...	8	...	21	35	...	17·14	...	22·86	...	60·
						Parsis ...	6	2	1	3	4	5	20	14	3	10	21	33	25	106	13·21	2·83	9·43	19·81	31·13	23·59
						Mahomedans ...	53	25	6	2	2	4	95	170	114	17	19	10	70	400	42·50	28·50	4·25	4·75	2·50	17·50
						Hindus ...	125	10	7	2	1	1	155	503	109	20	59	6	9	706	71·25	15·44	2·83	8·36	·85	1·27
						Jains ...	1	4	1	2	...	...	8	3	13	7	14	...	...	37	8·11	35·13	18·92	37·84	...	...
						Jews and others ...	1	...	1	...	...	...	2	2	...	4	...	...	...	6	33·33	...	66·67	...	...	...
						Total ...	881	193	32	7	5	15	1,132	3,337	1,538	108	30	46	65	5,124	65·12	30·02	2·11	·58	·90	1·27
		" ...	3	250	5,124	Christians ...	1	17	...	...	1	4	24	70	71	10	...	3	17	171	40·94	41·52	5·65	...	1·75	9·94
						Parsis ...	1	3	10	...	1	1	16	4	11	11	...	12	12	50	8·	22	22·	...	24	24·
						Mahomedans ...	9	12	1	...	1	1	24	30	13	3	...	1	7	54	55·56	24·07	5·56	...	1·85	12·96
						Hindus ...	807	153	19	6	2	8	1,055	3,227	1,419	79	27	30	28	4,809	67·10	29·40	1·64	·56	·63	·59
						Jains ...	3	7	1	1	...	1	13	6	5	5	3	...	1	40	15·	62·50	12·50	7·50	...	2·50
						Jews and others ...	...	...	...	...	...	...	...	...	...	...	...	...	...	...	...	...	...	...	...	...
						Total ...	684	207	24	21	7	8	951	2,875	1,085	125	194	64	83	4,426	64·96	24·52	2·82	4·38	1·45	1·87
		" ...	4	308	4,426	Christians ...	11	8	5	1	4	...	20	34	31	13	23	14	...	114	29·83	27·19	11·40	19·30	12·28	...
						Parsis ...	1	4	1	6	...	2	14	1	20	9	15	...	13	58	1·73	34·48	15·52	25·86	...	22·41
						Mahomedans ...	113	5	2	2	...	1	123	375	19	20	17	...	7	438	85·62	4·34	4·56	3·88	...	1·60
						Hindus ...	550	189	16	11	3	5	783	2,465	1,013	83	138	50	63	3,812	64·67	26·57	2·18	3·62	1·31	1·65
						Jains ...	...	1	...	1	...	...	2	...	2	...	2	...	...	4	...	50	...	50·	...	...
						Jews and others ...	...	...	...	...	...	...	...	...	...	...	...	...	...	...	...	...	...	...	...	...
						Total ...	273	109	44	20	12	17	475	1,279	513	217	209	75	127	2,420	52·85	21·20	8·97	8·63	3·10	5·25
		" ...	5	230	2,420	Christians ...	24	28	27	12	6	3	100	91	60	148	142	31	16	527	17·27	18·79	28·08	26·94	5·88	3·04
						Parsis ...	...	...	...	...	...	...	...	...	...	...	...	...	...	...	...	...	...	...	...	...
						Mahomedans ...	51	9	2	...	...	5	67	166	39	4	...	...	15	224	74·11	17·41	1·78	...	...	6·70
						Hindus ...	197	70	13	7	6	9	502	1,021	306	59	66	44	96	1,652	61·80	22·16	3·57	4·	2·06	5·81
						Jains ...	1	2	2	1	...	...	6	1	9	6	1	...	...	17	5·88	52·94	35·30	5·88	...	...
						Jews and others ...	...	...	...	...	...	...	...	...	...	...	...	...	...	...	...	...	...	...	...	...
						Total ...	372	94	28	13	5	14	525	1,967	484	210	163	38	110	2,992	66·41	16·18	7·02	5·45	1·27	3·67
		" ...	6	2,311	2,903	Christians ...	38	24	5	3	1	...	71	130	107	28	64	9	...	338	38·40	31·66	8·28	18·94	2·06	...
						Parsis ...	2	...	...	1	1	1	5	18	...	...	7	7	8	35	37·14	...	...	20·	20·	22·88
						Mahomedans ...	31	3	...	...	...	1	35	30	8	...	...	...	3	50	78·	16·	...	...	...	6·
						Hindus ...	297	65	21	8	3	10	404	1,778	361	179	92	23	67	2,519	70·58	14·33	7·11	3·65	·87	3·45
						Jains ...	4	3	2	...	...	2	10	27	8	3	...	...	12	50	54·	16·	6·	...	...	24·
						Jews and others ...	...	...	...	...	...	...	...	...	...	...	...	...	...	...	...	...	...	...	...	...
						Total ...	315	50	23	8	5	2	403	2,025	232	136	63	146	29	2,631	76·97	8·82	5·17	2·39	5·55	1·10
		" ...	7	232	2,631	Christians ...	31	30	12	2	1	...	68	146	130	61	18	19	...	374	39·04	34·76	16·31	4·81	5·08	...
						Parsis ...	...	...	...	...	...	...	...	...	...	...	...	...	...	...	...	...	...	...	...	...
						Mahomedans ...	30	...	...	...	3	...	33	157	...	...	...	5	...	163	96·31	...	...	...	3·09	...
						Hindus ...	259	10	11	6	1	2	299	1,709	102	75	45	122	29	2,083	82·19	4·90	3·60	2·16	5·60	1·39
						Jains ...	3	...	...	...	...	...	3	13	...	...	...	...	...	13	100·	...	...	...	...	...
						Jews and others ...	...	...	...	...	...	...	...	...	...	...	...	...	...	...	...	...	...	...	...	...

TABLE XV.

TOTAL POPULATION OF EACH RELIGION, ETC.

TABLE XV—*continued*.

TABLE SHOWING TOTAL POPULATION OF EACH RELIGION IN EACH CIRCLE AND ITS RELATION TO HOUSES AND TENEMENTS.

Ward.	Charge.	Section.	Circle No.	Total number of buildings.	Total number of persons.	Religion.	Total number of separate tenements occupied by persons of each religion with: One room.	Two rooms.	Three rooms.	Four rooms.	Five rooms.	Six rooms and over.	Total number of tenements of all kinds occupied by members of each religion.	Total number of members of each religion occupying tenements with: One room.	Two rooms.	Three rooms.	Four rooms.	Five rooms.	Six rooms and over.	Total number of members of each religion occupying tenements of all kinds.	Percentage of total population of each religion occupying each class of tenements with: One room.	Two rooms.	Three rooms.	Four rooms.	Five rooms.	Six rooms and over.
1			2	3	4	5	6	7	8	9	10	11	12	13	14	15	16	17	18	19	20	21	22	23	24	25
						Total ...	469	53	11	13	7	8	561	2,368	526	115	87	43	76	3,215	73·65	16·36	3·58	2·71	1·34	2·36
F.	26	Sion ...	8	210	3,215	Christians ...	15	5	1	2	1	...	24	121	23	15	8	7	...	174	69·54	13·22	8·62	4·60	4·02	...
						Parsis ...	11	...	...	2	1	5	22	115	...	...	26	19	53	211	54·50	...	...	12·32	8·53	24·65
						Mahomedans ...	15	1	...	...	1	...	17	64	4	...	...	4	...	73	88·89	5·56	...	...	5·56	...
						Hindus ...	415	37	8	5	4	3	472	2,034	434	85	21	14	24	2,619	77·66	16·72	3·25	·80	·53	·92
						Jains ...	19	10	2	4	...	...	26	34	61	15	20	...	...	139	24·46	43·88	10·79	20·66	...	...
						Jews and others ...	...	...	...	...	...	...	...	...	...	...	...	...	...	...	...	...	...	...	...	...
						Total ...	149	64	19	15	8	7	262	533	273	148	100	38	56	1,148	46·43	23·78	12·89	8·71	3·31	4·88
		" ...	9	136	1,148	Christians ...	13	4	3	...	2	...	21	26	33	29	...	9	...	97	26·80	34·02	29·90	...	9·28	...
						Parsis ...	1	...	...	...	...	1	2	6	...	...	...	...	8	14	42·86	...	...	...	...	57·14
						Mahomedans ...	1	2	...	...	...	...	3	5	11	...	...	...	...	16	31·25	68·75	...	...	...	...
						Hindus ...	132	53	14	13	5	4	221	487	207	100	96	20	42	954	51·05	21·70	11·11	10·06	2·73	4·40
						Jains ...	3	5	2	3	1	2	15	9	22	13	14	3	6	67	13·43	32·83	19·40	20·90	4·48	8·96
						Jews and others ...	...	...	...	...	...	...	...	...	...	...	...	...	...	...	...	...	...	...	...	...
						Total ...	170	55	10	7	4	24	270	652	281	83	63	24	210	1,312	49·69	21·42	6·25	4·80	1·83	16·01
		" ...	10	110	1,312	Christians ...	1	...	3	3	...	2	9	3	...	4	30	...	9	46	6·52	...	8·70	65·22	...	19·56
						Parsis ...	1	...	1	...	...	...	2	1	...	7	...	...	...	8	12·50	...	87·50	...	...	...
						Mahomedans ...	24	...	...	1	...	...	20	89	...	...	1	...	...	90	98·89	...	...	1·11	...	...
						Hindus ...	130	54	6	3	4	22	223	555	277	71	32	24	201	1,160	47·84	23·88	6·12	2·76	2·07	17·33
						Jains ...	1	1	...	...	...	...	2	4	4	...	...	...	...	8	50·	50·	...	...	...	...
						Jews and others ...	...	...	...	...	...	...	...	...	...	...	...	...	...	...	...	...	...	...	...	...
						Total ...	270	57	23	19	4	8	381	1,246	311	143	173	20	60	1,952	63·83	15·93	7·28	8·86	1·03	3·07
		" ...	11	218	1,952	Christians ...	2	...	1	3	1	1	8	25	...	10	30	5	3	73	34·25	...	13·70	41·09	6·85	4·11
						Parsis ...	1	1	...	...	...	...	2	4	9	...	...	...	...	13	30·77	69·23	...	...	...	...
						Mahomedans ...	65	18	10	...	...	...	93	172	97	45	...	...	...	314	54·78	30·89	14·33	...	...	...
						Hindus ...	201	37	12	16	3	7	276	1,041	201	67	143	15	57	1,544	67·42	13·02	5·64	9·26	·97	3·69
						Jains ...	1	1	...	...	...	...	2	4	4	...	...	...	...	8	50	50	...	...	...	...
						Jews and others ...	...	...	...	...	...	...	...	...	...	...	...	...	...	...	...	...	...	...	...	...
						Total ...	17,654	3,481	936	500	252	200	22,903	89,453	18,625	5,310	2,889	1,632	1,820	119,719	74·72	15·56	4·43	2·41	1·36	1·52
G.	...	Total for G Ward ...	...	6,067	119,719	Christians ...	611	284	156	118	62	63	1,319	3,893	1,425	777	610	358	406	6,529	44·31	21·83	11·90	9·34	5·49	7·14
						Parsis ...	274	104	121	41	14	20	577	1,105	484	510	177	93	133	2,502	44·17	19·34	20·38	7·07	3·72	5·32
						Mahomedans ...	1,793	411	102	55	25	28	2,413	8,857	2,070	611	201	241	269	12,348	71·73	16·81	4·95	2·35	1·95	2·18
						Hindus ...	14,610	2,561	491	261	150	83	18,186	75,919	14,165	3,264	1,701	937	912	96,698	78·35	14·62	3·37	1·75	·97	·94
						Jains ...	148	102	30	21	...	3	304	531	394	110	94	...	24	1,152	46·09	34·12	9·55	8·16	...	2·08
						Jews and others ...	69	19	6	6	1	3	104	147	79	38	7	3	16	290	50·69	27·24	13·10	2·41	1·04	5·52
						Total ...	3,410	1,147	548	334	184	92	5,715	17,692	5,956	3,178	1,630	1,125	672	30,253	58·48	19·69	10·50	5·39	3·72	2·22
		Total for Mahim ...	...	2,800	30,253	Christians ...	183	120	105	67	30	19	530	907	667	664	327	170	116	2,751	32·97	24·24	24·50	11·89	6·18	4·22
						Parsis ...	21	18	36	23	10	8	116	93	47	108	74	60	35	416	22·36	11·30	25·96	17·79	14·18	8·41
						Mahomedans ...	674	231	86	51	22	18	1,086	3,040	1,226	530	262	230	104	5,401	56·30	22·83	9·82	4·77	4·10	3·53
						Hindus ...	2,340	754	294	179	116	45	3,878	13,503	3,927	1,672	907	666	322	21,196	63·70	18·53	7·89	4·28	3·14	1·52
						Jains ...	40	18	25	13	...	1	97	143	84	67	68	...	1	373	38·34	22·52	23·32	18·23	...	·27
						Jews and others ...	2	2	2	1	...	1	8	7	5	9	2	...	4	26	26·92	19·23	30·77	7·69	...	15·38

TABLE XV—*continued.*

TABLE SHOWING TOTAL POPULATION OF EACH RELIGION IN EACH CIRCLE AND ITS RELATION TO HOUSES AND TENEMENTS.

Ward.	Charge.	Section.	Circle No.	Total number of buildings.	Total number of persons.	Religion.	Total Number of separate tenements occupied by persons of each religion with: One room.	Two rooms.	Three rooms.	Four rooms.	Five rooms.	Six rooms and over.	Total Number of tenements of all kinds occupied by members of each religion.	Total Number of members of each religion occupying tenements with: One room.	Two rooms.	Three rooms.	Four rooms.	Five rooms.	Six rooms and over.	Total Number of members of each religion occupying tenements of all kinds.	Percentage of total population of each religion occupying each class of tenements with: One room.	Two rooms.	Three rooms.	Four rooms.	Five rooms.	Six rooms and over.
		1	2	3	4	5	6	7	8	9	10	11	12	13	14	15	16	17	18	19	20	21	22	23	24	25
						Total ...	456	56	40	34	3	3	592	1,878	330	218	149	45	12	2,635	71·54	12·19	8·30	5·68	1·83	·46
G.	27	Mahim ...	1	294	2635	Christians ...	37	5	7	4	...	...	53	91	26	30	16	...	...	162	56·17	16·06	17·90	9·88	...	...
						Parsis ...	1	...	4	1	1	...	8	4	...	13	11	8	...	36	11·11	...	36·11	30·56	22·22	...
						Mahomedans ...	16	...	...	...	...	...	16	34	...	...	...	...	...	34	100·	...	...	...	...	...
						Hindus ...	400	50	21	19	2	3	503	1,741	280	147	122	40	12	2,351	74·06	12·20	6·25	5·19	1·70	·51
						Jains ...	1	...	6	...	...	...	7	7	...	21	...	...	...	28	25·	...	75·	...	...	...
						Jews and others ...	1	2	2	...	...	...	5	1	5	8	...	...	...	14	7·14	35·72	57·14	...	...	...
						Total ...	298	136	77	80	36	31	658	1,720	848	392	422	185	148	3,715	46·30	22·83	10·55	11·36	4·98	3·98
		„ ...	2	194	3715	Christians ...	33	25	33	35	10	11	140	142	89	147	167	49	63	647	21·95	13·76	22·72	25·81	7·57	9·19
						Parsis ...	1	1	...	...	...	...	2	1	3	...	...	...	...	4	25·	75·	...	...	...	...
						Mahomedans ...	8	...	...	...	...	...	8	17	...	...	...	...	...	17	100·	...	...	...	...	...
						Hindus ...	247	110	45	45	26	20	493	1,531	756	245	255	136	96	3,018	50·73	25·05	8·12	8·45	4·50	3·18
						Jains ...	9	...	...	...	...	...	9	20	...	...	...	...	...	20	100·	...	...	...	...	...
						Jews and others ...	...	...	...	...	...	...	...	...	...	...	...	...	...	...	...	...	...	...	...	...
						Total ...	446	121	32	26	6	11	652	2,240	605	245	155	52	113	3,440	65·12	17·59	7·12	4·58	1·51	3·28
		„ ...	3	310	3440	Christians ...	20	2	3	4	2	4	34	80	11	8	26	6	33	162	49·38	6·79	4·94	16·05	3·70	20·37
						Parsis ...	4	7	...	...	...	...	11	36	7	...	...	...	...	43	83·72	16·28	...	...	...	...
						Mahomedans ...	20	4	1	2	1	1	29	70	68	3	5	2	9	106	47·62	40·06	1·81	3·01	1·31	5·42
						Hindus ...	392	111	29	19	3	6	560	2,093	454	234	153	45	71	3,050	68·62	14·89	7·43	5·11	1·50	2·37
						Jains ...	10	7	...	...	...	...	17	40	34	...	...	...	...	74	54·05	45·95	...	...	...	...
						Jews and others ...	...	...	...	1	...	...	1	...	...	...	2	...	...	2	...	...	...	100·	...	...
						Total ...	193	95	81	43	35	6	413	1,066	455	364	178	150	50	2,313	46·05	20·07	15·74	7·70	6·48	2·16
		„ ...	4	394	2313	Christians ...	15	12	7	3	2	1	39	73	67	63	24	10	8	245	29·80	27·35	25·71	9·80	4·08	3·26
						Parsis ...	4	1	6	7	1	1	20	13	2	23	32	1	7	78	16·67	2·56	29·49	41·03	1·28	8·97
						Mahomedans ...	63	19	10	13	...	1	106	350	131	125	46	...	10	662	52·87	19·79	18·88	6·95	...	1·51
						Hindus ...	103	60	21	18	23	1	224	627	178	136	59	139	20	1,259	49·80	23·06	10·80	4·69	11·04	1·59
						Jains ...	6	3	7	5	...	1	22	17	7	17	17	...	1	59	28·81	11·87	28·81	28·81	...	1·70
						Jews and others ...	1	...	...	...	...	1	2	6	...	...	...	...	4	10	60·	...	...	...	...	40·
						Total ...	694	195	84	47	30	17	1,067	2,981	986	484	232	235	150	5,068	58·82	19·45	9·55	4·58	4·64	2·96
		„ ...	5	87	5068	Christians ...	17	8	7	6	1	1	40	161	56	39	31	6	5	298	54·03	18·79	13·09	10·40	1·66	2·01
						Parsis ...	8	3	2	2	2	1	18	31	15	9	5	20	5	85	36·47	17·65	10·59	5·88	23·53	5·88
						Mahomedans ...	415	144	41	22	10	11	643	1,792	730	220	143	146	97	3,143	57·02	23·51	7·10	4·55	4·64	3·09
						Hindus ...	247	37	25	11	7	4	331	976	167	173	30	64	42	1,452	67·08	10·89	12·	2·08	4·34	2·91
						Jains ...	7	2	9	6	...	...	25	21	19	37	23	...	...	100	21·	19·	37·	23·	...	...
						Jews and others ...	...	...	...	...	...	...	...	...	...	...	...	...	...	...	...	...	...	...	...	...
						Total ...	552	250	128	56	42	27	1,055	3,261	1,225	737	233	256	113	5,825	55·98	21·03	12·65	4·	4·40	1·94
		„ ...	6	308	5825	Christians ...	40	41	41	16	20	1	159	283	234	209	58	92	10	886	32·10	26·91	23·75	6·59	10·46	1·14
						Parsis ...	3	6	24	12	6	6	57	8	20	63	28	30	23	170	4·71	11·76	37·06	16·29	17·65	13·53
						Mahomedans ...	23	17	8	3	3	...	54	132	37	5	25	19	...	218	60·55	16·97	2·29	11·47	8·72	...
						Hindus ...	483	186	55	20	13	20	763	2,821	940	460	124	115	80	4,540	62·14	20·71	10·13	2·73	2·53	1·76
						Jains ...	4	...	...	...	...	...	4	17	...	...	...	...	...	17	100·	...	...	...	...	...
						Jews and others ...	...	...	...	...	...	...	...	...	...	...	...	...	...	...	...	...	...	...	...	...

TABLE XV.

TOTAL POPULATION OF EACH RELIGION, ETC.

TABLE XV—*continued.*

TABLE SHOWING TOTAL POPULATION OF EACH RELIGION IN EACH CIRCLE AND ITS RELATION TO HOUSES AND TENEMENTS.

Ward.	Charge.	Section.	Circle No.	Total number of buildings.	Total number of persons.	Religion.	Total number of separate tenements occupied by persons of each religion with: One room.	Two rooms.	Three rooms.	Four rooms.	Five rooms.	Six rooms and over.	Total number of tenements of all kinds occupied by members of each religion.	Total number of members of each religion occupying tenements with: One room.	Two rooms.	Three rooms.	Four rooms.	Five rooms.	Six rooms and over.	Total number of members of each religion occupying tenements of all kinds.	Percentage of total population of each religion occupying each class of tenements with: One room.	Two rooms.	Three rooms.	Four rooms.	Five rooms.	Six rooms and over.
		1	2	3	4	5	6	7	8	9	10	11	12	13	14	15	16	17	18	19	20	21	22	23	24	25
						Total ...	267	69	23	5	1	1	366	1,298	440	127	36	9	6	1,895	67.23	23.22	6.73	1.91	.48	.32
G	27	Mahim ...	9	139	1,895	Christians ...	36	28	9	1	1	1	40	50	113	60	6	9	6	253	19.81	44.65	27.38	2.38	3.57	2.30
						Parsis ...	...	...	...	...	...	...	...	...	...	...	...	...	...	...	...	...	...	...	...	...
						Mahomedans ...	69	13	2	1	...	...	85	105	30	7	9	...	...	151	74.71	19.35	3.49	2.45	...	...
						Hindus ...	164	54	10	3	...	...	231	1,031	279	43	21	...	...	1,363	74.81	20.40	3.15	1.54	...	...
						Jains ...	1	...	2	...	...	...	3	2	...	8	...	...	...	10	20.	...	80.	...	...	...
						Jews and others ...	...	...	...	...	...	...	...	...	...	...	...	...	...	...	...	...	...	...	...	...
						Total ...	585	205	118	53	50	6	915	3,208	1,047	611	195	190	80	5,281	60.85	19.46	11.35	3.62	3.53	1.49
		" ...	6	197	5,281	Christians ...	7	4	...	...	...	...	11	27	78	...	...	...	...	105	25.71	74.29	...	...	...	...
						Parsis ...	...	...	...	...	...	...	...	...	...	...	...	...	...	...	...	...	...	...	...	...
						Mahomedans ...	65	35	24	10	8	5	147	441	201	173	84	65	75	990	44.55	20.30	17.48	8.49	6.30	7.58
						Hindus ...	451	161	78	41	42	1	774	2,709	744	434	148	127	3	4,230	66.73	17.59	10.28	3.38	3.	.5
						Jains ...	2	5	1	3	...	...	10	10	24	6	16	...	...	56	17.86	42.86	7.14	32.14	...	...
						Jews and others ...	...	...	...	...	...	...	...	...	...	...	...	...	...	...	...	...	...	...	...	...
						Total ...	14,156	2,234	358	165	68	105	17,188	71,780	12,059	2,133	1,250	507	1,148	89,400	80.21	14.16	2.36	1.40	.57	1.28
		Total for Ward ...	...	3,307	89,406	Christians ...	459	184	51	40	26	44	780	1,966	754	213	203	128	330	3,776	52.37	20.05	5.41	7.40	4.26	9.25
						Parsis ...	353	93	35	21	4	12	484	1,012	467	403	103	34	95	2,080	48.51	22.35	19.27	4.94	1.63	4.70
						Mahomedans ...	1,114	180	16	4	3	10	1,327	5,817	853	73	39	11	75	6,867	84.83	12.44	1.06	.48	.16	1.10
						Hindus ...	12,354	1,800	197	82	34	38	14,308	62,417	10,238	1,398	794	271	590	75,708	82.45	13.52	1.84	1.05	.36	.78
						Jains ...	108	84	5	8	...	3	207	388	309	23	36	...	23	779	49.81	39.67	2.95	4.62	...	2.95
						Jews and others ...	67	17	4	5	1	2	96	140	74	30	3	3	13	261	53.65	28.35	11.83	1.30	1.14	4.98
						Total ...	578	12	3	3	...	1	594	2,594	84	19	3	...	6	2,685	96.61	3.13	.71	.11	...	.22
	28	Worli ...	1	206	2,685	Christians ...	17	...	1	...	...	...	18	37	...	3	...	...	...	40	92.50	...	7.50	...	...	...
						Parsis ...	4	...	1	...	...	...	5	11	...	8	...	...	...	19	57.89	...	42.11	...	...	...
						Mahomedans ...	26	...	...	...	...	...	26	128	...	...	...	...	...	128	100.	...	...	...	...	...
						Hindus ...	523	12	1	2	...	1	539	2,303	84	8	3	...	6	2,478	95.76	3.40	.32	.12	...	.24
						Jains ...	3	...	...	...	...	...	3	10	...	...	...	...	...	10	100.	...	...	...	...	...
						Jews and others ...	1	...	...	...	...	...	1	6	...	...	...	...	...	6	100.	...	...	...	...	...
						Total ...	1,805	233	14	12	5	8	2,077	9,270	1,287	71	58	9	69	10,764	86.12	11.96	.66	.54	.08	.64
		" ...	2	253	10,764	Christians ...	69	10	30	1	...	3	113	274	42	63	1	...	17	370	73.87	11.17	11.17	.27	...	4.62
						Parsis ...	34	1	...	1	...	...	60	304	1	...	1	...	...	306	99.31	.33	...	.33	...	...
						Mahomedans ...	326	36	1	1	1	3	368	2,717	169	8	9	3	40	2,964	91.67	5.67	.27	.27	.7	1.35
						Hindus ...	1,376	168	...	5	3	...	1,553	5,860	873	...	40	4	...	6,062	85.15	14.13	...	.57	.06	...
						Jains ...	7	8	...	...	...	...	15	37	28	...	...	...	...	65	43.86	57.14	...	...	...	...
						Jews and others ...	51	11	3	4	1	3	73	88	47	21	3	3	13	175	50.97	27.17	12.14	1.75	1.78	6.94
						Total ...	1,436	120	53	23	3	14	1,649	8,090	683	203	153	33	168	9,130	87.37	7.48	2.30	1.65	.35	1.11
		" ...	3	135	9,150	Christians ...	34	2	4	...	...	6	46	106	14	43	...	...	17	181	59.57	7.74	23.20	...	...	9.39
						Parsis ...	5	17	37	8	...	3	70	23	77	159	40	...	30	329	6.91	23.17	48.65	12.19	...	9.15
						Mahomedans ...	105	8	...	...	2	3	118	442	38	...	...	8	21	510	86.67	7.45	...	...	1.76	4.12
						Hindus ...	1,280	88	10	14	1	5	1,398	7,363	496	3	113	25	27	8,024	91.76	6.19	.4	1.30	.30	.34
						Jains ...	14	4	1	...	...	1	20	64	57	4	...	...	7	134	46.16	45.97	3.33	...	...	5.63
						Jews and others ...	8	...	...	...	...	...	8	23	...	...	...	...	...	23	100.	...	...	...	...	...

TABLE XV—*continued.*

TABLE SHOWING TOTAL POPULATION OF EACH RELIGION IN EACH CIRCLE AND ITS RELATION TO HOUSES AND TENEMENTS.

Ward.	Class.	Section.	Circle No.	Total number of buildings.	Total number of persons.	Religion.	Total number of separate tenements occupied by persons of each religion with One room.	Two rooms.	Three rooms.	Four rooms.	Five rooms.	Six rooms and over.	Total number of tenements of all kinds occupied by members of each religion.	Total number of members of each religion occupying tenements with One room.	Two rooms.	Three rooms.	Four rooms.	Five rooms.	Six rooms and over.	Total number of members of each religion occupying tenements of all kinds.	Percentage of total population of each religion occupying each class of tenements with One room.	Two rooms.	Three rooms.	Four rooms.	Five rooms.	Six rooms and over.
		1	2	3	4	5	6	7	8	9	10	11	12	13	14	15	16	17	18	19	20	21	22	23	24	25
						Total ...	787	120	3	...	...	...	910	4,056	737	19	...	...	...	4,812	84·29	15·32	·39	...	...	...
G.		Ward ...	4	53	4,812	Christians ...	20	1	...	...	...	...	30	90	4	...	...	...	...	94	95·24	4·76	...	...	...	...
						Parsis ...	40	20	1	...	...	...	61	171	96	6	...	...	...	273	62·64	35·16	2·20	...	...	...
						Mahomedans ...	38	3	1	...	...	...	39	94	11	3	...	...	...	108	87·04	10·18	2·78	...	...	...
						Hindus ...	667	69	1	...	...	...	737	3,601	584	10	...	...	...	4,205	85·64	13·93	·23	...	...	...
						Jains ...	16	5	...	...	...	...	21	50	16	...	...	...	...	66	75·76	24·24	...	...	...	...
						Jews and others ...	...	2	...	...	...	...	2	...	16	...	...	...	...	16	...	100·	...	...	...	...
						Total ...	2,280	359	59	23	11	15	2,727	10,457	2,107	359	171	62	141	13,327	78·69	15·81	2·69	1·28	·47	1·06
		,, ...	5	209	13,327	Christians ...	22	5	1	8	5	7	46	73	21	1	55	29	64	243	30·04	8·64	·41	22·63	11·94	26·31
						Parsis ...	63	34	38	6	2	5	133	200	173	168	38	16	11	675	29·63	25·63	24·89	5·63	2·37	1·63
						Mahomedans ...	251	28	3	...	...	...	282	709	314	17	...	...	...	1,130	62·71	27·79	1·50	...	...	...
						Hindus ...	1,022	284	22	7	4	3	2,242	9,294	1,572	173	66	17	66	11,188	83·07	14·05	1·55	·59	·15	·59
						Jains ...	10	7	...	2	...	...	19	40	25	...	12	...	...	60	66·66	20·67	...	13·95	...	...
						Jews and others ...	3	1	...	...	...	...	3	3	2	...	...	...	...	5	60·	40·	...	...	...	...
						Total ...	726	203	30	17	8	7	991	4,074	1,196	241	170	96	89	5,866	69·45	20·39	4·11	2·90	1·63	1·52
		,, ...	6	69	5,866	Christians ...	63	50	4	3	4	2	120	381	271	21	17	47	14	751	50·73	36·09	2·80	2·26	6·26	1·86
						Parsis ...	...	...	...	1	...	1	2	...	...	...	6	...	8	14	...	...	...	42·86	...	57·14
						Mahomedans ...	23	43	1	...	...	1	68	55	43	9	...	...	2	110	50·46	39·45	8·26	...	...	1·83
						Hindus ...	639	100	25	13	4	3	703	3,620	860	211	147	49	65	4,970	73·02	17·48	4·24	2·96	·99	1·31
						Jains ...	1	1	...	...	...	...	2	9	13	...	...	...	...	22	40·91	59·09	...	...	...	...
						Jews and others ...	...	...	...	...	...	...	...	...	...	...	...	...	...	...	...	...	...	...	...	...
						Total ...	3,200	230	93	24	16	25	3,591	14,049	1,317	507	155	127	357	17,412	85·86	7·56	2·01	·89	·73	2·05
		,, ...	7	610	17,412	Christians ...	152	5	11	1	...	10	182	529	22	6	7	4	102	665	79·40	3·31	·90	1·05	...	15·34
						Parsis ...	59	5	13	1	2	...	80	115	26	67	1	18	...	227	50·66	11·45	29·52	·44	7·93	...
						Mahomedans ...	227	17	3	...	...	1	248	850	76	8	...	...	8	942	90·23	8·07	·85	...	...	·85
						Hindus ...	2,718	182	67	20	14	13	3,041	13,469	1,170	415	136	100	231	15,470	86·68	7·56	2·68	·83	·71	1·49
						Jains ...	13	18	2	2	...	1	36	39	23	11	11	...	16	100	39·	23·	11·	11·	...	16·
						Jews and others ...	1	...	...	...	...	...	1	9	...	...	...	...	...	9	100·	...	...	...	...	...
						Total ...	3,374	1,047	101	66	25	36	4,649	18,310	5,279	714	542	181	384	25,410	72·06	20·78	2·81	2·13	·71	1·51
		,, ...	8	301	25,410	Christians ...	52	98	20	33	17	17	237	505	384	98	203	112	130	1,438	35·12	26·70	6·81	14·12	7·79	9·04
						Parsis ...	36	9	...	4	...	3	54	114	61	...	17	...	49	244	46·72	25·23	...	6·97	...	20·08
						Mahomedans ...	217	45	7	3	...	3	275	732	163	27	21	...	4	956	76·78	16·94	2·80	2·17	...	·41
						Hindus ...	3,019	561	71	21	9	13	3,693	16,808	4,501	573	285	69	196	22,430	74·93	20·07	2·55	1·27	·31	·87
						Jains ...	44	41	3	4	...	...	91	130	130	8	13	...	...	280	46·40	46·40	2·87	4·36	...	...
						Jews and others ...	4	2	1	1	...	...	9	12	9	9	3	...	...	33	36·37	27·27	27·27	9·09	...	...